About the author

Norman Rose was born and educated in England. He now lives in Israel and teaches history at the Hebrew University, Jerusalem, where he holds the Chaim Weizmann Chair of International Relations. His previous books include *Vansittart: Study of a Diplomat; Lewis Naimier* and *Zionism and Chaim Weizmann: A Biography.*

Churchill
An Unruly Life

NORMAN ROSE

TOUCHSTONE BOOKS
LONDON . NEW YORK . SYDNEY . TOKYO . TORONTO . SINGAPORE

First published in Great Britain by Simon & Schuster Ltd, 1994
First published in Touchstone, 1998
An imprint of Simon & Schuster
A Viacom company

1 3 5 7 9 10 8 6 4 2

Simon & Schuster Ltd
West Garden Place
Kendal Street
London W2 2AQ

Simon & Schuster Australia
Sydney

A CIP catalogue record for this book is available from the
British Library

ISBN 0-684-84034-0

Printed and bound in Great Britain by Cox & Wyman Ltd.,
Reading, Berkshire

Contents

List of illustrations   vii

Acknowledgements   ix

Prologue   1

1 'The Boy is Wonderfully Pretty'   3

2 Becoming Educated   17

3 In Pursuit of Fame   32

4 'I am an English Liberal. I hate the Tory Party'   49

5 Radical Politics   65

6 'The Biggest Thing that has ever come my way'   83

7 A Water Creature   98

8 'God Bless the Dardanelles'   108

9 Eclipse   124

10 Fighting Bolshevism   138

11 Running the Empire   152

12 'I will make you the Golden Chancellor'   166

13 Squandering the Treasure   179

14 Private Diversions   192

15 An Independent Voice   216

16 'What Price Churchill?'   234

17 His Finest Hour   252

18 Standing Alone   271
19 Grand Strategy   286
20 'Advance Britannia!'   301
21 The Great Commoner   322
    Epilogue   343

    Notes and References   347
    Bibliography   398
    Index   419

List of illustrations

1 Blenheim Palace
2 Chartwell Manor
3 Lord Randolph Churchill
4 Jennie, Lady Randolph Churchill
5 Clementine Churchill
6 On watch in India, 1896
7 The budding parliamentarian
8 Churchill at play to an appreciative audience, 1914
9 'The Two Romeos'. Churchill and Lloyd George about 1909
10 As First Lord of the Admiralty, 1912
11 Contemplating the Dardanelles
12 Churchill and F. E. Smith (Lord Birkenhead)
13 Guests of the duke of Westminster. Winston, Clementine, and Randolph out hunting
14 'The Golden Chancellor', April 1925
15 Churchill and his dog, Rufus
16 Churchill as Prime Minister and Minister of Defence
17 Churchill, November 1940
18 Inspecting the Home Guard in Hyde Park
19 Touring London's blitzed areas
20 Checking the coastal fortifications in north-east England
21 Watching a Boeing B-17 'Flying Fortress' arriving in Britain
22 Churchill and Montgomery entertaining the troops in Normandy
23 Triumphant in Berlin, July 1945
24 Electioneering in 1951
25 Addressing his supporters in Epping, October 1951
26 Carrying on in January 1954
27 Churchill's farewell dinner as Prime Minister to Queen Elizabeth II and the Duke of Edinburgh, April 1955
28 Relaxing at Lord Beaverbrook's villa September 1958
29 Churchill and 'Ari' Onassis aboard the *Christina*
30 Churchill's state funeral, January 1965

Acknowledgements

Realizing a project of this kind depends upon the good will and encouragement of many people. I would first like to record my thanks to the Chartwell Trustees for granting me access to the Churchill Archives at Churchill College, Cambridge. I am particularly grateful to Mr Ian Montrose, Mr Peregrine Churchill, and Mr Winston Churchill MP for their assistance in this matter. Mr Correlli Barnett, the Keeper of the Churchill Archives Centre, Mr Alan Kucia, its Archivist, and all the Search Room staff ensured that my stay at the centre was both profitable and pleasant. In the same connection, I would like to convey my thanks to the staff of the Cabinet Office, Historical Section, for displaying admirable flexibility in allowing me access to the state papers in the Churchill collection. My thanks are also due to the Warden and Fellows of St Antony's College, Oxford, for inviting me to spend a sabbatical year in the most agreeable and congenial surroundings. It was here that I began work on this book.

Crown copyright material at the Public Record Office is reproduced by kind permission of the Controller of Her Majesty's Stationery Office. I would also like to thank those authors and publishers (listed in the bibliography) for quotations I have used from works of which they hold the copyright; and to register in advance my apologies for those cases that I have inadvertently overlooked. I am also most grateful to the staffs of the numerous archives, libraries, and institutions that generously extended their facilities to me: the Library at St Antony's College, Oxford; the Bodleian Library, Oxford; the British Library of Political and Economic Science at The London School of Economics; the British Museum Library and its Newspaper Collection at Colindale; the Corrington Library, All Souls' College, Oxford; the Institute of Historical Research, Senate House, London; the Library for Humanities and Social Sciences and the National Library at The Hebrew University, Jerusalem; the New York Public Library; the Library at Nuffield College, Oxford; the Public Record Office, Kew; the Library at Rhodes House,

Oxford; The Royal Commission on Historical Manuscripts, Chancery Lane, London; the University Library, Cambridge; and the Weizmann Archives. Photographs are reproduced by kind courtesy of: Aerofilms, no. 1; Hulton Deutsch, nos. 4, 6, 8, 10, 11, 12, 18, 19, 20, 24, 25, 27; Punch, no. 7; S & G Press Agency Ltd., no. 9; Magnum Press, no. 15; *Daily Mail*, no. 16; Camera Press, no. 17; Imperial War Museum, nos. 21, 22, 23; *Daily Express*, no. 26; Paul Popper Ltd., nos. 28, 29; and *Times* Newspapers, no. 30. Every effort has been made to trace the copyright of the photographs reproduced, but it has not always proved possible to do so. My apologies to any such unacknowledged owner.

During the writing of this volume I have taxed the patience of many friends and colleagues, often picking their brains in what appeared to them, no doubt, as little more than casual conversations. For their forbearance, I wish to thank: Paul Addison; Sir Isaiah Berlin; Lord Beloff; Lord Blake; Lord Bullock; David Cannadine; Peter Clarke; Robin Edmonds; Timothy Garton Ash; Martin Gilbert; Gabriel Gorodetsky; James Joll; the late Eli Kedourie; Warren F. Kimball; Wm. Roger Louis; Sasson Sofer; Donald Cameron Watt; the late Charles Wenden; and the late Meir Verete.

Particular thanks are due to Ellis Joffe for cheerfully sustaining my all too often flagging spirits during our long and frequent walks through the streets of Jerusalem. And to the Cohen family of Hampstead Garden Suburb for their generous hospitality while I was engaged in my researches in England. I am also grateful to Dr Inbal Rose for pursuing various enquiries on my behalf, and for reading the manuscript and subjecting it to the most apposite comments.

Robert Ducas has been the most understanding and supportive of literary agents. Many thanks are due to the staff at Simon & Schuster: in particular to my editor, Carol O'Brien, for her expertise and tact in guiding this project to a successful conclusion; and also to Jessica Cuthbert-Smith, Jenny Olivier and Catherine Reed for their able assistance. I am also greatly obliged to Elfreda Powell whose skill and professionalism was invaluable in the final stages of the preparation of this book.

Finally, I wish to record my deepest thanks and admiration to my wife and daughter, Tslilla and Inbal, for their patience and understanding. All too often, while they were dealing with pressing family matters, my mind was elsewhere, preoccupied with distant and obscure historical controversies.

Ba'aka, Jerusalem,
October 1993

Prologue

On Saturday, 30 January 1965, at a quarter to ten on a cold wintry morning, the state funeral cortège of Sir Winston Churchill left Westminster Hall for St Paul's Cathedral. At that moment, Big Ben chimed, then remained silent for the remainder of the day. In St James's Park, the first of ninety guns began their salute, one for each year of Churchill's life. Borne by eight guardsmen, his coffin, covered by the Union Jack and bearing a black cushion on which rested his insignia of the Order of the Garter, emerged from the ancient hall into New Palace Yard, the Houses of Parliament windows ablaze. It was secured to a grey gun-carriage, with a guard of honour, including cadets from Harrow School, paying him tribute. A Royal Naval escort took up its position and the procession set off. Led by the bands of the Royal Air Force and Her Majesty's Foot Guards, it moved forward in slow time to the strains of Handel's 'Death March'. The principal mourners, led by Clementine, his wife, rode in the Queen's town coach, and Randolph, his son, on foot, followed the gun-carriage.[1]*

The procession made its way up Whitehall. As it passed the Cenotaph, the banners of the Danish resistance movement were dipped in honour. Rounding Trafalgar Square, it progressed down the Strand, along Fleet Street and up Ludgate Hill to the cathedral. Crowding the pavements were masses of people, some of whom had been camping out all night.

A great congregation of 3,500 waited at St Paul's. Queen Elizabeth II, contrary to convention, attended the service. Five other monarchs, five heads of state, and sixteen prime ministers were also in attendance. De Gaulle was present, as was Eisenhower and Marshal Koniev, conqueror of Berlin. One hundred and eleven countries sent representatives. Twelve pallbearers, among them Attlee, Eden, Harold Macmillan, Lord Mountbatten, and Sir Robert Menzies, carried the coffin through the nave to the catafalque. The service was conducted to the strains

* Notes and References begin on p. 347.

of Churchill's favourite hymns: 'Mine eyes have seen the glory of the coming of the Lord', 'Fight the good fight with all thy might' and, 'O God, our help in ages past'. From the crypt of the cathedral, Sir Robert Menzies broadcast to the world a heartfelt thanksgiving for Churchill's life.

> There were, in 1940, defeatists . . . In the whole of recorded history this was, I believe, the one occasion when one man, with one soaring imagination, with one fire burning in him, and with one unrivalled capacity for conveying it to others, won a crucial victory not only for the Forces (for there were many heroes in those days) but for the very spirit of human freedom. And so, on this day, we thank him, and we thank God for him.

After the service the coffin was taken to Bladen churchyard where he was buried, in a simple ceremony, next to his parents and his brother, Jack. Nearby, visible through the trees, stood Blenheim Palace, where Churchill had been born ninety years before.

1

'The Boy is Wonderfully Pretty'

Winston Leonard Spencer-Churchill, first child to Lord and Lady Randolph Churchill, was born on 30 November 1874 at Blenheim Palace, the Churchill family seat near Woodstock in Oxfordshire. The Churchills, despite Lady Randolph's advanced state of pregnancy, had left their London home – where all preparations for the birth had been made – to go shooting at Blenheim. Lady Randolph had been out following the guns when she took a nasty fall. An 'imprudent & rough' drive in a pony carriage brought on her labour pains, and her baby boy was delivered by the local doctor at 1.30 in the morning, after eight hours' labour and without the use of chloroform. 'She suffered a great deal poor darling,' Lord Randolph wrote to his mother-in-law, 'but was vy plucky . . . The boy is wonderfully pretty so everybody says dark eyes and hair & vy healthy considering its prematureness.'[1]

The marriage of Lord Randolph Churchill, second son of the seventh duke of Marlborough, to Jennie (Jeanette) Jerome, second daughter of a wealthy American entrepreneur, had been solemnized only seven months and two weeks earlier, on 15 April 1874, at a modest ceremony in the chapel at the British embassy in Paris. The occasion was not accompanied by any of the fanfare normally associated with marriages of this social distinction. It went unrecorded by *The Times*.[2] Only a handful of guests witnessed the union. Randolph's parents were notably absent, although they had sent a grudging letter of approval – 'She is one whom you have chosen with less than usual deliberation'.[3]

By all accounts – to coin a cliché – theirs had been a 'whirlwind romance', truly love at first sight. They had met briefly in August 1873 at the Royal Regatta at Cowes. In the course of three days they had waltzed (to Randolph's intense discomfort), contrived to meet by 'accident', strolled together, and dined in the company of Jennie's mother and eldest sister. On the third evening and at long last finding themselves alone in the garden, Randolph had proposed and had immediately been accepted. 'I love her better than life itself,' he wrote to his father, adding that 'my one hope and dream now is that matters may be arranged that soon I may be united to her by ties that nothing but death itself could have the power to sever'.[4]

The duke had received this startling news with a marked lack of enthusiasm, and haughtily dismissed Jennie's father, Leonard Jerome, as a 'sporting, and I should think vulgar kind of man', casting serious aspersions on his business ethics. Nor, in the first instance, were the Jeromes particularly ecstatic about Randolph, for news had reached them that he drank too heavily and was too fond of fast company.[5]

The major stumbling-block in the marital arrangement proved to be the financial settlement. Prolonged negotiations, sometimes acrimonious, led inevitably to verbal battles, misunderstandings, tears, and rash threats. 'He [Jerome] could do what he liked with his beastly money,' cried Lord Randolph, by now well at the end of his short tether. At last, just a week before the marriage was due to take place, the prickly obstacle of monetary remunerations was cleared. The final settlement provided for about £3,600 a year for the newly married couple, £2,500 guaranteed by the Jeromes, the remainder furnished by the duke who, in addition, generously cancelled all Lord Randolph's debts, estimated at £2,000.[6]

There were probably deeper reasons for the Marlboroughs' obvious distaste for their prospective daughter-in-law. Of ancient lineage, descendants of the great John Churchill, acclaimed saviour of his country during the wars of the Spanish Succession, created Duke of Marlborough in 1702 and a prince of the Holy Roman Empire three years later, their family origins have been traced back to Otho de Leon, Castelan of Gisor, whose youngest son was reputed to have fought alongside William the Conqueror at Hastings. By the mid-twelfth century, the name Jocelyn de Churchill appears in the parish register of Broad Clyst in Devon. Related by marriage to the Drakes of Ashe, one of more powerful families in the West Country, the family's fortunes fluctuated owing to their Royalist connections during the Civil War, and were not fully restored until John Churchill's famous victories raised them to great eminence.[7] As a tribute of the nation's debt to John, Queen Anne made over the royal estate at Woodstock near Oxford to him for posterity. It consisted of some 2,000 acres of park and farm land, including several villages and a half-ruined manor-house. On it John and his duchess, Sarah, commissioned Sir John Vanbrugh, assisted by Nicholas Hawksmoor, to build the imposing palace of Blenheim – named after the first duke's famous victory in 1704 at Blindheim, a small village in Bavaria. The palace buildings range over seven acres. 'How many rooms are there at Blenheim?' enquired one inquisitive lady. 'I am not sure,' answered the perplexed owner, 'but I know I paid a bill this spring for painting a thousand windows.'[8]

Over this splendid inheritance now reigned Randolph's father, the seventh duke, described by a critical, perceptive onlooker as 'a Tory of a narrow dispensation . . . a complete, full-blown Victorian prig'.[9] His initial reaction to 'an American connection' had been overtly hostile, a sentiment fully shared by his formidable duchess, Francis ('Fanny') Anne Emily, and other members of the family. 'You must allow,' his parents wrote to Randolph, 'it is slightly coming down in pride for us to contemplate the connection'.[10] Having already dismissed Leonard Jerome as a bankrupt New York speculator, the Marlboroughs ingrained prejudices would never fade entirely.

Leonard Jerome, as he wrote to Jennie, was quite aware of the aversion 'the English have against Americans socially'. His career in fact had been perfectly honorable and in many ways epitomized the American dream of the 'self-made man'. The Jeromes sprang from old Huguenot stock and could trace their arrival in America to the beginning of the seventeenth century. Beginning as a small-town lawyer and newspaper proprietor, he had graduated to Wall Street where he had made and squandered two fortunes, losing heavily in the uncertain years after the Civil War. Generous by nature – he was reputed to have contributed a quarter of a million dollars to the victims of the New York riots of 1863 – his extravagant lifestyle was a byword in fashionable Fifth Avenue circles. He had also been United States consul in Trieste, had, for a time, acquired the principal interest in the *New York Times* and the Pacific Mail shipping line, sailed across the Atlantic in small yachts, and founded two racecourses, Jerome Park and Coney Island Jockey Club. He was a philanderer, and devotee of the opera (Minnie Hauk, the celebrated opera singer, was reputedly his illegitimate daughter), his particular fads being horse racing and gambling, but, as Jennie was quick to point out, these latter were in any case 'decidedly English tastes'.[11]

Jennie was nineteen when she first met Lord Randolph at Cowes. With her mother and sisters, she had spent the previous six years in Paris. Mixing in social circles close to the Imperial court, Jennie, no doubt pushed forward by her family, succumbed readily to its alluring influence. Now known as Jeannette, she listened attentively, perhaps enviously, to stories of glittering receptions graced by the Imperial couple, Napoleon III and his Empress, Eugénie. She rode often, visited museums and exhibitions, and developed her natural skill for the piano, practising four hours a day, sharpening her talent to that of concert standards.[12] These pleasures, disrupted though not entirely halted by the collapse of the Second Empire in 1870–71, set the pattern for her future life.

Jennie was raven-haired, and her striking dark looks were set off by a lively, ebullient, high-spirited character. Rumour had it that she owed something of her exciting appearance and mercurial temperament to a strain of Iroquois blood, passed on to her through her mother Clara, referred to in family circles as 'Sitting Bull'.[13] Of independent mind and restless tongue, Jennie pursued life to the full, often exasperating her family and many admirers by her wilful behaviour. Her wild extravagances, already in evidence, were to become a byword for high living – one knowing friend later commented tartly that 'she was the sort of woman for whom life did not begin on a basis of less than forty pairs of shoes'.[14]

The Marlboroughs, on the other hand, did not consider themselves excessively wealthy, at least by the standards of some of the great aristocratic houses of the day – their estates brought in approximately £40,000 a year, most of which went on its upkeep and indeed they were soon to sell off some of the family treasures to boost their dwindling fortunes.[15]

For all that, they maintained the rigid lifestyle considered essential to those of their class and station. After a fashionable prep school, Lord Randolph was sent to Eton where he won for himself the soubriquet 'Scug', in his contemporary Lord Rosebery's bland expression, 'a pregnant word at Eton', but one that implies an unruly, ill-mannered, bumptious, lazy, arrogant youth. More charitable viewers saw him as 'bubbling over with fun and the sweetest deviltry'. Not so his father who remonstrated at his 'impertinence & overbearing disposition'.

As a student of Merton College, Oxford, Lord Randolph's reputation was scarcely better. Nicknamed 'Gooseberry', owing to his protruding eyes, he devoted himself to hunting, the exclusive Myrmidons dining-club, well-advertised drinking bouts, and aggressive high-jinks. Only occasionally did he reveal glimpses of the intellectual power and caustic tongue that were to flower, and sadly wither, later on.[16]

By the time of his marriage he had given little indication of the talents that only a few years hence were to electrify British politics. In a lacklustre campaign in early 1874, only two months before his marriage, he had duly been elected Conservative Member of Parliament for the constituency of Woodstock, virtually a pocket-borough of the Marlborough family.

In May 1874 Lord Randolph brought his bride to Blenheim on their first visit since their marriage. Despite a heavy thunderstorm that day, Woodstock was in celebratory mood. Flags and banners were flying, while the local pubs – at Lord Randolph's expense – ministered liberally to the village's thirst. Led by the gaily uniformed Woodstock Lodge of Foresters (of which Lord Randolph was a member), the local populace received the happy pair in traditional style, substituting themselves for the horses and triumphantly drawing the carriage through the town to the palace where they were welcomed by the Duke and Duchess and members of the family.[17]

On their return to London in May 1874, after their Continental honeymoon, they had established themselves first in Curzon Street, and then at a larger house in Charles Street.[18] Here they began to indulge in that lavish round of hectic socializing that was to dominate their lives for the coming three or four years. Overspending their income, they quickly ran into debt, a state of affairs that did not noticeably diminish their appetite for high-living. Entertaining on a lavish scale, with the Prince of Wales on occasion dignifying their table, and enjoying to the full the pleasures offered by the London season, the always fashionably attired Churchills – Lord Randolph, 'an archetypical Junior Carlton drone', was considered something of a dandy – cut grand figures in London society. This lifestyle 'of conspicuous and frivolous consumption',[19] was scarcely disrupted by the unexpected arrival of their first child, Winston Leonard Spencer-Churchill.

Young Winston was brought up as befitted a scion of an aristocratic family. Although the Randolph Churchills grumbled incessantly about their straitened financial circumstances, they had by no means descended to the level of genteel impoverishment. They entertained royally; kept a fine establishment in London, replete with the required number of servants – including a highly sought-after French cook; were among the top stars of the London season and were constant guests at the great houses of England. That they often ran into debt was not held against them. Among the circles in which they moved, indebtedness, provided it was not flouted ostentatiously, was not rated highly as a social impediment, particularly for the younger sons of noble families.

Winston's early years were spent in these highly privileged surroundings. Later he complained of parental neglect. He recalled that his mother appeared to him as 'a fairy princess', remote and inaccessible. 'She shone for me like the Evening Star . . . I loved her dearly – but at a distance.' In time, however, Jennie's influence on his career was to be considerable. As for Lord Randolph – whom Winston saw even less regularly than his mother – he steered well clear of a warm, affectionate relationship with his son. The young Winston idealized his father from afar. Stern and unpredictable in behaviour, Lord Randolph yielded little to the normal emotional ties that bind father to son. Substitute 'Father' for 'Papa' in your letters, he once suggested. Winston could remember only 'three or four long intimate conversations' with him.[20] His parents' attitude, frosty and capricious to an extreme, would have profound consequences on Winston's development. Nevertheless, the general pattern of his upbringing – governesses and nannies, prep and public schools – was, for someone of his background, very much the norm.

In large measure, it was his nanny, Elizabeth Ann Everest – known to Winston and his younger brother Jack, as 'Woom' or 'Woomany' –

who filled the emotional gaps in his life. Mrs Everest was first employed as Winston's nanny in early 1875, aged forty-two, and she remained in the family's service until she was summarily dismissed, in the most shabby circumstances, almost twenty years later. Winston's ambitions and hopes, his childhood frustrations and disappointments, found in Elizabeth Everest a ready and sympathetic listener. He depended on her and confided in her. She assumed for Winston the double role of surrogate parents. Two years after she died, Winston published his first, and only, attempt at writing fiction. The work, *Savrola*, is discernibly autobiographical in characterization. The hero, Savrola, a man of action as well as a man of letters, able to sway the masses by the magic of his words, clearly typecast Churchill in the role he dreamed of eventually playing. Of Savrola's Mrs Everest, he wrote from special knowledge.[21]

> He was all she had in the world; others dissipate their affections on a husband, children, brothers, sisters; all the love of her kind old heart was centred in the man she had fostered since he was a helpless baby. And he did not forget!

Elizabeth Everest's influence on his childhood can hardly be exaggerated. Reliable and sympathetic, she softened the sharp impact of his parents' neglect, providing him with a secure anchor in times of distress.

Winston Churchill's first conscious memories were of Ireland, to where his family had, in effect, been banished at the end of 1876. The origins of this affair were social rather than political. Early that year, Lord Randolph's brother, George Charles, Marquess of Blandford, had eloped with the wife of the Earl of Aylesford, a close friend of the Prince of Wales. In order to prevent messy divorce proceedings and to minimize the scandal and damage to the family name, Lord Randolph had chosen to intervene in this affair in a most reckless and insensitive manner. Threatening to expose publicly an alleged romance between the Prince of Wales and Lady Aylesford, he foolishly involved the Princess of Wales in his designs, assuring her that, if published, the letters would ensure that her husband 'would never sit upon the Throne of England'. Heated exchanges followed. 'I have the crown of England in my pocket,' Lord Randolph boasted. This was folly on a spectacular scale and retribution soon followed. The Queen, informed of these 'revolting accusations', thought Lord Randolph's conduct 'outrageous' and elected to stand by her son. The Prince demanded 'an apology or a meeting'. A duel 'was out of the question', Lord Randolph replied, and nothing came of this mad idea. Some months later he adroitly disposed of the Prince's first demand, so phrasing his apology as to render it worthless. As the Prince of Wales now made it plain that he would no longer tolerate their presence in his company, the Churchills were effectively blackballed from

London society, and their fall from grace reflected upon the entire family. These dismal circumstances finally convinced the Duke of Marlborough that it would be expedient to accept Disraeli's face-saving offer to accept the vice-royalty of Ireland, and take Lord Randolph with him as his unofficial private secretary, until tempers had cooled.[22]

The family's exile lasted until February 1880 – even though Lord Randolph's final reconciliation with the Prince of Wales did not occur until March 1884. On the surface, little seemed to have changed. From their base in Dublin, the Randolph Churchills continued their hectic social whirl. Jennie found Irish life 'very pleasant, with its various occupations and amusements', mainly hunting; but also, apparently, racing her sister, clad only in their nightgowns, on the lawns of the vice-regal lodge, to the astonishment of the servants. 'My picture of her . . . is in a riding habit, fitting like a skin and often beautifully spotted with mud,' Winston later recollected.[23]

But for Lord Randolph, the Aylesford affair and his enforced exile in Ireland had a sobering effect. It also enabled him to scrutinize from close quarters the Irish question, the most intractable issue in British politics. His own outlook had been shaped by a generation of Trinity College men, an institution thought by Gerald Fitzgibbon as 'the haute école of intelligent Toryism'. At Woodstock in September 1877, in a much criticized speech, Lord Randolph raised the banner of Tory radicalism by attacking successive British governments for creating and sustaining the Irish problem by their neglect and apathy. 'They must remember that England had years of wrong, years of crime, years of tyranny, years of oppression, years of general misgovernment to make amends for in Ireland.' Lord Randolph was pushing through the Irish door to burst upon English politics.[24]

Lord and Lady Randolph Churchill established themselves at 'The Little Lodge', some sixty yards from the vice-regal residency. 'Winston is flourishing,' reported Lady Randolph. There were walks in Phoenix Park, rides on his donkey, and stirring military tattoos to watch. Fleeting shadows darkened these pleasures. Once his donkey threw him, alarmed at an approaching band of strange men – perhaps the dreaded Fenians. Mrs Everest's nervousness about the Fenians, those 'wicked people' who would, apparently, stop at nothing, made a strong impression upon her young charge, a leaning that could only have been reinforced when an evening's entertainment at a pantomime was ruined owing to the theatre being burned down in mysterious circumstances.[25]

Towards the end of his three-year stay in Ireland, Winston, as he later typically put it, 'was first menaced with Education', personified in 'a sinister figure described as "the Governess"' – from whom he frequently sought refuge by hiding in the extensive shrubbery.[26] Over the years a popular legend has taken root, fostered not least by Churchill himself, that portrays him as the class dunce, struggling in vain to escape the scholastic strait-jacket imposed upon him by traditional academics and narrow-minded bigots; but who, despite his lack of formal academic prowess, went on to achieve great things.

The truth, naturally, was more prosaic. Doubtless Winston viewed the prospect of school, after the relative freedom of his nursery and Elizabeth Everest's benevolent regime, with a great deal of apprehension. But once there, like many bright, precocious boys, he tended to do well at those subjects that interested him and to respond to masters who stimulated him; and conversely, to neglect and shun those who bored him, usually the majority. He was, however, blessed with a phenomenal memory that he was to exploit to excellent profit throughout his long life.

At the age of eight, Winston's was sent to St George's preparatory school, a fashionable and expensive establishment at Ascot. Unwittingly, his parents had made an unfortunate choice. The headmaster, a tall angular person with red mutton-chop whiskers, inflicted a cruel regime upon his boys. Roger Fry, a near-contemporary of Winston's, recalled that every Monday morning, after assembly, those boys with bad form reports were summarily despatched to his study for a birching of fifteen to sixteen strokes that left 'the wretched boy's bottom a mass of blood', while the rest of the school, in Churchill's words, 'sat quaking, listening to their screams'. Fry, who as one of the headboys held down the victims, believed that the headmaster derived 'an intense sadistic pleasure' from these floggings. According to another pupil he was 'sexually excited by any boy with red hair', adding another dimension to poor Winston's beatings. Many years later, when Home Secretary, Churchill remarked, not entirely flippantly, that his sympathy for convicts stemmed from his spending 'eleven years of penal servitude in the private and public schools of England'.[27]

Winston's letters home pleaded for visits from his parents, pleas that in the main went ignored. Occasionally, the dependable and homely Mrs Everest would appear to lighten his burden, to listen to his troubles and tender him encouragement. His lot was further aggravated by lack of adequate funds. 'Send me a little,' he entreated, 'ten bob would do as I want to give a little to the chaple fund'.[28] This was the opening shot in a long war waged, often in vain, to prop up his desperately shaky finances.

By his last term, Winston had gained third and fourth places in classes of nine and eight. His history and geography were consistently 'very good', his classics 'very fair' to 'good', as was his French. Even his mathematical ability – never, alas, realized – showed signs of being 'very good', while his writing and spelling, after a slow start, were 'much improved'. Predictably, it was his conduct that gave cause for grave concern. 'Constantly in scrapes' and not to 'be trusted to behave himself', he lacked 'ambition' and proved to be 'a constant trouble to everyone', reported his teachers, who added that well-worn phrase: 'He might always do well if he chose.' As he did not always choose, the results were bound to disappoint not only his teachers – '[who] saw me at once backward and precocious' – but also his family, and in particular his father.[29]

Unruly and garrulous, Winston had also attained something of a reputation for lack of punctuality. 'He is rather greedy at meals', his masters also pointed out, while Maurice Baring recorded that Winston was once thrashed for stealing sugar from the pantry, a punishment that provoked him to kick the headmaster's straw hat to pieces in revenge.[30] Like his unpunctuality, his preoccupation with eating and drinking was to become a permanent feature of his behaviour.

But, already, the young Winston was showing signs of an independent, restless, stubborn, defiant character. It was with some justification that his peers regarded him as something of a self-advertising, bumptious scallywag.

Sentenced to spend the next ten years in the 'penal' colonies of England, and in the main bored by the academic fare they offered, particularly classical studies – 'no one ever succeeded in making me write a Latin verse or learn any Greek except the alphabet', he boasted – he went his own way. He devoured *Treasure Island*, acquired the works of H. Rider Haggard, reading *King Solomon's Mines* twelve times (according to his cousin, Shane Leslie, he believed the plot was true), and requested general Ulysses Grant's *History of the American Civil War (Illustrated)* for study. Later, he would learn by rote large chunks of poetry or prose – Macaulay or Byron, Longfellow or Milton – savouring the fine language while testing to the full his retentive memory.[31] Despite his obvious distaste for public school life – an aversion that deepened as his memory sharpened – he made the most of the few compensations it presented to him.

After enduring two years of the school in Ascot, Winston was transferred to the more gentle care of two Victorian spinsters, the Misses Kate and Charlotte Thomson, who ran a prep school in Brighton. He had, he recalled discreetly, fallen 'into a low state of health', and the sea air at Brighton – where Dr Robson Roose, the Churchills' family doctor was close at hand – was expected to restore him to full strength. Apparently, however, the reason for his move was more sinister. Mrs Everest, on discovering the scars of his beatings, had reported her findings to Lady Randolph who immediately removed him from the school.[32]

Life at Brighton left 'a pleasant picture' in Winston's mind.[33] In a more relaxed, flexible atmosphere his school work improved out of all recognition. One term he even headed his form in classics. But life under the Misses Thomsons was not wholly lacking in high drama. Three months after his arrival, Winston was attacked by a fellow pupil after a minor quarrel over the use of a penknife. But no serious damage was done. Was Winston blameless? Not according to Lady Randolph, for he had provoked the ruction by boxing his classmate's ear. Clearly his general behaviour still left much to be desired. Under the subject 'Conduct', one report read: 'Number in Class, 30 . . . Position in Class, 30'.[34]

Like most schoolchildren separated from their families, Winston still called repeatedly for visits from his parents; or alternatively to be allowed to come home as often as possible. For the most part, his cries went unanswered. Lord Randolph, by now fully engaged in politics, would not modify his crowded timetable for the sake of his son. 'I cannot think why you did not come to see me, while you were in Brighton,' protested Winston, 'I was very disappointed but I suppose you were too busy to come.'[35] Winston's complaint typified his one-sided relationship with Lord Randolph. His efforts to draw closer to his father, to gain his confidence, to strike an intimate note, to relate to him in a warm and meaningful way, as a father and son should, were met by a blank wall of indifference that must have seemed incomprehensible to a young and impressionable child. No doubt, the more Winston felt rejected, the greater he felt the need to prove his worth in his father's eyes – a drive that burgeoned after Lord Randolph's death and that flowed over naturally into the mature Churchill's career. By nature a complex, idiosyncratic, and volatile character, Lord Randolph's last years were tormented by what was most probably syphilis.[36] All his short life Lord Randolph was to remain a remote, cold figure to Winston, not only physically but also, more importantly, emotionally. Deprived of the contact he craved for, Winston conjured up his own image of Lord Randolph, one that bordered on the fantastic, that evoked a great folk-hero destroyed by lesser mortals actuated by petty motives. Virtually unattainable in real life, Winston placed his father on the highest of pedestals from which it would be impossible to dislodge him.

Lady Randolph's record was better, but only marginally. She too did not shrink from scolding Winston whenever she felt there was just cause – which was often! But Winston felt more confident in her company, more ready to open up, to reveal his feelings. He would express himself to her in a jolly manner that was in total contrast to the stultified relationship he had formed with his father. 'Jack send[s] you his love and 6,666,666,666,666,666,666,666 kisses,' he wrote, adding, 'And I send you double.' But Lady Randolph's preoccupation with her social obligations led Winston to conclude that she had muddled her priorities.

In fact, her neglect of Winston was neither premeditated nor malicious, but stemmed simply from lack of concern, of forethought, as she sought amusing distractions in a society in which such behaviour was fairly typical. There was little Winston could do but to nurse his grievances, occasionally airing his pain in public. And, as usual, he could always rely on the good Mrs Everest for encouragement and sustenance.[37]

Parental neglect, for all the frustration and anguish it caused, also had some advantages. Was it not a spur to ambition, an excuse to seek attention, to succeed at any cost? As a young man, Churchill wrote in *The River War* that 'Solitary trees, if they grow at all, grow strong; and a boy deprived of his father's care often develops, if he escapes the perils of youth, an independence of vigour and thought which may restore in after life the heavy loss of early days.' Thirty-five years later, when a great man of affairs, he added 'that famous men are usually the product of an unhappy childhood. The stern compression of circumstances, the twinges of adversity, the spur of slights and taunts in early years, are needed to evoke that ruthless fixity of purpose and tenacious mother-wit without which great actions are seldom accomplished.'[38] Although writing of other famous men, Winston surely found inspiration in his own case-history.

Winston counted the days when he could come home for the holidays and share his adventures with his family, and of course Mrs Everest, by far his closest and most intimate confidante. But Lord and Lady Randolph Churchill were frequently elsewhere, riding hard their social-political merry-go-round. 'I have no doubt you will try your best to make me happy,' came Winston's plaintive cry after one disappointment. And no doubt they did, according to their own stiff terms of reference. But they never met Winston halfway. 'Home', more often than not, was transferred either to Blenheim or to a seaside resort, Cromer, or Ventnor on the Isle of Wight, where, to his disgust, a governess would inevitably intrude to curtail his freedom.[39]

At Blenheim, Winston was put in the charge of his grandmother 'Fanny', the dowager duchess of Marlborough.[40] This, too, was not always to his liking; nor to Mrs Everest's, who, owing to Blenheim's frightful draughts, condemned the palace as 'unhealthy' and hence unsuitable for her delicate ward. Winston's own misgivings stemmed no doubt from his mother's reservations, who regardless of her fairy-tale reception, never felt fully at ease at Blenheim. Day-to-day life was conducted in a most stilted manner, quite out of keeping with her own quicksilver temperament. After dinner, no one, however sleepy, 'dared suggest bed until the sacred hour of eleven had struck. Then we would all troop out into a small ante-room and, lighting our candles, each in turn would kiss the Duke and Duchess and depart to our own rooms.' Misunderstandings and family squabbles were unavoidable. 'The fact is I *loathe* living here,' Lady Randolph recorded in her diary. The 'dullness' of the Marlboroughs' domestic regime was tolerable, just about. But her

relations with Fanny were decidedly not. Fanny was a forceful character
and ruled Blenheim with her narrow, even prudish code of behaviour.
'At the rustle of her silk dress the household trembled,' noted Lady
Randolph.[41]

Over the years, though, Winston was to form a deep affection for
Blenheim. But, for the time being, he was most certainly out of tune
with his grandmother, the redoubtable Fanny, who jibbed at the prospect
of the Marlborough inheritance dropping into Winston's fidgety hands.
'Your first duty is to have a child', she instructed her daughter-in-law, the
ninth duchess Consuelo. 'And it must be a son,' she continued, 'because
it would be intolerable to have that little upstart Winston become Duke.
Are you in the family way?' she enquired hopefully.[42] As for Winston's
beautiful but 'rather stupid' aunt Bertha – a Victorian practical joker
in the worst possible taste, wont to mix small pieces of soap with the
cheese or leave ink-pots balanced precariously on the top of doors –
she might have fired his imagination but must equally have sapped his
confidence in a secure, trouble-free existence in her household, a fact of
life compounded by the quirky behaviour of his uncle George, the eighth
duke.[43]

In 1890 Winston's parents rented Banstead Manor, a racing-box some
three miles from Newmarket where they hosted parties and from where
Lord Randolph gratified his new-found fascination in the joys of the turf.
Banstead was very much to Winston's liking. The grounds were spacious
enough for riding ponies and shooting partridges, or vermin – 'We have
slaughtered many rabbits . . . [and] Tomorrow we slay the rats'; and
for the more homely pursuits, birdnesting, raising guinea pigs, puppies,
kittens, and chickens. There were also winter sports. A pond that iced
up – eight inches in January 1891 – allowed for skating. Altogether, it
was a place where Winston could give full rein to indulge his urge to
play 'the Boss' with little fear of adult criticism. 'An almost ideal
existence,' Winston described it.[44]

Lady Randolph confirmed Winston's opinion as she saw her sons
'happy as kings riding and shooting', and having great fun 'building
a house'. The house was in fact the 'Den', a moated stronghold,
complete with drawbridge and thatched roof and carpeted with straw,
that Winston planned and built with the aid of some of the estate
workers. Together with his henchmen – brother Jack, visiting cousins,
and sundry local boys – he fortified and defended it against attackers
real and imaginary. For Shane Leslie, one of Winston's conscripts, those
days remained firmly etched on his memory.

> Winston already showed signs of a commanding nature. In his army
> there were only two rules but they were strictly enforced on the
> cousins: firstly Winston was always General and secondly there was
> no promotion. Our chief occupation was digging out the moated 'Den'

> ... which Winston had designed in a foreseeing moment. There in the
> damp straw we were told to await the enemies of England. Our artillery
> consisted of an immense catapult which discharged unripe apples and
> once struck an inoffensive cow.[45]

Not everyone waxed enthusiastic about the virtues of the 'Den'.
Mrs Everest, for one, had her doubts, always tactfully phrased. 'My
darling Lamb, I have never heard anything about you for a whole week.
Are you well dear?' she wanted to know. 'I am so afraid you will get ill
in that horrid little Den – be sure & open the window & door every
time you go out.'[46]

She had sound reason for concern. Winston was considered to be a
most delicate child. Frail in build, he was particularly prone to chills
and colds. But his ailments extended to other areas. As a teenager he
contracted a strain that led, apparently, to a form of incipient hernia. His
teeth also gave him much trouble; while at the same time, no doubt to
his extreme embarrassment, he found himself having to wear spectacles
for fine work. Later he suffered a painful attack of 'horrid boils'. 'Don't
neglect yourself if you don't feel well darling,' pleaded Mrs Everest,
'a stitch in time saves ninety-nine,' entreating him to try 'some Eno's
fruit salt' or 'the juice of a lemon & a bit of sugar' to settle his liver.
Winston's most serious illness occurred at Brighton, where he had been
sent to improve his health. Aged eleven, in March 1886, he succumbed
to a severe bout of pneumonia, so severe in fact that his life hung in the
balance for several days.[47]

With his temperature at 104.3 and his right lung badly inflamed,
Dr Robson Roose had good cause to feel 'anxious'. Lord and Lady
Randolph rushed down to Brighton to be at his side. 'Your boy is
making a wonderful fight,' Dr Roose assured them, leaving them hope
but not concealing the desperate nature of Winston's condition. After
three anguished days, the immediate crisis had passed. Fearful of a
relapse, Dr Roose advised 'nourishment, the avoidance of chill, rest and
quiet'. Not even Mrs Everest was allowed to see him for fear of exciting
him unduly. But by July things were back to normal: Winston resumed
his riding – and put in a gentle appeal for 'a little cash' as he was again
'bankrupt'.[48]

Winston's seemingly delicate constitution was, apparently, the deter-
mining factor in his parents' decision to send him to Harrow to further
his education and not, as originally planned, to Winchester. Eton,
situated in the low-lying Thames Valley and subject to a damp,
unhealthy climate, was ruled out, despite it being for generations
the Churchill family's public school – a fact hidden from Winston
by his father.[49] Winston received this news with a sigh of relief, for
Winchester, with its notorious reputation for academic excellence, was
a daunting prospect for a student of Winston's modest stature, whatever

his potential. Not that he coped all that easily with Harrow's entrance examinations. In a famous passage from *My Early Life* he described his predicament when confronted with the hateful Latin paper. Apart from his name and 'a blot and several smudges', he added nothing, he wrote sadly, to classical scholarship. None of this made much difference. The necessary arrangements had long been made. In response to Lord Randolph's request, Dr Welldon, Harrow's headmaster, had already — in October 1887 — expressed his pleasure at Winston's imminent arrival, '& I hope I may be useful to him, when he is here'. The authorities at Harrow were rightly apprehensive at antagonizing so powerful and unpredictable a figure as Lord Randolph, and this no doubt accounts for the 'broad-minded view' Dr Welldon took of Winston's Latin exam, a possibly controversial decision made easier by Winston's comparative successes in 'Algebra and Euclid. And a very easy Arithmetic paper'. He longed for Harrow: 'it is such a nice place — beautiful view — beautiful situation — good swimming bath — a good Gymnasium — & a Carpentering shop & many other attractions'. In April 1888 he arrived at Harrow-on-the Hill, hopeful that his favourable impressions would stand the test of reality.[50]

2

Becoming Educated

Fourteen months before Winston entered Harrow, in December 1886, his father, then Chancellor of the Exchequer, had resigned from the Cabinet in circumstances that gave rise to intense speculation. At the time, Lord Randolph was the most talked-of politician in England. His rise to the top had been quick and spectacular. The Tory defeat in April 1880, allowing Gladstone to form his second administration, gave Lord Randolph and other Conservative malcontents their opportunity. As a key figure of a Conservative opposition ginger-group, the so-called 'Fourth Party' (the others being Sir Henry Drummond Wolff, John Gorst, and Arthur Balfour), he joined the attack on the Conservative 'Old Gang' – those '"bourgeois" placemen, "honourable" Tadpoles, hungry Tapers, Irish lawyers . . . third rate statesmen just good enough to fill subordinate posts while Lord Beaconsfield was alive.'[1]

Lord Randolph proved himself a most formidable parliamentarian. On the surface, he possessed few natural characteristics to cast him for such a role. With popping eyes, a lisp and the stature of a pugnacious bantam, he was quick and fertile in thought, the cutting phrase tripped easily from his rasping tongue. No one could guarantee his behaviour, least of all, apparently, himself. One moment he would turn on his irresistible charm, the next he would astonish his friends with his impetuous, sometimes brutal, conduct. Nor, when he was out of control, did his conversation – laced with a biting sarcasm – smooth his path.

In the long run, this was not the most reliable formula for a successful politician. For the moment, however, he was riding high on a tidal wave of success. Although not a natural orator (he carefully wrote out and learned his speeches by heart before delivering them – as Winston would do in the future), he drew enormous crowds by virtue of his unrestrained, vigorous style. Nicknamed as 'the Champagne Charlie of politics', he was considered the coming man in British politics, widely tipped as a potential Tory prime minister.

Over the previous few years the franchise had been greatly extended from one to almost four million voters and parliamentary seats redistributed, allowing greater expression to the densely populated urban areas. In addition the introduction of the secret ballot in 1872 ensured that new voters would eventually be free from the corrupt practices that had characterized so much of British politics in the past. In this fluid, yet promising, situation Lord Randolph took up the Tory bid. With two others, he founded the Primrose League, a device for spreading the Tory gospel, and in particular Lord Randolph's version of it, among the newly enfranchised voters. Lady Randolph also joined in the fray as a Dame (number eleven) of the League, and even little Winston contributed his services to the cause.

Lord Randolph's Tory gospel was encapsulated in the slogan: Tory Democracy. And 'What is Tory Democracy?' a puzzled Wilfred Scawen Blunt asked Lord Randolph 'To tell you truth I don't know myself,' replied Lord Randolph, 'But I believe it is principally opportunism.' Lord Randolph's group spent its time probing the opposition's lines for weak points, only to draw back in the face of resistance. He displayed an admirable flexibility in his scouting the enemy positions for profitable political views. For a while he dallied with Fair Trade before abandoning it for the safer dogma of Free Trade. Generally assumed to be flirting with Irish Home Rule, he finally took the opposite stance, coining the slogan 'Ulster will fight, Ulster will be right', Lord Randolph was not always as consistent in his views as he liked others to imagine.

Still, his down-to-earth populist message rang out loud and clear. 'Trust the people,' he cried at Birmingham, 'trust the people and they will trust you . . . I have no fear of democracy.' In 1886 he elaborated a broad vision of economic, social, and financial reform, while he later claimed that he had orchestrated 'a complete change' in Britain's foreign policy.

In terms of public opinion his sparkling performances had a brilliant effect,[2] cutting into the Liberal-Radical vote and refurbishing the Tory image. For many Conservatives they had a dangerously subversive ring. To argue that the newly enfranchised urban working masses – almost by definition the sworn enemy of the ruling class – were in fact stable elements upon which the established parties might rest securely was indeed a revolutionary and far-sighted doctrine. In return, of course, the Conservatives would have to concede enough social and economic legislation to procure this strange alliance. Lord Randolph sensed that his party had to take this path if it were to prosper.[3]

Although his party leaders, Salisbury and Northcote, regarded him as something of a tub-thumper, an arriviste whose rantings compromised Tory orthodoxy, they could no longer ignore his huge popularity among the rank and file. He was given his due, first as Secretary of State for

India, and then, in 1886, as Leader of the House and Chancellor of the Exchequer in Salisbury's second Cabinet. Four months later he resigned. He had proved a most awkward colleague: domineering, haughty, self-opinionated. The final break came over the war estimates. He insisted on cuts. Ensnared by his own impetuosity, Lord Randolph could either have backed down or made good his threat. He resigned. He had gravely miscalculated. There was to be no turning back. Only thirty-seven years old, he had destroyed his political career by his own hand. It had terminated on as dramatic a note as it had begun.

By any reckoning, Lord Randolph's behaviour was bizarre, characterized by an over-bearing, aggressive self-confidence that had lost touch with reality. Queen Victoria thought him 'mad and odd' – and 'in bad health'. Lord Rosebery, who knew him well, regarded him as one of those 'tense spirits to be unduly elated and unduly depressed', espying in him a tinge of 'the eccentric, the petulant, and the unexpected'. Easily irritated, he would lash out ferociously at those who provoked him, signalling, thought Rosebery, 'a mind unbalanced and almost unhinged'. Lord Randolph spoke openly, almost light-heartedly, of his early death. Asked how long his leadership (of the House of Commons) would last, he replied: 'Oh, about six months!' 'And then?' 'And then? Why Westminster Abbey.'[4]

Lord Randolph was in fact terminally ill. It is practically certain that he was suffering from tertiary syphilis. His doctors, including a specialist in venereal diseases, certainly believed that his frequent breakdowns, his erratic, tempestuous behaviour resulted from the unremitting advance of the fatal disease, and treated him accordingly. So too did Lady Randolph. Just before Lord Randolph's death, she wrote to her sister: 'Up to now the General Public and even Society does not know the real truth & after all my sacrifice and misery of these six months it would be hard if it got out. It would do incalculable harm to his political reputation and memory.'[5]

Lord Randolph's remaining years were mainly devoted to travel, gambling on business ventures, and pursuing his racing interests. He stayed in politics, but his physical and mental decline were apparent to all. Spasms of violence were followed by displays of good temper. His orations lost their magic. Rambling of speech, clutching his notes with trembling hands, he stumbled from one sad performance to another. For his friends, such as Lord Rosebery, 'it was one long pain – pain of watching and listening, pain of thick and almost unintelligible delivery ... it was a waking nightmare' as 'he died by inches in public'.[6] He succumbed finally in January 1895.

The collapse of Lord Randolph's political career coincided with a mounting crisis in his personal affairs. After ten years, the Churchills' marriage had virtually broken down. Although not living apart, they were living practically separate lives. It is not clear exactly when Lady Randolph first learned of her husband's condition,[7] but she must have suspected for some time that all was not well. Her knowledge, or suspicions, coupled with Lord Randolph's inherent rudeness and short temper – considerably sharpened by his illness – must have put normal marital relations at a very low premium. Nor was Lady Randolph, by temperament, given to a policy of wait-and-see. Attractive to and attracted by men, she sought compensation elsewhere. She took lovers, the most serious of them being a friend of her husband's, Count Charles Rudolph Ferdinand Andreas Kinsky, an Austrian diplomat on service in London. Lady Randolph's 'Austrian alliance' was an open secret in society, even to Winston who once caught them breakfasting together, and towards whom Kinsky behaved like a benevolent uncle, sending him stamps and taking him on outings.[8]

The Churchills' marriage was swept along on an undercurrent of tension. Not only were Lady Randolph's affairs common knowledge, but also Lord Randolph's habit of taking long holidays in the company of his men friends fostered scandalous insinuations. Eye witnesses reported Lord Randolph as 'inclined to abuse his wife'. Stormy scenes, not always in private, gave rise to speculation. Rumours of a separation, or divorce, circulated the clubs and drawing-rooms of London, and were noted by inquisitive journalists. None the less the marriage survived, and Lady Randolph's touching devotion to her husband's welfare during his fast declining last years never flagged.[9]

Winston must have been aware of these political and domestic squalls, gusting, as they did occasionally, quite violently. He 'read every word [his father] spoke and what the newspapers said about him'. Fiercely partisan, he would stoutly defend him. He followed intently his rise to power, rejoicing in his electoral victories and triumphant speeches. Naturally, he refused to accept the fact that his father's star had fallen, and eagerly awaited Lord Randolph's 'reconquest of power'. Alas, the hope was little more than a pipe-dream. But Lady Randolph had no doubt who was to blame, and Winston followed suit. The Conservative Party leadership, the 'Old Gang', had revealed themselves in their true colours: mean-spirited creatures intent on preserving their own position to the exclusion of all else, unwilling to grasp the true significance of Tory Democracy for the revival of Tory fortunes. For Winston, his father, although 'small', would always be 'a great man'.[10]

In April 1888 Winston arrived at Harrow to spend the next four and a half years there. Eton being Tory, the great Whig families sent *their* sons to be educated at Harrow – Lord Randolph Churchill now conspicuously joining their ranks. At the first opportunity Dr Welldon moved Winston to his own house, from where he could keep a closer eye on his new charge's progress. Winston's performance as a scholar remained low key: nothing sensational, but not so undistinguished as popularly imagined. Once again, his phenomenal memory proved an enormous boon, allowing him, after only three months at Harrow, to bag an open school prize for reciting by heart 1200 lines from Macaulay's *Lays of Ancient Rome*. He was also most fortunate in three of his masters: Robert Somervell, who taught him 'the essential structure of the ordinary British sentence'; Charles Mayo, who led Winston, with some success, through the 'hopeless bog' of mathematics; and Louis Moriarty, who guided him, ultimately successfully, through his army class, and from whom he acquired 'the taste for history'. Dr Welldon coached Winston privately to improve his classical studies – though with less success, except in adding to Winston's anxieties.[11]

Still, Winston never rose above the Lower School. This was due mainly to his passing into the Army Class in September 1889. Winston's military tendencies had long been noticed. His first letter records his pleasure at receiving those 'beautiful presents' of 'Soldiers and Flags and Castle', the beginning of a magnificent collection of toy soldiers. Lord Randolph, impressed at Winston's skill in manoeuvring his division of 1,500 lead warriors, had concluded that his son's talents were more in keeping with an army career, as they were clearly not consistent with the more rigid intellectual requirements of the Bar. And Winston had agreed immediately, though some time later he did wonder briefly whether the Church might have suited him better. Henceforth, all his scholastic efforts were directed towards obtaining a place at Sandhurst.[12]

Winston never excelled at ordinary ball games, but took more easily to swimming – representing his house – and rifle-shooting; and in particular to fencing, winning in 1892 the public school championship, Harrow's only success, his performance being highly lauded for its 'quick and dashing attack'.[13] These exercises gave ample scope for his already manifest individualism, a triumph of self-reliance over reliance upon others.

Winston was a solitary figure at Harrow. Richard Meinertzhagen remembered him as a lonely, red-haired boy, 'usually walking by himself', whose face registered 'resentment and pride'. 'Uncouth, reserved ... precocious, bumptious, and talkative', Winston was little understood but respected; and definitely not someone to take liberties with. Meinertzhagen recalled how he had been edged into the gutter by Winston in a game of 'pavement-walking chicken'. Despite his lisp and a strange rattling noise that emanated from his throat, he was argumentative to an extreme. Once, as a junior and against all the rules, he intervened in a house debate to carry all before him 'with a magnificent speech'. Sometimes his antics boomeranged. Once a crowd of Harrovian bullies shoved Winston head-first into a fold-up bed, douching him with mixtures of hot and cold water. Rescued by a master, Winston emerged unpenitent and, parading up and down the dormitory, gave voice to his wrath, roaring that 'one day he would be a great man when they were nobodies and he would stamp and crush them!'

A strange, even eccentric figure, he seemed to lack the popular touch. He had one true friend: Jack Milbanke (later tenth baronet). Winston thought he had exceptional 'style and manner', in contrast to his own bumbling ways, and envied the manly bond Milbanke forged with Lord Randolph when they all met – a relationship that sadly eluded Winston all his life. What Lord Randolph thought of Milbanke went unrecorded, but Lady Randolph believed Winston's 'greatest friend' to be rather 'dull and stupid'. Winston never quite fitted into Harrow life. But for the protection afforded him by his cousin, Dudley Majoribanks (later Lord Tweedmouth), who 'fathered him', it was noted, he would have had a much stiffer time.[14]

The highest Winston climbed in the school hierarchy was to become Head of Fags for his House. More to his taste were his first essays in journalism, written for the *Harrovian* under the pseudonyms 'Junius Junior', 'De Profundis', and 'Truth'. In them he set out to expose the shortcomings in the school's administration, suggesting that 'something was rotten in the State of Denmark'. Despite it being heavily blue-pencilled by the editor, Leo Amery, it – and similar articles – were considered sufficiently seditious to rouse the ire of Dr Welldon. Summoning Winston to his study, he clarified the situation: 'As articles in the *Harrovian* are anonymous, I shall not dream of inquiring who wrote them. But if any more of the same character appear it may be my painful duty to swish you.'[15]

This flouting of authority was typical. At St George's 'dreadful legends' were told about Winston whose 'naughtiness appeared to have surpassed anything'. At Harrow he continued in the same vein. He was put under a master he 'hated & who returned that hate', with predictable consequences. Having once been 'whopped' by the head of school, Nugent Hicks (later Bishop of Lincoln), for whom he fagged, he told his chastiser: 'I shall be a greater man than you,' and promptly received another two strokes for his cheek. He was caught vandalizing factory windows and on this occasion Dr Welldon exacted his 'swishing'.[16]

On the whole, Lady Randolph found Winston's behaviour frivolous and exasperating. 'Dearest Winston,' she pleaded, 'do give up smoking. If you only knew how foolish and silly you look doing it'. Not only did he write 'in a pompous style', he was also in danger of turning into 'a prig'. 'Write!' she commanded him, 'You are a lazy little wretch!' She disapproved of the 'fitful inharmonious way' he went about his school work but was not above bribery. 'Work hard this term to pass yr preliminary [examination for Sandhurst], [and] I will get Papa to get you a gun and pony – & perhaps next season there will something to shoot at Banstead.' Winston paid his due and passed his 'preliminary', and the following summer, in 1891, the bribe was paid.[17]

Winston's scholastic success certainly surprised his parents, and surpassed even his own expectations. Out of twenty-nine candidates from Harrow, only twelve passed in all subjects, Winston among them. He outclassed his cousin, Dudley Majoribanks: 'Vive la joie,' he rejoiced. But Winston was still far from realizing his first house-master's verdict that 'as far as ability goes he ought to be at the top of his form'. However, it was undeniable that he had made considerable progress since his first gloomy days at Harrow.[18]

Winston possessed qualities that eluded his parents but not others. Sir Felix Seman, an eminent throat specialist whom Winston had consulted in the hope of finding a cure for his speech impediment, was quite categorical: 'I have just seen the most extraordinary young man I have ever met'. Semon concluded that there was nothing organically wrong with Winston. All he needed was to practise and persevere. He did. Over and over again, in the hope that he would master his lisp, he would repeat such tricky sayings as, 'The Spanish ships I cannot see for they are not in sight.'[19]

What Winston really needed, Lady Randolph hinted to her husband, was a man's hand, firm yet sympathetic. But Lord Randolph's disposition rendered him quite unsuitable for such a role. True, he radiated authority, but he did so in the most alarming manner. A stereotype of the Victorian father, Lord Randolph did not encourage familiarity. His nephew remembered him 'standing immobile by the fireplace, bearded and silent, a cause for trembling for all who passed'. Only once had Lord Randolph spontaneously opened his heart to Winston. 'Do remember things do not always go right with me,' he confessed, 'My every action is misjudged and every word distorted . . . So make some allowances.' An isolated incident, there were to be no other moments of such intimacy.[20]

Lacking faith in Winston's ability, Lord Randolph was incapable of giving him encouragement: instead there were sharp reprimands coupled with a perverse refusal to put things into perspective. Whatever Winston did it was never enough to satisfy his father's exalted standards. Naturally, as guardian of the family purse he joined in the strident protests about Winston's extravagances – though here he was on firmer ground as even the caring Mrs Everest thought fit to add her protest. The most trivial incident would be inflated to a crisis of major proportions. Lord Randolph chided Winston endlessly. A month before Winston was due to go to Sandhurst, he berated his wayward son's 'slovenly, happy-go-lucky harum scarum style of work', warning him that

I shall leave you to depend on yourself giving you merely such assistance as may be necessary to permit of a respectable life. Because I am certain that if you cannot prevent yourself from leading the idle useless unprofitable life you have had during your schooldays & later months, you will become a mere social wastrel one of the hundreds of the public school failures, and you will degenerate into a shabby unhappy & futile existence. If that is so you will have to bear all the blame for such misfortunes yourself.[21]

These censures pursued Winston to Sandhurst. When he damaged, purely by accident, a watch Lord Randolph had given him, the reaction was fierce and against all natural reason. The timepiece had fallen into a deep pool. Winston made phenomenal efforts to retrieve it. He dived in, but the freezing water soon drove him out. He then had the pool dredged, but with no result. Undeterred, he conscripted twenty-three cadets (costing him over £3), dug a new course for the stream, called up a fire-engine to pump the pool dry, and so recovered the wretched watch. In fact, he had exhibited admirable qualities of courage and perseverance. None of this had the slightest effect on Lord Randolph. Winston remained 'a young stupid' and definitely 'not to be trusted'.[22]

With the tension in his parents' marriage, Lord Randolph's fiery and explosive swings of mood, Lady Randolph's instinctive propensity for socializing on a grand scale, Winston felt deeply the lack of parental support. When in desperate need he would approach Lady Randolph. There is something unbearably sad in this seventeen-year-old's appeal to her after one contretemps.

Darling Mummy, do attend to my letter. I am so wretched. Even now I weep. Please my darling Mummy be kind to your loving son. Don't let my silly letters make you angry. Let me at least think that you love me – Darling Mummy I despair. I am so wretched. I don't know what to do. Don't be angry. I am so miserable.[23]

Winston no doubt carefully phrased his plea to squeeze the maximum of concessions out of Lady Randolph; yet for all that, his words betray deeper sentiments.

Visits from his parents were rare. Instead, breaking all the rules, he flaunted Mrs Everest – wearing an old poke-bonnet, her figure already of ample proportions – before his fellow Harrovians. Winston showed her all over the school, and, in a bold display of moral courage, paraded with her, arm-in-arm, up the High Street, ridiculed by some jeering boys as they went, kissing her good-bye in public. It was a noble gesture, but one that earned him little credit at the time. As most boys hesitated even before inviting their mothers to visit them, Winston's odd conduct only confirmed his schoolboy reputation as a misfit.[24]

He stood out as different. Undisciplined and insolent and indifferent to the accepted norms of school behaviour, he perhaps deliberately exaggerated his unconventional ways to force attention upon himself. At Harrow they left him strictly alone. In all his voluminous writings Winston singles out only one friend for special mention, Jack Milbanke, who was later killed on Scimitar Hill at Gallipoli. Moreover, his health was always suspect, another hurdle for him to surmount. Only weeks after entering Sandhurst he was told that he did not have a strong heart. 'I am cursed with so feeble a body, that I can hardly support the fatigues of the day,' he cried out in despair.[25]

By the normal, accepted standards of English public school life, Winston had little to contribute. It was a day-to-day existence full of frustration and tension. Held in low esteem by his family; criticized by his masters for his 'forgetfulness, carelessness, unpunctuality, and irregularity in every way'; regarded by his schoolmates as an awkward, outlandish character who behaved and spoke peculiarly, Winston deliberately set out to conquer their respect – and by so doing to repair his own badly dented self-image. He would stretch the school rules to breaking point, or casually perform the most foolhardy, daring acts, executing feats of juvenile heroism. On two occasions he almost lost his life playing the daredevil. Once, in a game of tag, he jumped off a 'rustic bridge' in a desperate attempt to evade capture, clutched at a fir tree, missed, fell twenty-nine feet, ruptured his kidney, and regained consciousness three days later. On the second occasion, in a boating and swimming incident on Lake Lausanne, he saw 'Death' close up, nearer than he had ever seen it before.[26]

He had a ready explanation for his foolhardiness. He sought, in a deliberate, calculated way, a reputation for courage. At school, he admitted to being 'in many ways a coward'. One humiliating experience cut deeply. Frightened by his school-mates aiming cricket balls at him, he had run away to hide behind some trees. Shamed by his 'cowardice', he resolved it would never occur again. Not endowed with the physical attributes of a traditional hero, he forced himself into the role. 'There is no ambition I cherish so keenly as to gain a reputation of personal courage,' he cried. Apparently, no price was too high to pay. 'Are you desirous of a reputation for courage?' asked his fictional hero, Savrola, who replied: 'You must risk your life.' He translated his fiction into real life. 'I rode my pony all along the skirmish line where everyone else was lying down in cover,' he wrote from the North-West frontier in India. Braving physical dangers was of supreme importance, but he was no less determined to demonstrate his moral courage – his flaunting Mrs Everest around Harrow is a case in point. Churchill was not content simply to act courageously: his courage had to be seen and acclaimed by all. 'Foolish perhaps,' Winston later admitted, 'but I play for high stakes and given an audience there is no act too daring or too noble. Without the gallery things are different.'[27]

Whatever he did, consciously or otherwise, he called attention to himself. And so it remained throughout his life. No matter what calling he pursued he sought the limelight. He would not pass unnoticed in the world. If he avoided doing 'unusual things', he reasoned, he would remain 'an average person'.[28]

Winston left Harrow with few regrets. Only later did he come to regard Harrow as an asset, and then mainly as a weapon to beat its rivals. Asked, in July 1940, how the public schools were getting on, he replied: 'Much as usual, Harrow has Amery, Gort and myself, Eton has the King of the Belgians and Captain Ramsey, and Winchester has Oswald Mosley to their credit.'[29] Or when, to roars of laughter, he offered to translate Latin expressions 'for the benefit of any old Etonians present' in the House of Commons. In the meantime, he was 'all for the Public Schools', but he did not want to repeat the experience again. In December 1892 Winston was seen departing from Harrow in haste, without the customary 'Leaving Breakfast', driving off alone to the railway station by cab, eager to shake loose the arbitrary restrictions imposed upon him by those designated to educate him.[30]

Winston passed into Sandhurst on the third attempt. After two failures, he was sent to the most successful of the 'crammers', an establishment run by Captain Walter Henry James in Lexham Gardens in Earls Court. It was whispered that only 'congenital idiots' failed to respond to Captain James's expert guidance who knew with 'almost Papal infallibility' the kind of questions likely to be asked. The good captain lived up to his reputation, even though his first impression of Winston was none too flattering: 'That lad couldn't have gone through Harrow, he must have gone under it.' Still, by the following August, he had successfully steered Winston through the ordeal. His results were sufficient to grant him a cavalry cadetship, but were eighteen marks short for a place in the infantry. Latin let him down badly. Otherwise his results were more than respectable, and he did outstandingly well in history, coming out top of his year.[31]

Lord Randolph had earmarked Winston for the 60th Rifles, a most prestigious regiment of the line, not only because cavalry cadets were 'always 2nd rate performers' but also because of the extra cost involved, an estimated £200. His response to the news was therefore almost hysterical. As it turned out he had raised a great pother about nothing. Winston was ultimately accepted for an infantry cadetship, moving up in the list as other, more successful candidates than he dropped out. Lord Randolph was pleased, if not fully assuaged, if only for the saving it made him. This raised the irksome question of Winston's allowance. Winston's spendthrift ways were beyond repair. No censure, however biting, put a stop to them. He would mortgage his allowance, patronize pawnbrokers, attract the attention of money-lenders, all in a vain attempt to stem the relentless drain on his purse. His parents were incapable of offering a solution. 'I am rather X,' grumbled Lady Randolph, going through the motions, 'all the same you fleece me!' Thwarted at home, Winston found a degree of solvency elsewhere. Sensing his predicament, Lady Wilton, a friend of the family, would regularly sent him £2 to boost his spirits. Of a generous nature, she sustained Winston in other, no less important ways, inviting him to spend his holidays at her homes near Windsor and in the south of France, and signing herself as 'Yr very affecte Deputy Mother'. Eventually, the dowager duchess Fanny stepped in and made him an allowance of £20 a month, alleviating Winston's chronic dearth of funds but not solving it.[32]

For the time being Lord Randolph promised a grant of £10 a month, pledging also to cover his tailor and haberdasher bills.[33] Winston found the work at Sandhurst congenial and 'extremely practical. Shot and shell of all kinds – bridges, guns, field and siege, mapping, keeping regimental savings bank accounts', and all that apart from the drill and parades. Absorbing work, but extremely fatiguing. So much so that he could hardly support the exertions of the day. He cursed his feeble body. Standing five feet six-and-a-half inches tall, his chest measuring thirty-one inches – swelling when required to another two-and-a-half inches – he did not meet Sandhurst requirements. Unless he could improve on his chest measurements, there was a real danger that his commission would be withheld. This did not occur. Gradually Winston adapted himself to the rigorous life. The day began at six o'clock with reveille and did not end until 'lights out' at eleven. In between there was hardly a free moment. The cadets attended lectures on tactics or fortifications; conducted drill and physical exercises; participated in mock battles; learned about the intricacies of army accounts; strengthened their bodies through gymnastics or on the sports field; and relaxed in the evening in idle chatter or reading, a game of whist or billiards, or even a communal sing-song. Through perseverance he survived these trials, his physical disadvantages overcome by sustained effort.[34]

Of all the diversions offered at Sandhurst, riding was the one he most enjoyed. Despite his father's ruling, he still had his eye on the cavalry. He had approached Colonel John Palmer Brabazon, commander of the 4th Hussars, a friend of the Churchill family, setting out the most telling reasons in favour of his joining a cavalry regiment. Lady Randolph was sympathetic, but Lord Randolph (who was unaware of his son's manoeuvring) would not hear of it. He positively declined to pay for any horses – and as if for good measure refused Winston 'unrestricted leave', allowing him to come up to London only when Lady Randolph was in town. His decision was irrevocable. Winston was not put off.

In any case, all cadets, infantry and cavalry, received riding training. But he went much further. Much of his allowance was spent on hiring horses at the local livery stables. And he moved in a circle of like-minded cadets who bent the rules and indulged in polo and fox-hunting, pony racing and point-to-point meetings, all forbidden at Sandhurst. Polo was Winston's particular favourite, but he also thought fox-hunting a most 'admirable and elevating sport'.[35]

The topics taught at Sandhurst suited Winston's style. 'Tactics', 'Fortification', 'Musketry', 'Riding', even, apparently, 'Military Administration' were to his liking. His teachers' main complaint was his chronic unpunctuality, a quirk he developed to a fine art in later years. At any rate, Winston applied himself. When he passed out at Sandhurst he came twentieth out of a class of 130, a most creditable performance. True, he developed early on a somewhat cavalier approach to questions of high strategy – a bias that was destined to cost him dear. It was just 'a matter of commonsense', he concluded. 'Put all the elements of a strategical problem before a clear-headed civilian of first-rate ability and enough imagination and he would come to the right solution.' There can be little doubt whom he had in mind.[36]

Winston blossomed in other ways. At Sandhurst he discovered a camaraderie that he had not encountered elsewhere. He made 'lots of friends'. Never embarrassed at playing to the gallery, he made the most of any chance offered him. An opportunity arose with a Mrs Laura Ormiston Chant, assistant manager of a private lunatic asylum, who led a 'Purity Campaign' to clean up the more sordid spots of London. She focused her crusade on the Empire Theatre, Leicester Square, or rather its bar behind the dress circle. It was here that the worthy Mrs Chant spotted young ladies of the night on the prowl. She had canvas screens erected to isolate the offending area from the attention of genuine theatre lovers.

Winston was outraged that prudes of Mrs Chant's ilk could thus challenge ancient liberties, and the Saturday evening after the screens had been put up, they were torn down in a burst of spontaneous anger by the two or three hundred young bloods present, including Winston's Sandhurst contingent and a number of university students. Appearing out of the débris, Winston addressed the victorious mob. It was his first public speech. For the first time he heard 'rapturous applause' greet his words. Did you see the papers? he asked Jack. 'It was I who led the rioters.' The Bishop of London put it differently: 'I never expected to see the heir of Marlborough being greeted by a flourish of strumpets.'[37]

On 2 November 1894, the day before Winston assaulted the barricades, he had written to Lady Randolph informing her that he had learned the truth about his father's illness. Dr Roose held nothing back, showing Winston the medical reports. Winston had previously no conception of Lord Randolph's critical condition. Shocked and anxious, he pleaded with his mother, 'Do, my darling mamma when you write let me know *exactly* what you think.' When he wrote this letter his parents were on their way from Burma to India. That June, against his doctor's advice, Lord and Lady Randolph had left England for a world tour, hoping to at least arrest the progress of the disease. But his health deteriorated rapidly. Apathetic and violent by turn, abusing his valets, his lower jaw partially paralysed, his speech garbled, his gait staggering and uncertain, it was no longer fitting that he be seen in society. Lord Randolph was hurried back to London. His life was flickering out. After a month, 'lingering pitifully', he died on 24 January 1895, a tragic figure, famous to the world but virtually unknown to his son. Thirty-five years later, Churchill wrote: 'All my dreams of comradeship with him, of entering Parliament at his side and in his support, were ended. There remained for me only to pursue his aims and vindicate his memory.'[38]

For the previous year calmer relations had prevailed between father and son. They went together on social outings, to the Empire Theatre, where Lord Randolph enjoyed the jugglers and acrobats. When home, Winston was allowed to sit in at luncheon or dinner where he would meet some of the leading political figures of the day – Arthur Balfour, Joseph Chamberlain, Lord Rosebery, or Henry Asquith. Occasionally, there were 'political parties' at Tring Park in the vale of Aylesbury, the country estate of Lord Randolph's banker, Lord ('Natty') Rothschild, where Winston was introduced to the up-and-coming men of the Conservative party. 'He has much smartened up,' thought Lord Randolph, 'and he has got steadier. The people at Tring took a great deal of notice of him but [he] was very quiet & nice-mannered. Sandhurst has done wonders for him.'[39]

In retrospect, Churchill detected the seeds of 'an Entente' forming, with 'an alliance or at least a military agreement' not inconceivable. But despite Winston's improved manners, Lord Randolph still shut him out from his political life, and any attempt by Winston to enter it was met by a frosty reception. In fact, nothing had changed.[40]

The grim reality of Lord Randolph's death profoundly affected Winston, more perhaps than the death of a father normally inflicts upon a son. The tragic story of his father's meteoric rise and fall from power was deeply engraved upon his mind. But it was a tale with twists of its own. Here was a man of superlative gifts who, according to Churchillian folklore, was hounded out of politics by second-rate, inferior men. Winston truly believed this version of events.[41] His was not an idle vow to 'vindicate' his father's memory. But he might equally have added that by so doing he would also 'vindicate' himself, finally and irrevocably, for a dutiful son could perform no greater service for his father than to redeem his squandered inheritance. By his own deeds he would force his father into the 'alliance' that he dreamed of. He had fashioned his own idealized image of Lord Randolph. Now, he was pledged to shape his own career in that image.

But there were other, more immediate, consequences. Lord Randolph's untimely death also liberated Winston from his father's tyrannical grip. In his own fashion, Lord Randolph no doubt loved Winston. But his love was qualified, conditional, contingent upon his own, too often irrational, expectations. Winston hardly ever lived up to these stringent requirements. Lord Randolph was wont to compare Winston, unfavourably of course, with Jack, his younger brother. Certainly Jack, of more amiable and pliant a temperament, was less of a handful.[42] Compared with Winston, he demanded far less attention, a commodity in scarce supply in the Churchill household. Winston, always likely to charge off in any direction, had to be held on a very tight rein. Clearly Lord Randolph was blind to any other alternative.

Lord Randolph's death allowed Winston to go his own way. 'I was now in the main the master of my fortunes,' he remarked.[43] His relationship with his mother took a fresh course. His new-found independence did not allow for excessive parental control. Nor was Lady Randolph anxious to govern in the old way. She too had inherited a new lease of freedom. Forty years old, still attractive and fascinating, she would continue to extract the maximum of pleasure from life. Her interest in Winston did not diminish. In some ways, it became more marked. She became his 'ardent ally', shamelessly exploiting her extensive contacts in society to further his career. Winston put it best: 'In my interest she left no wire unpulled, no stone unturned, no cutlet uncooked.'[44]

Of equally extravagant dispositions, Winston and Lady Randolph spent much of their time arranging and re-arranging their straitened financial circumstances, attempting to square a lavish standard of living with a considerably reduced income. For some years the Randolph Churchills had been living well beyond their means. They had been compelled to give up Banstead and, to effect even greater economies, they had evacuated their own home in Connaught Place, to share quarters with Lord Randolph's mother, Fanny. Lord Randolph's death brought them no substantial improvement. Although, owing to some lucrative South African investments, he left almost £76,000, this impressive sum was practically wiped out by his debts – £66,902 – to the Rothschilds. Nor was much left from Lady Randolph's private income. By their own exorbitant standards, they were living on a shoestring. Naturally, this caused some tension. But the positions were now reversed, with Winston chiding his mother for needless expenditures. 'We worked together on even terms,' he noted contentedly, 'more like brother and sister than mother and son.'[45]

Six months after Lord Randolph's demise Mrs Everest died of peritonitis, at the home of her relatives in one of the poorer districts of London. Almost two years earlier, when the Churchills moved in with Fanny, she had been unceremoniously discharged from service and sent packing elsewhere. Although the duchess had taken this initiative in the name of economy, Lord and Lady Randolph had meekly acquiesced. Winston was outraged. She was his 'dearest and most intimate friend'. He protested strongly, but to no avail. Alone in his adult world, Elizabeth Everest loved him with a touching spontaneous warmth. 'My poor sweet old precious lamb,' she would write, 'how I am longing for a hug – although you are not perfect I do love you so very much',[46] sweet words that were alien to his parents' style. She willingly gave Winston an emotional outlet that he found with no one else.

Whenever his own circumstances allowed it, he had sent her some money to ease her enforced retirement. The moment he heard Mrs Everest was critically ill, he hastened to her bedside. He spared no effort. He consulted the family doctor and engaged a nurse; but it was too late. Elizabeth Everest sank into a coma and died on 3 July. Winston went ahead with all the necessary arrangements. He ordered wreaths (also for Lady Randolph, who did not attend the funeral), a headstone – in his and Jack's names – and for many years afterwards paid for the upkeep of the grave. In later years, a portrait of 'Woom' adorned his study. 'She was so much to me in many ways,' he mourned, 'more than I had realized.'[47]

'Another link with the past gone', Winston reflected, immediately after the funeral.[48] The deaths of Lord Randolph and Elizabeth Everest released him from the last ties with his childhood. Winston was twenty-years old. Free at last to satisfy his giant ambitions in his own way, he was determined to make good in the army, if only as a gateway to first vindicating his father's place in history.

3

In Pursuit of Fame

Churchill's army career was little more than a breathing space before he got down to the real business of his life: politics. For much of the five years he held the Queen's commission he was darting about the world doing more interesting things than soldiering, exploring battlefields in remote corners of the Empire, dabbling in journalism, creating for himself a reputation as a war-correspondent – or even any kind of reputation. Consumed by the premonition of an early death, he was impatient to make his mark. But all for an express purpose. After only two years in uniform he had already seen 'three sharp skirmishes' and had been '10 complete times under fire'. 'Quite a foundation for a political life,' he thought.[1]

Churchill might have taken his chances in politics immediately after his father's death. He was inhibited from doing so mainly from lack of money, making a political career in those days out of the question. Lady Randolph was of no use here. Before long she herself was to become hopelessly enmeshed in financial mishaps – to such a degree that she had to seek Churchill's aid! Churchill would have to make his own way, by journalism and writing books and lecturing. Here was a further incentive to his feverish quest for action at any price.

He was also embarrassed by his lack of a formal university education. This rankled deeply. He believed it put him at a grave disadvantage. Sophisticates of the ancient universities ruled the political world he hoped to enter. He had met them at the Rothschilds and over his father's dinner-table, classicists and political economists, even philosophers, historical data or apposite quotations tripping easily from their lips as they resolved the great issues of the day.[2] Churchill craved 'a liberal education', certain that as a result his raw, untrained mind would receive 'that polish which for instance Oxford or Cambridge gives'. No sooner had he joined his regiment at Aldershot than he wanted to tackle economics or modern history, under Captain James's supervision. 'The more of I see of soldiering – the more I like it,' he wrote to Lady

Randolph in August 1895, after seven months with the 4th Hussars, 'but the more I feel convinced that it is not my *métier*.' Meanwhile, he declined to rush forward precipitately. 'It is a fine game – the game of politics – and it is well worth waiting for a good hand – before really plunging.'[3]

Colonel Brabazon commanded Churchill's cavalry regiment. An Irish landlord of few means, an intimate of the Prince of Wales, his dandified airs and graces, coupled with his inability to pronounce the letter 'r', inspired a fund of pleasing stories. 'Where is the London twain?' he enquired of the station-master at Aldershot. 'It is gone, Colonel.' 'Gone! Bwing another.' He took readily to Churchill.[4]

As a cavalry officer Churchill's life at Aldershot was dominated by horses. He would spend eight hours a day in the saddle training, two hours on stable duties, and then, 'indefatigably', on to polo. There was also horse racing. One such event – the 4th Hussars Subaltern's Challenge Cup involved him in a great scandal. The result had been a considerable upset. A rank outsider, Surefoot at 6–1, took the Cup, while the favourite had trailed in second; Churchill, riding a friend's horse, had crossed the line third. Almost a year later, owing to 'certain irregularities', Surefoot's 'victory' was declared 'null and void' by the stewards of the National Hunt Committee. They did not elaborate. But Henry du Pré Labouchère, a Liberal MP and journalist, picked up the story. Had a 'ringer' been substituted for Surefoot? he asked, suggesting that it had – and implying that the switch had been made with the full knowledge of the subaltern-jockeys. A rigged race! No more damning accusation could be levelled against officers and gentlemen in a land where the pleasures of the turf were held in such high regard.

While this damaging affair was breaking, Churchill's name was mentioned in connection with yet more scandal. Apparently Churchill and his cronies had decided that a candidate for their regiment, a second lieutenant Alan Bruce, was unsuited to join their ranks. After having feasted their prey at the Nimrod Club in London, Churchill, acting as group spokesman, bluntly informed Bruce that he was not wanted, and that his allowance of £500 was insufficient to meet the lofty standards of the regiment – as Churchill managed on £300 this was a piece of extra special pleading. Bruce refused to be browbeaten, making it perfectly clear that he still intended to join the 4th Hussars. Undeterred, Churchill's group placed Bruce under a general boycott at Aldershot.

Then, on Boxing night of 1896, told that he could meet a veteran of Balaclava, Bruce was lured to the Sergeants's Mess, normally out of bounds to officers. Innocently, he had raised a glass to the health of the mess before returning to his quarters. Three days later Bruce was arrested, charged 'with improperly associating with non-commissioned officers' and condemned as unfit to serve with the 4th Hussars. Given the choice of either sending in his papers or being cashiered, Bruce decided to leave the army.

Labouchère singled out Churchill – that 'amiable young officer who took a leading part . . . (and) whose bearing . . . (was) most offensive and insulting' – for special mention in the Bruce affair. Labouchère harried the authorities; his paper ran its own campaign. Questions were asked in Parliament; the War Office investigated the charges. Nothing happened. Was a powerful cabal at work out to whitewash Churchill's clique, an intrigue that extended to Colonel Brabazon and other senior officers and even touched the War Office? It appeared so.

By any reckoning, Churchill's behaviour had been reprehensible. Ruining another man's career – to say nothing of fixing races – cannot surely be judged in any other light. High spirits? Perhaps. But it seems that what lay behind Churchill's – in so many ways atypical – conduct, was the natural human desire to be wanted, to be accepted by his peers. At Harrow and St George's this had sadly eluded him. Three days after the Subaltern's Challenge Cup, he could note that 'Everybody in the regiment was awfully pleased at my riding . . . It has done me a lot of good here and I think I may say I am popular with everybody.' 'Having a really good time and enjoying life immensely', he wrote to Lady Randolph a month later. 'When I see how some fellows who are disliked are treated I feel very thankful I have been so fortunate to make my own friends and generally find my footing.' The group of young blades with whom he associated set their own dubious standards. Churchill surrendered to them, hoping to break into their world. He would compete with them on equal terms. Excelling at riding and shooting and polo, no one could doubt that his social connections were of the highest order. He would not jeopardize lightly these considerable advantages. He just tried too hard to be popular.

What bothered him most was the accusation of malpractices on the turf, rather than the fate of Alan Bruce. Unless challenged, such an imputation 'would be fatal to any future in public life for me'. In time, these scenes receded from his memory. Churchill passes over them in silence in his memoirs, My Early Life, perhaps embarrassed at raking up old and best-forgotten scandals.[5]

In the autumn of 1896, while still training at Aldershot, Churchill set out for the Americas on the first of his overseas adventures. Over the next four years, until his election as MP for Oldham in October 1900, he saw action in Cuba, battled against rebels on the North-West frontier, participated in the reconquest of the Sudan, and fought in South Africa: he also narrowly missed the Greek-Turkish war of 1897, but, unfortunately, it 'fizzled out' before he got there.[6] He accomplished all this not as an officer in command of troops, but as a journalist, covering these frontier wars for prestigious London newspapers and earning substantial fees. By any standard, this was an unusual arrangement, and aroused much hostile comment. He managed it mainly because of his name and background and some high-pressured social lobbying by Lady Randolph. But also because, with growing experience, he revealed latent talents as a war-correspondent. His outspoken articles and books brought him the attention he so craved for. Doors that might have remained locked, now opened. And Churchill was never too shy to barge through.

Churchill – accompanied by his friend, Reginald Barnes – travelled to Cuba in October 1896 to report for the *Daily Graphic* on the Cuban insurrection against Spanish rule.[7] Attached to Spanish military columns, they expended an inordinate amount of time and energy in chasing the guerrillas through the 'endless humid jungle'. Finally, on his twenty-first birthday, Churchill heard shots fired in anger, having been caught in a state of half-dress after bathing in a river – a predicament that seemed to personify the character of the war. He took a poor view of the martial abilities of both sides. The 'one conspicuous feature of this war', he claimed merrily to the *New York Herald*, 'is the fact that so few men are killed.' He sympathized with the rebellion, not the rebels. Ruling out Cuban autonomy, his preferred solution was for the United States to step in and 'take Cuba', hard though this might be on Spain. Churchill's instincts proved sound. Two years later, Spain was compelled to relinquish her control over Cuba to American influence.

When Churchill left Cuba, he took with him the *Rioja Cruz* (the Red Cross), a courtesy award by the Spaniards but one that provoked furious comment as newspapers – on both sides of the Atlantic – asked why a serving British officer was mixed up in a dispute so remote from British interests. Here was notoriety of the blandest variety.[8] In all, Churchill wrote five despatches describing the eight days he spent in the field. Lively and descriptive, and perhaps pruned by a skilful editor, they still read well. For his services, he received twenty-five guineas.

On his way to and from Cuba Churchill had passed through New York, his first visit to the United States. He had been the guest of Bourke Cockran (reportedly one of Lady Randolph's lovers) there. Cockran was a well-to-do Irish-American politician with a flair for high-flown oratory. A Democrat and 'Tammany Tiger' who had twice crossed party boundaries, and a fervent Free Trader, he made a strong impression on Churchill. Later, Churchill claimed that Cockran had inspired his own oratorical technique. In fact, he had never actually heard any of Cockran's orations – although he had learned some of them off by heart. At the time, what impressed Churchill above all else was Cockran's conversational style. 'In point, in pith, in rotundity, in antithesis, and in comprehension', it exceeded anything he had ever heard.[9]

Cockran also escorted Churchill around the New York social circuit. There were grand dinners, introductions to important personages, visits to points of interest. At West Point, he thought the strict discipline imposed on the cadets 'positively disgraceful'. To Jack, he summed up his general impression of the United States.

> Picture to yourself the American people as a great lusty youth – who treads on all your sensibilities perpetrates every possible horror of ill manners – whom neither age nor tradition inspire with reverence – but who moves about his affairs with a good hearted freshness which may well be the envy of older nations of the earth.[10]

Like many Englishmen of his class and generation Churchill held ambivalent attitudes towards the United States. Conscious of the need to foster friendly, or at least correct, relations with that country, they were yet tormented by the suspicion that ultimately America, crude and vulgar, an arriviste among the cultivated nations of the world, would call the tune. They were given to condescending graces and patronizing observations, and at times provoked by American unworldliness and egotism, their frustrations overflowed into intense suspicion or even outright hostility. Even Churchill – who was always careful to say in public the right things about America – although often carried away by the dynamics of his own rhetoric, could not disguise the equally genuine differences of opinion, often expressed acrimoniously, that emerged between himself and his would-be American brothers. To his mother he spoke of their 'odious' diplomatic manners. In 1929, his wife Clementine would write of his 'known hostility to America'.[11]

In September 1896 the 4th Hussars sailed from Southampton for Bombay. Churchill joined them, but most reluctantly. He would have preferred South Africa or Egypt, where things were hotting up.[12]

Only twenty-one years old, Churchill already saw his life in ruins as the years slipped by, one wasted opportunity following another. He believed ardently in his own star, boasting to incredulous listeners that one day he would become Prime Minister of England. At the same time he was convinced that his days were numbered. Would he survive to fulfil his fate? 'It is terrible to think how little time remains!' Churchill wrote in despair four years later.[13] Haunted by the prospect of an early death – like his father – his behaviour was characterized by a feverish scramble for position as he raced desperately against time.

Until the spring of 1899 Churchill was stationed at Bangalore in southern India. Much of his time however was spent in manufacturing his 'iron despatch box', with Lady Randolph's gracious assistance. Meanwhile, together with two friends, Hugo Baring and Reggie Barnes, he shared a 'magnificent pink and stucco palace in the middle of a beautiful garden'.

To maintain this residence a bevy of servants came to their aid: butlers, valets, grooms, gardeners, water-carriers, washermen, and a watchman. Time weighed heavily. He collected butterflies – a hobby that remained a lifelong passion; grew roses – fifty varieties – and orchids; and, inevitably, played polo – though now under a severe handicap, for when landing at Bombay he had dislocated his shoulder.[14]

After only a month in India Churchill concluded that 'life out here – is stupid dull & uninteresting'. With no one to talk to but soldiers, he would stay cooped up in India, completing 'his sentence', only until he could capture a parliamentary seat. Although occasionally 'very bored', he was not entirely unhappy. Books were now of particular importance to him. Churchill sat through the long hot afternoons studying, and adding his marginalia, to Gibbon's *Decline and Fall* (eight volumes), Macaulay (twelve volumes), Plato's *Republic*, Adam Smith's *Wealth of Nations*, Henry Hallam's *Constitutional History of England*, *Annual Registers*, supplementing these weighty tomes with the *Memoirs* of the Duc de Saint-Simon and Blaise Pascal's *Provincial Letters*.[15]

Churchill read with great enthusiasm and dedication, but without any intellectual yardstick by which to measure the concepts and themes other than his own powerful, unpolished mind. How far they affected his outlook, it is difficult to judge.[16] But Adam Smith's sanctification of free trade; or Gibbon's persuasive picture of a great imperial power corroded from the inside by the decadence of its ruling élite and the triumph of subversive doctrines; or Macaulay's peculiar, self-assured interpretation of English history that saw the victory of the great aristocratic Whig families and the enduring institutions they fashioned, a virile parliament and a compliant monarchy, as the fount and guarantee of all human improvement and freedom,[17] were ideas that surfaced later, time and again, in Churchill's writings and actions.

Winwood Reade's treatise, *The Martyrdom of Man*, now forgotten, was of particular interest. A Victorian classic (it ran to eight editions), it came highly recommended to Churchill as Colonel Brabazon's 'bible'. Reade, described as 'a traveller, novelist, and controversialist', examined, in quasi-Darwinian terms, the rise and fall of civilizations in Africa and the Middle East, assuming that the future lay with the more advanced, dynamic, energetic races, who would, by a process of struggle and conflict, triumph over those in decline. An atheist, Reade dealt in harsh terms with religion, reducing it to no more than a worthless superstition. The book certainly impressed Churchill, as it expressed much that he had 'for some time reluctantly believed'.[18]

Not surprisingly, Churchill's religious outlook changed. Hitherto, he had taken for granted the spiritual fare that had been offered him at school and home: he had been confirmed in the Church of England and had even considered, when sixteen, taking holy orders.

But after reading Lecky and Gibbon and Reade he began seriously to question the basis of his religious values. He passed, briefly, through 'a violent and aggressive anti-religious phase'. Later, he modified this extreme view. He compromised with what he termed 'The Religion of Healthy-Mindedness' – that is, provided you lived an honourable life, were faithful to friends and kind to the weak and poor, it did not matter much what beliefs you held.[19]

Lord Randolph would have been astonished at his son's powers of concentration, his seriousness of mind and purpose. Ideas and opinions flowed, conventional in themselves yet briskly put. Widespread reform at home – greater powers to local government, payment for MPs, and a progressive income tax – combined with 'Imperialism abroad' – India governed according to the 'old principles', a system of imperial defence, and a joint tariff policy. Opposed to European entanglements, he favoured reducing the army 'to a training depot for India with one army corps for petty expeditions'. 'A mighty navy', based on the double-standard, would guard the seas and guarantee British power. He advocated capital punishment as a 'great deterrent' and repudiated women's suffrage as 'contrary to natural law'. There could be no 'interference by Government with private trade' and he would extend the franchise only to the gainfully employed who happened also to be literate. As for universal elementary education: 'I should say that reading and writing, the knowledge of sufficient arithmetic to enable the individual to keep his accounts; the singing of patriotic songs and a gymnastic course is all that he may expect from the State.' He would enter parliament as a Liberal. 'As it is – Tory Democracy will have to be the standard under which I shall range myself.'[20]

He dismissed with contempt such Tories as Balfour and Curzon. But he found in Joseph Chamberlain 'a prudent Radical' and in Lord Rosebery 'an advanced Tory'. Together they would form a great centre party, a genuine national coalition, that would free the country from 'the fossils [the Conservatives] & the Fenians [the Liberal Home Rulers]'. Some of the ideas he now propounded were modified as circumstances changed – his strategic priorities, for instance. To others, he remained remarkably faithful – India, for example, or his ardour for Free Trade and his tireless labours in quest of a centre party.[21]

By the turn of the new century – little more than three years after he had begun his course of further studies – Churchill was a celebrated figure. He had seen action in three campaigns, published two books recounting his wartime experiences, composed a novel, and had leapt into the public eye after his spectacular escape from a Boer prison camp.[22]

I felt no excitement and very little fear. All the excitement went out when things became really deadly. Later on I used a rifle which a wounded man had dropped and fired 40 rounds with some effect at close quarters. I cannot be certain, but I think I hit four men. At any rate they fell.

Churchill wrote these words from the North-West frontier of India. They reflected accurately the exhilarating turn his life had now taken. A year later, after taking part in the last cavalry charge of the British army at Omdurman, he recorded:

> I pulled up and reloaded within 30 yards of their mass and then trotted after my troops . . . I am sorry to say I shot 5 men for certain and two doubtful. The pistol was the best thing in the world . . . The Dervishes showed no fear of cavalry . . . They tried to hamstring the horses, to cut the bridles – reins – slashed and stabbed in all directions and fired rifles at a few feet range. Nothing touched me. I destroyed those who molested me and so passed out without disturbance of body or mind.[23]

Churchill did not participate in these campaigns in the normal routine of his duties as a junior officer of the 4th Hussars. He forced himself upon them in the guise of a war-correspondent – in India for the *Daily Telegraph*, in the Sudan for the *Morning Post*. Only by a laudable single-mindedness of resolve – facilitated by Lady Randolph's deft petitioning – did he manage to secure these posts. It was not always easy. With Sir Bindon Blood, commander of the Malakand Field Force, he was on cordial terms; but General Sir Herbert Kitchener, commander of the Sudan expedition, did not want him, particularly in his role as a prying journalist. It was only by pulling wires at the very highest levels, including approaches to the Prime Minister, Lord Salisbury, and Sir Evelyn Wood, Adjutant-General of the army, that secured for Churchill (still as a war-correspondent) a temporary posting to the Sudan with the 21st Lancers.[24]

Churchill used many harsh words about the conduct of these campaigns, the methods employed and the politics that lurked behind them.[25] Vacillation was the hallmark of the Indian government's policy. The war was due to their 'criminal and cowardly' folly, their 'penny wise' policies. Having decided on a 'forward policy', it was imperative to press ahead without hesitation. Churchill also held that the 'Butcher and Bolt' techniques adopted, the system of punitive forays, although ferocious – demolishing house, blocking up wells, dynamiting fortified towers, cutting down trees, burning crops, destroying reservoirs, laying waste in vengeance to whole villages – was inevitable in the circumstances and should be carried out to the last letter.[26]

He was equally forthright when reviewing the Sudan expedition. But his arrows were directed more at Kitchener – 'a vulgar common man'

– than at the politicians who had authorized the campaign.[27] After the battle, Kitchener found himself at the centre of a great public commotion. Not only was he responsible for the 'inhuman slaughter of the wounded [Dervish]', he had also desecrated the Mahdi's tomb, cast his bones into the Nile, and, as a ghoulish afterthought, retained his skull as a trophy. These allegations were not without foundation.[28] That Churchill was shocked does him credit. But there was something entirely incongruous about a junior serving officer censuring his commander-in-chief in public. The Prince of Wales had warned him of the pitfalls in squaring his loyalties as a war-correspondent with those of an officer in the field. Letters were published in the *Army and Navy Gazette* protesting the spectacle of an influentially connected young subaltern[29] careering over the world, elbowing out of the way officers frequently more able and experienced than he, in order to criticize his superiors and sway public opinion. Have we not, in the case of lieutenant Churchill, reached 'the very utmost limit of absurdity?' contended 'A General Officer'.

But for Churchill the army was no more than a stepping-stone to the brilliantly lit stage of politics. 'My life here is not big enough to hold me. I want to be up and doing and cannot bear inaction or routine,' he wrote after Malakand, enthused by his own success. By April 1899 he had taken the crucial decision. Having fulfilled his last obligation to his regiment by playing, and winning, the Indian Inter Regimental Polo Tournament, he would now leave the army, earn his living as a writer, and pursue, what he termed, 'the larger ends of life'.[30]

In India Churchill discovered the Empire at first hand: the glittering, privileged world of the British Raj, then at the height of its power and glory. All doors were open to him, and he imbibed deeply the heady atmosphere of British India. He dined at the table of Lord Curzon, the most stately of viceroys, and fought in defence of the Raj in the most romantic of surroundings at the Malakand Pass.

It was axiomatic to Churchill's outlook that Britain had inherited this world as of right, by virtue of her superior powers, and she defended it as the representative of a more advanced, sophisticated civilization in conflict with 'the unpenetrated gloom of barbarism'.[31] Even when times and conditions had changed out of all recognition, in the 1930s and 40s, he was still bent on preserving the image of Empire he had formed as a young subaltern campaigning in the mountains and valleys of the North-West Frontier.

For Churchill, Malakand and Omdurman were little more than thrilling short-cuts to a political career. He was determined to squeeze the maximum advertisement from his exploits. How he railed at the decision of the *Daily Telegraph* to publish his articles unsigned. 'If I am to do anything in the world,' he clarified to his mother, 'you will have to make up your mind to publicity and also to my doing unusual things.'

Already he was being spoken of as 'pushy' and a 'medal-hunter', of being excessively ambitious and self-centred. 'Fame,' he wrote, although sneered at, melodramatized and degraded, was 'still the finest thing in life'. He asked Lady Randolph to keep on eye on the political situation in England. Should an vacancy occur, he wished to stand for election. 'They would probably elect me,' he forecast confidently in November 1897.[32]

In July 1897, on Claverton Down, near Bath, Churchill made his political début. The occasion was gay and lighthearted, an outdoor fête of the Primrose League, but he prepared his speech – of about twenty minutes – with painstaking care. He spoke in favour of the Workmen's Compensation Bill. Taunting the 'slap-dash, wholesale, harum-scarum policy of the Radicals', he maintained that 'the British workman had more to hope for from the rising tide of Tory democracy than from the dried-up drain-pipe of Radicalism. (Laughter and cheers).' His contrived phrases were well received. The press suggested that a new political figure had appeared on the scene. A year later in Bradford – a favourite haunt of his father's – he passed a severer test. He spoke for almost an hour, keeping rigidly to his notes, rousing and amusing the audience to prolonged bouts of applause. He was 'intensely pleased' with his performance: 'with practice I shall obtain great power on a public platform. My impediment is no hindrance. My voice sufficiently powerful – and – this is vital – my ideas & modes of thought are pleasing to men.' He spoke at two more Conservative meetings that October. Sure of his course, he resigned his commission the following March. He was gambling on his name and connections, and his conviction that sooner or later his literary skills would accord him independence.[33]

Still, his first attempt to win a parliamentary seat at Oldham in July 1899 ended in failure. Oldham was a working class, marginal constituency, the perfect setting for a Tory Democrat – in particular as Churchill, the aristocrat, was paired with a local trade unionist, James Mawdsley. Churchill proclaimed that he was 'Conservative', a 'Tory Democrat', and a 'Unionist'. He also proclaimed that 'To keep the Empire we must have a free people and an educated people, and a contented and well-fed people. That is why we are in favour of social reform.' As his campaign progressed, he became increasingly conscious of his 'growing powers – and facilities of speech'. Great halls packed with excited audiences fired his spirits. His speaking technique improved. At question time, his spontaneous answers were invariably received with cheers. For all that, he did not rate highly his chances of success. One reason was the Bill that Balfour had introduced giving preference to the Church of England and its schools. This had aroused fierce opposition among the nonconformists, who were strong in Lancashire. So Churchill abandoned it – a transparent manoeuvre which failed to save him.[34]

Three months after his minor setback, Churchill was on his way to South Africa to report on the Boer war for the *Morning Post*, fortified by sixty bottles of wines and spirits, a compass and field-glasses, a personal servant, and with all expenses paid and a salary of £250 a month. On board the *Dunottar Castle* he met the British commander, general Sir Redvers Buller, whom he found 'vy amiable', and 'well disposed' towards him. He also fell in with the special correspondent of t' e *Manchester Guardian*, John Black Atkins, who, almost fifty years later, recalled his first meeting with this

> most unusual young man. He was slim, slightly reddish-haired, pale, lively, frequently plunging along the deck with 'neck out-thrust' . . . sometimes sitting in meditation, folding and unfolding his hands, not nervously but as though he were helping himself to untie mental knots.

Struck by Churchill's intoxication with words, noting how he savoured them lovingly before committing himself, Atkins had never before encountered 'this sort of ambition, unabashed, frankly egotistical, communicating its excitement, and extorting sympathy'.[35]

Churchill's views of the Boer insurrection fed off his adventures in India and the Sudan. Now applied to South Africa, he saw 'a very great Power' defied by 'a miserably small people'. 'How long is the peace of the Empire to be disturbed by a party of filibustering Boers?' he had asked a Conservative fête at Blenheim. A week after his arrival at Capetown he revised his position. 'It is astonishing how we have underrated these people . . . A long and bloody war is before us – and the end is by no means as certain as most people imagine.' In order to stiffen British resolve, Churchill proposed punishing officers who surrendered to the enemy. 'And let us say at once – No exchange of Prisoners'.[36]

Five days later, on 15 November, Churchill was himself a prisoner of the Boers, eventually to be locked up in the State Model School at Pretoria.[37] Captured while accompanying an armoured train on a recon-naissance mission, he had acted with exemplary gallantry under fire. But it had been a gallantry born out of rashness and faulty intelligence. As Churchill put it at the time: '[We] ran confidently on to within range of the Boers, being unaware they had guns with them, and hoping to give them a lesson.' If his capture has been described as 'an inconceivably stupid incident',[38] his escape contains all the necessary ingredients of an adventure saga of high quality: roaming a hostile countryside alone; hunted by the Boers, a price of £25 on his head; stumbling by chance on to a friendly English family; drawing sustenance from Stevenson's heroes in *Kidnapped*; and finally smuggled to freedom among woolbales in a goods train. On 23 December he docked at Durban, welcomed as an authentic war hero.

The escape catapulted Churchill to fame; but it also had its sour side. The breakout had originally been planned by Captain Aylmer Haldane and a Sergeant-Major Brockie, who had been reluctant to take Churchill along. He was too talkative; his physical agility was doubted; and his value to the Boers would, they feared, compromise them. But Churchill had insisted. He promised Haldane 'a blaze of triumph'. And Haldane eventually succumbed.[39]

But it was Churchill who escaped and Haldane and Brockie were left behind. Haldane was 'surprised and disgusted' at having been left in the lurch since they had all planned to leave together. Reports circulated that Churchill had behaved dishonourably – having allegedly broken his parole and deserted his comrades. These allegations were given extra weight when the Boers released to the press Churchill's willingness 'to give any parole' that the Boer authorities might require, pleading his special 'character as a press representative' who had been 'quite unarmed'. All this was in startling contrast to Churchill's own accounts of the incident. (He later suggested that his brave conduct made him eligible for some kind of 'military mention or decoration'). These obvious inconsistencies were pounced upon by the British press, much to Churchill's chagrin. Still, there was no truth in the accusation that Churchill had broken his parole, for by the time the Boers had agreed to a deal it was too late: Churchill had already escaped![40]

And, in fact, Churchill had put himself at considerable risk by hiding in the close vicinity of the prison, waiting for Haldane and Brockie who had been unable to join him. However these dubious charges pursued him. In 1912 he felt compelled to sue *Blackwood's Magazine* for libel. The action fizzled out as Blackwood's backed down. But Haldane had refused to testify on his behalf, no longer feeling he could trust him.[41]

Churchill returned from captivity world famous. His election to parliament seemed assured as more than one (reportedly eleven) local Conservative associations sought his candidature. For the moment, however, Churchill decided to remain in South Africa. He secured a posting as a lieutenant (unpaid) in the South African Light Horse while continuing to report on the war for the *Morning Post*. His style was as uninhibited as ever. 'Are the gentlemen of England all fox-hunting? Why not an English Light Horse?' he asked, positive that the war should be pursued until victory. Victory certainly, but after the defeat of the Boer republics he counselled magnanimity: treat them with 'all generosity and tolerance', he proposed. This was taken badly by the authorities. No respecter of rank, Churchill possessed the unhappy knack of rubbing people up the wrong way – from the best of intentions. Buller he considered a dud general (an opinion widely held and compounded by the general's loose drinking habits). Field-marshal Lord Roberts, the British Commander-in-Chief, he thought 'a fortunate and very much overrated man', and incurred his severe displeasure after having made some tart comments about an army chaplain's sermon. Kitchener, Robert's Chief-of-Staff, was by now an old adversary. His closest ally among the generals was Sir Ian Hamilton whom he knew from India and who did much to smooth his troubled path.[42]

With his new regiment, Churchill participated in some famous battles. Although he was not actually present when the first squadrons galloped into Ladysmith, as he intimated in *My Early Life*, he did arrive there after darkness the same day. But he witnessed the horrific slaughter at Spion Kop; bicycled through Boer-occupied Johannesburg; and – sweet revenge – together with his cousin, 'Sunny' Marlborough, freed the prisoners from their 'cage' in Pretoria. At Hussar Hill, Churchill saw his brother Jack – who had arrived post-haste at the front that morning – receive a slight wound in his calf. Jack was immediately despatched to Durban where Lady Randolph, running her American-sponsored hospital ship, the *Maine*, tended to her youngest son, one of her first patients.[43]

By July 1900 Churchill was back in England preparing to stand as Conservative candidate for Oldham in the so-called 'Khaki election'. 'I entered the town in state in a procession of ten landaus, and drove through streets crowded with enthusiastic operatives and mill-girls.' But these elections revealed shaming undercurrents of anti-semitism – 'a ring of financiers . . . mostly Jewish, are really responsible for the war'. The Conservatives rode to victory on a clamorous, patriotic, anti-Boer swell. Churchill had no time for anti-semitism, but he did appeal blatantly to nationalist fervour: 'Be it known,' his election poster ran, 'that every vote given to the radicals means two pats on the back for Kruger and two smacks in the face for our country.' His campaign proved successful. He squeezed his nearest rival, the Liberal Walter Runciman, into third place, by only 222 votes.[44]

Before Churchill could devote himself fulltime to politics, he had to secure his finances. Nearly always on the verge of bankruptcy – on occasion his cheques bounced – 'Sunny' Marlborough had put up £400 to cover his election expenses. But over the coming months he succeeded in amassing £10,000 – from writing and highly successful lecture tours in the United States, Canada and Britain. This sum was entrusted to Sir Ernest Cassel, one of Lord Randolph's (and the Prince of Wales's) banker friends, with the instructions, 'Feed my sheep'. His 'sheep', as Churchill noted, did not multiply fast but they fattened steadily. And this was sufficient to keep him without undue care for the coming years. Lady Randolph, who had been a source of considerable financial embarrassment to Churchill some years earlier, had meanwhile settled into a second marriage. Her husband, George Cornwallis-West – a social butterfly at best – was but sixteen days older than Churchill. Neither he nor Jack were enthusiastic about this union, but Churchill promised to support Lady Randolph 'in every way', though he asked that she weigh carefully 'all the aspects of the question'. As for Jack, after a spell of soldiering, he had embarked on a life on the stock exchange.[45]

On his election to parliament, Churchill was two months short of his twenty-sixth birthday. His achievements were already impressive, by any standard: soldier-adventurer, war-correspondent, popular hero, author, and finally Member of Parliament. The key to his continued success was his writing. It would save him from a squalid life of poverty and guarantee his future in politics. He had faith in his pen. It did not come easily. For style he drew heavily on Macaulay – 'crisp and forcible' – and Gibbon – 'stately and impressive'. He slaved over his punctuation. 'Everything is worked out by hard labour and frequent polishing.'[46]

As with his writing, so with his oratory, that other indispensable tool of an effective politician. Rhetoric was his most valuable weapon, as he himself realized; but he was wont to brandish it with reckless abandon. For Churchill was of a rare species, a rhetorician in the precise meaning of the word: using language, often artificial and extravagant in nature, carefully designed to impress and to persuade. His was a long and enduring passion with the magic of words, particularly his own. He was quite aware of this 'mental flaw', as he called it. Only twenty-three, he admitted to Lady Randolph:

> It is quite true. I do not care so much for the principles I advocate as for the impression which my words produce & the reputation they give me. This sounds vy terrible . . . Perhaps to put it a little strongly, I should say that I vy often yield to the temptation of adapting my facts to my phrases.

Consoling himself with the thought that 'Macaulay is an arch offender in this respect', he went on: 'I think a keen sense of necessity or of burning wrong or injustice would make me sincere, but I vy rarely detect genuine emotion in myself.' Was this admitting that only naked ambition moved him? More than thirty years later he was able to say to a shocked research assistant, 'Give me the facts, Ashley, and I will twist them the way I want to suit my argument.'

Churchill, still only twenty-two, developed these themes in an unpublished essay he called 'The Scaffolding of Rhetoric'. He opened on a high note, uncannily prophetic of his own career: 'Of all the talents bestowed upon men, none is so precious as the gift of oratory. He who enjoys it wields a power more durable than that of a great king. He is an independent force in the world.' Churchill laid out the guide-lines for the successful public speaker. First, a striking presence. As long as he is invested with 'a personal significance', it matters not whether he be small, ugly, or deformed. 'Sometimes,' he thought, building on his own experience, 'a slight and not unpleasing stammer or impediment has been of some assistance in securing the attention of the audience.' The orator must employ the right word, the striking phrase, the colourful analogy, a wild extravagance of language, constructing sentences that are 'long, rolling, and sonorous', moulding them into a rhythmic whole, 'a rapid succession of waves of sound and vivid pictures', thereby electrifying the audience and preparing for the great climax when his final words would fall 'amid a thunder of assent'.

These were techniques that Churchill would nurse and foster. With time and experience, he would add others: humour, a biting sarcasm, a sense of timing. He possessed a marvellous, though highly dangerous, gift: an innate ability to bewitch himself by the potency of his crafted, dazzling phrases. Charles Masterman – later – wrote: 'In nearly every case an *idea* enters his head from outside. It then rolls round the hollows of his brain, collecting strength like a snowball. *Then*, after whirlwinds of *rhetoric*, he becomes convinced that it is right; and denounces everyone who criticizes it.' And Neville Chamberlain later made much the same point. 'I have often watched him in Cabinet begin with a casual comment on what has been said, then as an image or simile comes into his mind proceed with great animation, when presently you see his whole face suffused with pink his speech becomes more and more rapid and impetuous till in a few minutes he will not hear of the possibility of opposition to an idea which only occurred to him a few minutes ago.' Was Churchill merely a slave to his rhetoric? Perhaps. But without grasping this essential point, it is impossible to comprehend fully Churchill's life.[47]

Churchill's books as a war-correspondent are today little more than historical curiosities. *From London to Ladysmith* and *Ian Hamilton's March* are largely rehashes of his despatches from South Africa, served up again in more popular form in *My Early Life*. *The Malakand Field Force* and *The River War* are more serious attempts to write contemporary history: leading personalities were interviewed, sources collected and collated. Churchill wrote these works at tremendous speed, desperately anxious to corner the market. But too easily swayed by verbal testimony – particularly if put with force – he was reluctant to change his mind, even in the face of new evidence. Nor was he excessively careful in sifting his materials, once he had found a source that suited his purpose. But he revealed his talent to tell a good story in a vivid and exciting manner and he poured into them his own, highly personal experiences. They were touched with realism and passion.

Of all the books Churchill wrote, *Savrola* (published in 1900), his first and only attempt to write fiction, is of exceptional interest. 'All my philosophy is put into the mouth of the hero,' he revealed to Lady Randolph. His novel – whose sole purpose was 'to amuse' – would be free of 'squalor and animal emotions', but full of 'wild adventure and atheistic philosophy'. The resulting plot was a concoction of high drama, political intrigue and chaste romance set in a Ruritanian-style country called Laurania. Under the leadership of Savrola, 'the great Democrat', the progressive forces of unhappy Laurania were locked in grim struggle with the cruel autocrat, President Antonio Molara. No holds were barred: mass demonstrations and street massacres, great public meetings and revolutionary uprisings. The unscrupulous Molara even agreed to a plot to compromise Savrola, implicating his wife Lucille, 'the most beautiful woman in Europe', as bait. He partially succeeded, but the scheme came unstuck as Lucille and Savrola fall in love. '"Do you despise me very much?" she asks. "No, I would not marry a goddess." "Nor I a philosopher." Then they kissed each other, and thenceforward their relationship was simple.' Molara met his fate, gunned down by an extremist, to Savrola's displeasure. And although Savrola and Lucille were forced into exile, their banishment was temporary, for after a suitable period they returned to Laurania to general acclaim. Churchill's final sentence is Gibbon's: 'history [is] . . . little more than the register of the crimes, follies, and misfortunes of mankind'.

There is little literary merit in *Savrola*. Melodramatic in construction, the characterization is unconvincing, the dialogue false. But it tells all about Churchill: his Whig beliefs, the exile returning from abroad to establish democracy, to revive the old constitution, his total dedication to politics, his shameless ambition, his intoxication with words, with the power of oratory – 'his passions, his emotions, his very soul appeared to be communicated to the seven thousand people who heard his words; and they mutually inspired each other'. The books that lined Savrola's room were the books Churchill had read. A heavy smoker, Savrola loved polo and disliked dancing. He would catnap in moments of crisis, read his correspondence in bed in the morning, scribbling notes and marginalia. He yearned for praise and sympathy, 'like many highly wrought minds'. A lonely man, he had few close friends. Given to attacks of depression,[48] he had a strong premonition of an early death. His religious values were 'merely a jumble of formulas; seldom repeated, hardly understood, never investigated, and a hope . . . that it would be well with him if he did his duty as a gentleman'. And Savrola was inordinately brave, even reckless in the face of fire: 'I waved my hat at Fate,' he cried.

About Savrola's family background we are told little except that he was well-born and looked after by his devoted nurse, Bettina. Savrola's parents are not mentioned. A Freudian slip? What is abundantly clear is that Savrola, the spellbinder, the charismatic populist politician, was a driven man, driven inexorably towards his fate, his destiny to save his country in a moment of supreme crisis, whatever his private inclinations.

This was the young Churchill's fictional world. It merges effort-
lessly into his career. When Churchill took his seat in Parliament
in February 1901 he was prepared to live out the drama of his
imaginary hero.

4

'I am an English Liberal.
I hate the Tory Party'

In the Parliament of the early 1900s a sandy-haired youth was observed, 'fair, slight, with head thrust forward, eyes protuberant, eyebrows lacking, the whole air that of boyish audacity'. Winston was twenty-six years old when he entered Parliament in February 1901. Puny in physique – his chest measured only thirty-one inches – his unmuscular body was set off by a slight paunch. One observer called him 'a little, square-headed fellow'. A broad forehead accentuated his already receding hair. For a brief period he sported a light thin moustache, but he had little sense for fashion, or so thought his stepfather, George Cornwallis-West. Winston's skin was soft and delicate – he always wore silk underwear, although this might have been also out of vanity. His most attractive feature was his eyes, impish, cheeky, alive, a mood captured wonderfully by one of Spy's cartoons.[1]

Churchill was indeed prepared to take on the world. He flaunted his ambition. Three years earlier, he had wondered aloud whether a biographer would find him a fit subject. Perceived as a 'medal-hunter', his reputation as a pushy self-seeker blighted his fine achievements. Gentlemen of breeding did not cut corners so sharply or exploit their connections so breezily. His exploits, or so one reviewer of *Savrola* concluded, were no more than 'a gigantic advertisement of his modest personality'. When he was captured in South Africa, it was hoped in the clubs of London that the Boers would keep him! And when he escaped, unkind whispers circulated that the Boers had found his conversation so boring that they were glad to be rid of him![2] Now a Member of Parliament, would his magnificent egotism prove a barrier to normal political affiliations?

'Were it not for Home Rule,' he had announced in April 1897, 'I would enter Parliament as a Liberal.' Little had happened since then to change his mind. He was still wedded to his revamped version of Tory Democracy.[3] But would this be acceptable to the Tory leadership, and in particular to Balfour whom not so long ago he had despised, no doubt carried away by his father's comment that Balfour had effectively buried Tory Democracy. Churchill would breathe fresh life into the corpse, not only for the sake of rescuing contemporary politics from its torpor but also for posterity.

Shortly into his parliamentary career, in August 1902, Churchill began to write the official biography of his father, and reliving his father's struggles against the 'Old Gang' inspired his own career. He stepped into his father's old shoes. The political battles he now reconstructed on paper found expression also in those he fought in Parliament. He even thought of running his candidacy in central Birmingham, Lord Randolph's old constituency. 'In mind and manner he is a strange replica of his father,' remarked Wilfred Blunt, who had known them both well. 'There is just the same gaminerie and contempt of the conventional . . . As I listened to him recounting conversations he had with [Joseph] Chamberlain I seemed once more to be listening to Randolph on the subject of Northcote and Salisbury.' However, Blunt thought Winston more able than Lord Randolph.[4]

Anxious to startle the political world, Churchill sought advice from the Liberal journalist, John Alfred Spender. Deliver ferocious attacks on your own leaders, came back the reply. Like Lord Randolph before him, Churchill went blithely to war against his own front bench. In his first division in Parliament, he voted against his leaders. As an added affront he joined a Conservative ginger-group – shades of the 'Fourth Party'! In this way, again like his father, he cultivated hostility and suspicion. He was paid back in the same coin. Once, when Churchill rose to defend the principle of Free Trade, Balfour and a majority of Conservative MPs walked out of the chamber, a demonstration of studied insult.[5]

In 1900, at the general elections that had returned Churchill to Parliament, the Conservatives had a majority of 134 seats.[6] They had been in power since 1895. The Party leader, Lord Salisbury, three times Prime Minister, was now seventy and in marked physical decline; in July 1902, his nephew, Arthur James Balfour, replaced him. Although the achievements of Balfour's ministry were considerable,[7] the repercussions of the Boer war (which had dragged on till 1902) and internal dissension over tariff reform, gave the impression that the government was unable, and perhaps too tired after a decade in office, to cope. The Conservatives were perceived to be in decline and this reflected favourably on the Liberals, who had a wealth of untested talent on their benches. As the cohesion of the Conservative Party crumbled, Churchill found himself increasingly at loggerheads with his own leadership.

On 18 February 1901, at half past ten in the evening, Churchill rose from the gangway seat immediately behind the Treasury bench, his father's old place, to deliver his maiden speech. He chose as his topic the South African war on which he felt confident to argue or advise. Churchill was due to follow the up-and-coming David Lloyd George. As Lloyd George progressed in his pro-Boer oration, one colourful phrase following the other, Churchill became visibly nervous, at a loss to see how he would immediately counter the Welshman's animated arguments. Churchill made clear his policy: 'to make it easy and honourable for the Boers to surrender, and painful and perilous for them to continue in the field'. His phraseology, striking and provocative – 'if I were a Boer I hope I should be fighting in the field [to cheers from the Irish members]' – raised eyebrows as well as admiration. After the debate, he was introduced to Lloyd George, thereby beginning a friendship that 'persisted through many vicissitudes'.[8]

Churchill's speech was generally well-received. Henry Massingham, the Liberal publicist, thought he possessed one quality: 'intellect – and he can judge and think for himself'. But he also had many grave disadvantages. 'Mr Churchill does not inherit his father's voice – save for the slight lisp – or his father's manner. Address, accent, appearance do not help him,' pointing out that together with 'the wisdom and insight' there was also much 'claptrap'.[9] Churchill did not wait for his reputation to mature.

Three months after his maiden speech, he fired the House with a fierce attack on the government's policy of army reform. He prepared his ground thoroughly, working on his speech for six weeks. Every word had been chosen carefully and learned beforehand. Determined to extract the maximum publicity, he sent a copy of it to the *Morning Post* and it was in print even before he began to speak.[10] His message was precise. He raised again 'the tattered flag of retrenchment and economy' that his father had unfurled fifteen years ago. 'Is there no poverty at home?' he enquired. The war department's estimates, he suggested, was a drain on the country's resources. He opposed the minister's scheme to restructure the army into six corps, three to be ready for immediate use abroad. 'They are enough to irritate,' he pointed out, 'they are not enough to overawe.'

Churchill was in favour of preserving Britain's 'naval supremacy'. He would be satisfied with one army corps, 'quite enough to fight savages'.[11] This traditional view of British power, based on naval preponderance, commercial supremacy, and the might of the Empire was to be braced by 'a moral force – the Divine foundation of earthly power'.

> It is known alike by peoples and by rulers that on the whole British influence is healthy and kindly, and makes for the general happiness and welfare of mankind. And we shall make a fatal bargain if we allow the moral force which this country has so long exerted to become diminished, or perhaps even destroyed for the sake of the costly, trumpery, dangerous military playthings on which the Secretary of State for War has set his heart.[12]

This speech, it is often held, made Churchill's parliamentary reputation.[13] But it is difficult to detect in it any great originality of thought. Of course, Churchill had decorated his commonplace views with a racy, powerful style, uniquely his own, that improved with time. But the most significant feature of his speech was left unsaid, if understood. He had attacked his own Party's intention to reorganize the armed forces. Elected a Conservative, he was performing a Liberal's duty. Churchill detected in himself 'a divergence of thought and sympathy' from his fellow Conservatives over the entire range of government policy: South Africa, army reform, economies, above all, free trade, and he attacked them in an increasingly aggressive and unrestrained language. In this way, he sought the limelight and was reluctant to leave its seductive glare.[14]

In July 1901, Churchill and a number of other young malcontent Conservative MPs, joined together in a 'cave' known as the 'Hughligans' (named after their most prominent member, Lord Hugh Cecil, Lord Salisbury's youngest son), or more often referred to as the 'Hooligans'.[15] For Churchill, there was an element of 'great fun' in their activities that would allow him to develop 'that invaluable political quality – a desire for mischief'. He proclaimed their credo as 'High Imperialism nourished by a devilled sardine'.[16] Cecil, their outstanding figure, took his mission more seriously, defending with a religious certainty the standing of the Anglican Church and the dogma of free trade. More of a theologian in temperament, his intellectual arrogance and capacity for vitriolic oratory intimidated the younger Churchill, though during these years he became Churchill's most intimate political friend.[17]

The 'Hooligans' indulged in boisterous unparliamentary procedures – loitering in the 'No' lobby to ensure the defeat of an unwanted Bill, or even voting with the Liberals against the government. They also had a weekly dining-club where they entertained the leading political figures of the day. Of Churchill's four 'most pleasing and brilliant men', three – Lord Rosebery, John Morley, and Joseph Chamberlain – were hosted by the 'Hooligans' (the fourth, Balfour, was out of favour at the time). Among the 'Hooligans'' guests, Liberals seemed to predominate, particularly those on the right-wing of the party.[18] Lord Rosebery exerted a special fascination upon Churchill. Churchill saw him as the leader of a great Middle Party, 'upholding the flag for which my father fought so long & so disastrously'.[19]

Churchill's faith in Rosebery's staying-power was ill-judged. But his disenchantment with the Tories was deep-rooted.[20] The final break came in 1903–4 over tariff reform. Judging from his past record, Churchill might well have been considered a modest tariff reformer, or as he put it, 'a sober admirer of Free Trade principles'.[21] Previously he had advocated an imperial combination 'for Tariff & Commerce'. In 1902 he had voted in favour of import duties on corn, grain, flour, and meal as a source of extra revenue. But when Joseph Chamberlain launched his public campaign for 'a protected Empire' in May 1903, Churchill reacted vigorously. He emphasized to Balfour that he was 'utterly opposed' to it. He pleaded with Balfour to take a firm stand to preserve the essential character of the Tory Party. Otherwise, 'I must reconsider my position in politics'.[22]

No doubt Churchill's convictions took fire as the controversy flared up. He fed off his own rhetoric, until he became absolutely convinced of the rightness, and righteousness, of the cause he was preaching. The element of self-doubt was barely visible in his make-up. Nor was he tied to exclusive loyalty to a particular party machine. 'The only way a man can remain consistent amid changing circumstances is to change with them while preserving the same dominating purpose,' he was to write later.[23]

Once Chamberlain threw down the gauntlet, it was Churchill, among the Tory dissidents, who ran off with it, often outpacing the doctrinaire Cecil who, on more than one occasion, found cause to reprimand Churchill for adopting too extreme tactics or employing too caustic a tongue.[24] 'Your language alienates [like-minded Tories],' he despaired in December 1903. 'Your lamentable instability,' he went on, 'makes you quite impossible to work with; & will unless you can cure it be a fatal danger to your career.'[25] Churchill was also in trouble with the Oldham Conservative Association, where there were strong feelings in favour of a measure of protection. By January 1904 a vote of no-confidence had been passed against him, though he continued to sit for the constituency until the end of the present Parliament.[26]

Balfour's detached philosophical air masked a wily and ruthless politician, determined to stay in office, frustrated by the thought of opposition. In the autumn of 1903 he shed the Cabinet of its two extreme wings: the protectionist, Joseph Chamberlain, on one side; on the other, the free traders, Charles Ritchie, Lord Balfour, Lord Hamilton, and the venerable Duke of Devonshire. It was a carefully calculated act of desperation. Chamberlain was the real danger. His resignation from the Cabinet was widely seen as an act of rebellion against Balfour. In fact, he was Balfour's willing tool. The intention – agreed between them beforehand – was to test public opinion. Should it prove favourable to a measure of protection, Balfour would consider joining in. If not, Chamberlain could go his own way. It was an ingenious strategy but it came unstuck.[27] No prime minister could butcher his Cabinet on such a scale without leaving the impression that his administration was tottering.

Naturally, the Liberals took heart from these internal squabbles. They also pitched in, joined by the Unionist 'Free Fooders', a group of about sixty MPs including Churchill and Cecil. By the spring of

1904 Churchill's position was untenable. Balfour had no need to get rid of him. Churchill, quite indifferent to the dictates of party discipline, continued to assault Balfour in the press, in the House, and on the public platform. 'I'm going to put my mark on him,' he promised. His outrageous language provoked a response in kind. 'Your conduct in using words like "lie", "quack", "charlatan", "weak", "dangerous" of Mr Balfour and Mr Chamberlain has disgusted most people,' wrote one outraged Unionist MP.[28]

In April 1904 Churchill agreed to run as a free trade Liberal for North-West Manchester at the next elections. A month or so later he took the final step when he crossed to the Liberal benches, and sat down beside Lloyd George, in the same seat his father had occupied when in opposition.[29]

Did Churchill have any regrets? A day after he had broken with the Conservatives, he wrote to Lord Hugh Cecil, who had remained faithful to the party:

> What a wrench it is to me to break with all that glittering hierarchy & how carefully one must organize one's system of thought to be utterly independent of it. The worst of it is that as the Free Trade issue subsides it leaves my personal ambitions naked & stranded on the beach – & they are an ugly & unsatisfactory spectacle by themselves, though nothing but an advantage when borne forward with the flood of a great outside cause.[30]

Five months later he complained of being 'entirely isolated in politics'. In Tory eyes, he had betrayed his class and its values. It was not for nothing that he was referred to as 'the Blenheim rat'.[31] But he was scarcely better off with his new associates, the Liberals, whose cause he now championed with all the suspicious zeal of a new convert. 'Winston [has] no convictions,' thought Asquith. 'He has not got the art of playing in conjunction with others,' said Lloyd George; and always wants to be 'in the popular eye', added Charles Masterman. 'Churchill,' wrote Charles Hobhouse, 'is ill mannered, boastful, unprincipled, without any redeeming qualities except his amazing ability and industry. I doubt his courage to desert during a victorious cruise, but he would, without hesitation, desert a sinking ship.'[32]

The problem was that Churchill's belligerent ambition was always left 'naked and stranded on the beach', and it was, to most observers, 'an ugly & unsatisfactory spectacle'. For it was in Churchill's nature always to be 'borne forward with the flood of a great outside cause'. Destiny lay in wait for him at every corner. Like Bismarck, he heard all too often the steps of God sounding through events. Carried away by the impulse of the moment, he never flinched from a challenge, sweeping away problems in a manner that left most of his colleagues groggy. In this way, his strengths were also his weaknesses. He thrived in a crisis, stimulated to action by its excitement. His many detractors went further and presumed that if a crisis was not conveniently at hand, he would not be above fabricating one. This was the source of his inconsistency and the deep distrust it aroused. It was not until after his legendary achievements of the Second World War that even the Tory party came to love, honour, and respect him.

Churchill was by now a fully fledged Liberal, at least in his own eyes. In October 1903, he had declared to Cecil 'I hate the Tory Party, their men, their words & their methods': 'stupid' and 'ungrateful', they had, by 1904, forfeited all his respect.

It has been hinted that had Balfour, in July 1902, offered him a government post he might have remained a Conservative, seduced, as it were, by the lures of office. This is doubtful.[33] Despite his delight in his reputation as a Tory 'frondeur', Churchill was still too much of a political lightweight for Balfour to take that seriously. This is also to deny the sincerity of his feelings that mounted with every 'mark' he put on the government. 'My prognostication,' he wrote in October 1904, 'is that he [Joseph Chamberlain] and the Prime Minister will cut their own throats and bring their party to utter destruction ... [and] that the Liberals will gain a gigantic victory at the Election'.[34] In his own mind, he was already playing for the winning side.

In any case, Churchill had convinced himself that he had left the Tories for the purest of reasons, those for which he had entered politics.

> I admit I have changed my party. I don't deny it. I am proud of it. When I think of all the labours which Lord Randolph Churchill gave to the fortunes of the Conservative party and the ungrateful way in which he was treated by them when they obtained the power they would never have had but for him, I am delighted that circumstances have enabled me to break with them while I am still young and still have the energies of my life to give to the popular cause.[35]

Churchill spoke these words to an election audience in Manchester in January 1906. Six days earlier his biography, *Lord Randolph Churchill*, had been published to popular acclaim.[36] He was still chasing Tory Democracy – 'the popular cause' – seeking a platform for the heroic, populist policies that had died with his father. And where better to find it than on the radical wing of British politics. Lord Randolph, out of a sense of misguided loyalty, had shrunk from taking this step, to the ruin of his cause. Churchill would 'not fall into the same trap'.

On Balfour's resignation, an interim Liberal government had been constructed in early December 1905. At the general elections a month later Churchill was returned as the Liberal candidate for North-West

Manchester, and the Liberals swept into power with a massive victory.[37] Hoping for office in Sir Henry Campbell-Bannerman's new administration, he was rewarded with the post of Under-Secretary of State at the Colonial Office under Lord Elgin, after first having refused the financial secretaryship to the Treasury.[38] It was generally assumed that Churchill's preference of the Colonial Office sprang from dubious motives: that he wanted to monopolize attention in the Commons (Lord Elgin – who was not keen on the appointment of such a self-assured junior – sat in the Lords), particularly over the contentious South African settlement, and further that he had no stomach to play second fiddle to Asquith, Chancellor of the Exchequer. But this story,[39] impossible to discount, reveals only a healthy reflex for a budding politician.

It was Churchill's first administrative job. Lord Hugh Cecil had once depicted an Under-Secretary as 'a stipendiary echo'.[40] This was not Churchill's style. Rather, it might be said, he anticipated the echo. He demonstrated qualities that were to serve him for better or worse until the end of his career: phenomenal reserves of physical energy and concentration, a restless, refreshing mental vitality, and a wonderful ability to translate his thoughts, whether on paper or in speech, into lively, vivid language that enabled him to push his policies in government and defend them in Parliament and before the people. He was not however always capable of sorting the chaff from the wheat, and concentration on a particular topic often left him unable to take the wider view and impervious to contrary arguments. 'A typical missive, born of froth out of foam', Asquith once wrote, unkindly, of Churchill's interminable minutes.[41] Margot, his wife – possessor of an acid wit – noted that he had 'a noisy mind'. Later, she reflected on Churchill's recipe for success. Not his judgement, which was invariably wrong, but his 'courage and colour – his amazing mixture of industry and enterprise. He can and does always – all ways put himself in the pool. He never shirks, hedges, or protects himself – though he thinks of himself perpetually. He takes huge risks.' Churchill put it differently: 'Responsibility is an exhilarating drink'.[42]

Churchill was heavily involved in the most controversial question that confronted the Colonial Office: the South African settlement, acquitting himself with distinction and nursing government thinking towards responsible self-government for the Transvaal.[43] When he outlined the main features of the proposed Transvaal constitution to the House in July 1906, he pleaded with the Opposition to 'make it the gift of England'. It was a plea for magnanimity and reconciliation, but the Conservatives would have none of it. It was too 'audacious' a measure, they claimed, and denounced the scheme as 'reckless' and 'dangerous'.[44] Self-government was duly granted to the Transvaal in December 1906, and to the Orange Free State the following July. British interests were not imperilled.

In West and East Africa Churchill advocated greater railway development and 'imperial control', though he opposed military reprisals and the 'butchery' of local tribes. He expressed the Liberal view of 'using imperial power to secure the highest standards of justice in administration everywhere'. He defended Federation in Australia; criticized the leasing arrangements of the Ceylon pearl fisheries; refused to take immediate action on behalf of British firms in Shanghai who were concerned at the Chinese government's anti-opium edict; and pledged to guarantee adequate supplies of raw cotton to the mills of Lancashire 'by any method'.[45] He rapidly established a reputation, on both sides of the House, for hard work and high capacity.[46]

In the autumn of 1907 Churchill embarked on a tour of East Africa. Elgin had understood it to be 'a purely sporting and private expedition', but it quickly turned into 'an official progress'. Sailing through the Red Sea, where others would collapse from the sultry heat, he would work fourteen hours a day on his memoranda and correspondence and tourist articles for the *Strand Magazine*. Neither Elgin nor his Permanent Under-Secretary, Sir Francis Hopwood, were elated by Churchill's remarkable industry. But his proposals, mostly 'impracticable' and not pleasing 'either in style or substance', continued to swamp the office. He was irrepressible. Churchill's African 'progress' – captured in his slogan, 'sofari so goody' – lasted for four months. He landed in Uganda clad in a white uniform adorned by a galaxy of medals. He made a distinct impression on the Governor, Sir Hesketh Bell, who caught him once dictating his impressions of the country to a clerk while luxuriating in his hot bath, and to whom he crowed that within ten years he would be Prime Minister of Britain. 'He is a difficult fellow to handle,' confessed Bell, 'but I can't help liking him.'

Churchill and his party proceeded by foot, bicycle, rickshaw, motorcar, canoe, and steamer from Mombasa to Victoria Nyanza to Lake Albert and then up the Nile to Khartoum and Cairo. On the way he shot a white rhinoceros and hunted lions, indulged his passion for highly coloured butterflies, met local officials and native leaders, and inspected potential railway routes. He thoroughly enjoyed himself, like a child suddenly let loose in a fascinating toyshop. In one instance, he succumbed to temptation and ordered an advance of fifty miles into the country beyond Embo, a station lying north-east of Nairobi. 'This will bring 150,000 more natives under our direct control & add several English countries to our administration area,' he reported to Lady Randolph. 'Thus the Empire grows under Radical Administration.' Churchill's imperial concept of tighter control from the centre to develop these 'great estates' was strengthened as a result of these first-hand experiences.[47]

Churchill's propensity for voicing his opinions on any occasion and on every topic was already pronounced, and would take firm root with time, experience, and growing self-confidence. He could never quite grasp that what was for him perhaps no more than an intellectual exercise was interpreted by the recipients of his unsolicited advice as decisive proof of a pushy, assertive, abrasive character, whose levity was unbearable, and with whom it was virtually impossible to work. Hopwood remarked: 'He is most tiresome to deal with & will I fear give trouble . . . The restless energy, uncontrollable desire for notoriety & the lack of moral perception make him an anxiety indeed.'[48] Churchill lacked the necessary antennae to decipher this hostility.

His insensitivity to the feelings of others was certainly one of the reasons for the painful impression made by Churchill's first major speech as a government front-bencher, which condemned Lord Milner's role in the beating of Chinese labourers in South Africa. His speech was felt to be patronizing and offensive, particularly his references to Milner as a guilty Parnell who had ceased to be a factor in public life. The Liberals were disconsolate, the Unionists furious, the King thought it 'simply scandalous'. Churchill's private secretary, Edward March, who had been moved by the generosity of spirit of the speech in rehearsal, was convinced that his error was simply one 'of manner'.[49]

This lack of sensitivity extended also to his office routine. He had an unfortunate habit of running his pen, daubed in red ink, through the replies to parliamentary questions that his officials had so painstakingly prepared, and substituting his own wording. This no doubt improved their literary quality, but it implied, at best, lack of tact, and at worst, lack of faith in his staff's ability. With Elgin, his relationship has been described as one of 'qualified esteem'. Towards the end of their partnership, Churchill smoothed over their occasional clashes, admitting graciously that 'It would never be possible for me to quarrel with you, because your frank & invariable kindness always removes at once from my mind any trace of vexation which may arise from the tiresome course of business.' A month later, in March 1908, Churchill was brazenly angling to displace his chief.[50]

It should not be thought that Churchill's relations with his officials were always conducted on a razor's edge. He was also able to generate loyalty to an unusual degree. Edward Marsh first met Churchill at a Christmas party in 1904. Then a junior clerk in the Colonial Office, he found Churchill 'brilliant' but 'rather truculent and overbearing'. He was not therefore over enthusiastic when he learned that Churchill wanted him as his private secretary. But at a dinner party à deux, Churchill charmed him over. Lady Lytton (Pamela Plowden), an old friend of both, told Marsh, 'The first time you meet Winston you see all his faults, and the rest of your life you spend in discovering his virtues.' 'And so it proved,' concluded Marsh, who spent the remainder of his career accompanying Churchill from ministry to ministry. Eddie Marsh was the exception rather than the rule. Considering the length of Churchill's career, and his subsequent immense public popularity, he attracted remarkably few devoted followers of Marsh's quality. He was perfectly aware of this shortcoming and the fact that he had very few friends. 'I fail too often', he remarked, 'in the little offices which keep friendship sweet & warm.'[51]

'Why do you say I am incapable of affection?' Churchill asked Pamela Plowden, hinting broadly that his true love was reserved for himself. Much the same point was made by Gladys Deacon, 'Sunny's' second duchess: '[Winston] was incapable of love. He was in love with his own image – his reflection in the mirror . . . He was entirely out for Winston.' On the eve of his marriage, Churchill compared his personal destiny with that of his cousin, 'Sunny'.

> He is quite different from me, understanding women thoroughly, getting into touch with them at once, & absolutely dependent upon feminine influence of some kind for the peace & harmony of his soul. Whereas I am stupid and clumsy in that relation, and naturally self-reliant & self contained. Yet by such different paths we both arrive at loneliness.[52]

There was a bitter truth concealed in his frankness. He was too wrapped up in his own private world, too involved in his public duties, too much a captive of his demanding ego, blinded by its seductive pressures, ever to give himself up fully to another. And this would not change, only soften, with experience.

Churchill's experience of women was limited. Brought up in the cloistered, wholly male society of English public schools, and educated at Sandhurst, this was to be partially expected. During his early manhood, his name had been linked with a number of young ladies, but it is difficult to gauge the quality and intensity of these relationships. The thought of one, 'the beautiful Polly Hackett', consoled him, even though her correspondence – 'I am so sorry for writing such a dull letterkins' – was replete with nursery-like expressions. He had been envied by his contemporaries for his acquaintance, albeit passive, with Mabel Love, a well-known musical comedy actress. Of another, the shipping heiress, Muriel Wilson, he praised the 'tranquil *banalité*' of their companionship. Tongues had also wagged about Churchill and Helen Botha, daughter of the Boer leader. And at one time Lady Randolph thought that Churchill had designs – though, typically, 'not serious ones' – on Lady Gwendeline ('Goonie') Bertie, soon to become his brother Jack's wife.

At different times he had proposed and been rejected by Muriel Wilson, Ethel Barrymore, the American actress, and Pamela Plowden, daughter of the British Resident at Hyderabad. The most serious of these dalliances was with Pamela Plowden. He had first met her in India when he thought her 'the most beautiful girl I have ever seen'. Their affair deepened. 'She loves me vy dearly', Churchill confided to his mother. But by January 1901, their desultory affair had petered out. Pamela would not commit herself – to him! Still, penned Churchill despairingly, 'she is the only woman I could ever live happily with'. His family and friends were less certain. She had a somewhat skittish reputation in society. Jack thought her 'an awful humbug', noting that '[she] is the same to three other men as she is to Winston'.[53]

The impression remains strong that Churchill conducted these flirtations in a minor key, in a somewhat lackadaisical manner, as though he were going through the motions, doing what was expected of him. On one point at least there is a remarkable unanimity of opinion: Churchill was not a philanderer, neither before his marriage nor in after years. 'I always hear, that no one can nail Winston down to any particular lady,' wrote a lady friend to Lloyd George, '& that the opinion is that "he is not a lady's man" . . . [and] that he had a rather curious way of looking at a woman . . . Winston would become a million times more popular if it could be thought that he cared enough for some woman to risk even a little discomfort for her sake. Perhaps it will come but I doubt it.' Variously described as 'gauche' or 'romantic' or 'innocent' or 'clumsy' in his attitude towards women, his idea of 'a great woman' was that she should be 'sagacious and chaste'. His grandmother, the Duchess of Marlborough, concluded from his botched efforts that 'It is clear you have not yet attained a knowledge of Women – and it is evident you have (I am thankful to see) no experience of Love.'[54]

Clementine Hozier was the child of a broken marriage. Her parents, Lady Blanche and Sir Henry Hozier, had had a tempestuous relationship and had been separated since 1891, whereupon Sir Henry, a turbulent character, had disowned his family. Neither party was blameless. Both had openly indulged in extra-marital affairs. One of her lovers, Captain George 'Bay' Middleton, Lady Blanche told Wilfred Scawen Blunt, had fathered Clementine and her sister, Kitty. 'It is much wiser,' Blunt agreed, 'for a woman who has an inferior husband to choose a suitable sire for her children, and both these girls were delightful, refined and superior in every way'.[55] Left without means, Lady Blanche was forced to bring up her family of four children in reduced circumstances. Much of their time was spent at seaside resorts, Seaford in Sussex and Dieppe – 'the refuge of so much exiled English innocence' – across the Channel, in order to economize.

By chance, Lady Blanche and Lady Randolph were old acquaintances. And it was equally by chance that Churchill met Clementine for the first time at a London ball at Crewe House in the spring of 1904. It was not the most auspicious of meetings. When they were introduced to each other by Lady Randolph, Churchill simply stood silent, gazing intently at her. Notoriously short on small-talk, Churchill had nothing to say. 'He was very gauche,' Clementine later recollected, 'he never asked me for a dance, he never asked me to have supper with him.' Embarrassed by Churchill's clumsy conduct, Clementine went off to dance with another, less inhibited, admirer.

Four years passed before they next met, again by chance, at a dinner-party given by Lady Helier, Clementine's aunt and Churchill's benefactress from his army days. It was only by the purest fluke that either turned up. Churchill was caught soaking in his bath by Eddie Marsh, certain that what lay ahead would be an evening of utter boredom. It would be more amusing to remain at home, he settled. But Marsh jogged his conscience as to where his duty lay, and Churchill obeyed. Clementine too had no zest for an evening out. Her gowns were out of fashion; she could not find clean gloves; and she felt too tired to make an effort to entertain people she scarcely knew. As it happened, the evening went swimmingly. Churchill – by now a politician of some distinction – was far more attentive. Smitten afresh by Clementine's beauty and charm, he pursued her ardently for the next five months. At Blenheim, on 11 August, they were out walking in the rose garden when a sudden rainstorm surprised them. They took shelter in the ornamental temple of Diana that overlooks the lake. Clementine remembered the scene. They sat for half an hour and nothing happened. 'Well now, I looked down at the stone floor and noticed a beetle slowly moving across it, and I thought to myself, "If that beetle reaches that crack and Winston hasn't proposed, he's not going to."' Winston, apparently, won the race, for he proposed marriage and was accepted. Later, Clementine had second thoughts: but her brother Bill told her that she must stand firm by her commitment: she had already broken off two previous engagements and to do so a third time, with a prominent public figure involved, would be intolerable. Perhaps, to boost her own self-confidence, Clementine solicited a gentle nudge in the right direction. This time she was truly in love. 'How I have lived 23 years without you,' she marvelled. 'Everything that happened before about 5 months ago seems unreal.' Churchill was equally bowled over: 'There are no words to convey to you the feelings of love & joy by which my being is possessed.'[56]

At 2 pm on Saturday, 12 September 1908, Winston Churchill was married to Clementine Hozier at St Margaret's church, Westminster. He was thirty-three, she, nine years younger. Wearing Churchill's present of diamond earrings, and clad in a lustrous white satin gown, set off by a flowing veil of soft tulle and tiara of orange blossom, she was given away by her brother, Bill. Churchill, accompanied by his best man, Lord Hugh Cecil, did not present quite so stunning a sight. The *Tailor and Cutter* commented that his wedding suit was 'one of the greatest failures as a wedding garment we have ever seen', lending to Churchill 'a sort of glorified coachman appearance'. St Margaret's was crammed to capacity, mainly with family, but also with a sprinkling of politicians – it being the summer recess, most of Churchill's colleagues were away. Even at his wedding, Churchill did not lose his passion for politics. In the vestry, he buttonholed an astonished Lloyd George to settle one or two burning issues, no doubt connected with their insurance schemes.[57] The wedding was widely reported. One popular cartoon had Churchill clasping a stocking in his right hand, grinning mischievously at his public, over the legend: 'Winston's Latest Line – "Hoziery".'

After a honeymoon in Italy, the couple set up home, at first refurbishing Churchill's bachelor flat in Bolton Street, and later, in 1909, moving to a house in Eccleston Square.

Many years later, Churchill looked back gaily to September 1908 when he had married to live 'happily ever afterwards'.[58] Certainly their marriage proved solid enough to withstand the inevitable stresses in any marital union. But Churchill's fairy-tale ending, although true in general, does not tell the whole story. There was a clear incompatibility of temperaments, an in-built tension that on occasion bubbled over. Clementine was more reserved than he, more prone to worry, more puritanical by nature, more thrifty, more suspicious of people's intentions, less given to flights of groundless optimism. By contrast, Churchill was an unrepentant hedonist, he was more easy-going, more positive in outlook, more innocent in his ways. Clementine disapproved of most of his political cronies – F. E. Smith or Beaverbrook – and many of his habits – gambling, for example. Inconsiderate in small things, he would bring home unannounced his friends for improvised political dinner parties, a practice that set Clementine's nerves on edge. But also on major issues, such as acquiring their future home, Chartwell, he lacked sensitivity. He would charge ahead without taking into account Clementine's feelings, absolutely certain that his preferences would also be hers. Clementine was, in many ways, more wordly-wise than Churchill: her judgement was often sounder than his, her advice well-worth heeding – if he would but listen. If, as it is often claimed, most men marry their mothers, Churchill was the exception.

The Churchills' family grew steadily: Diana (b. 1909), Randolph (b. 1911), Sarah (b. 1914), Marigold (b. 1918, but who died tragically in 1921 of septicaemia of the throat), and Mary (b. 1922). One of the most endearing features of their family life were the nicknames acquired by each member of the family: Diana – 'Puppy Kitten' and the 'Golden-cream kitten'; Randolph – the 'Chum Bolly' and 'Rabbit'; Sarah – 'Bumble Bee'; Marigold – 'Duckadilly'. Winston and Clementine referred to each other as 'Pug' or 'Amber Pug' and 'Kat' respectively, and their letters to each other would be adorned with fetching sketches of the 'The Wow' or 'The Woo'. Some time after their marriage they ceased to share the same bedroom. 'Breakfast should be had in bed, alone,' said Churchill. As they kept different hours, this arrangement was convenient. Clementine was a morning person, an early riser whose energy was spent by late evening. Churchill was the exact opposite. Although he awoke early, he rose late. He would remain in bed during the morning, preparing his speeches and articles, working through his papers and correspondence, appear for lunch, and, fortified by his inevitable afternoon catnap, was then able to work well into the small hours of the morning. Clementine was wont to leave him little notes: 'Mrs Grimalkin [an old she-cat] presents her compliments & would appreciate a little visit with the Speech.'[59]

Lord Hugh Cecil, a confirmed bachelor himself, approved of the union on practical grounds: 'It will be excellent for you mentally morally & politically. A bachelor,' he bantered, 'is regarded as morally unprincipled.'[60] But it proved to be 'excellent' in every way. That it was a love-match there can be no doubt. That it survived harmoniously until his death was due also to Clementine's willingness to submerge herself in his career, to submit to the whims of his self-centred personality – or, as Goonie, her sister-in-law, once put it, to his 'pasha-like tendencies'.[61]

By April 1908 Churchill had acquired a family and a seat in the Cabinet. On Campbell-Bannerman's death, Asquith had assumed the premiership and in the ensuing Cabinet reshuffle had appointed Churchill as President of the Board of Trade,[62] at the young age of thirty-three. Few doubted his brilliance. Others thought him a shallow-minded and bumptious creature. 'This ridiculous jackanapes,' fulminated Leo Maxse in the *National Review*, styling him as 'a violent and reckless political adventurer, the pot-boy of Downing Street'. 'He would do well to study the drab heroes of life,' advised John Morley, 'Framing oneself upon Napoleon has proved a danger to many a man before him.' Yet Morley also saw in him, with his formidable energy and dynamism and powers of concentration, 'the most alive politician' he had ever met. Able, original, industrious – when compared with most Liberal ministers – he possessed a 'curious flair for all sorts of political cases as they arise, though even he now and then mistakes a frothy bubble for a great wave.' Sir Edward Grey, cool of nature and not given to overstatement, thought him 'a genius', his one fault being that 'phrases master him, rather than he them'. Still, Grey forecast presciently, 'his faults and mistakes will be forgotten in his achievements'.[63]

The journalist Alfred Gardiner described him as one of 'the two most arresting figures in politics [the other being Lloyd George]'. Was he democrat or aristocrat? asked Gardiner. And replied: 'we may . . . suspect that [in a crisis] his real political philosophy is the philosophy of Caesarism'. In normal circumstances, he remained an incalculable factor. The sympathetic Gardiner portrayed Churchill as a political gentleman of fortune, following politics as he would follow the hounds, holding no animus against the fox but wanting simply to be in 'at the kill'. Was he at heart just an outgrown Harrow schoolboy, wishing only to be in the thick of the fight and having a good time?' Was Churchill merely 'a wayward meteor' or 'a fixed star'? Gardiner offered no categoric answer. It remained an open question: but the most intriguing one in British politics.[64]

5

Radical Politics

'Winston Churchill is out, Out, Out!' rejoiced the Tory *Daily Telegraph*, overcome by the news of Churchill's defeat at the by-election held in North-West Manchester in April 1908, for it was then still the custom for newly appointed Cabinet ministers to vacate their seats and seek re-election. The blame was placed partly on 'those sulky Irish Catholics changing sides at the last moment owing to priestly pressure'. But there were deeper causes for his defeat. The seat was traditionally Tory. In 1906, in the heat of the debate on tariff reform, Churchill had won over a considerable number of Unionist free traders. They had now abandoned him and returned to their former allegiance. 'The surprise was not Churchill's defeat now, but his victory in 1906,' explained the *Daily News*.[1]

Still, he was greatly vexed: 'Defeat,' he reflected, 'however consoled, explained or discounted is odious.'[2] Happily, this setback was shortlived. By May, Churchill was back in the House as member for Dundee, a safe, working class Liberal constituency.

Another pressure group which claimed (largely without foundation) that it had defeated Churchill at Manchester was the Women's Social and Political Union. Withholding the right for women to vote in general elections was by now a glaring anachronism. For years women had been active in national politics: Lady Randolph and the Dames of the Primrose League were proof enough, as they canvassed on behalf of their husbands and relatives; and the Liberals possessed a similar organization.

When the Liberals came to power, acts were passed that enabled women to participate more fully in local politics. In the Commons, it was possible to muster sufficient support to pass suffragettist motions, but these remained demonstrations of good intent, thwarted by indecision at the top, and, after Asquith succeeded as Prime Minister, by a pronounced lack of conviction. For the Liberals, the suffragette movement presented a particular dilemma, for by ignoring it, or evading their demands, they tarnished their reputation as the progressive party of reform.[3]

As the Pankhursts' WSPU offices were quartered in Manchester, Churchill offered an easy target for their wrath when he attended Liberal meetings there. During the 1906 elections the suffragettes issued a manifesto opposing him 'on the ground that he is a member of the Liberal Government which refuses to give Women the Vote'. Churchill's meetings were disrupted, his speeches heckled, his character abused. Twice, in 1909 and 1910, he was physically attacked with whips by enraged suffragists. 'Take that, you brute! You brute!' cried Theresa Garnett, 'I will show what English women can do.' Churchill refused to press charges.[4]

As a young subaltern in India, Churchill had believed that women's suffrage was 'contrary to natural law and the practice of civilized states'. He vowed, rashly, to oppose unswervingly 'this ridiculous movement'. But by the time he entered Parliament he had begun to understand that women's suffrage could, however, yield material political benefits and in 1904 had voted in favour of women's franchise. Clementine was an ardent supporter. Her letter to *The Times* signed 'One of the Doomed', was, thought Asquith, that dyed-in-the-wool anti-suffragist, 'much the best thing' he had read for a long time on the question. In private she lobbied Churchill to adopt her broadminded views, but with little success. Close friends, Charles and Lucy Masterman, viewed him as a 'rather tepid' suffragist. He wavered, unable to raise any enthusiasm for the topic. But he refused to be browbeaten – or 'henpecked', as he put it – into submission by the distracted, unruly antics of the Pankhursts and their ilk. Lloyd George remarked that 'they make Winston very bitter . . . His perorations, prepared with the utmost care, are completely wrecked and spoiled by squeaky voices calling out, 'Mr Churchill! What about votes for women?'[5]

Although a majority of the Liberal Party were pledged to women's suffrage, few had thought seriously about it. As the government dithered, the suffragists escalated their campaign: mass demonstrations, arrests, hunger strikes, forced-feeding, vandalism, arson, even a martyr to the cause when Emily Davidson threw herself under the hooves of the Derby runners in 1913. On 'Black Friday', 18 November 1910, police and suffragists engaged in a six-hour battle in Parliament Square. There were accusations of police brutality: kicking, twisting arms, punching noses, gripping breasts, thrusting knees between legs. Fifty women testified to police violence. Churchill, who by then was Home Secretary, was singled out as having deliberately ordered the police to employ these barbaric methods, an accusation without foundation but which gained wide currency. Outraged, he considered prosecuting Christabel Pankhurst for libel, but eventually decided against it.[6]

At Dundee, a fortnight later, Churchill made clear he was 'in favour of the principle of women being enfranchised'. But he emphatically refused to vote for any Bill unless satisfied on two counts: that it would not favour 'the property vote', thereby tilting the balance towards the Conservatives (a condition it was impossible to guarantee) and that a genuine majority of the electors desired it (a condition requiring a general referendum).[7] Deploying these ingenious but entirely unrealistic alternatives, he was thus able to slip adroitly through the enormous loopholes he had fashioned in the name of democracy into a personal no man's land between the warring factions.

He employed wrecking tactics towards so-called Conciliation Bills of 1910–12, and resisted a further compromise by Asquith.[8] How ridiculous, he mocked, if the government were to go down 'on Petticoat politics!' Women would have to wait until June 1918, when Lloyd George passed his Franchise Act, before they finally gained the vote.[9]

Votes for women rated low on Churchill's list of priorities. In his four election campaigns of 1908 and 1910, he never once raised the issue in his prepared addresses.[10] Other, greater questions filled his mind: the Lords v. the People; Ireland; tariffs and free trade; national insurance schemes and social reform; army expenditure and naval estimates.

At heart, perhaps, Churchill felt that women had no real place in politics. Lady Violet Bonham-Carter wrote of his 'essentially romantic' approach to women. His inner circle of friends was exclusively male and remained so. Plain women rarely appealed to him. The intellectual attainments of 'blue stockings' left him cold. 'Beauty, glamour, radiance, innocence,' these were the qualities he sought. He divided women into two categories: 'the virginal snowdrops, unsullied by experience . . . and the mature who were at home among the seams'. He could, and did, enjoy their company, but they were not allowed to intrude into his political life, certainly not to challenge the ideas he held or the policies he advocated.[11]

The suffragettes battled vigorously against Churchill during his re-election campaigns in April-May 1908, but the main thrust of his arguments was to promote the cause of social reform, an aim that came to dominate his career for the next few years. As he moved from Manchester to Dundee, a working class constituency, his radical message became more pronounced. He swept into battle on behalf of 'the highest interests of the labouring classes'. Unemployment was 'the most urgent of our social problems'. The unemployed, the hapless victims of a cruel system, should not be cast aside and forgotten, but taken care of, prevented from becoming demoralized and broken, and restored to full vigour so that they might again 'take their place in the fighting line of industrialism'. The evils of unemployment and underemployment could be reduced, if not eliminated, by decasualizing unskilled labour and putting a stop to the exploitation of child labour. There was a need for greater government intervention, for the creation of state industries, afforestation schemes, work on the canals, the amalgamation – even nationalization – of the railways. He called for state pensions to alleviate the burdens of old age and an extensive revision of the Poor Law to cushion the hardships endured by the needy.[12]

These were advanced views. Was his new-found enthusiasm a sudden fad? Had Churchill 'just discovered' the poor? as his colleague and friend, Charles Masterman, haughtily put it. Only in the sense that he dived into the deep waters of social reform with the same abandon and fervour and pugnacity that characterized all of his labours. It was another well-lit stage for him to flaunt his talents for all to see and admire. 'Thou shall not muzzle the ox when he treadeth out the corn,' Churchill remarked.[13]

But his was not the enthusiasm of the ignorant. No working politician in Britain at the time, particularly an ambitious one, could have been unaware of the problems of the poor, the unemployed, and the elderly. These issues had been on the national agenda since the 1880s, and measures had already been enacted by Parliament that were designed to ease some of the distress.[14] Lord Randolph Churchill himself had taken a stand – not without characteristic touches of ambiguity – on the question and had gone on record as favouring 'a large amount of state intervention for the benefit of the masses of the people'. As a young Tory MP, Churchill had read Seebohm Rowntree's classic work, *Poverty*, a study of working class conditions in York. Its findings made his 'hair stand on end'; it was 'a terrible and shocking thing', he said, that the poor can only escape from their grinding destitution to either the workhouse or prison. 'However willing the working classes may be to remain in passive opposition merely to the existing social system, they will not continue to bear, they cannot, the awful uncertainties of their lives,' he wrote. 'Minimum standards of wages and comfort, insurance . . . against sickness, unemployment, old age – these are the questions, and the only questions, by which parties are going to live in the future. Woe to Liberalism if they slip through its fingers.'[15]

What drove Churchill towards his 'irresistible revolution'? Complaints have been levelled that his approach not only 'smacked' of paternalism, but was 'rooted and grounded' in it. He is reproached for seeing social reform as a means – not least to advance his own career – and not as an end in itself. But what could reasonably be expected of Churchill? He was, after all, a duke's grandson – a background he was trying to live down at the time, not up to. He had no intimate experience of the wretched and savage nature of life in the slums of the great cities.[16] 'You probably don't realize,' Clementine was to tell Lord Moran 'that he knows nothing of the life of ordinary people.' What are the English working class interested in? he once asked Lord Riddell, genuinely puzzled. Wandering through the squalid back streets of Manchester during an election campaign, he turned to Eddie Marsh and remarked, in a typical aside: 'Fancy living in one of these streets – never seeing anything beautiful – never eating anything savoury – never saying anything clever.'[17]

The findings of Seebohm Rowntree and Charles Booth – indicating that almost 40 per cent of the working classes in London and York were poverty-stricken or worse – were not for him cold statistics that could be amended by some clever accounting. They kindled his compassion, as they would any humane person, but they did not drive him to mount any revolutionary barricades. What was noted about his father and Tory Democracy in 1883 could equally have been written about him in 1908. 'Under the paternal sway of this nobleman, aided and supported by his brother nobles, we humble folk are to be given, as an equivalent for political power, better houses, a compulsory scheme of national insurance, commons, parks, museums, libraries and workhouses . . . We now know what a Tory Democracy is.'[18]

Churchill would dutifully raise up the standards of the lower classes. He would equip them to participate more fruitfully in the life of the country, to ensure that they served King and Country and preserved the greatness of the Empire. Thus social stability would be preserved, even strengthened, not torn down. Underlying Churchill's passion for social reform lay a deep vein of innate conservatism. He was appalled at Charles Masterman's 'revolutionary talk'. The Mastermans picturesquely saw him as an 'aboriginal and unchangeable Tory'.[19] He could not, nor did he wish to, escape from his own inheritance.

Although Churchill's reformist zeal took a strictly practical bent, it was not entirely devoid of ideological content. The link between imperial greatness and a healthy and well-educated population at home runs strongly through his declarations. He saw 'little glory in an Empire which can rule the waves [but] is unable to flush its sewers'. At the very least, he contended, minimum living standards must be attained – and then maintained. Not to do so could prove fatal to Britain's position as the dominant imperial power. In the great game of 'national efficiency' (then, as now, a popular pastime) Britain was losing out. For Churchill, the panacea was free trade which would guarantee prosperity at home, a prerequisite for financing social reform and raising the standards of the masses. Campaigning in Lancashire in 1909, he was more convinced than ever that his course was the right one. The 'stinted millions' crowded together in the ghastly urban slums of Britain were not fit to breed 'an Imperial race'. 'The seeds of Imperial ruin and national decay,' Churchill declared, were sown in the sprawling urban slums of Britain and in the denuded villages of the countryside, in 'the unnatural gap between rich and poor'. The true enemies of Britain were poverty and unemployment at one end of the social scale, and the shocking increase of frivolous luxury at the other.[20]

The problem was that other groups, more authentically radical than the Liberals, were now also bent on bridging Churchill's 'unnatural gap'. The newly formed Labour Representation Committee had twenty-nine MPs in the elections of 1906, although some parliamentary observers put the number of Labour-oriented members as high as fifty-four.[21] Rising industrial unrest and unemployment gave an added bite to Labour's claims.[22] The so-called 'Lib-Lab pact', an electoral arrangement whereby some Labour candidates went unchallenged by the Liberals, lent, on the surface, an air of respectability to the new Labour MPs. Not only were they a stable political element, but they also added greatly 'to the wisdom and earnestness, and consequently to the dignity of the House', claimed Churchill. But potentially the appearance of the Labour Party represented a real threat to the Liberals, a fact recognized by their leaders.

At Dundee in May 1908, Churchill, heckled forcefully by Labour supporters, appealed for their vote: pleading for unity, he drove a wedge between the responsible and respectable Trade Unions, and the revolutionary socialists, violent and extreme in their views, wild-headed in their actions.

> Socialism seeks to pull down wealth; Liberalism seeks to raise up poverty. Socialism would destroy private interests; Liberalism would preserve private interests by reconciling them with public right. Socialism would kill enterprise; Liberalism would rescue enterprise from the trammels of privilege and preference. Socialism assails the pre-eminence of the individual; Liberalism seeks, and shall seek more in the future, to build up a minimum standard for the mass. Socialism exalts the rule; Liberalism exalts the man. Socialism attacks capital; Liberalism attacks monopoly.[23]

Liberal social reformers drew their inspiration from the example of Germany. To Asquith, Churchill had spoken of instituting 'a sort of Germanized network of State intervention & regulation'. Lloyd George had visited Germany in August 1908 and had come away 'tremendously impressed' at what he had seen of the German social insurance system. He immediately passed on these impressions to Churchill. For the next few years Lloyd George and Churchill were to work in close tandem. It was the period of their most intimate collaboration. They were nick-named 'the two Romeos', or 'the Heavenly Twins'. It was only natural that Lloyd George should take the lead. As Chancellor of the Exchequer he outranked Churchill, his radical credentials were more impeccable, and his was the authentic voice of the common man. Nor had he blotted his copybook by betraying one party to seek preference with another. They were a formidable combination: dynamic, restless, visibly ambitious, blessed with brilliant powers of persuasion. Together they succeeded in pulling an often hesitant and suspicious Cabinet towards their goal of extensive social reform. But their fruitful partnership masked a rivalry no less acute because of their collaboration. Both considered themselves as potential leaders of the Liberal Party: Lloyd George with more cause, but with Churchill's confidence growing as he clambered up the political ladder. Apprehensive lest one snatch the glory from the other, they viewed each other with misgivings.

Two such ebullient personalities, egocentric, enamoured of their own abilities, could not fail, on occasion, to irritate each other. For all that, they appreciated and admired each other's talents. In time, through force of circumstances, Churchill accustomed himself to Lloyd George's pre-eminent position. He thought him 'the greatest political genius of the day', with more 'political insight than any other statesman', and admitted later that he had acted as Lloyd George's 'chief lieutenant'. He stood somewhat in awe of Lloyd George, at times intimidated by the Welshman's sharp tongue. 'You will see the point when you begin to understand that conversation is not a monologue!' Lloyd George once rapped out, tired of listening to Churchill's opinionated interruptions.[24]

When Asquith reconstructed the Liberal administration in April 1908, Churchill had first expressed a desire to replace Elgin and serve as Colonial Secretary. Although the Admiralty had been mentioned, and Churchill thought it 'the most pleasant & glittering' of all Cabinet posts, he declined it as Lord Tweedmouth, the incumbent First Lord, was his uncle. As for the Local Government Board, also on offer, Churchill thought it 'more laborious', and 'more choked with petty & even squalid detail' than any other government post; he had also turned it down on the reasonable grounds that he refused 'to be shut up in a soup kitchen' with Beatrice Webb.[25] Yet as President of the Board of Trade this was precisely the position he found himself in. He relied heavily upon officials and experts, like the Webbs, to prepare the groundwork for the measures he intended to execute. Often his own ideas did not ring true. Some detected a false note in Churchill's social crusade. Beatrice Webb, after their first dinner together, thought him 'egotistical, bumptious, shallow-minded and reactionary', even though endowed with personal magnetism, pluck, and originality. 'I never do any brainwork that anyone else can do for me,' he bragged, a boast unlikely to recommend him to the workaholic Webbs. Like most others who came to know him, she rated him 'brilliantly able', but doubted whether he ever fully comprehended 'the philosophy' behind his dazzling expositions on the social ailments that beset the country.[26]

Many of his Cabinet colleagues were no less troubled: they doubted his motives and were apprehensive lest his reforming zeal leave them stranded in deep waters. His appearance at Cabinet meetings, sending off electric shocks in all directions, disrupted its harmony. He remained supremely oblivious of the antipathy he aroused. By sheer persistence and rhetorical skill, he and Lloyd George prevailed over Cabinet vacillation. But they could not damp down entirely their colleagues' suspicion and hostility. They even taxed Asquith's patience. Churchill had no firm 'convictions', Lloyd George no firm 'principles', he held.[27]

The Liberals had made no unequivocal public commitment to social reform. At the previous general elections, issues such as free trade, imperial preference, retrenchment, the future of South Africa, had been to the fore. They resented being hustled into open-ended social policies that were not central to traditional Liberal doctrine. The harder Churchill tried, the more he was suspect. At a dinner party given by Sir Edward Grey, it was agreed that Churchill was 'hated', even though he was the second best known personality in the Cabinet (the first being John Burns). The Cabinet 'distrust everything they [Lloyd George and Churchill] advance,' recorded Masterman in October 1908. He does not 'inspire trust' and will 'never get to the top in English politics,' Asquith was to write. But this was precisely what most people believed fuelled Churchill's campaign. He wants 'to push to the front of the Cabinet,' decided Lord Esher. Suspected of harbouring Napoleonic ambitions, a fear reinforced by his undisguised admiration of the French autocrat,[28] few believed that he was moved by noble, generous motives. His conceit also gave rise for concern. 'The longer I live, the more certain I am I know all there is to be known,' he announced to Sir Edward Grey.[29]

Churchill forged ahead. After the impressive report on German insurance schemes and labour exchanges, he explained to the Prime Minister that Germany 'is organized not only for war, but for peace': Britain, on the other hand, '[is] organized for nothing except party politics'. In an article in The Nation in March 1908 and letters to Asquith, he set out a comprehensive programme of 'important legislation' that should include 'Labour exchanges & Unemployment Insurance: National Infirmity Insurance etc: Special Expansive State Industries – Afforestation – Roads: Modernised Poor Law i.e. classification: Railway Amalgamation with State Control and guarantee: [and] Education compulsory until 17.'[30]

Much of this programme was realized. The timing was right. In every respect, claimed a government report, trade conditions and the plight of the working man had worsened in 1908.[31] If the Liberals, or those among them so inclined, wished to corner the Labour vote, then they had to act expeditiously. And no one could act with more verve and drive than Churchill. As President of the Board of Trade, Churchill had involved himself intimately in major reforms. There was the Trade Boards Act which dealt with the shameful practice of sweated labour; two Acts that regulated working conditions in the coal industry; and two linked measures, the introduction of labour exchanges and a compulsory insurance scheme, to combat the misfortunes of unemployment in trades particularly prone to cyclical fluctuations.[32]

Having sketched out his strategy, Churchill then elaborated upon it. In the course of a year, from July 1908 until August 1909, he submitted twelve papers, not only 'intelligence reports' but also policy papers, for the Cabinet's instruction.[33] Of course, he did not act alone. He was dependent mainly upon his experts and officials, and also Charles Masterman, Under-Secretary at the Local Government Board who had worked among the poor of East London and had written a book, *The Condition of England* (1909), explaining his ideas. His commitment to social reform was deep-rooted, though no less 'patronizing' than Churchill's.[34] It was the Lloyd George-Churchill-Masterman combination that presided over the Liberal administration's grand design for social reform.

Some of the legislation was uncontroversial. Labour exchanges of a sort, run by local authorities and trade unions, had already been in existence for some time. The problem was to build on to the existing framework and turn it into a national, state-run system. This was the job of William Beveridge, an Oxford don who first met Churchill at a dinner-party at the Webbs.[35] The administrative particulars completed, Churchill introduced the Bill, with little trouble, to a poorly attended House of Commons on 20 May 1909, and it received the royal assent four months later.

Churchill's reliance on the experts did not mean that he was captured by them. He had long felt that the introduction of Labour Exchanges would enable the government to detect 'in what trades or in what places [unemployment] is acute', to trace 'its seasonal and cyclical variations', and to distinguish 'between the unemployed and the under-employed, between the worker and the loafer, between permanent contraction and passing depression'. And in this way, 'If anywhere in the British Isles there is a job for him, he can be conveyed to it as fast as the trains will travel.'[36] But unemployment insurance was a controversial issue. 'That old ruffian [John] Burns & that little goose [Walter] Runciman' queered his pitch in Cabinet. Before very long he had also fallen out with the Webbs and was at odds with his Permanent Under-Secretary, Sir Hubert Llewellyn Smith.[37]

Unlike the Webbs, Churchill had no wish to redeem society, to discipline it into adopting worthier habits. The Webbs thought that the use of labour exchanges should be compulsory for the unemployed, so that those entitled to unemployment insurance could be distinguished from the malingerers. This form of regimentation did not appeal to Churchill's freer spirit. 'I do not like mixing up moralities and mathematics,' Churchill wrote. 'Our concern is with the evil, not with the causes. With the fact of unemployment, not with the character of the unemployed.' Churchill was not concerned with saving the souls of sinners, but with rectifying concrete problems of acute hardship.[38]

When the National Insurance Act – a package-deal that incorporated both health and unemployment benefits – was finally enacted in December 1911, its unemployment clauses were framed roughly in accordance with Churchill's ideas.[39] By this time, Churchill had changed his Cabinet seat twice, first to the Home Office and then to the Admiralty, and he no longer held ministerial responsibility for the Act. This had passed to Lloyd George, who took the initiative for the most controversial aspect of the Bill, health insurance, and successfully guided it through a minefield of hostile opinion, both in and out of Parliament.[40] Naturally, Lloyd George took the glory, not only for health but also for unemployment insurance. Churchill was peeved. Lloyd George, however, was convinced that the credit was his by right, that he had actually fathered the scheme, but that in 'a weak moment' he had revealed his plans to Churchill who had then promptly run off to Asquith and gained permission to frame a Bill 'on the lines that I had proposed, and to introduce it himself'.[41] Churchill may well have picked Lloyd George's brain, given his penchant of never doing 'any brainwork' that others could do for him, as he had so disarmingly admitted. But one version of events does not entirely cancel out the other. Neither Churchill nor Lloyd George were above acting the political magpie, should the cause demand it and the opportunity present itself. It is clear enough that Churchill's drive and ardour carried unemployment insurance through its difficult and painful teething period. The Bill was a significant landmark in British welfare legislation; and Churchill's part in it was considerable and worthy of emphasis.

This massive programme of welfare legislation was contentious to an extreme,[43] and the coming years were among the stormiest in modern British politics. The Conservative attempt to stymie Liberal legislation by exploiting its built-in majority in the House of Lords opened a Pandora's box: 'the People's Budget'; two general elections in 1910; the reform of the House of Lords; and not least the resurrection of the Irish problem in all its contrariness. For the Liberals, the net cost of this casual chain of superbly dramatic events was prohibitive: at the end of it they had lost their majority position in British politics, as it turned out, for ever.

After the Conservative débâcle of 1906, Balfour laid out a strategy of recovery for his defeated Party. 'The two Houses shall not work as separate armies'. We must fight 'very stiffly' in the Commons, he believed, and use the Lords as 'the theatre of compromise'.[44] He soon abandoned this cautionary tone. The real business of an Opposition was to oppose, he contended. Bill after Bill – Education, Irish Devolution,

Land Reform – fell before the wrecking tactics of the Lords. Resentment mounted. An enraged Lloyd George chastised the Lords as 'Mr Balfour's poodle', ridiculing its claim to be 'the watchdog of the Constitution'. Churchill was equally outraged. He harangued a mass meeting at Hyde Park: 'This afternoon you must speak your mind as to who is going to rule this land, whether it shall be the masses through the elected members of the House of Commons, or whether it shall be an interested class through the instrumentality of the House of Lords.' In private, he was even more vigorous. At a dinner-party, he sat at the table, jabbing fiercely at his bread: 'We shall send them up a Budget in June as shall terrify them, they have started the class war, they had better be careful.' How long will this government survive? he was asked. 'If they survive the next Budget, two or three years. That'll be the teeth,' he answered.[45]

For two centuries the Lords had never thrown out a budget. They possessed, by precedent, the constitutional right to either adopt money Bills *en bloc*, or reject them wholly. But it was a right tolerated by the Commons; and it was taken for granted, however, that the sphere of finance was for the Commons alone to decide. In April 1909 the Lords rejected Lloyd George's budget. Provocative it might have been – its most draconian clauses, from the Conservative standpoint, stipulated a land tax of 20 per cent on unearned increment of land values, an increase in death duties and income tax, and a super tax on exceptionally high incomes[46] – but few believed that the Upper House would be lunatic enough to decimate it. Churchill warned that the government would tolerate 'No amendments, excision, modifying, or mutilating'. Should the Conservative diehards choose to ignore his advice, 'Parliament will be dissolved and we shall come to you in a moment of high consequence for every cause for which Liberalism has ever fought.' Churchill's forecast proved to be correct. By vetoing the budget, the Lords left the government with no alternative but to let the issue be 'determined by the people'. The country entered into a period of acute political turmoil, that came to a head with the passing of the Parliament Bill in August 1911 and simmered on until the outbreak of war in 1914.

This great drama was tailor-fitted to Churchill's barnstorming talents. As a lively chairman of the newly-formed Budget League, he did not forget that the original point of the budget was to finance social reform. Where was the money to come from, asked the doubters. Churchill provided the complete answer: the gospel of free trade. On the maintenance of this simple truth, he decreed, 'depends the happiness of millions'.

Standing in the way of this golden age were the Lords. Bereft of patience, Churchill itched to bring the issue to a head quickly and firmly. He took an extreme view. He was going off to war, leading 'an army' towards 'the right battlefield'. It was 'organized and aggressive reaction' against 'representative government'. The House of Lords was 'a played-out, obsolete, anachronistic assembly'. He proposed therefore to abolish it. This was too radical for most of his colleagues. So he urged on the faint hearts the creation of 500 peers to overawe the reactionary Lords.[47]

The succession of George V in May 1910 heralded a brief period when both parties drew in their horns. As the crisis hung fire, Churchill's appetite for a constitutional battle lessened.

> He cursed Charlie [Masterman] one night when they dined together
> a deux, swearing he would resign rather than accept the Veto policy
> again and spend four years with Sir Ernest Cassel, getting rich: then
> again and again repeating: 'No, no, no; I won't follow [Lloyd] George
> if he goes back to that d--d Veto.'

Lloyd George had finally to remind him 'that no man can rat twice'.[48]

In the summer and autumn of 1910 compromise was in the air. Talks were in progress between Conservative and Liberal leaders, although without Churchill's participation. Eventually, they came to nothing.[49] But another avenue of accommodation opened up. 'The time has arrived for a truce', wrote Lloyd George, 'for bringing the resources of the two Parties into joint stock in order to liquidate arrears which, if much longer neglected, may end in national impoverishment, if not insolvency.'[50] Churchill had always hankered after this prospect. If we stand together, he told Lloyd George, 'we ought to be strong enough either to impart a progressive character to policy, or by withdrawal to terminate an admin-istration which had failed in its purpose'.[51] Traditional party loyalties were not sacred to either man, particularly where issues of high national policy, as interpreted by them, were concerned. Should the situation warrant it, they would not hesitate to shatter the conventional mould of party strife. These two great mavericks of modern British politics were both to find final and lasting greatness in coalitions of sorts.

Churchill admitted that he could not take the lead in this matter. But his equivocal status in political life put Lloyd George in a dilemma, for it was quite certain that the Conservatives would not agree to any coalition that gave Churchill, the arch-heretic, a prominent role. When Lloyd George hinted that he might be excluded, Churchill exploded, 'pouring forth rhetorical denunciation of the whole project'. Churchill at heart was a coalitionist, but only on condition that his position was assured. Not surprisingly, F. E. Smith, Churchill's most intimate crony, was enthusiastic for the idea, and it was not dismissed out of hand by Balfour, while leading Liberals all expressed interest.[52] Eventually it was made clear to Balfour that he would face a split in Tory ranks should he persist in angling after a coalition. His position as leader in any case weak, he refused to 'become another Peel'. By November, all attempts at a compromise had died a predictable death, and with them Churchill's hopes of at least playing second fiddle to Lloyd George in the great Centre Party of his dreams.

As has been said, Churchill was curiously unaware of the distrust he fostered. His ego inhibited him from grasping the notion that anyone could actively dislike him. Accused of 'bad manners', he was wont to talk 'too much' and 'too loudly' in Cabinet. 'If he can jump another man's claim', grumbled Alick Murray, the Liberal Chief Whip, 'you can trust him to do it'. 'His great weakness . . . is his love of the limelight' recorded Masterman, a failing that 'is growing on him more and more'.[53] It was a verdict that most of his contemporaries would happily have concurred with, and was given added bite when a camera's eye caught him, clad in top hat and fur-trimmed coat, peering anxiously down Sidney Street, apparently directing operations against an anarchist gang trapped in a house there. 'I understand what the photographer was doing,' commented Balfour tartly, 'but what was the right honourable gentleman doing?'[54] In fact, Churchill was alerted to the scene in his capacity as Home Secretary; and, apart from instructing the fire-brigade to allow the house, with the anarchists still inside, to burn down, he went to satisfy his curiosity and took no part in directing the siege operations. Yet there he was, captured on film for all to see, surrounded by armed soldiers and police, in command of an armed assault on a gang of anarchists. The image of a pugnacious, somewhat irresponsible, perhaps childish, certainly impulsive, publicity-hound stuck; and no doubt he savoured the self-advertisement.

Despised by Conservatives as a turncoat who would sacrifice any principle on the altar of his shoddy ambition, regarded by the Liberal ideologues as 'not quite one of them',[55] he was, for a modern politician, acting in a vacuum, without the life-giving sustenance of a party machine or bureaucracy. He attracted devotees, but he commanded no party divisions. Nor did he seem capable of carving out for himself a party base through shady machinations and wheeler-dealing. 'He is an extraordinary transparent creature,' thought Masterman. 'I never heard or saw any attempt at intrigue by him that could have taken in a kitten; and his very vanity is somehow childish and disarming.' Apart from his exceptional talents, acknowledged but suspected by all, he was dependent upon the goodwill and patronage of others, for the moment, Asquith and Lloyd George. Constricted by narrow party politics, he would appeal to the people, as he did with telling effect during these years. At least in part, his social reforms were intended to court Labour voters and win over the working class. His record was impressive. The Webbs thought of him, together with Lloyd George, 'as the most advanced politicians' of the time. Having cast himself successfully as the People's Tribune, his electoral appeal, he hoped, would be also indispensable to the Liberals.[56]

But Churchill's public reputation as a broad-minded, progressive politician was to prove short-lived. As Home Secretary, despite his ardour for prison reform and righting various industrial and trading wrongs,[57] he alienated large sections of the working classes. His conduct during the great strikes of 1910–12 was the subject of much debate, and sometimes of much unfair criticism. The myth of Tonypandy – that, in November 1910, he had ordered the military to fire upon the striking miners of the Rhondda Valley – has no substance in fact. But the legend died hard, disproved but not dispelled. In fact, Churchill acted with admirable restraint in an explosive situation. Faced with widespread riots and looting, he ordered that the troops – who had been sent in – 'should not come into direct contact with rioters unless and until action had been taken by the police'. And even then, only to stiffen police action. His moderation brought him little credit. He was attacked by the Conservatives for his restraint and by Labour for his belligerence. Keir Hardie badgered him in Parliament, holding him responsible for police brutality and demanding a public enquiry. For the first time, Churchill figured as a prominent figure in the demonology of Labour rhetoric.[58]

In the summer of 1911 he was confronted by a more alarming situation. Widespread strikes broke out in the docks, from Southampton to London to Merseyside. Soon the railway workers joined in; and there threatened sympathetic strike action elsewhere. This was not a localized affair in the coal valleys of South Wales, but a national emergency. Militant trade unionism thundered the language of class conflict, forecasting the imminent breakdown of the existing social and economic order. Churchill reacted in kind. His words, at times stretching the limits of imagination, conjured up an image of Britain saved at the last moment – by his actions – from falling into utter collapse and ruin. Britain faced 'a new peril'. Had the anarchy been allowed to continue, 'it would have hurled the whole of that great community into an abyss of horror'. 'Absolute starvation' would have ensued. He asked 'whether in the history of the world a similar catastrophe can be shown to have menaced an equally great community?'

'Winston was in a very excited state of mind,' noted Charles Masterman, at the height of the railway strike. 'He has got rather a whiff-of-grapeshot attitude towards these matters; and he enjoyed intensely mapping the country and directing the movements of troops,' in his excitement sending them to several towns that 'did not in the least want them!' But on the whole Churchill had acted correctly, Masterman thought, though he went about it in 'an amazingly wrong way, issuing wild bulletins and longing for "blood".' Churchill did not yearn for 'blood'. But the situation was clearly deteriorating rapidly. Panic-stricken telegrams were arriving from the north speaking of 'siege', 'starvation', and 'revolution', and telling of pitched battles between violent mobs – or strikers – and the authorities.[59] As the minister responsible for the maintenance of law and order he had to act swiftly. And he acted in the only manner he knew how: with extreme vigour and ebullience, laced with a strong dose of impetuosity, and reinforced by an intense inner conviction that he was preserving the social fabric of the country from crumbling away. The HMS *Antrim* was despatched to Merseyside, in the eyes of the strikers a blatant show of strength intended to unnerve them. The same day that the strike was brought to an official end, Churchill ordered army commanders to use their own discretion as to whether or not troops were to be used in confronting the rioters. By so doing, he had tilted the civil-military balance dangerously in favour of the army, for he had suspended the army regulation that required a local authority to ask first for the use of troops and then only as a last resort. The following day, at Llanelli, the consequences of this precipitate move were felt. A furious crowd blocked a train operated by blackleg labour. Troops closed in, the riot act was read, shots were fired, and two demonstrators were killed. The chronology of these incidents is in itself a graphic indication of how far events had run out of control.

Lord Loreburn, the Lord Chancellor, thought Churchill's actions 'unstable' and 'irresponsible'. Alfred Gardiner, editor of the Liberal *Daily News*, accused him of playing at heroics, of Napoleonic posturing, of aping his great ancestor, Marlborough. Was Churchill after a showdown more than a compromise? 'The men have beaten us,' he protested to Masterman, looking 'absolutely prostrate'. When he heard that the strike had been settled, he immediately telephoned Lloyd George, whose mediatory skill had brought the bitter dispute to an end, to say: 'I am very sorry to hear it. It would have been better to have gone on and given these men a good thrashing'.

The labour uprising of those years was without precedent in contemporary memory; and it shook the Liberal administration. Widely seen as a revolutionary outbreak, it spawned fierce class antagonisms that were seemingly unbridgeable. This was not the Tory Democracy of Churchill's youth; nor even the gentleman's agreement enshrined in the Lib-Lab concord. This was class war as practised by a new, militant breed of trade unionist and socialist leaders. They did not want to tinker with the socio-economic base of society but to change it. This was foreign to the spirit of Churchill's social contract. He was prepared to countenance social reform, provided it was regulated and ordered by the government: he was not prepared to suffer dictates from below that threatened the social order he held dear.

Ironically, although his original, entirely genuine, intention had been to cultivate social stability, his actions and words contributed to a sharpening of class hatred. He could no longer convincingly promote himself as a benevolent aristocrat leading the thankful working masses into the promised land of greater social and economic equality. Whatever credibility he had accumulated, was dissipated – perhaps for ever. Labour leaders pictured him as being chiefly responsible for the bloodshed and violence. The precise historical truth is less important here than the image that stuck to Churchill as an unrepentant enemy of the working class, beating down the strikers with any weapon that came to hand. The myth of Tonypandy, and all it stood for, took on its own historical truth.[60]

In this way, Churchill began a long and troubled relationship with the Labour movement. He never retrieved the standing he had acquired as the social crusader of the mid-late 1900s. It has been suggested that his 'martial methods' in suppressing the strikes so embarrassed Asquith's government that his position as Home Secretary, responsible for the maintenance of internal law and order, became untenable.[61] He was certainly *persona non grata* with Labour, and perhaps Asquith felt it prudent to keep Churchill at arm's length from future labour disputes. When the coal miners struck in February 1912, and during the dockers' struggle five months later, Churchill was not included in the Cabinet negotiating team.[62] But by then he had been moved to the Admiralty.

The stormy events of 1910–12 were but the first in a series of episodes that ruined any prospect of his reforging his links with the organized working class. Unwittingly, he had emerged in the public eye as an implacable, not to say violent, opponent of Labour; and his angry, savage rhetoric thereafter confirmed this impression.

Churchill jumped out of social reform as quickly as he had jumped into it. Certainly, as has been pointed out with tedious persistence, it was a passing phase. But why should this be held against Churchill? Rather the contrary: it should be accounted to his credit. The reforms of 1908–11 were the first great upheaval towards the Welfare State in Britain. Comprehensive social insurance was an act of tremendous moment; as were the advent of labour exchanges, the legislation against sweated labour, and the move towards greater control in the coal-mining industry. Churchill's role in these matters was considerable.

His motives, however, will long remain the subject of endless and fascinating speculation. In the long run, they count for less than what he actually did. And what he did was not the result of a sudden whim. No doubt he saw in social reform a means of furthering his own career – a all-too-human incentive for a rising, ambitious politician. But this was not done in a fit of opportunistic abandon. He had been truly appalled by the revelations of Rowntree's report on the scale of poverty in York. He had called for 'minimum standards of wages and comforts, Insurance ... against sickness, unemployment, old age'. And later he had set out for Asquith a sweeping programme of social reform, much of which was later realized; he was absolutely consistent in his call for a 'comprehensive, interdependent scheme of social organization'.[63]

The charge that he was not driven by an overall conception of a more equitable, a more merciful and charitable society, does not stand serious examination. Of course, he did not act alone, nor in a vacuum. The times were never more ripe for serious movement in social legislation; and it is to Churchill's credit that he sensed this and acted accordingly. Without Lloyd George, whose greater authority he acknowledged, the movement would have been marginal, if at all. But the combination of their enthusiasm and conviction, their persuasive powers and combative qualities pushed the issue to a successful conclusion. All this was a far cry from the workings of a free market economy so beholden to traditional Liberal philosophy; or even from Churchill's original conception of Tory Democracy. Government was now intervening widely in the affairs of state. Churchill had no quarrel with the Liberal administration's increased role. He was reconciled to the fact that public works were now all permissible means 'for counteracting trade depressions', that state expenditure should be used to regulate the economy and to rectify social ills.[64] There is much to be said for the view that the Labour government of 1945–50 – so abhorrent to Churchill – was 'the lineal descendent' of the Liberal administration of 1906.[65]

In many ways, this period was the most extraordinary of Churchill's remarkable career, because it was so unexpected and out of character. His role of Saviour of the Nation in 1940 was well in keeping with his image of himself, with the heroic element in his personality, with his sense of history, his pride in his great ancestor, Marlborough, his feeling that destiny had preserved him for just such a crisis. The same could hardly be said of his role as a radical social reformer. For all that, his achievements were substantial and lasting and of immense benefit. His vision of a just and more equitable society did not fade away. But it remained shackled to the values of his upbringing and class. And however enlightened and progressive those values were, they were still hemmed in by his outdated, anachronistic dreams of a Tory Democracy from which all benefited but in which all knew their allotted place.

The First World War destroyed that world for ever, its ethos and its socio-economic structure. The Labour movement would not return to it, even if Churchill hankered after it. Alienated by the incessant, hungry demands of the organized working class, he in turn alienated them by the vigour of his reaction, by the uncompromising, flashing rhetoric he employed to dash their claims. Increasingly, however, he found himself adrift in a society that was foreign to his outlook, at once divisive, riven by class antagonisms, bent on sectional gain, unwilling to acknowledge the old master-servant relationship.

6

'The Biggest Thing that has
ever come my Way'

In September 1911, Asquith retired to Archerfield, a fine Adam house on the East Lothian coast where he and his family spent their holidays. Towards the end of the month, Churchill joined them. Neither Churchill nor his hosts were efficient golfers, although this in no way dampened their enthusiasm for the game, and much of their time was spent hacking and slicing their way up and down Asquith's private nine-hole golf-links. But Asquith was also preoccupied with public affairs, turning over in his mind the permutations of a Cabinet reshuffle and its consequences. This also bothered Churchill, who had his eye on the Admiralty, and who had come to Archerfield to stake his claim. His chief rival was Richard, Viscount Haldane, a highly successful Secretary of State for War who had managed partially to overhaul Britain's army establishment with a series of much-needed reforms. The navy was considered ripe for a similar shake-up and Haldane's experience at the War Office left him confident that he could fulfil the task. Haldane, who lived close by at Cloan, motored over twice to press his candidature. Surprised at seeing Churchill there, he must have been even more amazed at Asquith for closeting them in a room together to argue the point out. 'He is an importunate widow,' Asquith explained, 'begging to be given the Admiralty'. But 'Churchill would not be moved,' Haldane later noted ruefully. A day or two afterwards, Churchill, his face radiant, invited Violet Asquith (later Bonham-Carter), the Prime Minister's eldest daughter, for a walk. He was too excited to take tea. They strolled through the darkening woods down to the sea, where in the distance they saw dimly the silhouettes of two battleships steaming out of the Firth of Forth. 'Your father has just offered me the Admiralty,' he cried. 'This is a big thing – the biggest thing that has ever come my way – the chance I should chose before all others. I shall pour into it everything I've got.'[1]

A warlike mystique cloaked Churchill. His language was rich in military metaphors. On more than one occasion he was caught poring keenly over maps and planning troop or police movements. He seemed to revel in his martial image, as his performance at the Sidney Street siege indicated. He once told Asquith, in a fit of rash enthusiasm, 'that a political career was nothing to him in comparison with military glory'.[2]

Yet until the summer of 1911, Churchill had made no particular impact on questions of strategy or foreign affairs. Preoccupied with the affairs of the offices he held, they did not command his undivided attention. Indeed, judging from his sporadic incursions into these fields, it would be possible to conclude that he was something of an anti-militarist. Beatrice Webb thought of him in 1903 as at heart 'a little Englander'. He was still fighting his father's battles: for retrenchment, against bloated military budgets. The Times even referred to 'his hereditary tradition of hostility to the service estimates'.[3] For this reason, he had fought army reforms when he entered Parliament, and he continued in the same vein when he attained ministerial office.

Earlier, in June 1908 (the anniversary of the victory at Waterloo), he had proposed scaling down the army's strength, in answer to Haldane's plans to bring the army establishment up to scratch. Britain's military requirements were threefold, he argued: to maintain her army in India; to sustain a home-based army capable of repelling an invading force of 100,000; and to create the machinery necessary to expand the land forces in the event of war. 'Whether doubled or halved,' he contended, the existing army would be equally incompetent to meet a real threat.[4] Churchill's assault on Haldane's proposals was such as to give rise to rumours that he had been 'turned loose' on the War Office and that he would succeed Haldane, a prospect that horrified Lord Esher[5] and dismayed many senior officers on the active list. Haldane could barely conceal his displeasure at Churchill who proved 'as long-winded as he was persistent'.[6] And Haldane's reforms, necessary and long overdue, providing mainly for the creation of a General Staff and an Expeditionary Force of six infantry divisions and one cavalry division, were put into effect.

Churchill was no less persistent – but no more successful – in his demand to cut down naval expenditure. However, he certainly believed that British naval power was the key to imperial security. But in April 1908, at the height of the German naval scare, when the navy and public opinion were demanding more 'Dreadnoughts',[7] he expounded that the 'proper supremacy of the British fleet' would be secured by 'a patient policy of retrenchment, a sober policy in regard to armament, [and a] peaceful and conciliatory policy in foreign affairs'. All this, he went on, would enable 'considerable reductions to be made in the unproductive expenditure of the State', namely armaments. To John Morley he wrote that 'A resolute effort must be made to curb Naval expenditure ... It is an ugly & thankless job. Still I think I could do it.' It was a promise that he never fulfilled. Despite Lloyd George's premature delight at Churchill's aid in smashing the Admiralty's 'fatuous estimates', the radicals failed to carry the day.[8] The navy's case, skillfully put by the First Lord, Reginald McKenna, proved more than equal to the Churchill-Lloyd George combination, so much so that almost £3 million were actually added on to the naval estimates. McKenna's proposal called for the building of four Dreadnoughts, with four 'contingent' ships to be laid down later, should this prove necessary. In June 1909, three months after introducing his compromise programme, the necessity, apparently, arose. McKenna announced that the four extra Dreadnoughts would be laid down. A happy Admiral John 'Jacky' Fisher, the First Sea Lord, ribbed Churchill: perhaps they should be named *Winston*, *Churchill*, *Lloyd*, and *George*. Churchill and Lloyd George had been smartly outmanoeuvred. But it was their noisy persistence in 1908–9 that prompted Asquith to complain of their 'combined machinations'. Fed up at their antics, he admitted to moments when he was summarily disposed 'to cashier both of them'.[9]

If retrenchment and naval supremacy were two elements in Churchill's formula for national security, the third was a sober foreign policy. Arms expenditures beyond that deemed necessary to defend the country adequately – a flexible definition – would inevitably be accompanied by 'a sensational and aggressive policy in foreign and colonial affairs'. Democratic progress, to be guaranteed by the Liberal Party remaining in office, depended on the maintenance of European peace. He found no fault with the current themes of British foreign policy. He asserted that the Anglo-Japanese alliance (1902) secured British interests in the Far East, and brought great advantages to both powers. Although, on occasion, he railed against 'Russian despotism', he warmly supported the *entente* system, those arrangements with France (1904) and Russia (1907) that resolved a wide range of imperial, colonial disputes and that, on paper at least, did not commit Britain to take sides in the event of a European war.[10]

In his fight against Haldane's proposals Churchill had marked Germany down as a potential enemy, not because of any intrinsic clash of interests between the two powers, but simply because Germany was at odds with Britain's *entente* partners. At the time, this was a harmless assumption. When Churchill visited Germany, in 1906 and 1909, to observe the autumn manoeuvres of the Imperial army, he came away tremendously impressed. 'This army is a terrible machine,' he wrote to Clementine.[11] But these first-hand experiences did not lead him to conclude that it would be thrown against Britain; or that Britain would have to take action against it. Naval power was still sufficient to ward off any threat.

And what of the future? In 1909 he was supremely confident that it held no dangers. He decried the scaremongers, those alarmist 'Bismarckian statesmen' who predicted 'hideous and direful wars as imminent'. For him, these war-cries were simply 'nightmare nonsense'. Did Germany, widely perceived as powerful, ambitious, militaristic, unpredictable, set on outbuilding the British navy, constitute a threat to British interests? Churchill's answer was an emphatic 'No!'

By the summer of 1911 Churchill's perception of Anglo-German relations had radically changed. Certain people, in Germany, he would have insisted, had lost their heads. The catalyst for this *volte-face* was the arrival of the German gunboat, *Panther*, at Agadir, an obscure port on the Atlantic coast of Morocco, on 1 July 1911. The Germans, in their heavy-handed way, were signalling to the French that there could be no changes in the status of Morocco without their consent, or without their receiving compensation elsewhere. They had sound reason for complaint. In violation of previous international agreements, the French had occupied Fez in May, the first step, so it was assumed, towards claiming a protectorate over all Morocco.[12] Britain also was perturbed by the reckless nature of French moves and was equally determined not to be excluded from any deal; or as Asquith put it to the King, any settlement must concluded '*à quatre*' (the fourth power being Spain). But it was Lloyd George who gave public voice to these sentiments at a bankers' dinner at the Mansion House on 21 July, though not before showing his speech to Churchill and consulting Asquith and Grey as to its contents. Britain could not be treated, he said, 'as if she were of no account in the Cabinet of Nations ... peace at that price would be a humiliation intolerable for a great country like ours to endure.'

If this was a broad hint to the French, it was also an emphatic warning to the Germans. The prospect of German warships, based on a Moorish port, patrolling the western Atlantic and threatening British trade routes was an alarming one, though it was taken more seriously by the politicians than by the admirals. These fears were unfounded, but they magnified the growing tension and suspicion. The most pertinent question was how would the German challenge at Agadir affect the prevailing balance of power in Europe? The Foreign Office and some ministers, Lloyd George and Churchill among them, held that a French retreat in the face of German bullying would undermine the Anglo-French *entente* and lead to German hegemony in Europe, an outcome in the long run fatal to British interests. What had begun as a Franco-German squabble over colonial concessions developed into an Anglo-German row with talk of war on both sides.[13]

These danger-laden weeks roused Churchill. Grey, who saw a lot of him during these days noted 'that his high-metalled spirit was exhilarated by the air of crisis and high events'. 'Is it not horrible to be built like that?' he admitted. 'The preparations have a hideous fascination for me.'[14] This was to be a familiar theme in Churchill's career.

Stimulated by an emergency situation, he tended to slip into overdrive. He claimed that the current industrial unrest was being 'fermented by German gold', an assertion for which no evidence has yet appeared and which was regarded then as 'midsummer madness'.[15] On his initiative, troops and armed police were hurriedly despatched to guard the navy's cordite reserves. On 13 August he circulated a Cabinet paper entitled 'Military Aspects of the Continental Problem', based on the premise of a British army fighting on the Continent alongside France and Russia against the aggressor powers, Germany and Austria. Even though it was 'demolished' by General Sir Henry Wilson, director of military operations at the War Office, as 'fantastic and ridiculous', it predicted with astonishing accuracy the actual events of August-September 1914.[16]

There were also political ramifications to Agadir. At the end of August, Churchill proposed reconstructing the *entente* system into a full-blown Franco-Russian-British alliance. That October he seriously considered broadening the alliance to include Belgium, an act that would necessitate moving the British Expeditionary Force (BEF) from supporting the left wing of the French army to stiffening Belgian resistance against any oncoming German attack. Some of these ideas Churchill had garnered from Sir Henry Wilson, a voluble and persuasive Ulsterman who expressed a lively and arrogant contempt for all those who dared to disagree with him, particularly politicians. He insisted that the soldiers needed 'an actively friendly Belgium'.[17] Had these ideas been put into effect, they would have radically transformed British policy and military planning. But neither Grey nor Field-Marshal Sir William Nicholson, Chief of the Imperial General Staff, warmed to them, and British policy continued on its enigmatic course: no unequivocal commitment to France, but should circumstances force Britain into a continental war her forces would fight alongside the French army.

At least Churchill had a clear-cut policy. He would not shrink from a genuine alliance with France. But at a meeting of the Committee of Imperial Defence on 23 August, convened to discuss operational plans in the event of war, he encountered only confusion and muddled thinking.[18] Both army and navy were bent on implementing strategic plans that were wildly at variance. The navy argued for a blockade of German ports and capture of the Frisian Islands to serve as advanced bases for amphibious landings elsewhere. The British army would be merely 'a projectile to be fired by the navy'. The army, on the other hand, called for sending the British Expeditionary Force to France as

quickly as possible to be deployed on the extreme French left, with the
navy acting in a supportive role.

In this encounter, the navy was thoroughly worsted. The First Sea
Lord, Admiral Sir Arthur Knyvet Wilson, put his case clumsily. He failed
to produce a detailed, comprehensive war plan, nor did he seem to grasp
the implications that advanced weaponry, the submarine and torpedo,
would have on a strategy of close blockade.

It was a dismal performance. Churchill had subjected both Wilsons
to an intense grilling. But whereas Henry had answered with confidence, if not always with total frankness, Arthur had mumbled.
Churchill drew the perhaps inevitable conclusion that Admiral Wilson
lacked sagacity and imagination. As for the Admiralty, 'They are so
cocksure, insouciant and apathetic'. Asquith was equally disturbed.
'The present position,' he noted, 'is both ridiculous and dangerous'.

It was the need to sweep away the cobwebs at the Admiralty, to create
an effective naval war staff and ensure fruitful cooperation between the
two services, and to devise an effective plan for the swift and safe transfer
of the BEF to France that led directly to Churchill's appointment as First
Lord. It did not pass without criticism. The *Spectator* feared it because
Churchill 'is weak and rhetorical . . . [lacks] any principles or even any
consistent outlook upon public affairs. His ear is always to the ground;
he is a true demagogue.' Other opinion was more guarded, but no less
equivocal. His was a personality that attracted suspicion and fostered
mistrust.[19]

Asquith gave two reasons for his decision to move Churchill to the
Admiralty. 'The First Lord ought to be in the H of Commons,' he wrote
to Lord Crewe, a supporter of Haldane's candidacy, 'and the Navy
would not take kindly . . . to new organization imported directly from
the War Office.' He was certain that Churchill was 'the right man' for
the job.[20] So, apparently, was Lloyd George. 'I think I am entitled to the
credit,' he confided to Lord Riddell. 'I went to Archerfield in August, and
told the Prime Minister that we must make the change.' Lloyd George
himself was at one with Churchill in evaluating the extent of the German
threat at Agadir.[21] No doubt, he hoped also that Churchill, the radical,
would continue their alliance to prune the naval estimates. Asquith read
Churchill better. Appreciating his propensity for burying himself in the
affairs of his current office, removing him from the Home Office to a
service ministry would in effect weaken the radical wing of the Cabinet,
splitting the volatile Lloyd George-Churchill combination.[22] If this was
at the back of Asquith's mind, it proved to be a shrewd calculation, for
before very long 'the two Romeos' were squabbling openly over the size
of the naval budgets.

But whatever Asquith's motives, the decision to assign Churchill to
the Admiralty was a crossroads in his career. In terms of political kudos,

of the hierarchy of ministerial advancement, the Admiralty was a step down, for the Home Office was generally recognized as one of the three great offices of state. But Churchill never hesitated. The years he spent at the Admiralty were, he recorded, the 'most memorable' of his life.[23] They began on the highest of notes but ended on the harshest of discords; and they coloured his career until the end of the Second World War.

Agadir sharpened Churchill's political-military outlook. Germany had been earmarked as the enemy; France, Russia, and Belgium as allies. For years he had asserted that the army was little more than 'a training depot for India with one army corps for petty expeditions'. That notion had been abandoned. He was now committed to a European role for the army that, by the fortieth day of war, could muster 290,000 soldiers and enable Britain to play an effective part. Britain, as in the glorious days of his ancestor, Marlborough, would prevent Europe from falling under the sway of a single, dominant power. These ideas, as he recognized, 'underwent no change in the three years of peace that followed'.

But his current enthusiasm for the army did not mean that he had defected from the 'maritime school'. At any rate, as First Lord he began to have second thoughts about the defensive role that had been assigned to the navy. It would have been totally out of character for Churchill to lie back, and allow others to grasp the initiative while Britain was engaged in war. Still, it is somewhat ironic that Churchill soon began to endorse the close blockade strategy, to promote the 'seek out, hunt down, and destroy' school. He did so with such verve that he brought down upon himself the scorn of Captain Herbert Richmond, the scholarly Assistant Director of Operations at the Admiralty. Of Churchill's 'fantastic measures', he wrote: 'these are words only. They mean nothing: they will not affect well-considered plans of a thinking enemy any more than beating drums or waving flags would do.'[24]

Richmond's criticism did not resolve Churchill's problem: his chronic inability to sit still and wait upon events. His psychological make-up, no less than his physical impulses, rendered him incapable of playing a passive role. He was forever hungry for action. As First Lord he searched for ways to combine military intervention in Europe, that remained his 'decisive theatre', with an offensive role on the peripheries, either by the navy acting alone or by some form of combined operations. His labours, when put to the actual test in war, did not always meet with the happiest of results.

No other issue in British politics has aroused greater passions than the Irish question. Churchill had started out as a true Unionist. As a young man he had vowed that 'Were it not for Home Rule – to which I will never consent – I would enter Parliament as a Liberal.' But when he joined the Liberal benches he was duty-bound to soften his views. As the Liberal administration was dependent upon the support of the Irish Party for its parliamentary majority, Churchill was also tied to Home Rule by the principle of political survival. He wanted to allow the Irish a parliament in Dublin with full control over Irish affairs, including finance, while maintaining the customs union with England; and while control over foreign and defence policy would remain in Westminster. Earlier, he had told John Redmond, the Irish leader, that it was 'the ambition of his life to bring in a Home Rule Bill as Chief Secretary'. But when the job was offered to him, in February 1910, he turned it down. 'The office does not attract me now,' he told Asquith. 'There are many circumstances connected with it which repel me.' He did not elaborate. Except for the splendid task of preparing and passing the Home Rule Bill through Parliament, he had no wish to become enmeshed in the minutiae of Irish administration.[25] Few are the Chief Secretaries for Ireland who have emerged from office with their reputations intact, let alone enhanced. Instead, Churchill had taken the Home Office, a far senior post and a visible step forward into the front rank of the political hierarchy.

In November 1911, Andrew Bonar Law, to the astonishment of most observers, replaced Arthur Balfour as Leader of the Conservative Party. His unexpected elevation sharpened the inter-party debate on the future of Ireland. It also had a profound, almost wholly negative, effect upon Churchill's career. Despite the bitter rhetoric of Churchill's earlier clashes with Balfour, he was all too often ready to succumb to Balfour's whimsical charm, and at times regarded him with something akin to hero-worship. 'I love Balfour,' he confessed in 1923, and went on to explain that if only Balfour had taken more notice of him when he, Churchill, had started out in politics, 'he would probably have gone down with him. He longed to have served under him.'[26]

Bonar Law was a different kettle of fish. Of Ulster stock, he had been brought up in Glasgow where he made his way as an iron-merchant. His placid appearance and self-effacing temperament belied a caustic tongue, and a sharp political brain. He was to rule the Conservative Party until his death in 1923. The antithesis of the flamboyant Churchill in almost every way, he regarded the new First Lord with deep, unremitting suspicion. He admitted that Churchill had 'very unusual intellectual ability', but at the same time he thought him irresponsible, impulsive, imperious, the possessor of 'an entirely unbalanced mind'. Bonar Law also had not forgotten that Churchill had ratted on his party, holding up to an appreciative House 'the coat he has turned so often'.[27] Churchill neither forgave nor forgot Bonar Law's hostility towards him. For posterity's sake he recorded that his adversary would be recognized as 'the greatest political failure ever known in British politics'.[28]

Over Ireland, Bonar Law adopted the extreme Unionist view. In July

1912, at a mass rally at Blenheim, he denounced the government, in words that are impossible to interpret other than outright incitement to rebellion, as 'a revolutionary committee which has seized upon despotic power by fraud', and its deal with the Irish Nationalists as 'a corrupt Parliamentary bargain'. His final message excluded any compromise: 'I can imagine no length of resistance to which Ulster can go in which I should not be prepared to support them.' For Churchill, as for many others, this doctrine transgressed the bounds of legitimate political controversy. It was a menace to established order – perhaps more, judging from its source – than the labour unrest of the summer of 1911. Churchill was not averse to striking a bargain about the Ulster counties as the price of Home Rule, but he would take 'a very strong line' to counter violence against the elected government. To his mind, the provocative speeches of Bonar Law and the inflammatory conduct of the Ulster leader, Sir Edward Carson, bordered on 'treasonable activity'.[29]

Throughout 1912 both camps in Ireland – the Unionists and the Nationalists – were arming and drilling for an eventual showdown. The prospect of civil war threatened. In February, Churchill braved these dangers and went to Belfast to put the government case. He told Lord Riddell, emphasizing his points with a safety razor, that Carson had been stirring up trouble in Ireland. He would set the record straight. It was a typically courageous act, but the Conservative press forecast riots and bloodshed resulting from Churchill's provocative visit. No doubt their concern was fanned by Churchill's intention to speak at the Ulster Hall where his father, twenty-four years earlier, had encouraged Ulster in a policy of 'no surrender'. Churchill, wisely, agreed to change the venue of the meeting to the Celtic Road football stadium – shielded by a working-class Catholic area of Belfast.[30]

Accompanied by Clementine, who had refused all pleas to stay at home, Churchill sailed from Stranraer to Larne. It was a noisy crossing. Suffragettes disturbed their sleep as they rushed around the deck all night chanting 'Votes for women'. On their arrival, their reception was no less boisterous. Their car was almost overturned by a jeering, hostile crowd. Outside their hotel, effigies were burned, flags waved, staves brandished, all to the accompaniment of angry boos and curses. Four thousand policemen were on duty to protect them. In pouring rain, the huge crowd gathered to hear Churchill speak. He read his speech, while the fiercest interruptions came, yet again, from the suffragettes. Churchill, wittily, rephrased the celebrated words of his father.

> Let Ulster fight for the dignity and honour of Ireland; let her fight for the reconciliation of races and for the forgiveness of ancient wrongs; let her fight for the unity and consolidation of the British Empire; let her fight for the spreading of charity, tolerance and enlightenment among men. Then, indeed, 'Ulster will fight and Ulster will be right.'[31]

Churchill's Belfast speech put him in the front line of the Irish question, where he liked to be in any dispute. Later in the year, at Dundee, he depicted Home Rule for Ireland as the first step in a federal system for the United Kingdom, that, should it prove successful, could be expanded to include other areas, Yorkshire, Lancashire, the Midlands, and Greater London. An intriguing idea. Whether Churchill took it seriously it is difficult to say; the Unionists treated it with derision. But they reacted with open fury to the government's decision to force Home Rule through Parliament by use of the 'guillotine' procedure. On 12 November, the government was defeated on a snap vote on the financial resolutions of the Home Rule Bill. When, the following day, Asquith asked the House to rescind its vote, it erupted in boos, cheers and mutual insults. The Speaker was compelled first to suspend and then to adjourn the session. Churchill filed out of the Chamber with the rest of the ministers. He seemed in high spirits. Perhaps he heard the cry of 'Rat' directed at him. He took out his handkerchief and cheerfully acknowledged the slur. As he turned to leave, a book – a copy of the Standing Orders – struck him on the head, drawing blood. Ronald McNeill, an Ulster member, had been unable to contain his anger.[32]

At the beginning of 1914 it appeared to some of Churchill's Liberal colleagues as though his enthusiasm for Home Rule was on the wane. Churchill was then involved in a bitter dispute with Lloyd George over the size of the naval estimates. The crisis was not resolved until mid-February. But while it boiled the unity of the Cabinet was threatened. Churchill contemplated resignation, as did Lloyd George. Should the government have fallen, the future of Home Rule would also have hung in the balance. Lloyd George was in the stronger position, for while he still led the radical-economist wing of the Cabinet, Churchill had cut himself off from his former political base. Sir John Simon, one of Churchill's opponents, reckoned that if Churchill went the party would be strengthened. It could then fight for economies and pursue Home Rule unflinchingly, as befitted a true Liberal government. There was a distinct feeling that Churchill – like Lord Randolph before him – was playing 'the Orange card', hoping to gain an advantage from it in his struggle against the Treasury. If so, his timing was perfect. The Irish question had entered its last stage. Home Rule would come into law by the middle of 1914. The question could no longer be begged: if necessary, would the government use force to implement it? Churchill made his position clear. 'You understand,' he revealed to Lloyd George, 'that if a shot is fired I shall go out.'[33]

Churchill's letter of resignation justified his stand for an increased naval budget, but it was widely believed that he would go out, not over the estimates, but over Ulster, that symbol of Tory faith. What is the point of making concessions to you over naval armaments, enquired

Lloyd George, in the presence of Asquith, if in any case you will resign on the Irish question? Churchill, confused, at first denied the charge but later refused to 'commit himself in advance'. Suspicious minds envisaged Churchill as not merely leaving the government, but planning to desert the Liberals and return to his old party. 'Will you join the Tory Party?' he was asked. 'No, certainly not!', he replied. 'On no account. I am a Free Trader, and quite out of sympathy with their attitude to the working classes.'[34] But the fact that such leading questions could be asked at all indicates the automatic suspicion with which his every action was examined. For those, and they were many, who placed the worst possible interpretation on Churchill's actions, there were ostensible grounds for concern.

In October 1913 Churchill had publicly gone on record that Ulster's title for special treatment should not be disregarded, a claim that alarmed the Liberal purists. He also, he reported, had conducted 'a long & pleasant conversation' with Bonar Law at Balmoral. In fact, Bonar Law's tone was harsh and uncompromising. But he did not exclude a specific deal for Ulster. Neither did Churchill. He too believed that 'Ulster has a case. If Ireland has the right to separate government from England, Ulster cannot be refused similar exemption from government by an Irish Parliament.' What Churchill strongly resented was Bonar Law's sabre-rattling, of his wild talk of 'civil war' and 'rebellion'. Churchill approached other Tories, Austen Chamberlain, but particularly his bosom companion, F. E. Smith, an ultra Unionist. Again, the object was to seek a sensible compromise that would avoid bloodshed. Some Liberal leaders, Asquith – who was party to these negotiations – Lloyd George, Morley, Grey did not reject outright a special arrangement for Ulster. These feelers petered out. The idea of a kind of 'Home Rule within Home Rule' proved unacceptable to the majority opinion in the Unionist Party. The Liberals could go no further.[35] The Irish question drifted towards what seemed to be the inevitability of civil conflict.

The failure to obtain an agreed inter-party formula for Home Rule coincided with the government compromise over the naval estimates. Once again, Churchill's Liberal credentials were put in question, this time by Lloyd George, indignant at Churchill's refusal to countenance 'reasonable economies'. 'The truth is he is not a Liberal. He does not understand Liberal sentiment,' he complained to Lord Riddell. Churchill had acted from the best of motives. For all that, his standing among the radical-economist wing of the Liberal Party had been damaged, perhaps irreparably. Only five years earlier he – together with Lloyd George – had chosen to lead the Party from the left, fashioning a political base that would enable him to put in a claim on the leadership in the not too distant future. Now his constituents were disowning him. Weak on Home Rule, firm on swollen naval estimates, the impression was strong that Churchill was not really one of them.

Churchill needed to re-establish his Liberal qualifications. As he put it: 'In order to strengthen myself with my party, I mingled actively in the Irish controversy.' Prepared to meet 'force by force', he would no longer 'go out' if a single shot was fired.[36] Churchill was now a member of the Cabinet committee on Ulster. Lloyd George singled him out as the most effective spokesman for the tougher line. At Bradford, he spoke the language requested of him. 'There are worse things than bloodshed,' he warned, and made clear that 'law and order must prevail in this country at all risks'. A combative speech, it put the Liberals in fighting form. But for the Tories it expressed government policy in its 'most uncompromising and menacing form', virtually a declaration of hostilities.[37]

The same day that Churchill appeared at Bradford, General Sir Arthur Paget, Commander-in-Chief in Ireland, received instructions from the War Office to take special precautions to prevent 'evil minded persons' (namely, the Ulster Volunteer Force, the Unionist private militia) from seizing arms and ammunition depots. Paget took measures in the south, but balked from sending his troops into Ulster, feeling that this would not only test their loyalty but might also provoke civil disturbances. He was then summoned to London for consultations. This was the first act in a series of miscalculations and intrigues, compounded by incompetence and faulty leadership, that led to the so-called 'Curragh mutiny', an incident that embodied the intense passions and incurable suspicion that moved the main protagonists in the Irish emergency.[38]

If an agreed settlement proved unobtainable, would either side dare to execute a *coup de main*? The alternatives seemed frightening. Would Carson declare a 'Provisional Government' for Ulster? Or would the government 'coerce Ulster'? These conjectures were widely believed, and they coloured the events that were to follow. On 17 March Churchill's Cabinet committee on Ireland recommended that troops be deployed to protect the arms depots in the north, including, if necessary, additional forces from the mainland. And on 19 March a battle squadron was ordered to proceed to Lamlash, to within striking distance of Belfast Lough.[39] These measures inflamed the situation. Stormy scenes took place in the Commons. Bonar Law proposed a vote of censure, warning the government of the consequences of using force. Carson was more extreme. Attacking Churchill in person he charged the government of deliberately fomenting civil strife in Ulster.

At the same time, Churchill, Jack Seely, the Secretary of State for War, and Sir John French, Chief of the Imperial Staff, were conferring with Paget.[40] The precautionary troop movements for guarding the arms depots were confirmed. Should Paget's forces come under attack, or should widespread civil disturbances break out, 'large reinforcements' would be despatched, and Paget was granted 'full discretionary power' to deal with such emergencies. Officers who refused to carry out orders and act in support of the civil power would be summarily dismissed. But for those officers who resided in Ulster a special 'indulgence' might be shown, even allowing those officers domiciled in Ulster to 'disappear' if ordered north. This was the gist of Paget's report to his senior officers when they met in Dublin. 'Active operations' against Ulster were 'to be expected at any moment', he announced, and the country would be 'in a blaze' within twenty-four hours. In the light of this hysterical message, he put to the test the intentions of the officers under his command. That evening, Brigadier-General Sir Hubert Gough, an Ulsterman and commander of the 3rd Cavalry Brigade at the Curragh, informed Paget that sixty of his officers, including himself, opted for dismissal rather than move against Ulster.

This was the 'Curragh mutiny'. Its immediate cause, as Asquith recognized, stemmed from 'Paget's tactless blundering, and Seely's clumsy phrases'.[41] Gough and his officers had merely chosen between alternatives – the Churchill-Seely 'principles' – that should never have been put to them. Gough, summoned to London to justify his position, insisted on a written guarantee that the army would not be used to coerce Ulster, or as it was phrased, to suppress 'political opposition'. Seely, aided by John Morley, agreed, and the document was initialled by Sir John French. When the terms of this agreement were made known it produced an uproar. It seemed to confirm the opposition's worst suspicion: that the government – and in particular Churchill and Seely – had been planning all along to crush Ulster. Despite Churchill's denial, the impression remained strong that he longed for a showdown, that he wished to demonstrate that the Ulster Volunteers did not rule Ulster. After all, what was the point of deploying his battleships off Belfast? Simply to safeguard a few arms depots? The day after he ordered the battle squadron into Irish waters, he was reported to have told Sir John French that 'if Belfast showed fight "his fleet would have the town in ruins in twenty-four hours"'. The link between French, Wilson, and Bonar Law was sufficiently reliable to ensure that these words and sentiments reached the ears of the Tory leadership.[42]

By this time even Asquith, who believed that half the officers in the army 'would strike' if ordered to march on Ulster, had taken fright. He moved to restore civil authority over the military. He cancelled Churchill's orders to the battle squadron and disavowed Seely's document in the Commons. Seely resigned, as did Sir John French and Sir Spencer Ewart, the Adjutant-General; Paget and Gough returned to Dublin; Asquith took over at the War Office. Seely was perhaps a scapegoat for Asquith's inability to grasp the severity of the crisis at the outset. News of the Curragh incident had disturbed him at the bridge-table when he ventured the hasty opinion that the matter 'will be cleared up in a few hours'.[43] Asquith had also allowed Seely too much leeway in his dealings with the generals. But Churchill too cannot escape some share of the blame. Seely respected him and heeded his advice, and Churchill had been an active participant in the crucial talks with Paget. He was as responsible as Seely. It was of small consequence that the government had no plan to coerce Ulster. The Unionists believed it had; and Churchill's harsh words and actions did much to lend weight to this conviction. In Tory imaginations he established himself as the chief villain of the piece. From 25 to 30 March he made three major speeches in the Commons defending, to shouts of Tory disbelief and cries for him to resign, the government's position and his own conduct.[44]

Asquith's moves did not lessen the tension. It has been estimated that by the end of April he had answered some 500 questions, mostly hostile, relating to the Curragh episode.[45] The Unionists continued to accuse the government of 'plotting' to reduce Ulster.

On the night of 24 April, at Larne, the Ulster Volunteers successfully carried out a plot of their own. Drawing a cordon around the harbour, they prevented police and customs officials from entering the area and landed a cargo of 35,000 rifles and 3,000,000 cartridges. Gun-running on this scale and in this manner made sensational copy which the Liberals could exploit. It was undeniably illegal, clearly provocative, certainly warlike. Perhaps the government had been justified when it had ordered 'precautionary measures' in March. When Churchill replied for the government to a vote of censure he came down heavily on the Tories:

> Here they are committed to naked revolution, committed to a policy of armed violence, and utter defiance of lawfully constituted authority, committed to tampering with the authority of the Army and Navy, committed to obstructing highways and telegrams, to overpowering police, coastguards and Customs officials, committed to smuggling in arms by moonlight, committed to the piratical seizure of ships and to the unlawful imprisonment of the King's servants . . .

However, at the end of this tirade he called for compromise. He knew that in reaching out to the opposition he was in danger of being rejected by elements in his own party. But he went ahead. Addressing Carson, he pleaded with the Ulster leader to take 'some risk for peace'. Speak up boldly, he implored, for a settlement that would 'safeguard the dignity and interests of Protestant Ulster', yet leave 'Ireland an integral unit in a federal system'.[46]

Once again, Churchill's motives were of the noblest order. But once again he had sadly misjudged the prevailing temper on both sides. Not only did he madden the Tories with his biting admonishments, he also infuriated the more zealous of the Home Rulers by extending an olive branch to Carson. Many Liberals, and certainly the Irish Nationalists, were furious at his uncalled for gesture, and he was accused of betraying 'the Irish cause'.[47] Still, his call for a compromise found a faint echo, though renewed inter-party contacts failed to bear fruit. It seemed inevitable that the Irish problem, as intractable as ever, would be resolved, not by common sense and mutual compromise, but by bigotry and armed conflict. Such a catastrophe was to be delayed by the European crisis of July 1914.

Churchill's intervention in the Irish question brought him little political credit. The Tories still regarded him as a turncoat, a rank opportunist whose conversion to Liberalism was little more than a shabby disguise to hide his ambition. Regarded as impulsive, irresponsible, flamboyant by nature, his need to prove his Liberal credentials led him to adopt the most extreme of attitudes. Moreover, because of his considerable talents – his debating skills, his drive, his fortitude, his refusal to back down – he was considered an exceptionally dangerous opponent. In particular, his relations with Bonar Law were destroyed, really beyond repair. For the Liberals, despite his enthusiasm and resourcefulness, he remained something of an outcast, a rogue elephant. Superb in debate, brave in action, he often surprised and embarrassed them by his deeds and vivid phrases. His eagerness for compromise with political adversaries, admirable in itself, made him suspect in the eyes of the ever vigilant Liberal ideologues. At too many critical moments, he had wavered. There were those in both camps who thought out loud: was he a true Liberal? or, as the other side would have it, a political adventurer?

A Water Creature[1]

Life at the Admiralty suited Churchill. His office entitled him to reside at Admiralty House, a handsome building dating from the 1720s, situated between Whitehall and Horse Guards Parade, and overlooking St James's Park. Churchill wished to move in at once, but Clementine would not have it. She pleaded her case on grounds of economy. To maintain the splendour of Admiralty House in the required manner meant employing a staff of eleven or twelve, a daunting prospect, particularly as Churchill's new post meant a drop in salary of £500. It was not until early April 1913 that a compromise was reached. The first floor was closed off and the costs of running this magnificent establishment were reduced accordingly.

Another welcome bonus was the *Enchantress*, a beautifully appointed 3,800-ton steam yacht which was placed at the disposal of the First Lord, and which became 'largely my office, almost my home,' Churchill wrote.[2] Until the outbreak of war, he spent eight months aboard, inspecting shipyards and naval establishments, not only throughout the British Isles but also in the Mediterranean. But the *Enchantress* also allowed him to combine business with pleasure. There were Whitsun holiday cruises, usually to the Mediterranean. The social mix had to be right. Leading politicians – from both parties – mingled with family and favoured members of Churchill's staff. Lady Randolph and Margot Asquith were known as 'two rather explosive elements both singly and – still more – conjointly'. Asquith, a classicist, *Baedeker* in hand, would roam the museums and investigate the ruins, somewhat to Churchill's impatience. Violet Asquith found Churchill in combative mood. 'How perfect', she sighed, gazing at the sunlit Adriatic coastline.

> 'Yes,' Churchill replied. 'Range perfect – visibility perfect – If we had got some six-inch guns on board how easily we could bombard . . .! etc. etc.' – and details followed showing how effectively we could lay waste the landscape and blow the nestling towns sky-high.'[3]

The purpose for which Churchill was sent to the Admiralty was swiftly accomplished. By December 1912, little more than a year after taking office, Churchill had established a Naval War Staff of sorts; had set in motion plans to transfer the BEF to its prescribed battle position; had seen three Sea Lords quit the Board of Admiralty; and had presided over the retirement of two First Sea Lords, Sir Arthur Wilson and Sir Francis Bridgeman, before finally selecting a third, Prince Louis of Battenberg, with whom he felt he could work comfortably. The manner of Bridgeman's going raised much controversy and criticism of Churchill's methods. Bridgeman resented strongly Churchill's interfering ways. He wished to continue in office, but Churchill insisted on his resignation, claiming that the First Sea Lord was too ill to carry 'the burden' in the event of war. Since Bridgeman's doctors had given him a clean bill of health, and he was observed riding to hounds three days a week in Yorkshire, Churchill's arguments appeared even more threadbare.

This incident became the occasion for a most acrimonious debate in the Commons, when Bonar Law accused Churchill of being 'a dictator'. Churchill was hard put to justify his case, and to do so resorted to methods that were highly questionable, quoting in Parliament from Bridgeman's correspondence, including his 'private letters'. His manner of dispensing with Bridgeman showed that he was not above employing the most heavy-handed, even cruel, measures towards those who blocked his way or challenged his views.[4]

Complaints were widespread of Churchill's interfering, tactless, authoritarian ways, of his habit of airing firm – many would say, dogmatic – views on strategic and technical matters about which he possessed little expertise, and of meddling in appointments – at all levels – in such an maladroit manner as to sap the discipline of the navy. As he remarked to Violet Asquith, some admirals were 'to be "poached" and "scrambled" and others to be "buttered"'. 'His fatal error,' thought John Jellicoe, the Second Sea Lord, was his inability to comprehend that he was a layman 'quite ignorant of naval affairs'.[5] So much so that the four naval lords were on the point of mass resignation at the end of 1913. Only the general opinion among the admirals that Churchill 'was so much off his head' that his antics should be ignored resolved the situation.[6]

On the other hand, Churchill's ideas blew through the dusty corridors of the Admiralty like a fresh, if at times chilling, wind. Some were most appreciative of his initiatives. Churchill's 'quick brain and vivid imagination were invaluable,' affirmed Admiral Sir Roger Keyes, 'and, in the majority of cases, his intervention was in the best interests of the Services'. Churchill was quite aware of the ructions he caused, though he did little to contain himself. Later, he confessed that he had been 'a bit above himself' as First Lord.[7]

During these years Churchill relied heavily on the views of the seventy-year-old Lord Fisher, who had retired as First Sea Lord in 1910. More than any admiral of his time, he had dragged the navy into the twentieth century. But there had been a price to pay. Imperious and scornful of opposition, Fisher, like Churchill, was a controversial and divisive figure. His picturesque, often brutal language lent a frightening dimension to the ruthlessness and spirit of vengeance that lurked close to the surface of his character. To those who dared to defy him, he vowed, in one spicy phrase, that 'their wives would be widows, their children fatherless, and their homes a dunghill'. There was a certain inevitability in a clash between Churchill and Fisher, two overpowering personalities. But all the while that Fisher acted as Churchill's 'dry nurse', nurturing him but without sharing responsibility with him, their partnership flourished.[8]

Churchill was already friendly with Fisher during the naval estimates crisis of 1909.[9] They renewed contact immediately on Churchill's appointment to the Admiralty. 'I would offer to be your Chief of the Navy General Staff,' he wrote to Churchill, 'but I don't want to embarrass you.' His concern did not prevent him from filling the post by remote control. He left no aspect of navy life untouched. He proposed Battenberg as an 'ideal' First Sea Lord; Jellicoe, 'as great as Nelson', to command the Home Fleet; Hankey, 'he is Napoleonic', to succeed as secretary to the CID. Resolve the grievances of the lower deck, he stressed, or 'you will have a Mutiny at the Nore'. 'You must have cheapness & the big gun & speed!' he advised. The fifteen inch gun, he promised, 'will "stagger humanity"!' 'Oil fuel only', he cried enthusiastically. The navy would have no problem defending Britain from a German attack if it followed his orders. 'My beloved Winston,' he finally enthused, indicating his personal affection for a First Lord who was so willing to heed his advice.[10]

But Churchill was of too independent a mind to be an innocent tool of anyone. He took Fisher's advice because he believed in it. He had so much to do and so much confidence in his abilities to do it. 'I wish I had nine lives like a cat,' he confided to Clementine, 'so that I cd go into each branch thoroughly. As it is I have to trust so much to others – when I am pretty confident I cd do it better myself.' This did not deter him. The foundations of a Navy War Staff were laid; Jellicoe was advanced to second-in-command of the Home Fleet; while David Beatty was similarly brought forward to become Churchill's naval secretary. Churchill opened the lower deck to promotion; suggested competitive examinations for commissions; argued for higher widows' pensions and marriage allowances; achieved pay rises for the navy; and, in a typical Churchillian flourish, urged shipside sing-songs – to include popular music-hall choruses – with admirals and men singing in one voice to raise morale.[11]

Fisher also influenced Churchill regarding the preparation of the fleet. More heavily armed and speedier battleships were laid down. His fifteen-inch gun was installed on the Queen Elizabeth class, designed to sail at twenty-five knots. The most crucial move involved the switch from coal to oil. This was the bravest of decisions. The gains were considerable: faster ships, extra efficiency in re-fuelling, greater manoeuvrability, economies in manpower and space. But so too were the risks. Britain was rich in coal but possessed no oil, which meant relying on sources abroad and ensuring sufficient reserves at home. The initiative to buy into Anglo-Persian came neither from Fisher nor Churchill but from the oil company, intent on bolstering its status in the area from its rivals. It took the Admiralty six months to make up its mind. In July 1913, Churchill announced to Parliament the move over to oil. A year later, he initiated, for £2.2 million the purchase of a controlling 51 per cent share in the Anglo-Persian Oil Company, an arrangement that guaranteed the delivery of six million tons of oil over twenty years.[12] His achievements, intended and otherwise, were remarkable. Against much entrenched opposition and vested interests, he had guided the navy into a new era, symbolized by the Super-Dreadnoughts, the Royal Sovereign class, that were modified to oil consumption. As a contingent side-effect, British interests were extended throughout the Gulf area, for dependence on Persian oil meant deeper involvement in Persian affairs.

As early as March 1911 Churchill had been in favour of depleting the Mediterranean Fleet while retaining supremacy in 'decisive waters', the Straits of Gibraltar, the eastern basin of the Mediterranean centred on Alexandria, and of most significance, the North Sea. When the details of the new German naval law became known in early 1912, this need became even more urgent. Churchill regarded this 'remarkable expansion' as a most serious challenge to British naval supremacy.[13] It could be met in two ways: by reaching an understanding with Germany; or by expanding modestly and utilizing resources as efficiently as possible. The first option proved unobtainable. In a minor but characteristic way, Churchill contributed to the failure when he belittled the German fleet as 'a luxury', timing his declaration to coincide with Lord Haldane's presence in Berlin to negotiate a naval holiday. Naturally, the Germans reacted bitterly to this slur. So too did many of Churchill's fellow Liberals, including Lloyd George, who were incensed at his inept turn of phrase. Within days, Churchill floated the idea of a holiday himself. Anxious to avoid a naval confrontation, Churchill was willing to offer Germany concessions in the colonial sphere. But the German price of neutrality was too high to pay. Churchill used German obduracy to press forward with plans to prune the Mediterranean fleet and to ask the Cabinet for more money. It did not guarantee that he would get all that he asked for, but it did ensure that his claim would receive a sympathetic hearing.[14]

By early 1913, Churchill's programme, based on a naval arrangement with France, to reduce the Mediterranean fleet while ensuring a safety margin of sixty per cent against Germany in the North Sea, had been realized. But not before much hostile opinion had been overcome. Esher thought Churchill 'bold and courageous' but 'deficient in imagination'. He felt that control of the Mediterranean was a prerequisite for the preservation of the Empire. Extreme right-wing opinion was more forthright, describing the First Lord as 'a treacherous windbag'. And he also offended the Liberals who were apprehensive about what they termed 'an alliance' with France.

Churchill had to pick his way carefully. International developments came to his aid. As the Triple Alliance powers – Italy, Austria, and Germany – expanded their sea power and influence in the Mediterranean, so too did the need for Britain to make an adequate response. Although Churchill had favoured a French alliance during the Agadir crisis, and continued to do so, he needed to preserve at least the appearance of Britain's freedom of choice in the event of war. On paper, this was attained in a series of ambiguously worded exchanges with the French. There was an element of face-saving, even self-deception, in the British position. The latent dynamics of these accords – that called for co-operation in the Mediterranean and the English Channel and that included a British pledge to defend the north and west coasts of France – worked very much in the French interest, as Churchill well appreciated.[15]

One mark of a successful minister is measured by the degree he prevails in Cabinet in defending and advancing his ministry's interests. Churchill stood this test. He was adept in naval politics. In one sense, as a reforming First Lord he was enhancing his earlier role as a social radical. Reforms, of whatever variety, cost money. But whereas earlier he had worked hand in glove with Lloyd George to squeeze sufficient funds out of the government, he now found himself trying to force open the Chancellor's purse. This was a risky business. If Churchill had one ally in government, it was Lloyd George. Their partnership, although never devoid of inner stress, had strengthened over the years. Preserving it, while not guaranteeing Churchill's political future, ensured that he possessed a powerful benefactor in times of emergency. In April 1913 he had defended Lloyd George from charges of dubious transactions in shares of the Marconi Company, a scandal that developed into one of the gravest personal crises of Lloyd George's career.[16] Rumours that Churchill also was involved were easily demolished, but of equal importance he sustained Lloyd George.

Much of this political capital was squandered when they clashed head-on over the naval estimates in the winter of 1913. Feelings ran fever high. Churchill was bitterly attacked in the Liberal press for wasting public money on armaments. Politically, he was virtually isolated. Asquith, one patron, was annoyed at him for having blown up the issue into a great public debate; while the patience of Lloyd George, his other guardian angel, was visibly cracking: 'The PM must choose between Winston and me,' he told a colleague. In Cabinet, a cabal emerged to force Churchill's resignation.[17]

Churchill bombarded the Cabinet with papers, quoting chapter and verse, hoping that this avalanche of facts and figures would engulf his colleagues. But as Disraeli once remarked, there are 'lies, damned lies, and statistics'. It was possible to shuffle figures to suit everyone's purpose. In fact, there was no danger of Britain being overtaken by Germany. Not only had the British navy a head start in capital ships, but British shipyards could outbuild – by two years to three – their German counterparts. Churchill, perfectly aware of this, rightly observed that he had knocked Germany 'sprawling' in matters of naval construction.[18] What concerned him was to maintain a reasonable safety margin between the British and German navies, a flexible definition.

At the end of February 1914, a relieved Lord Riddell could write: 'And so ends a great struggle. No resignations and no drastic revision of the estimates.' Churchill was in 'high spirits'. The compromise gave him almost all that he had asked for: increased estimates of £2,750,000 for 1914–15, including the construction of four extra Dreadnoughts; while Lloyd George and the 'economists' were fobbed off with promises of substantial savings in the future. Asquith had averted a Cabinet split. With Ireland boiling, he could not afford any outcome that would imperil his beleaguered government. By spinning the crisis out and raising the spectre of general elections – in no one's interest except the Tories – he allowed saner counsels to prevail. But the manner of resolving the affair also indicated Churchill's standing in British politics. At the age of thirty-nine, with no party base, no faction to command, virtually bereft of political support, he had emerged as a force to be reckoned with.[19]

Churchill acknowledged that at the Admiralty he had never 'worked so hard nor been so happy'.[20] No subject escaped his interest: conditions on the lower deck, oil, guns, appointments, supplies, armour, re-deployment of the fleet, founding the Royal Naval Air Service.[21] Relying heavily on Fisher's advice, particularly in technical matters, he possessed the necessary vision and energy and courage to carry out a programme having once convinced himself of its necessity. Not all the deficiencies of the navy were overcome.[22] But the Churchill-Fisher combination was both creative and fruitful. The main tasks for which Churchill had been sent to the Admiralty were accomplished. Constant manoeuvres and training kept the Fleet on its toes. Its wartime deployment had been finalized to the last particular. Morale was high. Whatever its flaws, the navy, in Arthur Marder's words, 'believed itself to be ready'.[23]

Like most other working politicians, the European crisis caught Churchill, by surprise. They were, as he recalled, too busy toiling around the 'muddy byways of Fermanagh and Tyrone' to take much notice of the assassination of the Archduke Ferdinand in scarcely heard of Sarejevo. It was the Austrian ultimatum of 23 July that focused the Cabinet's attention on the possibility of a general European war. The Balkans were of little relevance to Churchill.[24] But this was true only as long as the fighting remained localized and did not drag in the great powers. In the event of a conflict, Britain's interests still lay in supporting France and Russia; Germany was still the foe. In April 1913 he had devized a 'Timetable of a Nightmare', a sensational tale that told of German landings at Harwich and Newcastle timed to coincide with the BEF sailing to honour its commitment to France; of a German army breaking into the suburbs of London; of the fall of the (Liberal?) government; and of the formation of an administration of national salvation.[25] In Churchill's wartime scenario, Britain was committed, whatever her contractual obligations, to fight against the German enemy.

On 28 July, the same day that Austria declared war on Serbia and Europe moved a step closer to general conflict, Churchill wrote pessimistically that 'we all drift on in a kind of dull cataleptic trance'. Although the preparations for war held 'a hideous fascination' for him, at the same time he felt exhilarated at the prospect of action.

Churchill drew up a seventeen-point crash programme, ranging from the worldwide disposition of the Fleet to positioning anti-aircraft guns at oil depots to shadowing enemy vessels on the high seas. On the authority of the First Sea Lord, Prince Louis of Battenberg, the Third Fleet, which had been on tactical manoeuvres, was ordered not to disperse, a measure approved immediately by Churchill and the Cabinet. On 28 July he took his 'most important step', ordering the Fleet north to its war stations at Scapa Flow, Cromerty, and Rosyth, again receiving Asquith's consent after the event. As the Fleet steamed through the Strait of Dover, under cover of darkness and without lights, Churchill reported to the King that 'all "precautionary measures" have been taken'. At the same time, he made clear his intention to appoint Jellicoe to command the Home (later Grand) Fleet, should hostilities commence. There was little more he could do now except wait upon political events.[26]

By 3 August Germany was at war with Russia and France. German armies were already deployed in Luxembourg, poised to move into Belgium and to fall upon France in a massive right swing that would skirt the Channel ports on their way to Paris. The same morning, news reached London that the Belgians would resist German attempts to cross their territory. Britain was compelled to reconsider her position. Since 24 July, when the Cabinet had been informed of the terms of the Austrian ultimatum, it had been in almost continual session.[27] What disturbed the Cabinet was how to preserve its unity while calculating the ramifications of the Anglo-French *entente*. Could Britain afford to sit by idly and witness the destruction of France as a great power without jeopardizing her truest and most basic interests? Sir Eyre Crowe, a senior official at the Foreign Office, put the case for intervention with devastating clarity: it was a struggle 'between Germany aiming at political dictatorship in Europe and the Powers who desire to retain individual freedom'. If England could not engage in a big war, she had to abdicate as an independent state, he added later.[28] Grey's position, as Foreign Secretary, was equally clear-cut. He too rejected half-measures. On 2 August, he asserted that 'either we must declare ourselves neutral, or in it. If we are to be neutral [I] will go'.[29] Asquith – after some dithering – backed him. Haldane took a strong line, and so did Churchill: 'it was not Belgium one thought of, but France'. From the outset, Churchill had adopted a militant attitude. Asquith saw him as 'very bellicose', moodily contemplating a 'bloody peace'.[30] The Grey-Asquith-Haldane-Churchill group was a formidable combination. As it happened, events also moved in their favour.

The options open to the Cabinet were strictly limited. Either the non-interventionists gave in to the Grey-Asquith bloc, or the government split, with incalculable consequences for the Liberal Party. Until the eve of Britain's entry into the war, the Cabinet agonized over this issue. The 'peace party' commanded a majority in Cabinet. Churchill put it as high as three-quarters, though this seems an exaggeration. The term 'peace-party', however, is something of a misnomer. Only John Morley and John Burns were dedicated anti-interventionists, the remainder wavered. Had they adopted a consistent anti-war line, they could have brought down the government, which no doubt was why Asquith reflected on 31 July that 'this Cabinet will not join the war'.[31] In the party and the Commons the situation appeared even grimmer, where over three quarters of the Liberals favoured 'absolute non-interference'.[32]

Unlike Grey, there is no indication that Churchill contemplated resignation should his views have failed to prevail. It was not in Churchill's nature to hum and haw in moments of crisis. Balancing the prospects of war and peace, he did not view the break-up of the Liberal government as an unmitigated disaster, and would have been quite prepared to resume his traditional role of 'maker' of national coalitions. Once again, his chief contact was F. E. Smith. But his initiative was frozen out by Asquith, no doubt encouraged by the fact that most Liberals assumed that if Churchill proposed anything – particularly a coalition designed to inflate his own role – it was necessary to oppose it. The Conservative response was equally negative, and for very much the same reasons. But Bonar Law led a Party united in its will to support France and Russia, and he promised Asquith 'unhesitating support' for the government in any measures it might take.[33]

On the afternoon of 2 August the Cabinet took the crucial decision to honour its obligation to defend the northern and western coasts of France against German attack.[34] For Morley this was a virtual 'declaration of war', while Burns asserted that it represented 'the symbol' of the 'alliance with France'. They resigned. (Two other ministers, John Simon and Lord Beauchamp, tendered their resignations but retracted immediately.) The following day, as Germany declared war on France and Paul Cambon, the French ambassador in London, was asking whether the word 'honour' should be expunged from the English language, the waverers reconsidered. Churchill had made every effort to bring them round. His main target was Lloyd George, who had emerged as the key figure, not only in Cabinet but also for Churchill's future. Shunned by Bonar Law and put off by Asquith, Churchill was left stranded. Once again, he needed Lloyd George; and he went some way towards meeting Lloyd George's enigmatic policies, trimming his own well-known leaning for war for tactical considerations. At the same time he prodded him forward. 'I implore you,' Churchill scribbled,[35] 'to come and bring your mighty aid to the discharge of our duty. Afterwards by participating in the peace we can regulate the settlement.' If not, 'All our lives we shall be opposed. I am deeply attached to you & have followed your instinct & guidance for nearly 10 years.'

Lloyd George's instinct, however, told him to hold back. For the moment, he refused to declare openly in favour of intervention. But he did not exclude the possibility should conditions change. Like Churchill, he was convinced that, unless Germany backed down, Britain would have no option but to intervene. But his political antennae were more finely tuned than those of his more hot-blooded associate. He would not go charging off to war unless certain that he could command widespread support in his own camp.

During these days, Lloyd George played his cards very close to his chest. Unlike Churchill, he was far more sensitive to mainstream opinion inside the Liberal Party. He was also a far more calculating politician and would not antagonize its radical, non-interventionist wing, the foundation of his political support. He would pull them in at the right moment. And that moment would arrive with the German invasion of Belgium, which he was certain would ensue, an act so emotionally charged as to sway even fair-minded and sober Liberals. The German ultimatum to Belgium brought the prevarication to an abrupt end, and with it collapsed the anti-war group in the government, as Lloyd George suspected it would.

By 3 August Lloyd George's waiting game was over. The Cabinet, now certain that Germany would march westwards, steeled itself to defend Belgium by force of arms, and by so doing save Europe from German hegemony. At about three o'clock that afternoon Grey rose to a tense and expectant House of Commons to explain why circumstances were forcing Britain to embark on war. His speech, 'almost conversational in tone', was generously received, punctuated time and again by cheers. 'It was a wonderful achievement,' remembered Balfour, 'he drew you on to the irresistible conclusion that war was inevitable for us.' Churchill, 'crying with excitement', was moved by the high drama of the occasion.[36] Afterwards, he rushed up to Sir Edward Carson and grasped his hand, a sign that parochial political squabbles were to be set aside to confront the German menace. The following day, as German troops poured into Belgium, Britain declared war on Germany. Due largely to Lloyd George's political acumen, his patience and refusal to be stampeded into precipitate action by wild advice, Asquith managed to bring his party, his government, and his country united into war.

'God Bless the Dardanelles'

When Churchill composed his account of his tenure at the Admiralty during the first nine months of war, he saw a 'sinister fatality' dogging his footsteps. 'The terrible "Ifs" accumulate,' he wrote.[1] As the tragedy at the Dardanelles cast a deep shadow on his future, heralding, or so he thought, the end of his career, he had sound psychological cause to seek the blame – even partially – in factors that lay beyond his control, rather than in the patterns of his behaviour and in the methods by which he sought to prosecute the war.

Churchill was not a militarist in the crude sense of that expression. But the expectation of battle excited him. 'My God!' Churchill exclaimed to Margot Asquith 'This, this is living History . . . Why I would not be out of this glorious delicious war for anything the world could give me.' 'But don't repeat that I said the word "delicious"', he added judiciously, 'you know what I mean . . .'[2]

Churchill's first signal to the navy was that it should 'Commence hostilities against Germany'. But what kind of hostilities did he have in mind? In the first instance to safeguard Britain from invasion and to protect her shipping-lanes; to transport the BEF to its battle stations in northern France and to impose a naval blockade on Germany. This naval war, he comforted Lloyd George, 'will be cheap – not more than 25 millions a year'. And even though he had initially assumed that the war would not last more than a year, the defensive nature of the Admiralty's contribution was totally out of character with Churchill's concept of waging war.[3]

There remained of course the greatest prize of all: to bring the German High Fleet to decisive battle. Churchill gave this prospect a priority of world historic importance: 'in the space of two or three hours [it] might nakedly decide who won the war'.[4] Despite some alarums, this did not occur. Nor was Churchill inclined to wait for it to happen. Even before the stalemate on the western front, his mind was picturing more dramatic ways of waging and winning the war. The main land battles would be fought between France and Germany. Britain would support her allies in Europe – a protracted business given her lack of a mass conscript army – and apply her naval strength by tightening the blockade and striking at points where he believed the enemy to be most vulnerable, on its peripheries. From the very outset of the war, his thoughts turned towards the Dardanelles, but also towards seizing the Frisian Islands off the Dutch-German coast to serve as bases to harry the Germans, perhaps also to tempt the German fleet into battle. 'If I did not interrupt him or ask questions he could capture Borkum in twenty minutes,' remembered Admiral Sir Henry Oliver.[5] The object of seizing an island base was to prepare the way for an assault on the Baltic that would lead in turn to an amphibious landing on the coast of Schleswig-Holstein, within easy striking distance of Berlin. The political benefits of a Baltic strategy were also deemed to be considerable: it would convince Holland and Denmark, so he hoped, to join the allied camp.

Although Churchill's name is linked irrevocably to the Dardanelles, his consistent, first preference was for action on the northern flank. Churchill distinguished between the 'decisive theatre' of war, 'where a vital decision may be obtained at any given time', and the 'main theatre', in which 'the main armies or fleets are stationed', these areas being not necessarily synonymous. 'If the fronts or centres of armies cannot be broken,' he maintained, 'their flanks should be turned,' and manoeuvres to turn them should be amphibious and dependent on sea power.[6] 'The Baltic is the only theatre in which naval action can appreciably shorten the war,' he told Fisher, another Baltic devotee, at the end of December 1914. However, this was not a view shared by many others. Most evaluations in detail of these schemes rendered them impracticable.[7]

Churchill did not intend his Baltic triumph, cheaper in manpower and resources, as a substitute for final victory on the western front – though he hints as much in his memoirs.[8] Churchill held no doubt that the 'decisive theatre' lay in Europe; it also happened to be where the great armies confronted each other. It was here that the war would be decided. Although he was sensitive to the butchery taking place in France, he was quite prepared to pay the cost, even though he might haggle about the price. On the eve of the Dardanelles campaign, he reminded Fisher that 'Germany is the foe, & it is bad war to seek cheaper victories & easier antagonists'.[9]

During the first five to six months of the war there was widespread criticism of the Admiralty's – and by implication, Churchill's – performance. Much of it stemmed from the public's high expectations of the navy, it being weaned for so long on the perception of absolute British naval supremacy. In fact, the navy carried out its immediate tasks competently and without mishap. Yet its shortcomings were soon apparent. On 10 August, two German battleships, the *Goeben* and the *Breslau*, after having successfully sprung a British naval trap in the Mediterranean, had slipped through the Dardanelles to anchor off Constantinople. Towards the end of September, the 'Cressys', three aged armoured cruisers, were caught by German submarines in the North Sea and sunk with the loss of 1,460 men. The same month there were submarine scares at Scapa Flow, panicking the Grand Fleet to put out to sea as a safety precaution. The following month the Dreadnought, *Audacious*, was mined and sunk off the north coast of Ireland – a loss that was kept from the public for some time. In the Atlantic and Pacific oceans, German light cruisers, the *Emden* and the *Karlsruhe*, were wreaking havoc with British merchant shipping. True, the British had claimed a splendid victory at the action off Heligoland Bight where four German vessels were sunk.[10]

But the battle of Coronel off Chile (1 November) saw the destruction of two armoured cruisers and the loss of British naval supremacy, albeit temporarily, in the South Pacific. German warships also appeared off Yarmouth (3 November), and Whitby, Scarborough and Hartlepool (16 December), the so-called 'tip-and-run' raids, resulting in loss of life and destruction of property. This sad tale was offset by a significant British naval triumph at the Falkland islands (8 December), sweet revenge for Coronel; and a less satisfactory one at Dogger Bank (25 January) where a combination of chaotic signalling and controversial tactics thwarted a major victory. In the words of one journal, these setbacks rendered Churchill 'a gasbag', Fisher 'a noodle', and Jellicoe 'an incompetent'.[11]

Asquith had early on concluded that the navy was 'not doing very well', and that the Admiralty had 'not been clever in their outlying strategy'.[12] Churchill's initial inclination was to blame the local commanders for the navy's relatively poor showing, harping on their temerity, their lack of drive and imagination, perhaps overlooking the fact that he had appointed many of them. Although there was some truth to these charges, they do not exonerate fully Churchill. Faulty staff work was all too often at the root of the trouble. There was too much centralization at the top, and too little delegation of authority to those remote from the First Lord's immediate circle. Directives from the Admiralty were generally long-winded and sometimes ambiguous; while the signalling between ships when engaged in action was frequently confused and muddled.[13]

But particular facets of Churchill's character also showed up to bad advantage. He was too impatient to make a showing. F. E. Smith, wrote of him during these days that 'No one department, hardly one war, was enough for him in that sublime and meteoric moment.' His brilliant gifts of persuasion, recorded one senior officer, 'hypnotized' the Admiralty staff into accepting opinions 'diametrically opposed to their own.' He intervened at the tactical and strategic level of Admiralty operations.

His rasping tongue also antagonized many of his officers. Angry at the German Navy for not coming out to fight, Churchill threatened that 'it would be dug out like rats from a hole'. His admirals complained 'that we have been dragged down to the level of boasting and breathing bombastic defiance, and we hate it'.[14]

Churchill's reputation was such that he was seldom given the benefit of the doubt. To the untrained public eye, and naturally to that of his more jaundiced colleagues, his image as a adventurer bent on self-glorification was more than confirmed by his flamboyant behaviour. No doubt, he thrilled to the ride on a perilous merry-go-round, believing that he would be able to descend gracefully to general applause. He was a avid gambler.

For example, Churchill's 'Dunkirk Circus' had developed from modest beginnings as an air-base sited at Dunkirk to attack hostile Zeppelins, to concentrating eventually a substantial land force for the defence of Dunkirk and to create 'a demonstration on the enemy's flank'. Churchill did not act independently, but responded promptly to requests from Lord Kitchener, with the full knowledge and consent of Asquith. But these operations had the Churchill imprint all over them. He was constantly in and out of Dunkirk; it was 'his little army'; and it appeared to some as though he were playing at soldiers.[15]

Antwerp was another case. Preserving its independence, this great Belgium port, commanding the approaches to the Scheldt estuary, had long been a prime British interest. After the Germans had been repulsed on the Marne, and the 'race-to-the-sea' begun, the necessity of securing Antwerp became critical. Churchill was prepared to go to great lengths to safeguard it, even to the extent of war with Holland.

But his advice was rejected. At the time, no troops were sent to Antwerp, though Churchill was allowed to send guns to stiffen its aerial defence.[16] A month later, the Belgians were preparing to evacuate Antwerp. At a hasty midnight meeting on 2 October, Churchill announced that 'the abandonment of Antwerp must be stopped . . . [and] he was going there at once to stop it'. Much discussion ensued. Finally, Kitchener agreed and Grey 'acquiesced'.[17] Churchill spent the next five days in Antwerp, masterminding his plan to stave off its surrender, but to no avail as the fortress-city fell on 10 October.

To most contemporary observers, Churchill's behaviour at Antwerp verged on the hysterical. The press, the *Morning Post* in particular, was scathing. Accused indirectly of 'deliberate murder', the costly 'Antwerp Blunder' rendered him 'unfitted for the office which he now holds'. His conduct was noticeably theatrical, enhanced by the bounty of 20,000 marks the Germans put on his head. One journalist on the spot noted 'a man enveloped in a cloak and wearing a yachting cap. He was tranquilly smoking a large cigar and looked at the progress of the battle under a rain of shrapnel . . . He smiled and looked satisfied.' Two days after his arrival in Antwerp, he offered to resign as First Lord and take command of the defence of the city, provided that he was given 'necessary military rank and authority, and full powers of a commander'. Asquith was astonished. Churchill's colleagues regarded his Antwerp performance as 'appalling', 'as a fiasco', the product of 'an unbalanced mind'. Lloyd George took the view that 'no strategic gain' would be yielded from the effort. Clementine, in the last stages of pregnancy (she gave birth to Sarah on 7 October), likewise thought that his 'sense of proportion had deserted him'.[18]

Whatever the merits of Churchill's intervention, his melodramatic performance played into the hands of his many detractors. He was not lacking in admirers, however. Lord Grey recognized 'his courage & gallant spirit & genius for war', and Lord Haldane thought him 'a figure for history'. James Garvin, editor of the *Observer*, defended him bravely in his papers. But their praise was muted when compared to the mounting swell of criticism, much of it unfairly hostile. For the undeniable fact was that Antwerp fell and 2,500 men – 'sheep to the shambles', in Asquith's caustic phrase – went into captivity or were interned by the Dutch. The considerable bonus of the Antwerp expedition was that it delayed the German advance sufficiently to save the Channel ports. Could this have been achieved without Churchill's stirring example? It is impossible to say with certainty. At the time, Churchill dug in, defending his actions, resting his case on the saving of Dunkirk, Calais, and possibly Boulogne, and blaming the loss of Antwerp on the War Office and Kitchener for their 'lack of foresight'.[19] Later, knowing the great damage his 'eccentric expedition' had done to his reputation, Churchill subjected his part in it to self-criticism. In 1932 he gave himself 'A Second Choice': 'I ought, for instance, never to have gone to Antwerp . . . Those who are charged with the direction of supreme affairs must sit on the mountain-tops of control; they must never descend into the valleys of direct physical and personal action.'[20]

This was a sensible ruling. But Asquith had seen him immediately after his return from Antwerp in a mood of high elation: he had 'tasted blood'; he 'ravened for more'; he had begged for 'some kind of military command'. Asquith dismissed this absurd request out of hand. But Churchill, enthralled at the prospect of a splendid military career, dismissed his desk-bound job at the Admiralty as one that had lost its meaning as 'the naval part of the business is practically over'. 'Are these "glittering commands" to be entrusted to "dug-out trash", bred on the obsolete tactics of 25 years ago?' Churchill entreated. 'A political career,' he told Asquith, 'was nothing to him in comparison with military glory'.[21]

This hyperbole betrayed a deep strain in his character. His unceasing search for instant 'military glory' explains his endless interference in affairs of high strategy and tactics, in the minutiae of military technology, often to the chagrin of his professional advisers. On the other hand, he had little taste for the humdrum and tedium of a military career. Once clad in uniform, he could not wait to shed it and take up politics. So it had been in India, and so it would be later.

Churchill's martial character was obvious to all. 'Winston is longing to be in the trenches – dreaming of war, big, buoyant, happy even. He is a born soldier,' observed Margot Asquith. Fisher listed his war attributes: 'Celerity; Courage; Audacity; Imagination.' But these qualities, laudable in themselves, could also be self-defeating. For like everything else he did, in his zest for attaining the aim he set himself, he stretched these traits to breaking-point. Imprisoned by the complexities of the immediate problem he was dealing with, he often failed to see the larger picture. He himself was aware of this shortcoming. A born soldier perhaps, but a flawed one. As he wrote to his friend, General Sir Ian Hamilton: 'I never look beyond a battle. It is a culminating event, & like a brick wall bars all further vision.'[22]

These qualities flowered during the Antwerp episode and they surfaced soon afterwards during the Dardanelles operation, the most dramatic incident hitherto in Churchill's career, and one of incalculable consequences.

The Dardanelles have exerted an eternal fascination, a naïve, almost mystical belief that whoever broke through the Straits to subdue Constantinople held the key to world power. Napoleon asked: 'Essentially the great question remains: Who will hold Constantinople?' Churchill shared this belief. 'This is one of the great campaigns of history,' he exulted in April 1915, as the struggle for Gallipoli raged. 'Think what Constantinople is to the East. It is more than London, Paris, and Berlin all rolled into one are to the West. Think how it dominated the East. Think how it will affect Bulgaria, Greece, Roumania, and Italy.'[23]

Long before Churchill actually fought for the Dardanelles, his romantic self-hero, Savrola, had watched in anguish as 'an ironclad fleet', consisting of two 'slow and out of date' battleships, 'two cruisers and a gunboat', rushed 'a sort of Dardanelles', daring the heavy cross-fire of the shore batteries, incurring severe losses, but pressing on to anchor victoriously before the 'rebellious capital' and shell it into submission, bringing the bloody civil war to an end.[24]

This was fiction. In real life, every enquiry whether or not to force the Straits had yielded negative results. A General Staff survey of December 1906, and recirculated in February 1915, left no doubt of the extreme foolhardiness of such a venture. Independent naval action would be 'dangerous and ineffectual' and 'much to be deprecated'. Even a joint operation would not guarantee victory. Lack of experience of amphibious landings in modern conditions would necessitate intensive training in a similar environment and would hence eliminate the element of surprise. Only if the Balkan countries would rise up against the Turks would there be a chance for success. But even then, who could guarantee that Turkey would surrender? These operations, it gloomily concluded, were neither militarily feasible nor of great political consequence, and were 'full of risk'.[25]

It is difficult to believe that Churchill did not read this assessment.[26] But in March 1911, in an altogether more tranquil atmosphere, he had reminded the Cabinet that 'it is no longer possible to force the Dardanelles, that nobody would expose a modern fleet to such perils.' Asquith, in August, had reiterated this warning, harping on the 'insuperable difficulty' of breaking through the Dardanelles. When war broke out, the entire question was re-examined by senior naval and military officers, with Churchill in attendance at some of the meetings. Their evaluations were entirely pessimistic. A 'fleet enterprise' alone was definitely discounted. It was not 'a feasible military operation' was their inescapable conclusion.[27]

Only once, in 1807, had a British fleet broken through the Dardanelles. But by the time they reached Constantinople, the Turks had sufficiently reinforced the city and Constantinople did not fall. The British were compelled to retire, incurring losses on the return passage. Since then, it had been generally assumed that more sophisticated artillery techniques rendered a naval assault through the Dardanelles as most perilous. 'Jackie' Fisher had seen earlier on that any naval action would be 'mightily hazardous', a judgement that upheld Nelson's maxim that 'any sailor who attacked a fort was a fool'.[28] Perhaps the only chance of delivering a decisive stroke at the Dardanelles would have been in a surprise, combined army-navy engagement. Even then, the chances of success would have been slender to an extreme. No British military force had ever attempted an amphibious operation on the scale and complexity demanded by landings on the Gallipoli peninsula, an area so confined and formidable in its topography as to exclude rapid maneouvre and invite, as one commentator later stated, 'terrible slaughter'. However one juggled the basic factors, misfortune beckoned.

Unfortunately, the crucial ingredient of surprise had already been frittered away, and it happened by Churchill's own doing. On 3 November, two days before Britain declared war on Turkey, he had ordered the bombardment of the Dardanelles' forts, an act, later much condemned,[29] that alerted the Turks to British intentions. He told the admirals that he intended to effect 'a demonstration' and to land 'a prompt blow'.[30] But he had long been eager to get in a first strike against Turkey. In August, incensed at the *Goeben*'s escape, he wanted to send a torpedo flotilla through the Dardanelles to sink the German warships that had so humiliated the Admiralty, a risky venture scotched by Asquith and Kitchener. At the end of November, with a hostile Turkey straddling imperial communications in mind, he returned to the Straits, now advocating that 'the ideal method of defending Egypt was by an attack on the Gallipoli peninsula', an audacious stroke that would gain command of the Dardanelles and enable the allies to dictate terms to Constantinople. No one took up his proposal. Churchill himself admitted that the operation was 'very difficult' and required 'a large force'. And that, for the time being, was an end to it.[31]

By the beginning of January 1915 Russia, her economy crumbling from the strains of war, her armies crushed by the Germans on the eastern front and now threatened by the Turks in the Caucusus, had appealed to London for aid. There were rumours that a separate German-Russian peace was in the making. Clearly, every responsible British politician felt dutybound to weigh up any move calculated to brace the Russian will to fight. At the same time, ways were sought to break stalemate on the western front – at least until sufficient power could be brought to bear to shatter the German lines – and yet to be seen to be engaged in hostilities.

Churchill joined in the consensus that the war would be decided in Europe. But this did not exclude the immediate need for action elsewhere to stem the awful carnage in France. The other main advocates of an oblique strategy, Lloyd George and Hankey, looked south-east, towards the Balkans and Constantinople. Lloyd George's preference was for employing an army of 600,000 at Salonika or on the Dalmatian coast, thereby 'knocking the props' from under Germany; Hankey, intent on 'weaving a web round Turkey', counselled launching a joint naval-army strike at Constantinople.[32] The hope was that, inspired by the example of the allied armies, the Balkan countries would take heart and rise up against the Turks.

Churchill too wished to avoid sending British armies to Flanders. He was torn between forcing the Skagerrak or rushing the Dardanelles. But his first priority was 'naval command of the Baltic', though when he read Hankey's proposal he thought that they were 'substantially in agreement'.[33] They became even more compatible when Kitchener suggested 'a [naval] demonstration' at the Dardanelles to relieve pressure on Russia, and Fisher proposed, as part of an overall Balkan drive, including the use of 75,000 seasoned British troops, forcing the Dardanelles with pre-Dreadnought battleships. This fired Churchill, and he rehashed the naval display and Fisher's exploitation of old battleships into one scheme. 'Do you consider the forcing of the Dardanelles by ships alone a practicable operation?' he enquired of Vice-Admiral Sackville Carden commanding the allied naval squadron off the Dardanelles, who replied cautiously that the Dardanelles 'might be forced', but it would take many ships to do so in an extended operation. Go ahead and produce a detailed plan, came back Churchill, 'Your view is agreed with by high authorities here.'[34] A sharp barrister would have considered Churchill's original question as 'leading' and his subsequent reply to Carden as tendentious. It remains unclear which 'high authorities' Churchill had consulted, unless one includes Admiral Sir Henry Jackson, whose essentially gloomy, non-committal report – that Churchill, in any case, read some days later – could hardly have excited him.[35] These cloudy beginnings were to thicken as the Gallipoli campaign progressed.

At its meeting on 13 January, the War Council directed the Admiralty to prepare for 'a naval expedition' that would systematically destroy the Dardanelles' forts, take Gallipoli, and proceed to Constantinople. There was general agreement, or at least no opposition. But neither was there any discussion as to what 'taking Gallipoli' implied. The assumption being that the naval bombardment would render the peninsula a wasteland, for as the Fleet advanced serenely to invest Constantinople it would have nothing to fear but the mere 'inconvenience' of 'field guns or rifles'. Planning went ahead and the date for the naval assault was set for mid-February.[36]

By then uncertainty had begun to creep in. The most conspicuous doubting Thomas was Fisher. In October, Churchill had appointed him as First Sea Lord, to replace Battenberg who had been hounded out of office by an ugly outburst of xenophobia. The combination of Churchill and Fisher looked unbeatable on paper, but in reality was too volcanic to stand severe strain. Matters were not improved by their different working habits.[37] Fisher would rise early and work throughout the morning, his energy flagging by afternoon; Churchill, a late riser, and refreshed by his afternoon cat-nap, would continue functioning until the small hours of the morning. Churchill's working habits certainly added to his reputation as a lovable, idiosyncratic character.

> He presented a most extraordinary spectacle, perched up in a huge bed, with the whole of the counterpane littered with dispatch boxes, red and all colours, and a stenographer sitting at his foot – Mr Churchill himself with an enormous Corona in his mouth, a glass of warm water on the table by his side and a writing pad on his knee.[38]

Soon enough it must have been abundantly plain to Churchill that Fisher was totally opposed to the navy going it alone. No doubt he read too much into Fisher's immediate response to send out the *Queen Elizabeth*, the latest super-Dreadnought, to practise its gunnery on the Dardanelles' forts; and took too much heart from Fisher's inability to stand up to his robust eloquence.[39] If at every conceivable opportunity

Fisher had to be won over, it must have been plain to Churchill that his First Sea Lord had no faith in a naval operation. Had Fisher wanted to be extra mischievous, he could with justice have asked: what plan? For throughout these weeks Churchill was also eyeing the coasts of Europe, looking for a suitable landing-point, harping as usual on Borkum and the Baltic, the 'only theatre in which naval action can appreciably shorten the war'. 'Winston [is] very brilliant, but too changeable,' grumbled Fisher, 'he has a different scheme every day'.

As ever, Fisher's feelings were passionately expressed, but to a restricted circle. To Jellicoe he revealed just how the Dardanelles' scheme had become an abomination to him. Only by converting it into 'a great military operation' could something, perhaps, be saved. To Churchill he damned the Dardanelles, forecasting they would drown them all. He argued cogently against risking valuable ships in questionable actions in secondary areas. Nothing, he stipulated, should be done to deplete or endanger British strength in the North Sea, the decisive battle area. Churchill did not see fit to circulate this warning to the War Council, though Asquith received a copy.[40] On 15 March, on the eve of the second naval assault, Fisher again solicited Churchill to combine the attack with military landings. Churchill declined. 'I don't think we want a War Council on this. It is after all only asking a lot of ignorant people to meddle in our business.'[41]

Fisher erred gravely in not spelling out his reservations more clearly to those in highest authority. He held his tongue on the grounds that it was improper for him to quarrel with his political chief in public debate.

At the Admiralty the weight of opinion for the projected operation was at best lukewarm and conditional, a fact that could not have escaped Churchill's notice. Jackson wrote that it was 'not recommended as a sound operation'; 'a strong military force' was necessary either to assist or follow it up. Richmond expressed himself more brutally: 'Winston very, very ignorant, believes he can capture the Dardanelles without troops'. Hankey held similar views, which led Asquith to the same conclusion.[42] Something of this must have rubbed off on Churchill. Only days before the first naval attack was due to begin, Churchill began to lobby Kitchener for a military force of 50,000, 'either to seize the Gallipoli Peninsula when it has been evacuated, or to occupy C'nople if a revolution takes place'. Until then he had given no consideration to a military force for action specifically at the Dardanelles.[43] It seems from this that he wanted these troops simply to mop-up Turkish resistance once the navy had broken through; but his persistence in insisting that the crack 29th division stiffen the military force hints at his own inner uncertainties, concealed from his colleagues. 'You get through! I'll find the men,' Kitchener told him.[44] The meaning was clear. Aware of the contradiction in his position, Churchill himself later conceded the point.

> I had no right at this stage to complain if Lord Kitchener had said, 'I am not going to land on the peninsula.' I could not have said. 'Oh! you have broken faith with the Admiralty.' On the contrary, we had said that we would try it without committing to him to that, and he would have had a right to complain if we had turned round and immediately demanded that he should undertake this very serious operation.[45]

Despite this widespread sense of unease, the preparations for the naval bombardment went ahead. At the War Council, no one opposed it. The politicians, Asquith, Grey, Lloyd George, Haldane, Balfour registered no dissent, preferring to see the dazzling rewards that would accrue from success. No doubt they were unduly swayed by Kitchener's confidence, whose reputation, though beginning to show signs of wear, was still formidable. The navy's strike was 'vitally important', he determined, the 'equivalent to that of a successful campaign fought with the new armies'. In the event of a setback, he promised them, 'the attack could be broken off'.[46] This ringing assurance left open an honourable way of retreat.

On 19 February the navy began its attempt to prise open the Dardanelles. The attacks continued sporadically for almost a month. Some progress was made. Some forts were silenced: some occupied and blown up by landing-parties of marines. There were moments when it appeared as though success was within reach. But the Anglo-French naval squadron was unable to clinch the issue. And as it faltered, the confidence of the Turks in their ability to resist hardened. On-the-spot military observers believed the navy did not possess the necessary power. Churchill was undeterred. Characteristically, his ardour flared up once the operation had got under way. Poor Carden, Asquith commiserated, he wanted, rightly, 'to proceed cautiously', but Winston was 'spurring' him on. Kitchener saw Churchill as 'too impulsive and headstrong'.[47]

Like any realistic field commander, Churchill was prepared to incur even 'severe loss' should the result justify it, having in mind the old ships that would not substantially alter the naval balance, and 'two to three hundred casualties' as a moderate outlay for sweeping the Straits up to the Narrows.[48] But this relatively cheap price-list took little account of the many operational flaws that were being revealed as the navy failed to make its decisive breakthrough. Still, Churchill remained optimistic. 'Our affairs in the Dardanelles are prospering,' he informed Jellicoe on 9 March, 'though we have not yet cracked the nut.'

Carden was anything but confident. But considered by both Fisher and Churchill as a lightweight who had arrived at his present high command by mistake, Carden's doleful reports of the lack of effective progress were taken by Churchill as evidence that his backbone needed stiffening. In fact, Carden identified genuine problems, and it would have been wiser to have thought them out than to discount them. Churchill, among others, had been over impressed with the ease by which the high-angle, heavy German guns had demolished the massive Belgium forts at Antwerp, Liège, and Namur, and the simplistic conclusion was drawn that battleships could reduce strongly entrenched shore batteries in the same way. It proved otherwise. Stationary ships were sitting targets for land forts; if they slipped anchor and moved out to sea, their firing-platforms became unstable and their gun-elevations too low, making scoring direct hits even trickier. Air reconnaissance to direct accurate fire from the sea was totally inadequate. Also, the Turks possessed movable howitzers, impossible to pinpoint for long. Nor was it safe to enter the Dardanelles without first clearing its waters of mines, the only sure way being to first destroy the Turkish artillery, which could not be done without the use of troops. There was no painless way to square this circle. Another complication emerged: lack of ammunition, Carden complained, would paralyse the navy's capacity to conduct heavy and protracted bombardments. All this, combined with faulty intelligence and lack of serious planning as to how the fleet would be supplied once it had pierced the Turkish defences, led Jackson at the Admiralty to warn that to enter the Dardanelles without first surmounting these obstacles 'must involve serious losses in ships and men', and Carden to propose military action 'on a large scale' to ensure fleet communications before entering the Sea of Marmora.[49]

Churchill must have been aware of these anxieties. Due also to his pressure, an army of around 80,000 troops was assembling at Lemnos, under the command of his friend, General Sir Ian Hamilton. Its instructions were to intervene only if the fleet failed to break through. Churchill did not exclude military cooperation. But trapped by his inability to decide on what form the intervention should take and its timing, and by his own freely avowed inclination for a great naval assault, he did not contest Hamilton's directive. At the War Council he had argued for military forces, but 'only to be utilized in case of necessity': they were there 'to reap the fruits of those [immediate naval] operations when successfully accomplished'. Hankey begged Churchill to wait and coordinate the strike with the army, 'but he wouldn't listen, insisting that the navy could do it alone'. His obstinacy, Hankey explained, was due to his desire to bring off a great naval coup to refurbish his damaged reputation after Antwerp. At any rate, Churchill was nothing if not decisive. The naval attack 'cannot be delayed for troop movements', he wrote to Kitchener. Press forward, he urged Carden, 'without hurry but without loss of time'.[50]

On 18 March an Anglo-French naval squadron of sixteen battleships opened its attack at the Dardanelles. By early evening, badly mauled, it withdrew. As feared, it had sustained heavy losses. Over 600 men had been killed; three battleships had been sunk and three others crippled. Drifting mines had inflicted the main damage. Five days later, after some hesitation, the new naval commander, Admiral Sir John de Robeck (Carden having resigned), conceded that a purely naval action was no longer practicable. The army would have to secure the heights dominating the Straits, thereby enabling the navy to sail safely through. It would take a month for the army to prepare itself. The War Council, with Churchill as its mouthpiece, left the final decision to de Robeck, who was in turn waiting for Hamilton. But it is clear from the phrasing of Churchill's original (and unsent) communication to him that he, Churchill, was unable to admit defeat; the navy could do it alone, he persisted, and he would be prepared to lose another '7 or 8 old ships' in the attempt. When Fisher read this uncompromising message he threatened resignation if it were sent off, and in consequence Churchill toned down his despatch.[51]

After the naval reverses, even the most relaxed of armchair strategists must have realized the need for a reassessment of the entire operation. Now, not only had no military headway been made, but the much-vaunted political aims that had prompted the campaign were no longer tenable. The immediate need to aid Russia had receded. The idea of a Balkan alliance rising up against the Turks, speculative at best, proved to be a will-of-the wisp. Their conflicting territorial ambitions would always divide them.

As though driven by a terrible internal dynamics, the British were sucked into an operation that spelled ruin from the moment the navy had failed in its mission. Amidst logistical confusion and inadequate staff preparations, flawed intelligence and security leaks, arrangements for amphibious landings went ahead, allowing the Turks a full month to take stock and reinforce their strongholds. On 25 April, as dawn broke, an armada of 200 ships put ashore 30,000 troops on choked-up beaches on the southern tip of the peninsula and to the north at Gaba Tepe on the Aegean coast. After two days of severe fighting and appalling butchery, the British force had failed to pierce the Turkish lines, although on occasion it had appeared to be on the verge of doing so. This futile exercise was repeated four months later, on 6 August, with the same grim returns. It was not until January 1916 that the spent British army was evacuated.

These reverses, if they troubled Churchill, did not deflect him. To the end he remained convinced that the operation was feasible. In the autumn of 1915 he drew up a full-scale plan to force the Dardanelles and capture Constantinople. The following September, in a draft statement, he was equally optimistic of success. Even after years of reflection, he wrote:

'the plan of British and Allied war which according to this account [in *The War Crisis*] would best have served our interests in the year 1916 would have been a surprise attack upon the Dardanelles.'

He saw it as 'a legitimate war gamble'.[52] Obstinate, yes. Perverse, certainly. But the element of true courage and integrity, of an indomitable spirit is also there. Like a legendary prize-fighter, he would never throw in the towel, no matter how badly thrashed.

Once the initiative had passed to the army, Churchill's role was drastically reduced, at least in the operational sense. In the eyes of all, however, he remained its most eloquent advocate; or, as it was put less kindly, its most intemperate promoter. An enraged Fisher blamed Churchill for having 'shoved' the politicians into the adventure.[53] To place the blame for the fiasco solely on Churchill's shoulders was unwarranted however. But his flamboyant, publicity-seeking style made him a soft target. He never evaded his responsibility as the prime mover in the adventure; nor, to his credit, did he wish to. The War Council's accountability, if less exposed to catchy headlines, was also considerable. The Dardanelles Commission exonerated no one: not Fisher, Kitchener, Churchill, nor the politicians. It accused the War Council of usurping the authority of the Cabinet, and by implication the politicians for having allowed it. Churchill explained: 'I have often heard the cabinet say: "We do not wish to be told about this – this is a secret matter, and the fewer who knew about it the better".'[54]

His influence on the wane, Churchill discovered an unexpected ally in Kitchener. Kitchener had previously argued that it would always be possible to retreat if the naval attack was repulsed. Now he changed course: 'A defeat in the Orient,' he pontificated, would have the most calamitous repercussions for a great imperial power. The campaign was now of 'the greatest importance from a political and military point of view,' and '[it] will be vigorously pushed to a conclusion.'[55] 'The Great Poster' (in Elizabeth Asquith's telling phrase) had already begun to fade, but his reputation and authority still allowed him to judge issues *ex cathedra*. Loss of imperial face was a factor that was impossible to prove but difficult to disregard. Kitchener's prestige; Churchill's resolution; the War Council's willingness to believe what it wanted to believe; the lack of a viable, alternative strategy; and the tantalizing hope that perhaps, despite all the Cassandras, the Dardanelles' offensive would prove to be the masterstroke that would bring the war to a swift end, led to the agony of Gallipoli.

One reason for Churchill's fixation on the Dardanelles, and his drive to bring the engagement to a triumphant conclusion, stems from his realization that, with defeat, his political future would be very much on the line. Three days before the April landings he spoke frankly to Lord

Riddell. He admitted that his initial calculations had been wrong. The idea of a naval breakthrough had 'proved impracticable'. The mobility of the Turkish guns, which enabled them to train easily on ships in narrow waters, had come as a surprise. The Turks were now defending from strongly fortified positions and he expected a 'great battle'. But the consequences of a successful operation were worth the gamble. 'It is better to risk lives in this way than to allow the war to drag on indefinitely.' And what if this colossal endeavour should terminate in disaster? '"They may get rid of me," he retorted. "My regiment is awaiting me".'56

In the immediate aftermath of the landings, Churchill exhibited his optimistic side. 'All is going on well,' he told Clementine on 5 May. Apparently, accurate reports of the losses sustained had not yet reached him. In no other way is it possible to explain his depiction of the events of 25 April. The incident of the *River Clyde*, when 2,000 men had been cut to pieces as they attempted to land, was described to Lord Riddell as little more than a gentle stroll on the beach: they had simply 'marched out of the collier on to the shore'. He was hopeful of eventual victory. Yet once again the disquiet crept through. 'I am not responsible for the Expedition,' he was careful to point out. Every detail had been approved by the Cabinet and the Admiralty Board. 'Fisher and I,' he asserted, with a gracious lack of candour, 'have a perfect understanding.'57

It would have been odd had Churchill's nerves not been on edge during these days. There were bad accounts of his health. He had quarrelled with Lloyd George who told Margot Asquith that Churchill had no judgement and 'no real imagination of the kind that counts'; he accused Churchill of responsibility for the war with Turkey – an absurd charge. With Kitchener, his relations, never cordial, also deteriorated. Churchill's intimacy with Sir John French – who disliked Kitchener intensely – and his habit of visiting French's headquarters at every opportunity and showering him with advice, aroused, rightly, Kitchener's ire. This was tactless, indeed foolish, behaviour, and it would have been wise for Churchill to desist, as Clementine more than once pointed out. Of more consequence was the nature of his relationship with Asquith, who found his manner 'noisy, rhetorical, tactless, & temperless – or – full'. Churchill was by 'far the most disliked man in my Cabinet by his colleagues', he told Margot. Churchill even managed to quarrel with the composed and ever-faithful Eddie Marsh over a trivial matter, a sure sign that his temper was frayed.58

The strain also filtered into his household. Clementine loyally supported Winston. But she was extremely wary about Fisher's role. Was he really loyal to her husband? Or was he consistent only in his erratic, wayward behaviour? His tantrums, she suspected, would end by hurting Churchill. Her worst suspicions were confirmed when, at a luncheon-party, Fisher told Clementine that Winston, ostensibly in Paris on government business, was in fact off 'frolicking' with his mistress. 'Be quiet, you silly old man,' she retorted, 'and get out'. He left quietly enough. But how was it possible ever to trust a man who could behave so irresponsibly, even viciously? Something of these pressures also darkened the snug, protected nursery-world of the Churchill offspring. They too were aware of 'the threatening cloud which seemed to brood over their parents' life'. In a touching gesture of solidarity, their children, Diana and Randolph, would pray every night for God to bless the Dardanelles, alas in vain.[59]

Eclipse

Only eight months after the Dardanelles fiasco Churchill was on active service in France. These months were the most painful of his life. One moment entrusted with great affairs of state, the next a political pariah, he believed his career was over. Fobbed off with a sinecure post in a new coalition government, he claimed to Lord Riddell to be 'the victim of a political intrigue'. 'I am finished!' he grieved, 'Finished in respect of all I care for – the waging of war; the defeat of the Germans.' Sir William Orpen's portrait of him, painted during these days, reflects all too clearly the crisis he was undergoing. The artist spoke of 'the misery in his face'. Clementine thought it too truthful. Later, she recollected that 'I thought he would die of grief.'[1]

His fall from grace had been swift and dramatic and humiliating. It would have destroyed a lesser man. It says much for his resilience and courage, for his enduring belief in his star, that he was able to survive what occurred and that, eventually, he went on to make a full recovery.

Discontent with the Liberal administration's conduct of the war had been mounting for some time. Most people had assumed the war would be over quickly, but it had degenerated into a futile slogging-match. The western front was frozen in a bloody deadlock, a pattern that threatened to repeat itself at the Dardanelles. New men and methods were needed, above all a fresh attitude, that would bring victory. Asquith, widely regarded as too lethargic and indecisive for a wartime Prime Minister, was a principal target. But for those in high places, who were able to observe at close quarters, Kitchener was the chief culprit. Autocratic in manner and disdainful of politicians, he was ill-equipped to cope with the exigencies of organizing a modern war from a Whitehall office, though, occasionally, he was given to flashes of strategic insight that eluded others and that he transmitted to his colleagues as revealed declarations. But however badly Kitchener was directing the war, nothing could dent the general public's faith in him. They needed a father-figure, and Kitchener, strong, reliable, impassive, provided it. As he pointed sternly at the man in the street from his poster, he imbued them with his own phlegmatic confidence in eventual victory. Asquith might have been disenchanted with Kitchener's record, but he could not afford to get rid of him.

Since March, Churchill's name had been linked to rumours of an intrigue to reconstruct the government. Churchill, apparently seduced by Balfour's 'superficial charm', wished to put him in the Foreign Office instead of Grey. Grey was ill and going blind. Fatigued from the strains of almost a decade as Foreign Secretary, he would have preferred retirement. But to aim at Grey was to strike at Asquith. Asquith had come to rely heavily on their long friendship. To widen the Liberal administration by including a leading Unionist, Balfour, meant, in effect, the realization of Churchill's old dream of a national coalition. Lloyd George thought the story 'substantially true', but Asquith was finally convinced that Churchill was loyal to him and the plot untrue.[2]

This did not clear the atmosphere of insinuation and suspicion. The chief conspirators were reputed to be Balfour, Lloyd George, James Garvin, editor of the *Observer*, and Churchill. Their intention: to overthrow the *ancien régime* of Asquith and Grey. When Kitchener refused to cooperate with them, the conspirators turned on him, quickly appreciating that Kitchener's ineptitude at the War Office left him vulnerable to attack. By discrediting Kitchener they would also damage Asquith, perhaps fatally. To this end they would exploit Sir John French, Commander-in-Chief of the British Expeditionary Force in France, with whom Kitchener was at loggerheads, highlighting the war minister's incompetence in supplying the BEF with sufficient manpower and munitions. At a Cabinet meeting, Kitchener offered his resignation in a fit of pique; and Churchill, coming to Lloyd George's rescue, 'went' for both Kitchener and Grey. But the session broke up with nothing resolved.[3]

Kitchener's hysterics could not cover up his shortcomings. Lloyd George admitted to Lord Riddell that they were 'very short of ammunition'. All the while this remained a topic for internal debate, it could not seriously damage the government. But on 14 May *The Times* published a powerful article by its military correspondent demonstrating that the army's failure to make headway was due to a lack of high explosives, and elaborated on the theme in its editorial. These sensational disclosures precipitated a crisis of confidence in the government, casting doubt also on Asquith's integrity, as he had recently denied such shortages.

Churchill's name figures prominently in these events. It was at a weekend in May, when he was a guest of Sir John French at his headquarters at St Omer, along with his cousin, Freddie Guest, a Liberal MP whom French used as a political go-between, that the damaging information was leaked to the *Times* correspondent. Was Churchill a party to these confabulations? Had he 'unquestionably inspired' the leak, as his enemies charged? No record of these meetings exists. But Churchill found it difficult to keep his mouth shut at any gathering. Charles Hobhouse, the Postmaster-General who was also in St Omer that weekend, believed that Churchill was the mainspring of the plot, and said so. Others too thought that he had 'arranged' the article.

From his viewpoint, Churchill 'intrigued' for the noblest of reasons. By removing the inefficient and slovenly Asquith-Kitchener regime and replacing it with a vigorous war ministry, his own position would be enhanced. It was unlikely that he sought the premiership. He knew his place in relation to Lloyd George. But 'a grandiose scheme' was attributed to him, the creation of 'a sort of Department of Public Safety exercising a general control over the War Office and the Admiralty', responsible also for the supply of munitions and war material, a post, incidentally, that Savrola had assumed to save his country.[4]

Was this a serious conspiracy? The case against Churchill is purely circumstantial. There were rumours, innuendos, hints, suspicions, insinuations aplenty – mainly put out by Churchill's enemies: Charles Hobhouse, Reginald McKenna, and Howell Arthur Gwynne. But Churchill was also a most improbable conspirator. Of course, he was embarrassingly ambitious, but he combined his assertiveness with a fetching naïveté. As Harold Nicolson once pointed out, Churchill made a bad intriguer, for 'he cannot really tell lies'. This is entirely to his credit; but it required that he steer clear from compromising situations, something he was temperamentally incapable of doing.[5] But the very fact that such tales circulated, and were given wide credence, brooked ill for Churchill's future.

The 'plot', if such it was, collapsed. The attack on Kitchener – and by implication on Asquith – boomeranged. Copies of Northcliffe's *Daily Mail* were burned on the floor of the Stock Exchange, a striking reminder of the vagaries of public opinion, and one that Asquith surely noted. Lloyd George confessed his fidelity to Asquith; while Balfour was said to be pressing Asquith for a general reconstruction of the government from which he, but not Churchill, would gain. But it was a crisis in Churchill's own ministry, over the Dardanelles' operation, an enterprise for which he was generally assumed to hold personal responsibility, that provided the final pretext for toppling Asquith's government. It also revealed the extent of Churchill's political isolation and the almost paranoid distrust which his every action kindled – and about which he remained curiously unaware.

Fisher's resignation, coming a day after *The Times'* revelations, strengthened the image of a government barely able to keep its head above water. The immediate reason was over the degree of naval reinforcements needed to sustain the battle for the Dardanelles. There was no immediate panic. Fisher met Asquith in what was reported to be a calm atmosphere. He did not bolt to the wilds of Scotland, as he threatened, but remained in London, at the Atheneum, accessible to all except Churchill whom he refused to see.

On 17 May Bonar Law, after first having been alerted by Fisher to his resignation, met Lloyd George. Bonar Law was blunt. He would not accept Fisher's resignation if Churchill remained. The scandal of Fisher's departure coming in the wake of the shells' crisis would injure the government, perhaps terminally. Lloyd George quickly grasped the point: 'Of course we must have a coalition for the alternative is impossible.' They retired next door to 10 Downing Street to meet Asquith, where, in a matter of minutes, they settled the deal. It remained only to decide on the composition of the new administration.

The idea of a coalition had never been erased from the political agenda since the great parliamentary and Irish battles before the war. It now suited both leaders' immediate needs – by definition the nation's – and they seized the opportunity in 'a quarter of an hour'. The speed at which the deal was concluded suggests that both were anxious to neutralize the voluble anti-coalition forces active in their respective parties.

Churchill's position was now desperate, though it took him some time to sink in just how desperate. He had every reason to believe that he would weather the storm. The previous day Asquith had refused to accept his resignation. He had managed to reconstruct an Admiralty Board, without Fisher, that would serve under him, an arrangement that Asquith had seemed to accept. But the Conservatives would not have it. And in fairness to Asquith, if he wanted the Tories in his government, he had to offer them at least one war ministry of consequence. Churchill's was up for the taking simply because he was more expendable than any other senior Liberal minister, with the possible exception of Haldane.[6] Bonar Law would have preferred to see Churchill excluded altogether: 'he seems to have an entirely unbalanced mind which is a real danger at a time like this'. When Lloyd George asked him in December 1916, 'Is he more dangerous when he is for you than when he is against you?' Bonar Law replied without hesitation: 'I would rather have him against us every time.'

Churchill fought valiantly to retain the Admiralty. Seemingly oblivious to Fisher's hostility, he suggested offering the old admiral a seat in the Cabinet – though how he would achieve this miracle remains a mystery; but Fisher refused 'to betray my country' for Churchill's '30 pieces of silver'. Clementine, suffering Winston's agony, wrote a pathetic appeal to Asquith, who did not even bother to reply, but remarked to Venetia Stanley that it was 'the letter of a maniac'. Churchill pleaded with Asquith: 'Let me stand or fall by the Dardanelles – but do not take it from my hands.' And solicited Bonar Law in the same vein. Their replies were menacing. His fate, Bonar Law spelt out, was 'inevitable'; while Asquith left him in no doubt that he could not stay at the Admiralty. He refused the Colonial Office, a hasty decision which he later regretted. He lobbied Asquith. But by now, Asquith was showing signs of impatience at Churchill's capricious behaviour. Finally, Churchill admitted defeat. On 21 May he informed Asquith that he would accept 'any office – the lowest if you like – that you care to offer me'. Asquith took him at his word. He was given, and accepted, the chancellorship of the Duchy of Lancaster, a sinecure with no responsibilities.

Margot Asquith mourned 'our wonderful Cabinet': it had been 'smashed! . . . and by the man whom I always said would smash it – Winston.' But in the same way, Churchill knew who had betrayed him: first, 'the odious Asquith & his pack of incompetents and intriguers'. He grieved that Asquith continued to reign, 'supine, sodden and supreme'. Next, Kitchener, with his incessant 'muddling' and incompetence, and finally Fisher, running them close, 'a very old man, without the nerve to carry on the war, not quite sane in moments of crisis'. From Bonar Law he expected and received nothing. About Lloyd George he was less certain. Lloyd George claimed that he had fought hard to procure high office for Churchill: the Colonies, the India Office, or the vice-royalty of India, but was thwarted by his hostile colleagues. He thought, somewhat patronisingly, that 'this blow will really be the making of him [Churchill]'. Churchill knew that Lloyd George held the key to his political future, and he instructed Clementine to cultivate him. But nothing could staunch his bitterness. The disgrace of his fall ate into his soul. 'I am learning to hate,' he divulged to Jack.

Churchill now paid the full penalty for having twice crossed the floor of the House, for his conspicuous talent of rubbing everyone up the wrong way, for flaunting his ambition in too aggressive a manner, for talking too much and listening too little, for meddling in affairs not his own, for pursuing his policies blinkered to the variations of mood of those around him, leaving little room for manoeuvre or compromise. 'It seems strange,' wrote Frances Stevenson, 'that Churchill should have been in politics all these years, & yet not have won the confidence of a single party in the country, or a single colleague in the Cabinet.'[7]

Asquith fired Churchill but did not exclude him altogether; yielding to a general interparty consensus, he cut Churchill down to size. Churchill's absolute confidence in his abilities blinded him to the political isolation that had dogged him from his first steps in politics. All his political life Churchill had dreamed of a great national coalition in which he would play a central role. It was his singular tragedy that when it arrived, at a moment of national crisis, he was contemptuously relegated to a minor role.

During the coming months, Churchill, politically, was going through the motions. He had nowhere to go and no one to turn to. Undeterred by the defeats of February-March, he proposed, in August, to renew a purely naval operation in the Dardanelles. That autumn, he presented to Kitchener a full-scale plan for taking the Balkans and polishing off Turkey. He had 'A Vision': the Dardanelles would be forced by Christmas.[8]

His vision, however brightly it shone on paper, held little appeal for the Cabinet. By November it was decided to evacuate Gallipoli. Churchill fought a valiant rearguard action, conjuring up the darkest of scenarios should such a calamity occur: 'No more terrible decision . . . has been wrung from a British government since the loss of the American colonies. All the specific disasters of our history, Calais, Minorca, Walcheren, Majuba, rolled into one, do not exceed the moral and material loss involved in it.'[9] But his colleagues had heard it all before and were not to be swayed.

In some ways, the remainder of his life was spent trying to clear his reputation over the Dardanelles fiasco. He did so with a quite manic obsession. He could never concede to himself that perhaps the operation had been conceptually unsound. 'My one fatal mistake,' he confessed to Jack, 'was trying to achieve a gt enterprise without having the plenary authority wh cd so easily have carried it to success.'

Afterwards he produced a torrent of speeches, articles, memoranda, letters and comments seeking to absolve himself from blame. This exercise in public relations reached its peak with the publication of *World Crisis*, the first volume of which appeared in 1923. In it he tried hard to justify his position. It was not for nothing that Balfour, when reading it, quipped that Churchill had written 'a brilliant autobiography, disguised as a history of the universe'.[10]

Churchill was not alone in believing that the Dardanelles were a short-cut to victory, and that it was only lack of vision and bungling all round that had prevented the accomplishment of a great coup. Beaverbrook saw no reason why Churchill had to be sacked, and others were equally unconvinced. For all that, the glaring failure of the Dardanelles, not its potential, clouded Churchill's life. His son, Randolph, discovered why his father was so controversial a figure when he was challenged at school with the charge, 'Your father murdered mine at the Dardanelles'. Repeatedly, the accusation, 'What about the Dardanelles?' was flung at him during his public meetings.

The abrupt change from intense activity one day to standing on the sidelines the next, left Churchill 'gasping' like 'a sea-beast' stranded on a beach.[11] These were desolate days for the Churchills: Clemmie, overcome by grief, 'crying all the time'; Churchill retreating from adversity into depression, his well-known 'Black Dog'. The causes of his depression are open to speculation. Perhaps it was hereditary. Certainly, the first duke of Marlborough complained frequently of 'despondency' and 'melancholy thoughts'; while his father, Lord Randolph, was renowned for his violent swings of mood. Five dukes of Marlborough, concluded the historian of the Churchills, suffered from melancholia. Churchill's depressive attacks have also been put down to his lack of inner self-esteem, a result of his deep anguish at being an unwanted, unloved, rejected child. He could not admit to himself that he had committed an irreparable error that might prejudice his future. He told his doctor, Charles Moran, that from his earliest days in politics 'He had to school himself not to think about things when they had gone wrong, for he found that he could not live with his mistakes and keep his balance.' Great men of high achievements are frequently subject to recurrent depression; and it may well be that one condition feeds off the other. Often, in order to avoid succumbing completely to their depressive state, it spurs them on to even more frenetic activity and the wild pursuit of more permanent successes.[12]

For these reasons, the more extra-curricular activities Churchill indulged in the better. And his varied callings – writing, bricklaying, polo, gambling, hunting, flying, painting – show just how urgent was the need not to allow his 'Black Dog' to devour him.

> When I was young, for two or three years the light faded out of the picture. I did my work. I sat in the House . . . but black depression settled on me. It helped me to talk to Clemmie about it. I don't like standing near the edge of a platform when an express train is passing. I like to stand right back and if possible to get a pillar between me and the train. I don't like to stand beside the side of a ship and look down into the water. A second's action would end everything. A few drops of desperation. And yet I don't want to go out of the world at all in such moments.[13]

It would not be too extravagant to conclude that painting saved his health, restored some light to his 'picture'. Here, at least, he could immerse himself entirely in creative work, responsible only to himself, without fear of contradiction. The 'plenary authority' he sought, he now assumed for each daub.[14]

Churchill came to painting by chance, a direct result of his leaving the Admiralty. At Hoe Farm, an estate in Surrey that Churchill had rented for the summer of 1915, and where he spent his weekends, he saw his sister-in-law, Goonie, exercising her talent. He was so enthralled that Goonie suggested he try. Hesitant about applying brush to canvas, he was rescued by Hazel Lavery, wife of the famous painter Sir John Lavery, and a gifted artist herself. She taught him that boldness and audacity, values that he admired most, were also essential for an artist.

The process of painting, as many have remarked, took on the aspect of a battle, as he fought to control his material.[15]

There was something typically grand in his painting routine.

> His coming was heralded by a procession of gardeners bearing an easel, a large canvas, a chair, a box of paints and a bristling bundle of brushes – the whole armoury of his new art. He followed in their wake clad in a white coat and hat, and having observed the light, chosen the sight, deployed his man-power and his apparatus, set to work.

He did so with 'fierce strokes and slashes' of a 'quite extraordinary decisiveness', with no apparent afterthought or hesitation. He was not above embellishing landscapes to conform to his purpose. 'Well,' he replied to a puzzled Violet Bonham-Carter, searching in vain for ranges of mountains rising dramatically over a dreary, flat countryside, 'I couldn't leave it quite as dull as that.'[16]

There can be no doubt that painting calmed the turbulence of his mind. It was the only occupation that Violet Bonham-Carter had seen him practise in total silence. A compulsive talker, he captivated and, or, exhausted his audiences, whether at play or at work. Painting was different. 'He painted silently, rapt in intense appraisal, observation, assessment of the scene he meant to capture'. Churchill, painfully aware of its therapeutic value, wrote:

> Painting is complete as a distraction. I know of nothing which, without exhausting the body, more entirely absorbs the mind. Whatever the worries of the hour or the threats of the future, once the picture has begun to flow along, there is no room for them in the mental screen. They pass out into shadow and darkness. All one's mental light, such as it is, becomes concentrated on the task. Time stands respectfully aside.[17]

Painting absorbed him for the remainder of his active life. How good was he? Opinions varied. Sir John Lavery, thought that 'he would have made a great master of the brush'.[18] For Churchill these reflections were irrelevant. Politics were his first and true love, the one passion sufficiently all-embracing to accommodate his overpowering ego. Into his paint-box he buried his misfortunes. At first, those that struck from the Dardanelles; later, whenever he encountered setbacks in his public life.

In early November 1915, Asquith disbanded the Dardanelles Committee and set up in its place a smaller war council, the Cabinet War Committee. Asquith had promised Churchill a place on it, but coalition politics intervened and he was finally excluded. This was the last straw. He tendered his resignation from the government and 'placed himself unreservedly at the disposal of the military authorities'. A dramatic act of this nature had been in his mind for some time. That September he had suggested to Asquith that he go to France, holding the rank of major-general, to command an army corps. It was, he wrote to Jack, 'odious to me to remain here watching sloth & folly with full knowledge & no occupation'.[19] Asquith's shameful capitulation gave him his opportunity. He went, however, with some misgivings. At the back of his mind lurked the case history of his father: resignation and political oblivion.[20] It is a mark of his intense despair that he was willing to take such a risk.

Early in the New Year, Churchill, newly promoted to lieutenant-colonel, arrived at the village of Moolenacker, some ten miles from the frontline at Armentières, to take command of the 6th Battalion of the Royal Scots Fusiliers. That a celebrated ex-Cabinet minister should take up a field command naturally created something of a local sensation. His soldiers were not quite sure how relate to him: as 'Lord Churchill', 'Viscount Churchill', even 'the Duke of Churchill'.

Churchill soon got down to business. 'War is declared, gentlemen,' he observed to his battalion, 'on the lice.' Riding 'a large black horse', and clad in a French helmet – which he wore 'chiefly for the appearance' – trench coat, Sam Browne belt and revolver, he would make his rounds. Intent on raising morale, he organized some 'most amusing sports – mule races, pillow fights, obstacle races'. An enthusiastic, if indifferent singer, he insisted on communal sing-songs. 'It was the one thing the lads dreaded,' one of the participants recalled, 'even more than the enemy shells. He always sang "My Old Tarpaulin Jacket" – and he couldn't sing a note!' Nor did he neglect his painting. Nor other luxuries. He wanted all the material comforts: a private bath-tub which he put at the service of others – and large towels to go with it, hot water bottles, food boxes from Fortnum and Mason, in particular 'large slabs of corned beef, Stilton cheeses, cream, ham, sardines – dried fruits . . . a big steak pie'; and, of course, his quality meals were laced with modest quantities of Champagne, brandy, port, or whisky.[21]

There was a more serious side to his soldiering. His battalion, considered to be the 'weakest' in the brigade, had been severely mauled at the battle of Loos. His job was to bring it up to scratch. 'I have been entirely occupied with practice points – gas helmets, rifles in good order, trench disicipline & routine . . . and vy precise drill and marching', Churchill reported. He also 'reduced punishment both in quantity & method'. Towards the end of January, he led his battalion into the front line at Ploegsteert. Churchill never led his men 'over the top', but neither was his section considered 'a cushy spot'. It attracted more than its share of enemy shells and on two occasions he narrowly escaped death.[22] Undeterred, he joined corporal John McGuire on his reconnoitring in no-man's land – thirty-six hazardous trips in all. 'They spent five hours in a muddy hole, so close to the Germans they could hear them talking.' Once, standing on the fire-step with 'whizzbangs' flying past, he asked one of his officers in a 'dreamy' voice: 'Do you like war?' Captain Andrew Gibb felt that Churchill 'revelled in it'. Not for its own sake, but as a challenge to combat his own inner anxieties. Exposing himself to danger – sometimes needlessly – was also a kind of safety valve.[23]

Churchill was reasonably content. Time did not hang so heavily at Ploegsteert as it had in London. He enjoyed the camaraderie of the trenches. His second-in-command, Sir Archibald Sinclair, a Scottish baronet with political ambitions, sixteen years his junior, proved a personable companion, and Churchill related to him almost as to a son. There were disappointments. It would have been out of character had Churchill not aimed at a command higher than a battalion. On the eve of his resignation from the government, he had proposed himself as commander-in-chief in British East Africa, complete with an offensive strategy against German forces there. His audience – Asquith, Balfour, and Hankey – either 'pirouetted' with delight or 'roared with laughter' at the suggestion. Put out, Churchill believed that Asquith had promised him a division instead. This notion proved too improbable to admit of execution. But he was on firmer ground in his ambition to command a brigade. He wanted this very badly, and pressed hard for it. Once again, he was let down, except for a brief period as a 'caretaker' brigadier. Asquith was held chiefly responsible for these reversals.[24]

But Churchill's greatest disappointment lay in his exclusion from active political life. He pined for politics. His mind never ceased planning his return to the Cabinet, turning over different permutations that would allow him to stage a comeback. His battalion was impressed by the string of eminent political personages who trekked out to Ploegsteert, among them F. E. Smith, Curzon, and Max Aitken (later Lord Beaverbrook) – who was of particular importance because of his closeness to Bonar Law. He confided to Clementine: 'The group I want to work with & form into an effective Governing instrument is LG: FE: BL: Carson: & Curzon. It is the alternative government, when "wait and see" is over.'[25]

Bonar Law was an essential element in Churchill's schemes, but he was known to be hostile and his support could not be relied upon. The key to Churchill's position was Lloyd George, particularly, so Churchill believed, because the Marconi scandal had placed Lloyd George in his debt. But however much he needed Lloyd George, he did not wholly trust him. A 'direct descendant of Judas Iscariot', Clementine called him, who would 'barter you away at any time, in any place'. Churchill was experienced enough to know the permanence and value of political friendships. Had not the 'odious Asquith' stabbed him in the back? For all that, he reckoned that Lloyd George was 'on the true trail . . . in this war'[26] and he continued to look to him. It was a shrewd decision. By building on their past intimacy, he would guarantee his political future.

Churchill returned to civilian life in May 1916. During his service in the trenches, he had made occasional forays on Westminster, not with the most conspicuous success. Egged on by James Garvin and C. P. Scott, he intervened in the debate on the naval estimates in early March, with disastrous results. He was pushed forward also by Fisher, who now flattered Churchill with the tempting prospect of becoming either 'LEADER of the OPPOSITION' or as a 'Certain Prime Minister'. Clementine was highly suspicious of this resurrected alliance. 'Keep your hands off my husband,' she warned Fisher. 'You have all but ruined him once. Leave him alone now.' Despite Clementine's misgivings, Churchill went ahead. In the House, he made a measured and impressive attack on Balfour's handling of the naval war. But he ruined everything by calling for Fisher's return as First Sea Lord 'to vitalize and animate' the Admiralty. The House heard this extraordinary demand in stunned disbelief. Balfour, however, had no difficulty in flicking aside Churchill's criticism. And he did so with a devastating mixture of scorn and derision, exploiting to the full Churchill's damaging *faux pas*. With his impulsive tongue, Churchill had ruined any possibility of staging a spectacular comeback as leader of 'an amazing Opposition'.[27]

This incident confirmed for many that Churchill, whatever his undeniable talents, lacked sensitivity. His speech encompassed all of his qualities: industry, marshalling of facts, clarity of exposition, mastery over words. Calling for Fisher's return reflected his magnanimity, if not his judgement. With the nation in peril, he was willing to cast past differences aside and conscript all those qualified and gifted into an administration of all the talents. Of course, he was carried away by his own ambition and impatience and spirit of adventure. He would have done better to listen to Clementine's sound advice than be led on by Fisher's seductive daydreams. But his motives were totally commendable. At the time, he was simply unable to combine them into a credible whole for the benefit of the House.

Churchill's qualities as a parliamentarian have been the subject of much comment, mostly highly favourable.[28] He respected the House and its procedures. His command of language, his wit, his compelling presence, endowed him with immense advantages. Never boring, always full of surprises, the House waited in keen expectancy for his perorations. In full flow, he would dominate it. It was not so much that he sensed the mood of the House, but rather that he overwhelmed it with his powers and personality, inspired by the occasion. Sometimes the magic did not work – often at critical junctures in his career. No doubt he fed off

Above: Blenheim Palace, Churchill's birthplace *(Aerofilms)*

Below: Chartwell Manor, Churchill's country estate from the 1920s *(Hulton Deutsch)*

Above, left: Lord Randolph Churchill
(Hulton Deutsch)
Above, right: Jennie, Lady Randolph Churchill
Right: Clementine Churchill

Above: On watch in India, 1896 *(Hulton Deutsch)*
Right: The budding parliamentarian — the father-son image
(Punch)

Churchill at play to an appreciative audience, 1914 *(Hulton Deutsch)*

'The Two Romeos': Churchill and Lloyd George around 1909 *(S&G Press Agency)*

Top: As first Lord of the Admiralty: inspecting naval trainees of the ship 'Mercury', 1912
(Hulton Deutsch)
Right: Contemplating the Dardanelles
(Hulton Deutsch)

Two old cronies at work: Churchill and F.E. Smith (Lord Birkenhead)

Above: Guests of the Duke of Westminster:
Winston, Clementine and Randolph out
hunting *(Associated Press)*
Left: 'The Golden Chancellor', April 1925
(Hulton Deutsch)

Churchill and his dog, Rufus, surveying the grounds at Chartwell
(C Phillippe Halsman/Magnum Photos Inc)

success, or the prospect of it. But when down and depressed, when under personal strain, he could lose touch. On these rare occasions, he would stumble, falter, retire from the debate confused, unable to grasp what had happened, convinced that he had dealt himself a mortal blow. The Fisher speech was one example; others would follow.

For more than a year, Churchill remained in a state of political limbo. Always the optimist, he believed Kitchener's untimely death at sea in June – 'a good exit', he called it, as 'the glory had departed' – would bring him back into the government as Minister of Munitions, the post Lloyd George had vacated to take over the War Office. But Lloyd George, although 'very sympathetic', thought it 'premature' to press Churchill's case. The Dardanelles expedition was under investigation, and to Churchill's way of thinking he was being set up as the guilty party. 'The best abused man in the country', the press was conducting an 'amazingly vicious' campaign against him. His frustration intensifed. He grumbled about his declining position. He fretted that his star was on the wane.[29] In November, he voted against the government. It was on a minor issue – the disposal of enemy property in Nigeria – but the government escaped defeat only by the narrowest of margins. In any case, its days were numbered. A month after the vote, Lloyd George formed his coalition government.

Churchill expected office. At Lloyd George's suggestion, he had attended a dinner-party at Smith's house, breaking off a moment of relaxation at the Turkish baths at the Automobile Club to attend. The company had discussed the composition of the new ministry. Why then should Churchill be left out? Lloyd George explained to Max Aitken that the pressure to exclude him was 'enormous'. If he defied the anti-Churchill forces, his administration, barely formed, 'might collapse altogether'. Would Aitken convey his dilemma to Churchill? He did. Churchill, as Aitken recalled, 'blazed into righteous anger', directed also at his closest political crony. 'Smith [he always referred to him as "Fred" or "F.E."], this man knows that I am not to be included in the new Government.' He stormed out of the house, pursued by Smith, endeavouring, in vain, to pacify him. As for Lloyd George, he had 'weakly & faithlessly' caved in to a 'malevolent' press campaign. Piqued at his political isolation, he still believed he could dictate terms. He would not take office 'in any subordinate capacity'. 'The War Office?' C. P. Scott asked. 'Yes, that would do very well.' For the time being, he remained outside. 'I am simply existing,' he confessed bitterly to a sympathetic Fisher.[30]

What were Churchill's views on the conduct of the war when seated on the opposition front bench? He spoke now under 'sentence of continued and indefinite inactivity', a setting he found 'almost unendurable'. This did not inhibit his oratory. At his suggestion, Lloyd George convened a secret session of the House in May 1917. Churchill opened for the opposition. He called attention to two events that had radically altered the whole situation: the entry of the United States into the war and the collapse of Russia. Victory, he assured the House, was guaranteed on one condition. 'If time is given, nothing can stand against Great Britain and the United States together . . . they could alone carry the war against the Teutonic Empires to a victorious conclusion.' Time was of the essence. It would take not months but years 'before this mighty force can be brought to bear'. In the meantime, his policy was to wait: 'we ought not to squander the remaining armies of France and Britain in precipitate offensives before the American power begins to be felt on the battlefield.'

Previously, 'the process of attrition' had not unduly unnerved him. 'As long as it works evenly on both sides,' he claimed in June 1915, 'we are on the road to victory.' His own experience in the trenches, together with two years of butchery on the western front, had had a sobering effect. The German generals had proved themselves more capable than their British counterparts. The Anglo-French armies no longer possessed 'the numerical superiority for such a successful offensive'. He wanted no more 'bloody and disastrous adventures'. 'Maintain an active defence on the Western Front,' he pleaded, until it was possible to 'Bring over the American millions'. Then the enormous weight of allied numbers would bring about a German collapse. This was a popular appeal, brilliantly put. Lloyd George was too astute to commit himself. But he was sympathetic to Churchill's case, and most sensitive to the large measure of endorsement it enjoyed. After the debate he told Churchill that he was determined to include him in his government. 'From that day,' Churchill recalled, 'although holding no office, I became to a large extent his colleague.'[31]

It was not until July 1917 that Lloyd George felt sufficiently secure to bring back Churchill as Minister of Munitions, the job he had sought a year earlier. Even so, Tory ministers vehemently opposed his inclusion in the government; one hundred of their backbenchers registered their disgust at his appointment. Sections of the Liberal Party were no less incensed. The *Morning Post* recommended that he be placed in an empty sea-mine and anchored off the German coast, though even this extreme measure would not prevent him from breaking loose and causing an explosion. All feared his unpredictability, his propensity to interfere in matters not his own.

Lloyd George did not allow this criticism to sway his judgement. Not that he was unaware of Churchill's shortcomings. 'His mind,' he wrote,

> was a powerful machine, but there lay hidden in its material or its make-up some obscure defect which prevented it from running true.

They could not tell what it was. When the mechanism went wrong, its very power made the action disastrous, not only to himself but to the causes in which he was engaged and the men with whom he was cooperating.

But Lloyd George was also deeply conscious of the damage a Churchill hungry for office might provoke in opposition. His own position was by no means secure. Bonar Law, placed before a *fait accompli*, backed him reluctantly, fearful lest a crisis lead to an alternative government.

Churchill remained. Oblivious of the degree of hostility he inspired, he later thanked Lloyd George for his 'warm-hearted & courageous act'. The Lloyd George-Churchill partnership was renewed, coloured by its customary mixture of mutual admiration and mistrust. Churchill, Esher mused, appealed to Lloyd George because of his ability to 'strike ideas into colour and imagery ... this strange toy [Churchill] amuses and fascinates L George, who likes and fears him'. The question was: could he control Churchill? Could anyone? His new colleagues, apprehensive at what lay ahead, would doubtless have echoed Churchill's aunt, Lady Cornelia Wimbourne, who gave her nephew the soundest possible advice: 'stick to munitions & don't try & run the Govt!'[32]

Churchill was still only forty-two. Ripe for a midlife crisis of sorts, it had sprung on him unexpectedly and from unforeseen directions. Painfully aware that his career had been strangled one moment and resuscitated – only just – the next, he was, in a very real sense, unable to grasp why it had happened. He believed implicitly in his ability to lead the country in war. He had so much to offer. What, then, inhibited others from believing in him? There remained the astonishing, seemingly unbridgeable, gap between his belief in his powers and how others perceived him. In this treacherous world, he clung to the one life-support system that he knew would never fail him: himself. To the ever-dependable Eddie Marsh, he wrote: 'I have fallen back reposefully into the arms of Fate, but with an underlying instinct that all will be well and that my greatest work is at hand'.[33]

Fighting Bolshevism

In the course of five years Churchill occupied three ministries – Munitions, War and Air, and Colonies – progressing steadily from one post to another but in a coalition that, after its initial popularity, rapidly lost direction, momentum, and lustre. Churchill may have deluded himself that he had joined the Great Centre Coalition of his dreams. In fact, as was apparent from the outset, the stability of the government depended upon widespread Conservative consent, a reservoir of support that almost by definition excluded Churchill. But mostly the survival of the administration – and Churchill's political future – depended upon the sharpness of Lloyd George's political wit to manoeuvre between the Tories and his own diminishing political base.

Churchill found his first ministry, set up by Lloyd George, already working at full flow. 'The whole island was an arsenal,' he recalled.[1] Even so, he overhauled its bureaucracy, scaling down its fifty departments into ten larger units and establishing an inner council to supervise its affairs. His job was then to ensure that it ran smoothly. But Munitions lacked the glamour of the Admiralty. Shuffling figures from one desk to another dented his self-image as a master strategist.[2] Excluded from the inner War Cabinet, he had accepted office in the 'subordinate position' he had vowed to decline some months earlier. However, the faintest of limelights was better than none at all. And Churchill was too robust a character to allow mere office regulations to limit his formidable energies.

Only a month after his appointment, complaints were rife that Churchill had intervened in excess of his authority at a session of the War Cabinet to which he had been invited. There was even talk of resignations if Churchill did not cease his interfering ways.[3] This was little more than a storm in a teacup. But it indicated the unrelenting suspicion that clouded Churchill's every act.

His natural restlessness also gave rise to harsh gossip. He was constantly on the move between the battlefields in France and his office in London, at times putting himself in great danger. Caught at a forward headquarters at the outset of the German March offensive, he narrowly escaped capture by a few hours. These expeditions quenched his thirst for adventure. Though he could also claim these trips were essential, his visits were both prolonged and frequent. Eventually, he was forced to set up a permanent headquarters at the Château Verchocq, near Hesdin.[4] Unkind tongues began to ask whether or not he was up to his old tricks again, trying to carve out from his relatively junior appointment a grander entitlement.

These feelings must have been reinforced when, in the spring of 1918, Churchill suggested to Lloyd George that he abandon the War Cabinet system for a 'proper Cabinet of responsible ministers'. Although clearly dissatisfied with his role as an administrator, Churchill was willing to exclude himself from a 'political Cabinet' should coalition politics dictate it. But that Churchill was aiming higher is quite apparent. 'I will never accept political responsibility,' he explained to Lloyd George, 'without recognized regular power'. These manoeuvrings may well have prompted Lloyd George to recall that although he had risked his government to appoint Churchill, he had occasionally 'reason to regret' his 'trust'.[5]

A pleasing aspect of Churchill's character was his ability to identify totally with his current ministry, immerse himself fully in its affairs, and to lend it greater weight in the general scheme of things than perhaps it deserved. This would preserve his self-confidence as well as ease his peace of mind. If the navy was the key to success in 1914–15, the outcome of the war now depended on procuring enormous quantities of munitions. War, and the mechanical means to wage it, had long fascinated Churchill. When running his 'Dunkirk Circus' he had been an early, perhaps the earliest, exponent of offensive air operations. In January 1915 he had proposed 'a caterpillar system' to carry men and machine-guns that would cross trenches and destroy barbed wire defences. Churchill was not the first to advocate these 'land ships'. But the novelty of the concept and its potential excited his imagination. It was his persistence and enthusiasm that fleshed out the idea. He had set up a Landships Committee at the Admiralty. This eventually produced a prototype tank.[7]

Churchill now laid emphasis on 'the four new arms of the highest consequence': aeroplanes, tanks, gas, and machine-guns. But when forecasting future production, he often got his figures wrong, allowing his drive to outrun reality. In December 1917 he urged a maximum annual programme of 10,000 tanks: two months later he proposed increasing aircraft production by fifty per cent, machine-guns by 100 per cent, tanks by 300 per cent and gas shells by 500 per cent. These numbers could not be met. In fact, from April to July 1918 the number of tanks actually produced fell to half the estimated number. Only Churchill's optimism was at fault; or his failure to recognize that the measure of improvization needed for such large-scale production was beyond the capacity of British industry.[8]

Much depended on the state of industrial relations. Churchill was not above dangling the carrot or wielding the stick. In July 1917, on assuming office, he tempted skilled time-workers with a twelve per cent bonus. But a year later, when the decisive battle on the western front hung in the balance, and industrial unrest threatened to cripple munitions' production in the Midlands and Manchester, he reacted harshly. Backed by Lloyd George, he recommended that the strikers be conscripted, a proposal that eventually persuaded the men to return to work. Once back at work, and with victory virtually assured, he called for a two-year truce in labour relations, a national effort to guarantee the post-war reconstruction of Britain. In short, Churchill's goal was to make certain that the factories kept working at full capacity and with a minimum of disruption. His efforts proved sufficient.[9]

If Churchill's most grandiose plans were not fulfilled, he had still accomplished a great deal. He was nonetheless disliked and distrusted in the political circles that mattered. Yet his current work had restored much of his self-confidence. His true ambition remained; but for the moment it was not placed on display, even in private. For all his ordeals, his war had ended on a more cheerful note. He wrote to Clementine in September 1918:

> It is just the sort of life I like – Coming out here [to Paris] makes me thoroughly contented with my office. I do not chafe at adverse political combinations, or at not being able to direct general policy. I am content to be associated with the splendid machines of the British army, & to feel how many ways there are open to me to serve them.

Hostilities came to an end on 11 November. Churchill was already pursuing Lloyd George about the formation of a new government. Aware of Conservative hostility and Liberal suspicion, he had little option but to place himself in Lloyd George's hands, a graphic indication of his real place in British politics. He played hard to get, hinting to Lloyd George that to join his new government would be 'a far-reaching political decision', one that he shrank from in advance unless he knew how it would 'be constituted'. This was mere shadow-boxing. What in fact Churchill was after was a 'legitimate share in political power'.[10] But first the elections had to be won.

Lloyd George appealed to the country as the man who had won the war and who would secure the peace, making Britain 'a country fit for heroes to live in'. On 28 December the final results were declared. He had achieved a resounding personal triumph. But he was entirely dependent upon the Conservatives who had captured 335 out of the coalition's 478 seats. The old Liberal Party no longer existed, split irrevocably between

Asquith's independents and Lloyd George's coalitionists. The Labour Party emerged as the main opposition party.[11] Churchill's demand to dismantle the War Cabinet was safely ignored by Lloyd George. When he came to divide the spoils of office, Churchill was awarded the War Office, with the Air Ministry added on. This prospect was not viewed with unmitigated enthusiasm in some military circles.[12]

Churchill's most immediate problem was in resolving the extent and pace of demobilization. And his swift and intelligent handling of what threatened to be a most ugly situation stands entirely to his credit. War Office demobilization procedures accorded preference to those workers most needed to rebuild a peacetime economy. This was an eminently logical economic theory. But as in many cases these key workers were the last to be called up, this ruling led to much ill-feeling. Disobedience spread among the troops. At Calais, the troops actually mutinied; while at Luton, the town hall was gutted by rioters. With Bolshevism menacing from the east, and acute industrial unrest paralysing parts of the country, revolution seemed to threaten. In one bold stroke, by applying the equitable principle of 'first in, first out', he averted a potentially ruinous confrontation. Order was soon restored. In April, he reported to Lloyd George that the army, previously debilitated by 'about twenty mutinies a week', was 'now a solid disciplined force'. By May, nearly three million men had been released from service. Churchill, as he put it, had preserved 'the general stability of British society'.[13]

Churchill's ministerial career in the 1920s was plagued by the need for retrenchment and by the overriding concern to give priority to revitalizing the home economy. Thrift, however, was not a Churchillian virtue. Cuts in military expenditure, thoughts of imperial pullbacks, defensive strategic postures, all went against his grain. Another limiting factor was the so-called 'Ten Year Rule' that presumed that Britain would not become involved in a great war for the next ten years. It took effect from August 1919. Churchill did not initiate this ruling, as has often been assumed. According to its author, Hankey, he found the prospect of 'curtailing expenditure distasteful'. But he supported the guideline, as did the Cabinet. In the short term, its execution proved beyond him. His enthusiasm for military intervention against Bolshevik Russia led him to press for more extensive commitments and hence greater expenditures. But in June 1928, when Chancellor of the Exchequer, he made the ruling 'a standing assumption'. It was this decision, governed by domestic constraints, and soon to be overwhelmed by crises in the Far East and Europe, that lent to the 'Ten Year Rule' its notorious reputation in later years.[14]

The estimates for 1919–20 cut to the bone the services under Churchill's authority. Despite some misgivings, he executed them with his characteristic determination, conviction (self-induced?) and energy. By November 1920 Britain's great armies had been reduced from three million to 370,000, excluding the Indian contingents. Stretched almost to breaking point, it had to find the resources to cope with internal disputes, the Irish emergency, armies of occupation, and the policing of an extended empire. The Royal Air Force suffered no less. At the close of the war it was the most powerful air force in the world. Severe cuts were inevitable in peacetime. That it managed to survive at all as an independent service was due in large measure to the planning of Sir Hugh Trenchard, Chief of Air Staff, and to Churchill's vigorous advocacy of it.[15] The military establishment never fully recovered from these hammer-blows. Churchill's brilliant, sustained, and noisy campaign for increased rearmament in the 1930s has tended to blur his role in the dramatic run-down of British armaments in the 1920s.

Apart from his evident distaste at slashing costs, Churchill suffered other frustrations. He took virtually no part in the most acute political issue of the day – the German question. He visited Paris only three times during the six months of the peace conference. Of course, Churchill had decided ideas on the terms of the settlement; but they too underwent change according to circumstances. During the emotive electoral campaign, he thumped the anti-German tub as hard as anyone. He did not trust the Germans and detested the Prussian military caste that had led them into war. He pronounced on the collective guilt of the German people. Reparations, he cried, would be paid 'to the uttermost farthing'. Nor, he promised, would the Kaiser and other war criminals escape trial and retribution. Alsace-Lorraine would be restored to France; Poland reconstituted as a free nation. The German Empire would be dismantled.[16] Outside the highly charged assembly halls he was more circumspect. Like Lloyd George, he too whispered his qualifications. He told the War Cabinet in February 1919 that he wished 'to see Germany treated humanely and adequately fed, and her industries restarted.'[17]

Compassion was a strong feature of Churchill's nature. His own deeply rooted patriotism enabled him to empathize with the patriotic sentiments of others. This awareness, perhaps sensitivity to their wounded national pride, was not entirely blotted out even when he was engaged in war. But before he would contemplate clemency he insisted on total victory.[18]

He was moved no less, perhaps more, by strictly pragmatic considerations. By now, Churchill was fully committed to excising Bolshevism from Russia and eliminating its threat to Europe. As his enterprise faltered, he came to see the German settlement as one part, increasingly an indispensable part, of his overall struggle against Bolshevik Russia. To isolate and humiliate Germany politically, to ruin her economically, would trigger off the most disastrous of domino effects: the fall of central Europe heralding the collapse of the western democracies. It became absolutely vital to prop up Germany as a bastion against the insidious menace from the east. Poland too had to be preserved, even though the Polish question had served to unite Germany and Russia in the past, as it would in the future. However, the most immediate challenge was to avert a Bolshevik Russo-German combination.[19]

One way was to press for a moderate and swift peace with Germany. He told the Aldwych Club in April 1919 that it was imperative to ease the allied blockade on Germany. If not, 'the orderly and stable forces' in Germany, deprived of the basic means to restore their economy and standard of life, would be swept into the Bolshevik camp.[20] In his mind, he had already re-arranged the balance of forces necessary to meet a potentially aggressive Germany. First, it was essential to maintain allied wartime unity; but no less, to secure 'a friendly [i.e. non-Bolshevik] Russia and a strong Poland'. As the United States retreated from Europe and the Bolshevik grip on Russia tightened, Churchill was thrown back on his 'strong Poland' – whose imperial policies were disrupting, not stabilizing, eastern Europe – and the French alliance. Churchill had long favoured a pact with France. He had first proposed it in 1911. Then it was to be directed against Germany. Now he argued for a defensive compact, but 'only if' France moderates her vindictive policy towards Germany and accepts, 'loyally', a British policy of 'help & friendship towards Germany'. The point was to bind together Britain, France, and Germany: 'we could then reconstruct Europe and Russia.'[21]

In his quest to raise an anti-Bolshevik bloc, he went much farther. He called, as a counterpoise to a Bolshevik Russia, for 'a policy . . . of real peace and appeasement' with Germany. In the summer of 1920, as a triumphant Red Army overran Poland and turned it into 'a Bolshevized area' on Germany's eastern frontiers, he proposed the 'early revision' of the Versailles treaty, including some of its disarmament clauses. In his own distinctive style, he defined his German policy: 'Kill the Bolshie, Kiss the Hun.'[22]

'Harsh and excessive' Churchill called the Versailles treaty,[23] but its consequences for Germany were not so catastrophic as he imagined. After a violent beginning, the Weimar Republic settled down, thriving economically, as it benefited from new reparations agreements, and returned to the international fold within the framework of fresh political and security arrangements in Europe. True, Germany pursued an eastern policy, and Soviet-German cooperation, consummated at Rapallo in April 1922, continued throughout the 1920s. But Germanic-Slav Bolshevik hordes did not overwhelm Europe. Germany pursued a cautious policy. Its material and political dependence on the west were too substantial to allow too radical a Soviet orientation.

Churchill was not alone in seeking a moderate peace for Germany; or in taking alarm at the Bolshevik peril. Most leading British politicians were of the same mind. But Churchill outdid them all in the virulence of his verbal onslaughts and fiery temper, and Bolshevism determined his outlook on politics, domestic and foreign, for the coming years. When he met the world leaders in Paris in February 1919, he told them that 'unless Russia [cleansed of Bolshevism] formed a living part of Europe, unless she became a living partner in the League of Nations, and a friend of the Allied powers, there would be neither peace nor victory.'[24]

Such was Churchill's exclusive identification with armed intervention against the Bolsheviks, that the British press dubbed it as 'Mr Churchill's Private War'.[25] When the initial steps to intervene were approved and implemented, in the spring and summer of 1918, he was already a minister, and if he was not involved at first hand in the decision-making process, he supported with alacrity the government's policy. With the war at a most critical stage in the west, and a separate Russo-German peace already signed, there were sound military reasons for doing so: most urgently, to prevent substantial military stores at Archangel and Murmansk from falling into enemy hands. But also there was the appealing prospect of resurrecting the 'eastern front'. This meant mobilizing all anti-Bolshevik forces who, it was thought, would continue vigorously to prosecute the war against Germany. In the Far East, Japanese and American allied forces and nearly 60,000 Czech troops (ex-Russian prisoners of war) stranded along the Trans-Siberian railway, would rally the 'true' Russians and combine and drive their way to the west. Churchill urged his colleagues to 'compel events'.[26]

The war ended without reconstituting the eastern front. But by then British forces were established in north Russia, in the arc between Archangel and Murmansk, and were active in the Baku-Batum area, and British warships patrolled the Baltic and Black Seas. With the war over, what, then, was the purpose of keeping them there? General Ironside, commander of allied force in the area, also pondered this question. 'We are now backing a White Russian Counter-Revolution against the Bolsheviks and are actually committed to staying here in Archangel.'[27]

By now, Churchill had changed the ground rules. With Germany defeated, he aimed now to topple the Bolsheviks, and, apparently, restore the Romanov, Nicholas II, whose murder at the time he described as 'absolutely fatal to the allied cause', and whose shallow character and corrupt regime he portrayed, after much time for reflection, in the most glowing terms.[28]

'Our first object,' Churchill later recalled, 'was to withdraw from Archangel and Murmansk without disaster and without dishonour.' How was this to be achieved? Not by half-hearted measures. Churchill informed the War Cabinet in December 1918 that only 'large forces, abundantly supplied with mechanical appliances' would produce the desired result. He reinforced this plea in February.[29] It was not only that Old Russia had to be restored. If the Bolsheviks were allowed to take over, he warned the Cabinet, the international consequences would be quite horrendous: a disaffected bloc, 'hostile to France, Britain, and America', would extend 'from Yokohama to Cologne'. To meet it, he proposed to the Council of Ten a more vigorous policy. President Wilson blocked him. Allied troops should be withdrawn. Not one allied power, Wilson laid down, was prepared to despatch extra troops to Russia. The following day, with Wilson on his way back to Washington, Churchill returned to urge setting up an Allied Council for Russian Affairs to coordinate the political, economic, and military struggle against Bolshevik Russia. He elaborated his plan 'for making war on the Bolsheviks, utilizing every available resource' some days later. This was Churchill 'at his worst', recorded Hankey. He alerted Lloyd George, who thoroughly incensed, swiftly quashed Churchill's irresponsible war-making.[30]

As the various stages of British intervention unfolded, one complication leading to another, Churchill revealed himself as always ready to raise the stakes, much to the annoyance of other Cabinet members. Nevertheless, a state of undeclared war did exist, as the Cabinet recognized reluctantly in the summer of 1919.[31] Had Churchill been given a free hand, the scale of intervention would certainly have been far more extensive than it was.

Churchill deplored the lack of 'a Russian policy'. His alternative was to employ 'an active defensive' type of strategy.[32] This term implied reinforcing those troops already under seige in order to cover their safe withdrawal; or authorizing Ironside to break out of the north to link up with friendly forces in the south; or encouraging the Czechs to fight their way through from Siberia to Archangel. In the short run, it did not limit the scale of British intervention. Quite the contrary, as Sir Henry Wilson, himself a rabid anti-Bolshevik, explained: 'Once a military force is involved in operations on land it is almost impossible to limit the magnitude of its commitments.'[33] The British contingent had by then reached 18,400.

All this smacked of the Dardanelles. A forceful, energetic, eloquent minister probing the vulnerable points of a Cabinet that was preoccupied with other business, no less urgent, and that although it admitted the validity of the enterprise, it did so without much inner conviction. It was high-pressure salesmanship of the first order. And Churchill never gave up. His consistency of purpose was remarkable. As one White Russian general failed him, he adopted another: Kolchak, Denikin, Wrangel, Yudenevitch, were all listed at one time or another among his saviours of Russia; as was Boris Savinkov, a Russian politician of the most dubious character. Such was Churchill's enthusiasm, that he even considered going out to Russia as a sort of roving ambassador to 'help Denikin to mould the new Russian Constitution'.[34]

Even when it became crystal-clear that the venture had collapsed, in January 1920, and the British evacuation was virtually complete, Churchill remained unrepentent. 'I will always advocate . . . the over-throw and destruction of that criminal regime', he said.[35]

Such was his disillusionment with the turn in British policy, that he contemplated resignation at the first hint of *rapprochement* with the Soviet Union. He opposed even the sending of humanitarian relief to Russia.[36] His main concern was still to throttle Russia by isolating her, to prevent her from linking up with revolutionary forces in the west, particularly Germany. His reputation as a right-wing extremist flourished. Just the thought of Bolshevism brought forth the most violent reaction.

Churchill justified this ultra-radical stand by embarking on what must surely be one of the fiercest, most unremitting campaigns of inflammatory rhetoric imposed on the British public in modern times. He aimed to whip up support for a militant policy against the Bolsheviks and to bring the Cabinet into line.[37] His purpose was clearly to demonize the Bolsheviks. He saw not only 'a wounded Russia' under the Bolsheviks, but

> a poisoned Russia, an infected Russia, a plague-bearing Russia, a Russia of armed hordes smiting not only with bayonet and cannon, but accompanied and preceded by the swarms of typhus bearing vermin which slay the bodies of men, and political doctrines which destroy the health and even the soul of nations . . . the mob are raised against the middle class to murder them, to plunder their houses, to debauch their wives and carry off their children . . .[38]

'Criminality and animalism', 'fungus', 'cancer', 'a horrible form of men-tal and moral disease', 'a plague bacillus', 'a deadly and paralysing sect', 'a barbarism . . . devoured by vermin, racked by pestilence', 'avowed enemies of . . . civilization', 'criminals', 'deranged and distraught', 'sub-human', were but a few of his choice expressions. 'Lenin,' he told the House of Commons, 'was sent into Russia by the Germans in the same way you might send a phial containing a culture of typhoid or of cholera to be poured into the water supply of a great city.'

If Bolshevism was a 'cancer . . . [a] monstrous growth swelling and thriving upon the emaciated body of its victim', it had to be eradicated. But to do so Churchill needed to de-legitimize the Bolsheviks and their regime. He never succeeded. Whatever the actual danger of Bolshevism to western civilization, these grim statements were listened to with increas-ing incredulity. After one of Churchill's more lurid expositions, Balfour quipped: 'I admire the exaggerated way in which you tell the truth.'[39]

Churchill also made the unfortunate, but common, error of equating Jews and Bolsheviks. He was outraged at the anti-semitic excesses perpetrated by his protégé White Russian generals and called repeatedly for restraint. But he could not help pointing out to Lloyd George that the Jews 'are regarded as being the main instigators of the ruin of the Empire, and who, certainly, have played a leading part in Bolshevik atrocities'. He even detected evidence of a 'very powerful' Jewish lobby in Britain. He continued to dub the Bolsheviks as 'these Semitic conspirators' or 'Jew Commissars', who are among 'the highest political intelligences of the world', turning on 'the international Jews' – Marx, Trotsky, Bela Kun, Rosa Luxembourg, Emma Goldman – as a 'world-wide conspiracy' dedicated to 'the overthrow of civilization and the reconstitution of society'.

Jews certainly played a leading part in the Bolshevik revolution, well out of proportion to their numbers among the Russian population. Four out of seven members of the first Politburo – Trotksy, Kamenev, Zinoviev, and Sokolnikov – were Jews. But this was a far cry from Churchill's intemperate conjectures. Apart from this outburst, Churchill was remarkably free from anti-semitic prejudice.[40]

Early on in his career, Churchill had given notice of his distaste for socialism, an authoritarian creed that trampled down individual liberties and encouraged cheap demagoguery.[41] The war had given rise to its extreme expression, Bolshevism, a doctrine that would destroy the society that had made him and replace it with values that were totally abhorrent to his outlook. In the aftermath of the First World War, the established European order had either collapsed or was at risk, no less in Britain than elsewhere, and the erosion of settled values haunted Churchill. He was consumed by a sense of deep foreboding at what the future held. His notes for a speech delivered in November 1922 reveal this all too clearly.

> What a terrible disappointment the Twentieth Century has been
> How terrible & how melancholy
> is long series of disastrous events
> wh have darkened its first 20 years.
> We have seen in ev country a dissolution,
> a weakening of those bonds,
> a challenge to those principles
> a decay of faith
> an abridgement of hope
> on wh structure & ultimate existence
> of civilized society depends.
> We have seen in ev part of globe
> one gt country after another
> wh had erected an orderly, a peaceful
> a prosperous structure of civilized society,
> relapsing in hideous succession
> into bankruptcy, barbarism or anarchy[42]

To this threat, Churchill reacted instinctively. He had no stomach for half-measures. Nor would he ever capitulate, particularly when the stakes were for preserving the traditional values that had made Britain supreme and which had moulded him. No less than protecting the Britain he cherished, and apart from saving Europe from chaos, he was engaged in an act of self-preservation. If Bolshevism represented the future, he spurned it.[43]

The notion of armed intervention to redress the balance of power in Europe could not have been foreign to Churchill. Belief in this so-called tenet of British foreign policy was common to practically all educated Englishmen. Certainly for Churchill, the descendant of the great Marlborough, and it came to dominate much of his thinking on foreign affairs. What would replace the old balance of power? Churchill had little faith in the League of Nations. It could never preserve the peace. At best, it would provide a convenient framework for the Powers to settle their disputes.[44] Nor was an Anglo-American combination feasible politics at the time. Although in August 1918 he had plumped firmly for an 'Atlanticist' option as 'the most solid guarantee of our common safety', these fraternal sentiments evaporated quickly in the aftermath of the war. The American retreat from Europe, her hardline stand on war debts, and her uncompromising position on naval disarmament led to much tension in Anglo-American relations, to which Churchill also gave harsh expression.[45] Churchill, therefore, was thrown back on the traditional balance of power, with Britain intervening in Europe, or not, as it suited her interest.

With the benefit of hindsight, it can be convincingly argued that Churchill had sized up the fundamental nature of Bolshevism with greater clarity and vision than his more hide-bound colleagues. For all that, there was an irrational element in Churchill's Russian policy. It is hard to conceive of a period less favourable for armed British intervention in Europe than 1919. The Treasury was empty, the country was war-weary. Who could contemplate another military ordeal when the memories of the bloodiest war in recorded history were still so vivid? Yet Churchill's apocalyptic vision of a Europe perishing on the Bolshevik vine drove him relentlessly forward.[46]

Owing to its manifest impracticability, Churchill's interventionist policy never commanded the unreserved support of the Cabinet, and in particular that of Lloyd George. That the affair dragged on for so long was due primarily to Lloyd George's preoccupation with other matters. Not always was he in sufficient control of his Cabinet. His absence from too many sessions allowed the persistent Churchill to push forward his policy, and, with Lloyd George away, it was not always easy to resist him.[47] Churchill might have dominated Cabinet discussions, but he did not determine policy. Lloyd George was the key figure. He set its parameters. In February 1919 he instructed Churchill not '[to] commit us to any costly operation which would involve any large contribution either of men or money'. The main idea being 'to enable Russia to save herself', and to that end he was prepared to equip the anti-Bolsheviks to do the job themselves. Lloyd George would not risk his career and reputation on a lost cause, so often a source of inspiration for Churchill.[48]

The Cabinet decided accordingly.[49] Churchill's job was to ensure the safe withdrawal of British forces from north Russia, a warrant flexible enough to empower him to despatch extra forces to shield a possible retreat. As British involvement showed no visible signs of lessening, Lloyd George's impatience and anger at Churchill grew. He found Churchill's mind 'so obsessed by Russia' that he was neglecting his main duty: to reduce expenditure. Churchill was in fact spending a lot of money, though just how much remains uncertain. Lloyd George feared it would be 'hundreds of millions'. Churchill scaled it down to 'only 40'.[50] Whatever the amount, it was too much for a policy of retrenchment abroad. Churchill eventually conceded defeat. Magnanimous as ever, he had nothing but praise for Lloyd George. 'You have gone on consistently, never varying, but always with the same fixed idea. I fought you & you have beaten me'.[51]

Churchill's anti-Bolshevik crusade was of cardinal significance to his career. He emerges from it as the original Cold War warrior. In this he never mellowed with time.[52] The rapprochement with the Soviets of the late 1930s and the Second World War was but a businesslike interlude brought on by circumstances beyond his control. Once the war ended, he returned to his old habits. In January 1949 he came full circle, echoing the opinion he had first voiced thirty years earlier: 'the strangling of Bolshevism at its birth would have been an untold blessing to the human race'.[53]

Intervention also confirmed his public image as a reckless adventurer. The *Daily Express* – a spirited advocate of overseas retrenchment – named the megalomaniacal Churchill as 'a military gamester'; a prominent Liberal, Sir William Sutherland, marked him down as the country's favourite 'bold, bad man'. It soured his relations with Lloyd George. They were at constant loggerheads. Over Churchill's political future hung a question mark. Churchill himself thought that Lloyd George would fire him from the War Office owing to their differences. In the autumn of 1919 Lloyd George was thinking in terms of a new progressive party – but without Churchill. 'You will have to have me in your new National Party,' Churchill said. 'Oh no!' retorted Lloyd George. 'To be a party you must have at least one follower. You have none.'[54]

To where would Churchill turn? Towards the end of the war he had entertained a desire 'of being top dog, by standing in with the Labour Party'. Later, he was reported to be planning 'a National & a Labour Party'. A National Party was the faintest of hopes at the best of times. To tack Labour on in the wake of his interventionist policy was little more than a pipe-dream. In public, he seemed to regard the Labour Party as the advance guard of Bolshevism in Britain. They are 'quite unfitted for the responsibility of Government', he proclaimed on more than one occasion. Labour reciprocated. Even the trade unionists, for whom Churchill retained a special soft spot as the genuine representatives of the working class now, 'thoroughly distrusted' him. Clearly, there was no salvation for him in the arena of National Coalition Politics.[55]

Churchill craved for a great healing Centre Party. Ironically, his Russian policy pushed him towards the extreme right and swung him into line in front of the Tory diehards for whom he became 'a fortuitous but lonely spokesman'.[56] More significantly, and also more dangerously for Lloyd George and his Conservative partners, he found himself at one with other, more mainstream Tory elements who had become increasingly unhappy at the coalition's policies in general and progressively more critical of their leadership for maintaining what they considered to be a damaging partnership with Lloyd George, one that was at odds with true Conservative principles.

By the beginning of 1922 the coalition's prestige was tarnished, its authority on the wane. Grassroots Conservative discontent mounted. In foreign affairs, the Russian problem served as a touchstone for much of its resentment. Sir Samuel Hoare, who declared himself dedicated to the 'destruction of Bolshevism', and Walter Guinness (later Lord Moyne), a close friend of Churchill's, led a ginger group of backbenchers – 'The Coalition Government Foreign Affairs Committee' – almost exclusively Conservative in composition, whose main aim was to foster government aid for the White Russians. Churchill admitted they were 'an invaluable aid' to his campaign. He worked with them, briefing them when necessary, stimulating them to greater activity. In turn, they saw him as their representative in government. It was more than just a marriage of convenience. As the coalition foundered, Churchill regretted its possible break-up. But, as he told Hoare, he possessed 'many natural affinities with the Conservatives'.[57]

Lloyd George found it increasingly irksome to work with Churchill. Not only was it a demanding chore to contain him, Lloyd George also feared the consequences of getting rid of him. As Britain moved closer to recognizing the Soviet Union, these issues came to a head. The Genoa conference of April 1922, planned by Lloyd George as a panacea for Europe's ailments, including a positive resolution of the Russian question, in the event resolved nothing. Its failure dealt Lloyd George another blow. The opposition to any kind of recognition with Russia focused on Churchill. The breach widened between him and Lloyd George. Again he hinted at resignation. It may well be that Churchill felt he was acting from a position of strength. 'Our position would be impossible if Winston retired because he was more Tory than the Tory Ministers,' Austen Chamberlain reminded Lloyd George. 'It would be quite fatal to us.' There could be no mistake: a substantial section of Unionist opinion sympathized with Churchill.[58]

Negotiations to restore trade relations between the Soviet Union and Britain had already begun, against Churchill's wishes, who characterized the Bolshevik representatives as 'ruffians and butchers', and refused to shake hands with 'the hairy baboon', Krassin. *De jure* recognition was another matter. Lloyd George, however, was adamant. On the eve of Genoa, he wrote to his mistress and secretary, Frances Stevenson, 'the Cabinet must decide between Winston and me . . . If the Unionists take Winston's view I go without any hesitation.'[59] In the event, neither went, both saved temporarily by the collapse of the conference. But it was already apparent that Churchill's political future as a Lloyd Georgite could no longer be guaranteed. The question was whether his reputation as a political maverick would allow him to find shelter among the Conservatives.

Meanwhile, Lloyd George was looking to move Churchill to a post where he could cause less trouble, not more. An opportunity emerged at the end of 1920 when the Colonial Office became vacant owing to Lord Milner's impending retirement. His coalition would be on safer grounds, perhaps, if Churchill were allowed to tidy up the the remains of the Ottoman Empire and develop British imperial possessions.

11

Running the Empire

For a capable and spirited politician the Colonial Office offered considerable latitude for advancement and publicity. Apart from running the old Dominions and the colonial dependencies proper, it now had under its control a vast 'informal Empire' straddling the Middle East from Egypt to the Persian Gulf (Clement Attlee's 'deficit areas').

If Churchill could have frozen the Empire as it was when he first experienced it as a young man, no doubt he would have done so. It was not that he was impervious to change. Not moved by a great imperial design, his views were often, not always, shaped on a strictly cost-benefit basis: territories that were too expensive to run, or were no longer economically profitable, or had outlived their strategic-political usefulness could be dispensed with. Nor did he possess a dyed-in-the-wool white settler mentality. The British Empire brought immense benefits to the home islands, but if it meant anything 'imperial power' had also 'to secure the highest standards of justice in administration everywhere', including safeguarding the rights of the indigenous peoples.[1] Churchill had most difficulty in adjusting to the scenes of his first imperial adventures: British rule in India and Egypt, in particular, but also the settlement in South Africa. Here he adopted the most entrenched of attitudes. He opposed the Milner report in 1920, that recommended a qualified form of independence for Egypt, conducted a great campaign on the same grounds for almost three decades over India, and stood firm on the British connection with South Africa, very much his own creation, until the last possible moment in the 1950s.[2]

As Colonial Secretary, and for the remainder of his career, he was acutely aware of the forces at large working to weaken, if not destroy, the British Empire. In the first instance, the Bolsheviks; later, the ambitions of the totalitarian regimes of the interwar period; and lastly, and most frustrating of all, the well-meaning, naïve intentions of the Americans. Against all he would speak out, employing a different language and tone according to the nature of the threat and those who made it. The early 1920s were dominated by the Bolshevik menace, 'a world-wide conspiracy' making 'a dead set' against the British Empire. 'They will not succeed,' he promised a cheering audience. 'We will not allow ourselves to be pulled down and have our Empire disrupted by a malevolent and subversive force, the rascals and rapscullions of mankind who are now on the move against us.'[3]

If Lloyd George had appointed Churchill to the Colonial Office to curtail his interfering ways, he was to be disappointed. Was the Colonial Office too cramped for his ambitions? In 1921 he proposed altering his title to Secretary of State for Imperial Affairs, denoting a grander and more extended domain. He was set on a little 'empire-building' of his own, protesting, with some justice, at the absurdity of 'the Arabian problem' being split between the India Office, the Foreign Office, and his own department, and suggested that it be placed under his jurisdiction. Placing the widest interpretation on 'imperial affairs', he sallied forth into foreign affairs in general, pronouncing on European and world matters, indeed on occasion pre-empting Foreign Office statements. 'He wants to be a sort of Asiatic Foreign Secretary,' Curzon complained, who found his interfering ways intolerable; and he was joined by Edwin Montagu, who also detected Churchill's finger stirring his Indian pie. Lloyd George too was most unhappy and promised Curzon 'to stopper his fizzing', a vow easier to make than to carry out.[4]

It has been suggested that Churchill's earlier spell at the Colonial Office 'very nearly exhausted' his interest in the Empire.[5] Despite his professed interest in its welfare, he visited little of it. He had last seen India in 1897 and South Africa in 1900. Australia and New Zealand (where his name was at a low premium after the Gallipoli disaster) never hosted him. Malaya and Hong Kong were denied his presence; while his last visit to a British colony in Africa had been in 1907. Only in Canada, Egypt, and parts of the Middle East was he a regular, if sporadic, traveller. He took the Colonial Office in 1921 as a stop-gap. He still eyed eagerly the Chancellorship, enough anyway to cut short an important mission to the Middle East in April 1921 and rush back to London to put in his claim – in vain.[6] Other matters, the Irish problem or the Greek-Turkish imbroglio, consumed almost as much of his time.

In March 1915 Asquith had recorded that 'Winston is very anxious ... to appropriate an equivalent [with Russia and France] share of the spoils' of the Ottoman Empire.[7] As a member of Lloyd George's coalition, Churchill had found himself responsible for some of those 'spoils', namely Palestine and Iraq [Mesopotamia], awarded to Britain as a result of allied wartime bargaining. But in the post-war world, Churchill's enthusiasm for retaining the prizes of war somewhat waned. Was the maintenance of a British presence in the region worth the effort and the cost? He was not certain. In October 1919 he proposed the reconstruction of the Ottoman Empire, its integrity to be preserved by 'a strict form of international control' under the stewardship of the League of Nations. He suggested that the European Powers abandon their interests in the Turkish Empire other than those which existed before the war. For Britain this meant abandoning Iraq and Palestine. When this solution proved impracticable, he was not adverse to turning these mandates over to a friendly power, the United States. His idea was hotly opposed by Curzon and Lloyd George.[8]

At first, it seemed as though the new British possessions in the Middle East held little attraction for Churchill. What was the point of retaining Palestine and Mesopotamia when 'we have far more territory in the British Empire than we shall be able to develop for many generations'. If Britain had spare cash to invest, he would have preferred to channel it into Africa where 'we have enormous estates of immense potential value which we have pitifully neglected'. In the summer of 1921, after several months' experience of dealing with the turbulent Middle East, he drew a comparison for the House of Commons between 'tractable and promising' African colonies and those areas of the Middle East, 'unduly stocked with peppery, pugnacious, proud politicians and theologians, who happen at the same time to be extremely hard up'.[9] Alas, the British could not wriggle out of their Middle East commitments so easily. Churchill floated these balloons with the same fluent facility that his mind worked. If they gained height, so much the better. If not, nothing much was lost except an exchange of memoranda, accompanied, usually, by angry gestures by his colleagues. Churchill's ideas were more in the nature of airing intriguing concepts than of unveiling a well-thought-out political programme. At best, Britain would have to be content with adapting her policy to the new forces at work in the region: a resurgent Turkish nationalism and a nascent but increasingly militant Arab nationalism; renewed French intransigence over Syria; Zionist claims and Palestinian Arab counter-claims. All this, coupled with crippling economic and financial constraints at home made imperative a policy that has been defined as 'defensive imperialism'. Churchill's task was to reconcile these often conflicting factors.[10]

However, he was also heavily involved in balancing white settler claims and Indian rights in Kenya, as well as deciding the future of Southern Rhodesia, where union with South Africa competed with settler demands for autonomy; or in general to foster interest and investment in 'our tropical colonies'.[11] But reshaping the Middle East took up an inordinate amount of Churchill's time and energy, setting a familiar pattern for future Colonial Secretaries. For this purpose he created a special Middle East Department, headed by Sir John Shuckburgh and staffed by such eccentrics as T. E. Lawrence – a particular favourite of Churchill – and Richard Meinertzhagen. The burning issues were 'the burden & the odium of the Mesopotamia [Iraq] entanglement', and the even more intractable problem of Palestine, a 'venture [that] is most difficult to withdraw from'.[12] He convened an extraordinary conference at Cairo in March 1921. The issues at stake were weighty, but Churchill, accompanied by Clementine, still found time to sketch and paint, visit the Pyramids, be photographed riding a camel, and in general cheer people up with a 'bottle of wine'.[13]

Of the two problems, the Iraq settlement proved the least controversial at the time. The overriding need was to reduce costs, military and administrative. There had been a great Arab insurrection against British rule in Iraq in 1920, which had gradually been suppressed by a combination of air power and the use of armoured car squadrons. Politically, Iraq was proclaimed a kingdom and Feisal, generally held to be a British tool, was installed as King. As Churchill delicately pointed out, the country would be run like 'an Indian native State', administered 'in general accord with the advice tendered by the High Commissioner, Sir Percy Cox'. These principles were enshrined in a treaty in the autumn of 1922, though not before it was necessary to protest at Feisal's more extravagant personal habits, fanciful political demands, lack of decision, and extreme incompetence of his advisers. Staying in Iraq, Churchill noted, was like 'living on an ungrateful volcano'. Churchill grumbled: 'Has [Feisal] not got some wives to keep him quiet?' He threatened to pull out of Iraq unless Feisal quietened down.

Churchill's policy of 'informal control' allowed for substantial savings, the whole point of the exercise. If peace could be maintained, he forecast that expenditure in Iraq would be reduced to £4 million, in comparison with £32 million in 1920. This was indeed imperial rule on the cheap. It did not completely satisfy Churchill. Later, as Chancellor of the Exchequer, he expressed a wish to cut Britain's losses there once and for all. 'I hate Irak,' he owned up, 'I wish we had never gone there.'[14]

Palestine was another matter. His concern for Zionism was an enduring one, and it re-appears at frequent intervals in his career.[15] The idea of the Return, the restoration of an ancient people to its historic homeland, appealed to Churchill's regard for justice as well as to his abiding sense of history. He explained to a hostile Arab delegation in Jerusalem in March 1921 that it was 'manifestly right' that the Jews should have a homeland, 'And where else could that be but in this land of Palestine with which for more than 3,000 years they have been intimately and profoundly associated?'[16] Of course, he was not blind to the imperial-strategic assets of a Zionist presence, beholden to Britain, in Palestine; but at this stage, it was not a decisive factor in his calculations. He never confused his duties as a serving British politician with that of advancing the Zionist interest. For Churchill, as for other gentile Zionists, it remained for him to narrow the gap to a minimum between Zionist expectations and the British capacity to fulfil them. Ultimately though, it proved beyond the wit of any British politician to bridge the 'expectation gap', including Churchill.

For a time, however, Churchill did have grave reservations about a continued British presence in Palestine. As early as 1915 he had suggested handing over Palestine to 'Christian, liberal, noble' Belgium. After the war, searching for expenditure cuts, he returned to the same theme. Should not Britain 'give up' Palestine, already costing Britain's taxpayers £6 million a year? There was also a political cost that he appeared unwilling to pay. 'The Zionist movement will cause continued friction with the Arabs,' he asserted. In the summer of 1921, he proposed that the Cabinet review Britain's 'profoundly unpopular' Zionist policy.[17]

Churchill was not pursuing an anti-Zionist policy. It was quite possible to be a dedicated Zionist without committing oneself to administering Palestine. The Balfour Declaration, however it be read, contains no obligation to do so.[18] Nor did Churchill rule out other possibilities. Only months after his questionnaire to Lloyd George, he envisaged 'by the banks of the Jordan' a state of three or four million Jews 'under the protection of the British Crown'.[19]

Lloyd George, however, was in no mood to relinquish any British gains from the war. And once it became clear that Britain was in Palestine (and Iraq) to stay, Churchill applied himself to the consolidation of British rule in those areas with all the energy and vision of which he was capable. At the time, he was under tremendous pressure to revise Britain's Zionist commitment. An anti-Zionist campaign, laced with strong doses of anti-semitism, was underway in the press, Parliament, and government. Richard Meinertzhagen detected a distinct 'hebrophobe' atmosphere emanating from the Colonial Office, while Churchill admitted to his friend, Chaim Weizmann, the Zionist leader, that nine-tenths of the British officials in Palestine were anti-Zionist.[20] Churchill's axe fell as heavily upon Palestine as elsewhere. At Cairo, he set up the emirate of Transjordan – or as he later elaborated, 'the Emir Abdullah is in Transjordan where I put him one Sunday afternoon' – thereby partitioning mandatory Palestine for the first time. But he would not renege on the essence of Britain's Zionist obligation, still anchored in the vague phrases of Balfour's declaration. To the Arabs, he defended staunchly, on moral and political grounds, Britain's Zionist oriented policy, and made it abundantly clear that 'we cannot abandon to Arab fanaticism Jewish efforts'.[21]

These months witnessed Zionist achievements no less considerable than the Balfour Declaration itself. In June 1922 the government issued the so-called Churchill White Paper; and the following month, the League of Nations ratified the mandate for Palestine. At the same time, Churchill guided a controversial scheme through Parliament for the electrification of Palestine – a major triumph for the Zionists.[22]

The mandate incorporated the Balfour Declaration and reconfirmed Britain as the mandatory power (a decision first taken at San Remo in April 1920). Churchill's, in fact, Sir Herbert Samuel's, White Paper was more contentious.[23] It reaffirmed the Balfour Declaration, but then redefined it, not in the enthusiastic, positive terms previously employed by Lloyd George and Balfour, but in more limiting phrases. A Jewish National Home, it laid down, 'is not the imposition of a Jewish nationality upon the inhabitants of Palestine as a whole', but the continued development of the existing Jewish community, that had already acquired 'national characteristics', into a centre which the Jewish people as a whole may take an 'interest and pride'.

However much the Zionists railed against the Churchill White Paper, they accepted it. Its phraseology was sufficiently flexible to satisfy both sides, after a hard argument. It enabled them to pursue their goals, building slowly and painstakingly their National Home, creating the economic and social and political foundations that would eventually lead to the Jewish state. If Churchill is to be held responsible for Zionist disappointments – the lopping off of Transjordan, for example – he must also be credited with current Zionist successes, less dramatic but more lasting. Having played no part in the Balfour Declaration negotiations, Churchill came to regard the 1922 document as the epitome of his, ergo British, commitment to Zionism.

During these years, relations between Churchill and Lloyd George were distinguished as much by tension and disagreement as by coopera- tion and harmony. Chilly relations had existed ever since Lloyd George had denied Churchill the Chancellorship, a post Churchill coveted as his. Churchill was not only at odds with aspects of Lloyd George's foreign and imperial policy – from the Bolshevik menace through the Middle East to the Greek-Turkish conflict – but he also voiced dissatisfaction with the government's domestic policy – particularly, housing and employment – or lack of it. The Prime Minister now believed his wayward minister was not above bidding for the supreme office. In May–July 1921, all this exploded into a first-class crisis, with complaints of intrigue and palace coups, particularly regarding Churchill's 'hostility' and 'treachery'. Their previous intimacy ceased. They now 'looked out at one another like two distant snow-clad peaks.' Churchill was not a natural intriguer (unlike Beaverbrook, one of his chief accusers). Still, he had never been shy from expressing himself in terms of great political blocs. He was known to favour National Combinations; his intimacy with Birkenhead was notorious; his party loyalty could never be taken for granted; his unbridled ambition was on continuous display. All this told against him. Lloyd George believed the assertions, or at least did not discount them, and this was enough to darken his relations with Churchill.

Churchill's increasingly independent line was not only a reflection of his mercurial nature, or an outcome of his eye always being focused on the main chance. It stemmed also from a growing realization that the days of Lloyd George's coalition were numbered. As he put it tartly in the autumn of 1922, 'The reign of our revered leader is I apprehend drawing to a close.'[24] The demise of Lloyd George, or even its prospect, severely limited Churchill's options. Hitherto, Lloyd George had acted as his political godfather. It would not be too fanciful to conclude that if Churchill thrived politically, he did so in Lloyd George's shadow. To bring him back after the Dardanelles fiasco was an act of extreme political courage. Deprived of Lloyd George, few other alternatives were open to Churchill. Almost by default, he was thrown back for support upon right-wing Tory elements. 'His tendency is all to the Right and his principles becoming more Tory,' thought Beaverbrook, who whatever his enthusiasm for plots was an acute observer of the political scene. Lloyd George, and others, had independently reached the same conclusion.[25]

Churchill's right-wing leanings also appeared to find expression over the Irish question. By the end of the war, the Home Rule Bill of 1914, to which Churchill thought Lloyd George's administration was 'absolutely committed', was in reality an anachronism. In effect, the Sinn Fein had already proclaimed its Republic, in much the same way that the successor states of the moribund Austro-Hungarian Empire had seized their independence. Its Parliament, the Dial, passed laws, levied taxes, meted out its own justice. Its military wing, the Irish Republican Army, defended its independence in a bitter campaign against the British authorities. Churchill's initial response to this challenge was typically belligerent. Martial law was his answer to violence. In May 1920 he proposed setting up a 'special force' of old soldiers to stem the bloodshed. Later, he defended staunchly the 'honourable and gallant officers' of the Black and Tans, who dealt with the Irish rebels in their own coin, reinforced by the 'Auxis', a semi-official terror squad. Whatever the provocation, these groups indulged in wild and brutal reprisals, responding to terror with terror. This was hard to justify.[26] Before long, Churchill was put on the kidnap list of the Sinn Fein and his personal bodyguard of pre-war days reinstated. At one stage, his concern was so great that he left the comforts of his bedroom and went to sleep in the attic, the door protected by a metal shield, with a loaded revolver at the ready, prepared for battle should the villains appear.[27]

Sir Henry Wilson thought it would need an army of 100–200,000 men to crush the uprising – an impracticable solution. Lloyd George, sensitive to the drifts in public opinion, was by now quite aware of the limitations of a repressive Irish policy. What remained was to conjure up a compromise sufficiently tempting to interest all sides. By the end of 1920, he presented the Government of Ireland Act that partitioned southern Ireland from the six Ulster counties, allowing each its own Parliament with representatives in Westminster, and a joint Council to deal with common matters. An ingenious formula, it was rejected by Sinn Fein, and only partially accepted by the Ulster Unionists, who adopted the principle of partition but would have nothing to do with a joint Council. Despite, this unpromising beginning, it proved to be the first step that led to the signing of the Irish treaty a year later.

Now fully in accord with Lloyd George, Churchill also began to think in terms of a 'truce'. He was lobbied by Clementine to do so, who pressed her husband for 'moderation' in Ireland, 'or at any rate justice'. 'Put yourself in the place of the Irish,' she pleaded. 'It always makes me unhappy & disappointed when I see you inclined to take for granted that the rough, iron-fisted "Hunnish" way will prevail.'[28]

Churchill was in favour of negotiations, but not if it would be interpreted as a sign of weakness. After months of murders and abductions, ambushes, arson, and summary executions, with martial law proclaimed in some areas, and all to no avail, he thought the time now opportune for a gesture of conciliation. Perhaps he too was moved by the more strident tone of public criticism: a Labour Party report concluded that Britain's Irish policy 'must make her name stink in the nostrils of the whole world'. At any rate, in May 1921 Churchill argued to the Cabinet, 'If you are strong enough you should make the effort. Where is the disadvantage?' This was not sufficient to convince the Cabinet, but two months later Lloyd George called a truce.[29] Negotiations began. De Valera, President of Sinn Fein, was received at 10, Downing Street, thronged with Irish supporters waving their green flags. This hard-headed decision reflected the situation on the ground. Both sides were exhausted, if not militarily then in terms of morale. Sir Nevil Macready, Commander of British forces in Ireland, reckoned that his troops could not be relied upon to campaign another winter, while Michael Collins, Commander of the IRA, astounded at the offer of a truce, said: 'You had us dead beat. We could not have lasted another three weeks ... We thought you must have gone mad.'[30]

The ensuing negotiations greatly boosted Churchill's parliamentary reputation. A member of the ministerial committee on Ireland, his performances in the House earned him much praise. Some Conservatives began to speak of him as a potential leader.[31] At the final stage of the talks, he and Birkenhead, together with Lloyd George and Austen Chamberlain, were practically running the negotiations. Beaverbrook has suggested that Lloyd George selected these two cronies 'because they were too dangerous to leave out'.[32] Birkenhead, after all, was known as an ardent Ulsterite. By rallying to Lloyd George's side, he would disarm the more extreme Conservative critics. As for Churchill, he would cause much trouble if left to roam about aimlessly. Still, there were limits beyond which even Lloyd George could not push Churchill. Churchill had not entirely abandoned a policy of repression. But he was prepared to accept 'Dominion Home Rule', even, if pressed, an 'all-Ireland Parliament', though he would not countenance 'physical force . . . against Ulster from any quarter'.[33]

These negotiations eventually worked themselves out into 'Articles of Agreement for a Treaty', signatured in December by Sinn Fein and British representatives. While maintaining special defence arrangements for Britain, it granted Dominion status to an Irish Free State, empowered to speak for a united Ireland, but shorn of the Ulster counties in the north which preserved the existing union with Britain. It was an exceptional personal triumph for Lloyd George. And Churchill acted as his back-stop.[34] Churchill was not above threatening 'a real war — not mere bushwacking' should the Sinn Fein not sign the Articles, a style very much in line with Lloyd George's promise of 'war within three days' at the final, dramatic scene of the negotiations. This was sufficient to convince the Sinn Fein finally to sign the treaty.[35]

Lloyd George rather meanly thought that 'Winston is contributing nothing', in sharp contrast to Birkenhead.[36] But the bad feeling that persisted between Churchill and Lloyd George during these months should not obscure Churchill's own substantial contribution. He came into his own after the Articles had been signed. As chairman of the Cabinet committee on Ireland, meeting almost daily, he dealt with the myriad of details that constituted the meat of the settlement. This was behind the scenes. In Parliament, he guided the treaty through clause by clause, earning much praise for his 'masterly performances'.[37] His accomplishments at Westminster were particularly impressive as in Ireland another outburst of ferocious fighting had broken out between rival camps in the Sinn Fein, which was also directed against the British. Would the treaty survive the renewed bloodletting? Churchill, now an active broker of the front rank, insisted that the signed treaty be honoured, even if it meant employing the British army to enforce it.

By December 1921 the Irish treaty went into effect; the Irish Free State, with Dominion status, officially proclaimed. Lloyd George, however, stuck obstinately to his previous verdict, rating Birkenhead as by 'far the best negotiator'. Others balanced the judgement. Before his assassination at the hands of former comrades, Michael Collins had sent Churchill a farewell message: 'Tell Winston we could never have done anything without him.' More than anything, however, the Irish treaty was a brilliant success for Lloyd George. At the time, Churchill 'rejoiced' to be associated with it. Later, he had second thoughts and vilified Lloyd George's 'wicked Irish treaty', arguing that the war should have been prosecuted 'for another winter' to gain better conditions.[38]

At the beginning of 1922, conscious that his fortunes were sliding, Lloyd George aimed at new elections to strengthen his parliamentary position. Austen Chamberlain saw no point in dissolution. Churchill, touchy at Lloyd George's allegedly pro-Bolshevik policy, also would not have it, fearing 'a new lease of life' on his leader's 'despotism'. Later in the year, this topic proved the occasion for a furious quarrel between them, so acrimonious that one observer wondered whether they could ever 'work together again'.[39] Lloyd George's failure to press the point home may well have been a fatal mistake, the last opportunity to retrieve his failing reputation. Relations between them worsened. Reports that Churchill had joined Birkenhead in bad-mouthing him must have reached Lloyd George's ears. He valued Churchill's worth but 'distrusted' him, particularly as rumours were circulating that Churchill was being pressed 'to come out as the leader of the Tory Party'.[40] However outlandish an idea, it indicated that Churchill was fed up with acknowledging Lloyd George as his patron and was seeking a new political framework. Within months of these skirmishes, in October 1922, Lloyd George and Churchill were both ousted from office, for Lloyd George a death-blow that despatched him into opposition for ever. Paradoxically, on the immediate issue that led to Lloyd George's downfall, the Greek-Turkish war of 1922, he and Churchill were once again working in tandem, though not before Churchill had performed a volte-face to get there.

Early on, Churchill had taken a definite stand against the Sèvres treaty of August 1920, intended to bring the war against Turkey to an end. Mustapha Kemal (Attaturk), hero of Gallipoli, had taken up arms to repudiate it. Who, then, would enforce Sèvres? Churchill asked. Only the Greeks, was the answer, who were being authorized to go to war to ensure their share of the spoils, Thrace and Smyrna and its hinterland. Any attempt on Britain's part to coerce the Turks, Churchill went on, ran counter to her interests. It meant an unwelcome increase in military budgets in an area for which Churchill held direct responsibility, and would strain relations with France and Italy who were currently toadying up to Turkey.[41]

As Mustapha Kemal's nationalists gradually took grip of the military situation, these questions became more acute. It appeared to many as though Britain was fighting the war through its proxy, Greece. And it was a losing war. As Churchill pointed out, it left Britain dangerously isolated, her prestige impaired. At odds with her European allies, and with little support evident in the Dominions, an anti-Turk policy contradicted Britain's position as 'the greatest Mohammedan Power in the world', stirring up passions in India, impairing the unity of the empire. Churchill made every effort to woo Lloyd George away from his shortsighted and reckless patronage of Greek ambitions. Greatly in Lloyd George's debt for bringing him 'a fresh horse' when he was 'dismounted in the war', Churchill hinted that the issues that now divided them were too acute for him to remain a member of his Cabinet.[42] These pleas had no effect. Lloyd George's sponsorship of the Greeks never flagged, a surprising blind-spot in his vision, usually so clear and far-sighted. But at least he was consistent in his foolishness. Churchill did not resign. Instead, he followed Lloyd George to the brink of war against the Turks, only to become 'dismounted' once again.

Why did Churchill suddenly abandon the Turks? Not out of any head-long passion for the Greeks, whom he had 'always hated'. Previously, he had feared that a Greek victory would throw the Turks into the arms of the Bolsheviks; now he presumed that the victorious Turks would cement their links with the Soviet Union to menace traditional British interests in the area. By mid-September 1922 the Turks had broken the Greek armies and were advancing in triumph on the Aegean coast and the Straits, cleansing Anatolia of their enemy in the most brutal manner. As they marched on the Dardanelles and Constantinople, violating the neutralized zone of the Straits agreed upon at Sèvres, Churchill took fright. He was compelled to throw in his lot with Lloyd George to avoid 'a complete Turkish walk-over and the total loss of all the fruits of the Great War in this quarter'. It was the Dardanelles syndrome come to life again. He was all for fighting the Turks, for encouraged by the Bolsheviks, Mustapha Kemal believed that the British could be 'trampled on and ignored'. Churchill was all for confronting him at Chanak, a small township overlooking the Dardanelles.[43]

Lloyd George failed to grasp that his Greek policy had opened up an unbridgeable divide between himself and those forces essential for his political survival. And his chief advisers, Churchill included, were either blind to the risks they were taking, or else, consumed by their own self-confidence, they cavalierly dismissed the opposition as being of small consequence. Matters were brought to a head by the bellicose press communiqué, drafted by Churchill, soliciting Dominion support in the event of a war with Turkey. Published in the press before the Dominions were informed, it backfired. The Dominions could no longer be taken for granted. Only New Zealand and Newfoundland were prepared to follow Britain. South Africa refused to become involved; Australia would not risk one soldier's life; Canada stood aside. If the Dominions would not make the necessary sacrifice, what could be expected of 'Our Allies [France and Italy],' Churchill acidly speculated, '[who] were prepared to take everything lying down.'[44]

Observers now began to note a disturbing development in Churchill's behaviour. The *Daily Mail* accused him of fabricating 'a new Gallipoli'. His pugnacious mood – 'Aren't you in luck to be at the Admiralty when there's a show on!' – was confirmed by Arthur Lee, First Lord of the Admiralty, who concluded that he positively wanted 'hostilities to break out'. 'Winston and F. E.'s warlike policy,' troubled most of his colleagues. Hankey too was bothered at Churchill's violent Turko-phobia and combat readiness. Fortunately, the calmer nerves of the British Field Commander, General Sir Charles Harington, prevailed. Ordered to issue an ultimatum to the Turks, he let the matter slide. The battle at Chanak was avoided, to Churchill's apparent distress.[45] One conclusion was self-evident: Britain was isolated. Some sort of compromise was inevitable. On 11 October it was concluded at Mudania in a convention between the allies and the Turks. By then, it was too late to save Lloyd George.

At home, a major political crisis was brewing. The Chanak confrontation acted as a catalyst for the widespread discontent with the coalition's performance over a wide range of issues, including the scandalous dispensation of honours by Lloyd George. In the eyes of many, a full-blown crisis in the Near East, with Churchill as his ardent partner, was added to Lloyd George's list of follies.[46]

Lloyd George reacted contemptuously to these rumblings. 'Does little [Stanley] Baldwin think he can turn us out?' In a last-minute attempt to maintain the unity of the coalition, Churchill convened a dinner-party at his home in Sussex Gardens. None of the leading Conservative ministers in attendance wished to break with Lloyd George. The Tory 'rebels' were looking for leadership. At last, Bonar Law provided it. 'We cannot alone act as the policeman of the world,' he had said.[47] Fortified by Beaverbrook, Bonar Law attended a meeting of Conservative MPs at the Carlton Club, called by Austen Chamberlain to crush the revolt and preserve Lloyd George. But the swelling dissatisfaction of the Conservatives spilled over in a vote to withdraw from the coalition.[48] That afternoon Lloyd George resigned and Bonar Law set about forming his first administration.

The day Lloyd George was tumbled out of office, Churchill was operated on for acute appendicitis. He remained incapacitated until the beginning of November, two weeks before general elections were due. Meanwhile, Bonar Law put together his government. Viewing it from his sick-bed, Churchill was not impressed. Incensed at 'the traitorous conduct' of his former Conservative allies, and especially at that 'lackey' Curzon, he prophesied that Bonar Law, who lacked the 'vital resourcefulness or constructive capacity' of Lloyd George, would be 'the greatest political failure ever known in British politics'. As for the rest of his ministers, they were merely 'duds and pipsqueaks'.[49]

For much of his political life Churchill had daydreamed of a great

Centre Party. This vision had now vanished. The closest he would ever approach it would be during the Second World War when he led the broadest based of coalitions. With Lloyd George gone, his own political future was very much on the line. He defended valiantly, though in a somewhat strained manner, the coalition's policies that had brought it political ruin. Past differences with Lloyd George were shelved. 'I take my stand by Mr Lloyd George . . . I am still his friend and lieutenant,' he announced. Although he had nowhere else to turn, it was a wholly admirable trait that inhibited him from abandoning his tarnished chief. (And it might be noted that one of Lloyd George's last acts as Prime Minister was to recommend Churchill to the Order of Companions of Honour.) So, 'Adopt me simply as a Liberal and Free Trader', he asked the Liberal Association in Dundee. But, perhaps thinking of the morrow, he added: 'if the public welfare requires it, I shall not hesitate to cooperate with sober, patriotic and progressive Unionist elements. These are no times when moderate-minded men can afford to dissipate friendship and support.'[50]

Churchill joined the campaign four days before the poll. Until then Clementine – although she was still feeding their seven-week-old baby, Mary – had conducted the fight, helped by Edward Louis Spears, a friend from the wartime trenches, and local supporters. But the organization, as she confessed, was 'in chaos'. The local press was hostile. She was heckled incessantly, even spat upon. Birkenhead came to give a hand. 'But he was no use at all, he was drunk,' she bitingly observed. Clementine gloomily reported to Churchill. 'The idea against you seems to be that are a "War Monger" but I am exhibiting you as a Cherub Peace Maker with fluffy little wings round your chubby face.'

Churchill finally arrived, in great pain, his features drawn, his expression dazed, groggy on his feet, and carried from platform to platform in an invalid chair. He was unable to campaign with his customary verve. He was jeered at, and met with cries of 'What about the Dardanelles?' The swing against him was considerable. He was defeated by 12,000 votes. It was rumoured that he wept at the trouncing, but he denied it. 'It wd not I think be difficult for me to obtain another seat quite soon,' he told a friend, 'But it is better to have a good holiday.' He spent the winter months on the Riviera, recuperating.[51]

What, now, were his 'main purposes'? Many of his constituents might have said warmongering, a view that would not have been seriously disputed by the electorate at large. And his *idée fixe* of expunging Bolshevism distorted his view of domestic politics as he came to see the Labour party as little more than its tool. It left him even more isolated politically. Most of his colleagues still regarded him as an exceptionally able man, but one consumed by his own ambition. There was also a deep-rooted suspicion that once having latched on to a concept, however unsound, he remained impervious to counter arguments, for to have abandoned it he would have had to eat humble pie. As Austen Chamberlain remarked, he was 'very much a man of one idea'. Naked ambition combined with mule-headedness is a most combustible compound. Once the dust had cleared, his reputation for recklessness, instability, lack of judgement, that dogged him to the end, was firmly implanted in the public mind.

This perception of Churchill – a political fact in its own right – was somewhat unfair. It tended to blur his successes and real achievements. He had done well at Munitions. His stint as Secretary of State for War and Air, in retrospect, became most controversial, as it set off that fateful run-down in British arms that Churchill himself so loudly condemned in the 1930s. But at the time, he discharged government policy to the letter. By September 1922 he had reduced expenditure in the Middle East from £45 million to £11. His endeavours to resolve the Irish and Palestinian problems were wholly to his credit, and at least achieved a breathing space in the hope that saner counsels would prevail. No one since has done better. The fact that he had to defend these controversial issues before the House consolidated his parliamentary reputation. His rhetorical skills were his most effective weapon. He could present his argument with almost surgical precision, often employing his wit to leave the House roaring with laughter, a most efficient and lively way of demolishing the opposition.

If the Dardanelles episode proved anything, it proved that Churchill was a survivor. His political courage was beyond question. But as regards controversial decisions he had taken, and for which he never shirked responsibility, he showed little, if any, flexibility of thought. He would not admit to mistakes. Criticism stirred him up. No setback, however severe, diminished his belief that eventually he would find political salvation. If many persisted in regarding him as a dangerous adventurer, his loyal, closed circle believed firmly in his star. And no one believed in it with greater intensity than Churchill himself. He must have inspired himself with the thought that he possessed all the attributes of a great Prime Minister. One, however, was lacking, seemingly beyond his capacity to procure: a firm political base. Still only forty-eight years old, and still a political orphan, the coming years would be spent in seeking political respectability.

'I will make you the Golden Chancellor'

'What a wonderful & terrible year this has been for you.' Churchill was no doubt comforted by Sir Archibald Sinclair's compassionate words, written at the end of August 1921. But nothing could deaden the pain of the tragedies he had endured during the past months. In June his mother had died. Lady Randolph had fallen and broken a leg. Gangrene set in and her leg had had to be amputated above the knee. She appeared to be recovering satisfactorily when she haemorrhaged suddenly and collapsed, never to regain consciousness.[1]

Lady Randolph had continued to live an independent life, extravagant, frivolous, exuberant. Her expensive tastes drove even Churchill − a hearty free spender himself − to distraction. She blazed her own path through society, regardless of any gossip or sniggers that might accompany her behaviour. In 1918, aged sixty-four, she took her wedding vows for the third time, marrying Montagu Phippen Porch, a country gentleman from near Glastonbury who was three years younger than Churchill. They lived happily together. For Churchill, she still shone brightly like the 'Evening Star'. He loved her dearly − but still at a distance. She had lobbied indefatigably, often shamelessly, on his behalf when he was a young man set on a great career. She had followed his political fortunes anxiously but with a growing pride. When he was down, she had defended him valiantly; when he was up, no one had applauded more loudly. 'I do not feel a sense of tragedy,' Churchill wrote to Lord Curzon, 'but only of loss . . . The wine of life was in her veins. Sorrows and storms were conquered by her nature & on the whole it was a life of sunshine.'[2]

Two months later, Churchill's youngest daughter, Marigold Francis ('the Duckadilly'), aged two years and nine months, died of septicaemia. Clementine, who with Winston was at her bedside at the end, reacted instinctively, emitting 'a succession of wild shrieks'. Prostrate with anguish, the parents travelled to Lochmore to join their children. After a fortnight, Clementine returned to London and Churchill went on to Dunrobin to stay with his friend, the Duke of Sutherland. As usual, he found solace in painting the wild countryside, 'a beautiful river', the 'crimson and golden hills in the background'. But their injury was 'heavy and painful'. Neither Churchill nor Clementine could ever forget 'the hurt of the Duckadilly'. As late as 1945, he and Clementine encouraged his secretary, Elizabeth Nel, who was about to be married, to have four children: 'One for Mother, one for Father, one for Accidents and one for Increase'.[3]

All that autumn, Clementine fretted. In December, her three children, Diana, Randolph, and Sarah were stricken with influenza; so was her house maid. The strain proved too much for her. Run down by a series of tragedies (her brother, William Hozier, aged thirty-four, had shot himself dead in a Paris hotel that April), Clementine collapsed from nervous exhaustion. Complaining of breathlessness, her blood pressure dangerously low, she was ordered to rest. Later, she joined Churchill in Cannes, recuperating in the luxurious surroundings of the Riviera. Ever since the death of Marigold, Clementine had wanted another child. While at Cannes, she found that she was pregnant again. 'I do beg you darling,' Winston implored, be extra careful not to 'fatigue' yourself. As Clementine's pregnancy neared its end, he prayed 'to God to watch over us'. 'I so look forward to seeing you safe & well with a new darling kitten to cherish.' On 15 September, Mary, their fifth and last child, was born.[4]

The calamities of 1921 took their melancholy toll on Churchill. Approaching fifty, he reflected: 'Another twenty years will bring me the end of my allotted span even if I have so long . . . I will take what comes.' By the end of 1922, recovering from his appenticitis operation and the shock of 'the most sensational defeat of the elections', he too began to show signs of wear. Less portly, balding, his high-domed forehead dominated his gaunt, more heavily lined features, denying him (at least temporarily) that cherubic aspect of his countenance that so many found so appealing.[5] In time, he would recover his buoyancy.

There was one bright spot on this otherwise dismal landscape. His cousin, Lord Henry Vane-Tempest, the victim of a railway accident, left him the property of Garron Towers in Country Antrim, a holding that realized an annual income of £4,000. By September 1922 he was able to purchase Chartwell Manor, an estate of about eighty acres, including a lake fed by a spring, near Westerham, Kent. It cost him £5,000. Churchill had first seen Chartwell the previous summer. Captivated by its location on a hill overlooking the Weald of Kent, he had determined to purchase it come what may. Clementine did not share his enthusiasm and was 'appalled' at the run-down state of the property. But Churchill was undaunted and completed the sale without consulting Clementine.

'Devastated', she believed that he had acted towards her with 'less than candour'. She had good cause to believe that she had been badly done by. Chartwell never excited her to same degree that it did Churchill; and she never reconciled herself fully to it. By contrast, his enthusiasm for his landed estate was pitched to the highest possible key. He positively basked in his role of country gentleman. Much of his energy and money went into rennovating the house and improving and expanding his domain. Chartwell came to occupy a central part of his life.[6]

Until October 1924, when he was returned for the Epping division of Essex, Churchill was without a seat in Parliament. To get back to the House, he had fought four elections and lost three – at Dundee, West Leicester, and Westminster, the latter by the narrowest of margins, after what he later described as 'the most exciting, stirring, sensational election' he had ever fought. Three successive failures must have come as a rude shock to Churchill's super-ego. During his Leicester campaign, he had been spat upon, insulted, his meetings disrupted, the windows of his car broken, and met with the haunting shout of the 'Dardanelles'. He might well have been forgiven for thinking that, despite his immense talents and the glorious future he had mapped out for himself, he had peaked as a politician. In fact, his own inclinations, buttressed by his sense of political realism that fed off deep currents of opinion, were pushing him towards political survival, though more slowly than he would have liked. At Dundee and Leicester he ran as a 'Liberal'; at Westminster, as an 'Independent and Anti-Socialist'. Finally, in October 1924, success came at Epping as a 'Constitutionalist', but with the full backing of the Conservative Central Office, winning a majority of just under 10,000. A year later, he officially rejoined the Conservative Party, allowing himself the ultimate accolade of being re-elected to the Carlton Club.[7]

Churchill was inhibited from switching sides too quickly. For one thing, Clementine did not trust the Tories. Do not sell yourself too cheap, she beseeched her husband, 'They have treated you so badly in the past & they ought to be made to pay.' He may also have been deterred by Sir Charles Dilke's warning that 'The rat may leave the sinking ship once, but not twice. The second time you're done for.' It took, as Churchill charmingly explained later, 'a certain amount of ingenuity to re-rat'. He commented at the time, 'the thing is to be "Conservative in principle but liberal in sympathy"'.[8]

By 1924 Bonar Law had gone, serving only 209 days as Prime Minister, having died tragically from cancer of the throat. Bonar Law had neither liked nor trusted Churchill. His successor, Stanley Baldwin, was more amenable. Baldwin thought of himself as a progressive Conservative.[9] Churchill was of similar mind. His first commitment in politics had been to his father's catch-slogan, 'Tory Democracy'. Once again, he took up its cause. 'I am what I have always been – a Tory Democrat,' he told the Conservative ex-Chancellor, Sir Robert Horne. Justifying to himself his departure from Liberal ranks, he confided to Clementine that a 'strong Conservative Party with an overwhelming majority and a moderate even progressive leadership . . . might well be the fulfilment of all that Dizzy and my father aimed at'.[10] To Baldwin he promised to bring with him between thirty to fifty like-minded Liberal MPs, a bait he dangled without Lloyd George's knowledge. He was aided in these efforts by Austen Chamberlain and Balfour, once Lloyd Georgian Conservatives but now returned to the fold, who were anxious to see Churchill join them, as well as by rising Tory rightists like Sir Samuel Hoare. By the summer of 1924, Baldwin felt able to reassure Austen Chamberlain that 'Winston, in private, accepts our policy'. This was but the consummation of his steady drift to the right, a trend, noted by many, that had begun when he was First Lord, and that solidified as a consequence of his relentless anti-Bolshevik campaign.[11]

Churchill was unexpectedly helped by a general election called in 1923 as a result of Baldwin's move to overcome unemployment 'by protecting the home market'. Protection was taboo to Churchill, who went ahead 'to criticize & attack this policy'. At the elections, the Conservatives dropped about 40,000 votes, but owing to the quirks of the British constituency system they lost eighty-seven seats.[12] As a result, Labour formed its first administration, propped up by the Liberals. Protection was vanquished, Free Trade, still an election winner, was vindicated.

Although Baldwin was roundly criticized, the first breaches in Free Trade had long been made. Like many rigid political-economic principles, this one too had been applied with a sensible degree of flexibility. Baldwin, shielded by the strong protectionist wing in his party, would not abandon the kind of 'creeping protection' that previous governments had indulged in. Churchill could not have been oblivious to these elementary political facts. Yet as for so many, there was a theological dimension to his faith in Free Trade.[13] He believed in it, so to speak, because it was there. At any rate, having deserted the Tories on this issue, he could not return to them until they had abandoned their schemes for protection. Now, he could argue, the issue had been decided once again. Perhaps Churchill turned a blind eye to these nuances of Tory protectionism. Or perhaps he wanted to return to active politics too badly. But he came to believe – or convinced himself to believe – that Baldwin, undone by protection, had learned his lesson. Tariffs, he proclaimed, were finally 'out of the way'.[14]

The spectacle of a Labour government, kept alive by his old ally, Lloyd George, however, was to live out his worst nightmare. For him the Labour government was 'a Socialist monstrosity . . . corrupting the character of the British nation', 'a vast monument of sham and humbug' that would reduce Britain to 'chaos and starvation'. Its supporters, he claimed, 'receive instruction in the Socialist Sunday school in the vilest garbage of atheism and revolution'.[15] Labour took note of these aspersions. In the demonology of the Labour movement, Churchill occupies a central place, with some justification.

Labour in power also signalled his break with the Liberals: by enthroning Labour they had dealt the country 'a serious national misfortune such has usually befallen great States only on the morrow of defeat in war'.[16] Hopelessly split, the Liberals had ceased to be an effective force in British politics. At best, they could act the role of spoilers.

In the final analysis, Churchill returned to the Conservatives because he had no where else to go. In terms of furthering his own career, he was acutely aware that after three consecutive defeats there was no place in the British system for maverick politicians leading splinter groups, whatever their gifts. Lloyd George would be a tragic example of this maxim. But although he returned to the Tory camp, it was never a happy association. Apart from Clementine's disapproval, his past record could not be expunged quite so easily. In August 1928, after years as Cabinet colleagues, Neville Chamberlain summed him up in terms that are uncannily familiar. Certainly a man of genius. Fluent, elegant in speech, a master 'of sparkling humour'. But equally 'there is no subject on which he is not prepared to propound some novel theory and to sustain and illustrate his theory with cogent and convincing arguments. So quickly does his mind work in building up a case that it frequently carries him off his own feet.' Chamberlain found him of indomitable courage and energy, and tremendous will-power, but his judgement was not to be trusted. Both brilliant and wayard, he was 'a very dangerous man to have in the boat'.[17] These feelings were common at every level of the Conservative Party.

No less intriguing a question, therefore, is why the Conservatives should have taken him back? Because if you do not, said Austen Chamberlain, one of Churchill's most persistent lobbyists, 'he will be leading a Tory rump in six months' time.' It would be more prudent to have Churchill in the Cabinet rather than roaming loose outside: to keep him so fully occupied that he could not interfere in the affairs of others, foment class dissension, or generally stir up trouble. Hence it was vital also to detach Churchill from Lloyd George, potentially the most dangerous of combinations. It appeared to work. 'You have done more for me than Lloyd George ever did,' Churchill gratefully told Baldwin, pledging his fealty when offered the Chancellorship of the Exchequer. 'Winston's appointment is genius – you have hamstrung him – so that his hairy heels are paralysed,' was one well-informed view. But Churchill was temperamentally incapable of limiting his talents to such modest proportions. No single office, however prestigious, was sufficient. He continued to tread heavily, and do battle. Worst of all, after six relatively quiet years as a front bench Tory, he would 're-re-rat', breaking with the Conservative Party leadership and going into opposition.

During Baldwin's Cabinet-making, Churchill's name was considered for practically every post, from India to the Admiralty to Health. In the event, he was given the Treasury, one of the three highest offices of state, mainly because Neville Chamberlain refused it, preferring the Ministry of Health, and because no other suitable candidate was found. The offer surprised Churchill, but he took it. Overcome with emotion, he told Baldwin: 'This fulfils my ambition. I still have my father's robes as Chancellor. I shall be proud to serve in this splendid Office.' Others were astonished. Francis Jackson, Chairman of the Conservative Party, nearly fell out of his chair when he heard the news, believing initially that Churchill had been offered the Chancellorship of the Duchy of Lancaster. Austen Chamberlain thought that Baldwin had gone 'mad'. Amery considered it 'disastrous'. Even F. E. Smith's response concealed a sting: 'Often right, but, my God, when he's wrong!!' Churchill had the last word: 'who am I to criticize the selective capacity of the Prime Minister.'[18]

It was perfectly natural that a combative, disputatious figure like Churchill, having recently rediscovered his Conservative past, and then having been rewarded for his pains with a senior Cabinet post, should attract much attention. Yet Churchill came to the Treasury no less prepared than other chancellors, Lloyd George, Snowden, Baldwin himself. Nobody doubted Churchill's capacity or his energy. The conventions of managing the national economy appeared to him incontrovertible. They had served Britain well for the past hundred years. 'Free imports', irrespective of how other countries behaved and heedless of the consequences upon 'any particular native industry or interest'; 'ruthless direct taxation'; 'rigorous economy' to cut wasteful expenditure; 'stern assertion of the rights of the creditor, national or private'; 'profound distrust' of state interference in the regulation of the economy; and 'absolute reliance' upon private initiative. In short, 'you have to pay your debts, you have to balance your Budget'.[19] If this was the acknowledged orthodoxy of running the British economy, Churchill had no quarrel with it.

Of course, there remained the perennial question of protection. Baldwin had inherited from his predecessors measures of disguised protection that remained in force, mainly enshrined in the Safeguarding of Industries Act of 1921 that imposed a thirty-three per cent tariff on 6,000 industrial goods, at the final count. Churchill had protested this Act, but not to the point of a crisis.[20] Although a noisy Free Trader, he had few qualms about restoring duties on luxury goods in his first budget. And he did nothing to reduce protectionist measures on other commodities. In fact, during his stewardship of the Treasury, Britain moved steadily forward towards more substantial measures of protection. Safeguarding was extended, though Churchill balked at including steel and iron and foodstuffs. There was a gap, small but noticeable, between his rhetoric and the premium the constraints of political reality compelled him to pay on this most vexatious of subjects.

Of course, Churchill did not move fast enough for the diehard protectionists, Amery, for example, or even Neville Chamberlain. The fierceness of his speech concerning some aspects of safeguarding confirm the impression that he was fighting a last-ditch, rearguard action, and made him a soft target for continual sniping from his critics, particularly Amery. But he was in retreat, nonetheless. Only a few years later, in 1931, under the impact of the world economic crisis, he told the electors of Epping that 'an effective measure of protection for British industry and British agriculture must hold a leading place in any scheme of national self-regeneration'.[21] Food taxes! For a free trade purist, this was the ultimate heresy.

One factor from Churchill's past certainly worked in his favour when he took up his new appointment: his commitment to social reform. No doubt in the past, his concern had been stimulated by many motives: ambition, opportunism, electoral considerations, compassion, not least by his romantic paternalism. But paternalism in this sense, apart from its somewhat derogatory connotation, also denotes a sincere, genuine regard for the welfare of the less privileged. An amused Herbert Morrison once likened him to an 'old benevolent Tory squire', full of sympathy for the plight of the British worker, who flinched from 'inflicting hardship on them', and who would spare no effort to alleviate their miserable lot, provided it did not destroy the existing class relationship.[22] This rings true. But it does not nullify his substantial accomplishments as a reforming Liberal minister. As a member of Lloyd George's government he had called for the nationalization of railways; a curtailing of monopolies; a heavy tax on war profiteers; a minimum wage; stern measures to combat unemployment; and vastly expanded housing programmes. In March 1924, he stood before the electors of Westminster because he felt that he would be able 'to assist in remedial legislation dealing with housing, and the extension of National Insurance, so as to give real security against the common hazards of life'.[23]

These questions were very much to the fore of Baldwin's administration, culminating in Neville Chamberlain's projected sweeping reform of the Poor Law.[24] If the government was to function properly, it was essential that these two leading ministers should see eye to eye and not compete. Churchill was looking for 'big landmarks' to distinguish

Baldwin's administration and to serve as points of cooperation with Chamberlain. He saw them in reducing unemployment, comprehensive pension schemes, and providing adequate housing – he was an early advocate of the mass construction of prefabricated housing. Churchill's principal private secretary, Percy James Grigg, believed that his chief intended to make the Treasury 'an active instrument of Government social policy'.[25]

But to finance these impressive schemes of social welfare meant imposing a rigorous policy of retrenchment elsewhere. The orthodoxy of the time, which Churchill also upheld, ruled out deficit budgeting. Grigg thought that his chief tended 'to overestimate revenue and underestimate expenditure', a habit that put in danger his 'brilliant projects' by not ensuring sufficient resources to carry them out. 'Even today a nought or two is sometimes misplaced', Churchill conceded two years after he had left office.[26] Unlike questions of strategy and military policy, economics and public finance were not subjects to which Churchill had devoted intense study. In this sense, he was more amenable to advice from his officials, if put persuasively and with vigour.[27] At times, he argued long and hard, trying to counter his officials' efforts to shoot down some of his wilder ideas. 'Don't be so controversial,' he would scold Grigg, after particularly heated discussions. While friends with Grigg, the same could not be said of his relationship with his Permanent Under-Secretary, Sir Warren Fisher, also head of the civil service and one of the most powerful public officials of the interwar period. It was replete with tension, mutual fault-finding, differences of opinion and judgement, with Fisher highly critical of Churchill's extravagant manner of calculating his sums.[28]

The main features of Churchill's first budget were an increase in contributory old-age, orphans, and widows pensions; a reduction in the standard income tax rate; supertax was marginally cut back while death duties were slightly raised; plus a reimposition of duties on some goods. Baldwin wrote to the King that Churchill 'rose magnificently to the occasion'. His one criticism being that Churchill floundered some-what when explaining the pensions' plans. The budget was generally welcomed, except predictably, by Labour. Churchill's most dramatic moment came when he announced that Britain would not renew the Act of 1919 that had suspended the gold standard, thereby restoring gold to its pre-war parity of $4.86. Years later, Churchill recalled this incident as the 'biggest blunder in his life', the result of Sir Montagu Norman's incessant 'blandishments'.[29]

Even at a distance of seventy-odd years, it is difficult to discover in Sir Montagu Norman, Governor of the Bank of England, any redeeming features. Austere in appearance and rigid in outlook, a believer in the occult, virulently anti-semitic, theatrical and highly strung, he projected an image of gloom, caution, and disagreeable eccentricity. A confirmed bachelor, Norman made the Bank of England his 'sole mistress', jealously shrouding her charms in mystery rather than revealing them in public. He had shamelessly flattered Churchill. 'I will make you the golden Chancellor,' he promised.[30] At the time, the decision to return to the gold standard provoked little controversy. Only when its return had so manifestly failed in its aims of stimulating the economy and reducing unemployment was it generally condemned.

Churchill had gone into the question most thoroughly. He held colloquiums, pitting the critics, Keynes and McKenna, against the protagonists, Sir Otto Niemeyer and Lord Bradbury, both Treasury figures. Was he out of his depth on this complex matter? He made clear that he had not arrived at any adverse conclusions. 'On the contrary,' he told his officials, not without a touch of irony, 'I am ready to and anxious to be convinced as far as my limited comprehension of these extremely technical matters will permit.' There were a few hostile voices, those of Leo Amery, Lloyd George, and Beaverbrook. Some academic economists, John Maynard Keynes and Hubert Henderson, forecast the direst of consequences: increased unemployment, a trade depression, a sharpening of class conflict – precisely the opposite effects that Churchill wished. But these were minority opinions. The overwhelming majority of responses to Churchill's investigation were positive. It was widely held that the British pound would be only slightly overvalued, not only in relation to the dollar, but more crucially towards other European currencies.[31]

Given the generally favourable consensus, why should Churchill, with his self-advertised 'limited comprehension', have opposed the decision? Apart from domestic considerations, other factors were at stake. The United States, Canada, and Germany were already on the gold standard; France, Holland, and Italy were about to decide in favour; South Africa, New Zealand, and Australia awaited a signal from London. Could Britain afford to remain outside this charmed financial circle? 'You have been a politician,' he finally challenged a sceptical McKenna, 'what decision would you take?' 'There is no escape,' came back the reply, 'you have to go back; but it will be hell.' Perhaps Churchill's enduring optimism vanquished the criticism of the few dissenting academics and politicians. Or perhaps, against his better instincts, Churchill succumbed to what Grigg called his 'great hankering to be considered orthodox', particularly to dismay his many critics in the City and among the Tories. At any rate, it is difficult to conclude that any other Chancellor, or government, would have decided differently.

It proved to be a most disastrous ruling; and for the very same reasons elaborated upon by the academics. An overvalued pound ushered in a period of harder times: high unemployment, a drop in exports, wage cuts, and fierce industrial strife, culminating in the General Strike.

Churchill's anger for leading him down this anti-social path was directed against his 'distinguished' officials.

'They have pursued inflexibly a strict, rigid, highly particularist line of action ... almost entirely unsatisfactory in its reactions upon the wider social, industrial and political spheres'. But his most withering scorn was reserved for Sir Montagu Norman. At one Cabinet meeting, he suddenly 'exploded' against Norman, his pedantry and his deflationary policies. 'I have gone the whole hog against gold,' he cried in February 1932, 'To hell with it!' adding, 'Surely it will become a public necessity to get rid of Montagu Norman. No man has ever been stultified as he has been in his fourteen years' policy.'[32]

It has been said that Baldwin sought to take 'all the heat' out of class conflict in Britain.[33] One of his motives in appointing Churchill Chancellor had been to keep him at arm's length from Labour. Even though Churchill had also proclaimed that the aim of his policy was 'the appeasement of class bitterness',[34] there were early indications that this would prove more difficult than envisaged. The 'Tonypandy syndrome' was too deeply engraved to be erased by well-meaning words. Philip Snowden, his Labour predecessor, had already marked him down as 'a menace to the national interest', and then went on roundly to condemn his first budget as 'the worst rich man's Budget ever presented', an inevitable political jibe, but one that went down well with the Labour voter. Churchill's careless tongue did not help matters. In his reply, he hinted that some of the unemployed were malingering in order to obtain relief, a clumsy remark that led to pandemonium in the House.[35]

Churchill's concern for the underprivileged, for the plight of the working man was entirely genuine. But as it was coupled with swingeing attacks on Labour and the deadly menace of socialism, assaults that never ceased, indeed grew in intensity, this became too fine a distinction for the unemployed and poverty-stricken to make. His compassion masqueraded in the guise of a crusty old Tory diehard – or so it seemed. Also, his aristocratic lifestyle and apparent disdain for the sensibilities of the lesser-favoured distanced him from those he sought to nourish. While Churchill was buying and refurbishing Chertwell, he was unable to comprehend 'the feeling of wrath among all people including old soldiers' at this rank extravagance, particularly when he and his government were inflicting heavier financial burdens on the people.[36] Whatever his good intentions and true feelings, he projected to the working masses and their representatives a tarnished image, and it was to be sullied even more by his, in their eyes, over belligerent temper during the General Strike of May 1926.

Churchill was fully involved in the coal dispute, that had been festering since the end of the war, and that led directly to the great strike. The pre-strike negotiations were prolonged and bitter. Churchill adopted a conciliatory position. He favoured granting a £19 million subsidy – that grew later to £23 million – an offer that blew a hole in his budget but which, together with an intensive enquiry into the ills of the industry, he hoped would preserve industrial peace. This proved to be the basis of a compromise that lasted until the spring of 1926.

In March, the Royal Commission chaired by Samuel reported its conclusions. Its author thought it 'very favourable' to the miners, but it brought no respite. Rejecting nationalization of the mines, it proposed state ownership of the mineral; the amalgamation of smaller, inefficient units; and extensive reforms for improving the health and safety of the workers. But the subsidy was to be stopped, on 30 April, and a temporary reduction in wage-rates was considered inevitable. The government, with considerable reservations, accepted the report, and promised to implement it on condition that the disputing sides could agree on its recommendations. But there was to be no enforcement. Given the parties' previous record of success or failure at the negotiating table, this was a sure recipe for disaster. The owners demanded cuts in wages and longer hours; the miners offered 'Not a penny off the pay, not a minute off the day'. Deadlock ensued. The owners retaliated with a lock-out. Nor did the government give a decisive lead. By now the Trade Union General Council had been brought into the picture and notices containing 'proposals for coordinated action' were sent out, though without specifically mentioning a general strike. The Cabinet considered this a direct challenge to the 'Constitutional rights and freedom of the nation'. In this manner, the talks broke down.

Labour ranks were divided: the miners wished the General Council only to direct the national strike, not negotiate their pay scales; the General Council was ready for a wages deal, but only if the government agreed to enforce the Samuel report; while the leaders of the Labour Party were opposed to a general strike and anxious for a compromise. For its part, the government was not prepared to dictate a settlement; and for their part, the owners refused to budge from their entrenched position. Nevertheless, contacts continued, each side hoping the other would break first. The muddled, clumsy nature of the negotiations left Birkenhead, one of the chief government mediators, with the clear impression that the sides were 'drifting' further apart. Whatever likelihood there was of a last-minute settlement was finally stymied by what the Cabinet defined as 'overt acts' on the part of trade union members. Compositors at the *Daily Mail* had refused to set up an editorial branding the general strike as 'a revolutionary movement' and calling upon all law-abiding citizens to place themselves 'at the service of King and country'. This gesture of defiance, made even without the knowledge of Labour leaders, led Baldwin to break off all contact. 'This is the end,' he said. On 4 May Britain woke up to its first, and last, general strike.[37]

Churchill, restive at not being involved in the day-to-day negotiations that led to the strike, was kept informed by Birkenhead, one of the negotiating team. As the prospect of a fight appeared inevitable, his mood, once conciliatory, turned militant. He was apprehensive lest a pressurized government, bereft of decisive leadership, strike a dishonourable compromise. His fears even led him to exchange sharp words with Birkenhead.[38]

Once the strike broke out, Churchill's attitude clarified. 'There are two disputes on,' he told Baldwin.

> There is the General Strike which is a challenge to the Government and with which we cannot compromise. Strike Notices must be withdrawn unconditionally. There is also a trade dispute in the coal industry: on that we are prepared to take the utmost pains to reach a settlement in the most conciliatory spirit.

The immediate issue was to terminate the General Strike – 'unconditionally'! Having committed itself, the government could not retreat. 'We are at war,' he shouted at Thomas Jones, 'We must go through with it. We must have the nerve.' It needed only 'three or four days of firm handling [to] bring the TUC to its senses'. 'Either the country will break the General Strike or the General Strike will break the country.'[39] His bellicose mood was noticed by others. Revelling in the warlike atmosphere, he treated 'this affair . . . as if it were 1914' all over again.[40] Churchill was now exhibiting all his former pugnacious characteristics, deploying troops, machine-guns, and tanks; still wanting to give the men 'a good thrashing' before settling with them. He seemed unable to grasp the fact that bargaining with humiliated and whipped British workers was not quite the same thing as dealing with a crushed foreign country.[41]

Judging from his statements, Churchill saw the current challenge to the constitution as a continuation of his crusade against Bolshevism. He saw every unemployed worker as 'a Bolshevik', recorded one colleague. Evidence of generous payoffs of 'Red Gold' from the Comintern to the miners, dating from the beginning of 1926, had come into his hands, confirming his belief that he was facing an international Communist conspiracy.[42]

Churchill found his niche in this epic struggle as editor of the *British Gazette*, the government's official strike journal. Baldwin put him there 'to stop him doing worse things'. He ran the *Gazette* with his usual flamboyance, and not without a touch of the military spirit for which he was so well known, promoting himself to commander-in-chief of the operation. He interfered at every level, infuriating the staff and leading to him being blue-pencilled on more than one occasion. To the King, who had been perturbed at Churchill's militancy, Baldwin spoke of his 'exuberant editorial enthusiasm'. At its peak, the Gazette put out an edition of 5 million copies, although, as one observer stressed, it was 'a paper for suburbia not the working man'.[43]

The strike ended unconditionally on 12 May, a triumph for constitutional government. Only the miners held out. Isolated, they were forced back six months later, impelled to endure longer hours and less pay. The following May, legislation was enacted making illegal sympathetic strikes or industrial action designed to coerce the government. Never applied, and repealed in 1946, it sharpened class antagonisms. Churchill thought it wholly in order, arguing that it would deliver the trade unions from their own excesses. In principle, he was no different from the rest of his Cabinet colleagues. What separated them was his style and manner of behaviour. As so often in the past, he appeared to spin out of control. It was as though he deliberately, perversely, played a game of one-upmanship at their expense.

This element of *gaminerie* in his make-up, so charming when flaunted in his more intimate circles, had a more deadly effect in his public life. The Labour movement found it impossible to take him seriously as a politician who would genuinely promote the interests of the working man. In one sense, this was quite unfair. Throughout the coming months, with the strike over, Churchill sincerely strove to bring miners and owners to a reasonable compromise; and he did not mince his words regarding the owners' obtuseness. But then, without warning, he would explode, 'bullying the miners'. If the proposed wage settlement 'is not good enough for them', he told Robert Boothby, then 'they ought to find something else to do', adding, 'There are too many miners.'[44]

In this way, he undermined his own salutary intentions, providing his numerous enemies with lethal ammunition to shoot him down. For Labour, he remained the leader of 'the war party', not averse to 'a little bloodletting' if necessary. Beatrice Webb marked him down as a potential Mussolini.[45] The myth, having solidified, refused to perish.

13

Squandering the Treasure

Baldwin's gamble to bring Churchill into the Cabinet as Chancellor paid off. He added lustre to the front bench. His expositions of the government's financial policies were invariably 'brilliant'. As a result, Churchill's stature as a parliamentarian and a competent Chancellor rose. Praise was always welcome, but criticism was also rife. Baldwin and Neville Chamberlain recognized him as 'a real man of genius', though a flawed, erratic, wayward one, faults that excluded him to all but the most devoted of his followers as a serious challenger to the leadership.[1] Amery, his most persistent detractor, fobbed off his 1927 budget as 'a footling affair of makeshifts and windfalls', repeating for the umpteenth time that Churchill 'still lives entirely in the 19th century in his outlook'. Baldwin detected a note of 'flippancy' in his otherwise perfectly crafted orations. But Neville Chamberlain accused him 'of reckless advocacy of schemes the effect of which he did not understand'. 'It is comic,' he reported to his wife, 'how he flounders directly we get to the difficult details'. Churchill sought instinctively 'for the large and preferably the novel idea', and then painted it in with 'the broadest brush'. For Chamberlain, this was a grievous fault; for Churchill, it stemmed naturally from a restless, curious mind. By temperament, Churchill was incapable of applying the high degree of pedantry and thoroughness that Chamberlain demanded.[2]

The background to their clash arose from Churchill's programme to revive the economy by relieving 'manufacturing and agricultural' producers from paying rates to local authorities. The original idea was not his: it was passed on to him by Harold Macmillan, then a young, radical Conservative MP for one of the most depressed areas of Britain. Churchill took it over. As he presented it to the Cabinet in January 1928, it reduced rates on industry by two-thirds – intended as a temporary expedient for five to ten years – and abolished them entirely for agriculture. The loss in revenue to the local authorities would be made up by a combination of better housekeeping and the

imposition of a liquid fuel tax. These monies would then be distributed
to the authorities in the form of newly calculated 'block grants'.[3] This
was to be a major reform: transforming relations between central and
local governments; resuscitating the economy; reviving the depressed
areas; combating unemployment. It also implied protection of the home
markets and a tighter, central – socialistic?[4] – control from Whitehall
over the autonomy of local authorities. Both these concepts were, in fact,
anathema to Churchill, but were glossed over in the excitement of the
moment.

Churchill's de-rating scheme, as it became known, could have been
enacted as a separate measure but it impinged upon Neville
Chamberlain's wider measures for Poor Law reform. If it was to have
any chance of entering the statute books, it would have to complement
Chamberlain's proposal, not rival it. Chamberlain himself was not averse
to reform. Quite the contrary. But he objected

> to any plan which completely severed all connection between industry
> and industrial interests and local Government. It appeared to me
> most dangerous if a large part of the community were given to
> understand that they were unaffected by any inefficiency, extravagance
> or corruption in Local Government. Moreover, seeing that industry
> required and is provided with certain costly local services, I thought
> it inequitable that they should pay nothing for them.[5]

Chamberlain was Churchill's most serious opponent; he also knew
local government from the inside, having been a successful Lord Mayor
of Birmingham. Now widely considered as Baldwin's most likely heir, he
wielded considerable political clout. During the early months of 1928
he conducted a war of attrition against the original Churchill proposal,
chipping away at its foundations until he was certain that it slotted into
– or at least did not damage – his own Poor Law reform. In this he was
abetted by Churchill's officials, in particular Sir Warren Fisher, who
calculated that Churchill's estimate of the Treasury's subvention was
far too low, and who mischievously remarked that his chief was like 'a
baby who must be handled as a child' and 'sat upon constantly'. Other
officials were reported to be on the verge of resignation, in despair at
Churchill's reckless ideas.[6]

However cogently Churchill argued his case, Chamberlain argued
his with greater authority – and support, particularly from Baldwin.
Churchill recognized the danger. Isolated in Cabinet, he would be a
soft target for any criticism. It conjured up memories of Gallipoli,
he told Chamberlain, and he would not have it. He admitted to
Chamberlain: 'I can make no progress in the face of your opposition.
You are therefore the master.' He was not defeated, however. Polite to
Chamberlain's face, he remonstrated to Baldwin in a most unseemly

manner, marching 'about the room shouting and shaking his fist', launching into 'a tremendous tirade' against Chamberlain who was evidently 'jealous' of him. Chamberlain brushed off his behaviour as 'childish & contemptible'.[7]

Eventually, a compromise was cobbled together, although the railways proved a sticking point. 'Be audacious', Churchill baited Baldwin, inviting him to include the railways, a measure that Chamberlain disapproved of. In its final form, the railways and industry were to be de-rated by seventy-five per cent. On the other hand, agriculture would be completely relieved of rates.[8]

If not a total victory for Churchill, it was still a considerable achievement. It was no less a triumph for Chamberlain. He had succeeded not only in toning down what he considered to be the wilder aspects of Churchill's de-rating scheme, but had also managed to integrate it into his comprehensive, far-reaching Local Government Act of 1929.[9] Here were the two most dominant personalities of Baldwin's government, brought together in a measure of teamwork that yielded immense benefits. Their association was replete with friction. But their political disagreements were more on points of emphasis than on broad lines of policy. Even these were eventually ironed out, to everyone's mutual advantage. It was a promising partnership. But although they cooperated, they never harmonized. Temperamentally, they were poles apart. Chamberlain found reasoning with Churchill was 'like arguing with a brass band'. He regarded Churchill as a kind of political magpie, flitting from one nest to another, making off with other birds' eggs, a highly 'amoral' creature. It was Churchill's judgement he distrusted most, as did almost everyone of note. 'Mercurial!', Chamberlain's damning indictment of Churchill, was far from being one of his character traits. Churchill, perversely, delighted in it. To him, Chamberlain was a 'rather inhuman figure' possessed of 'a certain arctic quality', too pedantic, too rigid, too aloof, too bleak for Churchill's more hedonistic tastes.[10]

To cover the added costs of his de-rating scheme and other social benefits, Churchill had to save money to balance his budgets. His plan for all-round cuts included a five per cent slash in pay for government and municipal employees; a phasing-out of a quarter of the civil service, a proposition that aroused Sir Warren Fisher's ire; trimming departmental overheads; the evacuation of Iraq; a freeze on Air Force expansion; a heavy cut in army estimates, while at the same time pressing for 'the complete mechanization' of the army; and considerable economies in naval expenditure – particularly in manpower, and the building of battleships and cruisers. This last proposal sparked off a heated controversy with the Admiralty. But Churchill was adamant.[11] He had turned full circle. As a reforming Liberal minister, he had stoutly resisted naval expansion; as First Lord, he had just as stoutly urged it. Now, responsible for the Exchequer, he again virulently demanded retrenchment.[12]

Churchill's battle to prune the naval estimates extended from 1925 to 1928. Inevitably, there was a compromise, though not before much ink was spilt in anger by the Treasury and the Admiralty. The main issue concerned the rate of building cruisers. Immediate construction would 'ruin' the government, let in the Socialists, and start a costly armaments race leading to 'a new vast war'. He wished to postpone the building programme until after 1931, when, he judged, the finances of the country would be much healthier. Let us have 'a twenty rule' for the navy, he suggested to Baldwin. The final settlement tilted decisively towards the Admiralty, with Neville Chamberlain finally intervening on its behalf.[13]

Churchill's differences with the Admiralty stemmed not only from his understandable wish to reduce costs, but also from an overall strategic concept that was more dubious. In 1922 he had accepted, with extreme reluctance, parity with the United States in capital ships, settled at the Washington conference in 1922, as 'the barest minimum' to maintain imperial needs. Other categories – cruisers, destroyers, and submarines – as yet unagreed were to be the subject of further talks. Naturally, the Admiralty began to frame its contingency plans. These were not in tune with Churchill's strategic conception of power-relations in the Pacific. What was the purpose of these vast naval provisions? he asked in December 1924, if not to prepare for 'a gigantic naval war in the Far East'. And against whom, Japan? He thought the very idea 'nonsense'. 'I do not believe Japan has any idea of attacking the British Empire, or that there is any danger of her doing so for at least a generation to come,' he assured Sir Roger Keyes.[14]

Since Japan was a non-existent menace there was no point in hastening to construct a great naval base at Singapore. Throughout the 1920s, he favoured the 'gradual and discreet' development of the base. He joined in the Admiralty war-games against Japan, but would not admit as 'a reasonably probable contingency' the fall of Singapore. Invoking, in July 1928, his own recommendation that the ten years' rule be made 'a standing assumption', he pleaded for 'indefinite postponement' of the project.

Even as late as 1934, after the Japanese conquest of Manchuria and advance on Shanghai, he was still reiterating that Japan posed no threat to 'our Empire' and lauding Manchukuo (the puppet state that had supplanted Manchuria) as rather 'a good thing'. Only three years later did Churchill detect, reluctantly, 'a somewhat different Japan', powerful, violent, ambitious, about whom her civilized neighbours must feel 'serious anxieties'. He now recognized the possibility of war. General Sir Edmond Ironside was left 'gasping', if in agreement, at Churchill's proposed strategy: to abandon Hong Kong and Shanghai and retire on Singapore. Churchill expressed complete faith in the navy. Not only was it 'absolutely efficient', it was also 'unassailable from the air', a ready match for the Japanese. Six months before the outbreak of the Second World War, he elaborated upon these ideas. He still thought it possible, though by no means certain, that Japan would join 'a hostile combination' against Britain. If so, and given the fact that the Mediterranean was 'the decisive battle-ground at sea', and Europe the more immediate danger, Britain must conduct a holding action in the Far East. He discounted the likelihood of a Japanese land assault on Singapore. As for a naval expedition, its exposed lines of communication, would invite failure, not success. 'Japan would not run such a risk', he reasoned. 'They are too sensible a people.'[15] Churchill's faith in the impregnability of Singapore, the proficiency of the navy, and the good sense of the Japanese was touching, but fanciful. Churchill was no more successful than anyone else in resolving Britain's chronic strategic dilemma of that time: how to balance Far Eastern against European needs, with the Mediterranean thrown in as an additional weight.

If, according to Churchill, Japan did not threaten British interests, who did? Not Germany, still bound by the Versailles restrictions. Nor France or Italy, middling naval powers at best. For Churchill, and for many in Britain, the United States appeared as the most troublesome of the naval powers. Disagreements remained; and despite protracted and acrimonious negotiations extending throughout the 1920s, they were not resolved. The Americans were certainly a considerable nuisance, but to the point of war? In the summer of 1927 Churchill did not think it 'unthinkable', however 'foolish and disastrous' it would be. 'I would neither trust America to command, nor England to submit.' The Geneva naval conference was then in session, with emotions on edge over American demands for 'parity' and heavy cruisers which Churchill considered ludicrous, little more than a euphemism for American 'supremacy'. 'Tell the Yanks sharply to mind their own business', he proposed to Amery.

After the final British proposals were rejected by the Americans,[16] the conference collapsed. Churchill was not sorry. Eddie Marsh had once told him that he favoured 'kissing [Uncle Sam] on both cheeks'. 'But not on all four,' replied Churchill.[17]

Given the capricious nature of the international system, Churchill was not, in general, over-sympathetic to disarmament plans. Security came from strength and independence of decision, not from ambiguous documents and paper agreements. In particular, France needed to protect herself against possible German aggression and Britain against 'American naval power'. Churchill was all for having no disarmament discussions for five years: disarmament talks, far from lowering international tension, stimulated 'ill-feeling and suspicion'.[18]

In the late 1920s Churchill could, with conviction, point to 'the present peaceable state of the world'. The Far East was quiescent. In Europe, Germany was down, France overwhelmingly powerful. Churchill regarded their quarrel as 'too bitter' for Britain to involve herself. He still mistrusted the Germans. But he would do nothing to encourage French intransigence. France should be left 'to stew in her own juice' for a few years. Britain could then 'impose anything whatever on her', meaning a reasonable settlement with Germany.

There was another alternative to these European entanglements. Provided Britain was strong enough, at sea and in the air, she could afford to ignore the Continent, even if 'all the Channel ports and all the Low Countries were in the hands of a vast hostile military Power'. In such a scenario, 'It should never be admitted . . . that England cannot, if the worst comes to the worst, stand alone,' he uttered prophetically.[19]

Little more than a decade later Churchill fiercely advocated (as in 1911) the Anglo-French alliance he now so eloquently rejected; and for the same reason: to 'over-awe' Germany. A success in 1925, a failure in 1938, one evolving from other. It was the same pattern in the Far East. In 1931, his 'sane and prudent' Japan of 1925 conquered Manchuria, the prelude to a protracted war that endangered vital British interests throughout the area. In retrospect, Churchill came to regard the Anglo-American 'naval war' of the 1920s, once a fact of international life for him, as 'that crazy time'.[20] Anglo-American cooperation, offensive to him in the 1920s, became a necessity in the late 1930s. The policies he advocated so passionately in the 1920s became serious shortcomings in the 1930s.[21] At the time, Churchill was taking a last, carefree fling at isolationism.

Churchill's gung-ho anti-socialism and his belligerent conduct during the General Strike, his firm stand against American naval supremacy together with his suspicion of disarmament placed him well to the right of the Conservative Party. It was rumoured that he had 'a complete stranglehold on the younger reactionary Tories'. His influence in the Party appeared to grow. He and Baldwin, neighbours in Downing Street, were in almost daily contact. Beaverbrook, no friend of Baldwin's, typically put the worst complexion on their good neighbourliness, confining the Prime Minister to Churchill's 'padded room'. A cruel exaggeration no doubt, but others also came away shaking their heads at Churchill's undue pull as 'chief adviser'.

One factor did much to gild his reputation: his impressive parliamentary performances. But there was a price to pay for these oratorical pyrotechnics. It was said that he was 'the best show in London', a performer with star qualities, a kind of sophisticated knock-about comedy turn.[22] Those who crowded the House came not only to be informed but also to be entertained. And he gave splendid value for money. Like the best of troupers, he played to the gallery and fed off its adoration. But too convinced of the force of his arguments, and too wrapped up in their structural beauty, he would not recognize when he had reached a point of diminishing returns. There would come a time when his listeners would weary of the relentless tempo of his oratory and lose sight of the weighty political messages he was so anxious to put across.

Churchill claimed to be at home and 'in genuine sympathy' with the Conservative Party. Yet he could not escape his suspect reputation. Churchill outshone his colleagues in ability but not in influence. In his own eyes, he was a potential Prime Minister. Five years as a spirited and competent Chancellor should have accorded him equal status in the leadership stakes. But Baldwin would not hear of it; nor would Neville Chamberlain; and neither would the rank-and-file Tories.[23] It was the old story: whatever his talents – or perhaps because of them – he was deemed too capricious, too untrustworthy, too much the rank opportunist. At the age of fifty-four, he still sought a firm party base.

As election day approached in 1929, Churchill's name was linked to other posts in a possible government reshuffle: at the India Office, as Lord President of the Council – with powers to coordinate the fighting services, in charge of 'Basic Industries', Minister of Agriculture, even Foreign Secretary. The reconstruction did not materialize. It was clear that in the event of a Conservative victory, Churchill would retain high office. He was not sanguine at the prospect. Beaverbrook reported that he was 'in despair' and had accepted electoral defeat in advance.[24]

'Safety First', Baldwin's solemn message to the country, asked the voters to keep faith with the proven record of sound Conservative government in contrasting it to the instability and recklessness of another Labour administration. This jaded slogan was not sufficiently attractive. The outcome of the elections was even worse than Churchill had feared: Labour won with a small majority over the Conservatives with the Liberals trailing far behind. Churchill followed the results at 10 Downing Street, checking his lists 'in red ink, sipping whisky and soda, getting redder and redder, rising and going out often to glare at the machine himself, hunching his shoulders, bowing his head like a bull about to charge'. Two-thirds of the 159 seats they lost were in industrial areas where, no doubt, working class Conservative supporters, alienated by the government's ineffectiveness in coping with unemployment (estimated at 1.2 million), and incensed by its handling of the General Strike and the anti-trade union legislation that followed it, polled their dissatisfaction. The Conservatives were out though Churchill himself held his seat on a minority vote.[25]

Apathy and boredom had clearly triumphed. One aspect of these elections, however, deeply intrigued Churchill. In 1928 women over the age of twenty-one had been given the vote, thereby widening the franchise to practically every adult in the country. Universal suffrage was to become for Churchill a universal apology for Britain's misfortunes. Churchill had not favoured the so-called 'flapper vote', but had made of it a 'virtue of necessity'.[26] For Churchill, what was absolutely clear was that the increased Liberal vote of almost 2.5 million were wasted votes that had to be won back if the Conservatives were going to regain power. He suggested doing so by weaning the Tories away from protection and forming a free trade bloc with Lloyd George.[27] This manoeuvre, however, had no chance of success.

Probably unwittingly, Churchill had touched upon the first of a series of controversies that would separate him from the Conservative leadership. In the meantime, he had to earn a living. Whatever his income, it was never enough to satisfy his expensive tastes. As a minister, he had been precluded from adding to his salary of £5,000 by writing, apart from honouring his contract for *The World Crisis*, the last sections of which appeared in 1927.[28] Now he returned in earnest to his work as a journalist and author. Even before election day, he was settling the details of a new undertaking, *The Life of the Duke of Marlborough*. He had first contemplated this in 1898; thirty-one years later he closed the deal with Harrap's, receiving £10,000 for the British Empire rights alone, and Scribner's, acquiring an additional $25,000 for the American rights. These were princely sums, estimated at about £180,000 at today's value. This was by no means his only project of the 1930s. His charming memoir, *My Early Life*, appeared in October 1930; two years later, he published *Thoughts and Adventures*, a series of essays, some autobiographical. There were three anthologies of his speeches, *India, Arms and the Covenant*, and *Step by Step*, the latter edited by Randolph; and in 1937 he brought out *Great Contemporaries*. At the same time, he contracted with Cassell's to write *A History of the English Speaking Peoples* for £20,000. By August 1939, four volumes of *Marlborough*, six other books and 530,000 words of the *English Speaking Peoples* had been completed. For any ordinary person, this was more than a full-time literary career. But it did not include his journalism. He was also composing articles for the *Daily Mail, Evening Standard, Daily Telegraph, Sunday Chronicle*, and *News of the World* in England; and *Collier's* and the Hearst chain in the United States. For these pieces, Churchill commanded enormous fees, as high as £300 an article. Only one newspaper was taboo, Labour's *Daily Herald*, for which he refused to write for 'at any price'.[29]

Immediately on losing office Churchill planned a prolonged trip to North America. He intended to lecture and promote his books, meet 'the leaders of its fortunes', and tour the country in leisure from coast to coast.[30] Accompanied by his brother Jack, his nephew Johnny (Jack's son), and Randolph, he sailed for Quebec on the *Empress of Australia* at the beginning of August. His party crossed Canada in royal style. Canadian Pacific Railway put 'a most palatial private car' at their disposal. Ninety feet in length, it contained 'a dining room, a sitting room, 3 bedrooms, two bathrooms, 4 lavatories & kitchen and an observation platform'. With a cook and waiter, refrigerators, fans, and a powerful wireless set, they lacked for nothing. This set the tone of the outing. Apart from one or two hotel bills, Churchill boasted, he expected no other expenses.

Traversing the continent at their leisure, they took in the usual tourist attractions: Niagara and Lake Louise, where Churchill painted, identified several species of butterflies, and climbed a glacier. His appearance was stunning. Clad in a 'Jodhpur riding suit of khaki, his ten-gallon hat, a malacca walking stick with gold knob, and riding a pure white horse,' he cut a magnificent figure. It was not all fun. He had talks with Mackenzie King, the Canadian Prime Minister. He lectured at the main stops: Quebec, Montreal (without notes), Toronto, Calgary, Vancouver, and Victoria; and inspected Winnipeg, Regina, and Edmonton from the observation box. At Calgary, Randolph chastized the oil magnates for 'pigging up' the countryside and amassing tremendous fortunes. Churchill would not have minded sharing the spoils, and considered buying shares in an oil company. 'Cultured people', he comforted his son, 'are merely the glittering scum which floats upon the deep river of production.' 'Damn good,' noted Randolph.

In the States they were guests of Charles Schwab, the steel magnate, William Randolph Hearst, the newspaper tycoon, and Bernard Baruch, the Stock Exchange wizard. Their style of travel scarcely altered. They visited San Francisco and San Simeon, Hearst's fantasy castle perched on 'the Enchanted Hill', overlooking the Californian coast at Estero Bay. Here and at Hollywood Churchill met the movie stars: Joan Crawford, Douglas Fairbanks jun., Ramon Navarro, Harold Lloyd, Pola Negri. Churchill made 'gt. friends' with Charlie Chaplin, a 'marvellous comedian, bolshy in politics & delightful in conversation'. The great comedian struck Churchill's imagination. If Chaplin would play the young Napoleon, he would write the film script. He also fished for swordfish off Catalina island, and managed to land a 188 lb 'monster'.

Churchill spent three weeks in southern California as a guest of Hearst and Louis Mayer. On his return journey, in Chicago and New York, he settled his literary and financial affairs. His initial optimism regarding his American investments was to be brutally short-lived. In late October, the assets that he had counted on were virtually wiped out in the great stock market crash. Even though these losses were set off by his magazine and newspaper contracts, transactions that earned him £40,000, his financial situation was now most precarious, and for a couple of years the Churchills were forced to economize.[31]

On 19 June 1930 Churchill delivered the prestigious Romanes lecture at Oxford University. His topic: 'Parliamentary Government and the Economic Problem'.[32] The background to his address was the deepening economic crisis. His theme was clear-cut. The current system of government was out of date. To meet the economic challenges of the hour, it needed a radical overhaul. He questioned whether institutions 'based on adult suffrage could possibly arrive at the right decisions upon the intricate propositions of modern business and finance'. Universal suffrage meant populism. Unless British parliamentary institutions met and resolved this threat, he warned, it might overcome them, as it had in other countries where the struggle had been abandoned for 'military chiefs or dictatorships'.

This was a harsh indictment of British democracy. What did Churchill offer as his 'remedy'? Not the present day House of Commons nor the 'classical doctrines' that had governed the economy for the past hundred years. The free market economy of the text books had been overtaken by events. He now proposed to build 'another storey' on the old institutions, an 'Economic sub-Parliament', capable of 'dispassionate or disinterested decision', and composed of detached economic experts. What was required was 'a new personnel', professional, specialist, authoritative, and unmoved by partisan considerations.

All this smacks of elitism. His profound distrust of universal suffrage – the most fundamental characteristic of modern democracy – stands out. He presents it as the overriding cause for the travails of contemporary Britain.

Churchill's plea was eloquent. But he was skirting the main issue. New ideas were needed, not new technocratic bodies. The overriding need was for politicians far-sighted and brave enough to break with the conventional wisdoms of the past. There were such men. Lloyd George went part of the way. Oswald Mosley, the author of the most comprehensive plan, went much further. Later dubbed 'the New Deal that Wasn't', it envisaged increased pensions and allowances, protection of the home market, bulk purchases from abroad, rationalization of industry, and greater use of credit to promote economic development.[33]

Churchill had no such blueprint. He floundered with the majority. He told Baldwin in no uncertain terms that it would be 'a disastrous error in Imperial statecraft to try to base the unity of the British Empire upon the protective taxation of staple foods or raw materials'. He hinted at taking the ultimate step: 'he would retire from politics and devote himself to making money', Amery recorded. Both Baldwin and Neville

Chamberlain thought it likely that Churchill would part company with the Conservatives on this issue. 'Politics', Randolph told Clementine, 'have taken an orientation not favourable to Papa.'[34]

Back in England, the Indian question had begun to consume Churchill. The government had ratified, and Baldwin endorsed, Lord Irwin's (the Viceroy of India) declaration of October 1929 defining India's 'natural . . . constitutional progress' as Dominion status. Churchill attacked it fiercely. 'Will the British Empire last?' he asked, castigating the policy of scuttle in India (and Egypt), ridiculing the notion that the Indians were a nation, and accusing the British of losing their self-confidence in their imperial mission. In the debate on the Declaration, he remained silent, but he was observed 'almost demented with fury' at its tone. About fifty per cent of Conservative MPs shared his concern, including his old coalitionist partners, Austen Chamberlain and Birkenhead. Was he out to 'make a corner for himself in Indian affairs', as Beaverbrook presumed? Would the struggle for India raise him to the leadership? This idea could not have escaped his attention – especially as it was put to him by others. Again, it was noticed that he was 'obsessed' with another coalition.[35]

Churchill's outbursts on India intensified. He wrote on 'The Peril in India'; told a friend that you must not delude 'a vain people with false promises'; said that Egypt and Ireland constituted bad examples, expressing the hope that 'the British Empire will arise in its old strength'; claimed that handing over power to the Hindus would reduce India 'to the deepest depths of Oriental tyranny and despotism'; denounced Gandhi as a 'malevolent fanatic'. For Churchill, 'the loss of India would mark and consummate the downfall of the British Empire.'[36]

There was another, equally distressing, dimension to the Indian quandary. Baldwin had not only abandoned the imperial mission of the Conservatives, he had allowed himself to be sucked into a joint policy of capitulation with Labour. Conservative delegates sat at the Round Table Conference – that convened in November – and lent their support to an All India Federation as the outcome of the constitutional *impasse*. Churchill dismissed this notion as entirely 'absurd and dangerous'. Baldwin was rapidly losing his patience. 'He has become once more the subaltern of hussars of "96".' Churchill was equally disenchanted with Baldwin. His lack of drive drove Churchill into 'a state of violent defeatism'.[37] Beaverbrook expressed the common view that Churchill had 'gone through too many shifting phases to be regarded with authority now. His voice lacks the proper note of sincerity for which the country listens.' Churchill led – perhaps – on 'one subject, namely India'. But it was the idea, not the man, who commanded support. Widely suspected of playing Indian politics to oust Baldwin, opinion had not changed that he would be 'disastrous' as a leader.[38]

At odds with his leadership, Churchill was becoming increasingly aware of his false position. His relations with Baldwin were 'chilly and detached', while his fellow Tories cared 'very little for else than food taxes'. By his own reckoning, 'most of the forces of the left and centre' had ganged up against him. He had stranded himself on the extreme right wing of British politics. However, he took courage from his isolated position! He preferred to remain on the side lines and fight 'à outrance'. But the real issue went much deeper than local political squabbles over protection or the future status of India. Britain had lost her imperial nerve, drowned in the ever-rising flood of populism and party factionalism. The crux of the problem was that eternal bugbear, universal suffrage, allowing the poor silly people to squander 'the treasure which five centuries of wisdom and victory had amassed'.[39]

Churchill's 'breaking-point' came when Lord Irwin released Gandhi, and thirty of his leading 'fellow-conspirators and revolutionaries' from detention, allowing them to participate in the negotiations. Two days later, on 27 January, Churchill resigned from the Conservative Shadow Cabinet, formalizing his break with the Tory leadership. The previous evening in the Commons, he had denounced Labour-Conservative Indian policy in the most scathing terms, describing it as 'a frightful prospect'. Churchill addressed a great meeting of the Indian Empire Society in Manchester three days later.[40] Although still formally a Conservative, he opposed in principle Party policy on the two major issues of the day, protection and India. Whatever political backing he obtained would derive from the appeal of his personality and the force of his arguments, not the manipulations of a party machine.

Events were now steering Churchill in different directions. The financial crisis of July-August 1931 had led to the formation of a National Government. As Churchill was 'painting at Cannes', as he put it, he took no part in these proceedings. At the general election that followed in October, the government secured a massive majority. Churchill supported this 'national concentration', mainly to avoid the 'evils' of socialism.[41] In the great economic debate, he had virtually capitulated. Reality had forced his hand. He foresaw 'the last expiring convulsion of Treasury Cobdenism', proclaiming loudly that 'I have thrown that off for ever.' Now convinced that 'national self-regeneration' would result from 'an effective measure' of tariff reform in industry and agriculture, he asked the electorate to cast aside the 'old disputes about Free Trade or Protection'. When a general Import Duties Bill was introduced in February 1932, he accepted 'with simple faith the new dispensation'. Some time later, he discarded yet another 'classical doctrine', calling for the development of public works to reduce unemployment.[42]

Churchill's conversion brought him into line with other, broader-based forces in British politics. Was he searching for a new political combination to ensure his return to office? It must have been intensely frustrating to be excluded from a great National Government at a time of acute crisis, a concept that was so central to Churchill's political philosophy. Contacts were maintained with Lloyd George. Feelers were even extended to Oswald Mosley, in 1930–31 thought to be a coming figure in British politics. Nothing came of these manoeuvres.[43]

In any case, Churchill was losing interest in social-economic problems. More pressing questions were taking their place. First, India. The passionate, unrestrained nature of his indictment of the government's Indian policy was sufficient to keep him out of its councils. But soon other, no less urgent, issues appeared: the German threat, rearmament, questions of high strategy. These were the topics that really caught his imagination, where he felt he had a distinct, perhaps unique, contribution to make. For the remainder of his political life, they absorbed him.

January 1932 found Churchill in the Bahamas, recuperating from a serious traffic accident he had sustained in New York. As he reviewed his last two years to Clementine, he became 'very sad'.[44] He had borne three 'very heavy blows'. He had lost a small fortune in the crash; he had almost lost his life in a foolish road mishap; and he had lost his position in the Conservative Party. He told Clementine that 'he did not think he would ever recover completely from the three events'. His friends had more faith. To celebrate his survival, and to ensure that he enjoyed it in physical comfort, they clubbed together – about 140 donors – to buy him a luxurious £2,000 Daimler.[45] His political future, however, was more difficult to guarantee.

14

Private Diversions

'All babies look like me,' said Churchill. And so they did. With his delicate bone structure, his natural pink and delicate skin, his fleshy cheeks and (deliberately ?) mischievous grin, with his lips slightly pursed, inviting instant gratification, he radiated a babyish innocence that was not entirely foreign to his character. By now, the mid 1930s, he was, however, a somewhat advanced infant, fast approaching retirement age, with the best part of his career seemingly behind him.

Weighing about fifteen stone he had a serious weight problem, not eased by his excessive eating habits. All attempts to trim his figure by exercises – which he detested – and settle his frequent attacks of indigestion by dieting – milk and biscuits being substituted for highly seasoned food – were in vain.[1] He was not given to disciplinary, self-denial ordinances. He believed that his needs took precedence over all others.

No act personified this aspect of his character more than the purchase of Chartwell Manor, the Churchill's family home for more than forty years. For most families, acquiring a permanent home is a joint venture, the result of endless consultations, careful scrutiny of the alternatives, and usually mutual compromise. These constraints were outside Churchill's terms of reference. He saw Chartwell, fell passionately in love with it, determined to buy it, and did so. Clementine was presented with a *fait accompli*. The house, quite derelict, overlooked a valley sloping away to the south, at the bottom of which rose the Chart Well, providing clear spring water for the estate that encompassed the upper reaches of the Chart coombe, and was bordered by a fringe of beech trees at its summit. Churchill transformed this rundown holding into a domain fit for a distinguished scion of one of the noble families of England to live and entertain in. He spent almost £18,000 in renovating the house. Its exterior was radically redesigned; its inside virtually gutted and restructured. Once he had taken the fateful decision, Churchill kept Clementine fully informed as to what was going on, in his frequent

Chartwell Bulletins, and made every effort to make her lot at Chartwell as comfortable as possible. In its final form, Chartwell Manor included a hall, five reception rooms, nineteen bed and dressing rooms, eight bathrooms, domestic offices, stables, three garages, a large studio, and three cottages. As the house was built on a slope, the dining room was situated on the lower level, allowing splendid views of the surrounding parkland.

On one occasion the house almost burned down. But it survived, to Churchill's immense relief. Although Clementine and their architect, Philip Tilden, had their say, the initiative, the drive, the daring, was Churchill's. His was the master-hand. He constructed an intricate system of waterworks, dams and lakes, and terraced gardens. He built cottages and garden walls; laid out a tennis court; installed an open-air, floodlit, heated and filtered swimming-pool.[2] He stocked his ponds with cranes and swans – black and white – and fish. He planted specimen trees, plum, pear, and apple trees – strawberries, and three hundred asparagus plants. He kept ponies and bred pigs, chickens, calves, and sheep. As he pointed out to Lloyd George he was determined to make his farm pay 'whatever it costs!'[3]

Financially, Chartwell bled Churchill dry. However crushing the expense, he refused to stint. To run his estate efficiently Churchill was helped by eight or nine indoor servants, a nannie or governess, two secretaries, a chauffeur, three gardeners, a groom, and a working bailiff. Constant improvement of the property, stocking the house with the essentials of his lifestyle, took priority over more mundane considerations. However, in the spring of 1938, as a result of badly placed investments, he felt compelled to put Chartwell up for sale at an asking price of £20,000, a traumatic reversal of fortune. In the event, he was rescued from this calamity by his financier friend, Sir Henry Strakosch, who consented to cover his share losses and assume control of his American investments, thereby stabilizing his finances for the coming three years.[4]

Chartwell was where Churchill held court. The guest-lists were long and varied. Members of his family, old cronies, financiers, scientists, historians, painters, authors, socialites, newspaper magnates, top civil servants, fellow politicians and foreign statesmen. War heroes, T. E. Lawrence, show business personalities, Charlie Chaplin, Laurence Olivier and Vivien Leigh, and the boxer, Freddie Mills, would also grace the company. All were selected with a careful eye. For them he put Chartwell on display, guiding them around his grounds, showing off his latest feat of engineering, the walls he had built, or the state of his livestock, revelling in his 'role of landed proprietor'.[5]

These tours were usually squeezed in between lunch and dinner. Meals were gay occasions, often lasting a couple of hours or more.

Here Churchill presided, the main course, so to speak. Food played an important part in his life. He would breakfast (alone) off melon, omelette or bacon and eggs, followed by a cutlet or a leg of chicken, toast, marmalade, and white coffee. Dinner, or lunch, would include some of his favourite dishes: oysters, possibly a soup, Petite Marmite Savoy, or an hors d'oeuvre, perhaps only sardines. Fried fillet of sole wrapped in smoked salmon and garnished with scampi would follow. Then a fillet of roast venison stuffed with *pâté de foie gras* served with a truffle sauce. Next a ripe Stilton and a vintage port, a baked tart or an ice-cream, coffee and brandy. Before retiring to bed, he would inevitably partake of a cold consommé. Particularly partial to cream with his dessert, he would enquire pugnaciously of his guests, after emptying the jug, 'Does anyone want cream?'

Churchill's drinking and smoking habits were also expansive. He stocked about 3,000 cigars, usually gifts from admirers, his favourite brand being Romeo y Julieta. He smoked eight or nine a day, but rarely inhaled. After piercing his cigar with a long Canadian match and wrapping its lower end in brown gummed paper, his 'Bellybando', to prevent it getting wet, he would then chew on the cigar, light and relight it until it was half finished, then discard it. 'His use of matches,' Beaverbrook noted, 'outstripped his consumption of cigars.' He first learned to drink whisky in India, where it flavoured the 'dirty water' usually served him. He would take his first whisky and soda soon after breakfast.[6] For the rest of the day the tumbler was rarely empty. But he lingered over every drink, weakened considerably by great splashes of soda and numerous ice cubes, making it last about two hours. 'Really a mouthwash' was how one aide described this particular refreshment. He would also, as he put it, enjoy 'buckets of claret & soda'.[7] But the real drinking was done over meals. He preferred white wines to red. Usually Champagne was served, virtually without limit. Port and brandy followed, passed around from right to left. Tens of thousands of bottles must have been consumed. Unlike his friend Birkenhead, Churchill refused to go 'Pussyfoot' [dry out] for a year. 'He looks sad,' Churchill reported to Clementine, adding, 'Not for Pig.' (Sadly, it proved also to be not for Birkenhead.) Churchill was tempted, however. Offered £2,000 by Lord Rothermere if he went teetotal for twelve months, he turned down this 'fine offer' as 'life wd not be worth living'. But he did accept a watered-down wager of £600 from Rothermere if he abstained from brandy or undiluted spirits for the same period.[8] It was a gamble he won – only to call the experiment to an immediate halt.

'Of course I am an egotist,' Churchill once told Attlee. 'Where do you get if you aren't?'[9] All the qualities associated with egotism, the too frequent use of 'I' and 'me' in conversation, preoccupation with one's thoughts and deeds, self-confidence, selfishness, a considerable dose of cockiness and self-admiration were to be found in Churchill's behaviour, inevitably in larger-than-life form. As a child, he remembered, he had never learned an instrument, though he had a 'feeling' for the 'big drum'. What he really wanted was to stand up on the podium and conduct, to be in absolute control.

Churchill rarely talked about other people except when they impinged upon his calling. He had little small talk. He was 'very bad at tête-à-tête' chats. It was all business, his business. 'He would talk endlessly about himself and what he was doing', visibly losing interest when the conversation drifted to other topics. He expected as of right to be the centre of attraction, fretting on the few occasions this did not occur. When moody, he would sit silent at a lunch or dinner-party, in splendid isolation, sulkily regarding the company, depriving them of his brilliant monologues. He did not like being contradicted, accusing those who dared to do so of 'impudence'.[10]

Even Clementine was not immune. 'I don't argue with Winston,' she complained, 'he shouts me down. So when I have anything important to say I write a note to him.' He could not admit to being wrong. After the age of twenty-five, he claimed, he had not changed his mind on a single subject. There could be no doubt: he was the star performer, the rest of the cast his 'straight men'. 'Oh, yes,' Clementine once snapped, 'he's very glad I've come, but in five minutes he'll forget I'm here.'[11]

Churchill once admitted that he had 'vy few friends'. 'Why should I have more?' he asked. 'With my busy selfish life – I fear . . . I fail too often in the little offices which keep friendship sweet & warm.' Of course, he was surrounded by a host of admirers, followers, acquaintances and hangers-on. He had no political intimates of the front rank, at least not in the sense of maintaining with them a sustained partnership on an equal basis. Although Churchill would call Lloyd George 'My dear', Lloyd George older, subtler, more seasoned, imposed upon him a 'master-servant' relationship, as Churchill well recognized. Between him and Bonar Law there existed a mutual antipathy, never bridged. On Baldwin, he fobbed off the dubious accolade of the Conservatives 'greatest Party manager', believing him to be a 'mediocre intellect'. With the socialist, Ramsey MacDonald, he had nothing in common. Despite his fulsome praise of Eden in his memoirs, he early on detected the hollow side to Eden's character: a 'lightweight'. Regarding Beaverbrook, never a major politician but a crony of many, Churchill conducted an ambivalent relationship. It has been noted that Churchill was attracted to 'flamboyant men of violent thought', like himself. Beaverbrook fitted this category. His incessant behind-the-scenes intriguing led Churchill to label him a 'Tammany Hall Boss', while, for his part, Beaverbrook recognized that Churchill, when riding the crest of a wave, 'has in him the stuff of which tyrants are made'. They disagreed on practically every major political issue. 'Yet throughout there ran a thread of intense personal regard.' Their mutual fascination with each other was such that they could rarely resist the temptation to get together, certainly to socialize, but, also, when conditions allowed it, to cooperate politically.[12]

There was, possibly, one exception to this list: Birkenhead. They had become friends in 1906 soon after Birkenhead (then F. E. Smith) had first been elected to Parliament, and remained so until Birkenhead's untimely death in 1930 at the age of fifty-eight. Although Churchill later defined their friendship as 'perfect', it was not free of tension. Birkenhead possessed a most powerful intellect. Intolerant of those who failed to measure up to his standards – a classification that included practically everyone – he would, on the slightest provocation, tongue-lash them to devastating effect. One unfortunate judge attempted to rebuke him: 'You are extremely offensive, young man.' 'As a matter of fact we both are,' Birkenhead retorted, 'the only difference between us is that I'm trying to be and you can't help it.' Churchill was quite aware of the 'brutal' strain in his friend's character and trod warily in his presence.[13]

Together, in 1911, they had founded 'The Other Club', with Lloyd George acting as a co-sponsor. Its membership consisted of MPs and peers and other 'distinguished' outsiders, press lords, authors, top military brass, even actors; its purpose was 'to dine' on alternate Thursdays when Parliament was in session. In time, Churchill became its *genius loci*. Not only Churchill's toadies were included, but if he wanted you in, you became a member. Their dinners were generally held in the Pinafore Room at the Savoy. Churchill invariably sat in the middle of the table, with his back to the window overlooking the Thames. By tradition, if only thirteen members attended, a large toy black cat was brought out and placed next to the chairman, challenging fate. No matter how preoccupied he was with other affairs, Churchill would make every effort to attend: he dined there for the last time just one month before he died.[14]

Apart from the American financier, Bernard Baruch, for whom he retained a lasting affection, and the South African, Jan Smuts, whom he held in enormous respect, the rest of his circle can be considered as devoted followers, a prerequisite for any friendships that later emerged. Like his marriage, these relationships were conducted on his terms. Outstanding among them were Frederick Alexander Lindemann (later Lord Cherwell), a physicist by training and professor of experimental philosophy at Oxford, known as 'the Prof', and Brendan Bracken (later Viscount), journalist, banker, and Conservative MP. Bracken latched on to Churchill's fortunes during the election campaigns of 1923–4 and thereafter never left his side as an adviser, a mine of information, and a weaker mouthpiece. A man of mystery, he enjoyed baffling society by muddying the truth of his origins. In fact, he was born in Ireland, spent some years of his youth in Australia, came to England to complete his education at Sedbergh, before breaking into the worlds of finance and journalism. One thing was certain: he was not Churchill's illegitimate son. An ebullient, exuberant, warm-hearted character, he was blessed with an enviable talent for conversation. At Chartwell, Sunday was known as 'Brendan Day', when he would descend upon the Churchills, talking 'like a fountain, without pause', and entertain them with a fascinating blend of anecdotes, gossip, and solid political data. Despite these charming attributes, he was generally judged to be a thoroughly bad counsellor and an inveterate political lightweight.[15]

Among Churchill's coterie, Lindemann, a well-to-do bachelor of American-Alsatian background, appears as the most bizarre figure. As a teetotal, non-smoking vegetarian, and less of an extrovert than his companions, his place at Churchill's opulent table, though assured, was somewhat incongruous. Even when he ate eggs, he would dispose of the yolks and consume only the whites. Occasionally, Churchill would force on him a 'cubic centimetre' of brandy. He was an unpopular figure: self-opinionated, fierce of argument, intellectually arrogant, keeping alive old scores, and also a social climber. Always welcome, he was Chartwell's most regular visitor.

Lindemann's original research had been in quantum physics. Later, he conducted experiments to overcome the effects of the deadly aeroplane 'spin'. In Oxford, his reputation high, he developed the Clarendon Laboratory into a world-class research centre. Many of his colleagues however questioned his professional competence. Rutherford, taking the extreme view, called him 'a scientist manqué'.

Lindemann first met Churchill at end of the First World War, but it was during the 1930s that their friendship matured. Violently anti-German, he was convinced that Churchill was one of the decisive historical figures of the age. He became indispensable to him, a kind of one-man 'think-tank', particularly on matters relating to air warfare, then a relatively unknown and scary field, but also for any question involving statistics. With his slide-rule always handy, he possessed the rare ability to explain complex scientific and technological matters in terms comprehensible to the layman. Much as Churchill valued Lindemann's talents, he attempted to regulate their relationship. 'Scientists,' he told Lindemann, 'should be on tap and not on top.' 'Now, now, Prof,' he warned, 'that's politics. You must not interfere in that.' These rules of the game were broken by Churchill himself, most publicly when he appointed Lindemann Paymaster-General in his Cabinets. The bond between them was unbreakable. 'Churchill loved Lindemann', recollected one observer, although his influence on Churchill was often believed to be deleterious. In retrospect, Lindemann emerges as a strange, even cranky, character, one who could easily have served as the prototype for Dr Strangelove.[16]

Lindemann apart, Clementine disapproved of most of Churchill's friends and mistrusted their judgement. Birkenhead, Beaverbrook, and Bracken she called 'The Terrible B's'. By the late 1930s Birkenhead had gone, while Churchill's relations with Beaverbrook were distinctly frosty. Only Bracken and Lindemann remained. To them were now added Bob Boothby and Churchill's son-in-law, Duncan Sandys. Sandys's loyalty endured. The flamboyant Boothby was not quite so tame. There was a frivolous side to his character that prevented him from realizing the great potential that all claimed to see in him. Churchill took him on as his Parliamentary Secretary when at the Treasury. He served Churchill well, though not blindly. The problem, from Boothby's viewpoint, was Churchill's flawed attitude to their intimacy, pursued not for its own sake but for the benefits it would bring Churchill. Churchill's most significant commandment, reflected Boothby, was 'Thou shalt have no other Gods but me.' In 1940, when Boothby was under investigation by a parliamentary select committee on charges of corruption and had need of him most, Churchill abandoned him. As the accusation was in essence unjust, Churchill's betrayal bit deeply. Boothby expressed himself vigorously, referring to Churchill as 'a tyrant' and 'a shit' touched by 'megalomania'. Other friends made much the same point, if put less colourfully.[17]

Wherever he happened to be, dictating his articles and books, or his speeches and memoranda at Chartwell Manor; building cottages and walls, or landscaping his estate; painting at Marrakesh or on the Riviera; whether gambling, hunting, talking, picnicking, eating, or sleeping, life centred upon him. His was the presiding genius of the household. Its style and timetable revolved around his whims and eccentricities.[18] When at Chartwell, his daily routine was rigid. Asleep in a draught-proof room, its temperature set at a constant 74°F, he would be woken at eight. The morning would be spent in bed, breakfasting, reading the newspapers – including the *Daily Worker* – dealing with his correspondence and other pressing matters. He then took his first bath, not stepping in until the bath thermometer registered 98°. Despite frantic entreaties from Clementine and his valets, he would arrive late for lunch, keeping his guests waiting, staging a grand entrance. After the meal he would sally forth to inspect his properties, towing along his admiring visitors. He rarely took tea. In the late afternoon, he would retire for his siesta. Rising after an hour or two, he would bathe again, dine sumptuously, and then disappear into his study to work until the small hours of the morning.

Of course, he did relax. There were his painting, bricklaying, farming, that allowed him to unwind, but were also carefully considered avocations. In his youth, he classified species of butterflies and grew roses. Until early middle age, he played polo. But, in general, he disliked extreme physical exercise. 'I hate all games,' he expounded, though he was prepared to consider golf, 'a good game for conversation'. He gambled constantly at casinos, sometimes winning, but usually losing small sums of money. Playing cards was another favourite diversion. At Bridge he would make 'every conceivable blunder', while he proved to be an 'erratic scorer' at Bezique – a habit he employed also when playing Mah Jong.[19]

Apart from all these distractions, he talked incessantly and brilliantly, itself 'a sort of spiritualized action', in Oscar Wilde's phrase. Through his speech and habits, he cultivated an engaging, archaic image. Preferring muffs to gloves, he described his motor car as 'the Cart', referred to his chauffeur as 'The Coachman', called for 'feats of arms', consulted his 'turnip' (old-fashioned silver pocket watch), and would solicit his aides with a 'pray' do this or that. Neither was he above using 'short Anglo-Saxon words' when particularly roused. 'Well, its the most absolutely fucking thing in the whole of my bloody life', he exploded, after losing his way in France at the end of the first war.[20]

Every minute of his day was put to a particular purpose. Even when travelling at speed by car he would direct his attention to business, reading or dictating to his secretary; or he would simply slip his black mask over his eyes and sleep. He put it succinctly, telling a friend that he was 'in a glorious mood', having written '2,000 words' and laid '200 bricks' in a single day. Did Churchill ever sit still doing nothing, gazing off into space, indulging in complacent philosophical quietism? The notion seems highly improbable. He was an intellectual fidget. His self-discipline, drive, dedication left ordinary mortals gasping.[21]

Although Churchill possessed a powerful intellect, he was not an intellectual in the accepted sense. 'His cast of mind . . . was always for action rather than reflection.' Smuts, with Churchill in mind, spoke of 'men of action' who 'live on the surface of things'. Even his literary projects were planned and executed with military precision. It was often noted that he acted 'entirely by instinct'. His mind, it was pointed out, was 'not really analytical', rather its 'darting processes' dominated.[22] He rarely saw, or looked for, two sides of a question. This was fortunate. Had he done so, his spectacular record as a statesman might have eluded him.

Churchill was not a religious man. In his youth, he had passed through an agnostic-atheistic stage, from which he never totally recovered.

His 'flippancy' when he spoke of religion irritated Smuts, a deeply religious man. You have never appealed to 'religious motives', Smuts said. Churchill countered smoothly: 'I have made more bishops than anyone since St Augustine.' Smuts was not amused. Known to attend church only for state ceremonials, or on family occasions, Churchill liked to think that there was a God in Heaven. Full of fascinating people, like Julius Caesar and Napoleon, he imagined it as the ultimate 'Welfare State', where everyone 'will have equal rights'.[23]

Churchill was fluent in no other language but English. He could perform in French, but the combination of his stout British accent and his bizarre phrasing proved generally to be beyond the grasp of all but his most dedicated listeners. As Asquith put it: 'Winston was very eloquent in the worst possible French.' Unable to penetrate any other culture but his own, his intellectual tastes remained very much those of the insular Englishman.[24] The authors he favoured most were those who wrote of high adventure, Robert Louis Stevenson, Rudyard Kipling, Sir Walter Scott, C. M. Forester's Hornblower tales. He much admired Somerset Maugham and Guy de Maupassant. Charlotte Bronte's *Jane Eyre*, George Orwell's *1984*, and Henry Fielding's *Tom Jones* were read with real pleasure. Strangely, he came to Trollope only at the ripe age of seventy-three. Appropriately, it was *The Duke's Children* he liked best, as it portrayed 'an extraordinary world that has gone'.[25]

In his youth Churchill was an avid fan of music-hall varieties, and remained so all his life. He enjoyed a good sing-song, his favourite songs being 'Me Old Cock Linnet', or wartime tunes such as 'Ta-ra-ra-boom-deay' or 'Run, Rabbit, Run'. The imperial 'Soldiers of the Queen' was another favourite. Jolly tunes like 'The Wizard of Oz', or from 'The King and I', would cheer him up. He adored Noël Coward's repertoire, and would partake enthusiastically of 'Mad Dogs and Englishmen' or 'Don't Let's Be Beastly to the Germans'. His record collections of Gilbert and Sullivan's comic operas and the martial airs of the Brigade of Guards Massed Bands were treasured possessions. In particular, he cherished the Harrow School songs, his first choice being 'Forty Years On'. But one song he would never listen to was 'Keep Right on to the End of the Road', because it made him so sad.[26]

Churchill was fond of the theatre, but not to the extent of disturbing his routine to attend. Shakespeare's historical cycle from *Richard II* to *Richard III* was much to his taste. But he seemed to prefer, once more, Noël Coward's lighter pieces, *This Happy Breed*, *Blithe Spirit*, *Private Lives*. *Journey's End* greatly impressed him, and he was vastly amused by *Arsenic and Old Lace*. Naturally, Sarah's career on the stage encouraged his theatre-going.

Churchill was a keen 'Film fan'. He enjoyed most of all adventure films, preferably costume sagas with historical themes, but also comedies, particularly Chaplin and the Marx Brothers. *Genevieve*, *Winchester 73*, *The Wooden Horse* or *The Battle of the River Plate*, were among his preferred movies. But nothing could eclipse *Lady Hamilton*. Rumoured to have seen it seventeen times, Churchill would sit enthralled, with tear-filled eyes, as he agonized over the drama of its heroine's rise and fall.[27]

Clearly, the households he presided over – Chartwell, his town house at 28 Hyde Park Gate, occasionally Chequers – were not ordinary ones. As the grandson of a duke, Churchill imbibed his standards from his noble upbringing. 'My tastes are simple,' he pronounced categorically, 'I like only the best.' He embraced the norms of aristocratic life – great houses, regal surroundings, servants waiting upon his needs – as his birthright. He never moved without a valet. Once he was compelled to do so. 'I came all the way from London [to the Riviera] without a servant,' he announced happily to Maxine Elliot. 'It was quite simple.' 'How brave of you,' rejoiced Maxine. Lady Gwendoline (Goonie), his sister-in-law, noted his 'tendency to orientalism'. Clementine compared him to 'a pasha', clapping his hands for his servants to appear as he entered the house. They pampered him, to his immense pleasure: they ran his bath, dried him, dressed him, fed him, nourished him with cigars and drink. He was 'never so happy' as when one of them put on his socks. For his part, he related to them as a kind of benevolent despot. When his 'Karsh look' crossed his face, trouble was brewing.[28] There was talk that he was coarse of tongue and brutal of habit towards his servants. On one occasion, his male nurse, not responding quickly enough to his instructions, narrowly escaped injury as a pair of hairbrushes whistled past his head. His inconsiderate work schedule left his principal secretary, Violet Pearman, in a state of mental and physical exhaustion. Typically, he made amends in the most magnanimous style, allowing her a year's recuperation with pay; and upon her death in 1941, he took care of her daughter's upkeep and education. Violet's case, although extreme, was typical. His aides during the Second World War had cause for similar complaints.[29]

Churchill insisted on nothing but the best. When on the move he was surrounded by an entourage of about twelve attendants – detectives, personal servants, researchers, doctor and nurse, and secretaries. He travelled first class; drove in his deluxe Daimler; stayed at the most luxurious hotels; ate at the most select restaurants; smoked the finest Havana cigars; drank vintage Champagne and the choicest brandies; and was a welcome guest at the stately homes, palatial villas, or opulent yachts of his friends. Living in this refined atmosphere, and enjoying every minute of it, cushioned him from the vicissitudes of everyday living. 'He knows nothing of the life of ordinary people,' Clementine revealed. He never shopped, never rubbed shoulders with the crowd, never rode on a bus. On the only occasion he tried the Underground, during the General Strike, he became hopelessly confused. 'He went round and round, not knowing where to get out, and had to be rescued eventually.'[30]

One problem, however, united him with the majority of his fellow countrymen: the need to make ends meet. Until the post Second World War years, Churchill teetered on the verge of bankruptcy. He inherited practically nothing from his father, Lord Randolph's assets being non-existent; Lady Randolph, a prodigious spender, proved a considerable burden. Nor did Churchill marry into money. Clementine came from a genteel, but impoverished, background. None of this inhibited him from living high. In early manhood, he regularly outspent his subsistence allowance and his cheques, now and then, bounced. Somehow his accounts would not balance. Did it matter? He was not prey to any middle-class obsession about falling into debt. Members of his social class traditionally kept tradesmen waiting. Among the local shopkeepers at Westerham, his name as a prompt payer of bills stood low.[31]

By any normal reckoning, Churchill's income was vast. His official salary when in office and an occasional directorship when not, his advances on books and the fees he commanded for his journalism, together with the odd legacy, should have left him and his family more than adequately provided for. In 1929, his journalistic contracts from his American trip alone netted him £40,000 (approximately £650,000 at today's rates). Two years later, a lecture tour in the United States yielded a further £10,000. As well as his writing income, he moved into other lucrative fields, writing film scripts for Alexander Korda. For a scenario on *The Reign of George V* they settled on a sum of £10,000.[32]

These were astronomical sums, but they never sufficed. With a standing overdraft of £7,000, a tax backlog of £6,000, and outstanding loans of £4,000, he made rather futile attempts at economy. The consumption of wine was 'strictly controlled', central heating was cut back, telephone bills were scrutinized for savings. This was scratching the surface. Nothing could diminish his appetite for living off the hog. Churchill was not built for parsimony. Hedonist by nature, he was unable to resist the lures of affluent living, whatever the objective constraints.[33]

Churchill's life was replete with idiosyncrasies – some of which must have been bewildering to the uninitiated. Nonsense words were very much in the mode as members of the family would greet each other to cries of 'Wow!' and 'Miaow!', before lapsing into normal conversation. His own preferences were varied. He abhorred whistling, loud voices, ticking clocks, telephones ringing – in fact his aversion to any kind of noise amounted to 'an obsession'. He disliked psychiatrists and aesthetes. His disregard of time was 'sublime', believing firmly that it waited for him, as, on occasion, the King himself discovered. He enjoyed driving at high speed, and was a dreadful backseat driver, rapping urgently on the glass partition, bellowing 'Go ON! Now!' to his chauffeur when he thought the moment appropriate to overtake. Fond of indoor party games, particularly competitive ones, he became 'childishly impatient' when prevented from winning. Every Christmas, the family played a terrifying game called 'Snapdragon', that he had devised, the aim of which was to extract raisins from a bowl of blazing brandy. At Chequers, he took up with youthful enthusiasm the pleasures of a pin-ball machine, though not before tampering with its mechanism to suit his advantage.[34]

Churchill was well-known for his sense of humour. Many of his spontaneous asides are of the highest order. Nancy Astor: 'If I were your wife I would put poison in your coffee!' Churchill: 'And if I were your husband I would drink it.' The House, inevitably, enjoyed his banter; his guests, usually, were amused by his quips. But Churchill's humour was turned outwards. He lacked the capacity to laugh at himself. Lloyd George grumbled: 'The worst feature about Winston is his vanity!'[35]

If Churchill was unable to ridicule his own behaviour, he noticed comic aspects in the relationship between other living things. 'Dogs look up to us. Cats look down on us. Pigs treat us as equals,' he once remarked perceptively.[36] Churchill kept many pets: Ginger, his marmalade cat; Toby, the green budgerigar; and his two poodles, Rufus One and Two. They were welcome everywhere, sharing his bed, waiting for scraps at his dining table. Equally attached to his livestock, Churchill shrank from delivering the *coup de grace*. 'You carve [the goose], Clemmie,' he instructed. 'He was a friend of mine.' Every afternoon, in a quaint ritual, he would feed his fish 'aristocratic maggots' to shouts of 'Hike, Hike – Hike, Hike'.[37] These were habits that befitted the model country gentleman. Naturally, his fondness for domestic pets did not inhibit him from gratifying other gentlemanly pursuits: he kept racehorses; rode to hounds; went pig-sticking in India; shot big game in East Africa; and hunted wild boar in Normandy.

Churchill's individuality was also emphasized by his style of dress. He was far from being a snappy dresser – apart from his pale pink silk underwear. With his time-worn apparel, he cut a singular figure. He recognized that every politician needed a 'distinctive mark'. Hats – though not only hats – were his. He called it 'all rubbish', an invention of creative journalists. But it wasn't. Army and navy headgear, pith helmets, an Australian bush hat, Russian Astrakhans, Homburgs, Panamas, tophats, six broad-brimmed Stetsons, an American Indian chieftain's feathered war bonnet, and countless others, were stacked in hatboxes in a special closet. Complementing his hat collection were his fifteen or so specially tailored siren zip-suits, striped worsted for lunch, green or black velvet for dinner. His bedroom attire – nightshirt, monographed purple velvet slippers, and green and gold dressing-gown embroidered with red dragons – was equally distinctive. Amery once had occasion to watch Churchill prepare for bed, donning his 'long silk nightshirt' and securing his 'woollen tummy band'. Even when swimming, Churchill stood out in his fire-red trunks.[38]

In this way he created his own unique private and public persona. In time, the affectations became the man, so firmly did they grip him. Conducting interviews 'clad only in a vest', he was recognized as 'a character', not above lending a hand 'to touch up the picture' when necessary. Clementine admitted his foibles. For all that, she knew, as did Churchill, that 'the common people love him for these faults – his cigars and extravagances'. And he in turn depended upon their adoration. 'When he sees a crowd at [Chartwell] gate he will go nearer and wave to them. Sometimes he takes them in and shows them his fish.' 'Are you happy?' Clementine asked him. 'Yes, as happy as I can be,' he replied.[39]

'Seven-eights Yankee and one-eighth Blenheim', wrote Shane Leslie of his famous cousin. 'The less he proved an old-fashioned Churchill, the more he showed a Jerome'.[40] In fact, Churchill was the quintessential English aristocrat, more akin to the fictitious Squire Western than to any real-life American robber baron.

The Blenheim-Marlborough connection was no less important to Churchill than Chartwell, perhaps more. For a brief period he was heir to this ducal estate. During the Edwardian heyday before the First World War, Churchill, according to a sympathetic Consuelo Marlborough, was 'the life and soul' of a 'young and brilliant circle' that met periodically at Blenheim. In the superb setting of the palace he could nurture his political contacts, conduct his historical research (on the Churchill family), pursue his social life, or simply relax. Pride in the family, its name, its tradition and history and future formed an integral part of his being. 'Yes, the spirit must continue,' he murmured on the occasion of 'Sunny's' death, 'It cannot all end here.'[41] Blenheim remained a constant reminder of his ducal ties, of his aristocratic inheritance. And he delighted in its pleasures, to the very end.

Chartwell was also a family home, left largely to Clementine to run on a day-to-day basis. To have viewed Chartwell in its original decrepit state and then to envisage its extraordinary potential required both considerable reserves of physical energy and a wildly optimistic nature. Churchill possessed these qualities in abundance. Clementine did not. Of an innately pessimistic disposition, and plagued continually by delicate health, she sometimes found the strain of managing the property, particularly on a shoe-string budget, beyond her. Not enamoured in the first place with her role as Chartwell's mistress, her unwelcome, onerous responsibilities led to some disagreeable scenes. On one occasion, differing about how best to regulate Chartwell's burgeoning accounts, Clementine threw a plate of spinach at Churchill. At times mentally and physically exhausted from the effort of matching up to his standards, she would take 'the cure' abroad. Churchill knew that her breakdowns resulted from the 'the work & burdens' he imposed upon her. They found partings painful, but inevitable. Clementine needed a respite, a few days of tranquillity free of the stress engendered by Churchill's overwhelming presence.[42]

For Clementine, one problem was that Churchill was never around when she most needed him. She often complained of his long absences, from her and the children. Of course, she recognized that politics dominated his life. Everything else took second place. And it was in his nature that, whether in or out of office, he was in the throes of one crisis or another. Clementine accepted these constraints, however reluctantly. But Churchill's habit of holidaying alone, neglecting family obligations, was more difficult to tolerate. Clementine exhausted and bedridden received a message from Churchill on the Riviera, admittedly 'a recreant', but still able to enjoy the 'flesh pots'. 'Poor sweet you have had a bad time – & all alone,' he empathized.

No doubt Churchill himself depended upon these interludes to recharge his own batteries, though unlike Clementine he usually took refuge among boon companions in the most congenial company. In one obvious way, these separations, highly upsetting for both, cemented their relationship, accentuating their need for each other. 'The most precious thing I have in life is yr love for me,' he wrote while Clementine was recuperating in Eze. 'You are a rock & I depend on you & rest on you. Come back to me therefore as soon as you can.' Their days without each other left Churchill desolate, drifting without anchor. 'Do you love me?' he would ask affectingly. After another spell apart, he penned: 'Your sweet love and comradeship is a light that burns the stronger as our brief years pass. Tender love my darling.'[43]

One complication, at least, never drove them apart. There is no hard evidence that Churchill indulged in extra-marital affairs. Early in their marriage, Clementine apparently entertained 'wild suspicions'. Churchill, deeply offended, repudiated her insinuations as 'unworthy of you & me', dishonouring 'all the love & loyalty I bear you'. And there is no reason to doubt him. Only one rumour dogged him, that Brendan Bracken was his illegitimate son. This piece of gossip, entirely without foundation, wounded Clementine, particularly as it was never denied by Bracken and was treated by Churchill in a most cavalier fashion, perhaps feeling that this tale gratified his male self-esteem. It seems as though physical sex was of minor importance to him. Perhaps he was inhibited by the behaviour of his parents, his father's terrible end, or his mother's notorious philandering. His young manhood was not punctuated by passionate affairs. He married late, probably a virgin. Churchill's energies, physical and mental, were directed inwards, upon himself. His ego was all demanding. He was reported to have said, 'The reason I can write so much is that I don't waste my essence in bed.' He admitted to Clementine: 'I am so devoured by egoism that I wd like to have another soul in another world & meet you in another setting, & pay you all the love & honour of the gt romances.' As the ninth duchess of Marlborough neatly put in: 'He was incapable of love. He was in love with his own image – his reflection in the mirror.'[44]

Clementine has been described by a lady acquaintance as 'the coldest woman I have ever met'.[45] Even allowing for normal hyperbole, there can be no doubt that she and Churchill were temperamentally poles apart. Puritan by nature, less given to disagreeable confrontations, and conditioned by a deep vein of pessimism, her disposition contrasted starkly with his outrageous hedonism and breezy, pugnacious optimism. It was not that Clementine was a totally passive partner, bowing to Churchill's every whim without a second thought. She often spoke her mind, on both personal and public matters, in a most forthright manner. The advice she tendered him was generally sound, revealing a healthy commonsense attitude. Usually it was ignored. 'You were right,' Churchill conceded, tears falling, during the Coronation of George VI. 'I see now the "other one" wouldn't have done.'[46]

Although in some ways disregarded, Clementine, for her part, never found solace outside her marriage, though she might well have sought it. However, given a softer clime and more exotic surroundings, she was susceptible to those random, but necessary, acts of thoughtfulness and admiration that were clearly less in evidence at home. In late December 1934, when on a five-month cruise to the Dutch East Indies on Lord Moyne's yacht, the *Rosaura*, she met and 'fell romantically in love' with Terence Philip, an attractive and sophisticated London art dealer. It was a fantasy flirtation, as Clementine readily recognized. But, she later recalled, with a touch of wistfulness, 'he made me like him'.[47]

Whatever strains were put upon their marriage, it endured. More than that, it prospered, because Churchill expected – and eventually secured – a marriage strictly on his own terms. The question of reciprocity scarcely arose. He required a haven, a refuge where he could conduct his busy, multi-faceted life without needless emotional turmoil. Clementine perfected a formula for holding their marriage together: 'If you find yourself in competition with men, never become aggressive in your rivalry. You will gain more by quietly holding to your own convictions. But even this must be done with art, and above all, with conviction.'

Not everything always worked out exactly in accordance with this recipe. After the Second World War, Clementine complained bitterly of being 'very unhappy', of 'our misery' together, of 'always having scenes'. But on the whole, Churchill's desires were fulfilled admirably. He prevailed because Clementine was willing to submerge herself into his life. Occasionally she would recite a couplet suitable, she claimed, for her own epitaph: 'Here lies a woman who always was tired, For she lived in a world where too much was required.'[48]

When the Churchills moved into Chartwell, Diana was aged fifteen, Randolph thirteen, Sarah ten, and Mary two. The house also echoed to the clamour of nursery sounds and teenage pursuits. This was to Churchill's liking. His schedule permitting, he relaxed with his children in an easygoing, indulgent manner that eluded Clementine. As 'a spoilt and naughty child' himself, he could relate to them at their own level. It was fun to be in his company. But growing up in Churchill's shadow had its family drawbacks. 'We soon became aware,' wrote Mary, 'that our parents' main interest and time were consumed by immensely important tasks, besides which our own demands and concerns were trivial'.[49]

Both elder daughters, Diana and Sarah, led troubled lives. Their relationship with Clementine was often clouded. Churchill was more forbearing, but his time was usually occupied with great affairs. Diana early on entertained stage ambitions. Treated with scorn at home, they were never realized. Two of her marriages were dissolved. Prone to ever more frequent bouts of depression, she suffered an extreme nervous breakdown in 1953. Diana never fully recovered. Ten years later, aged fifty-four, she committed suicide.[50]

Sarah was a more assertive personality, her gifts more on display. A skilful writer and more than competent painter, her greatest desire was to appear on the stage. Again, Clementine and Churchill were not over-enthusiastic, but she prevailed and joined Charles Cochrane's chorus line in the review, *Follow the Sun*. It was the start of a successful career as a stage actress – later to include the lead roles in *Peter Pan* and *The Philadelphia Story* – and also in the movies.

Sarah's first marriage to Vic Oliver (Samek), a stage and radio comedian of considerable repute, rumoured to be Jewish, and already twice married, was not the Churchills' ideal match for their daughter and Sarah eloped with him to New York where they married. Once the marriage was a fact, Churchill responded with typical generosity. 'Ah yes,' he remarked, 'I believe she inherited the adventurous spirit of her father.' In time, he even came 'to like and esteem [Oliver] greatly'.

Neither Churchill nor Clementine ever fully reconciled themselves to Sarah's second marriage to Anthony Beauchamp, a London photographer.

It survived until 1955, two years after which Beauchamp committed suicide. A year later, Sarah was arrested on a drunk and disorderly charge. She had acquired a drinking problem. Briefly married a third time, Sarah's remaining years were without design. Although she continued to act, her career was burnt out.[51]

Of the three sisters, Mary led the most settled life, a country life, mainly at Chartwell or nearby, though on her own admission 'tempestuous passages' passed between her and Clementine, and she dreaded 'the emotional, electric storms that could brew'.[52] In 1947 she married Christopher Soames, a professional soldier, soon to be a rising young Tory MP. Churchill took to him warmly. The stable nature of their marriage, their five children growing up in close proximity to Chartwell, gave her parents much pleasure.

The most glaring problem, however, was Randolph, perhaps because so much had been invested in him. 'Randolph will carry on the lamp,' Churchill had promised Clementine during the Gallipoli crisis. It was not to be. There were early warning signals that the burden might be too heavy. When Randolph was only ten, his preparatory school headmaster put the problem bluntly, describing him as 'very combative . . . on any pretext or excuse he mixes himself up in fights and quarrels'. It was a pattern of behaviour that intensified over the years. Churchill, remembering his own painful experiences, made every effort to develop Randolph's potential. It was said that, with a wave of his cigar, Churchill silenced the conversation at dinner to invite Randolph's opinion. Randolph was not excluded from his father's political life, but he took too much for granted. Or perhaps Churchill tried too hard. Obstinate, argumentative, self-opiniated, his overbearing conduct was 'intolerable for everyone'.[53]

At Christ Church, Oxford, he persevered for two uncertain years, departing finally without a degree. 'My son is very idle,' Churchill reflected. Randolph had chosen to inherit his father's egotism and self-confidence alone. 'He has great guns but no ammunition,' Churchill attested. In the course of one year, 1935–6, Randolph made three attempts to follow Churchill into Parliament, and failed ignominiously, severely embarrassing Churchill in his own career.[54]

Father and son rowed constantly. 'One's children are like a lot of live bombs. One never knows when they will go off, or in what direction,' Churchill wrote to Clementine after one altercation. Their explosive arguments, followed by touching reconciliations, lasted until Churchill's final years. One particularly 'gruesome evening' at Chartwell with Randolph drunk and out of control, had left 'Winston so shaken with fury' that Clementine feared another seizure. Randolph stormed off to pack, shouting he would never see his father again. 'Then at 1 a.m. Sir Winston padding down passage in pyjamas, saying: "I am going to die soon. I cannot go to bed without composing a quarrel and kissing them both.'"55

Randolph fashioned out a successful career in journalism, and later as an historian. A skilful writer and a sparkling impromptu speaker, he too possessed a gift with words. When he made an effort, he was not devoid of charm. On active service in North Africa and Italy, he served also with the British mission to Tito's Yugoslavian Army of Liberation, rising to the rank of major. He was elected Conservative MP for Preston, throughout the war years. But the greatest prize still escaped him: to become his father's shield, his champion, his rightful political heir. On three more occasions, in 1945, 1950, and 1951, he stood for Parliament, and lost.

The intense stress of Randolph's life found expression elsewhere. A notoriously heavy drinker, his offensive behaviour scandalized society. Rude and boorish to an extreme, it was said that waiters at the Savoy Grill competed not to serve him. At least, he was uncivil to all and sundry, without discrimination. 'One good thing you could say for [Randolph] was that he was as rude to ambassadors as he was to waiters.' When Randolph underwent surgery, Evelyn Waugh remarked acidly: 'So they've cut out of Randolph the only part of him that isn't malignant.' Randolph felt suffocated by the giant presence of Churchill. 'If I achieve anything they all say it's because of my father, and when I do something badly they say "What a tragedy for the Old Man!" I can never win.' His filial love and devotion was beyond doubt. But he could never bridge the gap between Churchill's accomplishments and the high hopes invested in him, not least by himself.56

For all that, Randolph's last years brought him the one lasting reward Churchill was still able to bestow upon him. After much hesitation, Churchill agreed that Randolph should be his official biographer. Unfortunately, Randolph completed only the first two volumes. In 1968, aged fifty-seven, he died of his own excesses. 'His liver and kidneys and lungs and guts have all packed up,' his doctor concluded. 'He's worn out every organ in his body at the same time.'57

When Ethel Barrymore, an old girlfriend, visited Chartwell in the early 1930s, Churchill waved his arms at the grounds and house and cried, 'Ethel, all this out of my pen!' Churchill never concealed the fact that he wrote for money. 'I do not believe in writing books that do not sell,' he proclaimed as a young man. The same could be said for many of the articles he churned out for the popular press. 'We shall not starve,' he promised Clementine, as he reviewed his literary earnings.58 And as he was forever hard up, his literary mill was forever at work.

Fortunately, Churchill thought 'the pleasures of composition' to be 'true happiness'. 'The pen,' he said, 'is the great liberator of men and nations.'[59] He wrote long books about complex matters, constantly moving between the battlefield and the inner circles of government. To maintain the pace, he needed considerable reserves of physical stamina and self-discipline. 'I did not grudge the twelve or fourteen hours of concentrated thought which ten thousand words of original composition on a vast, many-sided subject demanded.' No less impressive were his narrative gifts and his sense of structure. He possessed the skill to guide his reader through labyrinthine events, to persuade him that it was worth while and enjoyable to persevere to the last word. And his books sold extremely well – the ultimate test, he would claim.[60]

There was a sense in which History, or his version of it, was part of Churchill's very being, a second nature that merged into his first. In Sir Isaiah Berlin's words, he saw history – and life – as 'a great Renaissance pageant', a glorious, colourful procession of 'timeless symbols and embodiments of eternal shining principles'.[61] England's place in this spectacle was unique, a product of her own extraordinary past. For Churchill, England had won her political liberties, her wealth and prosperity, her imperial splendour, as a consequence of the enlightened struggle of the class to which he belonged. It had engaged the forces of darkness. Having tamed despotic monarchs at home and foreign tyrants abroad, it had worked hand in glove with a tolerant Parliament and a pliant Crown, forming an harmonious political whole, to raise England to her current exalted station. Whatever the exact historical truth of these articles of faith, Churchill could look back and claim, with some justification, that 'the ancient liberties' he so ardently championed were more deeply entrenched in England than elsewhere. Nor would he deny that his own family, the Churchills, had played a prominent role in this historic process. He said so, when mourning 'Sunny's' death: 'The three or four hundred families' that had for the past generations 'guided the fortunes of the nation from a small, struggling community to the headship of a vast and still unconquered Empire'.[62] This was a priceless national – but also personal – heritage that must be preserved, not squandered. These values also spilled over into Churchill's history writing. He did not come to history with an academic turn of mind, inquisitive, judicious, cautious. He was an historian with an axe to grind, an axe sharply honed on his Whig creed and the need to enshrine his family's place in its colourful mausoleum.

Churchill's early writings of imperial wars in India, the Sudan, and South Africa can be read as exciting adventure stories. They do not question Britain's imperial mission, or touch upon the squalid side of imperial rule. There is no mention of exploitation, of superior and inferior races. There is no hint of incipient nationalist sentiments that might, conceivably, dislodge British rule. It is a fixed world where a benevolent British empire marches forward for the greater good of all.

The biographies of his father and John Churchill, the first duke of Marlborough, so often described as 'acts of filial piety', are plainly arguments for the defence. Just as Lord Randolph had been spurned by his contemporaries, John Churchill had been maligned by history, in particular by Macaulay, who had portrayed the first duke as an unscrupulous political and social climber, greedy for power, a traitor to his royal masters, avaricious and grasping in money matters. Churchill was determined to set the record straight, to brand Macaulay 'a Liar'.[63]

Both these works contain much valuable evidence and documentation. But although Churchill went through an historian's motions, checking private papers, collating secondary sources, conducting interviews whenever possible, his critical faculties are blunted, and he lacked academic detachment. Instead, when the occasion demanded it, he employed his artist's eye, touching up the picture now and then as it suited him.[64]

With Marlborough, Churchill set out to write the biography of 'a hero', a formidable task. But he failed almost entirely to dent the essence of Macaulay's argument, although he did succeed in questioning the authenticity of some contemporary anti-Marlborough sources. Maurice Ashley, his research assistant, thought that his chief's fixation with '"exposing" Macaulay is like flogging a dead horse'.[65]

Churchill's more conventional histories are no less problematical. He admitted it. Of The World Crisis he wrote: 'It is a contribution to history strung upon a fairly strong thread of personal reminiscence. It does not pretend to be a comprehensive record.' The Times justifiably noted his 'remarkably egoistical' use of facts, particularly true of his account of the crucial Dardanelles episode. Of The Second World War Churchill would be even more emphatic. 'This is my case,' he would proclaim, seeing it as an 'anthology – with his own papers – not a history'.[66] Still, he succeeded admirably in ramming home his 'case'. His account of the war coloured its historiography for the coming generation. A History of the English-Speaking Peoples is generally acknowledged to be the least satisfactory of his books. It reads as a kind of pastiche that proclaims his 'secular [Whig] faith', its finest section (written as he read Gone With The Wind) telling the story of the American Civil War.[67] As he selected the landmarks of this chronicle, 'personal – and at times arbitrary', he stressed to his research assistant, Bill Deakin, the importance of historical myth in a nation's collective consciousness.

All this academic nit-picking would have had little effect on Churchill. The fact that Churchill was not a trained historian had its merits. As every scholar knows, in research it is necessary to be dogged in pursuit of sources, but also ruthless in sensing when to stop and to start writing.

Perhaps Churchill erred on the side of ruthlessness. But he was prepared to plunge in where more scholarly bodies would merely test the water. And he always wrote for the widest possible audience, and sensibly, about topics he knew best. Rarely does he touch upon social, economic, scientific or cultural affairs. 'The story of the human race is war,' he ruled,[68] and international strife and high politics were his themes. He insinuated their excitement into his prose. The most arresting passages in his books are those that capture the mood of set piece battles: the North-West Indian frontier, the charge at Omdurman, the missed opportunity at Jutland, the battle at Blenheim. No less compelling are the political wheeling and dealing of his subjects, from Salisbury's first ministry to the Grand Alliance in *Marlborough* to his his own efforts in *The Second World War*.

What motivated human activity was of marginal interest to Churchill. Lord Moran thought he lacked subtlety and was not 'interested in people' as such; he never threw new light on their activities, only elaborated on what they actually did.[69] It is this dimension that is lacking in his writings. His description of the Russian revolution, his characterization of its leading personalities, reads like a crude melodrama, bathotic, over-written, ultimately unconvincing. In his two biographies, for all his commitment, his heroes appear as unfinished, not to say hollow, characters. He was more successful in his pen-portraits. When he emphathized with his subjects, and when he was dealing with events that he had experienced, he was able to illuminate their careers in a vivid, credible, and succinct fashion, as he did in his portraits of Rosebery, or Morley, or Birkenhead in *Great Contemporaries*.

It was Balfour who ribbed *The World Crisis* as 'Winston's brilliant autobiography'. Indeed, an autobiographical strain runs through both of Churchill's war histories, though as a cleansing act of self-justification. Some inconsequential autobiographical material appears in *Thoughts and Adventures*; and also in a series of articles for the *News of the World*.[70] More enlightening is his novel, *Savrola*, which graphically reveals Churchill's image of himself.[71]

My Early Life was Churchill's only serious stab at autobiography. It is his most enchanting book, light-hearted, genial, spiced with touches of self-mockery – and comparatively short. It evokes the glittering, by now legendary world of his parents. It recounts his privileged, if frustrating, childhood, his adventures in Cuba and the outposts of Empire, ending as he triumphantly enters Parliament: a fabulous success story, told elegantly and with humour. A 'minor classic' of its genre, it still remains a marvellous read.

From his study and library at Chartwell, Churchill ruled over a literary 'cottage industry'. His extensive library, with its specialized collection on Napoleon, was used as a reference room.[72] But it was in his study, adjoining his bedroom on the first floor, the windows looking west and east across the gardens and lawns, that he wrote. The room had been especially prepared to suit his liking, its ceiling removed, revealing the building's old beams and rafters, and a Tudor doorway with a moulded architrave installed. His broad mahogany table with claw and ball feet, on which rested porcelain busts of Napoleon and Nelson, had once belonged to his father, though he often elected to work at his upright desk, similar in design to Disraeli's at Hughenden Manor, propped up against the wall between two windows. Here he organized and brought to fruition his articles, essays, and books.

As a young man Churchill noted that 'A syndicate may compile an encyclopaedia, only a man can write a book.' As a mature author, he combined both methods. But he adopted procedures denied most scholars. Once a contract had been signed, 'Camps were set up; intelligence gathered; reports compiled.' Batteries of research assistants – some of whom were later to be numbered among Britain's most distinguished historians – Maurice Ashley, Bill Deakin, Alan Bullock, for example – did the spade work. Their duties: to collect and marshal the bibliography, documents and books, with the relevant passages marked for his scrutiny; ferret out and check facts; prepare concise summaries of particular episodes; and 'to make sympathetic and cooperative noises' while he created. He would invite to Chartwell the Keeper of the London Museum, Mortimer Wheeler, for tutorials on early British history, or Keith Feiling of Christ Church to enlighten him on Restoration politics. He would farm out the work. Feiling received a first instalment of £500 for a year's labour, amending with his 'erudite pencil' Churchill's preliminary chapters.[73]

Eddie Marsh was similarly employed. Style and grammar were his forte. After the material had been submitted to him, endless exchanges would follow about correct English usage, proper spelling, the placement of commas and semi-colons, the role of the exclamation mark, or the function of hyphens. Churchill appreciated his immense debt to Marsh's expertise. He also took a stand on these controversies. He beseeched Clementine not to say '"very delicious". "Delicious" alone expresses everything you wish to say.' Marsh also relieved Churchill of the more tedious chores of preparing his newspaper money-spinners. For one series, 'The World's Great Stories Retold', Marsh composed 2,500 word outlines, at £25 a draft, that Churchill expanded to 5,000 words, to pocket £330 for each finished article.[74]

Once Churchill had absorbed all the material served him, and his capacious memory left little to chance, he would begin to dictate his first thoughts on the subject. Inevitably, these exercises lasted well into the small hours of the morning, usually to the dismay of his assistants and secretaries. As he recited his ideas, his imagination flowed. The politics of Marlborough's age would invite comparison with what he had experienced under Lloyd George or Baldwin. His rhetoric soared. Favourite words would appear, and re-appear: 'solid', 'courage', 'sultry', 'bleak', 'vast', 'grim', 'fearsome', 'immense', 'formidable', 'audacious'. Often, he could manage 3–4,000 words at one session. He preferred to get as much down on paper as possible. 'I write a book,' he bragged, 'the way they built the Canadian Pacific Railway. First I lay the track from coast to coast, and after that I put in all the stations.' Now, he would take up his pen to prune – or 'wood', in Chartwell vernacular – straight from galley proofs, sometimes up to five stages of proofs being required, a wildly expensive method of editing. At each stage there were corrections, additions, deletions to be made.[75]

Churchill never lost control, imposing a 'dictatorial' regime on his team of scholars and secretaries. Like a master conductor, he orchestrated the whole. Deakin recollected: 'Part of the secret was his phenomenal power to concentrate – the fantastic power of concentrating on what he was doing – which he communicated. You were absolutely a part of it – swept into it.'[76]

It was said of Churchill that he was enthusiastic for any audience, even an audience of one, for that was better than none at all. 'The rhetorician,' it was observed, constituted 'the master strain' in his character.[77] As he orated his drafts, his rhetorical flair often found excessive expression in his books. This was not to everyone's liking. One critic, Herbert Read, found his eloquence 'false' and 'artificial'. Evelyn Waugh thought Churchill's style 'sham Augustan, where the antitheses fall like hammers'. Isaiah Berlin rose to Churchill's defence. 'Heroic, highly coloured, sometimes oversimple and even naïve, but always genuine,' he countered, 'an inspired, if unconscious, attempt at a revival ... it was a deliberate return to a more formal mode of English utterance which extends from Gibbon and Dr Johnson to Peacock and Macaulay, a composite weapon created by Mr Churchill in order to convey his particular vision.'[78]

Isaiah Berlin's defence rings true. But to a later generation (including the present author) it is the more overblown, over-simple features that strike the eye. He was an exceptionally gifted and original phrase-maker. But at times, and with increasing frequency, his style moved into its florid, high-sounding mode. Of Nicolas 11, 'a dark hand, gloved at first in folly, now intervenes. Exit Czar.' Even when he yielded to this manner in speech, he struck a false note. 'Advance Britannia!' he appealed to the British people in May 1945, after the defeat of Germany. 'I don't think anyone but him could have got away with [it],' remarked Baffy Dugdale.[79] The idioms of Churchill's language, its narrative strength and catchy wording, its hyberbole and full-blown rhetoric, reflect his image of the world, how he viewed the past and envisaged the future, his place in this cosmos. It reflects the essence of the man himself. 'Words,' Churchill once said, 'are the only things which last for ever.'[80]

An Independent Voice

Churchill's struggle to impede the government's Indian policy increased in intensity and invective during the early 1930s. He was fighting a rearguard action, with flawed argument. He now claimed to assign 'no limits to the future potential development of our Indian fellow-subjects'. This was pure theory. In practice, he stopped short of accepting the logic of his own reasoning. Any extension of the India Act of 1919, he asserted, would be 'premature'. He could not conceive of India as not being controlled from London. 'The key to India is London', he quoted from Disraeli 'the majesty of sovereignty, the spirit and vigour of your Parliament.'[1] His was a last-ditch stand. 'Time' and 'facts', as he saw them, were anchored in the past: they would not admit of any precipitous legislation.[2]

India provided Churchill with the first of his Cassandra-like roles of the 1930s. His all too frequent outbursts were received with growing incredulity. 'Sooner or later we shall have to crush Gandhi and the Congress, and all that they stand for.' In a striking phrase, he described Gandhi as 'a seditious Middle Temple lawyer, now posing as a fakir of a type well-known in the East, striding half-naked up the steps of the vice-Regal palace' to negotiate on terms of equality with 'the representative of the King-Emperor'. Bracketing the Indian crisis with the General Strike, he denounced those gutless quitters who would inflict upon Britain 'a moral shame' and stain forever 'the reputation of the British Empire as a valiant and benignant force in the history of mankind'. He called the on-going negotiations 'monstrous' in their 'perversity'. He had little time for the Hindus, whom he described later as 'a foul race protected by their pollution from the doom that is their due'. He forecast a ferocious ethnic war. 'If we cannot do our duty in India,' he cried, 'we shall have shown ourselves unworthy to preserve the vast Empire which still centres upon this small island.'[3]

Indian nationalists were enflamed by his insulting, derogatory remarks. In February 1932, in Chicago, he escaped an assassination attempt from 'a correctly dressed Indian' who managed to elude the police in the confusion of the moment. Sam Hoare, responsible for guiding the government's Indian programme through Parliament, protested against his aggressive stance, while Lord Linlithgow, a future Viceroy of India, put his feeling in typically Churchillian style. 'My dear Winston', he began.

> Forgive me, then, if I say that it is not, it seems to me, so much I who am 'mouthing the bland platitudes of an age that has passed away, twenty years behind the times', but rather you who are hanging, hairy, from a branch, while you splutter the atavistic shibboleths of an age destined very soon to retreat into the forgotten past . . . All this in fun as well as seriousness.[4]

Churchill spoke freely about imperial surrender. But how did he intend to preserve Britain's imperial destiny? He philosophized about it in the most general terms. To think imperially, he once commented, 'means to think always of something higher and more vast than one's own national interests'. He had frowned upon every proposed measure of self-improvement. He saw the Statute of Westminster, which defined the status of the Dominions as 'autonomous communities . . . equal in status . . . and freely associated as members of the British Commonwealth of Nations', as 'repellent legislation', as applicable to the odious Irwin Declaration.

Yet Churchill offered no overall conception of how the Empire should adapt itself to the different values of a changing world. And although he pontificated endlessly about India, he was by no means conversant with the complexities of contemporary Indian life. 'He is badly informed,' concluded Ghanshysm Das Birla, who came away disillusioned by his lack of knowledge of the most basic of facts.[5] These lacunae emerged clearly in his frequent tussles with Hoare, who had mastered the details of his case. Reluctantly, Churchill conceded to India a measure of provincial autonomy, but he stopped short of any federal scheme. His strategy was that of a spoiler. The role of the British mission in India, he extolled, was to maintain 'our own control for our advantage and their salvation'.[6]

Churchill's image of India, its future and place in the Empire, was fixed in time and space. And to preserve this image he was prepared to fight the Government of India Bill 'inch by inch', badgering the government at every opportunity.[7] In March 1933 a parliamentary ginger group, the India Defence Committee, was founded, Churchill being among its inspirers. He refused to join the Select Committee on India, claiming that it was so 'packed' with pro-government supporters as to make its composition 'a scandal'.[8] When he gave evidence before it, he rehashed his old shibboleths: provincial government must be given 'a fair trial'; nothing must erode the 'inalienable' responsibility of Parliament for India; diarchy would only ruin the previous harmony of the Indian administration. These protests merely had a delaying effect.

In April 1934 Churchill made an all-or-nothing gambler's throw. Had he succeeded, he might well have ruined the government's policy. Documents had come into his possession that implied that Hoare and Lord Derby, members of the Joint Select Committee, had prevailed upon the Manchester Chamber of Commerce to postpone submitting its evidence and then finally to present it in a manner that materially differed from the original. In short, Hoare and Derby had doctored the evidence. After Churchill had raised the matter in the Commons, the Speaker ruled that a *prima facie* case existed for a breach of privilege and the matter was referred to the appropriate committee. This was a most grave accusation. To make it stick, Churchill needed to be fully conscious of the facts. He wasn't. He could hardly have been aware that Derby, a power in Lancashire, had induced the Manchester Chamber of Commerce 'to withdraw a dangerous and aggressive memorandum' – that he himself had suppressed – and that, according to Hoare, in its place 'a very harmless document' had been substituted.[9] On his own admission, he and Derby were not blameless. Their behaviour, had the entire story been known at the time, left them extremely vulnerable to Churchill's charges. But Churchill acted as much out of ignorance as of knowledge, and his flawed and inconclusive evidence was rejected unanimously by the Committee of Privileges and shot down unceremoniously in debate in the Commons.[10]

This humiliating reverse in no measure dampened Churchill's self-confidence. He operated in an environment of self-induced optimism. After the second reading of the India Bill, in February 1935, when eighty-four Conservatives had voted with him, he wrote to Clementine of his confidence at being able to control 'a fairly subordinate House', casting to the back of his mind the 400 or so members who had voted for the Bill. By May, he thought the government was 'absolutely shaken' and 'utterly discredited'.[11] In fact, as was apparent, the government was never more in control. A month later that 'beastly Bill' passed its third reading. Hoare had guided its 473 clauses and 16 schedules through Parliament, making 1,951 speeches, filling 4,000 pages of *Hansard* with over 15 million words. And Churchill had stalked him all the way. Finally, he had to concede defeat. In August, with a crisis brewing in Ethiopia and a rearmed Germany defying Europe, he assured Hoare that 'he regarded the Indian chapter as closed'.[12]

In one sense, however, Churchill succeeded. The Bill remained, as he forecast, 'a dead letter'.[13] He unquestionably delayed the passing of the Bill by months, possibly years. Had it been passed earlier, it would almost certainly have been operable before the outbreak of war. Not only had Churchill's violent agitation divided the Conservative Party, it had also fostered doubts in India as to Britain's actual intentions. Even so, it failed to satisfy the Indian nationalists, and even at one stage, the Indian Princes. Churchill's unbridled campaign fanned an already inflamed atmosphere. The government, it seemed clear, was intent on perpetuating British rule under a cloud of woolly phrases. This was a bleak legacy for any future attempt to settle the Indian question.

The Indian episode confirmed for many that Churchill had learned nothing from the past. Unable to make a rational decision, he was always shooting off at a precarious tangent, spouting the most dangerous nonsense. Widely believed that his aim was to topple the government, his ambition, apparently, knew no bounds. Nothing was sacred, not even the the unity of the Party that he had rejoined, barely ten years ago, professing his lasting allegiance. Matters were exacerbated when Randolph, in January 1935, resolved to fight the Wavertree by-election, ardently endorsing his father's Indian line. Churchill realized the dangers yet was unable to resist taking the plunge himself. Eventually, he spoke in Randolph's support, lashing out at the Socialists who had foisted their Indian Federal policy upon a spineless Conservative Party, claiming that the issues were too momentous to allow of 'loyalty to a party, or to a local organization, or to a Government, or to a leader like Mr Baldwin'.[14] Randolph lost. And as he had split the Conservative vote to put the Socialist in, Churchill's own position worsened. He confided to Clementine: 'It is nothing to me whether I am in Parliament or not, if I cannot defend the causes in which I believe'. He gained a vote of confidence at Epping in convincing fashion.[15] But observers drew the obvious conclusion: what was true for his irresponsible antics over India held no less for other controversial topics.

In the spring of 1933, Churchill warned the Commons of 'the tumultuous insurgency of ferocity and war spirit in Germany'. Given her current militant temper, nurtured by grievances that remained unresolved, he forecast a 'renewal of general European war' within 'a measurable distance' of time should Germany attain equality of arms.[16] In theory, 'equality of rights' in arms had already been granted by the Disarmament Conference the previous December. This prospect took on a most alarming aspect when Hitler, whom he was already convinced would 'resort to armed force' at the first available opportunity,[17] came to power at the end of January 1933. When Germany bolted the Conference and the League of Nations that autumn, his fear hardened. Churchill never faltered in his judgement: a resurgent, rearmed Germany, bent on reversing the decisions of Versailles in defiance of the other European powers, meant war. But many felt that some of Germany's complaints were justified. Questions such as the Polish Corridor or the ex-German colonies were frequently mentioned, also by Churchill. But he set stiff conditions for any treaty revisions. He wanted an overall European settlement within a system of collective security, but nothing 'just to keep the Nazi kettle boiling'.[18]

Nor were Churchill's first impressions of Hitler as clear-cut as generally assumed. Was Hitler 'a harmless lunatic or a gallant ex-corporal out to restore the morale of his country?' he asked his dinner companions at the Other Club. He admired Hitler's 'perseverance and the vital force' that enabled him 'to challenge, defy, conciliate, or overcome, all the authorities or resources which barred his path'. 'History,' he wrote, 'is replete with examples of men who have risen to power by employing stern, grim, and even frightful methods, but who, nevertheless, when their life is revealed as a whole, have been regarded as great figures whose lives have enriched the story of mankind. So may it be with Hitler.' For the readers of the *Evening Standard*, he expounded: 'One may dislike Hitler's system and yet admire his patriotic achievement. If our country were defeated I hope we should find a champion as indomitable to restore our courage and lead us back to our place among the nations'.[19]

Of course, Churchill was horrified by the barbaric nature of 'Hitler's system', its bogus racialist theories and virulent anti-semitism, its savage proscriptions of political opponents, the merciless crushing of any semblance of democratic political life. For Churchill, Hitler was also 'the gangster', a despot who fed off 'currents of hatred so intense as to sear the souls of those who swim upon them'.[20] But however much Churchill abhorred the Nazi regime, he was sophisticated enough to accept that other nations resolved their internal problems in their own way, in the context of their own past and tradition. He had also expressed misgivings at the manner in which Britain's established parliamentary institutions had failed to respond to the economic and social challenges of the time. Germany, without the benefit of Britain's infinitely flexible 'limited hereditary monarchy', pursued an alternative, more terrifying course. However unpalatable, Churchill could have lived with this. What he could not stomach was the combination of Nazism and a rampant Germany. Such a Germany would inevitably turn on its neighbours, upsetting the European balance, eventually dragging in Britain to defend its most basic interests. Churchill was more concerned with the dynamics of German rearmament than with the nature of the Nazi regime.[21]

In varying degrees, these views represented a broad spectrum of opinion among British policy-makers. Where Churchill differed was that he expressed his views in public repeatedly and vigorously, unshackled by the constraints of office. Moved by a deep foreboding that the inner momentum of Nazism, unless checked, would explode into a general conflict, his campaign took on the spirit of a crusade. Churchill wished to bargain from a position of strength. Time and again he made the point of not allowing 'diplomacy' to run ahead of 'preparedness'.[22] Increased rearmament, it was assumed, was a sure recipe for a more effective diplomatic posture.

By rearmament, he meant almost exclusively rearmament in the air. By now – 1933–5 – the government had reached much the same conclusions. The Disarmament Conference had petered out inconclusively; tentative Anglo-German negotiations for a convention of sorts had also run into the ground. And so a high-powered body, the Defence Requirements Committee (DRC) was set up, composed of Sir Robert Vansittart and Sir Warren Fisher (heads of the Foreign Office and Treasury), and Sir Maurice Hankey (Secretary to the Cabinet) – and the Chiefs of Staff. Germany rather than Japan was now designated as 'the ultimate potential enemy against whom our "long range" defence policy has to be directed'. This implied coming to an accommodation with Japan, even at the expense of the American connection. During 1934 an unsuccessful attempt was made to seek an Anglo-Japanese *rapprochement*. The foreclosure on the Japanese alternative severely restricted Britain's diplomatic and strategic options, particularly as the United States displayed marked reluctance to cooperate in Far Eastern affairs, and as 1935 progressed, the Mediterranean evolved into another area of potential conflict. The German threat intensified; but so did that of Japan and Italy.

To rectify Britain's defence deficiencies, the DRC proposed completing a fifty-two squadron scheme, the creation of an expeditionary force of four infantry divisions, one cavalry division, and one tank brigade, while the navy, bound by international agreements, would have its capital ships modernized and auxiliary services improved. Even this modest programme, planned to be executed within five years, proved beyond the means of the government. In July 1934, inspired by Neville Chamberlain, the DRC's proposals were recast, its resources re-allocated. The army, its portion cut by half, was the chief casualty. Chamberlain sanctioned clear priority to expansion in the air. 'Scheme A' was adopted, intended to increase the air force's strength to match projected German air strength for 1939.[23] The final report of the DRC in 1935 reflected the deteriorating international situation. Germany was openly rearming; Italy was on the rampage in East Africa; Japan was bent on dominating the Far East; France was divided and unreliable; and the United States was as isolationist as ever. The Report warned against any hostilities with Japan and any other power lying across the lines of communication with the Far East. Once again, accommodation with Japan was prescribed, together with every effort 'to promote and maintain friendly relations with Germany'. But in the final analysis, Britain could look only to her own strength. The navy was allocated a new standard: a fleet based in Far Eastern waters strong enough to deter Japan, while maintaining in all circumstances a home fleet powerful enough to ward off the German danger. Army strength was also increased and a territorial reserve added to be mobilized within eight months after the outbreak of war. In the air, yet another scheme was adopted, increasing it yet again by just over fifty per cent, three months later it was stepped up again.[24]

British rearmament had begun. The rulings reflected reasonably accurately Churchill's own strategic priorities. By December 1936, he was heartened by the navy's proficiency and strength. Overwhelmingly powerful in European waters, far stronger in fact than in 1914, he called for command of the Mediterranean, 'which Marlborough, my illustrious ancestor, first established', an aim he articulated many times throughout the 1930s. Not content with commanding the Mediterranean, Churchill sought also to dominate the Baltic, reviving his designs from the First World War, proposing to station there permanently a fleet based on the Russian port of Kronstadt. Hankey, echoing a widespread feeling in Whitehall, mocked these ideas as 'fantastic'.[25]

Nor did Churchill perceive an urgent threat in the Far East. 'Vain is the menace', he wrote in March 1939, that Japan would dare to despatch a force to conquer Singapore, and then advance on Australia. Such 'a wild adventure' would end in disaster, he promised. 'Do not therefore let us worry about this bugbear.' Only if Britain were 'decisively defeated' would the Japanese, an 'eminently sensible people', run the risk. From this assessment sprang a grave strategic choice. In the event of war, no 'powerful fleet' would be sent immediately to the Pacific, despite a definite obligation to Australia (and New Zealand) to do so. Banking on Singapore surviving, British holdings in the area would be secured with minimum resources, bearing 'losses and punishment', until a conclusive decision was reached in Europe; only then would Britain divert the full weight of her power against Japan.[26]

One reason for Churchill's confidence that Britain could dominate home waters, take the offensive in the Baltic, seize command of the Mediterranean, and simultaneously hold the ring in the Far East, was his belief that the navy was 'Absolutely efficient' and virtually immune from destruction. Chatfield, First Sea Lord and Admiral of the Fleet, had echoed the experts at the Navy Staff that the new sonar detection methods, ASDIC, were '80 per cent' efficient against the threat of submarines. Churchill himself had seen the new device at work in June 1938 and had come away suitably enthusiastic. The submarine threat, he concluded, 'has been mastered'.[27] He was also convinced that air power did not 'invalidate' battleships. Neither of these convictions went unchallenged by his confidantes, and neither stood the test of war. But they were the conventional naval wisdoms of the time. In adopting them, Churchill's faith in Britain as a great maritime power would dictate its strategy in a future war. And this fitted in with his romantic conception of sea-power. Perhaps in his mind's eye he still saw, in 'the fading light of evening . . . silhouettes of battleships steaming slowly out of the Firth of Forth', as he had when appointed First Lord of the Admiralty.[28]

Of the three services, the army came off worst. In 1927 Churchill had called for streamlining the army by reducing its cavalry complement in favour of mechanized units, a progressive, forward-looking outlook for the times.[29] Now, four divisions were cut to two, and then raised, tentatively, to five. This trend mirrored the so-called 'limited liability' doctrine in a continental war, that soon withered 'to one of no liability at all'. In the event of the Lowlands or northern France being over run by hostile armies, Britain would simply 'improvise an army' as in the last war.[30] Churchill did not rate a British Expeditionary Force (BEF) with the same urgency as he had shown before the First World War and he did not raise his voice in favour of expanding it.

Ironside 'could get nothing out of Churchill as to our need of sending an Army to France'. In a national emergency, he too would rely on improvisation. The French army would serve as a shield, warding off the enemy, allowing Britain sufficient breathing space to mobilize her own forces.[31] In December 1937, he was warned that the French army 'was sinking into a condition of chaos and confusion', reflecting the malaise of French political life. Even so, he had no doubt it was 'a stronger military organization' than Germany possessed. After a visit to the French lines in August 1939, he concluded: 'The French front cannot be surprised. It cannot be broken at any point except by an effort which would be enormously costly in life and would take so much time that the general situation would be transformed while it was in progress.' The full impact of his miscalculation did not strike home until the French débâcle of May-June 1940.[32]

Only a month before war broke out, Churchill envisaged a stalemate in the West, at least until one side had achieved overwhelming superiority in manpower and resources. For an offensive-minded strategist like Churchill, this blueprint seems strangely out of character. But this was a logical conclusion from the Great War. Later, he admitted that he had not fully grasped 'the violence of the revolution' in mechanized warfare.[33] Now, in the mid-1930s, he returned to his pre-1914 theme of an Anglo-French alliance to deter Hitler.[34] In August 1939, he also called for an increase in Britain's land forces, 'if we should unhappily be drawn into a great war'. Not 'upon the continental model', he stressed, but, as he clarified to Ironside, 'twenty Divisions by Christmas'. By then it was too late. On the outbreak of war, four divisions crossed over into France. When the fateful battle for France began in May 1940, only ten British divisions were stationed there to help check the irresistible German blitzkrieg, that fell also upon Churchill as 'one of the greatest surprises' of his life.[35]

As Vansittart put it, 'the real crux' of British rearmament in the 1930s was in the air. Churchill agreed. It was fear of the so-called 'knock-out blow' that spurred him on. He described London as 'the greatest target in the world, a kind of tremendous, fat, valuable cow tied up to attract the beast of prey'. He claimed '30,000 or 40,000 people would be killed or maimed' after a week's intensive bombing and once said that 'Through an accident of air power [Britain] will probably cease to exist.' If this was spreading panic, Churchill was not the only panic-monger. Most of his contemporaries shared his views. Even Baldwin contended that as 'the bomber will always get through', 'no power on earth' can protect the man-in-the-street. In a particularly blood-curdling passage, he elucidated: 'The only defence is in offence, which means that you have to kill more women and children more quickly than the enemy if you want to save yourselves.'[36]

As Churchill's Indian campaign petered out, so his air rearmament drive intensified. In three years he devoted at least thirty-five major speeches to this topic: Britain must not fall behind Germany in the air race. 'Parity' was the magic formula. In March 1934, in reply to a most forceful indictment by Churchill, Baldwin had vowed that Britain, 'in air strength and air power', would never be 'in a position inferior to any country within striking distance of our shores'. Exactly a year later Hitler announced that Germany had already achieved this capability. Many believed him, including Churchill, who promptly concluded that 'we cannot catch them up', and announced categorically, 'air parity lost'.[37] Unwittingly, Hitler had promoted Churchill's reputation, not as a messenger of doom, but as a seer whose predictions were startlingly accurate.

Parity was the loosest of terms. Did it mean the full 'establishment' of the air force? Or its total first-line complement? Or its 'strength', the number of machines actually available for service? Did it take into account the 'serviceability' of the aircraft for action, a percentage that never matched either its 'establishment' or its 'strength'? Did it refer only to the size of the bomber force? Should it include reserves? Or the capacity to manufacture aircraft and train air crews?[38] In the heated discussion that ensued between Churchill and his adversaries, no common language was found, or perhaps looked for. The subject was even more complicated by the variety of sources upon which the protagonists relied. Churchill was privy to the widest spectrum of information, much of it culled from official channels, but some of it highly dubious. Dissenters on the Air Staff, Vansittart and Ralph Wigram from the Foreign Office, Desmond Morton, head of the Industrial Intelligence Centre (an offshoot of the Committee of Imperial Defence), regularly leaked to him up-to-date intelligence data. Sir Henry Strakosch, the financier, was another source, as were businessmen visiting Germany, British expatriates, plain tourists, and the inevitable crank who all believed that Churchill was the proper recipient for their impressions.[39]

A great guessing game unfolded. The wildest figures were put forward with extreme confidence. By the middle of 1935, Rothermere informed Churchill, Germany will have 'between 10,000 and 20,000 aeroplanes', figures corroborated by another source.[40] Churchill estimated about half that number. In November 1934, he claimed that within three years German air power would be nearly double that of Britain's, unless the government rapidly accelerated its expansion programme. Baldwin repeating his pledge that Britain would not 'accept any position of inferiority', contended that Churchill's figures were 'considerably exaggerated'. Churchill would not be put off, however. In the spring of 1935 he claimed that Britain's first-line strength was still under 460 while Germany already possessed 1,500–2,000 'modern military machines', with the capacity to produce 2–3,000 more by March 1936. By the autumn, Germany would boast a first-line air strength of 'over 2,000'. Speaking to the Commons in November 1935, Churchill put British first-line strength at 960, comparing it to the German, now 'not less than 1,500'. Three months later, relying also on French intelligence sources, he refined the German figures to 4,000 with 2,369 as first-line machines. The strength of the Royal Air Force was but 'a fraction' of the Luftwaffe, its expansion plans well 'behind-hand'.[41]

The Air Staff took issue with Churchill's reading of the figures, as did others, who thought Churchill had exaggerated wildly.[44] Desmond Morton had warned him 'not to spoil a good case by anything which might later be revealed as gross or even ludicrous exaggeration'. 'The real disagreement,' Hankey commented, 'is not so much on the figures as on the deductions to be drawn from the figures.' Contesting 'these details', wrote Wigram, Churchill's chief contact at the Foreign Office, 'is idle'. 'This discussion of first line strengths is therefore not only endless, but also meaningless'.[42]

By the autumn of 1937 much of the heat had been taken out of what had turned into an acerbic debate. Churchill still called for 'a much more powerful Air Force', but there occurred a dramatic fall in the number of his speeches and the force of his rhetoric. Reluctantly, he came round to the opinion that rearmament 'is in full swing', although it was 'too little, too late' as 'we have at least two very dangerous years to go through'. At the Conservative Party conference that October he registered his full support for the government's defence and foreign policies – in the name of party and national unity. Judging from some of his public remarks, he had concluded that international tension was on the wane: he had told his constituents at Epping: 'I do not consider a major war in Europe imminent.'[43]

There were domestic reasons for this apparent volte-face, which in any case did not outlast the winter of 1937–38. His propensity for self-inflicted political injuries, highlighted by his Indian crusade and particularly by his disastrous intervention in the Abdication crisis, had left his reputation in shreds. At the time, Churchill was desperately trying to win his place back in the Conservative hierarchy, with his eye fixed on a possible seat in government. In the circumstances, it was perhaps more judicious to bicker less than to continue savaging the government, especially as the gap between them was being bridged, not widened.

Churchill's high profile campaign for air expansion had only a marginal effect on actual British air rearmament. As the debate turned on 'deductions', not 'figures', the Air Staff and other responsible government authorities had reached similar conclusions, as Morton and Wigram, Churchill's own private sources, had broadly hinted. Nor did German planning always stand the test of production. During the spring of 1939 a noteworthy shift in the relative power of the two air fleets was taking place. For the first time, Britain began to overhaul German aircraft production, a trend that continued into the war.

One aspect of the air question, Air Defence Research, saw Churchill cooperating actively with the government. In 1935 he was asked to serve on the ADRC, a sub-committee of the Committee of Imperial Defence that dealt with these issues. Although one of the initiators of this body, he was not its first choice. Only after Austen Chamberlain had refused the post did Churchill accept it, and then only on condition that he remained free 'to debate all the general issues' of the government's air policy. Of course, agreed Baldwin, 'my invitation was not intended as a muzzle'.[44] At the same time, his friend and scientific guru, Frederick Lindemann, had been included in a more specialized, technical body. Originally set up by the Air Ministry and chaired by Sir Henry Tizard, it worked in close tandem with the ADRC. In this manner, Churchill was privy to the secrets of Britain's air defence preparations, the establishment of a protective radar screen, for example.[45] However, despite Baldwin's consent not to 'muzzle' Churchill, inconsistencies remained. There was something patently incongruous in being a working member of a top secret government committee while simultaneously conducting a great public campaign on the very topic that this body was expected to adjudicate upon. This conspicuous conflict of interest disturbed more than one member of the government, Neville Chamberlain and Hankey included.

After three years' grind on the ADRC, Churchill regretted that he had agreed 'to take part in these studies'.[46] His association with the ADRC was replete with tension. As Lindemann was Churchill's man, Churchill was drawn willy-nilly into the almost daily feuding between Tizard and Lindemann, much of it centring on Lindemann's daily stream of ingenious brain-childs. And they were indeed ingenious, ranging from aircraft 'spewing out [aerial] mines like a fish lays eggs', to a belt of 'kite balloons', 4,000 in number, stretching from the Isle of Wight to Northumberland, and made lethal by clipping on to their cables tiny explosive devices, to lighting up clouds 'to silhouette bombers against the surface when viewed from below'. Much of this smacked of science-fiction, but some of his ideas had immense potential: the development of 'infra-red methods' to 'home onto enemy planes', or 'aerial torpedoes'.[47] For Churchill, these were fine distinctions. He backed Lindemann blindly, an allegiance that was to injure his own position on the ADRC.

In June 1936, Lindemann decided to contest the vacant parliamentary seat of Oxford to press home the realities of the German air menace. He lost. But as a consequence of his sortie into politics, it was decided to dissolve and then reconstitute Tizard's committee, without Lindemann's disturbing presence, considered to be a bad influence on Churchill. Continually raising 'wider issues', Churchill's contribution to the ADRC, according to Swinton, the Secretary of State for Air, was 'unhelpful' and 'very intransigent'. Not surprisingly, Lindemann defined the aggregate endeavours of the ADRC as 'nil'. Churchill agreed. It was generally admitted that Britain's air defences, to quote Churchill in the summer of 1938, were a 'horrid scandal'.[48] But Churchill, by not confining himself to the terms of reference of the Committee, had diverted it from its true purpose. This unhappy episode confirmed for many that Churchill, even when serving on the team and the recipient of state confidences, remained a most awkward partner: self-opinionated and bullheaded, a wrecker by nature. Neville Chamberlain, for instance, who had resisted Churchill's inclusion on the ADRC, might well have drawn the obvious conclusion that as the experiment had failed once, it should not be repeated again.

In a far more meaningful sense, Churchill had justice on his side. If his great public campaign had only a negligible effect on rearmament, it eventually paid off the richest political dividends. Germany did plan the most powerful air force in Europe, designed to be invincible against any combination of powers. And Hitler did intend to use it 'for terror purposes in international relations'.[49] It was unusual, to say the least, for potentially hostile countries to boast of their intentions and overstate their arms' strength – and this eventually worked to Churchill's definite advantage. So did the Munich crisis, when the spectacle of trenches being dug in Hyde Park revealed all too vividly to a fearful public Britain's acute vulnerability. Britain indeed lost the air race of the 1930s – though not by the margin Churchill envisaged. And as, from the winter of 1938–39, it appeared self-evident that the German peril threatened to consume Europe, so

Churchill appeared more than ever as the true prophet emerging from
the wilderness.

By the mid-1930s, although vociferously opposing the government in
public, Churchill had not abandoned all hope of office. 'Anxious to
cooperate' on other, no less compelling issues than those he had so
recently impugned, he strived hard to close the Indian chapter.[50] But
however much he yearned for office, his actions – or those for whom
he was held responsible, such as Randolph – blocked his return. In any
case, the scars over India healed slowly, if at all. Churchill's shining
talent for stirring up controversy, for raising his party's hackles, left his
appetite for power as hearty as ever, but unfulfilled. Whenever public
opinion appeared to move in his favour, his expectations mounted.
These ephemeral manifestations of popularity made little impact on the
party machine. After the elections of November 1935, it came as 'a very
great and bitter disappointment' to him when Baldwin, who had had a
massive victory, ignored his claim. Conscious of his sensitive position, he
appealed to Randolph to soften his journalistic attacks on 'the motives
& characters of Ministers, especially Baldwin and Eden'. In May 1937,
he seconded the resolution to nominate Neville Chamberlain as party
leader, and that autumn he registered public support for the goverment's
policies.[51] But Churchill's turn in humour was not awarded the
recognition he coveted. A note of frustration crept into his appraisal
of his fellow Conservatives. 'Worms', he called them, castigating
them as 'dirty Tory hacks who would like to drive me out of
the Party'. When under pressure, he claimed that he was 'still a
Liberal'. In moments of real desperation, he vowed to speak on
'every Socialist platform in the country against the Government'.[52]
    Optimistic by nature, Churchill, despite countless warning signals to
the contrary, believed himself still to be 'en jeu'. Initially, he wanted
to be put in charge of defence requirements but in March 1936, Sir
Thomas Inskip was appointed Minister for the Coordination of Defence.
By all accounts an extraordinary appointment, it left Churchill acutely
disappointed. Immediately, he shifted his attention to the creation of a
Ministry of Supply.[53] Until the outbreak of war, he never ceased to call
for this 'great Office' to be 'supervised by business men' and staffed
by 'a thousand', where, at any given moment, it would be possible
'to pull the lever and switch the whole of the munitions supply' to
its management. Clearly, with his achievements at Munitions from the
Great War in mind, he thought of himself as the man who would pull
the lever; as did many others.[54] But neither Baldwin – 'crafty, patient,
amazingly lazy, sterile and inefficient', nor Neville Chamberlain would
have him. The Cabinet, 'terrified' of Churchill's overbearing presence
and determined not to fall victim to his 'rash', 'notorious' judgement,

kept him firmly at arm's length. Churchill was fully conscious that his lobbying would probably yield nothing of consequence. He comforted Clementine, 'Destiny plays her part.' In this way he was excluded from the national governments of the 1930s, arguably the most maligned administrations of this century. Baldwin and Chamberlain rescued him from the ignominy to which they themselves were subjected without mercy.[55]

There were also the after-effects of Randolph's forays into politics to consider. In 1935–6, he ran three times for Parliament, splitting the Conservative vote to let in Labour on the first occasion, losing his deposit on the second, and narrowly saving it (by 200 votes) on the third. The official candidates he challenged – Duncan Sandys, soon to be his brother-in-law and one of Churchill's most dependable followers, and Malcolm MacDonald, the ex-Prime Minister's son – were not necessarily those Churchill would have chosen to dislodge. Randolph, Churchill told Clementine, wanted 'to smash up MacDonald and Baldwin'. Given Randolph's propensity for loud talk, it was difficult for some circles to imagine that Churchill was not party to his son's machinations. But of course Randolph waging guerrilla warfare on the government was the last thing Churchill needed and, ultimately, he had to disassociate himself from Randolph's escapades.[56]

Once the immediate excitement of these incidents had died down, Churchill's position improved. He remained disenchanted with the government, but in a less strident manner. Later, Neville Chamberlain identified 'his unwillingness to do anything which might prevent his yet receiving an offer to join the Govt'.[57] He sought a wider political base. Already identified with various anti-Nazi groups, Churchill was involved in forming a 'Focus in Defence of Freedom and Peace' in May 1936, a loose umbrella organization that aimed to coordinate the activities of these bodies and provide him with a public platform. It attracted a broad spectrum of support: dissenting Conservatives, a sprinkling of independent Liberal and Labour MPs, trade unionists, intellectuals, pacifists. There were problems. For one thing the press did not treat it too seriously; epithets such as 'Geneva gas-bags' or 'blood-thirsty pacifists' were all too often reported. Another was the embarrassing question of who would foot its bill. Fortunately, Eugen Spier, a German-Jewish refugee, had been invited to its founding meeting and discreetly provided over £9,000 to finance its activities.[58]

Although Focus did not live up to its original expectations, it functioned for three years and constituted a useful channel for Churchill to expound his views. By the end of 1936 he had regained a measure of political respectability. Already 'an elder statesman', he was asked by Lord Davies, founder of the New Commonwealth Society (Churchill was President of its British Section), 'to concentrate upon the role of saviour of Europe'. 'Winston is making a great recovery in the Conservative party,' recorded one diarist. 'Many regard him as only PM in a crisis.' This seemed particularly relevant as Baldwin, on the verge of a nervous breakdown that summer, had been compelled to take long absences of leave.

As Churchill's reputation solidified, so Baldwin's plummeted. His reply to Churchill, conveyed to the House with 'appalling frankness', that for narrow electoral considerations he had not 'gone to the country' on a platform of greater rearmament, was easily given to distortion. Baldwin had in fact been referring to the possibility of an election in 1933, not the elections of November 1935, that had provided him with a mandate for rearmament. But his lack of clarity enabled Churchill to highlight his own farsighted statesmanship in contrast to the Prime Minister's ruinous parochialism. Seemingly riding on a crest, Churchill was scheduled as the star attraction at a great mass rally to be held at the Albert Hall at the beginning of December. Organized by Focus, and intended to launch its campaign of 'Arms and the Covenant', all the signs were auspicious for another resounding Churchill success. To the cry of 'Baldwin should now make room for stronger leadership,' he rose to speak. His mind, however, was elsewhere, on the marital problems of Edward VIII and the likelihood of the King's abdication. He disappointed his audience. Churchill had intended to comment on the constitutional emergency, but Sir Walter Citrine, chairman of the demonstration, forbade him to do so. Focus suffered as a result of Churchill's clear-cut partisanship on behalf of the King. It also clouded Churchill's prospects of making a swift political recovery.[59]

The Abdication crisis broke in the press the same day the Albert Hall meeting convened. Although in England the press had maintained a discreet silence, the King's passion for the twice divorced Mrs Wallis Simpson of Baltimore – known to American newspaper readers as 'the King's Moll' – had been common knowledge in London Society and the international media for some time. While perhaps acceptable as Edward VIII's mistress, a divorcee was considered quite unsuitable as Queen to a King who was also head of the Church of England. A morganatic marriage was deemed equally undesirable. The Cabinet, led by Baldwin, was adamant that the King must comply with its advice.[60] It soon became clear that Edward would have to choose: the Crown or Mrs Simpson.

Churchill was conscious of these currents of opinion. He and the King – who had contributed to the financing of his Daimler in 1932 – were on friendly terms. With Baldwin's consent, they maintained contact throughout the crisis. Churchill pleaded for 'time and patience', for a 'searching constitutional debate'. Why panic? he argued. 'No pistol' should be held at the King's head, he asserted, particularly incensed at Baldwin's message to Edward that, if he resigned on the issue, both Labour and the Liberals had agreed not to form an alternative government.[61]

Four days after the Albert Hall demonstration, Churchill addressed the House on the emergency. Could Baldwin give an assurance that 'no irrevocable step will be taken before the House has received a full statement, not only upon the personal but upon the constitutional issues involved'? he asked. His intervention proved to be a fiasco. Twice called to order by the Speaker, he collapsed – according to one observer, 'the worse for drink' – waving his spectacles vaguely in the air, to shouts of 'Sit down', 'Drop it', 'Twister'. Unable to complete his statement, he fled the Chamber, visibly glowing with rage, escorted only by Brendan Bracken. Within moments, having retreated to the safety of the Lobby, he concluded that 'his political career was finished'. *The Times* called his performance 'the most striking rebuff of modern parliamentary history'. This was no off-the-cuff intervention. Quite the contrary, for weeks he had been cautioned by his friends, above all by Clementine, not to take too extreme a pro-King line. Only the day before, at Chartwell, he had agreed with Bob Boothby and Sir Archibald Sinclair on a common formula, drafting a declaration to the effect that the King would not contract a marriage in defiance of his ministers. As Mrs Simpson had recently issued a statement that she was prepared 'to withdraw forthwith from a situation that has been rendered unhappy and untenable', there appeared to be at least a slender chance of damping down the crisis. Any rational analysis of political gain or loss should have led Churchill to restrain his tongue and control his actions. Somehow, he was inhibited from doing so. Boothby wrote to him immediately after the Commons disaster, 'you have delivered a blow to the king, both in the House and in the country, far harder than any that Baldwin conceived of'.[62]

In landing his 'blow' against the King, Churchill had resurrected all the time-worn doubts about himself. An overwhelming majority of opinion was against the marriage, yet Churchill paraded his view that the King should be allowed '[to] choose his girl'. To what purpose? Was he, like Beaverbrook, out 'to bugger' Baldwin – to employ Randolph Churchill's preferred expression – and seize the premiership? Did he intend to lead a 'King's Party'?[63]

Rumours were rife that he was engineering a plot, exploiting the crisis for his 'own private ends'. These assumptions must remain highly speculative – although cutting Baldwin down to size might have been a desirable side benefit. But the fact that such theories were freely and confidently aired in public was a sound reminder of Churchill's suspect reputation.

Churchill's appeal for 'time and patience' was probably made in the expectation that Edward would eventually weary of Mrs Simpson and drop her, a fate shared by his previous lovers. 'A temporary passion,' Churchill surmised. 'Women play a transient part in his life. He falls constantly in and out of love.'[64] On this occasion, however, nothing could have been further from the truth, a reality crystal-clear to most observers but to which Churchill remained curiously blind. Edward was determined to marry Mrs Simpson, whatever the consequences. 'The king is insane about Wallis, insane,' noted Chips Channon, an insatiable society gossip. Once the dust had settled, Churchill also came round to this view. 'The Duke [of Windsor's] love for her is one of the great love stories of history,' he finally admitted. 'Make no mistake he can't live without her.' He swiftly realized that he was out of tune with popular opinion and was causing himself grave damage. Three days after being hounded out of the Chamber, on 10 December, the same day that King Edward signed the Deed of Abdication, Churchill again faced a hostile House, but 'in an admirably phrased little speech', thought Amery, executed 'a strategical retreat'. Highlighting his friendship with Edward, he justified his plea for more time while readily admitting 'the evils of prolonged controversy'. He also accepted 'wholeheartedly' Baldwin's version of events. It was a carefully balanced performance.[65]

It is often argued that it was Churchill's chivalrous temperament, buttressed by his romantic perception of the institution of monarchy, that warped his judgement in this affair. But it was not pure romanticism that moved Churchill. Although his relations with his monarchs, Edward VII and George V, were often less than harmonious, he believed passionately in the concept of constitutional monarchy, first as a vindication of British history, but also as a shield against the spread of totalitariansim. 'Danger gathers upon our path,' he said. 'Royalty,' he wrote, 'is the barrier against Dictatorship.'[66] Anything that eroded the monarchical principle, that tarnished its prestige, would cause Britain irreparable damage. In the 1930s, when despotic regimes were springing up like mushrooms in Europe, this seemed to him of particular relevance.

The Abdication crisis provided ample proof for many that Churchill remained a political adventurer, now aging fast. Potential supporters were saddened by his conduct. When given a choice, he could be relied upon, it seemed, to make the wrong move. Baffy Dugdale hoped that Churchill would disappear temporarily, 'so as to be uninjured until needed again'. Bob Boothby, who had been appalled by Churchill's cavalier treatment of the agreement made at Chartwell, distanced himself from his former chief. Although combating the German menace brought them together in common endeavour, their relationship had soured.[67] Ironically, even while Churchill's grass roots popularity flourished, he remained a vulnerable and isolated figure where it most counted, in establishment circles. His camp-followers in the House were narrowed down to Brendan Bracken, a lightweight controversial figure, and the young and inexperienced Duncan Sandys, coupled on the outside with the eccentric persona of Lindemann and the ever volatile Randolph. Despite the fact that international events were moving in his favour, justifying his direst predictions, Churchill's political career remained in the doldrums.

16

'What Price Churchill?'

In March 1936 Churchill set out the principles of his foreign policy, a classic exposition of the 'balance of power' doctrine: 'to oppose the strongest, most aggressive, most dominating power on the Continent, and particularly to prevent the Low Countries falling into the hands of such a Power'. Britain was following 'a public policy' to ensure 'the reign of law and freedom among the nations and within the nations'. It was self-evident that Germany, led by 'a handful of desperados', now sought to subjugate the Continent and establish 'a Germanized Europe under Nazi control'. Britain would be shirking her historic duty if she failed to prevent this calamity. 'We cannot afford to see Nazidom in its present phase of cruelty and intolerance, with all its hatreds and all its gleaming weapons, paramount in Europe'. An 'armed League of all the Nations, with Britain and France [in alliance] as the core of it' was his diplomatic formula.[1]

From the early 1930s, the German menace monopolized Churchill's attention. Its warlike temper, the resounding success over the Saar plebiscite, and the unilateral abolition of the disarmament clauses of the Versailles treaty in March 1935, followed by the reoccupation of the Rhineland a year later – a flagrant violation of the freely negotiated Locarno treaties – amply confirmed Churchill's fears. Other aggressors, Italy or Japan, or later Franco's Spain, were awarded a lower priority. Nor was Churchill at ease either with Sir John Simon, Foreign Secretary from 1931 until June 1935 or Hoare – who replaced Simon until the following December. When, during Hoare's term of office, Eden was appointed Minister for League of Nations Affairs, he railed against the system of 'two equal Foreign Secretaries'. In any case, although Churchill paid lip service to Eden's ability, he suspected that the glamorous image cocooned a man of straw. After Eden took over the Foreign Office, Churchill wrote: 'Eden's appointment does not inspire me with confidence. I expect the greatness of his office will find him out,' adding, 'I think you will now see what a lightweight Eden is'. Eden continued to disappoint Churchill. Even when both were in 'opposition', during the Munich crisis, Churchill found him 'very shy', a euphemism for Eden's reluctance to commit himself wholeheartedly to oppose Chamberlain.[2] Eden's usefulness to Churchill lay more in his general popularity than in his talents as a politician.

Denouncing Germany as a potential aggressor did not mean refusing to negotiate with her. Like the Foreign Office, Churchill appreciated that diplomacy cannot be conducted by shouting 'No!' to everything and everyone. In May 1935 he declined 'to close the door upon a revision of the Treaties', provided it was done 'under the authority and sanction of the League of Nations'. Six months later, his cry was faithfully mirrored in a Foreign Office memorandum, authored by two of the fiercest critics of Nazi Germany, Ralph Wigram and Orme Sargent.[3] Churchill, sooner than most, tired of this 'grovelling' to Germany, an attitude he characterized as 'Dear Germany, do destroy us *last*!' But in late 1937 he returned to the same theme. 'If sacrifices are to be made to lay the ghost of hatreds arising out of the late War', he told the House, they should be made all round, and all the powers who profited in territory during the Great War should be prepared to share in and contribute 'to any measure of appeasement to those who were defeated'.[4] He was referring as much to the vexed question of Britain handing back to Germany her ex colonies, as to the readjustment of the so-called 'lost provinces' in central and eastern Europe, now integrated into Poland and Czechoslovakia. On one point, however, he was adamant: there would no appeasement for appeasement's sake. Any new arrangement in Europe must be fortified by a dependable and genuine system of collective security.

In its first stage, this included Italy. There were sound reasons for this. Italy feared that German irredentism stretched to the South Tyrol via Austria. Engelbert Dollfuss, the Austrian Chancellor, was little more than Mussolini's protégé; his régime, Fascist and repressive, would be defended, so Mussolini had promised, against 'Prussian barbarism'. When the Austrian Nazis attempted to seize power in July 1934, killing Dollfuss, it was Mussolini who rushed troops to the Brenner Pass, an unambiguous warning to the Nazis to refrain from further aggression. Mussolini's denunciations of Hitler – a 'horrible sexual degenerate' – and Germany – 'a racialist lunatic asylum' run by pagans – left little doubt in the minds of western statesmen that an effective combination could be formed to deny Germany European hegemony. In the first half of 1935, an anti-German bloc appeared to be in the making. Franco-Italian agreements were signed, directed against Germany, that gave tangible strategic and political advantages to France, and hence to the West as a whole. At Stresa, this trend was reinforced when Britain joined France and Italy to safeguard Austria's independence and condemn

Germany's treaty-breaking over armaments, a public 'demonstration of comradeship', in Churchill's phrase, that brought him 'in closer relation to His Majesty's Government on foreign affairs' than ever previously.[5] In Churchill's calculations, the so-called Stresa front was too valuable an asset to be lightly squandered away.

Some might have found it morally repugnant to cooperate with Italy, a Fascist power. This was not a consideration that greatly troubled Britain's decision-makers or Churchill. Of course, he repudiated Fascism, certainly as a model for Britain. But he did not react with the same degree of enmity towards Mussolini's regime as he did towards Hitler's. Indeed, his first impressions had been rather favourable. 'If I had been an Italian,' he said in 1927, 'I am sure I should have been wholeheartedly with you from the start in your triumphant struggle against the bestial appetites and passions of Leninism.' Five years later, he was still able to refer to Mussolini as 'the Roman genius . . . the greatest lawgiver among living men'.[6] Clearly Churchill would not allow ideological differences to divide Britain and France from Italy on an agreed programme to check Nazi Germany. With the stakes so high, this might well embrace a flexible attitude towards Mussolini's territorial ambitions in East Africa. In all this, Churchill was merely echoing the conventional wisdoms of the Foreign Office and the government.

These promising signs soon faded away. One factor, certainly, was Mussolini's resolve to fulfil Italy's imperial destiny in Abyssinia, an ambition that severely narrowed Britain's options. But in Churchill's view, the latest twist in British policy, the Anglo-German naval treaty of June 1935, was no less instrumental in undermining the breakthrough at Stresa. Unlike those who negotiated this treaty, he did not regard it as a mere technical matter, an exercise in disarmament that limited Germany's capacity to resume the disastrous naval race of pre-war days. Churchill recapitulated the damage done: 'the League of Nations has been weakened by our action, the principle of collective security has been impaired, German treaty-making has been condoned and even extolled, the Stresa Front has been shaken, if not, indeed, dissolved.'[7]

Churchill was determined not to surrender the advantages of what had been achieved at Stresa, however elusive. In the face of Italian military movements in the eastern Mediterranean, and much loose talk of a 'mad-dog' strike, he reminded Hoare not to let 'diplomacy get ahead of naval preparedness'. At the same time, there could be no question of Britain acting 'individually and independently', of 'coming forward as a sort of bell-wether or fugleman to gather and lead opinion in Europe against Italy's Abyssinian designs'. The issue lay between Italy and the League. But Churchill balked at the use of armed force. 'It would be a terrible deed to smash up Italy'. Nor was he in favour of imposing economic sanctions, fearing this would lead to 'Germany and Italy coming together'.[8] These observations, voiced on the eve of the Italian invasion of Ethiopia, boxed in Churchill's policy no less than it did the government's. Short of slaking Italy's territorial thirst, little remained.

Even after Italian forces crossed into Ethiopia, on 3 October, Churchill saw no cause to modify his basic approach. Compared to 'the shadow of German re-armament', the war in Ethiopia was 'a very small matter'. He saw, briefly, a new and more vigorous League of Nations. Limited sanctions against Italy were being slowly applied. He was impressed. 'We are already in the presence of a memorable event,' he commented.[9] But he quickly switched tack when he realized they were proving quite ineffective. 'Futile half-hearted sanctions against Italy' should not be continued just to save the government's face. But if not sanctions, what else? In retrospect, Churchill concluded that 'resolute action', even at the risk of 'a single-handed war', would have deterred Mussolini.[10] During the summer of 1935, although he warned of the possibility of war, he spoke equally as resolutely against acting alone. 'We are not strong enough – I say it advisedly [to the Commons] – to be the lawgiver and spokesman of the world.'[11] No government spokesman could have expressed Britain's dilemma more plainly.

What remained was a policy of compromise, inevitably to Italy's advantage: and Churchill seized it, perhaps reluctantly, but no less firmly than those in authority. From the Zeila proposals of June 1935 to the Hoare-Laval plan the following December, the British offered Mussolini a way out, arrangements that awarded Italy territorial gain and political and economic primacy in Ethiopia.[12] Churchill felt that in general 'the gain would have outweighed the loss'. After much reflection, he judged: 'Everyone can now see that the Hoare-Laval agreement was a very shrewd, far-seeing agreement which would have saved the Negus of Abyssinia from ruin before his army was destroyed.' However, it was disowned, in Churchill's sarcastic phrase, to the 'splendid idealistic crusade' of the British people. 'Aggressor or triumphant,' he finally remarked about Mussolini, 'he will be rewarded with gains far beyond the Hoare-Laval proposals.'[13]

There was probably no way to appease Mussolini satisfactorily. Bent on martial glory and refurbishing Italy's tarnished prestige, he chose the path of military adventurism. But the consequences of failing to contain his ambition within the framework of a League of Nations deal, as envisaged by the British initiatives, were crystal-clear to Churchill. Everything stemmed from this setback. In Britain's 'spirited new mood', France was invited to share the unequal risks of a confrontation with Italy. Nothing positive, however, emerged from this display of excessive British pressure. He listed the sombre catalogue: British prestige plummeted, as did Anglo-French relations; the Franco-Italian accords, of inestimable value to France, were shattered; and Ethiopia, the hapless victim, was abandoned to the mercy of Italy. Only Germany profited, its isolation breached as Italy yielded to the German embrace. On 7 March 1936 German troops moved into the Rhineland, in clear violation of the Versailles and Locarno treaties, exploiting the estrangement of the western powers.[14]

In his memoirs, Churchill leaves the impression that Britain and France had only to act to win back the Rhineland, but that the British government laid down for France 'a velvet carpet for retreat'. Here, he explains, was 'lost irretrievably the last chance of arresting Hitler's ambitions without a serious war'.[15] But would Churchill have actually fought in March 1936? It is hardly conceivable that having ruled that Britain was not 'strong enough' to take on Italy in the summer of 1935, Churchill would have considered challenging Germany in the spring of 1936. And in fact he made no such proposal. While not belittling the gravity of the German coup, he still saw it as 'the smallest part of the whole problem'. The real peril, he elucidated, '[is] this enormous process of the rearmament of Germany.' He deferred passing judgement on the 'ultimate justice' of Hitler's lightning stroke. First, let the World Court at The Hague clear away the legalities of the issue. But for the League, there might have been war: France and her allies might have been tempted to fight. Instead, they were forced to appeal 'to a tribunal' that 'has in this matter shown once again its vitality'.[16] However his words are juggled, here is argument for deliberation, for delay, not for immediate action. His observations were muted not simply because he hungered after office, a natural enough desire. Like those he elected to fault, he too was unable to offer a convincing alternative. Shorn of its rhetoric, Churchill's proposals merged smoothly into the policy the government was actually pursuing.

There were longer term repercussions to the Ethiopian imbroglio, impossible to forecast with accuracy at the time but built into the situation. At odds with the League of Nations, isolated in Europe, Italy slowly, tentatively, moved into the German orbit, relinquishing its grip on Austria to Germany's advantage, a decisive shift in position that opened up south-eastern Europe to German pressure. Churchill was alive to these hazards, and began to call for the 'peaceful defensive encirclement' of Germany, a new Front that would include the Soviet Union. He was realistic enough to bury, at least temporarily, his anti-Soviet hatchet. Ivan Maisky, the Soviet ambassador to Britain, an 'agitprop-type' envoy given to intrigues and feeding half-truths to his contacts, and one of the less credible figures adorning the London diplomatic scene, had suddenly become 'a bosom friend'.[17] Constructing a Grand Alliance between Britain, France, and the Soviet Union became a constant theme in Churchill's overall design to deter Nazi Germany.

If these crises found Churchill in general agreement with government policy, the Spanish Civil War offered no break in the pattern. From its outbreak in July 1936, until its conclusion almost three years later, the war cast the deepest of shadows on international politics. The lines, apparently, were clearly drawn: a Popular Front coalition of Republicans, Socialists, Syndicalists, and Communists, after winning a decisive electoral victory, were facing an armed rebellion of their Conservative-Clerical-Monarchist rivals. Both sides were guilty of gratuitous violence, perpetrating the most awful atrocities. But did this imply that they should be treated with equal impartiality? This dilemma could be resolved by answering an elementary question: should a legally elected government, even if it let in Communists and their ilk, be protected against a rebellion of the self-proclaimed Fascist forces led by Franco and his generals? Here was the great ideological divide of the 1930s, and, despite his abhorrence of totalitarianism, Churchill was unable to cross it.

Churchill was not alone. The great bulk of the Conservative Party, anti-Bolshevik in sentiment, were 'very much inclined to cheer the so-called Spanish rebels', as Churchill phrased it. Tending to see the origins of the war as a Communist plot, and denouncing the International Brigade as 'the most fanatical revolutionaries in Europe', he applauded the 'progress' of the Nationalists and thought it better for 'the safety of all if the Communists are crushed', later wanting to award 'belligerent rights' to Franco. When Pablo de Azcarate, the Spanish Republican ambassador to London, offered his hand, Churchill turned away, allegedly red with anger, muttering, 'Blood, blood, blood'.[18] He found no fault with the government's declared policy of non-intervention, and encouraged Eden to persevere in these efforts. There was a definite rationale behind this strategy. Although the Spanish Republican cause gripped the imagination of an entire generation, particularly among the young intelligentsia and in left-wing circles, to have backed unequivocally one side or the other would have split public opinion. The Foreign Office took the view that true British interests called for a moderate, middle-of-the-road Spanish government with whom it was possible to conduct business. There were also wider implications. Intervention, it was feared, would fan a purely internal dispute into a general European conflagration, an outcome that the Chiefs of Staff strongly warned against. In theory, the case for non-intervention was sound. In practice, with Italy, to a lesser extent Germany, and the Soviet Union openly cheating on the non-intervention conventions, this so-called open-minded policy 'was to graduate from equivocation to hypocrisy and humiliation', as Hugh Thomas has put it. But equally it ensured that the fighting never escalated into the widespread conflict that British policy-makers dreaded, for them a considerable benefit.[19]

It took Churchill some time before he balanced his ideological hang-up against the political-strategic disadvantages that would accrue from a Nationalist victory. 'At heart,' recorded one observer, 'he is for Franco.' Yet he feared an Italian-Spanish alliance, a combination that would compromise Britain's position in the Mediterranean, and he even envisaged occupying and holding Minorca 'as Trustees for Spain'.[20] Despite his anxieties, Churchill stuck to his 'even-handed' policy, favouring 'formal diplomatic relations' with both sides, while at the same time declining to lend his name to a rally of rabid pro-Franco supporters. Gradually, he swung round to conceding that the strategic arguments against a Nationalist victory were 'unanswerable', although he continually harped back to a unifying constitutional monarchy, a by-now academic dénouement to the Spanish tragedy. By December 1938 he was compelled to conclude that British interests would best be served by a victory of the Spanish government, anything rather than see Franco and his Nazi backers triumph.[21] Never was a more reluctant bride dragged more unwillingly to the altar.

On the other side of the globe, another war was in progress. Renewed Sino-Japanese hostilities from July 1937 found Churchill resigned to 'a ceaseless encroachment upon our interests' unless Anglo-American cooperation – the most unrealistic of assumptions – could be guaranteed, but in any event not until the European situation had stabilized. His mind was not focused upon 'the quarrels of the yellow peoples'.

In the autumn Churchill registered 'general agreement' with the course of British foreign policy. He shrank from pursuing a line 'inimical to the legitimate interests of Germany'. Under no circumstances did these include the unconditional return of the former German colonies, or '[buying] immunity for ourselves' by allowing Hitler 'a free hand' in central and southern Europe, in his view a euphemism for the destruction of Austria and Czechoslovakia. Only by 'regional agreements' under a strong, reinvigorated League of Nations, he argued, would Germany 'be content to live within her own bounds in a law-abiding manner'.[22]

Little less than year later, all of Churchill's calculations came to nought. In any case, Churchill's reliance on a new-born League of Nations flew in the face of international realities. By late 1938 it had been shorn of all authority. It had watched powerless as Germany absorbed Austria in March; and stood by the following September, when the Sudeten German lands, hitherto part of Czechoslovakia, were handed over to German rule at Munich. On the other hand, regional agreements were very much in vogue, the Munich settlement being a prime example. But for Churchill, the government had stood his formula on its head. Regional agreements were intended first and foremost to deter Germany; only later, when tamed and more down-to-earth, would Germany be induced to enter into an overall arrangement. This prospect, in any case faint to an extreme, was finally destroyed by the events of 1938.

An intimation of the government's purpose emerged from Lord Halifax's visit to Germany in November 1937. During his conversations with the Nazi leaders, including Hitler, Halifax virtually extended the 'free hand', mentioning specifically Austria, Czechoslovakia, and Danzig as areas where treaty revision was possible. Churchill was not privy to the details of these talks, but the visit had provoked controversy even before Halifax set out. For Churchill too it sent out a storm signal about the extent of Germany's ambitions, an SOS that appeared totally justified when Germany stamped out Austrian independence. He inveighed against Hitler's bullying methods, but no less so than Neville Chamberlain and Halifax. Where they differed, at least in the immediate circumstances, was that Churchill believed that 'a fair plebiscite', the Austrian Chancellor's proposal, would have demonstrated the loathing of the Austrian people for Nazi rule.[23] Given the violent history of Austria's internal politics, this was somewhat in the nature of wishful thinking. At any rate, both Chamberlain and Halifax thought Kurt von Schuschnigg's move needlessly provocative; and so did Hitler, who launched his invasion as a result. But a more principled difference also separated Churchill from the government. Churchill had long held that a general war was unavoidable unless Germany's territorial goals were reined in, a view not endorsed by those directing government policy, some of whom were inclined to suspend judgement whether or not a German hegemony over central Europe would inevitably lead to an all-out European conflict.[24]

The Austrian coup was executed so swiftly that there was scarcely time to establish a position beforehand, except in the most general terms, or to fashion an effective response afterwards. How did Churchill react? He saw the Nazi conquest of Austria as yet another stage in 'a programme of aggression, nicely calculated and timed', but he could offer no immediate answer other than 'patient, determined, persevering discussion' by all the interested powers under the aegis of the League. Given the state of the League, this was merely a more sophisticated way of expressing Neville Chamberlain's clinical observation that the Austrian affair was so much 'spilt milk'.[25] Churchill persisted in this train of thought. Hitler's aggressive plans could be arrested by a spirited implementation of his two-pronged deterrent formula of rearmament and a Grand Alliance embracing the Soviet Union, a dynamic system of collective security drawing its strength from the League, at the core of which stood a military convention between Britain and France.

Rearmament was already underway, to Churchill's high praise. The government had also considered the Grand Alliance alternative, only for Neville Chamberlain to dismiss 'its practicability'.[26] And who could say that his was not a more realistic assessment than Churchill's? Of course, if, as a last resort, a militant, united France was determined on war to defend the integrity of the threatened nations in central and eastern Europe, and if a similarly disposed Britain was ready to back her, then the Grand Alliance was a feasible and preferred strategy. But this was far from being the case. France was not only rent by a permanent domestic political crisis, but its army chiefs displayed little enthusiasm to embark on pre-emptive military strikes without assured British support. As for Britain, its mood for compromise was markedly stronger than its appetite for an armed confrontation with Germany. Moreover, its military advisers, faced with the prospect of hostilities on three wide-ranging fronts, favoured postponing any armed clash, arguing incessantly for some kind of political arrangement to buy time. Only a week before the Munich settlement, they cautioned: 'To attempt to take offensive action against Germany until we have had time to bring our naval, military and air forces and also our passive defence services on to a war footing would be to place ourselves in the position of a man who attacks a tiger before he has loaded his gun.'[27] No responsible government could afford to ignore such advice. First, every diplomatic avenue would have to be explored.

As matters stood, there was much window-dressing in Churchill's propositions. He anticipated that his blend of rearmament and a grand coalition, if not sufficient in itself to warn off Hitler, would encourage 'all peace-loving and moderate forces in Germany' to re-constitute a more amenable government. Banking on the overthrow of Hitler was a will-of-the-wisp chased only by the most dedicated of optimists. But what if vigorous protest and resolute diplomatic action failed to call Hitler's bluff? What if Hitler was not simply posturing? Was not his rape of Austria decisive proof that his threats should be taken in deadly earnest? It remained highly speculative whether an Anglo-French-Soviet combination would have intimidated Hitler, particularly as he had seen the British and the French in action over the Rhineland and Austria, a performance that was to be repeated at Munich, and that he, together with his generals, consistently derided Soviet military power.[28]

In one sense, the logic of Churchill's own arguments worked against him. If Hitler was working to a carefully worked out plan of territorial expansion, no policy would deter him, no offer would appease him. Churchill, eventually and reluctantly, reached this conclusion.[29] But he could suggest nothing positive except more of the same. Somewhat like Neville Chamberlain, Churchill, more passionately and with far greater eloquence, hoped for the best, while preparing for the worst.

The Czech problem was a different case to the Austrian. Besieged on three sides by a bellicose Germany, and harbouring a disaffected minority of three million Sudeten Germans, it was self-evident to all that after the Anschluss, Czechoslovakia would be the next object of excessive German pressure. The Czech crisis simmered for six months, sufficient time for diplomacy and clarification. Of immediate concern were the claims of the Sudeten Germans. Churchill thought them 'the best treated minority in Europe', although most British politicians and officials, including Churchill's advisers, were highly critical of the Czech government's treatment of them. Churchill soon modified his appraisal. He did so, it appears, after he received Konrad Henlein, leader of the Sudetendeutsche Partei, a paid agent of the Germans who had been instructed by Hitler to pitch his demands too high for the Czechs to accept. Presenting himself as a moderate hemmed in by extremists, his carefully staged performances were sufficiently compelling to deceive even the most implacable of anti-Nazis, Sir Robert Vansittart, for example. Henlein urged that his people's legitimate rights, as guaranteed under the Czech constitution, be honoured, in effect a claim for greater autonomy. This highly laudable aim, he remonstrated, was being sabotaged by the obstinacy and short-sightedness of the Czechs. Churchill was impressed with this message. Encouraged by Henlein's 'attitude', and hailing him as 'a moderate', Churchill publicly took issue with Czech 'obduracy'.[30]

Like most of his contemporaries, Churchill saw the ideal solution in terms of greater autonomy for the Sudeten Germans. Regarding it as an internal issue, he did not exclude the role of honest broker for Britain, even to the point of gently persuading the Czechs to be more amenable to the idea of autonomy. But he felt that there could be no erosion of Czech sovereignty; and certainly no use of military force to extinguish it. There was to be no ceding of Czech territories to Germany.[31] In August, he began to have serious doubts about his own government's firmness of purpose. Given Germany's brutal, lawless record, at what point would it draw the limit? War having been ruled out by the military, the Cabinet was set on resolving the question by negotiations. Even the threat of war held out dangers. Might it not provoke Germany? Or encourage the French, or Czechs, or both, to adopt an embarrassingly militant line? Either way, the British would be dragged into a war for which they were singularly ill-prepared. The French, for their own reasons, met them half-way. In this sense, one policy fed off the other. Anglo-French contacts since the *Anschluss* were fashioned to ensure a diplomatic solution; and from the British perspective also to keep the French in line. Joint staff talks would continue, but not to the point of a full-blown alliance. The Cabinet, imprisoned in its own logic, drew the obvious conclusion: there would be no unequivocal public warning to Germany that war would inevitably follow if Czech sovereignty were violated.[32]

By contrast, this was precisely the policy that Churchill now proposed. As September 1938 passed, Churchill's alarm grew. The milestones are familiar: Hitler's Nuremberg speech; Chamberlain's flights to Germany; the western powers manipulation of the Czechs; the last crisis-laden days, leading finally to the well-timed appeal of Mussolini (and Roosevelt) for a conference at Munich where the concluding, humiliating scene was enacted, Sudeten German territories being ceded to Germany. Reported as having said that Neville's journey to Berchtesgaden to confer with Hitler (the first of his three trips) was 'the stupidest thing that has ever been done', Churchill, angling also after American backing, pinned his faith on an Anglo-French-Soviet statement that an attack on the Czechs would be immediately followed by 'common action', by which he meant war. At the same time, he pressed for 'fleet movements' to show firmness of intent, advice that was eventually adopted by the Admiralty. Perhaps he was encouraged by reports that some German generals were ready to oppose Hitler's adventurism – as it turned out yet another red herring. There also seemed to be a change of heart at the Foreign Office. On 26 September it issued a communiqué, which Churchill helped formulate, that 'Great Britain and Russia will certainly stand by France' in the event of war over Czechoslovakia. But this initiative died unobtrusively in yet another blind alley. Chamberlain disowned it; and Halifax, although he had approved it, lacked the required grit to stand up to his chief. Attempts were made to whip up support among oppositionist MPs, but to little effect. Divided and ineffectual, they were incapable even of issuing a joint declaration, Eden shying off at the last moment. In any case, Churchill, by far the major figure at these parleys, commanded the least support. On the other hand, Neville Chamberlain enjoyed virtual carte blanche from his Party for his peace efforts, and as it turned out from public opinion. When he told the Commons that he was going to Munich, the House rose to pay him tribute. Even Churchill congratulated him on his 'good fortune'. On his return, clasping the newly drafted Anglo-German agreement – that Hitler had scarcely looked at before signing – the crowds hailed him, ecstatic that he had brought them not war but 'peace with honour', 'peace for our time'.[33]

Sitting, 'lowering, hunched and circular', Churchill waited patiently to be called for the debate on the Munich settlement. Late in the afternoon of 5 October he rose to speak, his characteristic mannerisms, gently patting his trouser pockets and then gliding his hands up and down from groin to tummy, amusing his audience. His message, however, was deadly serious. He described Chamberlain's triumph as 'a total and unmitigated disaster' that also fatally endangered the safety, even independence, of Britain. Bidding farewell to Czechoslovakia as she 'recedes into the darkness', he pointed out that Hitler, 'instead of snatching his victuals from the table, has been content to have them served to him course by course'.[34] But his proposals to cut short Hitler's feast contained nothing new: rearmament, coalitions, a revivified League. For those pre-occupied with the making of British policy, tormented by the horrors of the Great War, inclined – also on moral grounds – to satisfy Germany's 'legitimate grievances', conscious of their own defence weaknesses and of French lack of will, this was insufficient. Given the basic facts as known to ministers, there was a tragic inevitability to the Munich agreement, however disgraceful the betrayal of Czechoslovakia.

Only one minister resigned over Munich, Alfred Duff Cooper, than First Lord of the Admiralty. In view of Churchill's ardent desire to join the government, the question whether he would have done so too, although speculative, merits enquiry. The terms of the settlement stuck in the throats of many ministers. Walter Elliot, one of the waverers, wrote on the morrow of the Commons debate:

> Being in the Cabinet, I am responsible for the fact that I am weaker than Germany. It is no use resigning – that does not get me out of my responsibility. That fearful timetable is a great crime and scandal, for which those of us who accepted it will be justly condemned, and I believe some day justly punished ... That does not get me away from my desperate question – if I could rub out that agreement, and get us put back to Tuesday night, would I do it? In the present state of our forces – French and British – I cannot say that I would. Therefore, I accept the Munich terms. Therefore re them, I do not, and cannot resign.[35]

These men were not cowards, neither were they indifferent to the German menace. Had Churchill been their colleague, he would have been subject to the same agonizing pressures. In the final analysis, neither Churchill nor the government could act out of free choice. Both would have operated in a limited, restrictive framework, bound by the same constraints.

Of course, Churchill, from the outset, had detected the deadly peril Hitler's regime posed. His keen prescience stands to his credit. But it was one thing to perceive the threat, as did others, and quite another to formulate an effective, practical answer when in office. Would Churchill's buoyant presence in Cabinet have been sufficient to boost its morale to the level required to risk resolving the German menace on the battlefield? A most unlikely proposition. Was he in a position to galvanize the French? Hardly. Churchill would have been trapped in the same cleft stick that Elliot had so graphically portrayed. Personal considerations also would have weighed heavily upon him. An elderly politician who had already resigned once from the Cabinet, with disastrous consequences, and who had abandoned the Shadow Cabinet some years later, with no less serious repercussions, would surely not have survived politically a third desertion. He would have been less than human had these thoughts not ran through his mind. Courageous though Churchill undoubtedly was, the signs appear less than auspicious that he would have quit over Munich.

Churchill's abstention on the Munich vote earned him little popular acclaim. At Epping, his constituency, at least two resolutions were approved that reprimanded him for his 'continued disloyalty' to the government. But by the beginning of November, he had mastered his constituency uprising. However, Chamberlain's success left the Conservative opposition in disarray. A bashful Eden had failed Churchill during the last critical days of September. He continued to disenchant his admirers. 'He is not a good leader', conceded one. Leo Amery, of sharp intellect and so often right, was too much of a windbag, too often boring his listeners with his cogent reflections, to command widespread appeal. As for Churchill, he continued to sparkle, but there were occasional disturbing indications of advancing years. Once, in the Commons, he flopped wretchedly, fumbling with his notes, confused in delivery. 'He is becoming an old man,' Harold Nicolson noted. 'He is certainly a tiger, who, if he misses his spring is lost.[36]

Less than a year after Churchill's Munich philippic, the war he had long anticipated broke out. Munich had earned eleven months of peace. Then, he had been prepared for war. Later, he came to admit that the intervening months had not been entirely wasted, the balance shifting gradually towards Britain.[37] By the summer of 1939 he found himself in general agreement with the government's rearmament programme and defence and foreign policies. 'In principle there are no differences between us,' he disclosed to Halifax (and through him, to Chamberlain), 'if differences remain, they will only be upon emphasis and method upon timing and degree'.[38]

Churchill was now speaking from a position of increased authority. Since Munich, events had borne out his direst predictions. Anglo-German relations had worsened. Hitler, frustrated at being denied a war at Munich, his self-confidence dangerously inflated, was less inclined to talk his way out of a crisis. Whatever the hope in some government circles, there were to be no more sealed bargains. Hitler took to abusing Churchill, verbal assaults that in the circumstances could only boost Churchill's reputation. In November, the Germans perpetrated their organized pogrom against the Jews, *Kristallnacht*, another indication of the barbarous nature of Nazidom. That winter, there were rumours of an imminent German strike into the Low Countries. In January, Chamberlain and Halifax returned empty-handed from Rome, after being contemptuously dismissed by Mussolini as 'the tired sons of a long line of rich men'. In March, German armed forces entered Bohemia and Moravia, tearing up the Munich agreement, destroying what remained of Czechoslovakia, despite the British guarantee of its frontiers. Shortly afterwards, Memel was annexed to the Reich. A month later Mussolini, who was also crying for the return of Nice and Corsica, occupied Albania. In May, the Pact of Steel was signed, signifying political-military cooperation between Germany and Italy. During the summer, German pressure on Poland, that had begun the previous autumn, mounted steadily, terminating in the war crisis of August 1939. Vindicated by this aggressive, brutal record, Churchill appeared before the British public, no longer as a panic-monger, but as a neglected and abused prophet who had finally come into his own.

To Churchill's satisfaction, the government met these challenges by adopting policies he had consistently advocated: increased rearmament; the opening of a 'national register', the first stage towards conscription; above all, his Grand Alliance strategy. After the decimation of Czechoslovakia, Britain erected its own eastern system: a guarantee to Poland and similar assurances to Greece and Roumania, rounded off by a mutual assistance pact with Turkey. Churchill applauded. Of course, he complained that it all came two or three years too late, but he would not deny the new robustness evident in British policy, and of no less significance, in public resolve. The greatest question mark hung over the Soviet Union. In Churchill's opinion, the newly constructed diplomatic front in the East made little sense without its inclusion. First, would the Poles agree? Churchill well understood their need to balance off Nazi Germany against Bolshevik Russia, and their fear of being swallowed up by either, or both, of their more powerful neighbours. Still, he pressed for 'a definite association between Poland and Russia', in the event a goal that proved impossible to attain.

At home, there were problems of a different sort. Since the wars of intervention, Anglo-Soviet relations, although regularized, also assumed the nature of an uneasy truce. In the long haul to induce the Soviet Union to join the western alliance system, confused signals predominated. Were the British encouraging Germany to drive eastwards, the Ukraine often mentioned as bait, as the Soviets repeatedly estimated? In fact, this made no sense at all, as it implied that Britain was out to sabotage its own policy, for any German move to the east would have triggered off the British guarantees in eastern Europe, provoking a clash with Germany, while the whole point of British policy was to deter, or at least defer, such a confrontation. Or conceivably the devious, machiavellian-like British were up to more sophisticated tricks? A Polish-style Munich, perhaps? As The Times had interpreted the Polish guarantee as an obligation to defend Poland's 'independence' but not 'every inch of [its] present frontiers' – a judgement upheld by Chamberlain in private, but condemned by Churchill in public as 'sinister' – there were, ostensibly, grounds for concern. Perceptions, clearly, were more compelling than reality.[39]

Many among Britain's ruling circles, Chamberlain included, regarded the

Soviet Union with profound suspicion: militarily incompetent, politically opportunistic, an implacable ideological foe. Not having brought the Soviet Union into play at Munich, Churchill constantly insisted, had been Chamberlain's 'fundamental mistake'. Would Chamberlain slip up again? The signs were inauspicious. Only with great reluctance did Chamberlain, at the end of May, accept a Cabinet decision to offer a pact (together with France) to Russia.[40] The on-going negotiations were conducted on both sides with much trepidation and distrust, not the most promising recipe for success, particularly as the Soviet Union was actively considering its German option.

Churchill was not beset by these doubts. Throughout the summer he agitated for a Soviet alliance, boosting his public image as a decisive, forceful, daring statesman, courageously bent on securing British interests. Any hint of defeatism roused his anger. At a dinner party in June 1939 he lashed into Joe Kennedy, the American ambassador, who had been impertinent enough to assert that Britain would be thoroughly licked in a war against Germany.

> It may well be true that this country will at the outset of this coming and to my mind almost inevitable war be exposed to dire peril and fierce ordeals ... Yet these trials and disasters ... will but serve to steel the resolution of the British people and to enhance our will for victory ... Yet supposing (as I do not for one moment suppose) that Mr Kennedy were correct in his tragic utterance, then I for one would willingly lay down my life in combat, rather than, in fear of defeat, surrender to the menaces of these most sinister men. It will then be for you, for the Americans, to preserve and maintain the great heritage of the English-speaking peoples.[41]

It was the first of his wartime speeches.

By this time the press had taken up Churchill's cause, pressing for his inclusion in the government. Posters appeared in the West End asking, 'What Price Churchill?' None of this was sufficient to convince Chamberlain. No matter how closely Churchill identified with the Party, or however high his reputation soared, he was not wanted. His personal following virtually non-existent, he could offer Chamberlain nothing but trouble. Said to be 'terrified' of the prospect of Churchill's return to office, Chamberlain harped back to his disruptive behaviour when in Cabinet. A perpetual irritant, Churchill monopolized its time, swamped it with lengthy memoranda and wild ideas, lost his temper when crossed. Churchill was also, Chamberlain made clear, 'Public Enemy No. 1 in Berlin', hinting that he would be an obstacle to a possible arrangement with Germany were Hitler to bid for Danzig 'in a normal way', pointlessly disrupting the guarded exchanges that were still in progress. To dash Churchill's hopes, Chamberlain was not above manipulating the press to discredit him.[42]

As the allied approach to the Soviet Union faltered, so the likelihood of a Soviet-German deal increased. Since Munich, the Soviet Union's sense of isolation had grown. Having been deliberately excluded from territorial settlements that directly affected its security, the Soviet Union could ask, with justification: to what purpose? To the Soviet mind, the answer seemed self-evident: another western deal with Germany to divert Nazi energies eastwards, an assumption basic to Soviet foreign policy throughout these months. To avert this calamity, the Soviet Union could itself arrive at a deal with Germany, in this way deflecting German bellicosity westwards. Even the prospect of such a compact would massively boost the stock of the Soviet Union in western eyes, impressing upon them the immense benefits a Soviet alliance would bring – or conversely the terrible cost to be paid should the Soviet option be shelved. In the aftermath of Munich, a hint of this kind had been dropped. The Soviet Deputy Foreign Minister had taken aside the French ambassador in Moscow: 'My poor friend, what have you done? For us I see no other way out than a fourth partition of Poland.' The following March, Stalin turned his invective on Britain and France, accusing them of warmongering, warning that he would not 'pull their chestnuts out of the fire for them'. Soviet-German contacts at an economic level were then expanded to include political matters, and pursued concurrently with the talks being conducted with the western powers. Playing off both sides against the middle, Stalin possessed a further advantage. Privy to information from highly placed Soviet moles in London, Warsaw, and Tokyo, he was able to orchestrate his moves in a manner denied his adversaries. It was as though, in the words of one commentator, he was playing poker 'with marked cards'.[43]

A Bolshevik-German bloc had been Churchill's greatest fear since his interventionist days. With the advent of the Nazis, the prospect assumed a nightmarish quality. In June 1939, a German source informed him that a Hitler-Stalin accord 'was imminent'. 'A more or less early war [was] certain!' he concluded. Perturbed at the lack of progress in the Russian talks, he urged Chamberlain to treat the Soviet Union as an equal, stressing its 'vital major interest' in the defence of the Baltic states, Poland and Romania, hinting at the need for flexibility to meet Russian requirements. Above all, it was imperative to bring the talks to a swift and successful conclusion. Whatever British intentions, the impression remained strong that they (and the French) were conducting the negotiations in a most off-hand manner. Did they really care about the outcome? The Russians kept all options open until the last moment. But no doubt they contemplated Chamberlain's three resolute flights to Germany and wondered why a delegation of officials, albeit senior in rank, who had proceeded leisurely – overland and by ship – to Moscow, had been foisted upon them.

This British lack of urgency was overtaken by the signing of the German-Soviet non-aggression pact on 23 August, its secret protocols providing for Russian primacy in the Baltic states and Besserabia, together with the partition of Poland, an irresistible bait for Stalin. War threatened, but was it certain? Chamberlain still held there was a slender chance of securing peace. Whatever form the current German-Soviet agreement took, he warned Hitler it 'cannot alter Great Britain's obligation to Poland'. It was, however, far too late for this kind of paper rattling. With Poland isolated, Hitler saw no reason to back down. He had already told his military commanders that he intended to crush Poland. 'All my life I have played for all or nothing.' He was set on war.[44]

While these events were taking place, Churchill was in France, inspecting the Maginot Line – 'very impressed with what he saw' – and relaxing at Consuelo Balsan's château, Saint Georges-Motel, near Dreux. Before he left England, he had had supported a motion to recall Parliament on 21 August. 'An odd moment . . . [for MPs] to go on a two months' holiday', he thought. There was an atmosphere of impending crisis: fleet movements; air defence preparations; allied precautionary measures; and in the East, German troop movements. But Chamberlain rejected the appeal. Parliament dispersed, only to reconvene hurriedly in the wake of the Nazi-Soviet pact. Churchill rushed back to London. Chamberlain, dignified but uninspiring, led the Commons through the ramifications of the Nazi-Soviet pact, 'exactly like a coroner summing up a case of murder'. In a deeply despondent mood, war expected at any moment, it passed an Emergency Powers Bill.

Churchill spent the last week of peace mainly at Chartwell. At 8.30 in the morning of 1 September he received a telephone call from Count Edward Raczynski, the Polish ambassador to London, informing him that German armies had crossed into Poland at daybreak. That afternoon he was summoned to 10 Downing Street. Chamberlain, pessimistic at the hope of averting war, invited him to join 'a small War Cabinet of Ministers without Departments'. Churchill agreed without comment. When the House met that evening, Chamberlain, visibly under tremendous emotional stress, read out 'very slowly' the allied despatch delivered to Berlin. It was in the nature of a warning: unless Germany gave a firm pledge to suspend all military activities and withdraw its troops from Poland, Britain would instantly honour its obligations. But why was no time limit set? wondered some members.[45]

The same question was repeatedly asked throughout the following day. One problem was how to work out a coordinated response with the French. Utilizing the Italians, Bonnet, the French Foreign Minister, slippery, evasive, not above lying when it suited him, was desperately searching for another conference formula. The French procrastinated all day. Bonnet put forward a twenty-four-, perhaps forty-eight-hour time limit to the proposed allied ultimatum. By now the temper of the Cabinet and the House was running far ahead of these fancies. The feeling of the Cabinet was in favour of a deadline at midnight. When Chamberlain met the House later that evening, his statement was loosely phrased. Was there to be another Munich? Arthur Greenwood, the Labour Party spokesman, rose to answer him. From the Tory benches, Leo Amery shouted, 'Speak for England'. Chamberlain turned round, 'as if stung'. To a scene that could hardly have been improved upon by any dramatist, the House adjourned in 'indescribable confusion'.[46]

Throughout this extraordinary day, Churchill was in a state of limbo. Was Britain at war, or not? Was he in the government, or not? All day he paced up and down, 'like a lion in a cage', waiting for Chamberlain's call. It never came. Churchill and his friends met at his flat at Morpeth Mansions to consider their position. Still undecided how to act, he telephoned the French embassy to stiffen their backbone. Later, around midnight, he contacted his 'friend' in the government (Leslie Hore-Belisha, the Secretary of State for War) who revealed to him that the Cabinet, which had reassembled at about the same time, had decided there would be no more delay in delivering the ultimatum. Churchill reported to his companions that it had been 'a very stormy Cabinet'. The metaphor was chosen with care. Outside, a fierce storm darkened London, blinding rain flooding its streets. Inside 10 Downing Street, the Cabinet had decided to present the ultimatum at 9 o'clock the following morning, to expire two hours later. 'Right, gentlemen,' said Chamberlain quietly, 'this means war.' No sooner had he spoken than a deafening thunderclap silenced the proceedings, accompanied by a blinding flash of lightning that lit up the Cabinet room.[47]

All morning the Cabinet waited for a response from the German government, but in vain. On Sunday, 3 September, at 11.15 in the morning, a bitterly disillusioned Chamberlain broadcast to the nation that Britain was at war with Germany. As the National Anthem was being played at the end of his speech, the air-raid sirens sounded – a false alarm, it later transpired. At Morpeth Mansions, Churchill, overcome by curiosity, went up to the roof and stood staring up at a cloudless sky dotted with barrage balloons. Being told to set an example, he retired to the basement shelter, a bottle of brandy tucked under his arm. Examining his surroundings, he pronounced them sadly ill-appointed. No telephone or portable radio, he cried impatiently, stamping his foot.[48] Churchill's second German war had begun.

His Finest Hour

Remember, Churchill once told Tito, the wielding of power keeps men young. Eight months before the outbreak of war, he had been dismissed as a tiger who had lost his spring. When, on 3 September, Neville Chamberlain offered him the Admiralty as well as a seat in the War Cabinet, the spring returned. The thought of action stimulated him. How much more 'agreeable' to have the right 'to act', to issue 'directions', than the privilege of rendering 'advice' and talking 'at large'. Of course, lacking all inhibition Churchill did both, on the grandest of scales, often to the intense annoyance of his colleagues and subordinates. But despite the obvious drawbacks of his behaviour, it also constituted one of his greatest contributions to the British war effort. An eye-witness to his ebullient presence compared him to a stone flung into a pond: 'the ripples go out in all directions, galvanizing people at all levels to "press on" – and they did'. On his taking over the Admiralty, the message 'Winston is back' was flashed to the Fleet. From that moment on, the ripples never ceased to ruffle the – to his fancy – sluggish waters of Whitehall.[1]

In 1915, he had been compelled to vacate the Admiralty in despair and disgrace. Now he returned to its historic board room in circumstances highly charged with emotion. The surroundings were all too familiar: his old high-backed mahogany and leather chair, the great octagonal table, his wooden map-case. But now as his First Sea Lord, he had Sir Dudley Pound, a far more staid figure than the brilliant Fisher. Conventional of mind, but highly ambitious and with a keen sense of duty, Pound suffered from arthritis of the hip and tired easily. In the spring of 1939, Churchill had publicly opposed Pound's deployment of the Mediterranean fleet. When they now met they 'eyed each other amicably and doubtfully'. At six o'clock the same evening he took office, Churchill welcomed his staff. With a portrait of Nelson eyeing the proceedings, he concluded his speech with the exhortation, 'Gentlemen, to your tasks and duties'.[2]

The first tasks that awaited Churchill must have reminded him of the opening days of the Great War. By the end of September more than

160,000 personnel of the BEF, complete with supplies and equipment, had taken up their positions in northern France, a complicated logistical exercise that was accomplished without loss of life. There was also a pressing need to secure 'command of the seas'. In 1939, Britain needed to import by sea fifty-five million tons of goods in order to survive, a figure that would rise dramatically with the exigencies of war. To ensure this major operation she possessed the largest merchant fleet in the world, some 4,000 ocean-going and coastal ships.[3] Guaranteeing that these supplies continued to sustain the British war effort was the job of the Royal Navy which, at the outbreak of war, enjoyed a marked numerical superiority over the German fleet.

Yet merely comparing the tonnage on both sides was misleading. For one thing, more up-to-date German naval technology cut down the margin. For another, despite Churchill's confident aside that the navy was 'absolutely efficient', its imposing complement of 220 surface war vessels concealed serious flaws. It lacked sufficient numbers of escort ships – a consequence also of Churchill's 'cruiser battles' of the 1920s – and mine sweepers. Nor were the defences of its main bases adequate. Highly vulnerable to air and submarine attack, in the first two months of hostilities the carrier, *Ark Royal*, narrowly escaped destruction from the air, while a German U-boat penetrated the booms at Scapa Flow and sank the battleship, *Royal Oak*, with the loss of 833 men, news that brought tears to Churchill's eyes. Until these deficiencies were made up, the Home Fleet, in Churchill's depressing words, was 'driven out of Scapa'. By the end of the year, only nine out of Britain's fifteen capital ships were still operational.

It was only by an immense effort, the employment of eight hunter-packs, that the navy succeeded, by December, in clearing the seas of two German surface raiders, the pocket-battleships *Deutschland* and *Graf Spee*. Churchill, of course, largely inherited this situation. But he too had optimistically championed the conventional wisdoms that had spawned some of the navy's defects. He still firmly believed that ASDIC (sonar detection) had 'mastered' the submarine threat and that air power did not 'invalidate' battleships.[4] By rapid introduction of the now non-controversial convoy system and through the sheer weight of its naval power, Britain gained command of the seas, though its greatest challenge was still to come.

Churchill was not only concerned with repairing the navy's short-comings, or infusing it with his defiant energy. A member of the War Cabinet, his eye ranged further. By end of September, Poland had been partitioned by the German-Soviet armies; two weeks later, the Soviet Union had firmly established itself in the Baltic states. As the western allies prepared for a German onslaught, Churchill's basic strategy remained constant. The power of the French army, coupled with British naval might and fortified by Britain's superior economic staying power, to be succoured, hopefully, by the United States, would eventually prevail. Churchill's restless, combative mind sought to put drive into this programme. In Cabinet, his interminable memoranda and wordy contributions sparked off old memories. Unkind tongues wagged. Remembering his *World Crisis* – his 'brilliant autobiography, disguised as a history of the universe' – they wondered whether he was not already composing the first chapters of his new memoirs. Equally, many were impressed by his irrepressible energy. Even Lady Astor, hard though she tried, could not cast out of her mind the treasonable wish that Churchill should replace Chamberlain.

Of course, not all were happy with Churchill's forays into spheres beyond his immediate domain, his 'Utmost Fish' order – intended to resolve the shortage of fresh fish – being a case in point. This carping did not deter him. It never had. Stickers labelled 'ACTION THIS DAY' gave added urgency to his instructions, while his ubiquitous prayers, 'pray do this' or 'pray do that', continued to grace his subordinates' desks. In any case, keeping a watchful eye on the overall picture was more in the nature of a vocation for Churchill, not merely a function of his standing as a member of the War Cabinet.[5]

Churchill generated vitality. The Admiralty buzzed with 'electricity' when he was present. When he was away 'it was dead, dead, dead'. His energy was phenomenal, conserved by his daily routine, perfected over the years, that recharged him but exhausted his associates. Much of his time, he spent on tour, inspecting the Fleet, its naval bases and stores. Each Tuesday, perhaps also to broaden his political base, he hosted a dinner at the Admiralty, inviting a bevy of public figures including politicians with whom he had so recently been at odds. When Neville Chamberlain recounted his youthful, alas unsuccessful, endeavours to grow sisal on a small island in the Caribbean, Churchill's heart warmed to him. Here, between soup and dessert, this sober Englishman reminded him of 'a hard-bitten pioneer from the outer marches of the British Empire!'

The pressures of his crowded timetable were countered not only by his extraordinary stamina, but also by the smooth running of his office machinery, in particular his map room, organized by Captain Richard Pim, who charted daily how the war was developing. Churchill also installed Lindemann as head of a private statistical section, whose mandate extended beyond the naval war. 'Let us have the cold-blooded facts,' Churchill pleaded. Although it was suspected that Lindemann sifted some of these facts from *Whitaker's Almanack*, or other handy reference books, and fed Churchill with as much nonsense as sound advice, his intimacy with Churchill allowed him influence given to few others. Like any enterprising, ambitious, successful minister, Churchill exploited his officials' expertise, moulding their talents to suit his will. Their job was to guide him. But it would have been quite out of character had he submitted meekly to their counsel. Sometimes he overstepped their mark, the strain of recklessness that had hindered him in the past showing through, offending not only their bureaucratic sensibilities but also their good sense. 'I have to be a sort of nurse at times!' grumbled Eric Seal, his principal private secretary, 'He's very like a spoilt child in many ways.' It was a sentiment that would be heard many times before the war came to an end.[6]

Naturally, Churchill's main preoccupation was in the realm of high strategy. He already had much to keep him occupied, but the impish spirit in him, perhaps moved by a prophetic intuition, anticipated more exciting scenarios than the 'Phoney War'. 'What a dull naval war this will be,' he remarked. 'We have only Germany to fight. Now if we fought Germany, Italy and Japan together, that would be much more interesting.'[7] Meanwhile, he concerned himself with the immediate realities. Nothing escaped his notice. But the most pressing need was to take the war to Germany. He called for a French strike in the West, with British air cover, to alleviate Poland's agony. Should Germany violate the Low Countries, he argued that the Ruhr would be a legitimate target for British bombers. He toyed with the idea of destroying the Kiel Canal. Sowing the Rhine with mines was his answer to the German magnetic mine. These warlike ideas were rejected by more timid – some might add prudent – minds on both sides of the Channel. At the same time, he urged the rapid expansion of the BEF – forty divisions by the end of the first year, fifty to sixty by 1941 – to prepare for 'decisive operations' the following spring.[8]

Churchill's temperament was not geared to the pace of the 'Phoney War'. 'While the Germans used bombs we only dropped leaflets', he told the War Cabinet. For all that, cool judgement dictated that Britain should not enlarge the number of her enemies. There was no point in needlessly provoking Italy or Japan into belligerent acts. Reluctantly, Churchill agreed that convoys should be re-routed from the Mediterranean to around the Cape; while from July to October 1940, Britain sealed off the Burma Road, the major supply route for Chinese nationalist forces fighting Japan. Nor had Churchill abandoned all hope of renewing relations with the Soviet Union. Paradoxically, he perceived some advantage in the Nazi-Soviet division of eastern Europe, regarding it as no more than a short-term truce that sharpened the historic Teuton-Slav conflict. Russian policy, he broadcast to the nation, 'is a riddle wrapped in a mystery inside an enigma', but 'the historic life interests of Russia', he continued, would never tolerate that 'Slavonic peoples' be subject to Nazi domination.[9]

For Churchill, this re-merging of interests against Nazi Germany would falter slightly in the heat of the Russo-Finnish war. Ultimately it stood the test of his analysis, as did his perception of the United States as Britain's trump war-card. There can be no doubt that he recognized that Britain's survival depended upon the intervention of the United States. With the encouragement of the Cabinet, Churchill carefully fostered his relationship with Roosevelt.[10] It was an intimacy based on genuine mutual admiration – even though later it was adorned with flourishes of artistic licence, particularly by Churchill. On closer examination, the 'special relationship', always more meaningful in London than in Washington, was highly ambivalent and concealed much tension. It proved to be one of the ironies of Churchill's war that his American friends, while adamant about maintaining Britain, displayed little patience with what they considered to be its archaic imperial pretensions.

At this stage, Churchill was reasonably optimistic about the outcome of the war. 'All will come right', was a favourite observation. 'Stand firm,' he told Halifax, and 'the Germans may themselves disintegrate.' 'We have only to persevere to conquer,' he reassured the House, in another morale-boosting oration. With the French army still intact, and the BEF gathering strength day by day, he could confidently preach perseverance. Despite some losses, he was also sure that the naval war was going well. Indeed, he was willing to give odds of 500 to 1 against any allied ship being sunk. The German fleet had been swept from the seas; convoys were on the move; the northern blockade, the navy's 'principal offensive naval measure', was being enforced; and the Americans had set up a safety-zone along their eastern seaboard, extending 300 miles into the Atlantic, in which belligerent activity was prohibited, an initiative that considerably eased the escort duties of the navy.[11]

But even if the naval war was not going as planned, a few cheerful proclamations for public consumption – that would incidentally also rub off on the bearer of good tidings – would be in order. In January, in another upbeat declaration, he claimed – perhaps under the influence of Lindemann's calculations – to be 'pretty certain' that half the U-boat fleet had been sunk; the true figure was closer to ten per cent. A first-class row erupted, with Churchill not only refusing to accept the correct estimation but also transferring the offending officer to another post, an act, as one admiral kindly put it, that revealed 'Winston in one of his naughtiest moods'. Early in the war he had directed that Admiralty bulletins should maintain a high reputation for 'truthfulness, and the tone should not be forced'. This commendable ruling proved, at times, too challenging for him to observe. His Director of Naval Intelligence had cause to note: 'He did not hesitate not to tell them [the public] the truth or to paint a rosy picture that had no connection with reality.'[12] Churchill would not tolerate pessimism or those who implanted it. Those who failed to live up to his high standards of expectation fell into instant disfavour and were moved to less sensitive, or more remote, posts.

Let Hitler 'stew in his own juice', Churchill recorded, meanwhile Britain would concentrate on rearmament and 'weaving-up [its] alliances'.[13] Having guaranteed Greece and Roumania and signed a pact with Turkey, Britain was already extended in the eastern Mediterranean. Still, beckoning from the Low Countries to Scandanavia and back again to the Balkans were other neutral countries, potential threads in Churchill's tapestry. Their faint-heartedness considerably irked Churchill. Why did they bow 'humbly and in fear' to German threats, hoping that 'if he feeds the crocodile enough, the crocodile will eat him last?' Pusillanimous and self-centred, the neutrals were playing Hitler's game. His broadcast was harshly received by his 'unfortunate neutrals'. It was certainly disowned by those in government who had been patiently wooing them and now held that Churchill's fulminations had set back their efforts three months. Halifax objected strongly. Churchill, full of charm, replied: 'Asking me not to make a speech is like asking a centipede . . . not [to] put a foot on the ground.'[14]

No neutral country heeded Churchill's counsel, not even 'the resolute Turk'. Ireland, a member of the Commonwealth, legally at war 'but skulking', was a particular bugbear. In the crucial struggle to maintain Britain's supplies, Churchill demanded the use of the treaty ports on its western coast, even to the point of seizing them should that perverse country, ruled by a 'malignant minority', persist in enjoying 'the best of both worlds'. The Cabinet turned down his suggestion, fearful of its effect on Ireland as a potential recruiting-ground and its repercussions on Anglo-American relations.[15]

But Churchill still sought areas where it would be profitable to probe German vulnerability. As during the Great War, his eye was drawn towards the peripheries, the Balkans and Scandanavia. Early on, he favoured mobilizing a Balkan front against Germany. He then saw Italy, although allied to Germany, as a candidate for an overall agreement, one that would reduce troops concentrations in the area and guarantee freedom of navigation in the Mediterranean.[16] Reasonable propositions, perhaps, but he sadly misjudged Mussolini's bloated ambitions. That left the Baltic.

'The command of the Baltic was vital to the enemy,' wrote Churchill.[17] Indispensable as a shield for Germany's long defenceless northern coast-line, it also ensured the smooth flow of vital supplies from Scandinavian countries to Germany, in particular iron ore from Sweden. Not only would Britain gain primacy of the Baltic, such an audacious feat would doubtless prompt the Scandinavian countries to join the allies, while its effect on the Soviet Union would be 'far-reaching'.

In essence, these arguments had been employed, in vain, by Fisher and Churchill in 1914–15. Three days after the outbreak of war, Churchill revived a scheme to send into the Baltic a self-supporting task force, composed mainly of old battleships, with escort and supply vessels, and preceded by specially prepared 'mine bumpers'. But daunted by its formidable logistic difficulties, his professional advisers were fearful of locking up much of their naval strength, without adequate air cover, in an enclosed sea from which there might be no escape. By mid-January 1940, the scheme was abandoned, a decision Churchill accepted 'reluctantly'.[18] But Churchill was drawn irresistibly to some form of action in the far north, against Norway, codenamed 'Jupiter'. It was never implemented, his military staff always shelving it with sound reason.[19]

If Churchill was not allowed into the Baltic, he sought other means to hurt Germany in the region. By mining Norwegian waters – or alternatively laying a barrage of mines across the entire North Sea! – Britain would cut off the supply of Swedish iron ore to Germany, thereby, Churchill argued, striking a decisive blow 'at Germany's war-making capacity equal to a first-class victory in the field or from the air'. Nor was Churchill averse to occupying Narvik and Bergen should Germany choose to 'fire back'.[20]

A new impetus was given to these ideas when, on 30 November, Russia launched a war against Finland. Coming to her aid would allow the allies both to control Narvik and to lay their hands on the Swedish iron-ore fields. Although Churchill had initially favoured concessions by Finland, once the shooting began his temper turned more militant. His anti-Communist fervour was roused. Most of the Cabinet shared his sentiments, as did their French allies, who cultivated a sharp thirst for action. But as usual, Churchill expressed himself more eloquently than his contemporaries. He forecast a return to 'the Dark Ages', 'every vestige of human progress' blotted out should the Finns, that 'splendid Northern race', succumb to 'the dull brutish force' of the Soviets. With such emotions running wild, it was hardly surprising that Churchill favoured action. By February, two divisions were put on the alert. Would these measures draw the Soviet Union into the war, widening the conflict with Germany? Churchill, concentrating very much on the issue at hand, elected to skip over this possibility, though it was real enough.[21]

The notion of opening a second front against the Soviet Union, however faint, is so surrealistic that it defies rational analysis. Ironside, chief of the Imperial General Staff 'thought it a half-cocked scheme'. 'We have no war policy whatever,' he grumbled, particularly as he was being asked at the same time to place forty divisions in the line alongside the French. Norway and Sweden remonstrated fiercely to the allies, fearful that Germany would fall upon them. Their opinion happened to be marginal to Churchill's calculations. As 'We are fighting to re-establish the reign of law and to protect the liberties of small countries,' he proclaimed, they must not 'tie our hands'.[22] His colleagues judged differently, swayed by the violent nature of their protest, the projected repercussions in the United States, and the firmly expressed reluctance of the Dominions to become involved. By mid-March, the Soviet Union had secured its aims, having at last overpowered the Finns. This finally put paid to the idea of allied armed intervention on their behalf, one of the most bizarre episodes of the war.

From the outbreak of hostilities, Churchill had urged these schemes upon the government, certain of the navy's capacity to thwart any effective German intervention.[23] Eventually his arguments made headway, though he was not party to the final decision. Chamberlain took it, at a meeting of the Supreme War Council on 28 March, not to appease Churchill, whom he could control, but to restrain the French who, incredibly, were pressing to expand the war against the Soviet Union, proposing operations in the Black Sea and the Caspian, the aim being 'to paralyse' the Russian economy and deprive Germany of its benefits. This was too much for Chamberlain, who preferred moving against Norway, another feature of the French proposals. A deal was worked out: the French agreed to the mining of the Rhine; the British would take similar action in Norwegian waters.[24] On 5 April 1940 a force sailed northwards, ground troops being held in reserve should the Germans respond. By then it was far too late. Four days later the Germans struck, ruthlessly and with frightening efficiency. By the end of the day, despite a strong British naval presence, they had occupied Denmark and were in control of all major Norwegian ports, from Oslo to Narvik.

'We have been completely outwitted,' Churchill admitted to Pound. In part, this was due to over-confidence, but also to a failure to evaluate correctly intelligence reports, that had been reaching Whitehall for some weeks, of an intended German blow in the region.[25] Having lost the initiative, the British never regained it. Reeling from the relentless pressure of German land and air strikes, they could only evacuate one bridgehead after another. The Norwegian campaign, that dragged on for almost two months, was a disaster. Flawed intelligence, poor planning, faulty logistics, divided command, muddle and improvisation, all contributed, and were crowned by the devastating – and largely unforeseen – effects of German air power.

At the time, Churchill believed that Hitler, by legitimizing a British riposte, had made a 'grave strategic blunder'.[26] It is impossible to sustain this judgement. Valuable resources in manpower and *matériel* had been drawn away – some would say, squandered – from the main theatre, western Europe, for the sake of a campaign whose military and economic benefits could only be marginal to the outcome of the war. Nor could it be denied that a great sea power had been humiliated by a major land power in an operation that depended for its success upon the exercise of naval strength.

Churchill's responsibility for this débâcle was considerable. He had been the most tenacious advocate of the campaign, while as First Lord he held a particular responsibility for the navy's performance. He had also succeeded to the chairmanship of the Military Coordinating Committee, a body concerned with directing overall strategy. This appointment was something of a disaster. Churchill turned it into chaos with his 'enthusiastic eruptions' and 'verbosity and restlessness'. Chamberlain's intervention averted 'a first-class political crisis'. Undone, but not intimidated, Churchill concluded that to make a success of the job he needed 'the necessary powers', broadly hinting that he could then 'concert and direct the general movement of our war action' more effectively. When Chamberlain floated this idea it was met by offers to resign by the Secretaries of State for War and Air, Sam Hoare and Oliver Stanley. Nevertheless, Chamberlain went ahead and eventually succeeded in improvising an arrangement that Churchill thought 'an improvement', but that was sufficiently pliant to rein his exuberance.

Churchill resumed his duties, chairing the Committee when Chamberlain was absent. He was also made responsible for 'giving guidance and directions' to the Chiefs of Staff. Ismay was appointed a full member of their committee to act as liaison and to reduce friction to a minimum. Ismay was dismayed when Churchill attempted to set up a defence think-tank manned by his own creatures – Lindemann, Desmond Morton, and Oliver Lyttleton – and much preferred using the Military Wing of the Cabinet Secretariat, which he already ran.[27] In retrospect, this was one of the most important decisions of the war, since it regularized Churchill's relations with the military. On becoming Prime Minister, Churchill built upon Chamberlain's system, and it worked extraordinarily well. It was perhaps Chamberlain's last significant, if largely unsung, contribution to the British war effort.

Later, in carefully guarded language, Churchill admitted 'the prominent part' he played in the Norwegian *débâcle*. 'Half-cocked as usual', noted one adviser, 'He will try to be a naval strategist if not an actual tactician.'[28] All this inevitably raised memories of the Dardanelles. Admiral of the Fleet Sir Roger Keyes, retired but still hungry for action, remarked harshly: 'The iron of the Dardanelles had entered into his soul.' 'It was a marvel that I survived,' Churchill admitted afterwards, doubtless disturbed by the same analogy.[29] But he not only survived another ill-fated action, he plucked from it the ultimate prize, the premiership, his personal Holy Grail. If luck is an essential ingredient to any successful politician's (or general's) career, then it smiled on Churchill in the days to come.

From the beginning of May 1940 it was apparent that a great political crisis was in the making. There was much talk of a National Government, but not with Chamberlain at its head. On 7–8 May the House convened, ostensibly to debate the Norwegian campaign but in fact to review the government's overall war record. It was an occasion packed with high drama. Sir Roger Keyes, in his full admiral's uniform decorated with six rows of medals, chastized the government in a devastating emotional outburst. Amery, looking at Chamberlain, quoted Cromwell's merciless words to the Long Parliament: 'You have sat too long for any good you have been doing. Depart, I say, and let us have done with you. In the name of God, go!' Set the country an example, Lloyd George implored Chamberlain, and sacrifice 'the seals of office'.

Labour forced a division. Chamberlain appealed to his friends, making a most unfavourable impression. Churchill gallantly defended the government's policies, with such vehemence that he was constantly heckled from the Labour benches. The House divided on a three-line whip. As the MPs entered the lobbies the Tory faithfuls howled 'Quislings' and 'Rats': 'Yes-men', shouted back the dissidents. The government scraped home by eighty-one 'Ayes'. Widely interpreted as a vote of no-confidence, Josh Wedgwood, the veteran socialist, was observed waving his hands and singing 'Rule Britannia', his victory chant being taken up by an almost tone-deaf Harold Macmillan. 'Go, go, go, go!' cried other delighted members, drowning out their duet. Chamberlain rose and walked out of the Chamber, 'pale and angry'.[30]

It was clear that the government would have to be expanded, that a real national coalition, with Labour included, would have to be formed. But who would lead it? Halifax was the establishment's choice, from Buckingham Palace to Whitehall to Westminster. Labour leaders – who refused to serve under Chamberlain – also favoured him, although they thought Churchill to be a 'tolerable' choice. Even a public opinion poll put Churchill in second place as Chamberlain's successor – to Eden, of all people. The reverse side of this coin were the grave misgivings, widespread among leading military and civil figures, voiced at the likelihood of a Churchill premiership. 'Everybody here [at 10, Downing street] is in despair at the prospect,' noted John Colville, Chamberlain's devoted private secretary (and soon to be Churchill's). 'Rab' Butler colourfuly expressed a commonly held view. 'The good clean tradition of English politics,' he railed, 'had been sold to the greatest adventurer of modern political history.' Surrendering to 'Winston and his rabble was a serious disaster and an unnecessary one', mortgaging to 'a half-breed American, whose main support was that of inefficient but talkative people of a similar type', the future of the country.

On the afternoon of 9 May, Chamberlain, Halifax and Churchill met at 10 Downing Street, with David Margesson, the government Chief Whip, in attendance. This conversation, that confirmed Churchill as

Chamberlain's successor, has since assumed legendary dimensions. Churchill – seven years later – set the scene. Chamberlain, concerned at Churchill's marred relations with Labour, implied that Halifax would be the better choice. 'Usually I talk a great deal,' Churchill recalled, 'but on this occasion I was silent . . . As I remained silent, a very long pause ensued.' Halifax broke it, explaining why, as a peer, he was unsuitable for the post – a technical obstacle that could easily have been cleared away. 'By the time he had finished it was clear that the duty would fall upon me – had in fact fallen upon me.'

Had there been 'a very long pause'? And if so, who had advised Churchill to bridle himself in this wholly uncharacteristic fashion? Or had Churchill himself sensed that his great moment had arrived? Halifax's account, written the following morning, makes no mention of it. Very much to the point, it reiterates Halifax's aversion to becoming Prime Minister, his stomach churning at the prospect. Finally and reluctantly, Chamberlain, 'and Winston evidently with much less reluctance, finished by accepting my point of view'. Perhaps the 'long pause' never occurred – though Brendan Bracken (a most unreliable source) and Sir Kingsley Wood both claimed its authorship – and was tacked on later for dramatic effect. Does it really matter? It is abundantly clear that had Halifax wanted it, the premiership was his for the taking. It was not Churchill's celebrated silence that earned him the job, but Halifax's recurring 'stomach ache'. He judged, with pinpoint accuracy, that he did not possess the necessary qualities to lead a country at war. Churchill, with his flair and extraordinary talents – and perhaps, also, because of his shortcomings – did. As compensation, Halifax reasoned that he would stand behind Churchill's shoulder to restrain him in his wilder moments. The civilized world can only remain thankful for Halifax's delicate stomach, for there can be no doubt that Churchill was the right man for the job.[31]

The following evening, with German armies driving into Luxembourg and the Low Countries towards France, Churchill kissed hands to become Prime Minister. Supported (in theory) by 607 MPs out of 615, his government, now including Labour, enjoyed an unprecedented majority. So 'the Bluebottle has become a Purple Emperor,' applauded Hugh Cecil (once thought of as a potential Prime Minister), 'Let us rejoice.'[32] Churchill had come to power not as the undisputed leader of a great party, guiding it to victory in elections, but as the result of a fluke set of circumstances, impossible to forecast in advance and unlikely to repeat themselves in the future. Aged sixty-five, he had fulfilled his greatest ambition. At the head of a broad based national coalition, always his preferred choice, he would lead Britain out of the most acute crisis in its history, jealously guarding its status as a great imperial power. Fate had preserved him for this moment, as he always knew it would. There is no reason to doubt that he went to sleep that night inspired by a sense of destiny.

> I was conscious of a profound sense of relief. At last I had the authority to give directions over the whole scene ... all my past life had been but a preparation for this hour and for this trial ... I thought I knew a good deal about it all, and I was sure I should not fail. Therefore, although impatient for the morning, I slept soundly and had no need for cheering dreams. Facts are better than dreams.[33]

The following months moulded the Churchill who would be venerated by posterity. There was little he could do to turn the war to Britain's advantage. The initiative lay wholly with Germany. On becoming Prime Minister he was greeted by crowds outside the Admiralty with cries of 'Good luck, Winnie. God bless you.' He put on a brave face, but once inside the building he dissolved into tears. 'Poor people, poor people,' he cried, 'They trust me, and I can give them nothing but disaster for quite a long time.' Only six weeks after he had assumed office, German armies stood poised to strike across the English Channel. Belgium had surrendered: France had fallen. What remained of the BEF, 224,000 soldiers, together with 111,000 of their French allies, had been evacuated from Dunkirk. Throughout that summer and autumn, invasion threatened. Deprived of a continental base, his army routed and bereft of equipment, Churchill was asked by Paul Reynaud, the French Prime Minister, 'And then what will you do?' Churchill, 'his jaw thrust well forward', had no cut and dried answer, but 'broadly speaking he would propose to drown as many as possible of [the Germans] on the way over, and then to "*frapper sur la tête*" anyone who managed to crawl ashore'.[34] This was typical Churchillian defiance, spontaneous, uplifting for the spirit. Ultimately, there might be no option but to follow his resolute example. But in the meantime more pragmatic minds were keen to explore other approaches. And Churchill too was compelled to apply himself to these unpalatable matters.

Churchill wrote in *Their Finest Hour* that 'Future generations may deem it noteworthy that the supreme question of whether we should fight on alone never found a place upon the War Council agenda ... There was no discussion. Heart and soul we were together.' The truth, alas, was more prosaic. The bare essentials of the danger had been graphically set out by the Chiefs of Staff. With the BEF bottled up at Dunkirk, it presented a grim scenario. Air superiority was 'the crux of the matter'. Should Germany attain mastery of the skies, 'our land forces would be insufficient to deal with a serious invasion'. In the light of this dire assessment, opinions were aired in Cabinet as to whether a negotiated peace could be squeezed out of Germany, one that would guarantee Britain's independence and status as a world power. The previous October, when he had been more confident about the prospects for victory, he had refused to 'close the door upon any genuine offer'. Now, the situation had changed dramatically. For Churchill, as for most others, the destruction of the French army as an effective fighting force came as a traumatic shock. Would Britain even survive? After a particularly depressing visit to France, he told Ismay: 'You and I will be dead in three months' time.'[35]

Neville Chamberlain's diary for the end of May records Churchill as telling the Cabinet that 'if we could get out of this jam by giving up Malta and Gibraltar and some African colonies, he would jump at the chance.'[36] He was responding to the possibility of an overture to Germany, with the Italians acting as sponsors. Halifax, the chief prompter of this initiative, was not advocating surrender at any price. The differences were of degree, of evaluating the probability of an agreed settlement. Churchill put the odds at a thousand to one, too high even for such an inveterate gambler as he. For if the talks broke down, as he expected, it would have a devastating effect on public morale. Churchill refused to be dragged down 'the slippery slope with France'. Britain, he insisted, had to hold on for another 'two or three months', to demonstrate to the world 'that Germany had not beaten us'. 'It was idle to think that, if we made peace now, we should get better terms than if we fought it out.' Only then, with Britain's battered prestige refurbished, and if Hitler was prepared for 'peace on the terms of the restoration of the German colonies and the overlordship of Central Europe', would he consider a settlement. But Churchill was certain that even this handsome formula would not satisfy Hitler. He would demand a virtual capitulation – 'our fleet, our naval bases, and much else' – that would relegate Britain to the status of a second-rate power, albeit with its Empire, for the time being, intact.

Churchill's natural inclination was to fight on, to be acclaimed as an illustrious war leader. But perhaps he also sensed the academic nature of this controversy. After all, why should Hitler accept as a gift from the detested Churchill what he had already taken by force of arms? Nor had Hitler ever given any indication that his word was to be trusted. Why should Hitler, drunk with victory, behave any better now? Would it also be too fanciful to apply a moral dimension to Churchill's – and his Cabinet's – deliberations? Even the most cynical of politicians would, in the final analysis, have balked from turning Europe over to Hitler's thugs. Although there was as yet no talk of the holocaust, the civilized world had already seen the bestial nature of Nazi rule in occupied Austria, Czechoslovakia, and Poland.

Eventually, Churchill's view came to dominate. In an emotionally charged meeting with his full complement of ministers – mocked by Halifax as his 'Children's Hour' – he electrified his audience: 'Every man of you would rise up and tear me down from my place if I were for one moment to contemplate parley or surrender. If this long island story of ours is to end at last, let it end only when each one of us lies choking in his own blood upon the ground.' Loud cries of approval greeted his cry of defiance. No one dissented. 'We shall never surrender'? Undoubtedly. But would it be 'Victory at all Cost'? No one could be absolutely certain, not even Churchill. That it was Churchill's preferred aim there can be no doubt, though how he would achieve it was by no means clear.

The main thrust of these exchanges took place as the troops were being evacuated from the beaches of Dunkirk, less than three weeks after Churchill was appointed Prime Minister. He soon recovered his equilibrium, or at least wobbled less in private. Despite – perhaps because of – the talk of a settlement, his gut optimism revived, and with it his vision of total victory. Towards the end of June, he chastized the Foreign Office for airing the idea that 'common sense and not bravado would dictate'.[37]

In the 'great trial of strength' in the air, the Luftwaffe had been 'beaten back', its purpose 'frustrated'. The battered troops at Dunkirk might have challenged Churchill's judgement, but the 'trial of strength' went on. Once again, the Royal Air Force beat back the Luftwaffe, although by the narrowest of margins.[38] On 15 September, the climax of the struggle, Churchill visited No 11 Fighter Group Headquarters at Uxbridge. 'What reserves have we?' he asked. 'There are none,' replied Air Vice-Marshal Keith Park. Churchill 'looked grave', as well he might. But the Battle of Britain had been won. From attacking RAF installations, the Luftwaffe switched the weight of its assault against London and other urban centres. The massive German air offensive had been broken, although Britain's great cities continued to suffer terribly from bombing. In mid-October Hitler finally postponed his plan to invade Britain. Since July, he had been considering another option – an attack on the Soviet Union.

Throughout these weeks, as the shadow of an invasion deepened, Britain looked to its own salvation. This often involved painful rulings. Stimulated by reports of cooperation between German parachutists and local fifth columnists on the Continent, Britain took action against its own suspect groups. Local Fascist elements, Mosley and others of his ilk, were interned with little regret. But the order also went out to round up 'enemy aliens', mainly German, Austrian, or Czech refugees, once victims of Nazism, now casualties of an ugly strain of collective hysteria. Approximately 70,000 in number, many of whom were Jews, they included distinguished academics, scientists, musicians, artists, as well as ordinary folk. 'Collar the lot', instructed Churchill, convinced that he was protecting them from 'outraged public opinion'. Some committed suicide rather than be confined in British camps. This unhappy affair reached a horrible climax on 2 July when the *Arandora Star*, carrying 1,200 aliens, was torpedoed in the Atlantic, 720 of whom were lost. At first 'strongly in favour' of expelling all internees from Britain, Churchill later relented. Rather than treat 'friends as foes', would it not be more humane, and profitable, to conscript these anti-Nazi refugees into public service, or even the Pioneer Corps, or perhaps as 'a Foreign Legion' to serve in Iceland? Most internees were released within eighteen months. But, all in all, this was a most unsavoury episode.[39]

'To be great one's actions must be understood by simple people,' Clementine had once written to Churchill. He followed this sound advice, as the summer of 1940 passed into autumn – and as his confidence grew. There were some eye-catching gestures. To keep France going, he told the Cabinet, 'some dramatic announcement was clearly necessary'. So he agreed, at first reluctantly, to an Anglo-French Union, the creation of one nation out of two, an extravagant idea that was eventually turned down by the French government. Two weeks later, desperate that the French fleet should not fall into enemy hands, he ordered with an 'aching heart' that it be seized, or destroyed if there was no other alternative. At Mers-el-Kebir, near Oran, a powerful French battleship squadron was obliterated. More than 1,200 French sailors lost their lives. Churchill explained later it was 'a hateful decision . . . unnatural and painful'. But as he made clear, not to have taken it would have meant utter ruin. Justified as a lifesaving expedient, it impressed upon all, at home and abroad, Britain's – that is, Churchill's – determination 'to prosecute the war with the utmost vigour' until victory.[40]

More and more Churchill became the indispensable man of the moment. This was not always smooth running. He still lacked a political base. He knew he had been foisted upon the Conservative Party. In the Commons, Tory backwoodsmen cheered Chamberlain and greeted Churchill with studied coolness when he appeared for the first time as Prime Minister. 'I shan't last long,' Churchill said, as he left the Chamber 'much disconcerted'.

But there were limits beyond which Churchill dare not go in reconstructing his government. With the exception of Hoare, whom he had once described as 'a snake', the Old Gang was not purged, as many hoped it would be. Chamberlain and Halifax remained as members of the War Cabinet, together with Attlee and Greenwood from Labour. Churchill's cronies, Bracken, Beaverbrook, and Lindemann were rewarded with office, as was Eden, who was placed in the War Office, Duff Cooper, at the Ministry of Information (compensation for his brave stand over Munich), and Amery, who was shunted off, protesting, to the India Office. Otherwise, among the nineteen Conservative ministers of Cabinet rank there were no great surprises.

Here was cause for concern for the purists. In June, Churchill quashed the so-called under-secretaries' plot, a cabal that called for a 'Committee of Public Safety' of all the talents. Clearly edgy, Churchill told Boothby and Amery, both heavily involved, that they had better 'stick to the job he had given them', to mind their 'own business', or perhaps they would find they had 'no business to mind!' This had been a clumsy attempt by his supporters to help him run the war more efficiently. Even so, Churchill may have suspected that the plotters were scheming to promote Lloyd George in his place, still regarded by many as a formidable figure. Churchill too wished to exploit his experience, but Lloyd George spurned his offer.[41]

Grappling with a grave national crisis, and with doubtful forces at work in Parliament, Churchill had to feel his way gingerly. He had defused Halifax's threat of resignation after angry words had been exchanged about a compromise peace. Lloyd George said: 'He will not smash the Tory Party to save the country, as I smashed the Liberal Party.' But Churchill had no need to if he worked hand-in-glove with Chamberlain, still leader of the Party, and still the object of popular acclaim from the Tory benches. On the other hand, their relations ran smoothly, one temperament complementing the other. Was Churchill flattering Chamberlain? 'I am up and down and you are steady. It is helpful to feel that my decisions are approved by your judgement.'[42] It was a remarkable dénouement to a hitherto blustery relationship.

Whatever lay at the back of Churchill's mind, he was too well versed in politics not to appreciate that as Prime Minister he needed, at the very least, the benevolent neutrality of a party machine. By now Chamberlain was fatally stricken with cancer. At the end of September he retired and died six weeks later. Churchill, having hated the Tory Party and railed against 'dirty Tory hacks' in previous battles, now assumed its leadership, though not without some inner hesitation. Finally, he convinced himself of the need to sacrifice 'Party interest and Party feeling' to defend 'grand human causes', discovering that both he and the Conservatives now shared 'deep conceptions lying far beneath the superficial current of Party politics and the baffling of accidental events'. He had also to overcome Clementine's passionate objections. Concerned that Churchill would impair his image as a great national statesman, rising above sectarian party politics, uniting all classes of the nation in its life and death struggle, several 'ding-dong arguments' ensued.[43] As usual, Churchill prevailed. Perhaps he sensed he was on a winning streak. The metamorphosis was complete. After forty years of the most extreme swings in his political fortunes, he emerged crowned with the accolade he had always yearned for, Saviour of his People – at least until the national emergency was over.

Survival, the Chiefs of Staff had suggested to Churchill, depended upon sustaining 'the morale' of the nation. Here was a mission singularly fashioned to suit his unique talents. The issue at stake was crystal-clear. 'Conquer or die', as Churchill put it. His historical imagination was also at work. Once again Fortress Britain stood alone. 'I have always faithfully served two public causes which I think stand supreme,' he told a Conservative audience in October 1940, 'the maintenance of the enduring greatness of Britain and her Empire and the historical continuity of our Island life.' When asked, 'what exactly Winston did to win the war?' Attlee replied: 'Talk about it. In Cabinet he spoke about practically nothing else.' This was Churchill's message, one that he proclaimed over and again with all the single-minded tenacity that was part and parcel of his make-up. The magnificent phrases poured out:

> I have nothing to offer but blood, toil, tears and sweat . . . You ask what is our policy? I can say: It is to wage war, by sea, land and air, with all the might and with all the strength that God can give us; to wage war against a monstrous tyranny, never surpassed in the dark, lamentable catalogue of human crime. That is our policy. You ask, what is our aim? I can answer in one word: It is victory, victory at all costs, victory in spite of all the terror, victory, however long and hard the road may be; for without victory, there is no survival. Let that be realized; no survival for the British Empire, no survival for all that the British Empire has stood for . . . But I take up my task with buoyancy and hope . . . Come then, let us go forward together with our united strength. (13 May)

> We shall go on to the end, we shall fight in France, we shall fight on the seas and oceans, we shall fight with growing confidence and strength in the air, we shall defend our island, whatever the cost may be, we shall fight on the beaches, we shall fight on the landing grounds, we shall fight in the fields and in the streets, we shall fight in the hills; we shall never surrender. (4 June)

> Hitler knows that he will have to break us in this Island or lose the war. If we can stand up to him, all Europe may be free and the life of the world may move forward into broad, sunlit uplands. But if we fail, then the whole world, including the United States, including all that we have known or cared for, will sink into the abyss of a new Dark Age made more sinister, and perhaps more protracted, by the lights of perverted science. Let us therefore brace ourselves to our duties and so bear ourselves that if the British Empire and its Commonwealth last for a thousand years men will still say, 'This was their finest hour'. (18 June)

> Never in the field of human conflict was so much owed by so many to so few. (20 August)[44]

Ed Murrow, the American broadcaster, said that Churchill had 'mobilized the English language and sent it into battle'. His verbal artistry raised commonplace events or horrendous experiences to a sublime and heroic level. Even today, two generations removed, his words retain their stirring quality. At the time, with the danger so immediate and the odious nature of the enemy so manifest, they struck a popular sensitive nerve that responded willingly to his touch. A London Club commissioner was overheard saying, 'Anyhow, sir, we're in the Final, and it's to be played on the Home Ground.'[45] It was the desperate occasion that fired the romantic, swashbuckling, audacious side of Churchill's character, and that endowed his speeches with their historic, memorable ring.

Parliament heard the great rhetorician in his natural setting. The people heard him over the radio, or read his exhortations in the press, not quite the same thing. How effective was he as a broadcaster? Opinions varied. 'Boastful', 'overconfident', 'indiscreet', and 'vulgar' believed some. According to others, they added 'the fire and stimulus which were so badly needed'. Politicians − Eden, Baldwin, Halifax − registered high praise after his first broadcast as Prime Minister. Some literary notables were downright critical. 'How we despised his orations,' remembered the acerbic Evelyn Waugh. 'Ghastly', pronounced the usually admiring Harold Nicolson when he heard the 'finest hour' speech broadcast. But his wife, Vita Sackville-West, even listening to an announcer read his 'we shall never surrender' oration, felt 'shivers (not of fear) down [her] spine', 'stirred by his Elizabethan phrases'.[46] It would be safe to assume that the silent majority felt the same. The audience was enormous. An estimated seventy per cent of the population heard his twenty-five broadcasts from May 1940 to December 1941. But if there was any doubt about his microphone personality, he impressed himself on the people in other ways.

Throughout these months, and well into the following year, Churchill travelled the country, inspecting the devastation wrought by the German blitz, sometimes brought to tears by what he saw. Huge crowds followed him, crying 'Good old Winnie'. 'Are we downhearted?' he would ask them. 'No!' they shouted back. At Bristol, a worker remarked: 'There goes the bloody British Empire.' Churchill's face expanded into an enormous smile. '*Very* nith,' he lisped appreciatively. He was full of bounce. One of his aides, watching him leaping from one girder to another, suspended five feet in the air, was astonished at his agility. Visiting the bombed areas invigorated him, they pumped him up, as they did the harassed populace he set out to comfort. He had found his true element. Like Midas, everything he touched turned to gold. Baldwin, over a breakfast of kippers at the Dorchester, observed that 'The furnace of the war has smelted out all base metals from him'.[47]

Everywhere he went, Churchill was accompanied by a bevy of press and newsreel photographers, recording for posterity his public persona, his John Bull image. Once again, the audience was phenomenal. Every week between 25–30 million cinema tickets were sold. Churchill, that splendid, irrepressible showman did not disappoint his fans. On the screen, larger than life, they saw his short, portly figure clad in a quaint, old-fashioned overcoat, the inevitable bow tie protruding, his beaming face topped by a funny hat. Marching from one bomb site to another, munching on a cigar, one hand clutching a cane, he would raise the other, two fingers extended in his famous V for Victory sign – a gesture full of earthy symbolism, decoded by all as a saucy 'Up Yours' to Hitler. Churchill's popularity soared to astonishing heights. In June 1940, eighty-eight per cent of the population approved of him as Prime Minister, a figure that remained remarkably stable throughout the war – even though, at times, a significant gap opened up between Churchill's stature and the standing of his government. Churchill's oratory, his broadcasts and walkabouts, his unprecedented press coverage and leading role in newsreels exposed him to a hitherto undreamt of audience. Unabashed, he played eagerly to this vast gallery, gratifying its needs, delighted to see himself 'featured' as a movie hero. Here was the Churchill that freedom-loving peoples all over the world came to recognize, to admire, to idolize, to love [48] Out of it all, Churchill emerged as a genuine Superstar.

18

Standing Alone

Already Prime Minister, but determined not to repeat the Dardanelles fiasco, where he did not hold 'plenary authority', Churchill made himself Minister of Defence, with undefined powers, a position hitherto unknown in British politics. Appointing Eden to the War Office, Sinclair to Air, and Alexander to the Admiralty was interpreted by most observers as a sure indication that 'Winston intends to run the War himself'. He streamlined the machinery set up by Chamberlain,[1] and established a Defence Committee of which he was chairman to liaise between the Chiefs of Staff and the War Cabinet. As the war progressed, its conduct was left increasingly to the discretion of the Chiefs of Staff and Churchill, the vital link being Ismay.

Despite occasional lapses, this system worked smoothly enough. Whether it gave Churchill 'the plenary authority' he so much desired was quite another matter. Like the Queen in *Alice*, he was capable of believing 'as many as six impossible things before breakfast'. On occasion, he even put forward Lindemann's ideas under his own signature, a practice that raised many eyebrows. His brain-childs, imaginative and enterprising, were all too frequently seen as brainstorms. Eden spoke of Churchill's 'devastating effect on planning' and called for a Minister of Defence 'independent of the PM'. Churchill's aides tackled his impatience and wilfulness in a war of attrition, paring down his extravagant schemes until either they passed noisily away or else assumed more realistic proportions. In this process, Churchill exhibited commendable flexibility.[2]

There was another aspect to the whittling down of his 'plenary authority' that caused him far more concern, frustration, embarrassment, even humiliation, and that he was largely powerless to avert. Once the Grand Coalition had been formed, with the United States and the Soviet Union assuming increasingly the major burden of the war, his ability to resolve major strategic decisions lessened dramatically. More than once he referred to himself as Roosevelt's 'lieutenant'.[3]

Churchill's work habits had scarcely altered over the years. Whenever possible, he spent the morning in bed. Propped up with pillows, his gaudy dressing-gown wrapped around him, he would bark, chewing on his cigar, 'Gimme my Box', and begin work on his papers. At times, Smokey, his Persian cat, would lie at the foot of his bed, fondly nibbling his toes. This could lead to embarrassing misunderstandings. 'Get off, you fool,' Churchill once shouted into the telephone, hoping to deter Smokey but causing grave offence to General Sir Alan Brooke, listening at the other end of the line.[4] Often his secretaries had difficulty in interpreting his 'inarticulate grunts or single words thrown out without explanation' as meaningful instructions. If they did not grasp his intention, he could be wounding: 'Where on earth were you educated? . . . Why don't you read some books?' He cancelled meetings to suit his own convenience but no one else's. Noise, particularly hammering resulting from building operations that he himself had ordered, provoked outbursts of rage. His daily routine exhausted the most robust spirits. To the dismay of all except himself, his work sessions would drag on until anytime between two and four-thirty in the morning.[5]

Churchill's intimidating personality tended to overwhelm those who worked for him. His ministers were likened to 'a lot of schoolboys frightened by the headmaster'. 'Impossible to argue with', resenting criticism, his 'egoistic and dictatorial manner' distressed his admirers. One wag suggested that Churchill appoint Vic Oliver – his son-in-law and a professional comedian – as Minister of Information.[6] At one stage Clementine felt compelled to intervene. 'My darling Winston,' she wrote:

> I must confess that I have noticed a deterioration in your manner; & you are not so kind as you used to be. It is for you to give the Orders & if they are bungled . . . you can sack anyone & everyone. Therefore with this terrific power you must combine urbanity, kindness & if possible Olympic calm . . . you won't get the best results by irascibility & rudeness. They *will* breed either dislike or a slave mentality.
> Please forgive your loving devoted & watchful Clemmie.[7]

No doubt, this affectionate appeal had an immediate, sobering effect, but it did not stem the flow of complaints.

Irascibility and rudeness were long-standing Churchillian traits, now sharpened by the stress of war. But the prickly side of his character never bred ill-will; or at least, hardly ever. 'He did not mean to be unkind,' explained Elizabeth Nel, one of his secretaries, 'He was just heart and soul engaged in the war.' In a curious way, his tantrums made him a more endearing figure, magnifying his idiosyncratic persona, projecting the image of a wayward urchin. His rages were normally short-lived. Inevitably, he would try to make amends, not by a direct apology but by an apposite witticism, a cheeky grin, or a word of generous praise for the aggrieved party, usually entirely out of context with the alleged offence.[8]

By October 1940 Churchill was sure that Britain would survive, but he confessed that 'he did not see clearly' how to win the war. Certainly, morale on the home front had to be maintained at the highest pitch. 'Wars are won by superior will-power,' he declaimed. As the heroic icon of victory, Churchill found abhorrent any hint of defeatism. This could lead to some odd incidents. On one occasion he expressed serious concern at the film portrayal of that hidebound snob, the cartoon character, Colonel Blimp, the embodiment of an effete and reactionary military establishment.[9] Nothing came of his fears.

On 20 June 1940 Churchill spoke to the Commons in secret session. He emphasized the need 'to get through next three months . . . three years', and looked to Britain's 'superiority in Air power', taking it as evident that Hitler was 'master of a starving, agonized and surging Europe'. Banking also upon 'Transatlantic reinforcements', Churchill had hit upon a formula that promised, perhaps, eventual victory.[10]

This prescription was wildly optimistic. With the possible exception of Yugoslavia, Nazi terror held occupied Europe in too savage a grip to allow it to surge. Nor, in the foreseeable future, would economic pressure undermine Hitler's New Order, if that was what Churchill meant by a 'starving' Europe. Intelligence reports held that Germany's Europe faced the prospect of something approaching famine; that the German economy was already fully stretched and was too 'brittle' to sustain a protracted war. These appraisals were without foundation. Able to exploit Europe as an 'economic playground', the German war economy, as it pulled in its slack, revealed considerably more staying power than anticipated, and did not fully peak until the summer of 1944.[11]

Employing effectively Britain's growing and superior air power was a vital element in Churchill's overall design. Air strikes would not only break civilian morale, they would also cripple Germany's war capacity. Persuaded that 'Bombers alone provide the means of victory', he told the Cabinet: 'We must . . . pulverize the entire industry and scientific structure on which the war effort and economic life of the enemy depend'. He was among the early advocates of area bombing: 'Let 'em have it. Remember this. Never maltreat the enemy by halves.'[12]

The results of this air offensive, however, were negligible. Bomber Command was ill-prepared and ill-equipped to launch and sustain a precision bombing campaign. An official report of August 1941 estimated that only one-third of all aircraft 'got to within five miles' of their assigned target; over the Ruhr – the hub of German industry

– this proportion dropped to one-tenth. 'We made a major assault on German agriculture,' commented one wit, after examining an aerial photograph of empty fields pitted with harmless bomb craters. Losses in machines and manpower rose to intolerable levels. During 1941 more British airmen were killed than German civilians. Churchill, Boothby reported, was 'loathed' by the bomber crews, who resented being sent on operations 'night after night', suffering casualties 'far too great for the damage they can do'.[13]

By the autumn of 1941, Churchill himself began to have second thoughts about the merits of strategic bombing. There was also a cost in human terms that disturbed him. In a haunting euphemism, he once spoke of the need to 'de-house' the German population. When he witnessed on newsreels the effects of 'de-housing', he suddenly sat bolt upright: 'Are we beasts? Are we taking this too far?' he cried.[14]

Despite these reservations, the bombing offensive was maintained, carried forward by the enthusiasm of its chief advocate, 'Bomber' Arthur Harris, but also in a kind of 'what else can we do?' mood. With experience, bombing techniques improved. By August 1943, Lindemann and the Air Staff were agreed that roughly seventy-four per cent of Hamburg and fifty-four per cent of Cologne had been levelled. These impressive figures – even if sometimes inflated – served a useful political purpose. After the Soviet Union and Britain became allies, Churchill employed them whenever possible to raise Stalin's spirits. 'Eighty per cent of the [German] houses are down', he once bragged. Here, at least, was decisive proof that Britain was on the offensive, making its own distinctive and substantial, if often costly, contribution to the Soviet Union's great land war against Hitler.[15]

Strategic bombing raids were stepped up during the last stages of war, not only to decimate the enemy's economy and military capacity, but also to intimidate Germany into laying down its arms. The policy remains controversial: was it sound strategy? was it not too wasteful in men and machines for the alleged benefits it brought? There was also the question of fair play, of descending to the level of Nazi methods. On the night of 14 February 1945 Dresden was attacked. It was raided with such ferocity that a fireball engulfed the inner city, razing almost sixty per cent of its total area. No one knows for certain how many were killed and injured. Estimates vary widely, from 25,000 to 135,000 to even a quarter of a million. Delicate questions of accountability were shouldered by Bomber Command and its commander, not by their political masters. No campaign medal was struck on its behalf, nor was it mentioned in Churchill's final victory speech. Alone among Britain's triumphant military chiefs, 'Bomber' Harris received no public tribute. As for the carnage at Dresden, its details seemed to have slipped Churchill's memory. He made no reference to it in his otherwise expansive war memoirs. And when asked by an historian, after the war, to verify some data about the incident, he replied: 'I cannot recall anything about it. I thought the Americans did it. Air Chief Marshal Harris would be the person to contact.'[16]

If Europe neither surged nor starved, and if strategic bombing proved a questionable policy, there remained Churchill's incessant petitioning for 'transatlantic reinforcements'. Churchill felt it vital that the Americans should be involved.[17] He promised to fight on until 'the New World reconquers the Old'. But would the United States intervene simply to rescue Britain, acknowledging her as an equal partner in the common struggle? Or had the Americans other, more dubious, motives? Churchill could not be absolutely certain. At any rate, he advised his ambassador in Washington, Lord Lothian, to discourage 'any complacent assumption' on Roosevelt's part that America would be allowed to step in and 'pick up the *débris* of the British Empire'.[18] This ambivalence, concealed by the staged displays of the 'special relationship', remained a constant factor throughout the war.

Much of Churchill's thinking on the nature of Anglo-American relations was distorted by an element of wishful thinking, a consequence, perhaps, of his family background and his optimistic disposition. Also, at the outbreak of war he was working on his book whose underlying theme was the unity of the English-speaking peoples, by which he meant primarily a solid, enduring Anglo-American partnership. This notion became something of a fixation. It determined his vision of the post-war world. As early as August 1940 he saw Britain as the link between a future European Federation and the New World which, however inspiring a concept, lent a lop-sided view to Anglo-American relations.[19] As the elected leaders of two Great Powers, Churchill and Roosevelt had a particular responsibility to preserve and advance their own national interests while engaged in a titanic global conflict. In fact, they were competitors united by a common goal. There was much discord. Differences over political and military strategies, coupled with tension and frustration, constantly emerged.

Churchill faced a special problem. Although he aimed at an exclusive relationship with Roosevelt, there remained a nagging doubt whether such a degree of intimacy was attainable. Roosevelt, no less a magician with words than Churchill, would lead him on: 'It is great fun to be in the same decade as you.' But unlike Churchill, what Roosevelt left unsaid or done was often more important than his messages or his actions. Some of this struck home. Roosevelt was 'a charming country gentleman', Churchill told Eden, whose 'business methods were almost non-existent'.[20]

How to understand Roosevelt, to get to the root of the man and the nature of the political environment in which he functioned? The complexities of American political life, its loosely structured parties, reflecting wide and disparate regional differences, its ethnic and economic lobbies placed upon Roosevelt constraints that he could not ignore, whatever his inclinations.

But what were Roosevelt's inclinations? Not even his closest advisers could say with absolute certainty. Charming, ruthless, soft, cynical, worldly, secretive, at times vindictive, at times loyal to his associates, he often baffled his aides with his abrupt about-turns. 'His character was contradictory to a bewildering degree,' wrote a shrewd observer, likening him to 'an artful dodger' who could not be hustled into specific commitments against his instinctive judgement.[21] By comparison, Churchill was almost a babe-in-the-woods.

Among Americans there was a widespread view that the inability of the western powers, particularly Britain, to abandon the bad old ways of colonialism and power politics was no less a factor in the collapse of the international system than the rise of the dictator states. Certainly Roosevelt regarded British imperialism with profound suspicion. He saw Churchill as 'pretty much a nineteenth century colonialist' spreading antiquated views.[22]

Roosevelt recognized the insidious nature of Hitler's Germany and the threat it presented to the United States. But he moved cautiously, at his own pace, not Churchill's. For Churchill, it was never fast enough. Every move that apparently brought the United States into line with Britain – zonal patrolling of the Atlantic, the destroyers for bases deal – was accompanied by complaints that the Americans were not doing nearly enough. Lend-lease, promoted by Harry Hopkins, Roosevelt's most favoured aide, as 'an endless assembly belt that stretches from our western coast to this island', was later publicly acclaimed by Churchill 'as the most unselfish and unsordid financial act of any country in all history'. In private, he was more forthright. 'As far as I can make out we are not only to be skinned, but flayed to the bone.' He wrote to Hopkins of a 'wave of depression through Cabinet and other informed circles' regarding Roosevelt's 'many assurances about no commitments and no closer to war etc'. Churchill might be forgiven for thinking that Roosevelt was using Britain as a shield – in much the same way as the British viewed the French army in the 1930s. Whatever the peril, Roosevelt 'was going to wait to be pushed in'.[23] And so it proved. It was the Japanese attack on Pearl Harbour and Hitler's declaration of war against the United States that realized Churchill's vision of an alliance between the two English-speaking peoples, not Roosevelt's abiding commitment to Britain's cause.

With Europe firmly in Hitler's grasp, and the Americans unwilling to play precisely according to his rules, how could Churchill prosecute the war with the necessary vigour he demanded? In September 1940 an Anglo-French force attempted to win over Dakar and French West Africa to the Gaullist cause. Churchill, 'determined to help the Free French', hoped to deny the enemy a naval base from which it could attack British shipping. Most of his Cabinet and military advisers held it an unnecessary distraction that would inflame relations with the Vichy authorities. After three days of indeterminate action, Operation Menace was abandoned. 'Why is it that we are never successful?' grumbled Harold Nicolson.[24]

For Churchill, the Middle East appeared a far more promising goal. Substantial British forces were already stationed there. There were also, it seemed, easier pickings to be had. Italy, never rated highly as a military opponent, had joined the war in June, threatening to outflank the British position in Egypt from Libya in the west and Ethiopia in the south-east. In October, Italian forces invaded Greece, inviting an immediate British riposte. Churchill was eager to take up the challenge. He refused to yield Malta, the eastern Mediterranean, or north Africa to Italian domination. In Cabinet, he was overheard to remark: 'Personally I should like to wage war on a great scale in the Middle East.' That August, even while invasion threatened, Churchill, to general consent, reinforced the British garrison in the area. He aimed at an 'Army of the Delta' numbering 56,000 by October, fortified by 212 heavy artillery pieces, an armoured force of 150 tanks, and as many modern aircraft as could be spared.[25]

A foolhardy gamble or an act of high courage? Probably a combination of both. Playing against the odds was a constant temptation to Churchill's bold character. But he was not acting on instinct alone. Reliable intelligence sources were revealing Hitler's intention to strike, not across the Channel, but eastwards. Still, his conscious decision to take the offensive in the Middle East also graphically illustrated his order of priorities, and what can only be termed as his obsession with the region as the main theatre of operations for British forces. The Mediterranean option came to dominate his strategic thinking. How important was it? Opinions differed – widely. Churchill held 'that the life and honour' of Britain depended upon it. 'The loss of Egypt and the Middle East would be a disaster of the first magnitude', comparable only to a successful invasion of the home base. To avoid such a catastrophe, there were to be 'No surrenders . . . unless at least fifty per cent casualties are sustained by the Unit or force in question'. The Chiefs of Staff however felt that 'the life . . . of Great Britain' depended upon winning the Battle of the Atlantic and preventing an invasion.[26]

Churchill's fixation with the Middle East – and later Italy – was to have far-reaching consequences. The more troops that were despatched to the area, the more were sucked in. This ongoing drain on resources and manpower greatly complicated his relations with the United States.

As early as the summer of 1941 the Americans railed against so large a proportion of their war supplies being swallowed up by the Middle East, claiming that it would be more beneficial to concentrate on other areas, particularly the Atlantic.[27] Once the United States joined the war, these arguments sharpened considerably.

In the short run, Churchill's preference paid off. At the beginning of November 1940, half the entire Italian battle fleet lying off Taranto was put out of action by British air strikes. For the moment, the navy commanded the Mediterranean. A month later, General Sir Archibald Wavell launched Operation Compass in the Libyan desert. It was a brilliant success. Urged on every step of the way by Churchill, he advanced 400 miles, taking 130,000 Italian prisoners. By mid-February he held all Cyrenaica. One last push by a relatively small force and Tripoli would fall and north Africa cleansed of enemy forces. Here was 'the glittering prize' that Churchill had prayed for earlier.[28]

The Balkans also attracted Churchill like a magnet. When the Italians attacked Greece, his attention re-focused on the area. His immediate reaction was to come to the aid of his beleaguered ally. Honouring a contractual agreement, thereby maintaining British prestige, was a legitimate aim in itself. It was also, Churchill thought, a necessary prerequisite for the formation of a British-inspired Balkan bloc – to include Turkey – that would dissipate Axis strength on another front. In theory, the concept was sound. But was it anchored in reality? As the crisis developed, all the signs showed that Churchill, who pulled his colleagues along with him, was chasing a will-o'-the-wisp.

Mounting Italian military setbacks complicated the situation. Intelligence sources reaching London indicated an overall German plan to move into the Balkans – an intolerable prospect for Churchill. Fearing a repetition of the catastrophes in Norway and the Low Countries and convinced that German troop concentrations signalled an impending offensive on 20 January, Churchill began to reverse his order of priorities. To Wavell, he wrote: '[the] destruction of Greece will eclipse victories you have gained in Libya.'[29] The order went out to concentrate an expeditionary force in the Nile delta for transfer to Greece, and possibly Turkey.

Initially, there was widespread opposition to Churchill's decision. The Greeks themselves were most wary at inviting British intervention lest it provoke a German attack. Nor was the force, approximately four divisions, considered sufficient to ward off a German strike. Was it to be Tripoli or Athens? The soldiers were adamant. Wavell told Churchill he was playing into German hands by halting the advance in Libya and dispersing his forces. In London, the view was forcibly put that control over the African coastline was infinitely preferable to seizing 'a bridgehead in Greece', running 'the risk of another

Dunkirk'. Sir John Dill, Chief of the Imperial General Staff, considered resignation.[30] Instead, with Wavell, he joined Eden's mission to Athens in late February to coordinate policy with the Greeks. According to Churchill's 'sealed orders', Eden was to ensure the necessary military and political conditions that would enable Britain 'to send speedy help to Greece'. Eden's report, now backed by the generals, was emphatically in favour of swift intervention, and this proved to be the source of the Cabinet decision of 24 February to aid the Greeks.[31]

By now the momentum for intervention was in full swing, despite some doubters in London. Churchill was certainly in favour. The lure of a Balkan combination – that had also been a factor in the generals' change of heart – was foremost in his mind. But he also hoped to impress the Americans by Britain's resoluteness; and even, by opening an additional front, to spread thin Germany's military capacity. No minister dissented.[32] But even as the last-minute preparations for British intervention were being put into motion, the Balkan front was crumbling. By March, Hungary, Roumania and Bulgaria had joined the Axis camp: Turkey, withstanding all pressure, remained neutral.

On 6 April German troops poured into Yugoslavia and Greece. The allied armies, fell back in confusion. Three weeks later, the Swastika was flying over the Acropolis. Ten thousand British troops were taken prisoner. By the end of May, German paratroops had overrun Crete, their planes inflicting heavy damage on the British naval force there. This was not another 'Norwegian fiasco', that Churchill had desperately sought to evade; it was a disaster of even greater magnitude. And it was compounded by the failure to exploit Wavell's desert victories, for on 3 April Rommel began to drive the British army out of Libya. Nor was there any substance to the claim that British intervention had delayed the German attack on the Soviet Union and perhaps saved Moscow, a point often used carelessly to justify the Greek action.

Churchill's responsibility for the débâcle was considerable. Later that year, he admitted that Greece had been an 'error of judgement', adding that 'he had instinctively had doubts', a remark that surprised his companion, John Colville, who recollected differently. Misreading intelligence data, succumbing to the illusion of a Balkan-Turkish alliance, he had not contested Eden's rosy despatches. (Nor is it inconceivable that Eden's optimistic reports, endorsed by Wavell and Dill, were partly fashioned to suit Churchill's perceived wishes.) When the Cabinet met to decide, his contribution, as Prime Minister and Minister of Defence, had been crucial. On 7 May 1941 he told the House that even with foreknowledge he 'would do the same thing again.'[33]

The humiliation of the rout cut deep. At home, the criticism was harsh, ranging from 'bewilderment' to 'anger', damaging Churchill's reputation. But in a series of speeches that tested all of his parliamentary skills, Churchill survived, even securing a vote of confidence. He left the Chamber, heartened by the burst of cheers that accompanied him.[34]

Churchill spent the week-end after his parliamentary success at Ditchley. On Sunday, 11 May, while watching a Marx brothers comedy, he received the astonishing news that Rudolf Hess, ranked third in the Nazi hierarchy, had parachuted on to the Duke of Hamilton's estate in East Scotland. Hess, a man of little ability, whose one distinguishing feature was his blind loyalty to Hitler, hoped to make contact with members of 'the peace movement' in Britain, oust Churchill's government, and negotiate a deal based on 'A free hand for Germany in Europe and for Britain in her own Empire!' If Churchill was astonished, Hitler was enraged. He ordered Hess to be stripped of his offices and to be shot should he return to Germany. A German official communiqué diagnosed him as suffering from hallucinations. His British interrogators reached roughly the same conclusion. Was there such 'a peace movement' in Britain, ready and able to overthrow Churchill, prepared to come to terms with Hitler, an international con artist who had honoured no previous treaty, and all on the basis of a vague, threadbare formula that Hitler had floated before with tedious repetition? Hess's troubled mind had conjured up 'a peace movement' that did not exist. Unlike in May-June 1940, no serious discussions took place regarding a negotiated settlement. By flying to Britain (on his fourth attempt), Hess had created a great sensation, easily given to speculative headlines. Bizarre and melodramatic, it remained, as Churchill rightly concluded, an escapade of no serious importance.[35]

Since May 1940 Churchill had been receiving highly classified information on a daily basis. The data derived from the success of the staff at Bletchley Park in breaking the codes of the German military cipher machine, Enigma. These decrypts came to be known as the Ultra Secret. Some German 'keys' proved easier to read than others. Those of the Luftwaffe were mastered first, a factor in Britain's air victory that summer. Army and some naval codes followed, as did those of other German military and civil organizations. At first the traffic in this material was limited, but as the war progressed it expanded enormously, until by mid-1942 Ultra was distributing between 3–4,000 decrypts daily, to say nothing of the Japanese and Italian offerings.

Initially, not content with reading the evaluations, Churchill wished also to examine the raw material itself. The sheer quantity of the material made this impossible. So each day a buff-coloured box would arrive, containing the choicest items, for his perusal. Whenever he travelled abroad, he insisted that 'good "C" [intelligence] stuff' accompany him, and a special liaison unit was set up to keep him in touch. Apart from Churchill, access to Ultra was restricted to a handful of ministers and soldiers. It was the most closely guarded secret of the war. Churchill attached to it cardinal importance. 'Make sure they [the team at Bletchley Park] have all they want on extreme priority.' As he put it, they were 'the geese who laid the golden eggs and never cackled'.[36]

Perhaps more than any minister this century, Churchill held a long-standing and consistent fascination with intelligence. But he tended to confer undue weight to clandestine activities. Apart from his round-up of aliens during the summer of 1940, he had sacked Sir Vernon Kell, head of MI5 for thirty years, for (among other reasons) not being sufficiently alert to the alleged menace. In much the same manner, he tended to over-estimate the capacity of the European anti-Nazi movements to 'set Europe ablaze'.

The Ultra products proved to be a tremendous bonus to the allied war effort, but they were not trouble-free. Often they contained information of a highly specialized, technical nature, logistical details that required continuous sifting, and inevitably editing, before they could be put to effective use. Once the evaluations were made, how would the decision-makers, political and military, interpret them? Churchill had experienced similar problems, though on a far smaller scale, in the 1930s when he had stood at the centre of a partially government-sponsored intelligence network. Then, some of his evaluations had missed the mark. On occasion, they were to do so again, as his misreading of the Balkan situation in early 1941 indicated; or later his impatience with his desert generals, exhorting them to embark on premature offensives. When they occurred, these failings were not merely a consequence of Churchill's positive, combative nature; they were also a concomitant of the rapidly changing war situation.

But whatever Churchill's shortcomings, his achievements were far more substantial. It was his drive that welded a hitherto splintered intelligence system into a coherent whole, honing its efficiency. Of no less importance, it was his enthusiasm that was instrumental in raising Anglo-American intelligence cooperation to a higher, more creative level, one of the more durable features of the 'special relationship'. Whether Ultra significantly modified the course of the war, or its duration, must remain speculative. But its successes were most impressive, among them the victory at El Alamein and the clearing of North Africa, phases of the Italian campaign, and the battle for Normandy.

Chartwell, its windows shuttered and grounds untended, was closed for the duration of the war. But it was never far from Churchill's thoughts. The calm and serenity of this great house, now lying silent, its rooms empty, held its own unique appeal. Churchill would find comfort in its sad tranquillity. Sometimes accompanied by Clementine, he would spend weekends there, at Orchard Cottage, visits that became rarer as the war progressed. More often than not he would retire to Chartwell for a few hours of leisure, to unwind from the tensions of office. Honking to alert his Canadian goose, he would tour the estate, with the birds waddling two or three paces behind.[37]

Chequers, a gloomy Tudor mansion, situated in the Chilterns not far from High Wycombe, was the Prime Minister's official country residence. It served as Churchill's main weekend resort, but its gravel approach roads leading like arrows to the house, made it vulnerable to air attack, particularly at full moon. Then, when in need of a country break, he would transfer the whole of his entourage to Ditchley Park, near Blenheim, the home of Ronald Tree, a rich Conservative MP. 'First come two detectives who scour the place from garret to cellar; then arrive valet and maid with much luggage; then thirty-five soldiers plus officers turn up to guard the great man through the night; then two stenographers with masses of papers; then . . . the Private Secretary on duty; and finally Winston and Clemmie.' And then would arrive the house guests, both Churchill's and his host's. Something of the gaiety of pre-war high society gatherings permeated these scenes. 'DARLING,' shrieked Lady Diana Cooper on one occasion, 'how glad we are to see you,' throwing her arms round Churchill's neck in an affectionate hug.[38]

Towards the end of 1940 the Churchills, to escape the structural defects of their residence in Downing Street, moved into a new, more secure apartment at nearby Storey's Gate. Known as No 10 Annexe, it lay directly above the series of underground bunkers that constituted the nerve centre of Britain's war effort. The flat overlooked St James's Park, its rooms, previously government offices, having been specially adapted to suit Churchill's needs. Under Clementine's supervision the Annexe was redecorated, and with their own pictures and furniture it became 'almost attractive'. As it also contained government offices, it turned into a kind of right-of-way for visitors and officials. This could lead to awkward scenes. Sometimes his guests, to their bewilderment, would be confronted by a corpulent figure, covered only by an enormous bath towel, padding across the main corridor from his bathroom to his bedroom, dripping water as he welcomed them with a stately wave. Churchill's unconventional behaviour took other forms. Together with some companions, he once went up to the roof to watch an air raid. Wrapped up against the cold, he found a comfortable, warm seat. Suddenly his party was dispersed by the arrival of a distraught official who complained that it had become impossible to work as the rooms downstairs had filled with smoke. Would the Prime Minister please mind not sitting any longer on the chimney.[39]

Even at the best of times Churchill worked hard at relaxing. But the constraints on a wartime Prime Minister were too onerous to allow for many diversions. Painting was put aside and *The English-Speaking*

Peoples project was postponed. For reasons of high policy he decided not to write a history of *Europe Since the Russian Revolution*. Late night films, distracting 'the mind away from other things', were 'a wonderful form of entertainment' that he did not forsake. He walked out of a 'sentimental' Mickey Rooney picture, but stayed for Bette Davis's splendid tragedy, *Dark Victory*, and was 'pulverized' by the emotional intensity generated by Rhett Butler (Clark Gable) and Scarlett O' Hara (Vivien Leigh) in *Gone with the Wind*. Once, at a showing of *Oliver Twist*, when Bill Sykes was coaxing his dog to the edge of the river to drown it, Churchill thoughtfully covered the eyes of his beloved poodle, Rufus, who sat on his lap. Politically correct movies fascinated him. Chaplin's brilliant satire, *The Great Dictators*, provoked great merriment, and thought. Over Olivier's magnificently patriotic *Henry V*, Churchill 'went into ecstasies'.[40]

Like other families, Churchill's was scattered during the war. All his children served in the armed services. When they met for family gatherings, he was able to relax in a familiar setting. In December 1940 he toasted the arrival of his new grandson, 'little' Winston (Randolph's son). Often they were reunited for lunch or dinner, but the inevitable appearance of generals and ministers at his table usually turned these occasions into self-styled working sessions. At times, his (contrived?) unpredictability added the flavour of a 'Mad Hatter's dinner-party' to these meals. This 'Wonderland of Chequers' was how one bemused general described Churchill's weekend gatherings.[41]

The war, however, had not diminished Churchill's appetite or regard for food. 'The way to lose the war', he informed Lord Woolton 'is to force the British public into a diet of milk, oatmeal, potatoes etc, washed down on gala occasions with a little lime juice.'[42] He set an example, one breakfast consisting of 'two eggs, ham and chicken, coffee, toast, butter and marmalade, two mangoes, and a glass of orange juice'. Now and then his hand slipped, as when he poured whisky on to his sardines and vinegar into his glass. To one of his private secretaries, he remarked that 'he was more likely to die of over-eating [than a heart-attack]'.[43]

For all that, the state of Churchill's health was a matter of national concern. At the Cabinet's insistence, Sir Charles Wilson (later Lord Moran), was appointed his personal physician in May 1940. In the American press Churchill gained the reputation of being 'the world's worst patient'. He was certainly perverse, sometimes cantankerous, always trying. Churchill took a serious view of his aliments. When sick, he obeyed orders. But convincing reasons had to be provided. Curious about the intricacies of the treatment prescribed, he was delighted to learn that his white blood cells – 9,900 per cubic millimetre! – were battling triumphantly against the microbes that had invaded his body.[44]

One night in December 1941, Churchill, while staying at the White House, suffered a heart attack. Trying to force open a window, he became breathless and felt a dull pain over his heart that ran down his left arm. Churchill, alarmed, put the incident down to a strained chest muscle. Moran did not enlighten him, fearing the repercussions if it became publicly known that 'the PM was an invalid with a crippled heart and a doubtful future'.[45] Churchill was far from being an invalid. But his outward appearance of eternal robustness was equally deceptive. Even as a child he had been prone to chills and high temperatures. As a wartime Prime Minister, bound to a crowded and rigid timetable, he was constantly on the move, travelling in all weathers, often in spartan conditions – between September 1939 and November 1943 he journeyed 111,000 miles, spending 792 hours at sea and 339 in the air. Clementine was worried at the real possibility of a coronary thrombosis, brought on by 'a long &/or high flight'.[46]

At the beginning of 1943, back in London after weeks of intensive travel, Churchill contracted pneumonia. He recovered. But the following December, after the exertions of the Teheran conference, he found himself stranded at an airfield in Tunis, utterly exhausted. He told Eisenhower, 'I am completely at the end of my tether and I cannot go on.' He was put to bed at Eisenhower's seaside villa on the outskirts of ancient Carthage. Once again, pneumonia was diagnosed, this time with complications. 'My heart is doing something very funny,' Churchill complained to Moran, 'it feels to be bumping all over the place.' His 'fibrillations' were treated with digitalis. As his illness approached its crisis, Moran feared for his life. 'If I die,' Churchill comforted Sarah, 'don't worry – the war is won.'[47] Fortunately, he rallied. But it took some time before he revived fully.

Apart from the strain on his heart – he suffered a third, mild bout of pneumonia in September 1944 – it was the overall effect on Churchill's stamina that was the chief causality of his hectic lifestyle. 'Can't you do anything for this horrible feeling of exhaustion?' he demanded of Moran. Some relief came in the form of the 'red tablet' he took each night to ensure that he slept soundly. Nonetheless, after Tunis, Moran considered that he was never 'the same man again'.[48] As the war progressed, his run-down state prompted a number of shrill observations. In March 1942 Eden and Cadogan agreed that the 'War Cabinet doesn't function ... There's no hand on the wheel'. 'Old, tired and very depressed', noted Colville at the beginning of 1944. Two months later, Cadogan feared that Churchill was 'breaking down. He rambles without pause.' In January 1945 a mini-crisis broke out in Cabinet. Churchill was making a 'deplorable impression', not reading the required papers yet 'talking on and on'. Attlee protested vigorously. Many ministers agreed with him, as did Clementine, who thought Attlee's criticism 'both true and wholesome'.[49]

Whatever the element of exaggeration in these strictures there can be no doubt that the war 'desperately taxed' Churchill's powers, as Mary put it. He was, after all, in his late sixties. No less, he was a hostage to his own temperament. 'If in the end he is defeated,' wrote Moran, 'it will . . . [be] brought on by his own improvidence.'[50] Churchill also carried the awful burdens of war with such burning intensity as to deprive himself of any 'self-protective mechanism', of the ability to retreat into himself, to cut himself off, to forget the anguish of the hour. The sensitive, emotional, artistic side of his character clashed with the man of action exercising supreme power, leaving its own distinctive mark on his physical well being, and on occasion, his functioning as a Prime Minister. But however harsh and just the criticism, no one dreamt of removing Churchill from office. He still remained the symbol of eventual victory.

Grand Strategy

During the months that Britain stood alone Churchill coined the dictum 'We must just KBO', by which he meant 'Keep Buggering On'.[1] In terms of Britain's military performance 'KBO' held well into 1942. Three days after Pearl Harbour, in December 1941, the capital ships *Repulse* and *Prince of Wales* were sunk off the Malayan coast. Assuming that they could roam the seas as an 'elusive menace', Churchill (and Eden) had urged that they be sent to the Far East. But they were caught and destroyed by Japanese bombers, and 600 men were lost. Churchill was deeply shocked. Nevertheless, he still assumed that Singapore was secure, and discussed on paper whether or not to ask the United States to base what remained of its Pacific fleet there.[2] But Singapore surrendered – its garrison of 130,000 (including 40,000 British troops, the remainder being Indian, Australian and local volunteers) yielding to a force less than half its number. The Japanese initiative never slackened. Hong Kong fell; Malaya and Burma were occupied; Japanese armies advanced to threaten India. By March 1942 the British Empire in the Far East had collapsed. In North Africa, Rommel, his army reinforced, struck westwards, driving British forces out of Cyrenaica. That June, Tobruk capitulated, again to an inferior number of enemy troops, 33,000 more British soldiers being led off into captivity. Axis armies, deployed on the borders of Egypt, menaced the Suez Canal and British possessions throughout the Middle East. These were military disasters of the first magnitude. They mortified Churchill: 'Defeat is one thing; disgrace is another,'[3] he recalled.

But in terms of high strategy Britain's fortunes had improved out of all recognition. Since January 1941 intelligence reports indicated that Germany intended to attack Russia. On 3 April Churchill sent a note to Stalin (who did not receive it until almost three weeks later) telling of German troop movements relating to the Yugoslav crisis: it was hardly an explicit warning; nor was it couched in a language of urgency. Stalin, however, had his own sources, and Stafford Cripps, the British ambassador in Moscow, having already passed on a similar message, thought it would be 'ineffectual' to belabour the point, and had delayed it. Cripps's alleged negligence immensely vexed Churchill.[4]

The Soviet Union was now an ally. On 22 June 1941 Hitler launched 'Barbarossa' (the code name for the attack on the Soviet Union). 'A smile of satisfaction' crossed Churchill's face. That evening he proclaimed his intention to recognize the Russians as full partners in the war against Hitler. His broadcast, unauthorized by the Cabinet, was a virtuoso performance. It contained touches of full-blown Churchillian rhetoric, picturing the Nazi war machine, 'with its clanking, heel-clicking, dandified Prussian officers' advancing on the villages of Russia where 'mothers and wives pray . . . where maidens laugh and children play'. But it also outlined the main themes that would complicate relations with the Soviet Union in the future.[5] Inevitably, he introduced himself as the seasoned anti-Bolshevik campaigner, refusing to 'unsay one word' of condemnation that he had uttered in the past. Politically, Bolshevik Russia was as objectionable as Nazi Germany; and, as shown in Poland and the Baltic states, would not hesitate to employ the most brutal methods to advance its interests. In all sections of Churchill's coalition there were many who balked at too close a political association with the Soviet Union, preferring to limit their cooperation to the military aspect. It was not always possible to separate these spheres. This discrepancy bedevilled Anglo-Soviet relations. In particular, it affected Churchill's behaviour, who often believed that through the forging of a special relationship with Stalin he could set matters right, when it was patently clear that they had gone wrong.

A day before 'Barbarossa' Churchill had remarked that Russia, if attacked, 'will assuredly be defeated'.[6] But for the moment, Churchill had little choice. 'Any man or state who fights on against Nazidom will have our aid'. The aid began immediately, though not on the scale that Stalin demanded. In July the Soviet leader called upon Churchill to open two additional fronts, in northern France and the Arctic. This was clearly impossible. But Stalin's demand stung Churchill. Conscious of the awful sacrifices of the Russian people, all he could offer in the way of military diversions was to step up the bombing offensive and promote secondary operations in North Africa, and later Italy. Anglo-Soviet military cooperation was successful in at least one area: Iran. In late August their forces occupied and partitioned the country, setting up a pro-allied regime to secure the transfer of men and supplies to southern Russia. The same month the first of the northern convoys sailed for Archangel. In all, until the end of the war, forty convoys hazarded this most perilous and daunting of routes, carrying a total of 4 million tons of equipment, including 5,000 tanks and 7,000 aircraft.[7] For Churchill, this massive effort was something of a gamble, depriving his own forces of invaluable supplies at a time when the war in the East hung in the balance and it was by no means certain that the Soviet Union would survive.

The Russian war stimulated greater American involvement in the conflict. Realizing the necessity of sustaining the Soviet Union, Roosevelt sent Harry Hopkins to Moscow with a message for Stalin promising 'all possible aid'. He also urged Churchill to scotch unpleasant rumours about nefarious 'trades or deals', to make it clear that 'no post war peace commitments as to territories, populations or economics have been given'. Mainly to assuage American opinion, he arranged to meet Churchill face-to-face. Churchill, of course, was delighted, confident that his exceptional powers of persuasion would convince Roosevelt to adopt more warlike measures. At any rate, he was all keyed up for the encounter. Hopkins, noted: 'You'd have thought Winston was being carried up into the heavens to meet God!'[8]

On 9 August 1941, they met aboard the warships USS *Augusta* and the *Prince of Wales* at Placentia Bay off Argentia, Newfoundland. The first of their nine wartime meetings, it turned into a eye-catching public display of Anglo-American solidarity. But the conference's best-known outcome, the Atlantic Charter, was little more than a tame statement of war aims. Even so, it generated an ironic agreement: Churchill, the veteran free trader, conceding to Roosevelt, an old protectionist, the advantages of an international trade order free of restrictive economic systems, for example imperial preference. Far more divisive was article three, respecting the rights of 'all peoples' to choose their own form of government. Churchill subsequently contended that it applied to the enslaved countries of Europe, but not to the peoples of the British Empire. Roosevelt thought differently. And so, apparently, did Churchill's deputy, Attlee, who told the *Daily Herald* that it embraced 'coloured peoples, as well as white'.[9]

Although the Americans still had no intention of involving themselves in fighting, Churchill was inclined to read much more commitment into their utterances than was actually there. Succumbing to his high expectations, he stretched Roosevelt's casually phrased intentions to breaking point. British observers at the meeting were clear there had been no 'secret commitments'. 'We wished to God there had been,' said one.[10] Nevertheless, the Americans did stiffen their naval activity in the Atlantic, extending their naval patrols to include the Iceland-America stretch together with a tougher policy towards German submarine raiders.

During these months the Americans were negotiating with the Japanese in an attempt to bring the Far East crisis to an end. Since July the United States, with the agreement of Britain and Holland, had steadily mounted a financial and economic embargo on Japan, freezing its overseas assets as a retaliation to Japan's virtual seizure of Indo-China, a move generally seen as the prelude to a wider campaign of aggression throughout south-east Asia. The British, naturally, had no desire to open a third front, and were prepared to allow the Americans to make the running. This required a delicate touch at the negotiating table. The Foreign Office contended that 'we must at least insist that the [negotiating] time isn't gained at China's or anyone else's expense'.[11] The image of appeasement returned to haunt the Foreign Office. Eden remained convinced that 'to show weakness' would not only 'invite Japanese pressure', it would also convince the Americans that 'our tactics were to appease the enemy'. Churchill employed the same language. He elaborated to Roosevelt: 'The firmer your attitude and ours, the less chance of their taking the plunge.' Churchill and his advisers were alarmed at the likelihood of war breaking out in the Far East and being left alone to face the Japanese onslaught.[12]

On 20 November Japan put forward its so-called *modus vivendi*, a deal that would limit the Japanese presence in Indo-China in return for raising the embargo, particularly on oil. Roosevelt was 'not very hopeful' that it would lead to anything. But it provided the starting-point for Cortell Hull to work out a series of counter-proposals. Churchill's initial, instinctive reaction was favourable and he felt that 'it would be worth while to ease up on Japan economically sufficiently for them to live from hand to mouth – even if we got only another three months'.

The Foreign Office was more truculent. Churchill, swinging into line behind it, took the same tone. After establishing that he did not want 'an additional war' and would let Roosevelt 'handle this business', he asked: 'What about Chiang Kai-shek?'[13] As the Chinese Nationalists' demands were the most extreme in these exchanges, the sense of Churchill's message was self-evident. Hull, already under pressure from the China lobby, reacted angrily to these interventions. Dropping his version of the *modus vivendi*, he delivered to the Japanese negotiators a bland statement of general principles. By then, 26 November, it was probably too late to avoid war, for that same day a Japanese task force set sail from the Kurile Islands in the direction of Hawaii. On 7 December it attacked Pearl Harbour, crippling the United States Pacific fleet. America was at war, forced into the global conflict by the Japanese assault and, three days later, by Hitler's reckless declaration of hostilities.

Almost two years after these events, Sir Robert Craigie, who had been the British ambassador to Tokyo, returned from Japanese internment and composed a final report on the course of his embassy. It was a harsh indictment of the Foreign Office and its political masters. British policy, he claimed, had been unrealistic, inflexible, and too dependent upon the Americans. By rejecting the overtures of Japanese moderates, they had played straight into the hands of the war party in Japan. Had a different policy been pursued, 'the day of reckoning' might have been postponed, and Britain 'might never have required an actual recourse to arms'.[14]

This highly critical paper struck a raw nerve. Churchill thought it 'should be kept scrupulously secret', and all copies were withdrawn from the Foreign Office files. He queried Cragie's main thesis that a more pliant attitude might have gained Britain a valuable breathing space.

> He [Craigie] . . . writes of the break with Japan as though it were an unmitigated disaster – It was however a blessing that Japan attacked the United States and thus brought America wholeheartedly and unitedly into the war. Greater good fortune has rarely happened to the British Empire than this event . . .[15]

In one crucial aspect, these sentiments were to be cruelly dispelled by events. During the first months of 1942 the Japanese dealt Britain's imperial standing a blow from which it never recovered. Hong Kong, Malaya, Singapore, and Burma were overrun; India was simmering with civil disobedience; Australia and New Zealand were turning to the United States to maintain their security. In any case, Britain's imperial mission, long under challenge, was entering its final spasm. These dramatic events merely hurried along the process. Did Churchill now sense that the Victorian Empire of his youth that he so much aspired to preserve was fast becoming an anachronism? That November, in a stirring testimony of imperial purpose, he pronounced: 'I have not become the King's First Minister in order to preside over the liquidation of the British Empire.'[16] This was the supreme irony of his life. In the wider political context of the decline and fall of the British Empire, with all its attendant consequences, this was precisely the role he had been conscripted to play.

But in another crucial aspect, he was absolutely right. United States intervention would guarantee that Britain 'would live'. This is not to suggest that Churchill schemed 'to drag' America into the war – and finally, after endless machinations, succeeded! Such an argument, surely, reads too much into even Churchill's abilities. Only a political innocent would deny that the active intervention of the United States was essential, perhaps not to Britain's survival, but certainly to its winning the war. If nothing else, the experience of the First World War confirmed this proposition. Fortunately, there emerged a coincidence of American and British interests to block Japanese belligerence. This worked to Britain's benefit, and Churchill would have been lacking in responsibility had he not taken advantage of it. Before very long, to his extreme anguish, he would discover that at various points their coincidence of interests no longer held. This was an unexpected price that he was compelled to pay. He paid it, reluctantly, for the infinitely greater benefit of United States involvement.

There was another account that Churchill was forced to settle. The 'plenary authority' he so much desired, in any case challenged repeatedly by his military advisers, would be further eroded by the intrusion of the Americans. Regarding the conduct of the war in Russia, Churchill was little more than a patient and hopeful observer. But also in the West, he could no longer direct the war from a purely British standpoint. Churchill shrouded the new Anglo-American relationship in a romantic glow. After many months of 'walking out', he told George VI, they were now 'married'.[17] It proved to be a stormy marriage, punctuated by fierce quarrels and affectionate reconciliations. Churchill was determined to make it work. Nowhere else would he find a mate of equal wealth and charm. But in the final analysis, it would be the stronger, more powerful partner who would force the pace. Typically, Churchill fought a valiant rearguard action. Nowhere was this more evident than in the great strategic debate of the Second World War, the place and timing of the second front in Europe, a debate that transcended routine military calculations to encompass the political future of post-war Europe.

Roosevelt himself had questioned the wisdom of defending at such great cost the British position in the Middle East, a view later put most strongly to Churchill by an American military delegation. Again, when the military staffs of both countries met at Placentia Bay, the Americans came away disappointed at the lack of a British plan to mount 'a major land campaign' in Europe beyond operations in support of 'a general uprising', proposed for the final stage of the war.[18] These two disproportionate thrusts of British strategic thinking, and the inter-action between them, were to prove the main sticking points in framing a harmonious policy with the Americans. In essence, as Churchill admitted, the distinctions were of emphasis, not substance. On the southern periphery of Europe, his 'war plan' for 1942 was to occupy and control north and west Africa. As for Germany, Churchill argued that 'the war can only be ended through the defeat in Europe of the German armies'. But the gist of his overall design remained constant: bombing, blockade, and subversion leading to the eventual weakening or collapse of Germany, to be followed by a large-scale invasion of western Europe. It was a theme unlikely to appeal to the Americans. This was pointed out by Brigadier Leslie Hollis, one of Ismay's aides, who urged his chiefs to think in terms of simultaneous Anglo-US landings on the Continent and to speak 'with confidence and decision upon the [European] liberating offensive of 1943'.[19]

Churchill went to the Washington (Arcadia) conference in December 1941 apprehensive lest the United States turn to the Pacific, relegating Europe to a secondary theatre of war. However, both Roosevelt and his Chief of Staff, General George Marshall, were determined to uphold the 'Europe First' agreement.[20] But it soon became apparent that the

American military staff displayed little enthusiasm for Hollis's ideas, now voiced by Churchill, for simultaneous landings on the European coastline. They had agreed to 'a return to the Continent' in 1943, but they conceived it as a major onslaught on north-western Europe. While Churchill's master-plan hinged upon Germany collapsing, the Americans asserted that a German collapse would result from a massive allied offensive across the Channel. It took much wrangling before this gap in outlook was finally bridged.

The Americans soon refined their ideas into a concrete operational plan. It called for 'the first great offensive of the United Powers' (later codenamed Overlord) to be staged in western Europe. The build-up for the invasion, scheduled for the spring of 1943, would include thirty American and eighteen British divisions. In the meantime, provision was made for a more limited action for the autumn. Churchill reacted in a lukewarm manner to this proposal. 'I am in entire agreement in principle', he wrote to Roosevelt. Roosevelt picked up the nuance contained in 'in principle' immediately. 'Mere acquiescence on the part of our friends is not sufficient', he countered.[21] These differences had not been resolved by the time the two leaders met again in Washington in June.

The second Washington conference was of crucial significance. Shortly before Churchill's arrival the American navy had halted the Japanese southward advance at the battle of the Coral Sea, and had then gone on to gain a decisive victory off Midway Island. Would these successes stimulate the Americans to switch their war effort from Europe to the Far East? Churchill could not be sure. As he himself was not enamoured at the American interpretation of 'Europe First', he had to feel his way carefully.

He offered the Americans an alternative: North Africa, perhaps combined with action in northern Norway. He did not present it as a substitute for a large-scale invasion of Europe in 1943, but as a necessary expedient to ensure that, as he put it, allied troops would not 'stand idle during the whole of 1942'. For Churchill, this had an additional advantage: here, at least, there was a British army intact and in contact with the enemy. Churchill put his arguments deftly and cogently. Paradoxically, the fall of Tobruk – news of which reached him during the talks – and the need to prop up the crumbling British position in North Africa came to his aid. Roosevelt asked: 'What can we do to help?' And to Churchill's reply, 'Sherman tanks', he ordered that three hundred be despatched, as they rolled off the production line, to Egypt.[22] Roosevelt finally swung behind Churchill's proposal for an Anglo-American landing in North Africa.

The ramifications of a decision to invade North Africa first were clear to military figures on both sides. Marshall and Admiral King argued that if the British persisted in their attitude, the United States should adopt a defensive posture against Germany and 'use all available means in the Pacific'.[23] Roosevelt refused. But American displeasure remained.

Churchill kept faith with North Africa, now backed by Field Marshal Alan Brooke, who had already decided that '1942 is dead off' for Europe. The decision to invade North Africa was finalized. Eisenhower, with uncharacteristic exaggeration, recorded this date as 'the blackest day in history'. As for Churchill, the Americans put down his indomitability to his incurable predilection for 'eccentric operations'.[24]

Some days later, as Churchill was waiting for his plane to take him to Cairo and then Moscow, he received a message from Dill, head of the British Joint Staff Mission in Washington. 'The American mind,' he stated, held that a North African landing in 1942 would render impossible a cross-Channel offensive in 1943. This warning could not have come as a great revelation. Only a week earlier, on 24 July, Churchill had presented to the War cabinet parallel findings of the Joint Chiefs of Staff, conclusions that he had found 'most satisfactory'. Yet perversely, he still offered the hope of a large-scale invasion of Europe in 1943, 'albeit much retarded', flying in the face of all the logistical evidence presented to him by his military aides.[25] No doubt Churchill was also moved by domestic support for a second front that was running at a high level. For a government that had recently overcome two votes of confidence on the conduct of the war, it was too popular a line for Churchill to ignore. Nor could he afford to alienate Stalin, or totally estrange Roosevelt.

Partly for this reason it was decided to go ahead with capturing Dieppe for a day, in the expectation of gaining data for a larger-scale landing in the future. Churchill thought it 'most important' that it take place that summer, and 'was carried away with optimism' at the prospect. Later, he called it 'a costly but not unfruitful reconnaissance in force'. It was certainly costly. Of the 5,000 attacking troops, mainly Canadians, 1,000 were killed and 2,000 taken prisoner. Nor was Dieppe secured. Churchill was highly critical of its operational details, to which he was clearly not privy, insisting on being informed more precisely about military plans in the future.

The failure of the raid unquestionably strengthened the reservations of those who were in any case hesitating about mounting a second front. 'Well, if we can't capture a port, we shall have to take one with us,' Mountbatten's naval adviser was reported to have said on his return from Dieppe. The origins of 'Mulberry', the floating, artificial harbour used on 'D' Day were more complicated, but the fiasco at Dieppe gave the conception, that had been germinating in Churchill's mind for some time, a great boost. But it did not, as Churchill maintained, hold down German reserves in the West, taking the weight off Russia and making the sacrifice 'not in vain'. Quite the contrary happened. The Germans assumed that after such a painful defeat, the allies would lie quiet in the near future, enabling them to send their better trained divisions to the East and replace them with lower grade units. In this odd manner, Churchill realized, unwittingly, one of his main conditions for a full-scale invasion of western Europe, the scaling down of German forces in the area.[26]

Later, Marshall would refer to the 'suction pump' effect, the steady draining of resources from the decisive theatre, western Europe, to the Pacific and, especially, the Mediterranean areas. Soon, the British would be complaining that the Americans were diverting increasing quantities of *matériel* to fuel their war in the Pacific.[27] Unconsciously or not, Churchill had helped prime this pump. But as far as Europe was concerned, he formulated a streamlined version of the second front. He explained to Ismay:

> The flank attack [North Africa] may become the main attack, and the main attack [Europe] a holding operation in the early stages. Our second front will in fact comprise both the Atlantic and the Mediterranean coasts of Europe, and we can push either right-handed, left-handed or both-handed as our resources and circumstances permit.[28]

On the surface this was an admirably flexible approach covering all options. But as it failed to give clear priority to western Europe, it disappointed the Americans, and the Russians. It also hinted at extended operations in Sicily and Italy, once north Africa had been cleared, for how else was it possible to interpret Churchill's right-handed push?

In Churchill's conversations with the Russians, he encountered the same kind of problems as he had with the Americans. He would register agreement 'in principle' to a second front and then go on to argue that to launch it in western Europe was, for the moment, impracticable. When Stalin heard this story in Moscow in August 1942 he 'began to look very glum', and the more Churchill pressed his point, the glummer he became. But he 'sat up and grinned' when he learned about the possible invasion of North Africa – not that he regarded it as *the* genuine second front. And he must have been greatly heartened at Churchill's promise of 'a very great operation in 1943'. But what did Churchill mean? Was he already thinking of Italy? Or even Norway? – only months later, in July 1943, he proposed operating in northern Norway, using icebergs as floating air bases.[29] To Stalin's mind he could only have meant western Europe, confirming what had already been said to Molotov in London two months ago. Churchill, perhaps wisely, did not elaborate, allowing the fog of war to thicken.

Churchill clarified his ideas to his colleagues in a paper that autumn.[30]

Left: 'Two Gun Winston': Churchill in twin roles of Prime Minister and Minister of Defence *(Daily Mail)*
Below: Running the War from the Cabinet Room: Churchill November 1940 *(Camera Press)*

Top: Inspecting the Home Guard in Hyde Park *(Hulton Deutsch)*
Centre: Touring London's blitzed areas *(Hulton Deutsch)*
Right: Making ready: checking the coastal fortifications in the north-east of England *(Hulton Deutsch)*

Victory in the air: Churchill watches a Boeing B-17 'Flying Fortress' arriving in Britain
(Imperial War Museum)

This Page
Top: Electioneering in 1951
(Hulton Deutsch)
Right: Addressing his supporters in
Epping, October 1951
(Hulton Deutsch)

Facing Page
Top: More cheerful after D Day.
Churchill and Montgomery
entertaining the troops in
Normandy. (*Imperial War Museum*)
Below: Triumphant in Berlin, July
1945. Accompanied by *(left to right)*
Lord Cherwell (Lindemann),
Montgomery, Ismay, Alexander,
Lord Moran, Eden, and Attlee
(*Imperial War Museum*)

This Page
Left: Carrying On. No resignation in January 1954 (Daily Express)
Below: Churchill's farewell dinner as Prime Minister to Queen Elizabeth II and the Duke of Edinburgh, April 1955 (Hulton Deutsch)

Facing Page
Top: Relaxing at Lord Beaverbrook's villa, 'La Capponcina', on the Riviera, September 1958. With Churchill are Randolph, Clementine, and Arabella, Randolph's daughter (Popperfoto)
Below: 'No philosophising, please.' Churchill and 'Ari' Onassis aboard the Christina (Popperfoto)

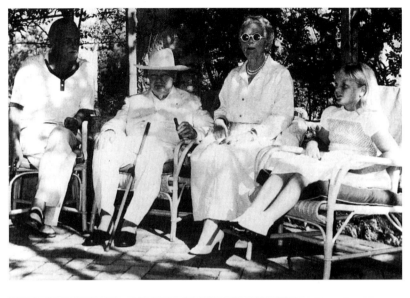

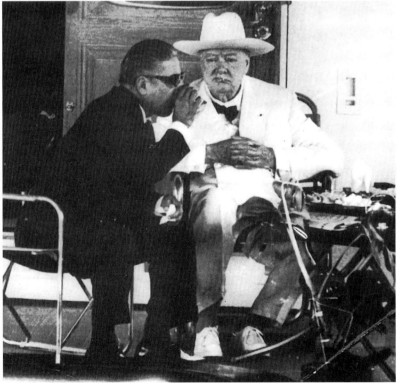

Churchill's state funeral, January 1965. Following the coffin down the steps of St Paul's Cathedral are Clementine and Randolph, Sarah and Mary, Christopher Soames and Winston Churchill, Randolph's son *(Times Newspapers Ltd)*

The main weight of British effort would be in the Mediterranean, first priority being given to the North Africa scheme. The success of these operations, he elucidated, 'will dictate our main action in 1943'. The inference was clear. And on this occasion Churchill had no compunction about expounding upon the options, employing that most inappropriate of metaphors, 'the soft underbelly of the Axis'. Sardinia, Sicily, Italy, the Riviera, even the Balkans, with Turkish aid, were pinpointed as possible targets; nor did he exclude an Arctic operation. As for western Europe, the allies must be ready to take advantage of a German collapse: the build-up for the invasion of Europe would continue at 'full blast', and it would not be discarded. It was not necessary to read too closely between the lines to realize where his real priorities lay.

Throughout 1943 the prospects for an immediate second front receded. The wars in the Pacific and the Mediterranean picked up impetus. In October 1942, at El Alamein, the British 8th Army under Montgomery achieved a hard-fought victory and began advancing – too sluggishly for Churchill's taste – westwards. The following month, the landings in North Africa were successful, allied forces establishing themselves in French Morocco and Algeria. These victories coloured Churchill's meeting with Roosevelt at Casablanca in January 1943. Inevitably, the next logical step was to drive the Germans out of North Africa, a campaign, it was estimated, that would commit the allied armies until the spring (in fact, until May). And then what? Sicily was decided upon as the next target, both to menace Italy and to free the Mediterranean to allied shipping. Winning the battle of the Atlantic was allotted top priority, a goal that was achieved during 1943, and that greatly facilitated the build-up in Britain for the projected invasion of Europe. As for the invasion itself, its future remained as cloudy as ever. The stock formula was trundled out again: only in the event of a German collapse, or a serious depletion of German forces in the West, would it be attempted. No date was mentioned.[31]

These decisions reflected accurately the British viewpoint. Pressed resolutely by Alan Brooke, and sanctioned by a willing Churchill, they confirmed that on this matter at least the general had gained a certain ascendancy over his Prime Minister. The Americans, on this occasion less united and resolved in debate, were persuaded. That April the British drew the obvious conclusion, ruling out a cross-Channel invasion in 1943. Sicily and Italy took precedence.[32] Assuming that Italy would collapse in chaos in the face of an allied assault, Churchill also presumed that the Germans would elect to fall back to the Brenner Pass rather than govern a rebellious country. This was a strange premise for Churchill to make, for if accurate it would surely have had the effect of strengthening Germany's strategic reserve in the West, cancelling out one of his basic requirements for the invasion of Europe.

The Americans, outwardly quiescent at Casablanca, remained unhappy at how the British calculated their strategic options. At their conference in Washington in May 1943, Alan Brooke felt the 'absolute hopelessness' of it all. Not only were the Americans urging an advance into Burma from Assam – 'without adequate resources', Brooke noted angrily – but he discovered that 'We are a long way apart in our strategy in the European theatre.' After one barren session, Brooke recorded the Americans as taking the attitude that 'we led them down the garden path by taking them to North Africa', and that 'at Casablanca we again misled them by inducing them to attack Sicily'. He concluded: 'They do not intend to be led astray again.'[33] Brooke had judged accurately. On this occasion, a timetable was fixed: the attack on western Europe was set for 1 May 1944. For Churchill, this was an ominous sign that the balance of Anglo-American power had moved against him. He left Washington ostensibly committed to the invasion, yet still hypnotized by Italy. Events moved in his favour. Sicily was occupied with comparatively little resistance; in Italy, there were clear signs that Mussolini's regime was tottering – it fell on 25 July. Armed with these facts, Churchill was able to entice the Americans to push on across the Straits of Messina, even though Marshall expressed grave misgivings.[34] So the allies, in particular the British, were drawn into a protracted campaign of highly doubtful utility.

By the second half of 1943 the outcome of the war had been decided. Two years earlier Churchill, declaring that the enemy were choking off Britain's food supplies and its links with America, proclaimed the opening of 'the Battle of the Atlantic'. The cumulative losses for 1941–42 – 7,893,000 tons of shipping; 623,545 tons for the peak month of June 1942 – were truly frightening. Gradually, this mortal threat was surmounted. At Bletchley Park, the cryptoanalysts succeeded in breaking the German Navy's 'Home Waters' Enigma codes, enabling the Admiralty to read its signals at almost real time and re-route convoys out of the danger zones. More sophisticated anti-submarine techniques and greater Anglo-American cooperation, together with a massive building programme – particularly at the staggeringly efficient American shipyards where, by October 1942, three standardized Liberty Ships were being launched daily – turned the Atlantic war decisively in the allies' favour. In May 1943 Karl Dönitz, commander of the U-boats, reported that his losses, forty-one that month alone, had 'reached unbearable heights'. Between June and September only one allied ship in convoy was lost.[35]

In the land war in the East, a similar process was taking place. At Stalingrad (November-February 1943) and Kursk (July) the Red Army won decisive victories. By October, it was deployed on the banks of the Dnieper. Stalin, like Churchill in December 1941, could presume that ultimate victory was only a matter of time.

With the Atlantic approaches securer than ever and the bulk of Germany's armies tied down in the East, the chances of pulling off a successful invasion of western Europe had improved out of all recognition. Nevertheless, Churchill hesitated. As the target date for May 1944 approached, so his attitude towards the European invasion stiffened. In July 1943 his sights were still fixed firmly on Italy, with the south of France or a drive to Vienna as the next step. Disturbed by 'the extraordinary efficiency of the German Army', he considered postponing the cross-Channel invasion. In its place, he resurrected the Norway operation, terming it 'a second string' to the allied bow. But once again, his pet scheme was damned by the Joint Planning Staff. He also encouraged the conquest of the Dodecanese islands of Cos, Leros, and Samos, to the intense annoyance of the Americans.[36] Their almost immediate reconquest by the Germans was, for him, a most humiliating experience.

At the Quebec conference in August 1943, he still claimed to be 'wholeheartedly in favour' of 'Overlord'. But he tacked on to his assent strict conditions that were intended to *guarantee* allied air and ground superiority before any landing was made. To Roosevelt, he stressed the operation's 'very grave defects'.[37] And to his Chiefs of Staff and War Cabinet he concluded that the current strategy was all wrong, exposing the allies to defeat 'in detail'. He feared that the crack German divisions would inflict 'a military disaster greater than that of Dunkirk', upon the Anglo-American forces, breathing new life into Hitler's regime. He spoke again of 'Overlord's' postponement. Alan Brooke chipped in: we cannot wage war bound 'by lawyer's contracts'. Churchill summed up: 'our priorities should be to reinforce Italy, enter the Balkans, hold our position in the Aegean islands, intensify the air war against Germany, and continue the build-up for "Overlord".' Like Evelyn Waugh's Brigadier Ritchie-Hook, Churchill wished 'to biff' the enemy wherever it could be found – except, apparently, in western Europe.[38]

When the Big Three met at Teheran in late November, Stalin asked: 'Did the Prime Minister and the British Staffs really believe in "Overlord"?' Churchill was still prevaricating, but in glorious style. 'Provided the conditions for "Overlord" were to obtain,' he replied to Stalin, 'it would be our stern duty to hurl across the Channel against the Germans every sinew of our strength'.[40]

Churchill had now to cope with joint American-Soviet pressure, for him an unfortunate, but foreseeable, by-product of the debate on the second front. Roosevelt was convinced that he could deal more effectively with Stalin without Churchill's unsettling presence. At Cairo, during the preliminary meetings to the Teheran Conference, Roosevelt had side-stepped Churchill's attempts to coordinate policy before the confrontation with Stalin, preferring to discuss Far Eastern affairs with

Chiang-Kai-Shek and his attractive spouse, matters that did not rate highly on Churchill's scale of priorities. At Teheran, the Stalin-Roosevelt bloc proved too strong for Churchill's scepticism. Italian operations were not shut down, a suggestion 'partly sponsored' by Roosevelt, but 'Overlord' was finally settled, its closing date fixed for 1 June.

The Teheran decision did not kindle any last-minute enthusiasm in Churchill. If anything, events must have confirmed his pessimism. The following January an attempt was made to outflank the German winter line at Monte Cassino by an amphibious assault at Anzio, south of Rome. Churchill, excited by the prospects of this operation, gave it his full support. But the enemy, far from being pressured into panic measures, reacted with lightning speed. Out of a total landing force of 110,000, 40,000 were left dead, wounded, or prisoners, while almost as many deserted or fell sick. After 125 days of bitter fighting, the allies were still confined to a small beachhead.[40]

This was a depressing rehearsal for 'Overlord'. But Churchill was committed and could not pull back. To Cadogan, he wrote in frank tone: 'This battle ['Overlord'] has been forced upon us by the Russians and the United States military authorities. We have gone in wholeheartedly, and I would not raise a timorous cry before a decision in the field is taken'. Hardly the words of a devotee. He confessed that he had become 'hardened' to 'Overlord', but his preferences had not altered. Only a month before 'D' Day he confided to the Dominion Prime Ministers his own 'inclination':

> [He] would have been in favour of rolling up Europe from the South-East, and joining hands with the Russians. However, it had proved impossible to persuade the United States to this view. They had been determined at every stage upon the invasion in North-West Europe, and had constantly wanted us to break off the Mediterranean operations.

Should 'Overlord' prove unsuccessful, he went on, 'we must either set our teeth and prepare for a longer war, or else reduce the severity of the terms which we were prepared to offer the enemy. He was in no doubt which course we should adopt.'[41] Churchill did not elaborate. But in view of his own record, and the constraints of the wartime alliance, it is clear that he envisaged – threatened? – a protracted, bloody campaign of attrition, something along the lines of Anzio.

'Rolling up Europe from the South-East' was a fine-sounding manoeuvre on a map. But not only the Americans balked at the prospect. Churchill's own Chiefs of Staff were no less adamantly opposed. Alan Brooke regarded an advance on Vienna as little more than a pipe-dream. At this stage – indeed, until the spring of 1945 – the much-vaunted Balkan strategy belongs to the mythology of the war, not its reality.[42] On the other hand, the Normandy landings of 6 June were carried out successfully and with comparatively few losses. By the end of August the allied armies had broken the German lines and stood on the Seine and the Loire, the great prize of Paris in their hands. Brussels was captured in early September. By mid-September patrols of the American 1st Army had crossed the German frontier near Aachen. Whatever blunders and mistakes were made, whatever strategic and tactical differences separated the generals, 'Overlord' certainly did not realize Churchill's direst expectations.

Was Churchill for or against a mass assault on western Europe? The records reveal that he was both. It depended largely with whom he spoke and in what circumstances. What is abundantly clear is that he did not give it overriding priority. When he spoke of it favourably, he imposed upon its implementation the most stringent conditions. Other, more inviting, options persistently beckoned. Was it simply coincidence that both the Americans and the Russians believed that he – the British – had misled them, were in 'breach of contract'? Clearly, Churchill's words were more meaningful in the telling than in cold print. Commentators have speculated whether or not 'Overlord' could have been mounted in 1943. For Churchill, this was never a tenable proposition. He had argued strongly and cogently against it. But had Churchill been given the 'plenary authority' over allied strategy he so desired, would he have mounted the invasion in 1944? The answer is by no means certain. 'Had we had our way,' wrote General John Kennedy, Director of Military Operations,' 'I think there can be little doubt that the invasion of France would not have been done in 1944.'[43]

Why was Churchill so ambiguous about 'Overlord', so hesitant until forced into it? Certainly, the Somme-Passchendaele syndrome took its effect, as it would on any veteran of the first war. From his days in the trenches at Ploegsteert he had held German military leadership in high regard – in contrast to the limited abilities of his own generals. On the eve of 'D' Day he spoke emotionally of the 'hecatombs of World War 1', of how 'An entire British generation of potential leaders had been cut off and Britain could not afford the loss of another generation.' But Churchill was too experienced a campaigner not to realize that tough battles meant losses, often on a considerable scale. If it would do any good, he told Stalin, for example, he would 'not shrink from throwing in 150–200,000 men on grounds of loss'. 'A military attack is not ruled out,' his Chiefs of Staff were instructed, 'simply because a fifth of the soldiers may be shot on the way', provided, he added, that 'the others get there and do the job'.[44]

But Churchill, evidently, lacked faith in the fighting ability of the British army to defeat the Germans – a belief that applied, equally, if not more so, to the Americans. His conviction, sustained by the painful series of British military setbacks, was compounded by his exaggerated opinion of the ability of the German General Staff. British commanders, chanting 'their stately hymn of "Safety First"', were badgered without mercy. Bereft of inspiration, they failed to inspire their armies. 'What were they doing? Why were they not fighting?' he complained to Alan Brooke. 'There is something deeply wrong with the whole morale of our army,' wrote Harold Nicolson, depressed by Churchill's verdict that 'our soldiers are not as good fighters as their fathers were'. No general escaped the rough side of his tongue, not even his favourites. Alexander, 'gay, smiling, debonair', lacked 'imagination and leadership'. As for the over-cautious Montgomery, 'He will bankrupt you. He will need 13 divisions before he'll ever make a move.'[45]

Something of this over-cautiousness had rubbed off on Churchill himself. With the success of 'Overlord', his natural pugnacity re-asserted itself. It did not signify the end of the strategic debate. But now, with the end of the war in sight, its political dimensions took on a greater significance. How did Churchill envisage the nascent world order and Britain's place in it? And what would be the nature of his – Britain's – relationship with his two over-mighty allies?

20

'Advance Britannia!'

Immediately after the Yalta conference, at a drawn-out lunch aboard the SS *Franconia*, 'a great argument' ensued. The war had been fought 'to secure liberty and a decent existence for the peoples of Europe', Field Marshal Alexander said. 'Not a bit of it,' retorted Churchill. 'We are fighting to secure the proper respect for the British people!'[1] For Churchill 'proper respect' was a highly prized commodity; it could also be ruinously expensive. But spurred on by his utopian vision of Britain's place among the nations, he bid extravagantly for its acquisition.

In large measure, it explains his infatuation with the Mediterranean area. In Italy, his basic assumption that the Germans would rapidly pull back had proved false. By April 1945, the Germans were still fighting an obstinate rearguard action all the way, and held a line just north of Florence. The strategic advantages of fighting along the Appennine heights were doubtful to an extreme. Far from tying down large enemy forces, at certain stages the reverse occurred. Churchill was quite aware of the failings of his Italian strategy. As far back as November 1943, he noted that the Germans had been able to withdraw several divisions from Italy to send to the Russian front. 'We have therefore failed,' he told the Chiefs of Staff, 'to take the weight of the attack off the Soviets.'[2]

Yet he persisted. Indeed, he attached to the Italian campaign an almost mystical quality. In the summer of 1944 a great controversy had erupted: whether or not to divert troops from the Italian theatre to invade southern France. Churchill responded to this proposal as if it were an act of perfidy. In a draft telegram to Roosevelt he refused to be party to 'an absolutely perverse strategy . . . to agree to the whole great Mediterranean scene, with all its possibilities, being incontinently . . . flung on one side'. He spoke of two distinct commands, the Americans in charge of 'Overlord', the British directing affairs in the Mediterranean. If it would 'ease matters' he would tender his resignation. This extraordinary message was never sent. Instead, a less threatening note was despatched stressing 'the dazzling possibilities' being thrown away in Italy for what he feared would be 'a costly stalemate' in France.[3]

Nothing of the sort happened. The invasion of southern France was launched successfully and with little opposition on 15 August 1944. In less than a month, American forces advancing from the south had linked up with Patton's Third Army, which had just broken out of Normandy, north of Dijon. Of course, Churchill could argue, as he did, that by depleting the Italian theatre the Americans had robbed him of 'dazzling possibilities'. But this remains a highly speculative proposition. What is absolutely certain is that while Churchill was absorbed with Italy, the German front in western Europe was crumbling. Allied armies now possessed a golden opportunity to roll up the German lines. Throughout the war, Churchill had waited for this moment. Yet he still could not rid himself of his Italian obsession. He unburdened himself to Clementine:

> The only times I ever quarrel with the Americans are when they fail to give us a fair share of opportunity to win glory.
> Undoubtedly I feel much pain when I see our armies so much smaller than theirs. It has always been my wish to keep equal, but how can you do that against so mighty a nation and a population nearly three times your own?[4]

Was he also stirred by latent emotions, stimulated once again by the exhilaration of war?[5] Driven to playing the illustrious warlord, he applied himself to high strategy as well as intervening in the tactical minutiae of great battles. He also assumed the outward appearance of a generalissimo. Churchill insisted on wearing military dress whenever possible, much like Stalin, a kind of posturing that has no precedent in British political tradition. But everyone tolerated his dressing-up. It was as though his military garb not only decorated his body, but also rounded out his personality.

By 1943–44 there were not two commands, as Churchill pretended, but only one; and the Americans were running it. As the war progressed, this dominance spilt over to encompass political and economic affairs as well. For someone who sought 'proper respect', this was a most disagreeable fact. But it could hardly have surprised Churchill. If there was one lesson to be drawn from the First World War, it was that Britain could not win a major conflict without American money, supplies, and ultimately manpower.

Galling though it was for Churchill, the Second World War tightened America's grip on Britain's fortunes. There was little he could do, except protest. And he did protest, most vigorously, whenever the Americans provoked him – which was quite often! He saw 'impossible situations' when negotiating the 'destroyers for bases' deal. He detected 'vainglorious ambitions' as a bitter dispute flared up over post-war civil aviation rights. The question of colonial trusteeship remained a running sore, masking, so Churchill suspected, American imperial aspirations. Nor was Roosevelt's impudent suggestion that Britain return Hong Kong to China received graciously. Over India, Roosevelt's accusation that Britain jibbed at conceding it 'the right of self-government' triggered off a paroxysm of extreme fury, Churchill's 'string of cuss words' lasting 'for two hours'. He was even prepared to retire from public life if such an eye-catching step would assuage American public opinion and preserve the wartime alliance. When Britain and the Soviet Union reached an agreement over Greece and Roumania in the summer of 1944, informing the United States after the event, another first-class row broke out. 'I cannot admit that I have done anything wrong in this matter,' he protested to Roosevelt. But probably the most vexed issue of all was lend-lease. Churchill had no doubt that he had mortgaged Britain's future. In a moment of frankness, he had alluded to Britain being 'flayed alive'. 'Are we, who alone saved the world during a whole year, to go short while Americans eat what they will?' he asked acerbicly. At Quebec, in September 1944, a most humiliating scene was witnessed. As the two leaders haggled over the second stage of the lend-lease agreement, Churchill, his patience at an end, snapped: 'What do you want me to do, stand up and beg like Fala [Roosevelt's dog]?'[6]

In these confrontations, Churchill was on the defensive, often forced to concede against his will. He suffered these indignities because the war could not be won without American aid. He was obsessed, rightly, with the power of the United States. Preserving, nurturing the Anglo-American partnership would assure Britain's future role as a Great Power. Churchill was particularly anxious to promote the image of a solid friendship, of two great allies walking hand-in-hand, chatting happily, confident that their outlooks had jelled into a 'perfect understanding'. He was not above suppressing contradictory evidence, so sensitive was he to this vision. When he came to write *Triumph and Tragedy*, he clarified to President Eisenhower that he intended to publish nothing that might 'impair the sympathy and understanding which exist between our two countries', and he carefully pruned the book, taking 'great pains to ensure' that it contained 'nothing which might imply that there was in those days any controversy or lack of confidence between us'.[7]

Despite Churchill's reluctance to formulate post-war solutions, he had sketched out a blueprint of sorts for the future. But it was drawn up in general, abstract terms. To contain German aggression he foresaw a 'World Council' comprising Britain, the United States, the Soviet Union, China (thrown in, no doubt, as a sop to the Americans), and delegations from Europe, the Pacific area, and the American continent. In Europe, no excessive demands would be made though Churchill did envisage the ceding of 'certain territories' and 'exchanges of populations'. However, Germany was not to be a 'pariah' nation, but would be partitioned. Prussia, the chief villain, would be isolated. Four confederations – the Danubian, the Northern, the Mitteleuropa, and the Balkan – would be established and France would be restored as 'a strong power'. In one way, Churchill had remodelled the classical nineteenth-century equilibrium, 'five great European nations: England, France, Italy, Spain and Prussia', balancing off 'the Bear' in the East.

Underwriting this concept was another: the special place in this world order of 'the English speaking world' which would command the seas, respecting the commercial and colonial rights of all peoples. Britain and the United States would enjoy naval parity. These two great democracies, while maintaining close connections with the Council of Europe would yet stand aloof from it. Perhaps, eventually, some form of Anglo-American union would be forged. But in any case, Britain would act as the vital link between the United States and a United States of Europe.[8]

If only this 'Grand Design' was workable. But Churchill had embellished Britain's true position in the world, distorting the issues rather than clarifying them. His on-going squabbles with the Americans only added to the confusion. Nor could he be certain of American long-term aims. As the war unfolded, it became increasingly apparent that America was intent on disengaging from Europe. Who, then, would stand with Britain against a resurgent Germany, or a belligerent Soviet Union?

Churchill's preferred option was to recreate France as a European factor. His preference was not guided solely by reasons of *realpolitik*. He had known and loved France all his life and was genuinely concerned with its reinstatement. But it proved to be a demanding process. The humours of de Gaulle, recognized as 'leader of all Free Frenchmen,' inflamed the situation even more.

Churchill recognized in de Gaulle many of his own qualities, another *homme du destin*. At times, he found the sight intolerable. In the summer of 1943 he wished 'to eliminate de Gaulle as a political force'. 'Anti-British', dragging behind him 'a trial of anglophobia', de Gaulle, who showed 'many of the symptoms of a budding Fuhrer', was 'animated by dictatorial instincts and consumed by personal ambition'.

Churchill had also been stirred up by Roosevelt who had developed a violent antipathy towards de Gaulle. Convinced that the French leader was a double-crosser and a menace, he called upon Churchill 'to break with him'. So strongly was Roosevelt swayed by his emotions, that he promoted Admiral Jean François Darlan, a Vichyite notorious for his anti-British opinions, and, after he was assassinated, the politically ineffectual General Henri Giraud as rivals to the detested de Gaulle. Churchill kept in step. Although he risked a mini-crisis with Eden, who hinted at resignation, he was not prepared to break with Roosevelt for the sake of de Gaulle.[10]

Even allowing for de Gaulle's provocations, Anglo-American policy towards France can only be called a shambles. Often brushing aside more judicious advice from his Foreign Office, Churchill followed where Roosevelt led. Eventually de Gaulle triumphed; but only in October 1944 was he acknowledged as leader of the official government of France. A month later, de Gaulle graciously hosted Churchill in his capital, staging a magnificent display of public solidarity on the anniversary of Armistice Day. After the parades – the Paris crowds chanting 'Churchill' – and the banquets and speeches – and after Churchill's tears of joy had dried – they dealt with more serious business: an Anglo-French alliance. De Gaulle, eurocentric in outlook, envisaged it as maintaining 'the equilibrium of Europe', of not allowing the Continent to become a plaything for 'disputes between America and Russia'; Churchill proved unwilling to sacrifice the American connection. No genuine *rapprochement* emerged, and old suspicions soon resurfaced. 'This menacing and hostile man', Churchill wrote to Eden, 'will be a great danger to peace and to Britain in the future.'[11]

Excluded from the councils of the Great Powers, treated as little more than an outcast, de Gaulle would not overlook these ongoing humiliations. Certainly, he could not be relied upon to dance to Churchill's tune. He would either adopt an independent line, or, in the tradition of French policy, turn eastwards towards the Soviet Union. Churchill was aware that de Gaulle had already signalled to Stalin, hoping to gain the recognition denied him by the Anglo-Saxons, implying that for all he cared the United States and Britain could keep to themselves. Ultimately though, Churchill fought hard to secure France a world role, arguing its case to serve as one of the occupying powers of Germany and as a permanent member of the Security Council. The Americans finally relented. But by then it was too late to appease de Gaulle.

Eventually, Churchill found that he could not manipulate the French in Europe and at the same time advance his Atlanticist conception of Britain's place in the world. In attempting to have it both ways, Churchill achieved neither. But the main factor disrupting Churchill's vision of an invigorated, politically stable Europe working in harness with an Anglo-American combination lay beyond his authority. If he could not handle de Gaulle, he could hardly hope to outmanoeuvre Stalin. As the Red Army advanced westwards, his options shrank. Who would restrain the Soviet Union?

Churchill abhorred the Communist system, but he hated Nazism even more. Since the late 1930s he had aimed at bringing in the Soviet

Union as a counter in the European balance against Nazi Germany. But unlike many, he had adopted a singularly broad-minded attitude towards the Nazi-Soviet pact, seeing it as a short-term truce that would not override the historic Teuton-Slav conflict. When the truce ended and Hitler attacked the Soviet Union, he refused to retract one word of invective he had said about Bolshevism. The choices before him had become simple: 'Any man or state who fights on against Nazidom will have our aid. Any man or state who marches with Hitler is our enemy. [The] Russian danger is therefore our danger, and the danger of the United States.'

But how was he to fashion the peace in cooperation with Russia after the fighting? Was Stalin merely defending legitimate Soviet national interests, or did he harbour aggressive ambitions? 'Trying to maintain good relations with a Communist is like wooing a crocodile,' he once pointed out, 'You do not know whether to tickle it under the chin or to beat it over the head. When it opens its mouth you cannot tell whether it is trying to smile or preparing to eat you up!'[12]

Part of the problem was Churchill's inability to fathom accurately the dynamics of the Soviet system. He saw it clouded by his late Victorian-Edwardian values (in much the same way that he was wont to regard Nazism as a malignant offshoot of Prussian militarism). Despotic, oppressive, illiberal, certainly. Yet so too was Tsarism, an authoritarian, autocratic regime with which his own Liberal Cabinet had hatched a deal in 1907. Nor was Churchill able to comprehend fully the gruesome nature of Stalin's absolutism, on occasion detecting 'a grim thing' inciting him. Nothing could be further from the truth. No radicals or conservatives jogged Stalin's elbow. Far from conducting a dialogue, Stalin and Churchill were speaking over each other's heads. Yet Churchill persevered. For one thing, lack of choice drove him on. But at another level, he genuinely held that he could trade with Stalin (as did Roosevelt). There was much to admire, even envy, in his baffling adversary. Stalin's 'plenary authority', his businesslike ways, his remarkable memory, his lavish hospitality, his personal cordiality, all must have greatly appealed to Churchill. Above all, Churchill believed in his mission as Defender of British interests and the potency of his words to realize his purpose. He caught a tantalizing glimpse of two Men of Destiny at work and at play. 'If only I could dine with Stalin once a week,' he remarked, 'there would be no trouble at all. We get on like a house on fire.'[13]

Stalin had one other advantage over Churchill: he seemed to know what he wanted from the outset. His demands, often phrased too stridently for Churchill's ears, were clear-cut: more convoys and supplies; the opening of a second front – Now!; and a territorial settlement that would reflect the substance of the Nazi-Soviet pact of August 1939.

Churchill, on the other hand, consistently shied away from committing himself on the nature of the post-war world. He set up demarcation lines between his military and political strategies, when in fact, as Stalin well knew, they go hand-in-hand, one feeding off the other. Preoccupied with the military dimension of the war, Churchill barely applied himself to its political aftermath – at least not until the late autumn of 1944, by which time it was perilously late to make amends for previous neglect.

According to Stalin, when he met Eden in 1941, the Soviet Union's western frontier would closely follow the line determined by the Nazi-Soviet pact. The Baltic states and areas of Finland and Roumania would revert back to Soviet rule; the Polish border would return to the so-called Curzon line.[14] As compensation, Poland would be awarded East Prussia; and as punishment, Germany would be broken up into three of four states. At the outbreak of war, Churchill had broadcast to the world that although he would have preferred the Red Army to be deployed on its 'present [Curzon] line as the friends and allies of Poland instead of invaders', he acknowledged that 'this line was clearly necessary for the safety of Russia against Nazi Germany,' an unambiguous message that, no doubt, Stalin picked up. By 1942 Churchill was bound by the principles of the Atlantic Charter, and anxious not to do or say anything that would disrupt the emerging American alliance, he inveighed fiercely against Stalin's frontier claims. To agree to Stalin's programme 'would be contrary to all the principles for which we are fighting this war and would dishonour our cause'. Anticipating that the Anglo-Saxon bloc will remain the most powerful force in the world, dispensing aid to a needy Soviet Union, he insisted that 'all questions of territorial frontiers . . . be left to the decision of the Peace Conference'.[15]

Stalin's terms varied little during the course of the war. It was for the western leaders to adjust to them – or not. Eden and the Foreign Office argued the case for 'stark realism' and the 'immediate recognition' of Stalin's demands. Cripps and Beaverbrook took a similar line. Churchill agonized. He appealed to Roosevelt: would it not be possible to bend, slightly, the principles of the Atlantic Charter so as not 'to deny Russia the frontiers she occupied when Germany attacked her'? But American sensibilities would not allow it. In Cadogan's words, Roosevelt sent over 'an out-size raspberry'.[16]

As negotiations for an Anglo-Soviet treaty went ahead, voices were raised against making far-reaching concessions. Churchill, still recovering from the political fallout of the Singapore catastrophe, took note. 'I am like a bomber pilot,' he said, 'I go out night after night, and I know that one night I shall not return.' A whiff of appeasement was in the air. After some additional American arm-twisting on the Russians, a treaty was agreed. Though it spoke in soothing phrases of twenty years of Anglo-Soviet post-war cooperation, it contained nothing on new frontier claims.[17]

By the spring of 1943, Roosevelt was also ready to approve the Curzon line, compensating Poland in East Prussia and Silesia. As Churchill had put forward an identical programme a year earlier, he had no cause for complaint. Neither was he prepared to remonstrate too loudly when the retreating Germans claimed that the bodies of some 10,000 Polish officers they had discovered in a mass grave at Katyn had been slaughtered by the Russians. But Churchill, although mortified by this grisly proof of Stalin's ruthlessness, would not allow it to cause a breach between the allies: 'There is no use prowling round the three year old graves of Smolensk,' he remarked. Nothing would be allowed to erode his game plan. In his graphic depiction, Poland would 'move westwards [to the Oder] like soldiers taking two steps left close'.[18]

Churchill later explained why he had revised his own feelings since his initial tirade against capitulating to Stalin's claims.

> The tremendous victories of the Russian armies, the deep-seated changes which have taken place in the character of the Russian State and Government, the new confidence which has grown in our hearts towards Stalin – these have all had their effect. Most of all is the fact that the Russians may very soon be in physical possession of these territories, and it is absolutely certain that we should never attempt to turn them out.[19]

Churchill's 'new confidence' in Stalin ran hot and cold until the end of the war. Needing a deal with Stalin, and wanting it so badly, he came to believe that it was feasible. But one fact overshadowed all others. The Russian's 'physical possession' of invaded territories was a reality impossible to deny, as was the obvious truth that neither Britain nor the United States could, or would, go to war 'to turn them out'.

When, therefore, Churchill, Roosevelt, and Stalin met at Teheran in late November 1943 – with Soviet armies deploying to cross Poland's eastern border – all they had to do was 'informally' endorse the expansion of the Soviet Union up to the Curzon line and then 'go to [impose it upon?] the Poles later'; which is what they did. Other significant decisions were taken: the date of the Normandy landings was settled, regardless of Churchill's hesitations; Stalin promised a renewed offensive westwards; once Germany was defeated, the Soviet Union agreed to enter the war in the Far East; and issues relating to a post-war international organization were raised. There was also much feasting and toasting. But behind the bonhomie – Churchill: "I drink to the Proletarian masses". Stalin: "I drink to the Conservative Party".'[20] – Churchill became painfully aware that he was gradually being shunted aside. The Big Two, seemingly, could manage without him.

For some time Roosevelt had been anxious to arrange a private tête-à-tête with Stalin. At Teheran, his wish was realized. To escape an alleged assassination plot – drummed up by Molotov – Roosevelt accepted Stalin's invitation to move into a villa in the Russian embassy compound. 'He will be well looked after,' was one caustic comment, 'for his servants are all members of the NKVD', and 'expressive bulges were plainly discernible in the hip pockets under their near white coats'. But while Roosevelt did not hesitate to see Stalin alone, he cold-shouldered Churchill. 'It is not like him,' Churchill grumbled. By-passing Churchill not only reflected Roosevelt's self-perceived flair for personal diplomacy, it also indicated his intuitive suspicion of British policy. He asked Stalin 'whether he would like to discuss the future peace of the world', a dialogue that he would conduct without being tied to Churchill's outmoded, Victorian outlook. Questioned whether the sessions had gone well, Churchill snapped back: 'A bloody lot has gone wrong.'[21] For the first time he realized 'What a small nation we are,' he confided to Violet Bonham-Carter. 'There I sat with the great Russian bear on one side . . . and on the other side the great American buffalo, and between the two sat the poor little English donkey . . .'[22]

Churchill's job was to persuade the London-based Polish government-in-exile to accept the Curzon line. 'We declared war for Poland . . . we have never undertaken to defend existing Polish frontiers', he wrote in a note to Eden in January 1944. After two wars, and 'between 20 and 30 millions of Russian lives', the Soviet Union has earned 'the right to the inexpungeable security of her Western frontiers'. If the Poles were unable to appreciate this, Britain would wash its hands of the affair, having 'discharged to the full her obligations'. He persisted: 'we might be overtaken by events which would be difficult to remedy'.[23] The hint was unambiguous.

To sweeten the pill of concessions, Churchill offered the Poles 'the prospect of a sure freedom and independence'. But was this a promise he was able to fulfil? As the allies were landing on the beaches of Normandy, Russian forces were preparing to cross the Curzon line into western Poland. From that point on, Stalin screwed up the pressure to ensure that his own creatures would rule in what was left of Poland. In August 1944, the Polish Underground Army, anti-Soviet in allegiance, rose up against their Nazi occupiers to liberate Warsaw. As German forces moved in to destroy the uprising, Stalin waited, although his armies were within easy striking distance of the beleaguered city. A report came into Churchill's hands describing German 'terror methods', how they were razing 'whole districts', brutally murdering the 'wounded and sick', butchering or deporting the inhabitants. Despite all Churchill's appeals, Stalin refused to come to the aid of what he termed 'power-seeking criminals'. Churchill, after much debate, decided not to reproach him, no doubt swayed by Roosevelt's refusal to join in a 'proposed message to Uncle J[oe]'.[24]

The Warsaw Uprising cast a dark shadow on Anglo-Soviet relations. Churchill was deeply moved by the spectacle of the Poles' heroic last-ditch stand. Equally, the callousness of Stalin's response strengthened suspicions long held about Soviet intentions. Churchill noted:

> If of course the view is adopted that Russia is going to present herself as a new Nazi Germany ideologically inverted, we shall have to make what head we can against another tyranny, and this would have to be borne in mind when considering the position which a chastened Germany would occupy.[25]

But he was not yet ready to include Germany in a western bloc to restrain the Soviet Union, even though this idea was already being widely canvassed in British post-war planning circles.

The discussion about the fate of western Poland was academic for another reason. At Casablanca, Roosevelt, with Churchill's consent, had proclaimed an allied policy of 'unconditional surrender'. However its other merits or drawbacks are calculated, 'unconditional surrender' ensured that the fighting would stop with Soviet troops on German soil. The only question was: at what point?

By September 1944 the German question had in effect been resolved, and largely in the Soviets' favour. That month, Britain, the United States and the Soviet Union signed a protocol that divided Germany into zones of occupation. Whatever happened, a Soviet military presence in Germany was assured, at some points little more than 120 miles from the Rhine. Churchill seems to have paid little attention to the political consequences of this decision. Not having read his papers, he was briefed by his private secretary, Jock Colville, while taking a bath, a somewhat complicated procedure as Churchill was inclined 'to submerge himself entirely from time to time and thus become deaf to certain passages'.[26] A day after this bizarre tutorial, Churchill agreed with Roosevelt to adopt the so-called Morgenthau plan that called for the dismantling of Germany's industrial base and its 'pastoralization'. Eden, when he heard the news, flew into a rage and reminded his chief that Morgenthau's ideas contradicted the Foreign Office's plans for Germany. The notion of turning Germany into an agrarian country was quietly dropped, with, as Churchill tactfully recorded, his 'full accord'.[27]

When Churchill went to Moscow in October 1944 he desperately needed some kind of *modus vivendi* with Stalin. To all intents and purposes, the fate of both Poland and Germany had been settled. With Russian troops entrenched in Germany, and the probability of the Soviet Union acting 'as a new Nazi Germany ideologically inverted', who would restrain the Soviets? The idea of mobilizing Germany for this task was still repugnant to Churchill. And as he derisively noted: France was down and out; the Belgians were 'extremely weak'; the Dutch 'entirely selfish'; and Denmark and Norway were 'helpless and defenceless'. In these circumstances, Britain would have to shoulder the main burden, about fifty to sixty divisions, which was quite preposterous.[28]

So Churchill elected to take what was on offer. It amounted to the division of Europe. With Poland and half Germany in any case lost, perhaps he could salvage something in the Balkans, a region that from Britain's Mediterranean-imperial interest ranked far higher than the outer marches of eastern Europe. It was the best Churchill could hope for. Even an old-fashioned spheres of influence agreement was better than nothing. And it would carry the added bonus of avoiding outright hostility at a time when the allies could least afford it.

Stalin, of course, had his own ideas. On the day Churchill arrived for the Moscow Conference, he told his Lublin Poles not to fret. 'The alliance will not break up over Poland,' he assured them. 'Serious politicians should ignore parliamentary gobbledygook.'[29] In fact, the Lubliners had little to worry about. Although Eden, not wishing to go down in the history books as 'an appeaser', argued that Poland 'must be allowed to settle her own affairs', Churchill countered that he had already settled them at Teheran with Stalin and Roosevelt. Nothing would disrupt their bargain. 'Anyone who raises difficulties,' noted Lord Moran, 'gets short shrift.' This was certainly true of the London Poles. Mikolajczyk, the Prime Minister of the Poles-in-exile, was brought to Moscow to be browbeaten into accepting the Curzon line. Churchill shook his finger: 'Unless you accept the frontier, you're out of business forever,' he cried. 'Our relations with Russia are much better than they have ever been. I mean to keep them that way.' 'Should I sign a death sentence against myself?' Mikolajczyk asked. As the exchanges grew more furious, Churchill – who had meanwhile developed a fever – lost his temper.

> This is crazy! You cannot defeat the Russians! . . . You wish to start a war in which twenty-five million lives will be lost! The Russians will sweep through your country and your people will be liquidated . . . If you want to conquer Russia, we shall let you go your own way. You ought to be in a lunatic asylum! . . . You hate the Russians. I know you hate them.

Mikolajczyk held out to the end, but to no avail. The following month he resigned.

At the Moscow conference, the fundamental question was not the Polish question – for all its high drama – but the Balkans, the British fears for Greece and the Adriatic. At their first session Churchill had pushed across the table to Stalin 'a half-sheet of paper'. Stalin had glanced at it, ticked it with 'a fat blue pencil', and passed it back. This was, in Churchill's description, the 'naughty document' that divided by percentages the Balkan countries into spheres of influence, apportioning Britain – in accord with the United States – primacy in Greece, the Soviet Union in Roumania and Bulgaria, and earmarking equality of status in Yugoslavia and Hungary. Churchill was uneasy about the cynical nature of this deal, about the impression it would leave of two chieftains disposing of the fate of millions in such a casual, offhand manner. Still, he had achieved his main aim. 'Britain,' Churchill had explained to Stalin, 'must be the leading Mediterranean power.' With footholds secured on the Adriatic and Aegean seas, this objective at least was attained.

But was Stalin to be trusted? Whenever Churchill was in 'Uncle Joe's' company, whenever they were wining and dining together, toasting each other, attending the Bolshoi ballet, flattering each other in public, Churchill's optimism rose, a vision forming of how the Great Men of History can determine world-shaking events. He assured both Attlee and Roosevelt that the Balkan 'arrangements' were 'the best' possible: Greece would be saved, Yugoslavia preserved.[30] And in a curious way the notorious 'percentages agreement' worked. By now Churchill had lent his full support to Tito in Yugoslavia, throwing over the monarchists in a manner considered by many to have been dishonorable.[31] When Tito himself broke with the Soviet Union in 1948, Stalin held back, tolerating Yugoslavia's growing links with the West. This was an unforeseen outcome that must have raised, albeit belatedly, Churchill's spirits.

In Greece – where the British had procured a ninety per cent interest – the dividends were more immediate. Churchill spent his Christmas holidays of 1944 in Athens, settling the civil war that had broken out between the Communist dominated National Popular Liberation Army, the military wing of the National Liberation Front, and the forces of the royalist provisional government of Georgios Papandreou. Churchill was determined not to let Greece slip from his grasp. Treat Athens as a conquered city where a rebellion has broken out, he instructed the local British commander, General Robert Scobie. Restore order, he directed, 'without bloodshed if possible, but also with bloodshed if necessary'. He secured the confidence of the House, and pressed by Eden and his advisers, he eventually and reluctantly agreed to a compromise of a temporary regency under Archbishop Damaskinos. Churchill would 'hold and dominate Athens', as he had set out to do, establishing Britain's position in the eastern Meditteranean.

But although Stalin adhered 'strictly and faithfully' to the agreement over Greece, Churchill had an irritating suspicion that the Soviet leader's territorial appetite knew no bounds. These fears hardened as Churchill viewed Stalin's actions from afar. Deprived of the personal chemistry that he believed their meetings triggered off, Churchill's anxieties grew. He explained to de Gaulle:

> At present Russia is a great beast which has been starved for a long time. It is not possible to prevent her from eating, especially since she is now in the middle of her herd of victims. But she must be kept from devouring everything.[32]

As he prepared to leave for the Yalta conference of February 1945, his prognosis turned even gloomier: 'All the Balkans, except Greece, are going to be Bolshevised; and there is nothing I can do to prevent it. There is nothing I can do for poor Poland either.'[33]

Yalta was the most famous and notorious of the wartime summit meetings.[34] There, so the myth goes, United States policy floundered in the hands of its mortally stricken President; the British, hamstrung by their hopelessly gullible American partners, were powerless to foil the .machinations of the Soviets; the French, conspicuous by their absence, believed that their presence would have made all the difference; and most vivid of all, Stalin, patient, devious, determined, waited impassively for half of Europe to fall into his hands like a ripe fruit. It was the classic sell-out. Like most myths, this one too contains a grain of truth. But if Yalta was a sell-out, the main goods had been eyed, appraised, and bought long before the Big Three met at the Crimean resort; only over the final packaging would there be some extra haggling.

The trappings of the conference were on a magnificent scale. The British delegation was housed in the Vorontzov palace, a mixture of Gothic and Moorish styles with carved white lions guarding its entrance, its gardens and terraces, adorned with sub-tropical plants and cypresses, falling away to the Black Sea. There were gargantuan meals and endless tongue-in-cheek speechifying, reminding Alan Brooke of an 'insincere, slimy sort of slush!' There were some moments of contrived light humour. When Churchill began to sing a few choruses of 'Keep right on to the end of the road', Roosevelt quipped: 'this singing by the Prime Minister is Britain's secret weapon'.[35]

Neither Roosevelt nor Churchill appeared to be functioning properly. The President's physical condition had deteriorated so badly that even his most loyal adviser, Harry Hopkins, doubted whether he heard 'more than half of what went on'. As for Churchill, Cadogan, at one session, saw him as 'a silly old man . . . knowing nothing whatever of what he was talking about'. Roosevelt 'flapped about' and Churchill 'boomed', he recorded, but Stalin, 'quiet and restrained', never uttering 'a superfluous word', was by far 'the most impressive of the three'. To make matters worse, Roosevelt and Churchill quarrelled among themselves. At the same time, Roosevelt buttered up Stalin, who naturally played along. Churchill felt left out. He complained that he was constantly being 'beaten up' as a reactionary. But he was also troubled by Roosevelt's statement that American troops would evacuate Europe within two years of Germany's defeat. How would the European balance be maintained? he asked. 'Such a task would be far beyond our strength,' he concluded.[36]

At Yalta, last-minute military moves were coordinated for the final onslaught on Germany. It was settled that German industry would be shorn of its military potential; that major war criminals would be tried; and that a commission would sit in Moscow to determine the reparations' settlement. The zoning of Germany was confirmed. Voting procedures for the Security Council and the United Nations Organization were finally agreed upon. In the Far East – where all feared a prolonged and bloody battle with the fanatical Japanese – the Soviet Union promised to enter the war two to three months after Germany's surrender, receiving in return territories it had lost during its war with Japan in 1904–05. Over Poland, Stalin would not budge, except to scatter paper promises. Nor did he disguise his intention to extend Poland's frontier with Germany up to the Oder-western Neisse line. It was the same story in the Balkans, where, even as the parleying at Yalta continued, the Soviets were tightening their grip. Finally, a 'Declaration on Liberated Europe' was signed, affirming 'the right of all peoples to choose the form of government under which they will live.'

At the end of the conference Churchill expressed a wish to inspect the battlefields of the Crimean war. He was taken to the field of Balaclava. Gazing down at the valley where the Light Brigade had charged so valiantly – 'Into the jaws of Death,/Into the mouth of Hell' – he remarked to his Russian escort that he was studying 'a war of dynasties, not of peoples'. 'Our host gave no sign of comprehension, but seemed perfectly satisfied.'[37] Here was a symbolic finale for his own efforts at Yalta.

Churchill returned to London to justify the Yalta settlement. He thought that the agreement would be honoured while Stalin was alive. He felt convinced that Stalin 'meant well to the world and to Poland', and 'had confidence' him.[38] He told Colville that 'Chamberlain had trusted Hitler as he was now trusting Stalin (though he thought in different circumstances)'.[39] Colville felt that Churchill 'was not convinced of the strength of our moral position'. But if Churchill convinced himself of Stalin's 'utmost loyalty', so too did his Cabinet and Parliament. Opposition was muted, confined mainly to discredited 'Munichites' who now sprang to the defence of Poland. When the Commons voted 396 to 25 in favour of his policy, he was 'overjoyed'. It boosted his fighting spirit. 'I have not the slightest intention of being cheated over Poland,' he proclaimed to Colville, 'not even if we go to the verge of war with Russia.'[40]

The reckoning swiftly followed. Unlike in 1940, the issues were not clear cut. Contemplating the destruction of Germany, he asked, 'What will lie between the white snows of Russia and the white cliffs of Dover?' With the Americans about to abdicate their responsibility, he resurrected his 1930s' formula. 'The first principle of British policy in Western Europe is a strong France, and a strong French army,' he told the Commons. Matters worsened when, in April, he heard that Roosevelt had died. As he informed the Cabinet, 'he must now take the lead' in reining in Soviet ambitions.[41] Three months later, at the Potsdam conference, he finally met the new President, Harry Truman, and came away most favourably impressed. Truman, previously a haberdasher from Kansas City, was quite different in temperament and background from the East Coast patrician, Roosevelt. 'A more typical American,' it was whispered. 'Very blunt' and 'means business', Churchill thought, he 'can hand out the rough stuff'.[42]

By now, the war in Europe had ended. German generals had signed the instrument of surrender on 7 May. Since Yalta, the Soviets had been imposing their own version of the Crimean Declaration. Churchill appealed to Stalin, 'my friend', not to 'tear the world to pieces' or to 'under-rate the divergencies which are opening about matters . . . which are symbolic of the way the English-speaking democracies look at life'.[43] It was as though he appreciated for the first time the full horrors of a Soviet dominated eastern Europe; as though, finally, the lamentable repercussions of the zoning agreement combined with the Red Army's conquests had struck home. He saw 'the tide of Russian domination sweeping forward 120 miles on a front of 300 or 400 miles', an event that 'would be one of the most melancholy in history . . . [and] to which there has been no parallel'.[44] To Truman he twice invoked the image of 'an iron curtain' descending 'between us and everything to the Eastward'. 'We do not know what is going on behind.'[45] Stalin had redrawn the map of post-war Europe.

However Churchill railed against this outcome, he had been an active party to the wartime decisions that had shaped the new Europe. It was Churchill's way to immerse himself in the pressing questions of the hour – and these were of a military nature. Throughout, he revealed little disposition to think through to the end the political aftermath of the war he was fighting. When he awoke to the terrible reality, it was too late. But even had he been more prescient, or less accommodating, would it have made any essential difference? In the long run, there was nothing he could have done. Stalin's domination of eastern Europe was built into the exigencies of the wartime situation. As two exiled Soviet historians laconically put it: 'The presence of 6.5 million Soviet soldiers buttressed Soviet claims.'[46]

But by the same token that half of Europe was absorbed into the Soviet orbit, the other half was liberated, or saved, from Nazi terror, a considerable bonus for the hundreds of millions of people who happened to live in those countries. In western Europe at least, the principles of the Yalta declaration would be upheld. If Churchill's conscience was troubled by the fate of those peoples cut off by the 'iron curtain', he could rest easy in the knowledge that the remainder of Europe, including his own country, would maintain the democratic traditions he so valued. It was, as Churchill recognized in the theme of the final volume of his war memoirs, both 'Triumph and Tragedy'.

Anything that distracted Churchill's attention was regarded as little more than an intrusion upon his main business of running the war. In the 4,230-odd pages of his war memoirs there is virtually nothing on domestic issues; the Beveridge Report, the seminal text for post-war social policy, is dealt with in less than two pages of placid officialese.[47] But Churchill could not simply wish these affairs away, or even relegate them to the background whenever he so desired. In a very real sense, his political survival depended upon how he calculated the day-to-day politics of Westminster.

As Churchill's prime ministership had been foisted upon the Conservative establishment, he had to move cautiously. The 'Old Gang', in the figures of Chamberlain and Halifax, had been retained as members of his first War Cabinet and their unsettling presence was a constant reminder to Churchill that, should he fail, there were other, more popular, alternatives among the Tory backwoodsmen. By the end of 1940, he could feel more secure. Chamberlain had died; Halifax and Sir Samuel Hoare were shipped off as ambassadors to Washington and Madrid; while Sir John Simon was given the Lord Chancellorship, without a seat in the War Cabinet. The 'Old Gang' had been effectively neutralized. But above all, Churchill had consolidated his role as the indispensable man.

Despite Churchill's intimidating authority, he was subject to continuous criticism about his management of the war, not only its strategic aspects but also what seemed to be the creaking machinery of his government. Setbacks in the war inspired speculation about Churchill's future. Alternative figures appeared. Lloyd George, although aging visibly, menaced Churchill by virtue of his prestige and parliamentary skills. In the spring of 1941 Robert Menzies, the Australian Prime Minister, appeared in London. Bitterly critical of the débâcles at Dakar and Greece, and the government's Far Eastern policy, he made a 'tremendous impression, 2nd only to Winston'. On 7 May Churchill met and demolished these potential rivals. 'Pungent, amusing, cruel, hard-hitting' – comparing Lloyd George's diatribe with 'the sort of speech' to be expected from Marshal Pétain – he dominated the House with 'all his inimitable wit and venom'.[48] Sir Stafford Cripps, an eminent barrister and left-wing

Labour politician, lasted longer. Austere in appearance, he was decidedly not fashioned in the Churchillian mould. Churchill, on his return from a visit to the Libyan desert, was alleged to have quipped, 'There are miles and miles of nothing but arid austerity. How Cripps would like it.' He had returned from his ambassadorship in Moscow a popular character, turning to good account the surge in pro-Soviet sentiment. Intellectually curious and committed to running the war 'scientifically', he schemed for the premiership, but overplayed his hand. After placing on record his 'fundamental disagreement' over defence policy, Churchill insisted on his resignation and moved him from the War Cabinet to Aircraft Production in November 1942.[49]

Criticism continued. Papers like *Tribune* and the *Daily Mirror* constantly sniped at Churchill, while *Time-Life* found that 'a great many people', when invited, would 'begin to tell all kinds of things that they dislike about him'.[50] But the main forum of dissent was Parliament. In one debate, Aneurin Bevan called across from the Labour back-benches, in a manner worthy of Churchill himself: 'The Prime Minister wins debate after debate and loses battle after battle. The country is beginning to say that he fights debates like a war and the war like a debate'. Other well-known parliamentary characters, Labour's 'Manny' Shinwell and the Tory, Lord Winterton – a pair whom Churchill dubbed 'Arsenic and Old Lace' – and the more serious, Leslie Hore-Belisha, joined the dissidents.[51] But Churchill's position was never in real danger. He dominated Parliament, at times aided by an unusually inept opposition.

As a young, uninhibited politician, Churchill had confessed that he hated the Tory Party. Now that he was leader of it, he realized that the 'bulk of Tories hated him'.[52] In the autumn of 1942, he had already chosen Anthony Eden as his heir apparent.[53] Yet despite Eden's high station and glamorous public image, Churchill did not rate highly his successor designate's abilities, a fact that deepens the suspicion that his choice was a matter of form rather than actual intention.

Churchill and Eden clashed over many issues: the Soviet Union, the role of de Gaulle and the Free French, but also Yugoslavia and Tito, Portugal, the Morganthau plan, the British action in Greece, the future of Germany, and the question of India. Not only differences of approach in foreign affairs separated them. Eden was equally unhappy at Churchill's manner of running the war, of Churchill's fondness, as he charmingly owned up, of surrounding himself with 'obedient mugwumps'. Churchill's late-night habits, his verboseness, his obstinacy, his lack of skill in guiding a committee through its agenda, added to Eden's discontent. At one point, in February 1942, Eden felt that Churchill was 'losing grip'. He was not alone in this belief. In government and the press there were those who held that Churchill ought to turn the Ministry of Defence over to someone else. But Churchill would not hear of it. Cabinet changes were made: Attlee was appointed Deputy Prime Minister, but with no claim as successor, who 'must be a Tory'; and Cripps joined the government as Leader of the House. None of this was to Eden's liking. But whether out of good sense or lack of stomach for a fight, or both, he did not elevate any of these issues to crisis point.[54]

However harsh the criticism, and from whatever its source, Churchill showed no intention of resigning. Why should he have done so? In the final analysis, Churchill knew, as did his detractors, that no satisfactory successor could be found.

Labour came to power together with Churchill, and gradually advanced to dominate the home front. Starting out with sixteen government posts, by the end of the war they had progressed to thirty-seven. Their most prominent ministers, Attlee (Lord President and Deputy Prime Minister), Herbert Morrison (Minister of Supply, later Home Secretary), Ernest Bevin (Minister of Labour), were also members of the War Cabinet; and together with Hugh Dalton (Minister for Economic Warfare, subsequently President of the Board of Trade), and William Jowitt (Minister of Social Insurance), they constituted a powerful group. But Labour's influence also extended to those Cabinet sub-committees that dealt with social and economic policy and post-war reconstruction. Of the five key domestic committees, Labour initially headed four of them: Food, Home Policy, Economic Policy, and the Production Council. Eventually these bodies passed into the safe hands of Sir John Anderson, later Chancellor of the Exchequer, a dour, efficient, ex-civil servant, known as 'Pompous John'. Anderson's standing did not hamper Labour. Its opinion, particularly when expressed by the forceful and compelling voices of Morrison and Bevin, continued to be heard on the widest range of domestic issues and problems of post-war reconstruction.[55]

On the home front, the rise of Labour squeezed out the Tories. Irrespective of whether this resulted from an overall design, or whether Churchill allowed it to happen simply from lack of interest, it was probably the most sensible, down-to-earth line that his coalition could have taken. The mood of the country was moving towards the left, with a feeling that there could be no return to the bad old days. There was a climate of expectancy, of better times to come, that the end of the war would bring not only victory over tyrannies abroad, but also, as it was called, a 'New Jerusalem' at home. '[When] is Churchill going to realize that this war belongs to the Ernest Bevins of England, not to the Old Gang?' an American commentator recorded the Common Folk as asking.[56]

Churchill, similar to his approach in matters of grand strategy, preferred to delay long-term planning in domestic affairs until the end of the war. In these instances, his political instinct may have been sound. One major piece of legislation, 'Rab' Butler's Education Bill, encountered considerable difficulties in the House. The main features of his Act called for general secondary-school education, raising the school-leaving age, and equal pay for women teachers. Over one of the amendments, concerning equal pay, the government was defeated, by a single vote. Churchill upgraded this setback into a vote of confidence, worried lest the enemy interpret it as a sign that the country was weary of war. He reversed the failure, by 425 to 23 votes. There was clearly something to be said for avoiding controversial, divisive legislation at a time when national unity was all important.

Whatever Churchill's gut reaction when confronted with innovative social legislation, his twin roles as Prime Minister and Minister of Defence left him little time to devote to these issues. But as the war progressed, these matters took on an increasing significance. There was a curious dimension to Churchill's thinking, archaic yet attractive in its own way. Contemplating the soulless features of town and country planning,' he remarked, 'Give to me the romance of an 18th-century alley, with its dark corners, where footpads lurk.'[57]

The discussion on post-war social policy came to a head with the publication of the Beveridge Report in December 1942. Hailed as a new declaration of human rights, it provided for a comprehensive system of insurance to combat the adversities of poverty, ill-health, and unemployment. A National Health Service, family allowances, and benefits for the out-of-work would establish the 'national minimum', a slogan appropriated by the younger Churchill when he had been President of the Board of Trade. The Report was an instant success. Churchill was not hostile, but he did not wish to float 'airy visions of Utopia and Eldorado'. Let us 'work from now till the end of the war,' he told the Cabinet, 'polishing, reshaping, and preparing for the necessary legislation. We cannot however initiate the legislation now, or commit ourselves to the expenditure involved . . . or tie the hands of future Parliaments in regard to social matters.' Attlee later thought that Churchill was playing a devious game, that 'Winston planned to come in as the first post-war Prime Minister and thought it would be a nice thing to have the Beveridge Report to put through as an act of his government,' but not 'by the war-time Coalition'.[58]

At the time, his stonewalling paid off, at least in the sense that he managed to impose his views on the Cabinet and the House. But in a wider context, he had not only misjudged a widespread feeling in the country, he had also chosen to ignore many rebellious voices in the government and the Commons, lending credence to the view that 'vested interests' were out to kill the Report. For Labour, it was a veritable windfall.[59] Morrison and Attlee argued for an immediate commitment to the Report. At the grassroots level, Labour activists were demanding 'Beveridge Now!' Even the newly formed Tory Reform Committee, a group of forty-five MPs, called for the early establishment of a Ministry of Social Security, an indication that the more forward looking Tories appreciated that their Party could not afford to ignore the Beveridge bandwagon. But the Churchill government's anodyne commitment in principle to a future Welfare State was just the kind of 'pie in the sky' attitude most likely to offend a long-suffering population waiting eagerly to enter the gates of a 'New Jerusalem'.

Churchill must have sensed something of the inadequacy of his response. A month after the Commons had put Beveridge's plan into cold storage, Churchill went on the air to expound on post-war planning.[60] Presenting to the people a 'Four Year Plan', he covered all bases: 'the amalgamation and extension of our present incomparable insurance system'; 'a National Health Service'; a 'broader more liberal' educational system, with facilities for advanced learning 'evened out and multiplied'; 'the replanning and rebuilding of our cities and towns'; and as a last Tolstoyian flourish, 'a vigorous revival of healthy village life'. There is no reason to doubt Churchill's sincerity. Yet it was in vain that he sought to repair his crumbling reputation as a social reformer. In March 1944 there took place a series of heated exchanges in the House over a wide range of post-war issues: housing, civil aviation, national health, education. The *Economist* drew the harshest of conclusions: 'for every one elector who, two months ago, suspected that the government was needlessly obstructing reform or who doubted whether Mr Churchill is the man to lead the country in peace as well as war, there must now be three or four'.[61] According to Mass-Observation surveys, approximately sixty per cent of the population were opposed to Churchill staying on as a peacetime Prime Minister. Many believed him to be 'no man of peace, domestic policy, or human detail.'[62]

Churchill's credibility as a social reformer was seriously, perhaps irretrievably, damaged. And his manifest unwillingness to initiate concrete reforms deepened this impression. It also rubbed off on the Conservatives, a party whose past record underscored its badly flawed public image on these issues. Nor was Churchill a good party manager.[63] More at ease with his acolytes and cronies than with Party functionaries and leaders, his relationship with the Tory rump remained problematical. One backbencher thought that the Party had become 'a cheap joke'. By-election results confirmed this gloomy appraisal. In fourteen by-elections, from February 1943 to May 1945, the swing was notably towards Labour identified candidates. In some Conservative circles, there was a feeling of impending disaster. Harold Macmillan and Leo Amery were of the opinion that 'Winston should really give up and write his book and let the Conservatives get just beaten and come back reinvigorated by opposition four of five years hence'.[64]

By the winter of 1944–45 there was mounting concern about Churchill's capacity to run the government. His Cabinets, according to Attlee, 'were not good for business', though 'they were great fun'. Others thought that 'his work has deteriorated', that he was irritating and verbose. But Churchill was impervious to criticism. In a fit of pique, he put it all down to 'a socialist conspiracy'.[65] Had Churchill become, as Harold Nicolson, one of his most fervent admirers put it, 'an electoral liability' rather than an asset? Nicolson was horrified to find scrawled in the lavatory at Blackheath station the graffito, 'Winston Churchill is a bastard.' His companion assured him that 'the tide has turned. We find it everywhere.'[66]

Somewhat depressed at 'the prospect of the end of the war and the problems it will bring', Churchill greeted 1945 as 'this "new, disgusting year"'. His spirits soon picked up. At the Conservative Party conference in March he delivered 'a good fighting speech' to 'a tumultuous reception'.[67] But in mid-May Labour decided against renewing the coalition and polling day was set for 5 July. No doubt, Churchill believed that he could take the country by storm, as Lloyd George had done in 1918. After all, he was the 'Bulldog of Battle' who had secured the peace. 'This is your victory,' he told a vast throng gathered in Whitehall, 'No,' the crowd roared back, 'it is yours.' He was still an inspiring phrase-maker. To the gasps of the crowd, he cried: 'Advance, Britannia!'[68] But what lay behind these thrilling words? A few months earlier he had confessed the sad truth to Lord Moran. 'I have a very strong feeling that my work is done. I have no message. I had a message. Now I only say "fight the damned socialists." I do not believe in this brave new world.'[69]

21

The Great Commoner

'I never think of after the war,' Clementine reflected in the winter of 1944, 'You see, I think Winston will die when it's over.' In one sense she was right. As nothing could match his wartime triumphs, everything that came after was 'all anticlimax', as he put it.[1] Churchill spent his last days as Prime Minister at Potsdam, participating in 'Terminal', the final wartime summit.

The map of Europe had changed. Despite his frustrated cry that he was 'sick of the bloody Poles', Churchill fought a valiant rearguard action on their behalf.[2] To no avail. Stalin's Polish goose would be fed to the full, gorging itself with Germany territory up to the western Neisse. Measures were approved to ensure the democratization of Germany and to wipe out the last vestiges of Nazism, while the German economy was to be shorn of any military potential. Reparations policy was left flexible, but it was already clear that the Soviet Union, devastated by the war, intended to claim its due from the Germany economy. The Red Army's advances into Europe included East Prussia, the port of Stettin, and Silesia, rich in resources: roughly eighteen per cent of Germany's pre-war industrial capacity were already effectively in Russian hands. It was later agreed that a quarter of the capital assets dismantled in the western zones were to be transferred to the Soviet Union in exchange for deliveries of other goods. A year later, the Americans stopped this procedure, and the Russians were compelled to strip the territories they controlled in the East.

In his memoirs, Churchill insisted that he would never have tolerated the western Neisse line, preferring 'to have a show-down' with the Soviets: a noble afterthought, prompted, no doubt, by a troubled conscience. But it was hardly conceivable that any theatrical gesture of official disapproval would have deterred Stalin. Eden, who felt that Churchill was under Stalin's spell[3], was, like others, pressing him to take a more forthright stand against the Russians. But Churchill's handling of the conference came under widespread criticism. 'Confused

& woolly & verbose' in debate, he 'refused to do any work or read anything ... [yet] he butts in on every occasion and talks the most irrelevant rubbish, and risks giving away our case at every point'.[4] The few concessions Churchill did achieve – regarding Turkey's eastern border, the evacuation of foreign forces from Persia, Britain and America's right to a role in the occupation of Vienna – although important in themselves, were unlikely to shake the world balance of power. As Cadogan cautiously summed up: 'Joe has got most of what he wants'.[5]

But Churchill had also to contend with the condition of Britain. Virtually bankrupt, it was estimated that the war had destroyed a quarter of Britain's national wealth, some £7,300 million. Overseas assets amounting to £4,200 million had been either sold or lost; income on both foreign investments and exports had been halved; and the external debt had soared to £3,300 million.[6] This bleak situation was not eased by the cutback of lend-lease supplies in May. Truman listened 'attentively and with great sympathy' to Churchill's exposé but promised nothing. Churchill, confident in his ability to work with the President whom he liked 'immensely', thought Truman's attitude 'warm and comforting'.[7] This impression was too sanguine. In August, immediately after the conference, lend-lease was cut off altogether, so that an insolvent Britain had now to pay on the nail for the essential raw materials and manufactured goods it desperately needed for its post-war recovery.

On 16 July 1945 the first atomic device had been successfully detonated at Alamogordo in New Mexico. Churchill was told only the day after it had taken place. In its own way, this episode reflected accurately the unfolding of Anglo-American relations in general. The scientific basis of the bomb had been developed by British, and refugee, scientists. By mid-1942 the Americans had totally outstripped the British effort. The 'Manhattan Project', and the investment of $2,000 million, gave them a virtual monopoly over the enterprise. An agreement – 'Tube Alloys' – was reached in May 1943, followed, in September 1944, by a much hazier arrangement. These understandings were made, ostensibly, to guarantee continued cooperation in the project. Alan Brooke later recalled Churchill's initial, almost fanciful reaction to news of the bomb. 'He at once painted a wonderful picture of himself as the sole possessor of these bombs and capable of dumping them where he wished, thus all-powerful and capable of dictating to Stalin!' On a more sober note, it had been assumed that the war in the Far East would drag on for another twelve to eighteen months, and would cost up to a million and a half American and British lives, 'or more'. Moreover, there were the adverse repercussions of Russian intervention to take into account. 'Now all this nightmare picture had vanished.' In Churchill's account, 'there was never a moment's discussion as to whether the atomic bomb should be used or not'. But the decision to drop it was American. However reviewed, the British were very much the junior partners in this affair.[8]

Earlier, in May, the election campaign had begun in Britain. As it heated up, Churchill admitted that he felt 'very lonely without a war'. (Of course, the war in the Far East was still in progress, but *the war*, for Churchill, was over). When men were fighting he had known instinctively what to say. Suddenly there was a blank. Stranded without a war and without a message, he could have retired from politics in a blaze of glory. Clementine pressed him to step down. But loath 'to be put upon a pedestal', he was bent on fulfilling his destiny to the end.[9]

Churchill's electioneering struck a wrong note from the outset. His speeches sounded 'confused, woolly, unconstructive and so wordy'.[10] Booed at Walthamstow, a squib thrown at him at Tooting Bec, he returned to the free-for-all of the hustings. He scored sensational headlines with a singularly inept remark that a Labour government 'would have to fall back upon some sort of Gestapo'. It was a gaffe of monumental proportions. Clementine had pleaded with him to cut out this monstrous comparison. He refused. He also claimed that if Attlee got into power he would be under the control of Harold Laski, a professor of political science and chairman of the Labour Party's National Executive, who, in a misguided observation, had intimated that Labour had a foreign policy of its own and would not be bound by the decisions of the forthcoming Potsdam conference simply because Attlee was to accompany Churchill to the summit. Churchill detected here 'grave constitutional issues'. This style of campaigning was unlikely to appeal to many of the electorate.[11]

Churchill sensed something was going wrong. 'He is very low, poor Darling,' Clementine wrote to Mary, 'He thinks he has lost his "touch" & he grieves about it.' Sarah warned him of the dangers ahead. After all, she pointed out, 'Socialism as practised in the war, did no one any harm, and quite a lot of people good . . . So why, they say, cannot this common feeling of sacrifice be made to work as effectively in peace?'

In the event Labour was returned with an overall majority of 146 seats. At Epping, Churchill's previous majority of 20,000 was reduced by 3,000 votes, even though he was only challenged by an independent, 'somewhat "crack-pot" opponent'. On 26 July, the day the results were declared, Churchill tendered his resignation and advised the King to send for Attlee, declining the offer of the Order of the Garter.[12]

The bread and butter issues that were at the heart of the election failed to stir Churchill's imagination. In his appeals to the electorate, housing, the great issue, came last on his list of his priorities. Failing to judge the mood of the voters, it was noted that he fell back on 'abuse', 'vituperation', and 'cheap' shots. Perhaps he was over-confident. Or, as Clementine suspected, that he was being led astray by the ruinous influence of Beaverbrook, whose papers were conducting a robust campaign, and Brendan Bracken.[13] But it would be too simplistic to blame Churchill's intemperate language, or his over-confidence, or the alleged influence of the 'Two B's', for the Labour landslide. The Conservatives lost because, by 1945, they lacked credibility. Rightly or wrongly, they were held responsible for the bitter experiences of the inter-war years.

However interpreted, the defeat was a cruel blow. 'Yes,' Churchill remarked, 'I won the race – and now they have warned me off the turf.'[14] Some weeks later, his spirits somewhat revived, he was heard entertaining the doorman of Claridges Hotel with an old music-hall ditty.

> I've been to the North Pole,
> I've been to the South Pole,
> The East Pole, the West Pole,
> And every other kind of Pole,
> The Barber's Pole,
> The greasy Pole,
> And now I'm fairly up the Pole,
> Since I got the sack,
> From the Hotel Metropole.[15]

Churchill's return to private life, with its abrupt change of tempo, left its mark on his relations with Clementine. However much she had learned to cushion herself against his occasional dark moods, his unpredictability, his self-centred behaviour, Clementine still found these traits 'very tiring to cope with'. Often nervous and depressed, on edge and testy, she longed for Churchill to quit politics. Rows were frequent. 'In our misery', she wrote to her youngest daughter, Mary, 'we seem, instead of clinging to each other to be always having scenes . . . I'm finding life more than I can bear.'[16] Perhaps as therapy for these scenes, they still spent much time apart, holidaying separately or waiting for each other while Churchill travelled the world. When apart, Churchill would regale her with wonderfully descriptive letters of his adventures, expressing his deep love for her. Their relationship was still fulfilled on his terms. And as usual, Clementine generously took the blame for this state of affairs.

These days found Churchill in a generally grumpy mood. His relations with Randolph were always balanced on a razor's edge. 'We have a deep animal love for one another,' he once said, 'but every time we meet we have a bloody row.' Randolph's divorce from Pamela Digby and remarriage to June Osborne added to the family tension. As did Sarah's love affair with a man whom Churchill heartedly disliked. His boorish behaviour wounded Sarah deeply. 'I do not understand how you can say you love me – when you are so very unkind . . .'[17] By contrast, the marriage of Mary to Christopher Soames in February 1947 brought him much joy, their relationship dignified by a stability that was lacking in his other children's personal lives.

Amid the family storms, there were interludes of calm. In September 1945, accompanied by Sarah, he holidayed at Field Marshal Alexander's villa on Lake Como, Clementine, 'exhausted emotionally', staying behind. The weather was perfect, a cool breeze from the lake breaking up the heat. Opulently appointed, the villa was 'a palace of mirrors'. Pink from his bath and clad in a spotless white suit, Churchill would dine at the head of 'an enormous green glass table in an oval pale green room', attended to by four white-coated batmen. The days were filled with picnics and painting. One evening, offended by the drabness of one of the villa's landscapes, 'the worst picture that has ever been painted', he committed an act of 'artistic rape', restoring it to glory with some lusty daubs of vivid reds, greens, and blues. 'Painting is a wonderful cure,' Churchill added, 'because you really cannot think of anything else.'[18]

'How it melts,' Churchill was wont to say, referring to his capital assets. All his life he had lived in princely splendour, a consequence of his artistry in deficit budgeting. This now changed radically. Chartwell, always a steady drain on his resources, was bought from him by a group of admirers for £43,800 and turned over to the National Trust with the condition that the Churchills be allowed to spend the remainder of their lives there. Churchill rejoiced at this arrangement. Not only had he acquired a considerable capital sum, but he had also obtained a fifty-year lease on the estate at an annual rent of £350.[19] With Chartwell secure for his lifetime, and for posterity, he looked to his own personal fortune.

Churchill had always been counted among the most highly paid journalists and authors of his time. Now his current status as a world historical figure allowed him to command the most fabulous sums. He possessed three extremely valuable literary properties: his war memoirs, his private archives, and his own future biography. To protect these assets from death duties, and to ensure that maximum financial benefits accrued to his family, a trust was set up. In 1947 the *Daily Telegraph* group agreed to pay the trustees £555,000 for the publication of his memoirs. By it, Churchill would receive £175,000 – in five equal instalments; the trust, £375,000; and £5,000 would be retained by the *Daily Telegraph* for stamp duties. As an additional bonus, the *Daily Telegraph* would grant Churchill an interest-free loan of £15,000 on completion of the agreement. The American rights on the project had also been negotiated, yielding $1,150,000 for serial rights to *Life* magazine and the *New York Times*, and a further $250,000 from Houghton Mifflin for book rights. There were other extras. Henry Luce, owner of *Life*, purchased his *Secret Session Speeches* for £12,500; Alexander Korda paid him £50,000 for the rights to *English-Speaking Peoples*; London

Film Productions sent him the final payment of £10,000 for the rights to *Savrola* and *The River War*; while some years later, he received a cheque for £100,000 from Columbia Studios for the film rights to *My Early Life*.[20]

Virtually overnight Churchill had become a rich man. He estimated that he needed at least £12,000 a year to live. For the first time, he could maintain his expensive standards without going into the red. Investments in Argentinian railway stock, in South African shares, in building societies and other securities ensured that his bank balance stabilized at around £120,000.[21] His new-found wealth enabled him to buy about 500 acres of farmland surrounding Chartwell, a veritable squiredom. He raised Shorthorn and Jersey cows, bred pigs, grew vegetables and fruit. To Clementine he described corn-fields, 'cut and stooked', lettuces being sold off at a nice profit, hothouses 'dripping with long cucumbers', grapes 'turning black', and 'a continuous stream of peaches and nectarines' being sent to the London markets. 'I have one [nectarine] a day,' he owned up, '"le droit du seigneur".'[22]

Churchill's other valuable 'property', his wartime memoirs, began to be developed in the spring of 1946. He invited Bill Deakin, now an Oxford don, to take charge of 'the political and diplomatic side'; Ismay was conscripted to look after 'all military questions'. Two young historians, Denis Kelly and Alan Hodges, were picked to join the research group. More specialized briefs were dealt with by General Sir Henry Pownell, Commodore G. R. C. Allen, Air Chief Marshal Sir Guy Harrod, Professor R. V. Jones, and Lord Cherwell. Sir Isaiah Berlin read some of the drafts and advised on the style and the structure of the work, while the proofs were scrutinized by the 'ruthless eye' of Charles Wood.[23] It was a formidable team, and it functioned according to Churchill's time-honoured system. His assistants served him, researching, commenting, providing the necessary feedback. But he dictated the narrative and polished draft after draft until he felt that he had got it just right. Planned as a five-volume work it expanded to six, the first appearing in 1948, the last in 1954.

Churchill never disguised the fact that he was not writing a history of the Second World War, but his version of it. 'This is my case,' he told Deakin. He explained to Denis Kelly that 'if you are trying to influence peoples and nations', establishing and collating data was not sufficient. So, Kelly noted, he took 'immense pains' in 'dishing them up'.[24] The finished product was not to everyone's liking. Clementine took volume III to task: 'it was too full of minutes and memos and was all rather dull'. Churchill glowered, reddened, and barked out his irritation.[25] Clementine, however, was merely expressing what his publishers and literary agent were trying to impress upon their author. The final work's greater readability owes much to Clementine's courage.

The Second World War succeeded superbly in putting Churchill's case. Its sales were phenomenal: a run of 200,000 copies for the first volume in Britain, 600,000 for the American edition.[26] With five more volumes to come, and foreign language rights in the pipeline, Churchill was assured of the widest possible audience.

Forty years on its shortcomings stand out more clearly. It resembles a kind of historical painting, impressionistic and suggestive. Its account of the controversies and personalities – mainly of his opponents – of the inter-war period muddies rather than clarifies. All too often, he portrays the complexities of the issues, the debate on appeasement, for example, as a battle between the Children of Light and the Children of Darkness. The volumes dealing with the Second World War are crowded with his own memoranda and letters, invaluable testimony in itself. But as, in general, the replies to them are omitted, the evidence 'dished up' is somewhat loaded. Individuals who failed to meet his requirements are given short shrift, Wavell being the most pertinent example. His treatment of key issues – the second front; the nature of his relationships with Roosevelt and Stalin; the aims of his Mediterranean strategy; his misconceptions regarding the Far East; his handling of the domestic scene – is selective and hence misleading. As a whole, the work leaves a slanted impression on the events it covers. Yet even today, as any working historian will bear witness, it is difficult to escape its pervading influence – which is exactly what Churchill had set out to do.

As Leader of the Opposition, Churchill could, with justification, claim to be the most famous man in the world. The symbol of Victory, his personal prestige unblemished, he was headline news whatever he did or said. As a world statesman, Churchill's attention was naturally drawn to the complexities of the international scene rather than to the nuts and bolts of domestic politics. But after the débâcle of 1945 – the Conservatives most humiliating defeat since 1906 – there was a pressing need for the Party to convince the electorate that it had a viable alternative policy to socialism. Harold Macmillan saw Churchill as 'sadly miscast' in this role. Flinching from these matters, Churchill wisely left them in the hands of his lieutenants. The Party, under the skilful management of its new chairman, Lord Woolton, underwent a radical facelift; a more forward-looking programme was formulated,[27] largely the product of young, talented Conservatives recruited by 'Rab' Butler and working under his guidance. This new breed of Conservatives, with their modern ideas, was not always to Churchill's liking. 'They are no more than a set of pink pansies,' he once said of them.[28]

At first, Churchill appeared to be contemplating retirement, but he quickly recovered his appetite. 'Winston is in very good fettle,' noted Brendan Bracken in October 1946, 'and is determined to lead the Tory

Party until he becomes Prime Minister on earth or Minister of Defence in Heaven.[29] As it happened, it was a forecast very close to the mark.

He formed a kind of Shadow Cabinet, fifteen members in all, that met every Thursday in his room at the House to coordinate parliamentary strategy. His own contributions from the opposition front bench were uneven, and he tended to attack Labour policies in shrill diatribes, describing them as 'positive folly'. Rab Butler recalled this '"magnificent animal" bursting with vigour and vengeance', trotting out 'the Bolshevik bogey' and doing 'much harm'. But he was at times as effective as ever. 'A stupendous performance,' enthused Chips Channon, when the House debated the devaluation of the pound, 'audible, polished, unanswerable, and damning'.[30]

As a life-long Gentile Zionist, Churchill was an ardent supporter of the Balfour Declaration, viewing it as not only serving British interests, but also as an act of historical justice. In 1944, his own government, with his full approval, resurrected the Peel partition plan, with its promise of a Jewish state. But his scheme was wrecked as a result of the brutal murder of Lord Moyne by Jewish terrorists in Cairo. Moyne (Walter Guinness) had been a long-standing friend of Churchill, and his senseless murder affected him profoundly. From then on, it proved most difficult to draw Churchill back into active Zionist work.

As Churchill witnessed the collapse of British policy in Palestine, his pronouncements reflected his conviction that Britain, weak and isolated, bereft of power and lacking authority, could not by itself impose its will to resolve the conflict – or indeed any other world crisis. Only two alternatives remained: either joint responsibility with the United States, or else Britain should return its mandate to the United Nations. Now a firm advocate of partition, he watched with satisfaction as the Zionists seized their chance to create their state. And once Israel had been established, he delivered, in the winter of 1948, a series of telling speeches calling for its recognition. For the remainder of his active life, he cultivated his Israeli interests. He advised Eden, 'Israel is a force in the world & a link w the USA'.[31]

If the Palestine imbroglio had worked out, eventually, to Churchill's satisfaction, it is difficult to envisage any nationalistic solution to the Indian problem that would suit his taste. But as in so much else, the war proved to be a catalyst also for the question of India. In February 1942, with Singapore besieged, Churchill hatched a scheme to turn the Indian Defence Council into a more representative body, allowing it even to frame future constitutional proposals. Worked on by Amery and his experts, and with Labour's support, this plan soon expanded into far wider reaching proposals. New measures envisaged complete independence for India after the war; acknowledged India's right as a

Dominion to secede from the Commonwealth; and provided safeguards for the principalities and the dissident, that is Moslem, provinces to remain outside the new Indian state.[32] In effect, the principle of the partition of the sub-continent into a Hindu Indian state and a Moslem Pakistan was recognized. These were radical conceptions. After some humming and hawing, Churchill accepted them.

Cripps flew out to India to test Indian opinion. He found it too intransigent even for his taste. In the autumn of 1942, India lapsed into a period of extreme civil disobedience. While Churchill deplored the violence and loss of life, politically the outcome was convenient for him. Its failure allowed the government to unite and to rule India with an iron hand until the end of the war. In the long run, however, Cripps had provided the framework for an eventual solution to the problem.

This episode emphasized yet again Churchill's split personality when faced with the vexed Indian question. One side of him, harassed and coerced by the force of circumstances, gradually, resentfully, complied with the inevitable. So in 1935 he saw 'the Indian chapter as closed', and in 1942 he surrendered, without marked enthusiasm, to his own government's advanced proposals. Once the immediate pressure eased off, his other side took over. Giving vent to his innermost feelings, he let loose. 'I hate Indians,' he blurted out in September 1942, and railed against the 'humiliation of being kicked out of India.' A year later, at a government reception, he glorified the British Raj, reiterated his opposition to Indian self-government, and hoped that Britain would never relinquish its responsibility for India.[33]

The same pattern was repeated when Attlee came to redeem the pledge that Churchill's government had given. Churchill had felt that Indian self-government would be a mistake and that imposing caste Hindu domination upon the ninety million Moslems and the sixty million Untouchables would lead to chaos and inter-communal violence; he had repeated his warning of 1931 of 'a ferocious civil war'. Partition, at least, would reduce the bloodshed and safeguard Moslem interests.[34] In May 1947 he pledged Conservative support to the creation of a Hindu India and a Moslem Pakistan, both with Dominion status, and both free to claim full independence of the crown.[35] Once the decision had fallen, Churchill attempted to square his circle. 'Should all these parties decide to remain within the British Commonwealth of Nations, the theme of the unity of India will be preserved, and the many nations and States of India may find their unity within the mysterious circle of the British Crown.'[36]

It was not quite the end of Churchill's Indian journey. Over the years, his attitude mellowed. In 1950 India became a republic, but, under the guidance of the 'caste Hindu' Nehru, now Prime Minister, it maintained its Commonwealth links. This was to Churchill's liking. 'Sir, I have done you great wrong,' he admitted to Nehru, 'You are like the prodigal who has returned to the fold of the family.'[37]

Churchill's frequent absences from Parliament were commented upon but tolerated. Much of his time was spent at Chartwell, working on his memoirs. Long periods were spent abroad; either holidaying, or else playing the role for which he was best suited, that of senior world statesman. Of course, he had no official standing, but his massive reputation allowed him to intervene with an authority denied to others. In March 1946, in Fulton, Missouri, in the presence of Truman, Churchill delivered his most acclaimed speech of the post-war years. Broadcast throughout the United States, he drove home two connected themes: the imminent Soviet threat and hence the need to reforge the links between the English-speaking peoples. He claimed that:

> Nobody knows what Soviet Russia and its Communist international organization intends to do in the immediate future, or what are the limits, if any, to their expansive and proselytising tendencies . . . From Stettin in the Baltic to Trieste in the Adriatic, an iron curtain has descended across the Continent. Behind that line lie all the capitals of the ancient states of Central and Eastern Europe.

And went on:

> Neither the sure prevention of war, nor the continuous rise of world organization will be gained without what I have called the fraternal association of the English-speaking peoples. This means a special relationship between the British Commonwealth and Empire and the United States . . . Eventually there may come – I feel eventually there will come – the principle of common citizenship, but that we may be content to leave to destiny.[38]

However prescient its message, Churchill's 'Iron Curtain' speech aroused almost universal hostility. Predictably, the Soviet Union maligned it as typical Churchillian sabre-rattling, as an attempt to liquidate the United Nations and secure 'Anglo-American rule throughout the world'. Stalin, branding Churchill as a racist propounding the supremacy of the Anglo-Saxon nations, detected in it a plot to wage war against the Soviet Union. But also in America, Churchill's heavy emphasis on Anglo-American cooperation was widely interpreted as an attempt to sidestep the United Nations and a call for an Anglo-American military alliance. Influential American opinion reacted as if it was being hijacked for an anti-Soviet crusade. It also fanned opposition to the loan Attlee's administration was lobbying for in Congress, a life-saving device for the British economy. This was an unanticipated fallout that Churchill attempted to rectify in later statements.[39]

In Britain, the general reaction was no less hostile. Attlee had had no prior knowledge of the speech, and some Conservative leaders, Eden, Macmillan and Butler in particular, registered unease at the extravagance of Churchill's language. Whether by coincidence or not, in the immediate months after Fulton a strong current of Conservative opinion began to see Churchill as an embarrassment. Butler came to dread what 'Winston will say'. Over luncheon at the Walter Elliots, the guests, Peter Thorneycroft and Smuts, concluded, sadly, 'that Winston must go'. Eden, wholly in character, refused to declare open war on his chief, but he gave 'private encouragement' to those of his friends who were less inhibited.[40] A year later, the discontent had not died down. Pierson Dixon, Bevin's private secretary, was told by 'Rab' Butler's wife, Sydney, that 'There is a Tory game' to replace Attlee with Bevin in a coalition government and that 'Winston would have a rude awakening' when he discovered that he had also been ousted as Leader of the Opposition.[41]

Nothing came of these manoeuvres. Churchill stayed on as Leader. He also continued to travel widely, scattering his ideas on how best to rebuild the post-war world. At Zurich University, in September 1946, he offered a vision of a new 'European Family', 'a kind of United States of Europe' to be based on the astonishing proposition of a reconciliation between the historic enemies, France and Germany. And what of Britain's place in this golden age? Britain should exert every effort to bring it about, but would not be part of it. Britain and its Commonwealth, together with 'mighty America', and he trusted the Soviet Union, would act as 'the friends and sponsors of the new Europe and must champion its right to live and shine'. Churchill never deviated from this attitude.[42]

As Opposition Leader Churchill spoke often on the theme of European unity.[43] But he had no intention of including Britain in an integrated Europe. Thanks to a creative sleight-of-speech, many gained a different impression. They were to be rudely awakened when Churchill returned to office. From October 1951 his pronouncements on Europe petered out. Supported by Eden and the Foreign Office, he made no effort to reverse Attlee's policies. Britain remained outside the Coal and Steel Community (the Schuman plan), and refused to commit its troops to the European Defence Community, derided by Churchill as 'a sludgy amalgam, infinitely less effective than a Grand Alliance of national armies'. When he was reminded of his warm statements on Europe, he retorted that Britain 'should be with it though they could not be of it'. The genuine Europeans felt betrayed.[44] But Churchill would not be moved. 'Unite', he preached to the Europeans in July 1957, while making it clear that nothing would induce Britain to sever its bonds with the Commonwealth.[45]

If his Fulton and Zurich speeches can be interpreted as a bait to tempt the United States into a more active role in world politics, he succeeded. In one sense he was pushing through a door that was already swinging open. American irritation at Soviet policy was already noticeable. At a rally in Central Park in October 1945, Truman made clear that the United States, 'together with other friendly countries, would be willing to employ its military power to ensure peace'.[46] These thoughts meshed with Churchill's. Unrestrained by the duties of office, he gave them a great public boost. Churchill stormed Western public opinion and captured it on behalf of the Cold War. It was a task eminently suited to his unique talents.

The Truman Doctrine (March 1947) and the Marshall Plan (June 1947) followed, the latter, so George Marshall revealed, stimulated by Churchill's Zurich discourse.[47] Two years later, the North Atlantic Treaty was signed in Washington. The United States was now fully involved in confronting world Communism and reconstructing western Europe. Churchill approved. But the 'special relationship' he so hankered after would never materialize. Whenever a showdown occurred, most notably over Berlin in 1948, but also in distant Korea, the two powers cooperated. But it was always apparent which partner held the upper hand. Churchill now looked to American nuclear superiority to guarantee the old freedoms. Occasionally, he gave the impression that to teach the Russians better international manners the Americans should not rule out dropping the bomb. 'I was deeply impressed by your statement about not fearing to use the atomic bomb if the need arose,' he wrote to Truman.[48]

In October 1951 Churchill's six years in opposition came to an end.[49] If it had been proper to ask in 1945 whether he should have retired, the question arose with greater urgency in 1951 when he returned to 10 Downing Street. Now almost seventy-seven, he was tired and exhausted and found difficulty in functioning at full stretch for long periods. He already had a heart condition and had survived three bouts of pneumonia, one 'a damn near thing'. He was being treated for increasing deafness, a violent irritation of the skin, and a particularly sensitive eye condition. Then, in August 1949, while staying at Beaverbrook's villa near Monte Carlo, he suffered his first minor stroke. Five months later, during the election campaign of 1950, he complained that suddenly 'everything went misty'. Moran now referred to a 'spasm of the cerebral arteries', 'to some instability in the cerebral circulation, which must be increased by excessive mental effort'. At Monte Carlo, Moran had prevaricated when Churchill asked: 'Will I have another?' allowing Churchill's ingrained optimism to prevail. But in his diary he penned: 'This is the beginning of trouble . . . but there can only be one end to it. How long it will last is only guesswork'.[50]

Moran's prognosis proved all too tragically accurate. In February 1952 Churchill suffered another 'spasm'. For about three or four minutes he was unable to string his sentences together, the 'wrong words' forming in his head. Later, he found great difficulty in grasping the point of the numerous memoranda put to him. 'Can't I read?' he cried out to Jock Colville. In Cabinet, his mind wandered. Lord Salisbury complained that he would 'talk about something for two and a half hours without once coming to the point'. In June 1953 he endured his most serious stroke. Paralyzed down his left side, he remained incapacitated until August. Unable to walk, his speech slurred, his memory began to fail him. A leading neurologist, Sir Russell Brain, doubted whether he would be alive in a year's time.[51] Although there was a media black-out regarding his true condition, rumours were rife about his survival. At the end of the month, Harold Nicolson prepared his obituary for the *Observer*.[52] To relieve the pressure on him, it had been suggested that Churchill go to the Lords and remain, nominally, Prime Minister, while Eden led in fact from the Commons. But when this idea was put to him, he had dismissed it with a joke: 'I should have to be the Duke of Chartwell, and Randolph would be the Marquis of Toodledo.'[53]

So Churchill stayed on. To deprive him of his red boxes, of the trappings and reality of power, would only compound his private agony. Politicians and advisers who surrounded him argued that his name and reputation still constituted Britain's 'greatest asset'.[54] Above all, there was Churchill's appetite for power, despite everything, as sharp as ever. If he had to go, he would end his career in the blaze of an Indian Summer, and not as the leader of a defeated party, picking his way through the barren wasteland of opposition.

It was also true that even in advanced age Churchill showed a most astonishing resilience, bouncing back quickly from adversity. With his 'Macaulay phrases pouring out', he could still electrify an audience. In October, four months after his 1953 stroke, he appeared before the Conservative Party Conference. Promising to stay on in office to build 'a sure and lasting peace', he scored a 'triumphant achievement', dispelling spiteful gossip about his future. In November, he rose, 'amidst cheers', to address the House. 'It was an Olympian spectacle. A supreme performance,' recorded Chips Channon. Flushed with pride, Churchill sat for two hours in the Smoking Room, 'sipping brandy and acknowledging compliments', beaming 'like a schoolboy.'[55]

Scenes such as this were dangerously deceptive. He was not, as many claimed, 'gaga', nor did he act irrationally. But it proved impossible to arrest his physical and mental decline. The human dynamo was simply running down. From time to time his will-power gave it an impressive boost. But it operated in fits and starts. In April 1954 he made a disastrous speech on the implications of the hydrogen bomb, losing control of the House, leaving Attlee 'quivering with rage', the opposition 'booing and shouting'. 'Things didn't go as well as I expected. When one gets old one lives too much in the past,' he noted.[56]

Governments cannot be run effectively for sustained periods in this way. At times, Churchill's administration coasted along without him, propelled forward by the efficiency of his top ministers. Throughout his second premiership the movement to induce him to retire gathered steady momentum, but convincing reasons, at least from his point of view, were always discovered to put off the unhappy day. And Churchill's bursts of energy, usually reserved for great public occasions, were sufficiently uplifting to convince those who wished to be hoodwinked, including Churchill himself.

Bevan once remarked that Churchill reacted to 'peace-time problems' like 'a dinosaur at a light-engineering exhibition'.[57] But if Churchill had little patience for the details of home legislation, he held an overall conception of the character of British society for the 1950s. When he first addressed Parliament as Prime Minister, he proposed to give the country 'several years of quiet steady administration, if only to allow Socialist legislation to reach its full fruition'. No more 'party brawling', he promised the nation in his 1951 Christmas broadcast. Its 'social services' were a common heritage of successive governments, and in foreign affairs 'Nine-tenths of the British people agree on nine-tenths of what has been done and is being done and is going to be done.'[58] These ideas sprang from his constant yearning for coalition politics and his image of himself as a national leader rising above partisan political calculations. This theme runs throughout his career. It is somehow fitting that this motif should find positive expression in his last years as a politician.

Churchill's government left Labour's domestic legacy virtually intact. The Welfare State was left to reach 'fruition'. He was also wise enough to choose empirical, pragmatic, forward-looking ministers to lead in domestic affairs, most notably Butler at the Exchequer and Macmillan at Housing, and allow them to get on with their job. Churchill was also bent on removing the sting from industrial disputes. He had long regarded the trade unionist as the authentic expression of the British working class, far more so than the middle-class, often public school, products to be found among Labour's leaders. His appointment of Walter Monckton as Minister of Labour was widely interpreted as a sign of goodwill towards the trade unions, guaranteeing negotiated deals, even at the cost of inflationary wage settlements.[59]

If there was continuity in domestic affairs, the same trend was noticeable in imperial policy. Churchill made every effort to wriggle out of another agreement with Egypt. Crying 'scuttle' and 'appeasement' all the way, he ached to give the Egyptians 'a military thump'. To avoid the evacuation of British troops, he floated a most eccentric idea: a kind of Anglo-American-Egyptian condominium for the Canal zone. This notion, preposterous in Egyptian eyes, was also rejected firmly by Eisenhower. Grudgingly, he conceded the formula whereby British forces would be permitted to return to the zone in the event of an attack by an outside power on Turkey or any Arab state.[60]

The retreat from Empire went on. Pakistan became a republic; Nigeria and the Gold Coast (Ghana) moved towards self-government. Kenya and Malaya witnessed messy police actions, but his policy could by no means be categorized as one of high imperialism. No gunboats were sent to the Persian Gulf to retrieve the British oil complex at Abadan after its nationalization by Mossadeq in 1951, though Churchill noted with delight his overthrow and the return of the Shah two years later. 'Young man,' he told the CIA operative who had organized the coup, 'if I had been a few years younger, I would have like nothing better than to have served under your command in this great venture.'[61]

During the election campaign Churchill had been accused of war-mongering. Yet, ironically, from the beginning of 1953 he sought 'new prospects to the security and prosperity of all nations and every continent',[62] and he pursued this aim unremittingly. It was his most significant venture in foreign affairs. He argued that Stalin's death in March 1953 called for a fresh approach to be made to the Soviet Union[63]. Churchill also acted out of a sense of urgency, for he was convinced that by now the world had become a much more dangerous place. Thermonuclear devices had changed everything. 'This ghastly invention,' he told Jock Colville, 'might perhaps present humanity with a real chance of a lasting peace, since war would now be impossible.' At the Bermuda Conference in December 1953, he was shocked to learn that the Americans were prepared to drop the atomic bomb in the event of a breach of the truce in Korea. Churchill protested: this was an 'entirely new and terrible' weapon. But not in Eisenhower's opinion. The enormous gap in outlook between himself and Eisenhower gave Churchill an added incentive in his search for 'world easement', as he preferred to call it.[64]

One other factor moved Churchill: his insatiable passion to revive the Anglo-American relationship. His basic attitude had not changed. Peace could only be founded 'upon the moral unity of the English-speaking world'. Britain would still act as 'the vital link' between the Old and the New Worlds, a role that must be jealously guarded. On his first visit to America as Prime Minister, Churchill had not found Truman responsive to his petitioning.[65] Eisenhower would prove no more amenable. In New York, in January 1953, Churchill's 'almost childlike faith . . . in British-American partnership' cut no ice with Eisenhower – nor with John Foster Dulles. America's better interests would be served by treating 'every country as an equal'. Nor could Eisenhower have had much faith in Churchill's ability to carry through any project to the end. Walter Gifford, the retiring American ambassador to Britain, had told him with 'complete conviction' that Churchill was 'no longer a real power in the Conservative Party'.[66] On the other hand, Churchill thought American diplomacy 'very clumsy' and Eisenhower a man 'of limited stature'.[67] But without him, there would be no summit meeting.

Churchill's efforts continued. But he was like a one-man band, unable to find anyone to accompany him. The Russians were correct but non-committal; Eisenhower inventively evasive. In July 1954 Churchill executed a bold stroke. Returning from Washington, and without first notifying either Eisenhower or his Cabinet, he sent off a message to Moscow suggesting a bi-lateral 'friendly Meeting, with no Agenda and no object, but to find a reasonable way of living side by side'. Eisenhower reacted coolly.[68] At home, the Cabinet revolted. Cries of 'unconstitutional' were heard. Macmillan thought there was a danger of the government 'breaking up'. These pressures were too strong even for Churchill. When the Cabinet met on 23 July, he equivocated. Three days later, Churchill abandoned his proposal. He had not changed his mind; the Russians had changed it for him. By proposing an all-European conference, they had cut through his ideas – at least for the time being.[69] That December he was still hopefully inquiring about 'a top level meeting' with the Malenkov regime. But Eisenhower, undaunted, turned it down.[70]

Churchill's handling of this affair raised with greater urgency the question of the succession. It seemed to personify the vintage Churchillian qualities of capriciousness and lack of judgement, now aggravated by increasing old age. Macmillan, speaking for other senior colleagues, approached Clementine, relaying the message that Churchill ought now to retire. Churchill's immediate response was to 'soldier on' as there were several things that he wished to 'see through'. But throughout the autumn of 1954 the pressure for him to go never slackened, with Macmillan taking the lead. As his Russian initiative slipped away, Churchill himself began to lose interest in his position. In a moment of truth, he had admitted to Butler: 'I feel like an aeroplane at the end of its flight, in the dusk, with the petrol running out, in search of a safe landing.'[71]

There was no serious public discussion as to who, eventually, would succeed Churchill. Eden was the acknowledged heir-designate. For Churchill, this posed certain problems, snags that perhaps sharpened his desire to cling to office. Eden was in bad health. Indeed, it was highly questionable who was more indisposed, Churchill or Eden, so there was a bitter – unintended – twist to his remark that 'I must retire soon. Anthony won't live forever'.[72] Churchill too had long possessed grave doubts about Eden's competence to hold the highest office. Was he capable of rising above the duties of a Foreign Secretary? Churchill's reservations remained until the end.'[73]

Churchill's last Cabinet met at midday on 5 April 1955. It was a brief, nostalgic affair. Anthony Eden, who would succeed him, paid him the final compliments. As Churchill left the Cabinet room, someone reminded him, not too subtly, that he personified almost sixty years of British history. 'General X died this morning,' he was informed, 'except for yourself the last of the survivors of Omdurman.' 'How very *civil* of him!' Churchill responded. Whatever else, he retained his sense of humour. That afternoon he tendered his resignation to the Queen. Was he finally reconciled to retirement? So it seemed. 'I am tired of it all,' he said to Colville. But only days later, with a smile on his face, he was planning a comeback.[74]

Three months after Churchill left office, in July 1955, the Big Four – Eisenhower, Eden, Faure, and Bulganin – met in Geneva. Churchill's summit had finally taken place, but without him. He had failed to realize the last great mission of his political life. Yet his vision to save humanity from a nuclear holocaust by a great power settlement was a noble one. But neither at home nor abroad could he find partners with sufficient faith in his ability to carry it off. For them, he had become *passé*. It was a sad, even pathetic, finale to his career as a world statesman. Paradoxically, in the fields where he took least interest, the achievements of his last administration were more substantial. Was this because of Churchill, or despite him? In fact, a mixture of both. The minutiae of home legislation were of little concern to him. But he spoke again of national unity, invoking the spirit of Dunkirk to repair the fabric of Britain's social and economic life. He provided the inspiration, the impetus to 'move forward into broad, sunlit uplands'.[75] This is what he did best. Divisive policies were avoided. Consensus policies that commanded broad popular support – a mixed economy, limited government interference, the maintenance of an extended Welfare State – were made fashionable.

In the immediate months after his retirement, Churchill was noticeably depressed. Bored and lethargic, he also suffered another 'spasm'.[76] He took little part in the elections of May 1955 that returned the Conservatives to power. At Woodford, he maintained his substantial majority, and he continued to serve the constituency until 1964. But if Churchill felt despondent, there were always stimulating distractions to reinvigorate his jaded spirit. Besides his writing and painting, he had developed a new pastime, breeding and racing horses. His grey French colt, Colonist II, won thirteen races and more than £13,000 in prize money, though Churchill hesitated at living off 'the immoral earnings of a horse' when it was suggested that he put it out to stud.[77] There would also be longer vacations on the Riviera, idyllic interludes at La Capponcina (Beaverbrook's villa), La Dragonière (Rothermere's), and La Pausa (Emery and Wendy Reves's).

From the late fifties, these diversions were complimented by long voyages aboard *Christina*, the luxury yacht of the Greek shipping tycoon, Aristotle Onassis. 'Ari', overwhelmed by Churchill's reputation, put *Christina* at Churchill's disposal, even adapting its sailing schedules to suit the great man's timetable. Churchill was grateful for Onassis's exceptional generosity, but their friendship was conducted strictly on his terms. Once, 'Ari' tried to engage him in general conversation. Churchill, impatient and hard of hearing, cut him short: 'Would you like to play a little cards instead of talking philosophy?'[78]

A sense of satisfaction also came from the honours that were now bestowed upon him. Already a Companion of Honour, in 1946 he was awarded the Order of Merit. In April 1953 Churchill accepted the Order of the Garter, and became known as Sir Winston Churchill, even though Clementine would have preferred them to remain as plain Mr and Mrs Churchill. The same year he received the Nobel prize for literature, the announcement citing his 'mastery of historical and biographical description as well as [his] brilliant oratory in defending exalted human values'. '£12,000 free of tax. Not so bad!' he disclosed to Clementine. On retirement, in a carefully staged mise-en-scène with the Queen, he refused a dukedom, wishing 'to die in the House of Commons'. During these years, at Jock Colville's initiative, the plans were laid to found Churchill College, Cambridge, to be formally opened in 1964.[79]

In November 1954, he celebrated his eightieth birthday. The nation applauded him: 23,000 congratulatory messages poured in. The climax came at a special session of Parliament, convened to unveil its commissioned portrait of Churchill by Graham Sutherland. Churchill detested it on sight. In private, he denounced it as 'filthy' and 'malignant'. Clementine was equally appalled at Sutherland's portrayal of her husband as 'a gross & cruel monster'. Later, she had it secretly destroyed. Small wonder that two months after the Sutherland fiasco, Clementine rejected Salvador Dali's considerate offer to paint another portrait.[80]

Churchill had begun to think about his official biography towards the end of the war, stipulating that nothing should appear until at least five years after his death.[81] The subject continued to bother him. To whom could he entrust this major literary and historical enterprise? Randolph was the obvious choice, but Churchill was uncertain whether he was stable enough, or possessed sufficient talent, to carry the project through. Only in 1960 did Churchill finally agree that Randolph should write the story of his life. Randolph, 'proud and happy', promised to devote his declining years exclusively 'to what will be a pious, fascinating and I suppose, a remunerative task'.[82]

The overall sum paid for the biography was £421,000. Five volumes were planned accompanied by eight ancillary tomes of documents, each of approximately 230–250,000 words. Quoting Lockhart, the Scottish biographer and critic, Randolph revealed his methodology: Churchill 'shall be his own biographer,' and hence intended to include as much 'direct quotation' as possible. Would this not make it 'too indigestible for the general reader', 'too spasmodic in style'? queried Anthony Montague Browne, Churchill's private secretary. No, replied Randolph optimistically, brushing aside these complaints.[83]

By the time of his death in 1968, Randolph had completed two biographical and five companion volumes. Martin Gilbert, one of his team, undertook the formidable task of completing the work – which he did by 1988, adding six more volumes; at the same time, he published a further eight volumes of letters, memoranda, and extracts from diaries, documenting Churchill's life until 1939. And with even more companion volumes in the pipeline, the project has turned into the greatest biographical enterprise ever carried out in Britain, a monumental tribute to Churchill.

The last scenes of Churchill's life impose a feeling of immense sadness upon the observer. Noel Coward's cruel eye caught him 'obsessed with a senile passion for Wendy [Reves]', chasing her 'about the room with his brimming eyes', wobbling 'after her across the terrace, staggering like a vast baby'. Harold Nicolson saw him at a Royal Academy banquet: 'He is frightfully old. His eyes are bleary and immobile.' Montgomery, who unfailingly cheered him up during these years, recorded that 'he just lies in bed all day doing nothing'. In his later years, recalled Sarah, 'a certain silence descended upon him and he spoke rarely'. 'Sometimes when I used to sit with him in the long afternoons he would repeatedly ask the time. I would tell him. He would sigh deeply. About half an hour later he would ask again. "What is the time now?" I would tell him. "Oh Lor," he would say.'[84]

'I'm not afraid to die,' he had once confided to Moran, adding after a long pause, 'At least I don't think I am.' His death had long been expected. Since 1958, preparations for his state funeral – code-named 'Hope Not' – had been in progress. But where would he buried? Not in Westminster Abbey, where he would have to share his last resting place 'with so many people he did not like'.[85] Finally, after Chartwell was considered, he decided on Bladen churchyard, where his parents and his brother Jack were buried.

On 30 November 1964 Churchill celebrated his ninetieth birthday. The previous day, crowds had gathered outside 28, Hyde Park Gate, hoping to catch a glimpse of him. Ever the showman, he leaned out of the window beaming and waving, responding to the shouts of 'Happy birthday sir!' On the morning of his birthday, he was awoken by Clementine singing 'Happy Birthday to You'. 'That was lovely,' he purred. Over 70,000 birthday greetings arrived, from heads of state as well as ordinary people. In the afternoon he rested, lying in bed listening to Harrow school songs. At dinner, a family affair with some close friends, a special menu was prepared: consommé, Whitstable oysters, partridge, ice-cream and fruit, cheese and biscuits, all washed down by the appropriate wines. Over brandy, his guests toasted his health. And to round off a perfect day, he cut his birthday cake.[86]

Appropriately enough, Churchill's last public appearance was at a dinner of the Other Club in early December. It met at its usual place, the Pinafore Room at the Savoy hotel, and he sat at his usual place, in the middle of the table, his back to the river. For the other diners, it must have been a melancholy occasion, for it was 'increasingly difficult to light the spark, formerly so vital; all that could be said was that he knew where he was and was happy to be there'.[87] Exactly a month later, on 10 January 1965, Churchill suffered a severe stroke. For fourteen days he lay motionless, his strength slowly draining out of him, attended to by his family already in mourning. Blocking the narrow street outside, distraught crowds and journalists waited anxiously. At his bedside, Christopher Soames offered him a glass of Champagne, hoping to rekindle a flame. Churchill, semi-conscious and vague in thought, murmured, 'I'm so bored with it all,' his last coherent words. On Sunday, 24 January, at eight o'clock in the morning, he died.[88]

Seventy years ago to the day, his father, Lord Randolph Churchill, had also died. Of his final moments, Lord Rosebery had written: 'Why recall those last days, except to recall the pity of them? – his devoted [family] hoping against hope for his future, his own feverish energy, the brilliant light fluttering out in the full glare of day. There was no curtain, no retirement, he died by inches in public.'[89]

Two days later Churchill's coffin, draped by the Union flag, was escorted to Westminster Hall to lie in state. For three days and nights, in bitterly cold and windy weather, 321,000 people passed by the catafalque to pay him tribute. On Saturday, 30 January 1965, he was accorded a state funeral, the first for a commoner since the Duke of Wellington's in 1852. After the service in St Paul's Cathedral, the coffin was taken to Tower Pier.

As it was piped aboard the *Havengore* and the bier laid on its deck, the cranes on Hay's Wharf opposite dipped their jibs in an eerie, impressive civilian salute. The launches, carrying the family, turned upstream to the sound of 'Rule Britannia' and a nineteen-gun salvo. Overhead, sixteen Lightning jet fighters swooped down in box formations of four, peeling off over north-west London, their grey, exhaust trails marking the sky. The tiny flotilla of craft sailed up the Thames until it reached Festival Hall Pier. From there, the coffin, still flag-draped and bearing the black cushion on which rested the insignia of the Order of the Garter, was taken to Waterloo Station.

The train that took the family party to Long Handborough, the station nearest Bladen, was drawn by 'Winston Churchill', a Battle of Britain locomotive. As it passed through the countryside, an observer noted two figures who epitomized for him what Churchill really meant to ordinary people: a man standing to attention in his old RAF uniform, saluting; and in a field, a farmer stopping work, motionless, head bowed, cap in hand.[90]

Churchill was finally laid to rest in Bladon churchyard.

Epilogue

The years of Churchill's life spanned the rise and fall of the Victorian British Empire. The mid-1870s saw Disraeli acquiring a controlling interest in the Suez canal (1875), declaring Victoria Empress of India (1876), and sharing the honours with Bismarck at the Congress of Berlin (1878). By the time Churchill died, Harold Wilson's administration was beginning the debate on the size of a British presence East of Suez. If nothing else, Churchill was a child of his time. He knew it. 'The Victorian era,' he reflected, 'eighty years which will rank in our island history with the Antonine age.'[1] By upbringing, instinct and temperament he would have made a magnificent nineteenth-century Prime Minister. But by one of history's oddities, after waiting forty years, he was called to this task in the period of Britain's decline. He proved to be a superb war minister; but war, the great catalyst, only quickened the process of his country's fall from the ranks of the Great Powers.

An historical experience that could not be stayed? Not for Churchill. He spent most of his public life denying it, bringing into play his most formidable weapons: his rhetoric; his charisma; his refusal to recognize reality. It was Bevan who noted that his greatest talent was 'to persuade people not to look at the facts'.[2] Probably a majority of his countrymen succumbed to his vision. In this sense, his passing away truly marked the end of an era.

If Churchill's perception of Britain's imperial mission was obsolete, could the same be said of his other guiding tenet, the union of the English-speaking peoples? By this Churchill meant primarily a 'special relationship' with the United States. But except in a vague, sentimental, but politically meaningless way, it meant nothing to Roosevelt, Truman, or Eisenhower. In the final analysis, it was the American century, and they would not share it with what they considered to be a dilapidated, decaying Empire. Nor would they allow Britain to sustain its greatness by clinging on to their coat-tails, which is what Churchill hoped for when he offered Britain's services as 'the vital link' between America and Europe.

Two world wars, fought to maintain Britain's great power status, only heightened Britain's dependence upon the United States. But if Churchill drew meagre political dividends from the 'special relationship', he scored a major personal triumph. His figure came to symbolize the union. He was, after all, half-American. There was, therefore, something most appropriate when, in April 1963, he received an Honorary Citizenship of the United States.

Turncoat, adventurer, opportunist, irresponsible, were just some of the epithets commonly used to describe Churchill's political behaviour. Distrusted for most of his career, he did not fit into any general pattern. Party machines held little appeal for him. In turn, Conservative, Liberal, Independent, Conservative again, Oppositionist, and finally to return, almost by default, as Leader of the Conservative Party, a role that sat heavily upon his shoulders. Although he took a positive delight in savaging his political opponents, he hankered after national coalitions, perpetually fascinated by their possibilities. He rose to greatness presiding over one, confirming his image of himself as a statesman and not a mere politician. When he returned to power in 1951, he aimed to damp down the old political rivalries, preaching national unity, wishing to allow Labour's programme to reach 'fruition'. A scion of Britain's ruling class, he helped to undermine its traditional basis to govern, another of the paradoxes of Churchill's life.

If Churchill did not fit exactly into the stereotyped image of the stern Victorian patriarch, some aspects of his behaviour came close to it. Patrician by birth, outlook, and behaviour, those around him were left little option but to subordinate their wants to his whims. Nor did he find this strange; it was simply the natural order of things. His super-ego would allow nothing else. He could be rude to his servants, abrupt to his friends, inconsiderate to his colleagues. As he matured, he honed his idiosyncrasies, projecting himself as a character to be reckoned with, and one certainly not to be forgotten. His family learned to live with his quirks, the long-suffering Clementine and his children, all of whom, apart from Mary, seemed to live on an emotional high wire. None of this should disguise the fact that he was a caring and loving husband and father. But his personal relationships, like his political ones, were conducted strictly on his own terms.

Whenever Churchill gave offence, a sixth sense alerted him that he had overstepped the mark. A winning smile, some appropriate words, a touching gesture, and he would swiftly make amends, repairing the damage, appeasing the aggrieved party. In a curious way, he was respected and loved all the more for these transgressions, for his wayward behaviour was cushioned by a disarming naïveté. Blessed with a generosity of spirit, he did not bear grudges for long. But above all, people tolerated Churchill's often inexcusable conduct because they recognized that they were dealing with a man of extraordinary talents, a man of destiny.

Was Churchill the greatest Englishman of his time, of all times? No doubt, this question will continue to delight academic colloquia, in much the same way that medieval theologians relished debating how many angels could dance on the point of a needle, and with the same barren results. All that can be said with absolute certainty is that between 1940 and 1941, at a moment of his country's greatest peril, and by virtue of his unique abilities, Churchill saved his country from a dreadful tyranny. And by so doing, through his courage and leadership, he inspired the rest of the free world and gave fresh hope to those already crushed under despotic rule.

Viewed against his career as a whole these few months might be judged as an aberration. But it was sufficient to elevate him on high, to a position so remote, so impregnable that he has never ceased gazing down upon his contemporaries and rivals. Bismarck once said: 'Man cannot create the current of events. He can only float with it and steer'. Churchill put it in another, more personal way: 'It was a nation and race dwelling all round the globe that had the lion heart. I had the luck to be called upon to give the roar.'[3] For once, Churchill was being over-modest. No man was ever more prepared, more fitted, more willing to fulfil this historic task, one that he accomplished with consummate artistry. If the test of true greatness is that a statesman leaves a positive imprint on the course of history, then Churchill passed that test with flying colours. Surely that must be enough to satisfy even Churchill's colossal ego and the most fanatical of his admirers.

It would have been unnatural had Churchill not agonized over aspects of his career. In the years of his decline, he sat with his daughters contemplating his life's work. 'I have achieved a great deal to achieve nothing in the end,' he said. 'How can you say that? responded Diana. 'There are your books,' added Sarah. 'And your paintings,' noted Diana. 'Oh yes,' Churchill admitted, unconvinced, 'there are those.' 'And after all, there is us,' continued Diana and Sarah, 'Poor comfort we know at times: and there are other children who are grateful that they are alive.' Churchill acknowledged their remarks with a smile. Some years earlier he had told Bob Boothby that he worried about the position he would ultimately occupy in history. 'Historians are apt to judge war ministers less by the victories achieved under their direction than by the political results which flowed from them. Judged by that standard, I am not sure that I shall be held to have done very well.'[4] He need not have worried. Historians will go on chipping away at his monumental statue, reshaping, remodelling it, but the essential structure will remain unaltered. In his own way, Churchill had explained why.

In the late 1930s, when working on *A History of the English-Speaking*

Peoples, an exchange took place between Churchill and his professional advisers. Should the story of King Alfred and the burnt cakes be included? 'No', said they. 'Yes', he insisted. 'Why?' they asked. 'Because', Churchill explained, 'at times of crisis, myths had their historical importance: the cakes symbolized a myth of British resistance in their sternest hour against the foreign invader, and were the source of inspiration to those dim distant figures, the Counts of the Saxon shore, striving to defend the island.'[5] Who can say that he was wrong? Unwittingly, Churchill had dictated his own epitaph.

Notes and References

Abbreviations have been used throughout, see under author in Bibliography for full version. The following abbreviations have also been used:

Alanbrooke War Diaries – see in Bibliography under Arthur Bryant
Amery Diaries – see Barnes and Nicolson (eds.)
Asquith Letters – see M. and E. Brock (eds.)
BD – Documents on British Foreign Policy
Bertie Diary – see Lennox (ed.)
Bridgeman Diaries – see Williamson (ed.)
Cadogan Diaries – see Dilks (ed.)
Channon Diaries – see R. R. James (ed.)
Noel Coward Diaries – see Payn and Morley (eds.)
CSWC – see Churchill's Speeches under R. R. James (ed.)
CV – Companion Volumes to the Official Biography, see under Randolph S. Churchill and Martin Gilbert
Dalton Diaries – see Pimlott (ed.)
Davidson Memoirs – see R. R. James
Dugdale Diaries – see Rose (ed.)
FRUS – see *Foreign Relations of the United States*
Hobhouse Diaries – see E. David
Ironside Diaries – see Macleod and Kelly (eds.)
MEL – see under W. S. Churchill, *My Early Life*
Nicolson Diaries – see Nicolson, N. (ed.)
Sanders Diaries – see Ramsden (ed.)
Scott Diaries – see Wilson (ed.)
Stevenson Diary – see A. J. P. Taylor (ed.)
Waugh Diaries – see M. Davie (ed.)
WC – W. S. Churchill, *World Crisis*
Webb Diaries – see under Cole (ed.)
Webb, OP – Cole and Drake (eds.) *Our Partnership*
Whitehall Diary – see under Middlemas (ed.)
Wilson Diary – see Callwell

WSC – Official Biography, see under Randolph S. Churchill and Martin Gilbert

Prologue

1 From the *The Times*, 1 Feb 1965, and transcript of Richard Dimbleby's television broadcast. I am grateful to Tom Bower for making this available to me.

Chapter 1. 'The Boy is Wonderfully Pretty'

1 CV/1, i, 1–2. One of Lady Randolph's biographers concludes that *The Times*'s announcement of a premature birth 'caused some snickers'. (See Ralph Martin 1969, i, 111).

2 News of their impending marriage, leaked to *The Court Journal* in September 1873, brought a swift denial from the Jeromes in the following issue. See P. Churchill and J. Mitchell, 1974, 45–46

3 See W. S. Churchill, Lord Randolph Churchill, i, 57; R. R. James, 1959, 47; Anita Leslie, 1969, 37; R. Martin, i, 95. See CV/1, i, 11, 22

4 See R. Martin, i, 65

5 See CV/1, i, 12; R. F. Foster, 1981, 18; and P. Churchill and J. Mitchell, 44

6 See CV/1, i, 18–19; R. R. James, 1969, 43; R. Martin, 90; and Foster, 18. The sources differ as to exact sum involved. But Jerome put aside a capital sum of £50,000 for investment while the Duke raised his son's yearly allowance to £1,100.

7 See A. L. Rowse, 1966, and WC, 1, 6–14. The Spencer connection resulted from the marriage of John's favourite daughter, Anne, to Charles Spencer, 3rd earl of Sunderland, in 1700.

8 See D. Green, 1951

9 See D. Green, 1984, 109, and Rowse, 320

10 Quoted in R. Martin, 74

11 See Mrs George Cornwallis-West, 1908, 1–2; Anita Leslie, 1954; Lord Moran, 629–30; R. Martin, i, 24; and P. Churchill and J. Mitchell, 45

12 Jennie was a personal friend of Ignace Paderewski and organized his first London appearance. On occasion, they played duets together in private. See R. Martin, i, 45, 279, and A. Leslie, 1954, 273

13 See WSC, 1, 16, and R. Martin, i, 15–16

14 CV/1, i, 9; Edward Marsh, 1939, 154; and quoted by P. Churchill and J. Mitchell, 21

15 WSC, 1, 96, and Rowse, 328–29

16 See Lord Rosebery, 1906, 33–36; R. R. James, 1959, (1969 ed.), 20–32; Foster, 10–12; and R. Martin, i, 62–63. Winston Churchill, 1906, i, 8–38, gives a much blander account of his father's career at Eton and Merton.

17 From the *Oxford Times* and *Oxford Chronicle and Berks and Bucks Gazette*, 30 May 1874

18 See WSC, 1, 24, and R. Martin, i, 97, 333

19 See Foster, 24. See also Winston Churchill, 1906, i, 72–73; R. R. James, 1959 (1969 ed.), 50–53

20 See CV/1, i, 439, and MEL, 12–13, 39, 54. Also R. R. James, 1959 (1969 ed.), 259

21 *Savrola*, 197, also 32–33

22 See *WSC*, 1, 25–34; CV/1, i, 36–38; Philip Magnus, 1964 (1967 ed.), 184–93; Foster, 31–32; R. R. James, 1959 (1969 ed.), 57–59; A. Leslie, 1964; P. Churchill and J. Mitchell, ch. 4

23 See Foster, 55, and *MEL*, 12

24 See Mrs George Cornwallis-West, 1908, 72; *MEL*, 12; Foster, 40–57; R. R. James, 1959 (1969 ed.), 60–64; W. Churchill, 1906, i, 80–94

25 See *MEL*, 9–10, and *WSC*, 1, 37

26 *MEL*, 11, 16

27 See *MEL*, 19–20, also *WSC*, 1, 54–55, and Shane Leslie, 1966, 21. For his 'penal servitude' remark see Randolph S. Churchill, 71, also Moran, 464. See article of Nov. 1931, *Daily Mail*, where he railed against 'the Spartan life' of the public schools, bastions of 'privilege of temporary wealth'; 'an insult to the past and a danger to the future'. See *WSC*, V, 417

28 See CV/1, i, 89

29 See CV/1, i, 90–96, and *MEL*, 20

30 See CV/1, i, 6. For the sugar incident see S. Leslie, 1966, 21, Maurice Baring, 1922 and 1936

31 See *MEL*, 20, 24–25; CV/1, i, 125, 136–37, 147; and S. Leslie, 1929, 137, and 1966, 18

32 See *MEL*, 21, and *WSC*, 1, 56, 60. The family avoided St George's after this episode. Winston's brother Jack and his Leslie and Frewen cousins were sent to other preparatory schools.

33 See *MEL*, 21, and *WSC*, 1, 60.

34 Three of his school reports at Brighton are in CV/1, i, 97–99, and 129, 141, 146; for penknife incident, see P. Churchill and J. Mitchell, 127–28

35 See CV/1, i, 113

36 See also Ch. 2

37 CV/1, i, 124, 128

38 See W. Churchill. *The River War*, 24, and his *Life of Marlborough*, vol 1, 33. Also CV/1, ii, 1002

39 See *WSC*, 1, 116, and CV/1, i, 111, 149

40 In 1883 John, the seventh duke, her husband, died. He was succeeded by his eldest son, George, the Marquess of Blandford, whose sensational affair with Lady Aylsford had reinforced his dubious reputation. In 1888 George divorced his first wife, Bertha, daughter of the first Duke of Abercorn, and married Lilian Hammersley, an American heiress.

41 P. Churchill and J. Mitchell, 110; also Rowse, 336, quoting from Lady Randolph's *Reminiscences*. Another American, the heiress Consuelo Vanderbilt, when ninth duchess of Marlborough, experienced similar difficulties in acclimatizing to the stiff, unbending atmosphere at Blenheim. See her memoirs, 1953

42 See Consuelo Vanderbilt Balsan, 1953, 57. For twenty-three years Winston remained heir presumptive to the dukedom and Blenheim until, in 1897, a son, John Albert (the future tenth duke) was born to Consuelo

43 See Rowse, 346–47. Also *WSC*, 1, 206, 257, and CV/1, i, 373, 431

44 See CV/1, i, 219, 235, 264, 270

45 See CV/1, i, 66, 270; and S. Leslie, 1929, 129, and 1966, 17

46 CV/1, i, 64, 292

47 See *WSC*, 1, 140, and CV/1, i, 230–31, 245, 325, 427, 429, 485

48 The fluctuations in his illness may be followed in CV/1, i, 116–123. See also P. Churchill and J. Mitchell, 135–36

49 It too seems that Lord Randolph's unhappy experiences at Eton hardened his opinion against that institution. In consequence, he took his revenge by sending his sons to its great rival, Harrow. See S. Leslie, 1966, 20

50 See *WSC*, 1, 96, and CV/1, i, 143, 157–59; also *MEL*, 23–4

Chapter 2. Becoming Educated

1 See Foster, 63, 74, 113. Material on Lord Randolph is taken from biographies: by Winston, 1906 (later edition, 1951); R. R. James, 1959 (1969 ed.), and R. F. Foster, 1981. There is also a memoir by Lord Rosebery, 1906

2 His speeches, particularly the Dartford peroration, contained 'many ambivalences and omissions' and were stronger in verbal acrobatics than substance. See Foster, 292–97

3 See Edith Finch, 1938, 210, and Rosebery, 136, 160

4 See Rosebery, 42, 47, 49–50, 112–14

5 See CV/1, i, 545. Some authorities have doubted whether syphilis was the cause of Lord Randolph's death [see R. R. James, 1978, 113, and his biography of Lord Randolph where he refers to a 'rare and ghastly disease of the brain' (p. 361), following closely Winston's wording in his life of his father (p. 746)]. Treated with the utmost delicacy, Lord Randolph's case was shrouded in Victorian discretion. No autopsy was performed on the body; some of the symptoms displayed can also be attributed to a brain tumour or multiple sclerosis. There is no authoritative account of how and when Lord Randolph contracted syphilis. Shane Leslie, Lord Randolph's nephew, claims that his uncle contracted the disease from a chambermaid at Blenheim shortly after Winston's birth, and that once syphilis had been diagnosed he ceased sleeping with his wife. The precise details will probably never be known. But the evidence, circumstantial and otherwise, is overwhelming that Lord Randolph died of syphilis, or as his physicians put it, from 'General Paralysis of the Insane', the accepted euphemism for syphilis. (See Foster, 59, 96–97, 217–19.)

6 Rosebery, 72, 99

7 One of her biographers puts it soon after her marriage (see R. Martin, 1969, 113), a date that fits in with Shane Leslie's account; another, as late as October 1886 (see A. Leslie, 1969, 108)

8 Lady Randolph's affairs can be followed in any of her, or Lord Randolph's, biographies, listed above. For 'the Austrian alliance', see Foster, 270; and for Kinsky's warm relationship with Winston, CV/1, i, 226, 256–58, 266

9 See Foster, 163, 270 and n.2, 318–19, and n.14, 349–50; R. R. James, 1959, 312; A. Leslie, 1969, 97; P. Churchill and J. Mitchell, 142, 156–57; R. Martin, 220–21

10 See CV/1, i, 106, 122, 123–25

11 See G. A. Hatham, 1929, 22; E. D. W. Chaplin (ed.), 1941, 16; MEL, 25, 29–30, 33; CV/1, i, 336–37, 350–52, 354. A rumour was circulated that Winston was once in danger of being expelled from Harrow for lack of academic progress (see Marvin Rintala 1984), but this seems highly unlikely.

12 See MEL, 27–28, and CV/1, i, 78, 259. And Shane Leslie, 1929, 129.

13 See CV/1, i, 131, 163, 328, and Charles Eade (ed.), 1953, 20

14 See CV/1, i, 157, 293; MEL, 47; R. Meinertzhagen, 1964, 175–77; Chaplin, 28, 87; and Shane Leslie, 1966, 21. For his speech impediments, see CV/1, ii, 1089, 1091

15 See MEL, 28. For his contributions to the Harrovian, CV/1, i, 308–319, and Amery, i, 39–40

16 See CV/1, i, 214, 234–35, 237, 247; S. Leslie, 1966, 21; and Eade, 19

17 See CV/1, i, 204, 207, 264–65, 364

18 See WSC, 1, 135–35, and CV/1, i, 168, 217–18, 220

19 See CV/1, i, 101, 205, 294. Also Felix Semon, 1926. And WSC, 1, 293

20 See S. Leslie, 1966, 17, and MEL, 39

21 See CV/1, i, 268, 328, 338, 390–91

22 See CV/1, i, 468–71

23 CV/1, i, 295

24 See CV/1, i, 184. The Mrs Everest incident may be followed in S. Leslie, 1966, 21; Eade, 20; and Chaplin, 45

25 See CV/1, i, 414, 421

26 See CV/1, i, 168, and MEL, 36, 45

27 For this paragraph, see CV/1, i, 833–34, CV/1, ii, 793, 812, 835; MEL; Savrola. In this connection, Anthony Storr has written: '[Churchill's] courage was not something that he himself took for granted, but rather something which he had to prove to himself; a compensation for inner doubts about his own bravery.' See his essay 'The Man', in A. J. P. Taylor (ed.), 1969, 210–211,

28 See CV/1, ii, 812

29 Leopold Stennet Amery, MP for Sparkbrook, who had been 'ducked' by Churchill at Harrow, was then serving as Secretary of State for India in Churchill's administration, and General Lord Gort had commanded the British Expeditionary Force in France until its evacuation at Dunkirk, bringing honour to their professions. On the other hand, Leopold, King of the Belgians, had capitulated to the Germans on 27 May 1940, an act that earned him much obloquy; Captain Archibald Henry Maule Ramsey, MP for Peebles and South Midlothian, an extreme right-wing Conservative, founder of the Right Club, had been imprisoned under the emergency 18B defence regulations in May 1940; and Oswald Mosley, leader of the British Union of Fascists, was also imprisoned under the 18B regulations.

30 See N. Rose, 1973, 174; MEL, 47; Chaplin, 28, 75, 83–84; and Harrow School Songs

31 See MEL, 33, 36; WSC, 1, 193–94; and CV/1, i, 384, 392.

32 See CV/1, i, 386, 402, 404, 457, 488–89, 520–21. For Lady Wilton's contributions, ibid., 210, 215, 229, 240, 349, 359, 372

33 See CV/1, i, 404

34 See CV/1, i, 402, 404, 409, 411–12, 414, and Winston's article in the Pall Mall Magazine (Dec. 1896) on 'The Royal Military College, Sandhurst,' in CV/1, i, 548–552. Also WSC, 1, 212

35 See MEL, 53; WSC, 1, 225–26; and CV/1, i, 413–14, 433–34, 515, 550–51

36 See WSC, 1, 231, 242–43; and Chaplin, 68

37 Churchill covered this incident in some length in MEL, 58–66. Also WSC, 1, 232–34, CV/1, i, 526–28, 530, 532–33, and Halle, 19

38 See CV/1, i, 531–47; also WSC, 1, 240; and MEL 70

39 See MEL, 41, 53–54, and CV/1, i, 423

40 See MEL, 41, 54, and CV/1, i, 413–14

41 Thirty years after Churchill wrote the official life of his father, he recognized 'the fatal character' of his father's resignation, and showed more of a mature understanding of Salisbury's position, understanding that it would have been politically unwise to divide power with 'a restless rival, entrenched in the leadership of the House of Commons and the control of the public purse'. See MEL, 54–55

42 It has been suggested that John Strange [Jack] Churchill's natural father was not Lord Randolph, but one of Lady Randolph's lovers, Lieutenant-Colonel John Strange Jocelyn, and that this somehow explains Jack's un-Churchillian characteristics. (See Ted Morgan, 1983, 27, 66, followed by William Manchester, 1983, 136). While this possibility cannot be entirely excluded, the evidence is far from convincing.

43 MEL, 70

44 MEL, 70, 159, 170

45 See Foster, 349, 379. Also MEL, 70

46 See MEL, 80, and CV/1, i, 424–25; and, CV/1, i, 283–84

47 See WSC, 1, 253–54, CV/1, i, 578–79, 586, and MEL, 80–81

48 CV/1, i, 579

Chapter 3. In Pursuit of Fame

1 See CV/1, ii, 804
2 CV/1, i, 423
3 See CV/1, ii, 583–85
4 See *MEL*, 69–7–, 75–79, and CV/1, i, 553–54, 626–27
5 The Alan Bruce and racing-ring affairs may be followed in detail in CV/1, i, 625–662. For Churchill's desire for popularity, see CV/1, i, 565, 571; his concern about his career, CV/1, ii, 701, 703. And for Lady Randolph's opposition to his racing, see *WSC*, 1, 308–11
6 See CV/1, ii, 768
7 His Cuban adventures may be followed in CV/1, ii, 589–624, also *MEL*, 82–95
8 See *WSC*, 1, 276
9 See W. Churchill, *Thoughts and Adventures*, 52–53; *WSC*, 1, 282–83; and Robert Boothby 1947, 45
10 See CV/1, i, 597–600
11 For Churchill's care in not annoying the Americans in public, Moran, 57, 103, 135–36; for his call for a 'common citizinship', Harvard, Sept. 1943, Moran, 135–36
12 CV/1, i, 676
13 See *WSC*, 1, 352–53, and CV/1, ii. 1084, 1152–53. Also Violet Bonham Carter, 23
14 See CV/1, ii, 688, 690, 695, 722, and *MEL*, 107–08
15 For his disillusionment with life in India, see CV/1, ii, 697, 753, and for his process of self-education, *ibid.*, 715, 724, 730, 742, 744, 746–47, 757–68, 776. Also *MEL*, 115–19
16 See also Paul Addison, 1980a
17 See J. H. Plumb's compelling essay, in A. J. P. Taylor (ed.), 1969. See also Plumb and Maurice Ashton, 1968, 138–45
18 See *MEL*, 121, CV/1, ii, 724–25, and P. Addison 1980a
19 See *WSC*, 1, 157–58, CV/1, ii, 839, 969, 1083, and *MEL*, 119–22
20 See CV/1, ii, 709, 751, for his 5-point programme for Tory Democracy
21 For his comments on Balfour and Curzon, CV/1, ii, 734–35, and his attitude to Chamberlain and Rosebery and national coalitions, *ibid.*, 698. For Lord Randolph's remark about Balfour, see *WSC*, 1, 86
22 S. Leslie, 1966, 23–24
23 For these quotations see CV/1, ii, 792, 973–74
24 For his appointment to the Malakand Field Force, see CV/1, ii, 774–75, 780–84, 786; to the Sudan and his relations with Kitchener, *ibid.*, 729, 733, 813, 948–49, 951–52, 971; and Lady Randolph's lobbying, *ibid.*, 854, 856, 911, 915. Also *MEL*, 128–54, 168–77
25 See Frederick Woods, 1972. See also CV/1, ii, chs 12, 13. And his books, *The Story of the Malakand Field Force* (1898) and *The River War* (1899). Churchill later drastically pruned his remarks in both subsequent editions of *The River War* and in his public speeches. See also Maurice Ashley, 1968, 46–47; *CSWC* 1, 31–32; also W. S. Blunt, 1932, 322
26 See CV/1, ii, 788–89, 803, 807, and Woods, 51. Also *MEL*, 154
27 See CV/1, ii, 968, 997, also 979
28 See Philip Magnus, 158–59, 164–68, and Ashley, 48–49
29 Churchill was not the only soldier-journalist active at the time. Lord Fincastle, a lieutenant in 16 Lancers, represented *The Times*, and R. T. Greaves, *The Times of India*, who was killed in action. Neither drew fire like Churchill. See CV/1, ii, 865 n1
30 See CV/1, ii, 813, 1011, 1015, 1023

31 This imagery is very pronounced in Churchill's writing about India during this period, see Woods, 39, 52, 65, and CV/1, ii, 791

32 See CV/1, ii, 811, 814, 828, 839, 924; and WSC, 1, 340, 396

33 See CSWC, 1, 25–30; CV/1, ii, 770–74, 922, 949–50; WSC, 1, 345–45, 395–96; and MEL, 209–13.

34 See CV/1, ii, 1030–36; MEL, 225–33; and CSWC, 1, 32–50.

35 For his wine list, CV/1, ii, 1054; comments about Buller, ibid., 1055, and MEL, 240; and J. B. Atkins 1947, 122.

36 See CSWC, 1, 50–51, for his speech; and CV/1, ii, 1059

37 See MEL, 245–304; CV/1, ii, 1060–1136; WSC, 1, 461–506

38 Quotations from Thomas Pakenham, 1979, 172, 290–91. Churchill's own account makes no mention of these aspects of his adventure, see MEL, 245–59; nor are they noted in WSC, 1, 461–75

39 See CV/1, ii, 1101–02; and for Churchill's previous opinion of Haldane, ibid., 908

40 For this episode see CV/1, ii, 1104–05, 1106; and WSC, 1, 497; CV/1, ii, 1077–78, 1085, and 1069–70; MEL, 305–08

41 For the libel charge, see CV/1, ii, 1109–15, and WSC, 1, 486–87, 501; CV/1, ii, 1115. Haldane, it should be noted, made good his escape the following April.

42 For Churchill's newly acquired fame, MEL, 304, WSC, 1, 505–06; and report that eleven constituencies sought him, Halle, 31. For his 'fox-hunting' remarks, WSC, 1, 507; and for his brush with the generals and Hamilton's attitude, CV/1, ii, 883, 1114, and WSC, 1, 522–24, 530

43 See also Pakenham, 384–85; MEL, 305–60, and Woods, 155–341; CV/1, ii, 1149–51. And his two books on the South African war, London to Ladysmith and Ian Hamilton's March

44 See MEL, 362; for the anti-semitic, nationalist climate at the 'Khaki election', R. R. James 1978, 201; for Churchill's election campaign, Pakenham 492: his speeches are in CSWC, 1, 53–62; and for reactions to his victory, CV/1, ii, 1203–06

45 On Churchill's financial situation, see CV/1, ii, 1183, 1190, 1214, 1225, WSC, 1, 329–32, and MEL, 309; and for the Churchill brothers doubts about their mother's marriage, see CV/1, ii, 922, 1044, 1046, 1188, and R. Martin, ii, 171–72. In 1896, Lady Randolph, together with her sisters, had been embezzled, considerably worsening their precarious financial situation. Lady Randolph was compelled to borrow £17,000 to clear her debts; using life insurance policies on hers and Churchill's lives as security. Churchill was required to pay the premium of £700 per annum. As Lady Randolph had made these arrangements without consulting Churchill, he was quite naturally put out, but eventually agreed, conditioning his consent on Jack sharing the burden. See CV/1, ii, 685, 745–46, 834, and WSC, 1, 370–72

46 For See CV/1, ii, 726, 835, 895, 927, 929

47 See CV/1, ii, 816–21 and 933; Also Ashley 1968, 18, and Lucy Masterman, December 1964, 823–24, and WSC, V, 297. See also R. R. James, 1970, 25–31.

48 See Storr, 219–21

Chapter 4. 'I am an English Liberal . . .'

1 Quotes from A. G. Gardiner, 1908, 227; WSC, 1, 212; Wilfred Scawen Blunt 1932, 488; Atkins, 122; and George Cornwallis-West, 1930. See also R. R. James, 1970, 4–5; Anthony Storr, 210–12; Randolph S. Churchill and Helmut Gernsheim (eds.) 1955; and Martin Gilbert, 1974. Storr defines Churchill as endormorphic.

2 For finding a biographer, CV/1, ii, 882; his 'modest personality', WSC, 1, 514; the clubs of London quote in S. Leslie, 1966, 23; also Gardiner, 1914, 231–34

3 See Ch. 3 and CV/1, ii, 751

4 See, CV/2, 1, 454; and CV/2, i, 16, 257, 260. Also Blunt, 488–89; and Fred Urquart, 1955, 2

5 See Wilson Harris, 1946, 79; WSC, 2, 77–79; and CSWC, 1, 269–71, 274–76.

6 See David Butler and Anne Sloman (eds.), 1975, 182

7 R. C. K. Ensor, xiii. Among the government's more solid achievements may be included the Education Act of 1902; the Licensing Act of 1904; Irish land reform; the alliance with Japan in 1902 and the *entente* with France two years later; and the reorganization of the country's defence machinery with the creation of the Committee of Imperial Defence in 1904.

8 CSWC, 1, 65–70; also MEL, 370–73

9 See CV/2, i, 8–19

10 *Morning Post*, 13 May 1901

11 In his programme for Tory Democracy, set out in April 1897, Churchill thought the army should be 'reduced to a training depot for India with one army corps for petty expeditions'. See CV/1, ii, 751

12 CSWC, 1, 76–86

13 See WSC, 2, 22; also R. R. James 1964–65, [18]

14 See CV/2, i, 69; WSC, 2, 21; MEL, 375; CV/2, i, 68

15 The founding members were Churchill; Ian Malcolm, a family friend; Lord Henry Percy; the hon. Arthur Stanley; and Lord Hugh Cecil. Other names were linked to the group: Ivor Guest (later, Lord Wimborne), Churchill's cousin; Jack Seely (later, Lord Mottistone); George Kemp (later, Lord Rochdale); Edmond Beckett (later, Lord Grimthorpe). See L. S. Amery, vol., i, 195, and Consuelo Vanderbilt Balsan, 113–14.

16 CV/2, i, 146, and Halle, 41

17 CV/2, i, 346. See also Churchill's *Thoughts and Adventures*, 55–58.

18 For example, Lord Rosebery, Sir Henry Campbell-Bannerman, Henry Asquith, Sir Edward Grey all dined at the 'Hooligans' table. John Morley, Gladstone's biographer and a pacifist in outlook, was another prominent Liberal. See also Churchill's *Great Contemporaries*, 71. Also, WSC, 2, 23–26, 42–47; CV/2, i, 75–78, 113–117, 139, 146, 154, 163–68; MEL, 206–08, 376–78; Amery, i, 195; Ronaldshay, ii, 175

19 For his search for a centre party, CV/2, i, 168, 212–13.

20 See CV/2, i, 114

21 CV/2, i, 174

22 CV/2, i, 174–75, 183–84

23 See Gardiner 1914, 234–35; and Churchill, *Thoughts and Adventures*, 39

24 Nationwide it was a different story. Here it was Asquith who made the most impact, shadowing Chamberlain on his public campaign, refuting his arguments fact for fact, disputing the logic of his case. See Roy Jenkins, 151–54, and S. Koss, 1985, 59–60.

25 CV/2, i, 188–89, 267–68

26 See CV/2, i, 122, 169, 269–71

27 See Alfred Gollin, 1965

28 See WSC, 2, 64, 87, and CV/2, i, 307, 310–11, 322; and Lucy Masterman, November, 1964

29 See CSWC, 1, 238; and CV/2, i, 336–38, 343.

30 CV/2, i, 346

31 See Eade (ed.), 359

32 See WSC, 2, 247, for Asquith's comment; Lloyd George's in Lord Riddell,

1934, 106; also Lucy Masterman, 1939, 154; and *Hobhouse Diaries*, 1977, 121.

33 Writing in 1924, Churchill's close friend, F. E. Smith, vividly embroidered this argument. Smith harboured no doubt that Churchill had 'bitterly regretted' his decision to abandon the Tories, for by so doing he had inadvertently backed the losing side with disastrous results. See Birkenhead, 1924, 117–18

34 CV/2, 1, 366–67

35 CSWC, 1, 550–52

36 The first edition was published in two volumes by Macmillan and Churchill received an advance on royalties of £8,000, an enormous sum for those days. See WSC, 2, 135–43, and CV/2, i, 434–94.
    The biography has since been subject to a searching review (see Foster, 382–403). And the conclusion is inescapable that Churchill's attempt to vindicate his father's career coloured the historical methods he employed.

37 He gained a majority of 1,241 over the Conservative candidate, William Joynson-Hicks.

38 See R. Hyam, 1968, 43, and Brett, 1934, ii, 215–16.

39 As in Wilson Harris, 1946, 82

40 CSWC, 1, 514. Also John Wilson, 1972, 459

41 WSC, 2, 246, and Hyam, 1968, 500

42 See R. Hyam, 1968, 500; WSC, 2, 246; and CV/3, i, 284; CV/1, ii, 731

43 See WSC, 2, 144–193, and CV/2, i, chs 8, 9. Also Hyam, 1968, 84–153

44 See CSWC, 1, 662; Denis Judd, 1968, 209–10, and Arthur Murray, 1945, 15

45 See Hyam, 1968, 198, 207–08, 215, 218–23, and CSWC, 1, 627–29, 662, 695–99, 797, 813. The pearl fisheries dispute occasioned Elgin's famous minute: 'It is his [Churchill's] opinion and he has stated it in the House – but it is not mine.'

46 His Cabinet memoranda included nine papers on the South African problem, 2, 25–27, 30 Jan., 5 Feb., 15 March, 20 Jul. 1906 in CAB.37/82, 83, and 28 Apr. 1907, CAB.37/88; on Colonial Marriages, 17 Apr. 1906, CAB.37/83; the Colonial Conference, 30 Jan. 1907, CAB.37/86; on Cyprus and Somaliland, 19 and 28 Oct. 1907, CAB.37/89; and Certificates of Naturalization, 6 Mar. 1908, CAB.37/91; also Hyam, 1968, passim.

47 See Hyam, 1968, 349–66, and also WSC, 2, 226–36; CV/2, ii, ch. 10; F. A. Dickenson, 1910, 65–104; Hesketh Bell, 1946, 166–73; and Edward Marsh, 1939, 265–67.

48 CV/2, ii, 730

49 CSWC, 1, 594–601. Also WSC, 2, 185; and E. Marsh, 151. See also A. M. Gollin, 1964, 82–84

50 See Master of Elibank, 1934 118–19; CV/2, ii, 751, 754–57, 797; Hyam, 1968, 488–97; Almeric Fitzroy, i, 290; Christopher Hassall, 122; and Elibank, 118.

51 See Edward Marsh, 148–49, and CV/2, ii, 678–79. Marsh was an unusual choice for Churchill's private secretary. A generous patron of the arts, particularly literature, painting, and poetry, and wont to appear at the theatre attired in a cape with a red silk lining, it has been stated with some authority that he stood 'at the centre of a large homosexual artistic colony in England'. (See Douglas Plummer 1963, 34.) However, his biographer, Christopher Hassall, (1959, 23) wrote that a boyhood illness (unspecified) left Marsh impotent – and with a falsetto voice – and that he 'died as chaste as he was born', enabling 'his affections to grow more intensely in the mind'.

52 See CV/1, ii, 989; CV/2, ii, 800; and D. Green, 1984, 141

53 See WSC, 1, 231–32; CV/1, i, 474; CV/1, ii, 697, 1044, 1143, 1209, 1224; CV/2, i, 656; CV/2, ii, 705. Also A. Leslie 1969, 263–64, and P. Churchill and J. Mitchell, 191

54 See CV/1, ii, 908, 989–90; WSC, 2, 209; Violet Bonham-Carter, 150; and

Savrola, 157. Also J. Grigg 1978, 184. The lady friend is identified only as Miss G- G-, whose family was quite well-known in Liberal circles.

55 See Elizabeth Longford, 1967, 386. Margot Asquith later told Blunt, in 1916, that she had heard that Clementine was Lord Redesdale's daughter, but Blunt discounted this rumour. Clementine's unsettled early history may be followed in Mary Soames, 1979, 4–10

56 CV/2, ii, 781–820; *WSC*, 2, 248–75; Soames, 30–49; also D. Green, 1984, 228. Most sources (*WSC*, 2, 268 Soames, 42) have the happy couple seeking shelter from the rainstorm. But Green (p.228) relates – based on Clementine's memory – that it was in fact a sunny day and that they were escaping from the heat.

57 See Riddell, 1934, 1

58 *MEL*, 378

59 Halle, 221, and Soames, 88. Churchill's valet called him at 5 or 6 o'clock at which hour he commenced his work (Riddell 1934, 1). This spartan habit was not kept up in later life.

60 CV/2, ii, 808

61 CV/2, i, 672

62 See Ch. 5

63 See *WSC*, 2, 243, 247, 451; Leo Maxse quoted by Gollin, 1964, 83; for Morley's evaluation, Margot Asquith, 251, and Hyam, 1968, 502; Grey and Esher's assessment in Brett, ii, 344

64 Gardiner, 1914, 233–36

Chapter 5. Radical Politics

1 Other factors – tariff reform, the brewers' monopoly, reform of the House of Lords – also worked against Churchill and in favour of the Conservatives. The radical Social Democratic Federation had also drawn away from the Liberals 276 crucial votes. Churchill's 'sulky Irish Catholics' remark (CV/2, ii, 787) refers to Catholic indignation at the government for introducing the Education Bill of April 1906. Intended as a conciliatory gesture, it had the opposite effect, and was seen as further undermining the independence of the voluntary religious schools system. The Lords killed the Bill, and in consequence Asquith dropped it. See Elie Halevy. Vol. vi: 64–69

2 CV/2, ii, 787

3 See Andrew Rosen, and David Morgan, 1975. Also Halevy, 514–27

4 See *WSC*, 2, 121, 393; *WSC*, 2, 394; CV/2, iii, 1457–64; and Rosen, 126.

5 See CV/1, ii, 765; *CSWC*, i, 544; Soames, 59, 79. Also Lucy Masterman, 1968, 166; *Scott Diaries*, 59, and Riddell, 36

6 See Rosen, 140–41; and CV/2, iii, 1468–69

7 See his discussions with the Women's Liberal Association and its militant off-shoot, 2 Dec. 1910, in CV/2, iii, 1465–67

8 See PD, C, 5th series, v.xxxvi, c. 615–731; *CSWC*, ii, 1582–87; CV/2, iii, 1483; and *WSC*, 2, 407. Also Rosen, 135–37; and *Scott Diaries*, 58–59

9 See CV/2, iii, 1473–77; Arthur C. Murray, 1945, 100–01, and also *CSWC*, ii, 1650, 1653.

10 See *CSWC*, 1, 939–1042, and 2, 1356–1488, 1633–44

11 See Violet Bonham-Carter, 152–53, and CV/2, iii, 1998

12 From his campaign speeches in Manchester and Dundee, in *CSWC*, 1, 959, 965, 969, 974, 978, 1015, 1040. The nationalization of the railways was a pet idea of Churchill's.

13 Masterman, 1938, 97–98

14 B. B. Gilbert, 1966, and Halevy, 98–103

15 See R. R. James, 1959, 347, and Foster, 165, 368–70, for Lord Randolph. For

Churchill's impressions of Poverty, CV/2, i, 105–111, and WSC, 2, 30–32; the letter to Spender in W. Harris, 80–81

16 See, for example, the searing impressions it left on George Bernard Shaw and Leonard Wolff (Michael Holroyd, 1988, 69–70)

17 Marsh, 150

18 See Ronald Hyam's review, 1969, XII; Riddell, 22; and Foster, 117–18

19 See CV/1, ii, 768; Masterman, 1939, 140, 152, 165; Gardiner, 1914, 234; and Birkenhead, 1924, 116

20 See CV/1, ii, 751; CV/2, i, 104; CSWC, 1, 40–41, 862–63; and W. Churchill, The People's Rights, 139–40

21 See Halevy, 91–92

22 In 1908 the number of working days lost through industrial disputes rose to 10.785 million, an increase of almost five-fold on 1907. Until 1915, with the exception of 1909, the number did not drop below 9.8 million, while in 1912 it reach the staggering level of 40.89 million. See British Political Facts, 299–300; and B. B. Gilbert, 1966, 246–48.

23 See CSWC, 1, 625, 1015, 1023, 1028–31; and W. Churchill, Budget Issues, 150–52

24 Churchill to Asquith, 14 Mar. 1908, CV/2, ii, 756. Also J. Grigg, 1978, 163; Frank Owen; Riddell, 18–19; and Stevenson Diary, 41–42

25 See CV/2, ii, 754–55, and Marsh, 163

26 See Violet Bonham-Carter, 166; Webb, Our Partnership, 1948, 269, 404, 417; and Lord Beveridge, 1953, 87

27 See Hobhouse Diaries, 73, 76; Masterman, 1939, 112; Roy Jenkins, 216; Brett (ed.), ii, 324; Fitzroy, i, 377, 383; WSC, 2, 247; to 'cashier' Churchill, Scott Diaries, 37–38; and R. Hyam (1969)

28 Churchill kept a statuette of Napoleon prominently displayed on his desk. 'He is always comparing the position he has reached with what Napoleon was doing at his age and gets worried,' remarked one observer. See Lucy Masterman, November 1964

29 See Masterman, 1939, 127–28; Asquith Letters, 508; and Brett (ed.), ii, 327

30 See his article 'The Untrodden Field in Politics' in The Nation, 7 Mar. 1908; and his two letters to Asquith, 14 Mar. and 29 Dec. 1908, CV/2, ii, 754–56, 862–64

31 CAB.37/95, PRO

32 See CV/2, ii, 896, letter to Lloyd George, 20 Jun. 1909. And for the same point, his memorandum on 'Unemployment Insurance and Labour Exchanges', 30 Nov. 1908, CAB.37/96

33 See his papers, 8 July 1908, CAB.37/94; 10 Oct. 1908, CAB.37/95; 2 and 30 Nov., and 11 Dec. 1908, CAB.37/96; 2, 26, and 27 Jan. 1909, and 1 Feb. 1909, CAB.37/97; 12 March 1909, CAB.37/98; May and 4 Aug. 1909, CAB.37/100

34 See Lucy Masterman, 1939 and her two articles, Nov.–Dec., 1964

35 See William Beveridge, 1953, 66–79

36 'Unemployment Insurance', 11 Dec. 1908, CAB. 37/96

37 See CV/2, ii, 886–887; also Webb, 430, 435

38 Churchill's letter to Llewellyn Smith, from which this is taken, is quoted by B. B. Gilbert, April 1966. It is interesting to note that for those men unfortunate enough not to be insured, or to have no savings to fall back on, the Webbs had devised a rigorous programme of 'vocational training centred on the labour exchange; compulsory attendance at labour depots; farm colonies for those unable to find work in cities; and finally, detention centres for those who remained stubbornly unemployable'. See B. B. Gilbert (1966), 260

39 Both schemes were based on the worker, the employer, and government contributing towards a general fund. In return for 6⅔d. per week (2½d. from the

worker and employer, and the remainder from the government), the unemployed would receive seven shillings per week for a maximum of fifteen weeks after a one-week waiting period. Health insurance was financed in much the same way. Details in B. B. Gilbert, 1966

40 For Lloyd George's success, see John Grigg, 1978, 315–51

41 See WSC, 2, 306; and Arthur C. Murray, 1945, 88–89
Other evidence strengthens Lloyd George's version. In Oct. 1908 Lloyd George, after his return from Germany and confiding his thoughts to Churchill, had spoken in public on the need to insure the unemployed, while at the same time he had suggested the outline of a scheme to his friend, Lord Riddell. Later, Sidney Buxton, who took over from Churchill at the Board of Trade, claimed in Parliament that the 'first idea' for unemployment insurance had come from Lloyd George. See B. B. Gilbert, 1966, 267 n: 75

42 See Beveridge, 87. The Churchill-Lloyd George unemployment scheme was never fully tested. As Britain moved into a period of revived economic activity before the outbreak of the First World War, the need for such benefits lessened. The aftermath of the war left Britain in a state of chronic economic crisis, too severe for Churchill's modest ideas to cope with. Another measure – a means-test unemployment benefit – was introduced.

43 It included, apart from labour exchanges and comprehensive social insurance schemes, also Old Age Pensions, a Workingman's Compensation Act, an Education Act (for the provision of school meals), Road Improvements and Development, a Coal Mines Regulation Act, the highly controversial Licensing Bill, and other measures. See Halevy, vol. 6; R. R. James, 1978, ch.8; B. B. Gilbert, 1966, and B. B. Gilbert, April 1966. Also Beveridge's memoirs and Webb, OP

44 Quotations in Blanche E. C. Dugdale, 1939, ii, 24–25; also Kenneth Young, 1963, 265

45 See K. Young, 1963, 263, 267; CSWC, 2, 1072–73; and Masterman, 1939, 114

46 For details of the budget, see J. Grigg, 1978, 176–77, Halevy, 291–96, and R. R. James, 1978, 241

47 For his attacks on the Lords, see CV/2, ii, 965–66, 968–71, 1030–33, 1037; also The People's Rights, 40–41, 57, 61, 63–64, 65, 68–69, 170, 173. For abolishing the House of Lords, see his memorandum of 15 Feb. 1910, CAB.37/102

48 Masterman, 1939, 173

49 The 'Constitutional Conference' met from June–July, and again in October and November, some twenty-one sessions in all. For details of the conference, see Halvey, 335–339; R. R. James, 1978, 249; and J. Grigg, 1978, 262–64

50 The memorandum, dated 17 Aug. 1910, is printed in J. Grigg, 1978, 362–68. It listed twelve 'arrears': housing; drink; insurance; unemployment; the poor law; national reorganization [that is, education]; national defence; local government; trade; land reform; imperial problems; and foreign policy.

51 Churchill to Lloyd George, 6 Oct. 1910, CV/2, ii, 1024–25

52 It has been suggested that Lloyd George floated the proposal with the intention of displacing Asquith, which might explain Asquith's neutral attitude. See S. Koss, 1985, 123, and Jenkins, 240–42

53 See A. Murray, 40, 47; Masterman 1938, 154; and also Hobhouse Diaries for this period.

54 See R. Churchill and H. Gernsheim, nos. 50, 51. This photograph was later released as a postcard entitled 'The Battle of Stepney', while the siege was filmed for a contemporary cinema newsreel. Audiences received the spectacle of Churchill directing operations with 'unanimous boos' and shouts of '"shoot him"'. See WSC, 2, 409

55 Charles Scott recorded that Churchill had expressed regret at having left the

Conservatives as he would now be in the running for the leadership of the Party. Naturally, this only reinforced fears that he was considering defecting from the Liberals. See *Scott Diaries*, 63–64, 72–73. See also Birkenhead's opinion on the same subject, 354, n.33

56 See Masterman, 1938, 154–55; Webb OP

57 See his papers on 'Prison Reform', 25 Oct. 1910, CAB.37/103; 'Trade Unions', 27 Mar. 1911, CAB.37/106; 'Child Employment', 1 June 1911, and 'Intimidation during Trade Disputes', 8 Aug. 1911, CAB.37/107

58 See *CSWC*, 2, 1599–1603, 1614–21; Paul Addison in J. M. Winter (ed.), 1983; Nevil Macready, 1924, i, 137–55; Emrys Hughes, 205–06; Kenneth Morgan, 1975

59 See *WSC*, 2, 381–83

60 See *CSWC*, 2, 1870–76; Hughes, 205–06; David Marquand, 1977, 144–45; *Amery Diaries*, 595; *Webb Diaries*, 165

61 See Halevy, 583

62 See Koss, 1985, 132; Jenkins, 2661

63 See CV/2, i, 105–111; CV/2, ii, 754–56, 862–64; also Hyam, 1969, 170–71; and *WSC*, 2, 304–05

64 For the original Tory Democracy, see CV1, ii, 751; for 'Development Grants . . .', CV/2, ii, 895. See also Henry Pelling, 1974 (1977 ed.), 128–29,

65 See Marquand, 79

Chapter 6. 'The Biggest Thing that has ever come my Way'

1 Violet Bonham-Carter, 246–50; Haldane, 1924, 228–29; *Whitehall Diary*, i, 239; and Churchill, 1938, i, 49–50

2 For his remarks to Asquith, CV/3, i, 178. And A. G. Gardiner, 1914, 229. See R. Hyam, 1969, on his military way of thinking.

3 'Webb, OP, 269. For *Times*' comment see Amery, i, 337

4 See CAB.37/93. He followed it up with two more papers putting the case against increased military expenditure.

5 Reginald Baliol Brett, second Viscount Esher. Esher moved ubiquitously behind the scenes in late Victorian, Edwardian England. Admitted to Queen Victoria's private circle and the confidant of her heirs, he was a strong advocate of army reform. In 1904, although holding no official position, he joined the Committee of Imperial Defence and came out strongly in favour of Haldane's proposals.

6 See Brett, 11, 324–25. Also S. Koss, 1969, 56–58. And Haldane, 1929, 217

7 The famous 'all-big-gun' battleship. The first of its class, HMS *Dreadnought*, was launched in Feb. 1906. She carried ten 12-inch guns and had a speed of 21 knots. Able to outrange and outpace any other vessel, she represented a revolution in naval design. The appearance of the *Dreadnought* led to a full-scale naval race, allowing rival fleets to begin the construction of capital ships on almost equal terms. When, in July 1907, the Germans began work on the *Nassau* class, their answer to the *Dreadnought*, the worst British fears were confirmed.

8 See *CSWC*, 1, 990; CV/2, ii, 928; and *WSC*, 2, 515

9 For the 1908–09 naval scare, see Arthur Marder, 1961–70, i, 159–71

10 See *CSWC*, 1, 671, and 11, 1284, 1286–89; 1, 171–72, 375; 11, 1288–89; and 111, 2257. And CV/2, iii, 1512

11 See CV/2, i, 582, and CV/2, ii, 907, 910–12

12 In 1904 the British had agreed to establish the French in such a position, in much the same way as they had consolidated themselves in Egypt with French consent. See B. B. Gilbert 1985

13 See Asquith to King, 4 Jul. 1911, CAB.41/33/20; For Lloyd George's Mansion House speech, T. Boyle, 1980, and J. Grigg, 1978, 309. For background to Agadir crisis, see Z. Steiner, 1977

14 See CV/2, ii, 1109, and iii, 1989; and Viscount Grey, i, 238
15 Fitzroy, ii, 462
16 The paper is in the CID files, CAB.38/19; for Wilson's opinion, see *Wilson Diaries*, i, 99.
17 See Churchill to Grey, 30 Aug. 1911, CV/2, ii, 1116–17, for the triple alliance proposal. Also K. M. Wilson, 1977, and *Wilson Diaries*, i, 98–103, for the Churchill-Wilson contacts.
18 Minutes in CAB.38/19
19 Based on minutes of 114th CID meeting, 23 Aug. 1911, in CAB.38/19; for Churchill's account see WC, i, 38–42. For army as 'projectile' of navy, see Ruddock F. MacKay, 1973, 369. For Churchill's opinion of Wilson and Admiralty, CV/2, ii, 1121, 1124, and S. Roskill, 1970, i, 102; for Asquith's views, Jenkins, 268, and Koss, 1985, 146. See also Marder, 1961–70, i, 392–93; Roskill, 1970, i, 102; and M. Hankey, 1961, i, 78–82. Reactions to Churchill's appointment, CV/2, ii, 1303, and *WSC*, 2, 538–39
20 Text of letter in CV/2, ii, 129
21 See CV/2, ii, 1109, 1118–19; B. B. Gilbert, 1985; and J. Grigg, 1978
22 Asquith may have wished to permanently detach Churchill – 'and perhaps Lloyd George as well' – from 'the "economist" wing' of the party, in order to weld the government (see Jenkins, 269). Lloyd George, however, remained 'undetached'; even though Churchill behaved roughly in accordance with Asquith's desire. For Lloyd George's comment, see *Riddell Diaries*, 25
23 WC, i, 51
24 See in detail in Marder, 1961–70, i, 373–77, 403; Nicholas J. D'Ombrain, (1970); and Tuvia ben Moshe, 1989
25 See Blunt, 698, 702–03; CV/2, ii, 1132–34; and Brett, ii, 451–52
26 R. R. James, 1976, 101
27 Robert Blake, 1955, 95, 234
28 R. R. James, 1976, 83
29 Quoted in Blake, 1955, 130; Churchill's reaction in CV/2, iii, 1393–1400, and *WSC*, 2, 469
30 For background to Belfast incident, see CV/2, ii, 1380–92. Also *Riddell Diaries*, 35; Fitzroy, ii, 475–76, for Morley's attitude; and Foster, 256, for Lord Randolph's Belfast speech.
31 For descriptions of Belfast visit, see *WSC*, 2, 466–68; Violet Bonham-Carter, 297–98; and Henry W. Nevison, 280–81. His speech is in *CSWC*, 11, 1899–1909.
32 For Churchill's Dundee speech, *CSWC*, 11, 2021–28. See also *Bridgeman Diaries*, 62; Violet Bonham-Carter, 300–01; Charles Petrie, 1939, i, 323; *WSC*, 2, 472–73.
33 Simon's letter to Asquith, CV/2, iii, 1859; and Churchill's remark to Lloyd George, *Riddell Diaries*, 194. See the *Scott Diaries*, 72–81, and *Riddell Diaries*, 189–202, for general background questions.
34 See *Scott Diaries*, 76, and *Riddell Diaries*, 198
35 For Churchill's talks with Bonar Law, F. E. Smith, and Austen Chamberlain, see CV/2, iii, 1399–1401; Blake, 1955, 155–57; Birkenhead, 1965, 225–30; Charles Petrie, 1939, i, 347–49. The government had been severely embarrassed when the *Daily News* published in advance details of the plan. At Asquith's request, ministers denied in writing their responsibility for the leak. The source was never discovered, but Lloyd George, and apparently Asquith, suspected Churchill.
36 WC, i, 142; and *Scott Diaries*, 78
37 Bradford speech in *CSWC*, 111, 2222–32
38 For Curragh incident: James Fergusson, n.d., and A. P. Ryan, 1956
39 CV/2, iii, 1414–15
40 See CV/2, iii, 1411–13. Churchill's undated account of these talks must have

been written towards the end of the month as the text corresponds closely with Churchill's speech to the Commons on 30 March, in *CSWC*, 111, 2275–91. Seely's version of the talks in Jenkins, 342–43; see also Blake, 1955, 190, quoting from War Office orders.

41 *Asquith Letters*, 60
42 See *Wilson Diaries*, i, 141–45; *CSWC*, 111, 2274; Blake, 1955, 189, and *Asquith Letters*, 59
43 Quoted in Koss, 1969, 110
44 *CSWC*, 111, 2267–91
45 Blake, 1955, 204
46 *CSWC*, 111, 2292–2305
47 CV/2, iii, 1418–19

Chapter 7. A Water Creature

1 Lloyd George to Churchill, *Riddell Diaries*, 78: 'You have become a water creature . . .'
2 *WC*, i, 91
3 See Violet Bonham-Carter, 274ff.
4 For Churchill's differences with the admirals, see CV/2, iii, 1653–56; and for Churchill-Bridgeman affair, 'Correspondence regarding Retirement of Sir Francis Bridgeman', 30 December 1912, CAB. 37/113, and CV/2, iii, 1675–93; also Marder, 1961–70, i, 258–59
5 See Marder, 1961–70, 254–55, 260–61; S. Roskill, 1977, 21; Dudley de Chair, 149–52; Violet Bonham-Carter, 251
6 See CV/2, iii, 1796–98
7 See Marder, 1961–70, 255; Roskill, 1977, i, 104; and Churchill's confession in a diary note by Hankey, 22 Jul. 1917, *ibid.*, 414
8 See Ruddock F. MacKay, 1973, 423ff; also Marder, 1961–70, 83–88, 205–07, 264; and Chalmers, 1951, 179
9 CV/2, ii, 957–58
10 These suggestions to Churchill were written between Oct.–Dec. 1911, see CV/2, ii, 1298–1303, 1316–21, 1323–33, 1341–44, 1347–53, 1364–67
11 CV/2, iii, 1530. See, 'Naval War Staff', 1 Jan. 1912, CAB.37/109, and CV/2, ii, 1303–1312, 1321–23; 'Pay in Navy', 17 and 21 Oct. and 11 Nov. 1912, CAB.37/112, 'Widows' Pensions, 15 Sep. 1914, CAB.37/121, and CV/2, iii, 1632–33, 1967, 1971–73; 'Oil Supply for His Majesty's Ships', 16 Jun. 1913, CAB.37/115; 'Arrangement with Anglo-Persian for Supply of Oil', 4 Jul. 1913, CAB.37/116; 'Anglo-Persian Oil Co.', 10 Mar. 1914, and 'Agreement', 11 May 1914, CAB.37/119; 'Oil Supplies', 9 Jun. 1914, CAB.37/120, and CV/2, iii, 1926–27, 1932–65, and *CSWC*, 11, 2125–47, and 111. *WC*, i, 100–105, 136–37; Marder, 1961–70; 268–71, 439–441; and Marian Jack, 1968
12 Marian Jack, 1968; Also *PD*, Commons, v. L1X, 10 March 1914.
13 See 'The Mediterranean Fleet', 15 Mar. 1911, CAB. 37/105, and 'Details of the New German Naval Law', 15 Feb. 1912, CAB. 37/109
14 Churchill proposed a naval holiday on three separate occasions, in March 1912 and in March and October 1913, see *CSWC*, 11, 1924–25, 2071–73, 2174–76. For Churchill's colonial concessions policy, *WC*, i, 71
15 See Churchill's papers of 15, 22, 24, 25, 26 June, and 2, 6 20 Jul. 1912 in CAB. 37/111, some of which are printed in CV/2, iii, 1564–79, 1585–91; also Marder 1961–70, 287–311; and Brett, iii, 100–05; and for Churchill's evaluation of the accords, CV/2, iii, 1639.
16 In April 1912, Lloyd George, together with, Rufus Isaacs, the Attorney General, had purchased shares at preferential rates in the American Marconi Company. The deal had been negotiated through Isaacs's brother, managing director of

the British Marconi Company and a director of the American firm. Since both companies were closely linked and the British company's shares had recently boomed, charges of corruption, touched by anti-semitism (directed against the three Jews involved, the Isaacs brothers and Herbert Samuel, the Postmaster-General, who had accepted the tender of British Marconi) were widespread. To still these suspicions Lloyd George and Isaacs instituted a libel suit against a French newspaper. They disingenuously denied transactions in shares of 'the Marconi Company' (a term intended to refer only to the British firm, but generally assumed to cover the American company as well). A select committee of the House of Commons investigated the charges. It cleared the ministers, but the scandal stained Lloyd George's reputation.

17 See *Riddell Diaries*, 190–91, 196, for his position in Cabinet; 'German Naval Law and Comparisons with Strength of Royal Navy', 10 Jan. 1914, CAB.37/117, for his resignation comment.

18 From Dec. 1913 to Feb. 1914, Churchill submitted eleven papers relating to the naval estimates debate, see CAB.37/117, 119; also CV/2, iii, 1818–73. For 'sprawling' Germany, *Riddell Diaries*, 51

19 For the estimates dispute see also, Asquith's letters to King, 20 Dec. 1913, CAB.41/34/39; 29 Jan. 1914, CAB.41/35/1; 11 Feb. 1914, CAB.41/35/3. Also *Riddell Diaries*, 201–02; and Violet Bonham-Carter, 15

20 *Riddell Diaries*, 51

21 See 'Ariel Navigation', 9 June 1913, CAB.87/115

22 For the navy's shortcomings, see Marder, 1961–70, i, chs. X11, X111, 435–36; also Roskill 1977, 24.

23 Marder, 1961–70, i, 435

24 For reaction to assassination, WC, i, 155, and CV/2, iii, 1987–88; and attitude towards Balkans, CV/2, iii, 1991, and Masterman, 1939, 245

25 See WSC, 11, 613–25. The decade before the outbreak of war in 1914 saw the publication of many similar works of fantasy, the most notable being, William Le Queux, *The Invasion of 1910*, and P. G. Wodehouse, *The Swoop, or How Clarence Saved England: a Tale of the Great Invasion* (1909).

26 His letter to Clementine in CV/2, iii, 1989–90; and to King, also regarding Jellicoe, *ibid.*, 1992, 1994. For postponment of dispersal of the Fleet, Asquith to King, 28 Jul. 1914, CAB.41/35/21, Marder, 1961–70, 433, and WC, i, 159–60, where the impression is given that the initiative was Churchill's. His crash programme is in WC, i, 156–57. For ordering the Fleet to its battle stations, WC, i, 171–72, and CV/2, iii, 1992

27 For Cabinet meetings, see Asquith's letters to King in CAB.41/35/20–24; also, *Asquith Letters*, 122–52

28 Quoted in Zara Steiner, 1969, 156, 161

29 Quoted in K. M. Wilson, 1975. See also Grey, i, 312–13; ii, 2–3. 36–39; and G. M. Trevelyan, 253–54

30 See WC, i, 163–64. Also *Asquith Letters*, 129, 140; and Morley, 24. One reference questions Churchill's bellicose line. Masterman (1939, 265) records Grey as saying: 'We can't desert France,' and Churchill as replying: 'I don't see why we need come in if they only go a little way into Belgium.' But apart from this aberration, Churchill took a consistent line in favour of intervention.

31 See Cameron Hazelhurst, 1971, 55–57, 85

32 For Churchill's assessment of balance of forces in Cabinet, WC, i, 161; it contradicted that of Morley's. For strength of Liberal peace-party see Morley, x, 5. Also *Asquith Letters*, 146; and Koss, 1985

33 See Violet Bonham-Carter, 34, 288. Churchill's contacts with Smith and the attitude to coalition, see CV/2, iii, 1990; *Asquith Letters*, 147; Blake 1955, 220–22; K. M. Wilson July 1975; and Morley.

34 See CAB. 41/35/23–24, for Asquith's letters to King; *Asquith Letters*, 145–51; CV/2, iii, 1996–99, and CV/3, i, 51; *Riddell War Diary*, 31; *Scott Diaries*, 91; *Hobhouse Diaries*, 179; Morley; Violet Bonham-Carter, 330; G. M. Trevelyan, 265; Countess Lloyd George, i, 635; *Sanders Diaries*, 79–80; and Frances (Stevenson), Countess Lloyd George 1967, 73–74. Also K. M. Wilson, July 1975; Trevor Wilson, 1979; and B. B. Gilbert, 1985. For general studies see Zara Steiner 1977, chs 9–10, and Hazlehurst, 1971, part 1

35 These exchanges took the form of notes passed across the Cabinet table on 1 Aug., see CV/2, iii, 1996–97

36 *Sanders Diaries*, 80

Chapter 8. 'God Bless the Dardanelles'

1 *WC*, i, 208–09

2 See Earl of Oxford and Asquith, 1928, i, 21, 25; 314; and CV3/i, 400

3 See CV/2, iii, 1990, 1997, for hostilities against Germany, and a cheap naval war; CV/3, i, 21, for war lasting a year

4 *WC*, ii, 1015

5 Quoted in William James, 1956, 144

6 For his use of these definitions, see memorandum of 13 Aug. 1911 in CAB.38/19; and for his general strategic principles, *WC*, i, 489. See also Tuvia Ben Moshe, 1992 ch. 2,

7 Churchill's Baltic strategy, CV/3, i, 326; and for its impracticability, Tuvia ben Moshe, 1992, 10, 25

8 See *WC*, i, 488

9 CV/3, i, 371

10 Marder, 1961–70 ii, 53

11 For details of these incidents, see Marder, 1961–70, ii, chs I–VIII, passim; S. Roskill, 1977, 26–40; Prior, 1–25; D. Brownrigg, 1920, 32–33; and *WC*, i, 575. The journal in question was *Land and Water*, quoted in Marder, 1961–70, ii, 130. From Nov. 1914 the Admiralty had a tremendous advantage. At the beginning of the war, Churchill, on the advice of Vice-Admiral Henry Francis Oliver had set up a special department – Room 40 – to intercept and decode enemy signals, and after the Russians captured a document containing the secret German naval ciphers Room 40 was able to crack the German codes. This gave the Admiralty advance notice of German naval sweeps into the North Sea – the 'tip-and-run' raids and the Dogger Bank action, and, later, the battle of Jutland – that the navy was unable to exploit to the full. Churchill gave every encouragement to the work of Room 40. Its findings were top secret, known only to a highly restricted group at the Admiralty, and Asquith, who sometimes brought Grey into his confidence but regularly passed the information on to Venetia Stanley. See William James, 1956, 128–29; *Asquith Letters*, passim; *WSC*, 111, 179

12 *Asquith Letters*, 253

13 It was only in 1914 that the Admiralty was able, for the first time, to telegraph direct to its naval squadrons dispersed worldwide, thereby exercising a degree of control over naval operations previously unknown. This was a tool of tremendous potential, if used correctly. But it took some time before the Admiralty arrived at the degree of precision and clarity of expression in its signalling to enable the Fleet to benefit from this technical advance. See Robin Prior, 1983, 1

14 For inadequacies of War Staff, see Marder, 1961–70, ii, 37–40, and Roskill, 1977, 32–34. Richmond quoted by Marder, *loc. cit.*, ii, 50. For Birkenhead, see Birkenhead, 1924, 118. For being *persona non grata* and 'hypnotizing' Admirals, Marder *loc. cit.* ii, 8. His 'rats from a hole' speech in *CSWC*, 3,

2337: for King's comment, CV/3, i, 128; and the Admirals' reaction, Marder *loc. cit.*, ii, 48.

15 For details of 'Circus', see CV/3, i, 86, 88, 97, 117, 121, 126–27; *WSC*, iii, 65–75; and *Asquith Letters*, 227–28, 230, 247, 253

16 See Churchill's memorandum of 7 Sept. 1914, CV/3, i, 97–99; and Asquith to King, 8 Sept. 1914, in CAB. 41/35/41. Also Hankey, 1961, i, 200.

17 See Grey, 1925, ii, 78–80

18 Ransom price in Marder, 1961–70, ii, 83–84. For contemporary journalist's impression, Violet Bonham-Carter, 356. Churchill's vow to defend Antwerp, *Riddell War Diaries*, 51–52. Churchill's letter of resignation and cabinet's reaction, CV/3, i, 163; *Asquith Letters*, 262–63; and *Riddell War Diaries*, 34; Asquith's reaction in *Asquith Letters*, 262–63, 275–76. For Clementine's reaction, see Soames, 109–10, 113. Lloyd George's opinion in *Scott Diaries*, 112. And for press reports, *WSC*, iii, 125–29

19 For his defenders see CV/3, i, 178, 191–92; for Asquith's remark, *Asquith Letters*, 275. For his digging in, his two articles in *Sunday Pictorial*, 19 and 26 Nov. 1916, in Wolff, i, 172–82; and WC, i, 280–323. His criticism of Kitchener in *Stevenson Diary*, 5

20 W. Churchill, *Thoughts and Adventures*, 16–17

21 See *Asquith Letters*, 266

22 Margot Asquith's comments in CV/3, i, 284; Fisher's, CV/3, ii, 1544; and Churchill's confession to Hamilton, CV/3, ii, 1081

23 *Riddell War Diaries*, 82–83

24 See *MEL*, 161, and *Savrola*, 220–25, 239–40

25 The paper is in CAB.38/12, or CAB.4/2/92B

26 *Riddell War Diaries*, 80

27 See 'The Mediterranean Fleet', 15 Mar. 1911, CAB.37/105; and Asquith's comment made at CID meeting of 23 Aug. 1911, CAB.38/19. From 1–3 Sep., Maj. General Callwell (War Office), Captain Herbert Richmond (Admiralty), and other senior officers, discussed these issues, along with Churchill and Prince Louis of Battenberg. See CV/3, i, 61–62, 91–92

28 Marder, 1961–70, ii, 200

29 For Lloyd George this was, apparently, the last act that led him to the conclusion that Churchill was partly responsible for bringing Turkey into the war, the first act being Churchill's seizure of two Turkish battleships under construction in British shipyards on the outbreak of war. (See *Scott Diaries*, 112). This accusation was entirely without foundation. The Turks, in early August, had concluded a military alliance with Germany.

30 CV/3, i, 236, 243

31 See *Asquith Letters*, 171, and CV/3, i, 278. Also T. Ben Moshe, 1992

32 These memoranda, Hankey's of 28 Dec. 1914, and Lloyd George's of 31 Dec. 1914, are printed in CV/3, i, 337–43, 350–56

33 Churchill's remarks, *ibid.*, 344, 346

34 See CV/3, i, 361, 367–68; 380–81

35 Churchill claimed, (*WC*, i, 531–33, and is followed by *WSC*, iii, 237–38), that the 'high authorities' he had in mind were Sir Henry Jackson and Admiral Henry Oliver, both of whom conveyed verbally their feelings to him, adding that at the War Council meeting of 5 Jan. 'Everyone seemed alive to all its advantages'. Jackson was highly sceptical; Oliver's later supported the plan, though at the time – apart from Churchill's evidence – his view remains obscure.

36 Minutes of the meeting in CV/3, i, 407–11

37 *WC*, i, 363

38 Quoted in Marder, 1961–70, ii, 267

39 *Asquith Letters*, 387

40 For Churchill's preoccupation with Baltic, CV/3, i, 326, 465, 737; for Fisher's

feelings, CV/3, i, 436, 452–54, 770; and Churchill's unwillingness to circulate his memorandum, CV/3, i, 458. Also Brett, iii, 212, for Churchill's different schemes.

41 CV/3, i, 604–05, 698–99
42 Jackson's memoranda, and others by Carden and Oliver, in CV/3, i, 376–77, 405–06, 419–21, 489–90, 506–12; Richmond quoted by Marder, ii, 212; also Marder, ii, 227, for admirals' view that the success of the operation would depend on sufficient ammunition, effective mine-sweeping, good weather, bad Turkish morale, and efficient reconnaissance. For Hankey's and Asquith's opinions, CV/3, i, 500, and Asquith Letters, 429
43 Churchill's call to Kitchener, CV/3, i, 518–19
44 Brett, iii, 217
45 From Dardenelles Commission Report, quoted by R. R. James, 1970, 71
46 From meeting of War Council, 28 Jan. 1915, in CV/3, i, 463–70
47 For Asquith's comment, see Asquith Letters, 474. Kitchener's remark quoted from French's diary, 23 Mar. 1915, in Gerald French, 1931, 288. For army's pessimistic estimation of navy's ability, CV/3, i, 637, 643
48 See CV/3, i, 367, 687
49 For Carden's reservations, see CV/3, i, 661–62, 676–77, 693, 695; and for Jackson's warning, ibid., 677. Also Marder, 1961–70, ii, 214–18 And see above, n42
50 See CV/3, i, 560, 568, 629, 695. For Asquith on Hamilton, see Asquith Letters, 257. And Roskill, 1970–04, i, 168
51 For de Robeck's change of heart and Churchill's unsent despatch, see CV/3, i, 723–26; and for the Churchill-Fisher clash, ibid., 724–26, 728–30
52 See CV/3, ii, 1003–04, 1242, 1320, 1373, 1553–57, and WC, ii, 983, quoted in Prior, 211. For his 'legitimate war gamble' and justification of the operation, CV/3, ii, 1553–57, CSWC, iii, 2378–84, 2390, 2650–51, 3086; Wolff (ed.), i, 277–82, 334–37, iii, 191–99; and Thoughts and Adventures, 126
53 See CV/3, i, 808–09; Marder 1969–70, ii, 259; and Duff Cooper, i, 252
54 Cd. 8490
55 CV/3, i, 555–61, 1213–14, War Council meetings of 24 Feb. and 11 Oct. 1915; Riddell War Diaries, 86
56 Riddell War Diaries, 80, 80–82. The conversations took place on 22 and 29 Apr. 1915
57 Churchill's attempts to conscript another 20,000 men for the campaign, CV/3, i, 816–17, 830; and his remark to Clementine, ibid., ii, 845–46. Between 25 April and early May, Churchill was receiving information from, among others, Hamilton, Josiah Wedgwood, de Robeck, and his brother Jack, who was serving on Hamilton's staff and who had watched the landings from the bridge of the Queen Elizabeth. No doubt these reports, some of which were wildly optimistic, took some time to arrive in London. It was only by 5 May that Jack Churchill wrote that the situation 'gives cause for great anxiety'. See CV/3, i, 816–29, 834–35; and ii, 842–45
58 French's comments about his health on 9 April 1915, CV/3, 785. For his spat with Lloyd George, Stevenson Diary, 41–42, and CV/3, 769–70, 776; and for Lloyd George's accusation over Turkey, CV/3, ii, 849. Asquith's comments in Asquith Letters, 449–50, and WSC, iii, 329. And for his dispute with Marsh, WSC, iii, 401
59 See Soames, 118, 120

Chapter 9. Eclipse

1 Passage on the May 1915 crisis is based, unless stated otherwise, on the following: CV/3, i, 855–56, 858, 874–83; CV/3, ii, 887, 891–92, 898–99,

901–02, 906–07, 914–14, 921, 925–27, 932, 1082, 1350–51, 1384, 1530–31; WSC, iii, 473

Also: Moran, 1966, 782; Riddell War Diaries, 81, 87, 89–90, 93–94, 97; Stevenson Diary, 42–43, 44–45, 52–53; Asquith Letters, 423, 508–09, 517–19, 523; Hobhouse Diaries, 231, 237–38, 240–41; Bertie Diary, i, 162–63; Nicolson Diaries, i, 308; S. Koss, 1969, 184–218; C. Hazlehurst, 1971, in particular, Part 111; Hankey, 1961, i, 314–19; Violet Bonham-Carter, 427; Soames, 123, 126; Fitzroy, ii, 594; A. J. P. Taylor, 1965, 30; Marder, 1961–70, ii, 277–93; Blake, 1955, 234–49. And, S. Koss, 1968; and Martin Pugh, 1974

2 See Asquith Letters, 495, 508, 523

3 Stevenson Diary, 44–45

4 Fitzroy, ii, 594; Savrola, 203

5 In the 1920s he was again involved in a similar incident when rumours circulated that he was 'plotting' against Baldwin. These too were eventually discounted. See CV/5 i, 161 and n.1, 1451

6 For Asquith, the most distressing episode was the sacrifice of Haldane, victim of a shameful public campaign that identified him as a pro-German. Asquith let him go to preserve the coalition. As it was, he retained for the Liberals the key posts: the Premiership, the Foreign and Home Offices, and the Chancellor of the Exchequer: the Admiralty went to Balfour, while Bonar Law, modestly, took the Colonial Office.

7 Quoted in Pugh, 1974. For further evidence of Liberal backbench pressure to oust Churchill, see CV/3, ii, 919

8 See CV/4, iii, 1752, for his blaming Asquith. All these military commands and political posts had been in the offing during 1915–16, CV/3, ii, 1151–55, 1242. For his conviction that the Dardanelles could and should have been forced, CV/3, ii, 903, and CV/4, i, 5

9 CV/3, ii, 1221

10 CV/3, ii, 1373, for his comment to Jack; and WC, ii, 983, for his 'surprise attack' on the Dardanelles in 1926. For some examples of his justification of the operation, see CV/3, ii, 1003–04, 1242, 1320, 1373, 1553–57; CV/4, i, 53–55, 329–30; CSWC, 111, 2378–84, 2390, 2650–51, 3086; Wolff (ed.), i, 277–82, 334–37, iii, 90–92, 191–99; and Thoughts and Adventures, 126. Balfour's quip in Blanche E. C. Dugdale, Arthur James Balfour, 1939, ii, 247

11 'Painting as a Pastime', in Thoughts and Adventures, 307; to Clementine, CV/3, ii, 1350

12 For Clementine's state after Churchill's departure from the Admiralty, Soames, 121–24. Marlborough's depressive moods in W. Churchill, Marlborough, i, 474, and ii, 84, 201, 696–97; Lord Randolph's rapid changes of mood in Foster, passim. For the Marlboroughs' melancholia, see Rowse. And for the psychological background to Churchill's depression, see Moran, 203, and Anthony Storr, 205–46.

13 Quotations from Moran, 141, 187, 441

14 Of his other main discipline, writing was of a quite different order. Also, he wrote as the undisputed chief of a team. Of course, the final word was his. But he was surrounded by batteries of research assistants and secretaries waiting on his every command. He could dominate, bully, cajole, persuade, placate, and soothe others into fulfilling his wishes. Not so with painting.

15 See 'Painting as a Pastime', 308–12

16 Bonham-Carter, 492–93; 'Painting as a Pastime', 308; and Charles Eade (ed.), 1953, 416

17 Bonham-Carter, 494; 'Painting as a Pastime', 318–19. Also Moran, 325

18 Eade (ed.), 421; and Lavery, 177

19 See CV/3, ii, 1171, 1180, 1249–50

20 CV/3, ii, 1405

21 See Capt. 'X' (Andrew Dewar Gibb), 1924, and *Sunday Post*, 25 Feb 1990, some reminiscences of John McGuire, who served with Churchill in France. I am most grateful to Dr Paul Addison for bringing this article to my attention. Also CV/3, ii 1276, 1311, 1327, 1332, 1336, 1339, 1347, 1358, 1376, 1400, 1420, 1430

22 Described in *Thoughts and Adventures*, 99–120

23 From Capt. 'X', 1924, and McGuire, 1990; also CV/3, ii, 1374, 1375, 1394

24 See *WSC*, iii, 563, and CV/3, ii, 1251–53, for his East African command; for his division and brigade ambitions, CV/3, ii, 1276, 1279, 1298, 1311, 1312, 1314, 1317, 1415; and for blaming Asquith, CV/3, ii, 1309

25 CV/3, ii, 1279, 1310, 1409, 1453

26 For these quotations, see CV/3, ii, 1366, 1369, 1397, 1482 and n1, and *WSC*, iii, 623. Also Capt. 'X', 1924.

27 See CHAR 1/118, pt 1; *Scott Diaries*, 186–92; *Riddell Diaries*, 163; Violet Bonham-Carter, 472–82; CV/3, ii, 1439–45. Churchill's speech in *CSWC*, iii, 2405–2413

28 See, for example, R. R. James, 1964–65, and Woodrow Wyatt, 1954

29 See CV/3, ii, 1517–18, 1519; *Scott Diaries*, 234–35; and *Bridgeman Diaries*, 110

30 See Beaverbrook, 1928–32, ii, 286–91. For Lloyd George and Fisher remarks, CV/4, i, 36, 41. Also *Scott Diaries*, 268, 285

31 See *WC*, ii, 1141–44. For the shifts in his 'attrition' policy, CV/3, ii, 979, and CV/4, i, 330–31

32 For quotations, see CV/4, i, 64, 77–99, 101, 108; Esher, iv, 121; and *WC*, ii, 1142–44. The crisis resulting from Churchill's appointment, *Sanders Diaries*, 88; Frank Owen, 1954, 412–16; and Blake, 1955, 360–61. Lloyd George's remarks in his *War Memoirs*, i, 637–38

33 See CV/3, ii, 1290–91, 1329

Chapter 10. Fighting Bolshevism

1 See Churchill's high praise of Lloyd George, Wolff, iii, 92–96.

2 See *WC*, ii, 1170–77

3 See CV/4, i, 133, 134, 137, 139–40, 143

4 *WSC*, iv, 79, 113, 131

5 Churchill's proposal to disband the War Cabinet see CV/4, i, 302–03, 309–10, 314–16

6 See *Thoughts and Adventures*, 243–52

7 For Churchill's ideas about the tank in general, see CV/3, i, 552–54, 377–78, ii, 1185, 1187, 1303–08, 1422–23; CV/4, i, 27, 33, 159; *WSC*, iii, 534–48. Prior, 1983, 231–48, examines these questions in convincing detail.

8 Churchill's production memoranda are printed in *WC*, ii, 1179–84, 1189–98, 1251–56, 1265–74. Also Prior, 246–48

9 For his tempting and conscripting the workers, Christopher Addison, 1934, ii, 466–67, and CV/4, i, 354–62, 402–03. Lloyd George's praise in his *War Memoirs*, i, 638, ii, 1877; and in same connection, Brian Bond, 1980, 5

10 See CV/4, i, 408–11

11 In fact, the Sinn Fein party had won 73 seats, but as half of their members were in prison and the remainder refused to participate in the affairs of an English Parliament, Westminster was abandoned to Labour.

12 *Amery Diaries*, i, 248; Wilson's remark in Richard Meinertzhagen, 1959, 96

13 See Winston S. Churchill, *The Aftermath*, 60–64; CV/4, i, 458–59, 462–67, 610, 648; Bond, 1980, 20–22

14 See Cabinet sessions of 5 and 15 Aug. 1919, CAB.23/15. Also, S. Roskill March, 1972, and 1970–4, ii, 107, 112; and Bond, 1980, 24–26 1970–4

15 For the restructuring of the army, see CV/4, i, 458–59, 463–67, 459–60; CSWC, iii, 2674–92, 2897–2904; and Bond, 1980, 20–22. For the Royal Air Force, Cmd. 467, for Trenchard's programme, and CSWC, iii, 2886–97, for Churchill's defence of it. Also, Charles Webster and Noble Frankland, 1961, i, 52–53; and H. Montgomery Hyde, 1976, 72–75. And CV/4, 517–18, 563–65, 682–84; CSWC, iii, 2666–70

16 See his speeches at Dundee and Newcastle, Nov.-Dec. 1918. CSWC, iii, 2642–47; and Aftermath, 47

17 CV/4, i, 557 (minutes of War Cab., 28/2/19); and Aftermath, 47–49

18 CV/1, ii, 1162

19 See CSWC, iii, 2773, and his appearance before the Supreme Council in Paris, 15 Feb. 1919, FRUS, iv, 15

20 Aldwych Club speech quoted in Donald Graeme Boadle, 1973, 34–35; his remark on reparations, CV/4, iii, 1899

21 CV/4, ii, 1053–55; and Whitehall Diaries, 116–17

22 See CV/4, i, 613, ii, 1131; WSC, iv, 278; Aftermath, 267; CSWC, iii, 2935–36; Boadle, 1973, 122, 129, 135

23 CV/4, ii, 1191

24 Churchill's comment to Council of Ten, FRUS, iv, 15; also Hankey, 1963, 69–71

25 WSC, iv, 349

26 Churchill's remarks in CV/4, i, 326, 333. Also Richard H. Ullman 1968, ii, 6–7

27 Quoted in Ullman, loc. cit., 6

28 CV/4, ii, 919; WC, ii, 1119–20; and Aftermath, 71

29 For Churchill's object, Aftermath, 237; and his policy of large-scale intervention, Cabinet minutes, 23 Dec. 1918, CAB.23/42, CV/4, i, 521, and Ullman, 1968, 90

30 For his disaffected hostile bloc, CAB. 25/15, 15 Feb. 1919. The incident in Paris, 14, 15, 17 Feb. 1919, is described in Hankey, 1963, 67–73, and Roskill, 1970–4 ii, 62. Churchill's version, CV/4, 1, 555–56

31 International consequences quoted in Ullman, 1968, 119; for declaring war, CV/4, i, 525, ii, 729

32 CV/4, i, 532, 549

33 Quoted in Boadle, 1973, 77

34 For instances of his support of the White Russian generals, CV/4, i, 681–82, 685–86. ii, 757–64, 816–18, 1004, 1131, 1146; on Boris Savinkov, CV/4, ii, 973, and Churchill's laudatory essay in Great Contemporaries, 93–101. On his going to Russia as Denikin's adviser, CV/4, ii, 921

35 His unrepentance in Ulmann, 1968, 333; also his speech to the Oxford Union, WSC, iv, 440

36 CV/4, ii, 1005, iii, 1814, 1942; CV/4, iii, 1874–75, 1884–85; and for not sending famine relief, CV/4, iii, 1794

37 CV/4, i, 549

38 From his article, 'The Poison Peril from the East', Evening News, 28 July 1920, in Wolff, i, 234–37. In 1929, he repeated this passage in Aftermath, 263

39 These quotations are taken from CSWC, iii, 2771, 2822, 2920, 2918, 3025; Wolff (ed.) i, 205, 234–38, ii, 58–62, 79–84, 156–60; PD Commons, 6 Nov. 1919; CV/4, i, 479, 609. Balfour's comment, CV/4, ii, 949. Churchill did not mellow with time, at least not regarding the Bolshevik phenomenon. His references in Aftermath, 1929, 1941, 1944, 70–85, 232–76, are as harsh as ever.

40 Quotations from CV/4, ii, 860, 912, 1010–12, iii, 1699, 1874; CSWC, iii, 2918–19; and his article, 'Zionism verses Bolshevism', Illustrated Sunday

Herald, 8 Feb. 1920, in Wolff (ed.), iv, 26–30. These issues are discussed more fully by the author in 'Churchill and Zionism', Blake and Louis (ed.) 1993

41 See p. 70
42 *WSC*, iv, 915
43 *Stevenson Diary*, 196–97
44 CV/5, i, 286; also his article, 'British Foreign Policy', *Weekly Dispatch*, 22 June 1919, Wolff (ed.) i, 214–17; and Boadle, 1973, 44–47
45 CV/4, i, 366, ii, 1353; also Ch. 12
46 Repugnant though it might be to make the analogy, Churchill's ferocious rhetoric and imagery bears comparison with Hitler's, the most notorious anti-Bolshevik agitator of the period. Hitler too described Bolshevism in terms of 'poisonous bacilli', 'menacing hordes', 'plague', 'infection', 'a veritable world sickness which threatens to infect the peoples, a plague which devastates whole peoples ... an international pestilence', as 'the incarnation of the human destructive spirit', 'a foe of humanity', 'a ghastly ideology of annihilation, 'a world peril for which there must be no toleration' for it corrupts 'mankind with its thoughts and deeds'. See Norman H. Baynes (ed.), 1942, i, 667, 677, 682, 691, 693, 702, 710, ii, 1333, 1338, 1339, 1395, 1396
47 *Whitehall Diary*, i, 85
48 CV/4, i, 537–38
49 Sessions of 4 Mar. and 25 Jul. 1919, CAB.23/11, 15
50 CV/4, ii, 867, iii, 1892; *CSWC*, iii, 2872; *Scott Diaries*, 421; and Ullman, 1968, 210–11, 304. Apparently, these discrepencies arose from all too familiar book-keeping devices, see Ulmann 1968, 365–68

Bernard Shaw told Hesketh Pearson that on his visit to Russia he had asked Stalin if Churchill would be more welcome in the Soviet Union than Lloyd George. Stalin replied in the affirmative. During the wars of intervention, he argued, Churchill had inadvertently armed and clothed the Red Army by handing over £100 million of equipment voted by Parliament to help the counter-revolutionaries. The Bolsheviks had triumphed also thanks to Churchill's generosity. See Halle, 98

51 *Whitehall Diaries*, i, 105, and *Stevenson Diary*, 197–98
52 See Wolff (ed.), ii, 58–62, 79–84, 156–59, iii, 96–98; and *Amery Diaries*, i, 505, 569. In *Aftermath*, 1929, his references to Bolshevism are as unrelenting as ever.
53 *CSWC*, vii, 7774
54 *WSC*, iv, 311, 430. For Churchill's deteriorating relations with Lloyd George. CV/4, ii, 771–73, 867, 870–72, 874, 1004–05, 1010, 1035, 1319; also *Stevenson Diary*, 197
55 See *Bertie Diary*, ii, 271, quoted in *WSC*, iv, 71; CV/4, ii, 995; *CSWS*, iii, 2921, 3019, 3026, 3164–65; *Whitehall Diary*, i, 94, 119. For his special feelings towards trade unionists, see *CSWC*, i, 1030; his article, 'Red Fever', *Illustrated Sunday Herald*, 25 Jan. 1920, Wolff (ed.) ii, 58–62; and Paul Addison, 1980, 43
56 Kenneth O. Morgan, 1986, 135; and for the 'Die-Hards', *ibid.*, 235–54
57 See J. A. Cross, 1977, 60–61, 71; also CV/4, i, 675–76, ii, 669–70, 774–76
58 CV/4, ii, 874, iii, 1814–15, 1819–20; also Kenneth O. Morgan, 1986, 310
59 CHAR 16/53A; CV/4, iii, 1814–15, 1213; Beaverbrook, 1966, 292

Chapter 11. Running the Empire

1 Ronald Hyam, 1968, 225. Hyam brings many examples of Churchill's essential humanity and fairmindedness, *ibid*, 207–08, 215, 225–26, 239–62, 433–35. See also Hyam in Blake and Louis (eds.). I have relied heavily on these works for these passages.

2 For his opposition to Milner report, CV/4, ii, 1171–81, 1318, 1361–62; his struggle over India in CV/4, 3, passim; and for his position on South Africa, Hyam in Blake and Louis (eds.), 1993

3 From his speech to the United Wards Club, London, 4 Nov. 1920, CSWC, 111, 3024–26; and Hyam in Blake and Louis (eds.), 1993, 13

4 These matters in CV/4, ii, 1305–06, 1310–11, 1313, 1349; iii, 1502–06, 1509–10, 1542–43, 1665–66, 1743–47; CV/5, i, 294; and Hyam, op. cit.

5 See Hyam 1968, 505, and Hyam in Blake and Louis (eds.) 1993

6 CV/4, ii, 1397, 1404–05, 1418; and WSC, iv, 572

7 Asquith, 1928, ii, 69

8 For reconstituting the Turkish Empire, CV/4, ii, 937–39, and for handing over the mandates to the United States, CV/4, iii, 1498–1501

9 Memorandum in CV/4, ii, 937–39; speeches in CSWC, 111, 3088–90, 3115–21, quoted in Hyam, Blake and Louis (eds.). His Manchester speech also quoted in Henry Pelling, 1974, 266

10 See John Darwin, 1981, 204–05

11 These issues are discussed more fully in Hyam, Blake and Louis (eds.)

12 As he told Lloyd George CV/4, ii, 1119–20, 1289–90

13 Minutes of Cairo Conference in CAB.24/122, C.P.2866; for his cheering people up, WSC, iv, 557

14 For the passage on Iraq, see CHAR.2/147; CV/4, iii, 1471–72, 1577–81, 1554, 1675, 1973–74, 2074; CV/5, i, 625; also Hyam, Blake and Louis (eds.) For a devastating critique of Feisal in particular and British policy towards Iraq in general, see Eli Kedourie 1970, 236–82

15 These themes are discussed in greater detail in Rose, 'Churchill and Zionism' Blake and Louis (eds.)

16 CAB.24/126

17 His Belgium proposal is in a minute of 18 March 1915, F.O.800/88; for giving up Palestine, CV/4, ii, 937–39, 1119–20; CV/4, iii, 1498–1501, 1585–90; also Notes of a Meeting at Balfour's house, 22 Jul. 1921, Weizmann Archives, Rehovoth

18 The Declaration, a letter from Balfour to Lord Rothschild issued on 2 Nov. 1917, promised that Britain 'would view with favour the establishment in Palestine of a national home for the Jewish people', though without prejudicing 'the civil and religious rights of the existing non-Jewish communities'.

19 From his article, 'Zionism versus Bolshevism', Illustrated Sunday Herald, 8 Feb. 1920, in Wolff (ed.) iv, 26–30

20 Richard Meinertzhagen, 1959, 99; and Meeting at Balfour's House, 22 Jul. 1921.

21 Churchill's defence of Zionism, CO. 733/17B, nos.41298, 43805; Cmd 1700; PD, Commons, v.143, c.266–96; ibid., v.151, c.1547–72; ibid., v.156, c.337–340, v.310, c.1114; CSWC, iii, 3102–09, IV, 3342–51; also CV/4, iii, 1592–1601, 1610–18. His suggestions on behalf of Zionism, CV/4, iii, 1585–90. Of course, not all these ideas were implemented; others were carried out in a half-hearted manner. But they do indicate Churchill's turn of mind.

22 PD, v. 156, c. 328–40; and CV/4, ii, 939, and iii, 1926. Also Hyam, Blake and Louis (eds.)

23 It was inspired and drafted by Samuel, Palestine's first High Commissioner. See his draft of 24 May 1922, CO.733/34, published as Cmd. 1700; also CV/4, iii, 1491. Final terms of the mandate in Cmd. 1500

24 CV/4, iii, 1986

25 See CV/4, 1005–05; iii, 1656, 1772, 1794, 1806–08

26 CV/4, ii, 1149, 1195, 1206, 1217; Wilson Diary ii, 262, 267, 269; Whitehall Diary, 118

27 WSC, iv, 734

28 Wilson's views, Callwell, ii, 283, 296, 305; for the Ireland Act and truce, *Aftermath*, 285–295, CV/4, ii, 1277; and Clementine's intervention, *WSC*, iv, 471

29 For the swing in public opinion, Beaverbrook, 90–92; *Scott Diaries*, 390; and Charles Loch Mowat, 81–83; Cabinet minutes for 12 May 1921 in CAB.23/25

30 Macready's report in *Aftermath*, 293; Collins' remark in Amery, ii, 230

31 *Sanders Diaries*, 157, 178

32 Beaverbrook, 93

33 *CSWC*, 111, 3131–34, and CV/4, iii, 1667

34 *Aftermath*, 302–04, and CV/4, iii, 1666–67

35 R. R. James, 1970, 130; Mowat, 92–93; A. J. Taylor, 1965, 158

36 For Smith's and Churchill's contribution, *Stevenson Diary*, 236, also *Aftermath*, 301–02. The Smith-Collins relationship in Margery Forester, 231–32

37 Speeches in *CSWC*, iii, 3191–92, 3219–32, 3291–96; iv, 1 June 1922; and CV/4, iii, 1837, 1908–09

38 For Churchill's view of the treaty, CV/4, iii, 1846–50, 1852–53, 1855–57, 2095; Collins's message in *Aftermath*, 348 – the only source for this quotation; Cosgrave's praise, CV/4, iii, 2099. Vilifying Lloyd George, CV/5, i, 389. In public, Churchill was more circumspect, writing that Lloyd George differed from all English statesmen in that he had achieved 'a solution' to the Irish problem. *Aftermath*, 307

39 See Beaverbrook, 125, 128, 151–52

40 *Whitehall Diaries*, 197, 220

41 From his Cabinet memorandum, 7 Jun. 1920, CV/4, ii, 1114–16. The Sèvres treaty was particularly harsh. All non-Turkish territories – Arabia, Syria, Lebanon, Palestine, and Mesopotamia – were handed over to Britain and France, as mandates, and local Arab rulers, as quasi-independent entities. These measures were non-controversial, accepted by the Turks as inevitable. Not so the awards given to Greece – Thrace, and Smyrna and its hinterland, until a plebiscite could be held after five years, and islands in the Aegean; and to Italy – the Dodecanese and Rhodes. Armenia was declared independent; and the Straights were to be internationalized, its coastal strips of land demilitarized. What remained was in every sense a rump Turkey.

42 Churchill's differences with Lloyd George in CV/4, ii, 1249–50, 1260–62, 1267–69, 1319, 1324, 1369–70, 1343–44; iii, 1436, 1482, 1488–91, 1498, 1583–84, 1628–29, 2051

43 Quotations in CV/4, iii, 1489, 1584, 1980, 1988–89, 2029, 2051, 2053; Beaverbrook, 161, 166

44 Text of communiqué in CV/4, iii, 1993–95; other quotation. *ibid.*, 2085. For the fall of the Coalition, I have followed in general, Blake, 1955, 436–58; Keith Middlemas and John Barnes, 1969, 95–124; James, 1969, 100–133; Mowat, 112–42; and Beaverbrook, for an inside but partisan view.

45 Alan Clark (ed.), 1974, 229; CV/4, iii, 2082; Roskill, 1970–04, ii, 298, 295

46 CV/4, iii, 1934, 1986, 2073; also *Scott Diaries*, 425–29

47 Blake, 1955, 447–48, and CV/4, iii, 2079

48 Voting figures in R. R. James, 1969, 129–33

49 R. R. James, 1976, 83; CV/4, iii, 2092–93, 2099; *Thoughts and Adventures*, 213

50 CV/4, iii, 2093, 2095–96

51 For the Dundee election, Soames, 207–08; *Thoughts and Adventures*, 211–13; CV/4, iii, 2123, 2125, 2127; and *WSC*, iv, 880, 885.
    Churchill was beaten by 'a quaint and dim figure', a Mr Edwin Scrymgeour, an independent prohibitionist, who first contested the seat against him in 1908, gaining 655 votes. At his sixth attempt, in 1922, Scrymgeour emerged victorious with 32, 578 supporters.

Chapter 12. 'I will make you the Golden Chancellor'

1 CV/4, iii, 1502, 1523

2 CV/4, iii, 1525, 1532,

3 Soames, 201–02; *WSC*, iv, 613; CV/4, iii, 1618, 1623; and Elizabeth Nel, 187

4 See CHAR. 1/139, 158; CV/4, iii, 1706 and n2, 1712, 1757, 1956–58; and Soames, 203–04

5 Quotations in *WSC*, iv, 614, 887. His physical appearance from his photographs of the period, in Randolph S. Churchill and Helmut Gernsheim, and Martin Gilbert, 1974

6 For the purchase of Chartwell, see CV/4, i, 392 n2; ii, 1334 n1, 1365; iii, 2014–15, 2027–28, 2118; and Soames, 217–20

7 For the elections CHAR. 7/1; *Thoughts and Adventures*, 213–15, CV/5, i, 74, 78, 110, 127, WSC, v, 21; and for Carlton Club, CV/5, i, 563

8 Clementine and the Tories, CV/5, i, 111; for 'ratting', Halle, 42; and for 'principle' and 'sympathy', R. R. James 1976, 77

9 CV/5, ii, 114–15

10 *Riddell Diaries*, 30 May 1923, and CV/5, i, 424

11 For leading his Liberal wing to the Conservatives, CV/5, 138–39, 157; Baldwin to Austen Chamberlain, *ibid*, 170; and his longstanding intention to switch camps, CV/4, iii, 1794

12 Baldwin's protection policy in John Barnes and Keith Middlemas, 1969, 229–49. For Churchill's opposition, CSWC, iv, 3396–97, 3398–3412 passim, and CV/5, i, 69. The election results, at Leicester, CV/5, i, 74, and in general, David Butler and Anne Sloman, 1975

13 *Amery Diaries* ii, 49

14 CV/5, i, 89

15 CV/5, i, 90, 94, and CSWC, iv, 3453–55

16 CV/5, i, 94

17 See CV/5, i, 1047, 1328–29, and David Dilks, 1985, i, 449

18 This account of Churchill's appointment as Chancellor is based on, CV/5, i, 234–40; *WSC*, iv, 59–60; *Whitehall Diary*, i, 301–03; *Stevenson Diary*, 485–86; *Amery Diaries*, i, 390–91; Brett (ed.) 297; R. R. James, 1969, 202; Dilks 1985, 398–401; Barnes and Middlemas, 280–81; Amery, 1953 ii; 299–300; P. J. Grigg, 174

19 From Churchill's Romanes Lecture, 1930, printed in *Thoughts and Adventures*, 233–34, and Peter Clarke, Blake and Louis (eds.)

20 CV/4, iii, 1917–18

21 CSWC, v, 5085

22 A. J. P. Taylor (ed.), 1973, 323, quoted in Paul Addison, Blake and Louis (eds.)

23 See CSWC, iii, 2648, 2941, 3024; iv, 3443; and CV/4, i, 217, 225–26; ii, 791; iii, 1495

24 The legislation governing the relief of the destitute and defining local government authority had developed gradually and unsystematically since the English Poor Law of 1601. By the early twentieth century, there existed an extensive, often conflicting, bureaucracy dealing with these matters, from Boards of Poor Law Guardians to trade unions to national schemes of health and unemployment benefits. The need for overall reform was obvious. Royal Commissions had been set up. The Webbs had investigated the question with their usual thoroughness. Now Neville Chamberlain aimed to cut through the confusion by transferring to public-assistance committees of the counties and county boroughs the authority to deal with these questions, while at the same

time re-organizing urban and rural district councils. Much power was now to be concentrated in the hands of these local bodies: from general welfare and public health to education, local transport, and street lighting.

25 CV/5, i, 264, 172–73, 418–19; *Whitehall Diary*, i, 305, 307; and P. J. Grigg, 174, 194

26 P. J. Grigg, 194–95, and *Thoughts and Adventures*, 291. His remark about misplaced noughts was made in a different context, in an essay on 'Moses'. But the wider meaning is clear.

27 *Great Contemporaries*, 229

28 CV/5, i, 600–03, 682, 689–90, 1087–88, 1148; Dilks, 448, 540, 543

29 Churchill's budget speech in *CSWC*, iv, 3556–83; Baldwin's comments in CV/5, i, 472–73; his 'biggest blunder' in Moran, 330

30 Quotations in Ron Chernow, ch.6

31 Even Keynes balked more at returning at the old rate of parity, believing that there was now a 10% disparity, than at the actual decision itself.

32 The above passage is based on: CV/5, i, 329, 997–98; CV/5, ii, 339, 399; CV/5, iii, 2; *WSC*, v, 94–95, 119; *Amery Diaries*, i, 547; P. J. Grigg, 180–86; P. Clarke; R. R. James 1978; and J. Redmond 1989

33 P. J. Grigg, 174, and Barnes and Middlemas, 296

34 *CSWC*, iv, 3635, quoted in *WSC*, v, 120

35 *CSWC*, iv, 3586–88, and *WSC*, v, 116

36 CV/4, iii, 2070

37 Churchill's conciliatory proposal in Cabinet minutes, 30 Jul. 1925, CAB.23/50. Quotations in *Whitehall Diary*, ii, 28, 30, 34–36; Viscount Samuel, 1945, 184–87; Amery, ii, 483–84. See also Mowat, 284–310, for an excellent general account of these events; and Dilks, 1985, 458–65; Barnes and Middlemas, 378–408; and Alan Bullock, 1969, i, 308–15

38 See Dilks, 1985, 463; for alleged plot, *Whitehall Diary*, ii, 28

39 Quotations in *Whitehall Diary*, ii, 36, 41, and 44. Also *CSWC*, iv, 3951–52, and CV/5, i, 703–07, 880

40 Dilks, 1985, 466–67, 473

41 See CHAR. 2/147; *Davidson Memoirs*, 243

42 *Davidson Memoirs*, 242, and CV/5, i, 880 n1, 882

43 See *Whitehall Diary*, ii, 44, 54, *Davidson Memoirs*, 238, 242, and CV/5, i, 717

44 For Churchill and the Trade Disputes Act, CV/5, i, 1000; his attempts at compromise and sympathetic attitude towards the miners in the post-strike negotiations, in CV/5, i, 781–807, 808, 843, 856, 863, 865–67; his propensity to bully, CV/5, i, 809, 855, and *Amery Diaries*, i, 545; and as leader of the war party, CV/5, i, 726 n1

45 *Webb Diaries*, 106

Chapter 13. Squandering the Treasure

1 See CV/5, i, 471–74, 499, 533–34, 743, 985, 1045–47, 1050, 1239, 1328, 1463; and T. Jones, 1969, 204

2 Amery's comments in *Amery Diaries*, i 503, 542; Baldwin's and Neville Chamberlain's criticism, CV/5, i, 745, 986, 1327–29, and Dilks, 1985, 546; and P. J. Grigg, 175

3 See his Cabinet paper of 20 Jan. 1928 in CV/5, i, 1128–37, 1187–94 (see CAB.24/192, 193); for Cabinet decision of 20 Jan. 1928, CAB.23/57

4 In the grim circumstances of Asquith's funeral, Churchill told Thomas Jones that 'it really was the Communist principle, from each authority according to its ability, to each authority according to its need'. *Whitehall Diary*, ii, 132

5 CV/5, i, 1328. For Chamberlain's immediate reaction to the proposal, CV/5, i

1151–54; also Dilks, 1985, 534 passim

6 CV/5, 1147–48, 1327; and Dilks 1985, 448, 540

7 Quotations in CV/5, i, 1155, 1220, 1227, 1263–64; and Dilks, 1985, 539, 542

8 CV/5, i, 1250, for being 'audacious'; Cabinet compromise of 20 Apr. 1928, CAB.23/57, and CV/5, i, 1265–66; also Dilks 1985, 555–56. Churchill's budget speech in CSWC, iv, 4372–4405, and 4405–4410; also Churchill's report to George V, CV/5, i, 1267–70

9 The details of the Act may be followed in Dilks, 1985, 570–77, and Mowat, 340–41.

10 See CV/5, i, 534, 1046–47, 1239, iii, 686; Dugdale Diaries, 39; also Dilks, 1985, 420, 440–41, 449

11 CV/5, i, 304, 548–51, iii, 696

12 William Scott Chalmers, 1951, 403

13 Quotations in CV/5, i, 304–07, 1120–21. For the debate, CV/5, i 357–76, 359–68, 373–76, 383–88, 935–97, 944, 946, 1035–36, 1062–63, 1082, 1089–95, 1097–1100, 1106–09, 1120–21; Bridgeman Diaries, 179, 188; Chalmers, 402–03; Dilks, 1985, 436, 527. Naval expenditures and cruiser building figures in S. Roskill, 1968, 581–82, 586, and also for a general account of these affairs.

14 Accepting parity, Cabinet minutes, 15 Feb. 1922, CAB. 23/29; CV/5, i, 387; and CSWC, iii, 3125. Decrying the 'gigantic naval war', CV/5, i, 286 n1, 830, 1174; assuring Sir Roger Keyes, CV/5, i, 442–443; and in same vein, ibid 305–07, 349, 384, 443–44 (only in the event of Japan threatening to invade Australia could Churchill envisage a war against Japan).

15 The Singapore controversy in CV/5, i, 286, 315, 330, 361–62, 373, 379, 451–52; ii, 51 n1; iii, 854–55, 1414–17; Amery Diaries i, 549–50; and Roskill, 1968, 282, 289–92. His 'standing assumption', CV/5, 1, 1302. See his speech to Oxford students, CV/5, ii, 726 n1; and a 'different' Japan, CV/5, iii, 389 n1; and abandoning the Far East, iii, 855, 1414–17

16 Details in Roskill, 1968–81, 510–13

17 Quotations in CV/5, 1030–35, 1038 n1, and Amery Diaries, 519. See also, Bridgeman Diaries, 205–10; CSWC, iv, 4323–25; D. C. Watt, 1984, 58–59; Roskill 1968–81, 433–66, 498–516. Ref. to his Cab. memo, 20 Jul. 1927, on Cruisers and Parity, CV/5, i, 1030–30; and C. Hassall, 484

18 CV/5, i, 1348–49, 1384.

19 Quotations in CSWC, v, 4521, and his papers on 'French and Belgian Security' [CP, 118] and 'Anglo-French Relations', 24 Feb. and 12 Mar. 1925, CV/5, i, 413–17, 430–32

20 See CV/5, i, 384, and iii, 1003 n1

21 This was precisely the point Admiral of the Fleet and Minister for the Coordination of Defence, Sir Ernle Chatfield, made in March 1939: 'the British Fleet is an old Fleet, largely due to his [Churchill's] own action when he was Chancellor . . .' CV/5, iii, 1465

22 See CV/5, i, 650, 735, 744–45, 1050, 1319, 1468

23 See CV/5, i, 744–45, 1050, 1327; Davidson Memoirs, 296–97; and Whitehall Diary, ii, 244

24 For Churchill's posts, see Whitehall Diary, ii, 172, 174, 179–80, 183, and Amery Diaries, i, 584–86. His pessimism about electoral victory, CV/5, i, 1410, 1451

25 Election figures in Butler and Sloman, 183, 187–88; Churchill at Downing Street, Whitehall Diary ii, 186–87; his last budget with the elections in mind, Amery Diaries i, 589, and CV/5, i, 1468; and for Poor Law and De-rating as non-election winners, CV/5, i, 1328

26 For Churchill's attitude towards the flapper-vote, see CV/5, i, 958–66, 1066, 1245, 1376; *Amery Diaries*, i, 504; and P. J. Grigg, 202

27 For Churchill's approach to Lloyd George and Baldwin, CV/5, ii, 8, 10–11

28 CV/5, i, 741 n1

29 See CV/1, ii, 927; CV/5, ii, 2–3, 4 and n1, 12–13, 131; CV/5, iii, 114 and n1, 1601. See also pp. 202, 213

30 For his North American trip, see Randolph Churchill, 1965, 73–93; CV/5, ii, 10, 16, 46, 54, 57–58, 61, 68, 94–95, 96–97; John Spencer Churchill, 1961, 65–69, 72; and Anita Leslie, 1985, 16–18

31 For his financial position, see CV/5, 86–87, 108 n3; and Soames, 216

32 Printed in *Thoughts and Adventures*, 229–41. See also his speeches in the Commons, 16 Dec. 1930, and at Liverpool, 2 Feb. 1931 (*CSWC*, v, 4941–42, 4971–73); his rectorial address at Edinburgh University in Mar. 1931, and his memorandum of Jun. 1931, where he repeats the themes of his Romanes lecture, (CV/5, ii, 281 n2, 324–25).

33 For details of Mosley's programme, see Robert Skidelsky, 1975, 187–89, 192–95, 199–220

34 See CV/5, ii, 191–93, 203–04, 226; and *Amery Diaries*, ii, 49

35 His article, 'Will the British Empire last?' in Wolff, ii, 172–76. For remaining silent in debate, CV/5, ii, 111; having support for his views on India, CV/5, ii, 111, 285, and Sarvepalli Gopal, 1992, Blake and Louis (eds.); and his 'bid' for the leadership and ideas of coalition, CV/5, ii, 254, 269

36 'Peril in India', *Daily Mail*, 16 Nov. 1930, CV/5, ii, 112 n3; for other violent 'anti-Dominion status' articles, see Wolff, ii, 228–33, 266–68, 292–95, 348–52. His comments to a friend, Lord Lytton, and Irwin, CV/5, ii, 254, 269. Other quotations from his speeches at Thanet, 20 Aug. 1930, Woodford, 6 Nov. 1930, and to Indian Empire Society at Cannon Street Hotel, 11 Dec. 1930, *CSWC*, v, 4913, 4927, 4938

37 For Baldwin's comment, *Davidson Memoirs*, 354, and *Amery Diaries*, ii, 97; other quotations, CV/5, ii, 156, 222

38 Beaverbrook's comment, CV/5, 242 n1; leading on India 'only', CV/5, ii, 293; and 'disastrous' as a leader, CV/5, ii, 294

39 Relations with Tories and Baldwin, CV/5, 243, 295; letter to Randolph and fighting India 'à outrance', CV/5, 242–43

40 Letter to 'Sunny', CV/5, ii, 246; his 'breaking-point', Churchill, 1948, i, 27; resignation from Shadow Cabinet, CV/5, ii, 250–51; and his speeches in Commons and Manchester, *CSWC*, v. 4947–56, 4966–71

41 Churchill 'at Cannes', *Second World War*, 29; avoiding 'evils' of socialism, CV/5, ii, 361, 366, and *CSWC*, v, 5087–88

42 For Churchill's abandoning Free Trade, see his speeches at Chingford and in the Commons, 11 and 15 Sept. 1930, and at Epping, 11 Oct. 1931, *CSWC*, v, 5074–75, 5085, also his appeals to the electors of Epping, 10 and 20 Oct. 1931, CV/5, ii, 361–64, 366–67; his acceptance of Import Duties Bill, CV/5, ii, 399; and his call for public works, *CSWC*, v, 5218

43 Contacts with Lloyd George, CV/5, ii, 281, 334, 336; feelers to Mosley, *Nicolson Diaries*, i, 78–79, 86–87

44 CV/5, ii, 393

45 CV/5, ii, 394 n2

Chapter 14. Private Diversions

1 Howell, 72; John Martin, 32; McGowan, 86; CV/5, iii, 320–21, 1095

2 CV/5, ii, 979, 1130 nl, 1243

3 Quoted in Beaverbrook, 1966, 306

4 See CV/5, iii, 971 and ns. 2, 3, 972–76

5 Quotations in Soames, 219, and CV/5, iii, 655. For the passage on Chartwell in general, Robin Fedden, 1986, 15–19; Soames, 217–220; Moran, 702, 713, 757; CV/5, i, 18–19, 178, 423–24, 542, 642, 655, 850, 1012, 1055, 1375; CV/5, ii, 1039, 1127, 1130; CV/5, iii, 528, 673, 1088 and n2, 1132, 1323, 1381 and n1, 1575 n1; and for samples of Chartwell Bulletins, CV/5, ii, 987, 1031, 1093–95, 1104–05. Much of the information on Chartwell in CHAR1/166–68, 173, 332, 350, 393A

6 See *Observer*, 85; *Dictionary of National Biography, 1961–70*, 205; and Moran, 469

7 *WSC*, vi, 33 n1, and CV/5, i, 145

8 Quotations in CV/4, 1340, 1381, and CV/5, ii, 1367

9 *Observer*, and Eade (ed.), 25

10 Has 'vy few friends', CV/2, 678–79; no small talk, R. R. James, 1970, 245; as centre of attraction, Walter Graebner, 1965, 105; when crossed and 'impudence', Moran, 812, and R. R. James, 1976, 248

11 Clementine 'simply listens', CV/5, 1243, and sends Winston 'notes', Moran, 121; never apologizes, *Observer*, 98; forgets Clementine, Moran, 175

12 Has 'vy few friends', CV/2, ii, 678–79. For Lloyd George, *Nicolson Diaries*, i, 387; Baldwin, i, 26, and CV/5, iii, 143; Eden, CV/5, ii, 1363, iii, 11, and Moran, 581; Beaverbrook, see Kenneth Young, 1966; quotations in CV/4, iii, 2101, Beaverbrook, 1959, 284, and Sarah Churchill, 39; and 'flamboyant men', Moran, 753

13 Quotations in CV/5, i, 13, 229; Birkenhead, 1965, 98; R. R. James, 1991, 36; and W. Churchill, *Great Contemporaries*, 135–37

14 See CHAR 2/137,201; Colin Coote, 1971, and CV/5, iii, 63 n4. Lloyd George's role in the founding of the Other Club is mentioned in CV/5, iii, 506 n1, and Vansittart, 1958, 123

15 For Bracken see Andrew Boyle, 1974; quotation in Sarah Churchill, 38, and CV/5, ii, 289

16 For studies of Lindemann, see Birkenhead, 1961, and Roy Harrod, 1959. Quotations in Soames, 229; R. R. James, 1970, 242; Sarah Churchill, 37–38; Randolph Churchill, 1965, 127; and CV/5, iii, 557

17 Quotations in Soames, 252; R. R. James, 1990, 252, and CV/3, ii, 1332; Boothby, 1947, 46

18 These aspects of his life may be followed in McGowan, Howells, and Graebner.

19 His attitude to games, Moran, 288; and golf, Bernard Darwin, 1952, 172. For his gambling habits, CV/2, iii, 1698, CV/4, iii, 1713, CV/5, i, 436, iii, 575, 1059 n1, and Howells, 105–06

20 Ellman, 112; Howells, 70, 116, 176; *Observer*, 66; Coote, 41; and *WSC*, iv, 154

21 Driving habits, Nel, 60–61; his 'glorious mood', R. R. James, 1976, 125

22 Quotations in *Observer*, 76; Meinertzhagen 124; and Moran, 69, 129, 328

23 See *Savrola*, 84, 186; Moran, 14, 69; *WSC*, viii, 367; Soames, 426, and P. G. Reid, 1969, 62; *The Times*, 2 June 1988 (review of *WSC*, viii, by John Grigg); Graebner, 25

24 Asquith in CV/5, i, 497; also Spears, 1954, 312

25 Literary tastes in Sarah Churchill, 26, and Moran, 394, 423, 442, 450, 453, 462, 470, 474, 757–78

26 See CV/2, iii, 1967; John Martin, 37, 149; Graebner, 26; McGowan, 48; Howells, 152, 166–67, 176; and Soames, 388

27 See Howells, 97, 153; McGowan, 52; Graebner, 37, 41; Soames, 338; and CV/5, i, 683, 1247

28 Churchill's smouldering, dogged, determined, bulldog look, probably his most famous expression. It was captured by the well-known photographer, Karsh

of Ottawa, in 1941, the result of having snatched Churchill's cigar from his mouth, without permission, though 'ever so politely'. See *The Times*, 20 Feb. 1988; also Howells, 76

29 His 'simple tastes' in Graebner, 57; Maxine Elliot's remark, McGowan, 71; 'oriental tendency' and as a 'pasha', CV/2, i, 672, and Moran, 436, 456; as coarse of tongue, Moran, 139, Elizabeth Nel, 33–34; for throwing hairbrushes, Howells, 77; Violet Pearman, CV/5, iii, 22 n3, 443–45, 1032–33, 1096–97, 1253; and Second World War aides, *Alanbrooke Diaries* and *Ismay Memoirs*

30 For entourage, Graebner, 73–74; lost on Underground, Moran, 269

31 For his allowance, cheques bouncing, and money-lenders, WSC, i, 328, CV/1, i, 402–03, 489, CV/2, i, 102–03; Lady Randolph's scolding, CV/1, ii, 741; his extravagant wine bills, CHAR. 1/318, and his reputation at Westerham, Soames, 426

32 His directorships in CV/5, iii, 576 n1; lecture and journalist fees in United States, WSC, v, 349, 420; his book advances, CV/5, ii, 3, 4 n1, 502–03; and for film script, CV/5, ii, 876

33 For his financial situation in general, CHAR.1/212, 229; his cry of despair, CV/1, ii, 879; for debts, share losses, and attempts at economy, CV/5, iii, 438, 517, 572, 807, 950 n3, 959; rushing *Malborough*, CV/5, iii, 576; for projected sale of Chartwell and Strakosch's rescue, CV/5, iii, 950 n3, 959, 971 ns. 2, 3, 972–76

34 For this passage, see Howells, 111, 136, 149: Elizabeth Nel, 60–61; Halle, 91; Moran, 423; Randolph Churchill, 1965, 20; Marsh, 259; Graebner, 36; and Philip Zeigler, in Blake and Louis (eds.)

35 See CSWC, iv, 3348; Consuelo Balsan, 162; *Observer*, 47; McGowan, 138–46; *Stevenson Diary*, 198; Moran, 206, 756, 812

36 WSC, viii, 304

37 Howells, 123; Graebner, 102–03

38 His clothes, CV/1, 169, and his tastes in dress, Bonham-Carter, 230, *Thoughts and Adventures*, 34–35, Howells, 119, 164, 174, Graebner, 23, McGowan, 93, Elizabeth Nel, 43, 105; Amery's observation, *Amery Diaries*, ii, 49

39 As 'Edwardian survivor', Sir Michael Howard's remarks at Churchill Conference, Austin, Texas, 20–23 Mar. 1991; quotations in Moran, 757, 811–12, and J. Martin, 11

40 S. Leslie 1966, 15, 20, and CV/4, i, 127

41 Quotations in Consuelo Vanderbilt Balsan, 103, and Leslie, 1966, 238–39

42 Spinach throwing incident, Soames, 232. Quotations in CV/4, ii, 1009, CV/5, iii, 1095, 1098–99; also Soames, 254

43 For above passage, CV/5, i, 434, iii, 1316, and CV/4, iii, 1709

44 William Manchester asserts (1988, 15) that Churchill committed 'one act of infidelity' with 'a divorced, titled Englishwoman'. The evidence provided, however, is at best highly circumstantial. Clementine's suspicions in Soames, 63. For a decisive refutation of the Bracken story, see Andrew Boyle. Fisher's allegation and Churchill's 'gt romances', WSC, iii, 419, 745. For not wasting his 'essence in bed', A. J. P. Taylor, quoted in Manchester, 15. And 'incapable of love', in David Green, 1984, 141

45 Quoted in R. R. James, 1991, 86

46 Quoted in Soames, 274

47 CHAR. 1/273; Soames, 266–67

48 Clementine's formula, Howells, 129; quotations in Soames, 92, 236, 253, 391

49 CV/5, iii, 1254, 1348, and Soames, 238, 397–98

50 See CV/5, ii, 491 and n3, 495, 1078–79; Soames, 238–39, 243–45, 412–15, 443, 455, 480

51 For Sarah, see CHAR.1/288; CV/5, ii, 1295–96, 1315–16, CV/5, iii, 53–54,

60, 123–24, 344–45, 360, 372, 388, 422 and n1, 520, 1065–66, 1115, and Soames, 243–45, 295, 305, 412–15, 419, 444, 463–64, 478–79

52 Soames, 248–49

53 Quotations in CV/4, ii, 1351, and CV/5, i, 896, 1254, 1402; and cigar waving in Anita Leslie, 34

54 Quotations in CV/5, ii, 145, iii, 1569; WSC, v, 435

55 Quotations in CV/5, ii, 1096, 1137, iii, 921; and Waugh Diaries, 732, also CHAR. 1/273

56 This passage based on, CV/5, ii, 405–06; A. Leslie, 1985, 44, 110, 118, 176; and Randolph Churchill, 1965, 86

57 Leslie, 207

58 Ethel Barrymore, 1955, 274; CV/2, ii, 901; and CV/5, i, 55, 1014

59 CSWC, i, 903–04, from his address to the Author's Club, London, 17 Feb. 1908

60 Trevelyan in CV/5, ii, 207, also CSWC, i, 903–05

61 Isaiah Berlin, 1949, 12, 13. This passage relies also on: Maurice Ashley, A. J. R. Taylor (ed.); J. H. Plumb's essay 'The Historian', 1969; F. W. Deakin, 1970; Robert Blake, 1990; R. R. James, 1970, 307–16

62 CV/5, ii, 820

63 Deakin, 11

64 Foster, 389. Lord Randolph has been subject to two modern biographies, by R. R. James (1959, 1969 ed.) and R. F. Foster, that balance Churchill's picture. See in particular Foster's critical but judicious summary of Churchill's historical methodology, ibid., 382–403

65 Quotation in CV/5, ii, 15 n3, 7

66 Quotations in WC, i, v; WSC, iv, 14–15, 224, and viii, 315. Both these works have failed to satisfy the more meticulous academic mind and have been subjected to vigorous investigation. See Robin Prior, 1983. Regarding The Second World War books and articles continue to appear non-stop (see references), but see in particular Tuvia Ben Moshe, 1992

67 Although the first draft of 530,000 words of English-Speaking Peoples was completed in August 1939, its final volume was not published until 1958. By then Churchill was eighty-four years old, perhaps too weary, too far gone in years to accord it the demanding application a work of this nature required.

68 Ashley, 228

69 Moran, 69, 146–47, 328

70 They can be seen in Wolff (ed.), iii, 127–212

71 Savrola, 5, 31, 41, 52, 62, 81–82, 89, 107–08, 111

72 Details of his study in Fedden, 42–48

73 For 'syndicate' writing, CV/2, i, 441; his research assistants and their tasks, Ashley, 26–28, and Deakin, 4; Mortimer Wheeler in WSC, v, 959; Feiling, CV/5, ii, 454–55, 485, 511, 874–75

74 See, CV/5, ii, 459, 461–62, 463, 488 n1, CV/5, iii, 305 and n1, 315, 1532. The 'Great Stories' series was eventually upgraded to twelve articles. It appeared in the News of the World in Jan. 1933. For Churchill's English usage, Moran, 450, and Observer, 98

75 See in general the articles by Deakin, 1970, and Robert Blake, 'Churchill as historian,' 1990, and Ashley, 24–25. 'Favourite words' in CV/5, ii, 601, 614–15; 'Canadian Pacific Railway', Graebner, 69, also CV/5, ii, 438, 455 n1

76 WSC, v, 729–30

77 Said by Arthur Christiansen, then editor of the Daily Express, CV/5, iii, 1433; observed by G. W. Steevens, war correspondent, in his portrait of Churchill, Daily Mail, 2 Dec. 1898, reprinted in Eade, 65

78 Quotations in Herbert Read, 172; Foster, 389; Mark Amory (ed.), 1982, 627; Pelling, 1974 (1977 ed.), 623, 634; Isaiah Berlin, 9–10

79 See *Dugdale Diaries*, 221, and Kenneth Rose's review of 'Never Despair', *WSC*, v, viii, *Sunday Telegraph*, 29 May 1988

80 *CSWC*, i, 905

Chapter 15. An Independent Voice

1 Quoted in R. R. James, 1970, 187 n3

2 See *CSWC*, V, 4951, 5111; and *CSWC*, 111, 3525. Also his evidence before Joint Select Committee on Indian Constitutional Reform, 23 Dec. 1933. CHAR. 2/195

3 Quotations in CV/5, ii, 434, 436, and *CSWC*, V, 4986, 4987, 4996, 5004, 5245, 5507. His judgement on the Hindus in John Colville, 1985, 563

4 Linlithgow to Churchill, CV/5, ii, 603; Hoare's remarks, *CSWC*, V, 5000, and Templewood, 1954, 88; for attempt on his life, CV/5, ii, 3999 n2

5 Thinking imperially in *Nicolson Diaries*, i, 396–97. For his attitude towards the Statute of Westminster, *CSWC*, V, 5475, 5517–18, and VI, 5648. For being 'badly informed', CV/5, ii, 1243–44

6 CV/5, iii, 827

7 CV/5, ii, 592

8 CV/5, ii, 568

9 CV/5, ii, 678. For the additional evidence that has since come to light, see *WSC*, v, 511–48, and Carl Bridge, 1979

10 Churchill raised the question in the House on 1 Apr. 1934. *CSWC*, V, 5353–58; the Committee's report was debated on 13 Jun. *CSWC*, V, 5359–73; also *Amery Diaries* ii, 382–83

11 To Clementine, 21 Feb. 1935, CHAR. 1/273; 'shaken' and 'discredited', CV/5, ii, 1128

12 For Hoare's mammoth effort, Templewood, 100; and Churchill's defeat, CV/5, ii, 1240

13 CV/5, ii, 1140

14 For Churchill's attitude to the Wavertree by-election, see CV/5, 1034–35, 1044–45, CHAR. 1/273, 1064–65; his speech supporting Randolph, *CSWC*, V, 5469

15 For the 'revolt' at Epping, CV/5, ii, 1107, 1124

16 See his speeches 23 March and 13 April 1933, *CSWC*, V, 5236, 5261–62

17 Reported by Prince Bismarck, counsellor at the German Embassy in London, after a conversation with Churchill in Oct. 1930, CV/5, ii, 197

18 Regarding 'treaty revision', see his speeches of 13 Apr. 1933, *CSWC*, V, 5262; 2 May 1935, and 21 Dec. 1937, *CSWC*, VI, 5596, 5908–09. See also Churchill, *Great Contemporaries*, 205

19 The Other Club quotation in Coote, 81. His article, 'Friendship with Germany', appeared in the *Evening Standard*, 17 Sep 1937 and in *Step by Step*, 167–70. Other quotations from *Great Contemporaries*, 203–210. This essay first appeared in 1937, and remained substantially unaltered in subsequent editions

20 These quotations from *CSWC* V, 5377, CV/5, ii, 627, and *Great Contemporaries*, 208

21 Quotations in *CSWC*, VI, 5680, and *CSWC*, V, 5262

22 For example, CV/5, ii, 1248, 1251

23 For discussions and recommendations of the DRC, see CAB. 16/109–112; for 1933–34 negotiations with Germany, Vansittart to Sir John Simon, 9 Jan. 1934, and correspondence between Vansittart and Hankey, FO. 800/291, 9294, also W. N. Medlicott, 1969, 9–10; for Cabinet decisions of Jul. 1934, CAB. 27/514 (minutes of Cabinet sub-committee), and CAB. 23/79 (Cabinet minutes).

24 DRC's final report of 21 Nov. 1935, with its military recommendations, in CAB. 16/112. Two other air schemes were approved in 1938, the second, to

be completed by March 1942, to bring Britain's home defence force to 2,549 machines. Figures of air expansion schemes in, Charles Webster and Noble Frankland, 1961, iv, 103–04, and Malcolm Smith, 1984, 328–35

25 His belief in the strength of the navy, CV/5, iii, 467, and CSWC, VI, 5896; seeking command of the Mediterranean, CV/5, 114, 767, 1231, 1392 n1, 1414; and Baltic plan, CV/5, iii, 108, 1416–17, 1576–77

26 These quotations from his address to the 1922 Committee, 8 Dec. 1936, CV/5, iii, 466–67; his conversation with General Sir Edmond Ironside, 6 Dec. 1937, Ironside Diaries, 41; and in particular his memorandum on sea power, 27 Mar. 1939, CV/5, iii, 1414–17

27 See CV/5, iii, 854, 1064, 1414. Also Tuvia Ben-Moshe, 1992, 113

28 For his views on the invulnerability of the battleship, see CV/5, iii, 467, 854, 1414; Ironside [see Diaries] and Desmond Morton challenged these views, CV/5, iii, 854, 1417; and WC, i, 49, for 'silhouettes of battleships'. Also Ben-Moshe, 1992, 114, and Roskill, 1977, 89

29 Bond 1980, 92, and CV/5, i, 940, 945, 1024–25

30 See Brian Bond, 1980, 258–59

31 See Ironside Diaries, 41; and his speeches of 23 Mar. 1933, CSWC, V, 5236

32 For the warning about the state of the French army and his vigorous denial, CV/5, iii, 865–66, 869, 875; his conclusions of Aug. 1939, CV/5, iii, 1593–94

33 For a stalemate, CV/5, iii, 1593–96. And for his lack of understanding of mechanized warfare, Second World War, ii, 39, quoted in Ben-Moshe, 1992, 116. General Spears, who accompanied Churchill on his tour of the western front, recalled later that Churchill was conscious of the possibility of German armoured columns breaking through the Ardennes (WSC, v, 1101). This estimation, however, found no expression in his notes, written only five days later. See CV/5, iii, 1593–96

34 See Ironside Diaries, 51, and CV/5, iii, 937 n3

35 His call to expand the BEF, CV/5, iii, 1053; Ironside Diaries, 90, 106; CSWC, VI, 6069–70; and Ben-Moshe, 1992, 110; for deployment of BEF, Bond, 1980, 336, and J. R. M. Butler, 1957, ii, 177; and Churchill's 'surprise', Second World War, ii, 42–43

36 Quotations from Norman Rose, 1978, 127; CSWC, V, 5384, 5441; CV/5, iii, 557; and Barnes and Middlemas, 1969, 735. For official statistics, Malcolm Smith, 1984, 78, and for a general discussion of the 'knock-out blow', Uri Bialer, 1980

37 Churchill's speeches on this subject are in CSWC, V, V1. Quotations in CV/5, ii, 1134, and CSWC, V1, 5590

38 For this passage, R. J. Overy, October 1975, and 1984; Williamson Murray in B. Bond and I. Ray (eds.), 1977; Malcolm Smith, July 1980, and 1984; and Wesley K. Wark, 1982

39 For some of these evaluations, see CHAR. 2/274, 275, and CHAR. 16/53B

40 Rothermere's claim, CV/5, ii, 845. Corroborating evidence by Captain Norman Macmillan, a famous test pilot, in his memorandum of May 1935, CHAR. 2/243; see also CV/5, ii, 1161

41 Churchill's estimates from CSWC, V, 5446, 5448, and V1, 5812; CV/5, ii, 1156–1601, 1276, and iii, 500–02, 767; also Ironside Diaries, 42. CHAR.1/273, and CV/5, ii, 1140

42 See CV/5, iii, 218, 531–34; CHAR. 2/243, 244, and CV/5, ii, 849–50, 1172–73, 1310–11, 1314, CV/5, iii, 116, 121–22; CV/5, iii, 586; CV/5, iii, 617; CV/5, ii, 1356

43 Quotations in CSWC, VI, 5894–96, 5898; CV/5, iii, 635; Basil Liddell Hart in A. J. P. Taylor (ed.), 1969, 183

44 See CV/5, ii, 1207–08, and iii, 325

45 CV/5, iii, 1521–22, 1533–34
46 CV/5, iii, 1057
47 The Lindemann-Tizard feud may be followed in Roy Harrod, 1959, Birkenhead, 1961, Ronald Clark, 1964, Swinton, 1948, and (with J. Margach), 1966. For Lindemann's 'brain-childs', see CHAR. 16/53B, and 25/10, 16
48 Quotations in CHAR. 25/16, and CV/5, iii, 62–63, 235, 1053, 1054–55, 1057
49 See R. J. Overy, 1980
50 CV/5, iii, 1240
51 His 'bitter disappointment', CV5, iii, 1324, also Channon Diaries, 179; pp. softening attacks on Baldwin, CV/5, iii, 1364; for Neville beginning 'very well', CV/5, iii, 767; and supporting government, see pp 246, 247
52 Quotations in CV/5, iii, 679, 1050, 1189, 1344
53 Throughout this period, the top job was, apparently, never far from Churchill's thoughts. During an after dinner guessing game, he was asked to confess his most cherished desire. His response came without a glimmer of doubt: 'I wish to be Prime Minister and in close and daily contact with the President of the United States'. See CV/5, iii, 733 n1
54 Quotations in CV/5, iii, 236, 1040–42; also CV/5, iii, 1028–31, where Inskip sharply criticizes his proposals. In the same connection, see also CSWC, VI, 5732, 5749–56, 6019–30, and CV/5, iii, 107, 1034–35, 1456
55 For Baldwin's and Chamberlain's hostility, CV/5, iii, 55, 1280, 1456, 1541, 1545; Churchill's opinion of Baldwin, CV/5, ii, 1097: Clementine's conditions, CV/5, iii, 4; 'destiny' and 'invisible wings', CV/5, iii, 62, and Second World War, i, 141
56 For Randolph's political game plan, CV/5, ii, 1070 n2, 1086, 1095; and Churchill's reaction, CV/5, ii, 1095, and iii, 35
57 CV/5, iii, 1456
58 These details in Eugen Spier, 1963, and CV/5, iii, 162 n3
59 As 'elder statesman', CV/5, iii, 304; the diarist, Sir Robert Lockhart, quoted in CV/5, iii, 349 and n3; details about Focus in Eugen Spier, 1963; for Churchill's 'remarkable triumph', CSWC, VI, 5805–13, and his damning Baldwin, Second World War, i, 615; and for Baldwin's health and 'appalling frankness', Barnes and Middlemas, 1969, 963, 970–73
60 R. R. James, 1969, 413
61 Material concerning Churchill's role in the crisis is to be found in CHAR./264, although some of it still remains classified. Quotations also in CV/5, iii, 455, 457–58
62 See CSWC, VI, 5820–21, for his speech. Also Nicolson Diaries, i, 276; Davidson Memoirs, 415; Channon Diaries, 121; and WSC, V, 824. For Boothy's role, also about the alleged state of his intoxication, see R. R. James, 1991, 166–67; also CHAR./264 and CV/5, iii, 482–84, 486
63 See Nicolson Diaries, i, 276; Philip Ziegler, 1993; Channon Diaries 186–87; and Amery Diaries, ii, 431–32. Amery later changed his mind about Churchill's motives.
64 Quoted in Ziegler
65 Channon Diaries, 96, 107; Mabel, countess of Airlie 1962, 201; Amery 1955, iii, 216; and CSWC, VI, 5821–22
66 CSWC, VI, 5822, and CV/5, iii, 519 n1; and in the same vein, CSWC, VII, 6796, 6930
67 See Dugdale Diaries, 11 Dec. 1936 (unpublished), and R. R. James, 1991, 165–67, 170

Chapter 16. 'What Price Churchill?'

1 CSWC, VI, 5694–96, and Churchill, Second World War, i, 162–65. See also

his speeches of 24 Oct. 1935, *CSWC*, VI, 5680, and 26 Mar. 1936, *CSWC*, VI, 5720

2 Churchill opposed to 'two equal Foreign Secretaries', *CSWC*, VI, 5655; and for his opinion of Eden, CV/5, ii, 1363, and CV/5, iii, 11, 1270

3 Churchill and treaty revision, *CSWC*, VI, 5596, also pp. 219–20. The Foreign Office memorandum of 21 Nov. 1935 in FO.371/18851, C.7752/55/18. Composed by Orme Sargent and Ralph Wigram, it gained almost universal support in the Office. Wigram, head of the Central Department, was particularly close to Churchill and leaked much classified information to him.

4 'Grovelling' to Germany, CV/5, ii, 1140, and 'any measure of appeasement', *CSWC*, VI, 5908

5 For Mussolini's attitude towards Hitler, and the Franco-Italian agreements, see Denis Mack Smith, 211, 215, 221–22, 22. On Stresa, *CSWC*, VI, 5652

6 Quotations in CV/5, i, 916 n2, and *WSC*, V, 457

7 *CSWC*, VI, 5655; also *ibid*, 5661–64, and *Second World War*, i, 146

8 Reminding Hoare, CV/5, ii, 1239–40, 1248–49, 1251–52; not acting alone, *CSWC*, VI, 5654, 5673; no use of force, CV/5, ii, 1278; or sanctions, *ibid*, 1252

9 See his speech to the Commons, 24 Oct. 1935, *CSWC*, VI, 5679–86

10 Quotations in *Second World War*, i, 138, and CV/5, iii, 105

11 CHAR. 1/244; CV/5, ii, 1251; *CSWC*, V1, 5654

12 Zeila proposals in FO. 371./19113, J.1459, 2435/1/1; and Hoare-Laval plan, by which roughly two-thirds of Ethiopia would fall under Italian control, in CP. 235(35), CAB.24/257

13 On resurrecting the Stresa Front, CV/5, iii, 144; justifying Zeila and the Hoare-Laval plan, CHAR. 2/251, CV/5, iii, 2–3 & n4, *CSWC*, VI, 5654, 5724, 5747; and the British 'crusade', in a letter to *The Times*, CV/5, 102

14 This was the tenor of Churchill's contemporary statements. See his speeches of 10, 14, and 26 Mar. 1936, *CSWC*, VI, 5698–5704, 5704–05, 5717–21, and his letter to *The Times*, 20 Apr. 1936, in CV/5, iii, 101–03

15 *Second World War*, i, 151–53

16 Quotations from his speeches of 14 and 26 Mar. 1936, *CSWC*, VI, 5704–05, 5717–21, and his article of 13 Mar. 1936, 'Britain, Germany and Locarno', in *Step by Step*.

17 For 'encirclement' of Germany, *CSWC*, VI, 5720, and Churchill's Soviet oriented policy, CV/5, iii, 108, and *WSC*, V, 737. For Maisky's reputation, see D. C. Watt, 1989, 119, 217–18

18 Cheering the rebels, CV/5, iii, 297; the war as a 'plot' and 'belligerent rights' to Franco, CV/5, iii, 397, 718; on the International Brigade, see his article, 'This Agony of Civil War – To What End?', *Evening Express*, 2 Apr. 1937, in CHAR. 8/569. The incident with Azcarate in Hugh Thomas, 1961 (1965 ed.), 289 n1

19 For Churchill's encouragement of Eden, CV/5, iii, 307, 649 ns1, 2 and 714 n1. On formulation of non-interventist policy, Avon, 1962, 401–03; Lawrence R. Pratt, 1975, 41–44; David Carlton, 1971. See also Thomas, 1961 (1965 ed.), 338

20 His confusion, CV/5, iii, 800, and *Nicolson Diaries*, i, 252

21 On gradually swinging round, *Step by Step*, 188–91, 312–16; CHAR. 2/328; and CV/5, iii, 940

22 On Churchill and the Far East, CV/5, iii, 755–56; on Anglo-American cooperation, CV/5, iii, 733, n1; for his 'general agreement', CV/5, iii, 812–13; and for British attempts to seek a settlement with Germany, see W. N. Medlicott, 1969

23 See CV/5, iii, 934

24 Halifax, voicing a common view, spoke in this sense immediately after

the Anschluss, see minutes of Foreign Policy Committee, 18 Mar. 1938, CAB.27/623. This point is elaborated in David Dilks, 1987

25 Churchill's quotations from his speeches of 14 and 24 Mar. 1938, CSWC, VI, 5923–27, 5939–45; see also 'The Austrian Eye-Opener', Step by Step, 223–26. For Chamberlain, Keith Feiling, 1947, 347–48, and CV/5, iii, 952

26 Churchill and rearmament, see 'Is It Peace?', Step by Step, 335–39; for Chamberlain, Feiling, 347

27 For military-civil relations in France for this period see Robert J. Young, 1978, in particular ch. 1. Quotation in Chiefs of Staff paper, 23 Sept. 1938, CAB.53/41, COS. 770

28 Quotation from Churchill's broadcast to the United States, 16 Oct. 1938, CV/5, iii, 1216–27. See also Donald Cameron Watt, 1992, his general conclusion being that 'It would seem unlikely that it [Churchill's programme] would have actively deterred him [Hitler] let alone have resulted in his overthrow'. See also his How War Came, 44–45, and David Dilks, 1987, 345–46

29 CV/5, iii, 1529

30 Churchill and 'best treated minority', CV/5, iii, 1018. For the Sudeten problem and Henlein in general, R. M. Smelser, 1975; and for Henleins's contacts and conversations in Britain, BD, Series 3, vol, i, 633–35, and appendix 11; CV/5, iii, 1021–24; Keith Robbins 1969; and Norman Rose, 1978, 222–26. Churchill's impression of Henlein, CV/5, iii, 1025, 1112, and taking Czechs to task, Step by Step, 265–66

31 For his criticism of Czech policy, Step by Step, 265–66; and for Britain's mediatory role, his speech of 27 Aug. 1938, CSWC, VI, 6001, where he registers support for Lord Runciman's ill-fated mission. His drawing the line, Step by Step, 266

32 French policy may be followed in R. J. Young, 1978, 192–213; for examples of Anglo-French contacts, see talks of 28–28 Apr. 1938, BD, 3, i, no. 164, also Cadogan Diaries, 71–73, and Young, 200. Cabinet decision of 30 Aug. 1938 in CAB.23/94, and Inskip Diaries, 30 Aug. 1938 (deposited at Churchill College, Cambridge)

33 'Stupidest thing' in CV/5, iii, 1162; Great Power 'common action', CV/5, iii, 1130–31, 1155, 1156, 1177, and Step by Step, 284; 'fleet movements', CV/5, iii, 1184–85; German generals, BD, 3, ii, 683–86, and CV/5, iii 1119–20; Foreign Office communiqué, CV/5, iii, 1181–82, and A. Roberts, 1991, 114–19. For oppositionist MPs and congratulating Chamberlain, see Nicolson Diaries, i, 357–72, and Amery Diaries, ii, 517–26; and for a general review of Conservative opposition, Neville Thompson, 1971

34 Churchill's speaking mannerisms in Nicolson Diaries, ii, 32, 322; his speech, CSWC, VI, 6004–13; for Czechs' incapacity, Young 1978, 210, 212

35 Quoted in Dugdale Diaries, 112

36 Churchill's constituency troubles, CV/5, iii, 1213–15, 1229 and n2, 1239, 1240, 1248; on Eden's ability, Nicolson Diaries, i, 354, 365–66, CV/5, iii, 1270, 1293; and Churchill losing 'his spring', Nicolson Diaries, i, 375–76

37 In favour of war in Sept. 1938, CV/5, iii, 1156, 1342. But see his reflections of Jun. 1939, CSWC, VI, 6139–40, and CV/5, iii, 1527–31

38 For his general agreement with government policy, see his speeches of 10 Mar. and 21 Jun. 1939, CSWC, VI, 6071–72, 6139–40, and CV/5, iii, 1527–31; also his article of 9 Mar. 1939, 'Is It Peace', Step by Step, 335–39. His cautious optimism regarding rearmament may be gauged from the following estimates. From 1938–39 the percentage of GNP devoted to military expenditure rose from 8% to 21%, while the actual sums spent on the armed services jumped from £400.239 million to £700.538 million. See David Dilks, 1987, 349–50, and G. C. Peden, 1979, 205, appendix lll, table A2.

39 Churchill's support for the eastern system, CV/5, iii, 1429–30, 1446–48, 1494,

and *CSWC*, VI, 6091–96, 6100, 6104–05; for it coming years too late, *CSWC*, VI, 6012; his arguing for 'definite' Russo-Polish connection, see 'The Russian Counterpoise', *Step by Step*, 357–60; for the complexities of Anglo-Russian relations, Watt, 1989, 44–45, 117–18, 221, and Watt, 'The Initiation of the Negotiations Leading to the Nazi-Soviet, C. Abramsky and B. Williams (eds.), 1976, also Robert Manne, July, 1974; *The Times* and Chamberlain's assessment, CV/5, iii, 1438 n1, and Churchill's verdict, *CSWC*, VI, 6093

40 For Chamberlain's views on Soviet Union, see Feiling, 1947, 403, 408, and Dilks, 1987, 344, 346; and for Churchill's, CV/5, iii, 1179, and his call for an alliance, *ibid*. 1525 n2, 1530. For the pact with the Soviet Union and Chamberlain's reluctance. Cabinet minutes of 24 May 1939, CAB.23/99, *Channon Diaries*, 182, and Manne 1974

41 *Nicolson Diaries*, i, 396–97

42 Chamberlain's reluctance to bring back Churchill, CV/5, iii, 1540, 1544–46; and for his discrediting Churchill, Richard Cockett, 1989, 112–15

43 Potemkin's remark in Robert Coulondre, 1950, 165; and for Soviet moles, Watt, 230–31, and Alan Bullock, 1991, 667–78, 674. The diplomacy of 1939 can be followed in greater detail in Watt, 1989, also Bullock, ch. 14.

44 Churchill's German source, CV/5, iii, 1524; urging Chamberlain, *CSWC*, VI, 6118–23; Chamberlain's letter in Nevile Henderson, 1940, 301–03, and BD, 3, vii, 127–28; and Hitler's remark, BD, 3, vi, 692

45 Churchill's trip to France, CV/5, iii, 1591–92; his appeal not to disperse Parliament, *CSWC*, VI, 6145–49, and *Channon Diaries*, 256; despondent Parliament reconvened, *Channon Diaries* 258, and *Nicolson Diaries*, i, 406; summoned to Downing Street, Churchill, *Second World War*, i, 317, and *WSC*, V, 1106; and Chamberlain under stress, *Nicolson Diaries*, i, 410–11, and *Amery Diaries*, ii, 570

46 The events of 2 Sept. may be followed in great detail in Watt, 1989, ch. 30. For Cabinet decision. CAB.23/100; and scenes in House of Commons, *Amery Diaries*, ii, 570–71, *Nicolson Diaries*, i, 412–13, *Dugdale Diaries*, 150–51, and *Channon Diaries*, 263–64

47 Waiting for Chamberlain's call, *WSC*, V, 1108. For the meeting at Morpeth Mansions, see Duff Cooper, 1957, 259–60, and CV/5, iii, 1603–04. The description of the Cabinet session from Reginald Dorman-Smith's recollections, *Sunday Times*, 6 Sept. 1964, quoted in CV/5, iii, 1607–09

48 Churchill at Morpeth Mansions, CV/5, iii, 1609–11

Chapter 17. His Finest Hour

1 Tito in *NY Times Book Review*; story of mankind, Moran, 355; as 'Warlock' in Anne de Courcey, 1992; his recollection in *Second World War*, i, 320; 'galvanising people' and 'Winston is back', quoted in Arthur Marder, 1969, Supplement 5

2 The scene is described in *Second World War*, i, 320–21; *WSC*, VI, 4; Correlli Barnett, 1991, 58; and Marder, 1969

3 For transfer of BEF, Bond, 1980, 366; figures for Britain's survival at sea John Keegan, 1989 (1990 ed.) 104

4 'Driven from Scapa' quoted in Barnett, 1991, 72, and for navy's deficiencies in general, Roskill, Marder, and Barnett, and *WSC* VI, 17; and for Churchill's 'conventional wisdoms', see pp. 222–23

5 For Churchill as potential Prime Minister, see *Amery Diaries* ii, 571, 584, *Nicolson Diaries* ii, 32–33, and *WSC*, VI, 88; for apprehension at his activities, Dilks, 1978, 68, and *WSC*, VI, 15, 32, 59–60, 165–66

6 'Electricity' quote in *WSC*, VI, 157; his timetable and office organization, *Second World War*, i, 329, *WSC* VI, 159–62; dinner with Chamberlain,

Second World War, i, 389; Lindemann's activities in *WSC*, VI, 162–64; and Seal's comment, *WSC*, VI, 223

7 *WSC*, VI, 165

8 For Churchill's proposals, War Cabinet minutes, 20 Oct. 1939, CAB. 65/1; *Second World War*, i, 323–24; and *WSC*, VI, 5, 14–15, 17, 19, 66

9 'Bombs' and 'leaflets', *WSC*, VI, 192; reluctantly closing the Mediterranean, *Second World War*, ii, 391–92, and *WSC*, VI, 731–32. Renewing relations with Soviet Union, see his paper, 25 Sept. 1939, CHAR. 20/15, and his broadcast of 1 Oct. 1939, *CSWC*, VI, 6061

10 Churchill's remark in *WSC*, VI, 358. The Churchill-Roosevelt wartime relationship has been scrupulously recorded in Warren F. Kimball (ed.), 1984, 3 vols.

11 'All will come right' and 'stand firm' to Halifax in *WSC*, VI, 13, 73; his 'persevere to conquer' speech, *CSWC*, VI, 6160, and *Nicolson Diaries*, ii, 32–33; for enforcement of blockade, *Second World War*, i, 323, and *CSWC*, VI, 6183–84; odds of 500–1 in *CSWC*, VI, 6183; and American safety-zone in Kimball (ed.), 1984, i, 25–27

12 For U-boat incident, *CSWC*, VI, 6183, and Marder, 1969, 15–17; telling the truth, *WSC*, VI, 11; Godfrey quoted in Paul Addison, 1977, 79

13 See his paper of 25 Sept. 1939, *op.cit*. Also, *CSWC*, VI, 6160,; *WSC*, VI, 45; and *Nicolson Diaries*, ii, 32–33

14 Churchill's broadcast of 20 Jan. 1940, *CSWC*, VI, 6183–86; his 'centipede' reply, quoted in Roberts, 1991, 189; see also *WSC*, VI, 136–40

15 'Resolute Turk', in *CSWC*, VI, 6184; on Ireland, Cabinet minutes, 24 Oct. 1939, CAB.65/1, and *WSC*, VI, 43, 67–68

16 Churchill's proposed Balkan front in Cabinet minutes, 21, 22 Sept. 1939, CAB.65/1; his Italian agreement, *WSC*, VI, 57; and for sensible Italian claims, minutes of 24 May 1940, CAB.65/7

17 *Second World War*, i, 323

18 Quotations in Marder, 1969. Details of Baltic scheme in Marder, Roskill, Barnett, and *WSC*, VI, 25–27. See also R. A. C. Parker, October 1976, and David Dilks, 1977

19 Churchill's fixation with a Norway operation may be followed in his minute of 15 Jun. 1942, PREM.3/333/2; record of his talks with Stalin, 15–16 Aug. 1942, PREM.3/76A/12; his memorandum, 'Policy for the Conduct of the War', 24 Oct. 1942, CAB.66/30; Churchill to Ismay, 19 Jul. 1943, and minutes of Quadrant Conference, 23 August 1943, PREM.3/257/4

For rejection of scheme, see 'Report by Chiefs of Staff, COS(42) 278, 24 Sept. 1942, J.P.(43), 4 May 1943, and Ismay to Churchill, 11 Aug. 1943, PREM.3/257/4

20 Quotations from his memorandum, 'Norway – Iron-Ore Traffic', 16 Dec. 1939, in *Second World War*, i, 430–33, and Marder, 1969, 41 n2

21 Churchill's speech in *CSWC*, VI, 6184; for widening the conflict, see his confused remarks in Cabinet on 11 Dec. 1939, CAB.65/2; also *WSC*, VI, 99–100, 103, 136

22 Quotations in *Ironside Diaries*, 189–92, also 195–97; and Churchill's memorandum of 16 Dec. 1939, *op.cit*

23 The gist of his remarks to Cabinet, 3 Apr. 1939, CAB.65/12. This was also the view of the Chiefs of Staff, see Ismay, 1960, 119, 153

24 Minutes of the meeting in CAB.99/3

25 'Outwitted' in *Second World War*, i, 474. For prior knowledge of an intended German move, see F. H. Hinsley, 1979, 115–25; also Barnett, 1991, 104–06. It is now known that since Oct. 1939 the German navy had proposed seizing bases along the Norwegian coast.

26 *WSC*, VI, 251, 296

27 For developments relating to the Military Coordination Committee, see *Second*

World War, i, 463–65, 505–07, where Churchill is particularly discreet; Ismay 1960, 111–14, 158–59; *Action This Day*, 48. Also Dilks, 1978, 75–78

28 Quotation in *Second World War*, i, 511; as 'half-cocked', *WSC*, VI, 231. Several incidents have been convincingly recorded regarding Churchill's propensity to interfere in these matters. Among the most conspicuous was the order, on 8 Apr. to disembark troops being held on alert, leaving them stranded without transport ships or escorts, thereby delaying an immediate response to the German strike the following day; and also Churchill's special concern with the particulars of the Narvik operation. See Roskill, 1991, 1954–61, i, 1977, 99, 105–08, 116, 289, 293–94, and Roskill, December 1972; Barnett, 1991, 117–18, 120–23; Marder, 1960, which takes a more lenient view, but does not deny the essence of the charges; and Piers Mackesy, 1970, and 1985

29 Keyes quoted in Marder, 1969; also Ironside's similar conclusion, *Ironside Diaries*, 192. And Churchill, *Second World War*, i, 511

30 The above scenes are based on: *Channon Diaries*, 299-303; *Nicolson Diaries*, ii, 71–76; *Amery Diaries*, ii, 592–93; *Dugdale Diaries*, 168–69; and Alistair Horne, 1988, i, 139. Churchill's speech in *CSWC*, VI, 6212–18. The actual figures for the division were 281 for the government, 200 against. Among those who voted against were 33 Conservatives and 8 other supporters, while another 60 Conservatives abstained.

31 This account derives from: Churchill, *Second World War*, i, 523–24; Lord Blake in Blake and Louis (eds.); Roberts, 1991, 198–207; *Cadogan Diaries*, 277–80; Hugh Dalton, 1957, 306–07; Wheeler-Bennett, 1969, 162; Ismay, 1960 116; and Colville, 1985, 122. For public opinion poll, Dennis Kavanagh, 1974. The poll was taken in March 1940, but there is no reason to assume that two months after the Norwegian fiasco the results would have been significantly different. See also, *WSC*, VI, 288–305

   David Carlton, 1986, 161–62, takes a different view, arguing that Chamberlain preferred Churchill, believing Halifax to be a more serious rival should, once the war was over, a leadership race break out again. This is an intriguing, though not entirely convincing, thesis.

32 CHAR.2/393

33 *Second World War*, i, 526–27

34 Quotations in Ismay, 1960, 116, 140

35 Churchill quote in *Second World War*, ii, 157, 79; the Chiefs of Staff memorandum, 26 May 1940, in CAB.66/7, also printed in *Second World War*, ii, 78–79; and for his October conditions, *WSC*, VI, 56–57. Comment to Ismay quoted in David Reynolds, 1985, 154

36 Dilks, 1978, 82. And for following passage, see War Cabinet minutes for discussions of 26–28 May 1940, CAB.65/13. Also David Reynolds, 1985 and 1993; Jonathan Knight, 1977; *WSC*, VI, 412–13, 418–22; Dalton, 1957–62, 335–36; Roberts, 1991, 212–24, 227–29; and Norman Rose, 1978, 194–95

37 'Common sense . . .' quoted in David Reynolds 1985

38 As the RAF sustained heavier losses in the Battle of France than it did in the Battle of Britain, the months of May-June were more critical for its survival than the more dramatic weeks of Aug-Sep. It has been estimated that from 10 Jul. until 31 Oct. overall air losses were 915 British aircraft to 1,733 German. See R. J. Overy, 1987, 34

39 See François Lafitte, 1939; *WSC*, VI, 342, 378, 389, 586; and Angus Calder, 150–53

40 Clementine's remark, 6 Apr. 1916, in CHAR. 1/118, Part 1; Anglo-French Union in Cabinet minutes, 16 Jun. 1940, CAB. 65/7, also Avi Shlaim, 1974; and for disabling of French fleet, minutes of 22 Jun. 1940, CAB. 65/7, *Second World War*, ii, 206, and *CSWC*, VI, 6241–47. Apart from the action at Mers-el-Kebir, all French ships stationed at Plymouth and Portsmouth were

seized, a French naval force based at Alexandria was commandeered, and at Dakar, the battleship *Richelieu* was torpedoed and crippled.

41 Churchill's reception in Commons, and Cabinet-making, *Nicolson Diaries*, ii, 81–82, *Dugdale Diaries*, 170, and *Channon Diaries*, 309; for composition of Churchill's government, *Second World War*, ii, 13–14, and Paul Addison, 1975 (1977 ed.), 106 and Appendix; the under-secretaries plot in *Amery Diaries*, ii, 625–26, *Dugdale Diaries*, 173, and R. R. James, 1991, 256–61; Lloyd George's remark quoted in David Reynolds, 1985: in same connection, see also Paul Addison in A. J. P. Taylor (ed.), 1971

42 Halifax's resignation, *WSC*, VI, 413, and *Cadogan Diaries*, 291; Lloyd George's comment quoted in Addison in Taylor (ed.), 1991, quoting Thomas Jones, 1969, 465; for the Churchill-Churchill-Chamberlain relationship, Dilks, 1978

43 Defending 'grand human causes', *WSC*, VI, 836–37; and 'ding-dong arguments', Soames, 299–300

44 For 'morale' and survival, and 'conquer or die', *Second World War*, ii, 79, 146. Two 'public causes' in *WSC*, VI, 836; Attlee quoted in *Observer*, 16; Churchill's speeches, *CSWC*, VI, 6218–20, 6225–31, 6231–38

Some of Churchill's more famous phrases echoed those of two of his favourite historical figures, Garibaldi and Clemenceau. In Rome, July 1849, Garibaldi offered 'neither pay, nor quarter, nor provisions': he did offer 'hunger, forced marches, battles and death'. In March 1918, in Paris, Clemenceau told Churchill: 'I will fight in front of Paris; I will fight in Paris; I will fight behind Paris.' To the National Assembly, he said: 'My formula is the same everywhere. Home Policy? I wage war. Foreign Policy? I wage war. All the time I wage war.' See Churchill, *Great Contemporaries*, 246, and A. J. P. Taylor, 1965, 475 n1

45 'Home Ground', *Second World War*, ii, 228. Murrow quoted in D. J. Wenden, 1993.

46 See *WSC*, VI, 80–81, 365; Mark Amory (ed.), 630; and *Nicolson Diaries*, ii, 90, 93–94. For radio audiences, Wenden, 1993, and Angus Calder, 112–13

47 Churchill on tour and his agility, *WSC*, VI, illustration 13; *Colville Diaries*, 296, 341; and Ismay, 1960, 184. Baldwin quoted in *Nicolson Diaries*, ii, 307

48 Cinema tickets sold, Calder, 423; Churchill's wartime popularity, Kavanagh, 1974; 'featured' in newsreels, *WCS*, VI, 354

Chapter 18. Standing Alone

1 'Plenary authority' in CV/3, ii, 1373; and Churchill's defence machinery, Ismay, 158–76, and *WSC*, vi, 323–26

2 Ismay, 1960, 164–65; Lindemann's ideas, *WSC*, VI, 593; Eden's comments from John Harvey (ed.), 1978, 15, quoted in *WSC*, VI, 1112. For his behaviour in committee and 'brainstorms', see also Ismay, 159, passim; *Alanbrooke War Diaries*; John Kennedy, 1957 and Ian Jacob, in Wheeler-Bennett (ed.), 1969, 158–217

3 Quoted in Wheeler-Bennett (ed.), 207, and Kimball (ed.), 1984, i, 594

4 See Elizabeth Nel, 1958, 27–28, 74

5 'Inarticulate grunts', Martin, 1991, 11, and Wheeler-Bennett (ed.), 219; as wounding, Nel, 68; cancelling meetings and hammering, *Colville Diaries*, 280–81; and 'going to bed', Nel, 28. In same connection, see Nel, 33–34, 50–53; *Colville Diaries*, 126–27; and Ismay, 1960, 176

6 As 'headmaster', Moran, (1966), 201–02; 'egoistic and dictatorial', *Amery Diaries*, ii, 637, and *Nicolson Diaries*, ii, 250; Vic Oliver, *Colville Diaries*, 415; and *Second World War*, iv, 78. For similar comments regarding his brusque manner, see *Nicolson Diaries*, ii, 171, 384; *Colville Diaries*, 428; *Cadogan Diaries*, 339; Martin 1991, 43; and James 1991, 252, 275–76

7 *WSC*, VI, 587–88

8 'Just heart and soul', Nel, 34; violently offensive and making amends, *Colville Diaries*, 126–27, 280–81

9 Unclear how to win the war, *Colville Diaries*, 266; 'superior will-power', Ismay, 1960, 195; for preserving public morale, see his speech notes to a secret session of the Commons, 20 Jun. 1940, *WSC*, VI, 578–80; Colonel Blimp episode, Wenden, 1993

10 Eade (ed.), 1946, 8–16. His speech notes are printed here.

11 'Set Europe ablaze', Dalton, 1957–62, 366; economic intelligence reports and Chiefs of Staff assessments, Hinsley, 1979–90; 232, 237–38; 'economic playground', *Cadogan Diaries*, 316; and for Germany's war-time economy, see Alan Milward, 1965, and R. J. Overy, 1982; also D. Reynolds, 1985, 157–60

12 Bombers as 'means of victory', quoted in D. Reynolds, 1985, 156; as advocate of area bombing, Overy 1987, 38–39; and 'letting 'em have it', *Colville Diaries*, 230, 249, and *WSC*, VI, 803

13 See the official (Butt) report printed in Charles Webster and Noble Frankland, 1961, iv, 205–13; assaulting 'German agriculture', Fussel, 1989, 16; air losses, Lord Carver, 1993, and John Keegan, 1990, 420; and Churchill as 'loathed', *Dugdale Diaries*, 186. For more detailed accounts of the limited effects of the bombing offensive, see Overy, 1987 37–39, and Webster and Frankland, i, 167–87, 190–212, 299–306, 473–92

14 Doubts about strategic bombing, *WSC*, VI, 1205, and *Second World War*, iii, 451–52, v, 456–65, vi, 598; 'de-housing', quoted in Paul Fussell, 1989, 16; and 'Are we beasts?', Richard Casey, 1962, 166

15 Impairing enemy's morale, *Second World War*, iii, 451; Lindemann and Air Staff in agreement, *WSC*, VII, 468 n4; and reporting to Stalin, *WSC*, VII, 178–79, 356–57, 375–76, 468, 599–600

16 Churchill protesting *WSC*, VIII, 178; details of Dresden, *WSC*, VII, 1220 n2. British aircraft, dropping some 2,700 tons of bombs, led the raid on Dresden. Several hours later an American second wave followed, raining another 700 tons on an already shattered city.

17 Involving the United States in war, see *WSC*, VI, 485

18 New World reconquering the Old, *WSC*, VI, 444, 486; also *CSWC*, VI, 6231. 'Pick up the *débris*', *WSC*, VI, 486; for further evidence of Churchill suspecting the United States of wishing to dismember and inherit the British Empire, see W. R. Louis, 1978, 7–8, 26, 351

19 *Colville Diaries*, 215–16

20 *WSC*, VI, 564

21 Quotation in Robert E. Sherwood, 1948, i, 10, 298–99, 365

22 Quoted in Warren Kimball, 1993. For American attitudes towards Britain, David Reynolds, 1981, Louis, 1978, and Kimball (ed.), 1984, i, 14–15

23 Harry Hopkins' remarks in PREM.3/224/2; Churchill's reactions to lend-lease, CSWC, VII, 7140, *WSC*, VI, 1041, and PREM.3/224/2; and Sherwood, 1948, i, 299

24 See *WSC*, VI 719, 722; *Colville Diaries*, 211, 241; Kersuady, 96, 100–01; and *Nicolson Diaries*, ii, 116. There is an amusing and perceptive account of the Dakar operation in Evelyn Waugh's masterly *Sword of Honour*.

25 Waging war in *Colville Diaries*, 252. For details of reinforcements to Middle East, J. R. M. Butler, 1957, ii, 308; *Second World War*, ii, 378–79; *WSC*, VI, 735–36; and *Colville Diaries*, 266

26 For intelligence sources, see pp. 280–81, Churchill's correspondence with the Chiefs of Staff in Butler, Appendix IV, 577–80

27 See *WSC*, VI, 1140

28 *Second World War*, ii, 480

29 Quotations in Hinsley 1979–90, i, 354, and Tuvia Ben-Moshe 1992, 137;

Churchill's arguments to prevent a German takeover, CAB.65/21, No.12., also WSC, VI, 1006–07; For the passage on Greece, see in particular Kennedy, 1957, 69–76; Ben Moshe, 131–53; and Martin van Crevald, 1974

30 Wavell's objection in Hinsley, 1979–90, i, 354; 'another Dunkirk' and Dill, *Colville Diaries*, 356. See also *WSC*, VI, 1007, 1011; Ben-Moshe, 1992, 137, 140, 146; Kennedy, 1957, 73–74

31 Churchill's 'sealed orders', Avon, 1964, 192–93; and clarification, *Second World War*, iii, 63; Cabinet decision in CAB.65/21, Confidential Annex.

32 See minutes of 24 Feb. 1941, CAB.65/21, Confidential Annex, and *WSC*, VI, 1014

33 *CSWC*, VI, 6391

34 Churchill's parliamentary triumph, *Nicolson Diaries*, ii, 163, and *WSC*, VI, 1083–83; his speeches in *CSWC*, VI, 6385, 6388–99, 6401–05, 6408–23

35 See Alan Bullock, 1952 (1969 ed.), 643–46; A. J. P. Taylor, 1972, 483–85, and 1973, 220–21; Record of meeting between Churchill and Stalin, 15 Aug. 1942, PREM. 3/76A/12; *Cadogan Diaries*, 376–80, 386–88; *Second World War*, iii, 43–49

36 Quotations in Christopher Andrew, 1988. For Churchill, Ultra and intelligence matters in general, see also Sir Harry Hinsley, 1993; Martin Gilbert, 1990; Hinsley, 1979–90; Keegan, 1989 (1990 ed.), 497–502; and *WSC*, VI, 609–13

37 See Gerald Pawle, 1963, 118–19; Soames, 316; and *WSC*, VII, 99

38 CHAR. 20/32; Churchill's entourage in *Nicolson Diaries*, ii, 126, and Lady Diana quoted in *WSC*, VII, 357

39 Nel, 55, 58

40 See *Colville Diaries*, 316, 509, 529, 554, and *WSC*, VII, 428, 949–50, 1285; and for Rufus incident, Halle, 1987, 157

41 'Mad Hatter's Dinner Party', *WSC*, VI, 683–85.

42 Letter of 14 Jul. 1940, CHAR. 20/2, and *WSC*, VI, 663

43 His breakfast and hand slipping in *WSC*, VII, 317, 1271; and 'over-eating', J. Martin, 1991, 13

44 Moran, 19, 108–09, 171–72

45 Moran, 31–32

46 Miles travelled, *WSC*, VII, 552; and Clementine's worry, *WSC*, VII, 288

47 For this episode, see *Second World War*, IV, 650–51, and V, 372–73; Moran, 108–09, 173; and *WSC*, VII, 606

48 See Moran, 197, 202, 261

49 Quotations in *Cadogan Diaries*, 438, 621, and *Colville Diaries*, 474, 537, 554–55

50 Quotations in *WSC*, VII, 69, and Moran, 117–18

Chapter 19. Grand Strategy

1 *WSC*, VI, 1273

2 The *Repulse* and the *Prince of Wales*, Correlli Barnett, 1991, 397–400, 415–21; and Churchill's 'shock', *Second World War*, iii, 551. For Singapore and US fleet, see his paper of 18–20 Dec. 1941 in PREM. 3/499/2; it was written while on his way to America. Exhorting defence of Singapore, *WSC*, VII, 48, and sending reinforcements there, *Second World War*, iii, 564–66, iv, 10–11

3 *Second World War*, VI, 344

4 Churchill's account, including text of his note, in *Second World War*, iii, 319–23. But see also Gabriel Gorodetsky, 1984, 112–25; Martin Kitchen, 1987; and *WSC*, VI, 1051

5 His initial reaction to 'Barbarossa', *Colville Diaries*, 405–06, and Avon, 1965, 270; text of his broadcast in *CSWC*, VI, 6427–31

6 *Colville Diaries*, 404

7　See Correlli Barnett, 1991, 693–95, 748
8　Roosevelt's message for Stalin in Sherwood, 1948, i, 321–22, and his urging Churchill, Kimball, i, 221–22. For Churchill going to 'meet God!' Sherwood, i, 351 (ed.) 1984
9　Text of Charter in Second World War, iii, 393–95; Attlee's quotation in Louis, 1978, 122–125; and hitting 'it off', Cadogan Diaries, 399
10　Churchill's statements to the Cabinet, 19 Aug. 1941, CAB.65/19, and to the House, 27 Jan. 1942, CSWC, VI, 6563; see also Kimball (ed.), 1984, i, 229–31. British observers in Sherwood, 1948, i, 356, Ted Morgan 1985, (1986 ed.), 598, and WSC, VI, 1166
11　Cadogan Diaries, 399
12　These quotations are taken from Professor D. C. Watt's unpublished paper 'Could War in the Far East have been Prevented in November 1941?' I am most grateful to Professor Watt for making available to me this stimulating article.
　　Churchill's message to Roosevelt also in Kimball (ed.) 1984, i, 265
13　Above quotations in Watt (unpub.). Churchill's minutes also in WSC, VI, 1260, and for his exchange with Roosevelt, Kimball (ed.), 1984, i, 275–76, 277–78
14　Quotations in Watt, (unpub.)
15　Quotations in Watt (unpub.)
16　CSWC, VI, 6695
17　WSC, VII, 44; also Kimball, 1993
18　The Americans and the Middle East, Second World War, iii, 377–79; and no 'major land campaign', Gwyer 1964, iii, part i, 127, quoted in Ben Moshe, 1992, 171
19　See memoranda from Churchill, 16 Dec. 1941, his 'war plan', and 18–20 Dec. 1941, and his review of 'The Atlantic Front, the Pacific Front, The Campaign of 1943'; Chiefs of Staff to Churchill, 20 Dec. 1941; and Hollis to Chiefs of Staff, 21 Dec. 1941, all in PREM. 3/499/2. See also Ben Moshe, 1992, 172–76
20　For the Arcadia-Washington conference, see Gwyer, 1964, iii, part 1, 353–65, and Ben Moshe, 1992, 180
21　For details of the American military proposals, Churchill's reaction to them, and Marshall's impression, see Sherwood, 1948, ii, 523–28; Churchill's message to Roosevelt in Kimball (ed.), 1985, i, 448–49; and Roosevelt's response, Hopkins Papers, Box 308, file 5, quoted in Timothy Garton Ash, 1987. See also WSC, VII, 85–86, and Ben Moshe, 1992, 181–85
22　See J. R. M. Butler 1964, iii, Part II, 624–31, and Second World War, iv, 344
23　Butler 1964, 631
24　Brooke's remark in Alanbrooke War Diaries, i, 352; Eisenhower quoted in Walter Scott Dunn, Jr, 1980, 17, also S. Ambrose, 1970, 76; and Churchill's 'eccentric operations', Sherwood, 1948, ii, 594
25　Dill's message, WSC, VII, 160; a 'much retarded' Round-Up, Churchill's memorandum, 'Policy for the Conduct of the War', 24 Oct. 1942, CAB.66/30; Churchill's 'most satisfactory' quoted in Ben Moshe, 1992, 192–93; and for Beaverbrook, A. J. P. Taylor, 1972, 522–47
26　For the Dieppe passage see, Second World War, iv, 457–59; Philip Ziegler, 1985 (1986 ed.), 186–92; Moran 85; WSC, VII, 211; Taylor, 538; and Dunn, 1980, 196. For an eccentric view that presents Mountbatten as the undisguised villain of the piece, see Brian Loring Villa, 1990
27　'Suction pump', Ben Moshe, 1992, 210; for complaints about diversion of American resources, Bryant i, 499, 512, 505, 508
28　To Ismay, 23 Jul. 1942, PREM. 3/257/5, quoted in Ben Moshe, 1992, 191
29　Minutes of Molotov's and Stalin's meetings with Churchill in PREM. 3/333/8, 3/76A/12; and Stalin not accepting North Africa as the second front, WSC,

VII, 280–81. For northern operations see Churchill to Ismay, 19 Jul. 1943, PREM. 3/257/4, and WSC, VII, 444–46

30 Churchill, 'Policy for the Conduct of the War', 24 Oct. 1942, CAB.66/30

31 Proceedings of the Casablanca conference in FRUS, 'Conferences at Washington, 1941–42, and Casablanca, 1943, 1968. See also CHAR. 20/127, Michael Howard, 1972, IV, ch. XIII, XIV. And Churchill, Second World War, ii, 619–21, and Minutes of Combined Chiefs of Staff, 23 Jan. 1943, CAB.80/67

32 See Chief of Staffs meeting, 13 Apr. 1943, CAB. 79/60, and Ben Moshe, 1992, 217; also WSC, VII, 383

33 Alanbrooke War Diaries, ii, 506–08

34 See Ben Moshe, 1992, 221–22

35 Quotations and figures in Correlli Barnett, 1991, 276, 573, 607–12, also Keegan, 1989 (1990 ed.), 113, 118–19

36 Quotations in Churchill to Ismay, 19 Jul. 1943, Ismay to Churchill, 11 Aug. 1943, and Minutes of Quadrant Conference, 23 Aug. 1943, PREM. 3/257/4; for Dodecanese islands, Second World War, v, 185–200

37 Kimball (ed.), 1984, ii, 541, 556

38 Minutes of the War Cabinet and Chiefs of Staff meeting, 19 Oct. 1943, CAB.79/66; also Ben Moshe, 1992, 250–252. I am grateful to Timothy Garton Ash for providing me with the Ritchie-Hook image.

39 Proceedings of the conference in FRUS, Conferences at Cairo and Teheran, 1943, 1961. Also John Ehrman, 1956, v, 173–83, and Alanbrooke War Diaries, ii, 76–78

40 For the latest account of the Anzio operation, see Carlo D'Este, 1991

41 Churchill to Cadogan, 19 Apr. 1944, PREM.3/197/2; Churchill 'hardening', Colville Diaries, 483; and Minutes of Dominion Prime Ministers Meeting in WSC, VII, 767–68

42 See Alanbrooke War Diaries, 177–79, 182; Ehrman, 1956, V, 111–12, 393, and Ben Moshe, 1992, 293, 295–96, 298–99

43 Quotations in Kennedy, 1957, 309, 305

44 Churchill and German generals, WSC, iii, 755; and 'hecatombs', WSC, VII, 760 remarks to Stalin, PREM.3/76A/12; and to Chiefs of Staff, quoted in Ben Moshe, 1992, 263

45 Quotations in WSC, VI, 1227, and VII, 167, 169, 369, 913; Alanbrooke War Diaries, ii, 184, 349; Nicolson Diaries, ii, 208–09; Halle 1987, 288

The question of the second front has attracted much attention. See also, Mark Stoler, 1977; Walter Scott Dunn, Jr 1980; John Grigg 1980; Ross Graham 1975; Keith Sainsbury, 1978; Joseph L. Strange, 1982; and Tuvia Ben Moshe 1990

Chapter 20. 'Advance, Britannia!'

1 Cadogan Diaries, 711

2 Comparison of enemy and allied forces in Ben Moshe, 1992, 216, 254. Churchill's note to Chiefs of Staff, 21 Nov. 1943, PREM.3/76/12

3 See Kimball (ed.), 1984, iii, 225–29

4 WSC, VII, 1283

5 See also Ben Moshe, 1992, 241

6 'Destroyers for bases' in Kimball (ed.), 1984, i, 138–42; civil aviation dispute, ibid., i, 17; colonial trusteeship is thoroughly explored in W. R. Louis, 1978; the return of Hong Kong, Louis, 7, 229; for India and resignation threat, Kimball, 1984, i, 446–47, and Sherwood, ii, 535–36; the Greece-Roumania crisis, Kimball, 1984, iii, 178–80, 201–02; 'going short', Cadogan Diaries, 462; and begging like Fala, John M. Blum, 1970, 598–99

7 See Second World War, i, vii; letter to Eisenhower, quoted in Martin Gilbert

29 July 1980. See also David Reynolds, Louis and Bull (eds.), and Kimbal, 1984, i, 5

8 This passage is based on *Colville Diaries*, 215–16, 312–13, 363; Churchill's 'Morning Thoughts. Note on Post-War Security', 1 Feb. 1943, in M. Howard 1972, IV, 637–39; and Ben Moshe, 1992, 281–82.

9 See Douglas Johnson in Blake and Louis (eds. 1993)

10 Churchill's anti de Gaulle paper, 13 July 1943, in PREM. 3/181/8, and Roosevelt's, 17 June 1943, in Kimball (ed.), 1984, ii, 255–56.

11 Paris crowds, *Cadogan Diaries*, 679; alliance discussions and suspicions resurfacing, Kersuady, 388–9, 395; and reporting to Roosevelt, Kimball (ed.), 1984, iii, 390

12 'Wooing a crocodile', *Alanbrooke Diaries*, ii, 114, and Kitchen, 1987

13 *WSC*, VII, 364, 1027

14 The Curzon line (after the British Foreign Secretary, Lord Curzon) had been agreed upon by the victorious powers at the Paris Peace Conference as the Soviet-Polish frontier. It was disregarded by the Poles in their war against the Soviet Union. Flushed with nationalist fervour, they imposed a new border at the treaty of Riga in 1921, about 150 miles east of the Curzon line, incorporating into the enlarged Polish state substantial Ukrainian and Belorussian minorities. Stalin, therefore, came not only upholding his deal with Hitler but also as defender of the Versailles settlement.
     Of course, the London Polish government-in-exile resolutely rejected the Curzon line, and in particular refused to abandon the city of Lvov that lay within the Russian area.

15 Churchill's broadcast, *CSWC*, VI, 6161; and reacting fiercely, Churchill to Eden, 8 Jan. 1942, PREM.3/399/7, also M. Kitchen, 1987

16 *Cadogan Diaries*, 444

17 Eden's 'stark realism', PREM.3/399/7; Churchill appealing to Roosevelt, Kimball (ed.), 1989, i, 394, also *Cadogan Diaries*, 442–44; 'like a bomber pilot', *Nicolson Diaries*, ii, 221; 'Munich over again', quoted in Carlton, 1986, 197; arm-twisting, *Cadogan Diaries*, 455; and text of Anglo-Soviet treaty in CAB.66/24

18 Roosevelt's change of heart in Sherwood, ii, 706–08, 713, and Kimball (ed.), 1984; ii, 178; on Katyn, quoted in Kitchen, 1987; and for Poland moving westwards, *WSC*, VII, 576

19 Churchill's minute to Eden, 16 Jan. 1944, CHAR.20/152, also quoted in *WSC*, VII, 652

20 Proceedings of Teheran Conference in *FRUS*, 1961; the toasting in Moran, 165

21 For Teheran, see Sherwood, ii, 771–72; Kimball (ed.) 1984, i, 12–13; and Moran, 155–57

22 Quoted in Wheeler-Bennett, ed., 1969, 96. To Eduard Benes, president of Czechoslovakia, he employed the more flattering image of 'a small lion . . . talking between a huge Russian bear and a great American elephant, but perhaps it would prove to be the lion which knew the way', *Colville Diaries*, 564

23 Note to Eden in CHAR.20/179, also *WSC*, VII, 641–42

24 Stalin's moves in Poland west of the 1939 partition line after the opening of second front in June 1944 may be followed in Vojtech Mastny, 1979. Quotations in Kimball (ed.), 1984, iii, 254, 292–94, and *WSC*, VII, 861, 926

25 See his minutes of 15 Feb. 1944, FO.954/20

26 *Colville Diaries*, 513; and for Churchill and the zoning of Germany, see Tony Sharp, 1975, 7, 82–91

27 For the Morgenthau plan, see Blum 594–99; Moran 199–201; and *Second World War*, VI, 138–39

28 Quoted in Kitchen, 1987

29 See Antony Polonsky and Boleslaw Drukier (eds.), 1980, 298, quoted in T. G. Ash, 11 June 1987; Churchill's speech, CSWC, VII, 7007–08
    For the passage on the Moscow ('Tolstoy') conference, see PREM.3/434/7, FO.800/302 (Inverchapel papers), and FO.800/414. Also Second World War, 197–212; Kimball (ed.), 1984, iii, 359; WSC, VII, 989–1033; Kitchen, 1987; Stanislaw Mikolajczyk, 1948, 97–99; Moran, 1966, 215–16, 221–23; and Carlton, 1986, 246
30 Letters in WSC, VII, 1028, and Kimball (ed.), 1984, iii, 359
31 See Colville Diaries, 479, 484, 550, 551; and Cecil Parrott, 1975, 112–15. I am grateful to Professor D. C. Watt for bringing this reference to my attention.
32 Quoted in Kersaudy, 389
33 Colville Diaries, 555
34 T. G. Ash, 11 June 1987
35 Quotations in Alanbrooke War Diaries, ii, 324, Moran, 247–48, and WSC, VII, 1209
36 Quotations in WSC, VII, 1175; Cadogan Diaries, 706; Sherwood, ii, 844; and WSC, VI, 308.
    The proceedings of the Yalta Conference are in FRUS, Malta and Yalta, 1955
37 Second World War, VI, 346
38 Churchill's report to Cabinet, 19 Feb. 1945, CAB.65/51
39 Colville Diaries, 562. Hugh Dalton sharpened Churchill's analogy, and reported him as saying: 'Poor Neville Chamberlain believed he could trust Hitler. He was wrong. But I don't think I'm wrong about Stalin.' Dalton Diaries (deposited at The London School of Economics), 23 Feb. 1945
40 See Churchill's speech to the Commons, 27 Feb. 1945, CSWC, VII, 7107–24; Colville Diaries, 565–66; Nicolson Diaries, ii, 439–42; and Channon Diaries, 485–86
41 'White snows of Russia,' in Colville Diaries, 563; his remark to the Commons, CSWC, VII, 7109; and to the War Cabinet, 13 Apr. 1945, CAB.65/52
42 Quotations in Moran, 307, 310, 371
43 His telegram of 29 Apr. 1945, PREM.3/356/6
44 Quoted in WSC, VII, 1329–30
45 See his messages of 12 May 1945 (in Second World War, VI, 498–99), and 4 June 1945 (in PREM.3/356/13)
    For the genesis of this well-known phrase, that was not coined by Churchill though it was monopolized by him, see Henry B. Ryan, 1979, and Martin Gilbert, April 1981
46 Quoted in T. G. Ash 11 June 1987
47 Second World War, IV, 861–62
48 Menzies's 'impression' in Cazalet Diaries, 259; Churchill's speech to the Commons, CSWC, VI, 6389; and demolishing rivals, Channon Diaries, 371
49 For Cripps, see Addison, 1975, (1977 ed.), 205–06, 209–10, and Addison 1992, 348 and Calder, 1969 (1971 ed.), The People's War, 311–13
50 Quoted in Calder, 280
51 Bevan quoted in WSC, VII, 138; 'Arsenic and Old Lace' in Halle, 167
52 Tories hating him and yielding to another, WSC, VII, 49
53 See WSC, VII, 125, 141. Was Churchill as clear-cut in his choice as indicated? Churchill, Eden reported to his private secretary, Oliver Harvey, had told the King that if he 'fell down dead . . . [the King] should choose either A. E. or [Sir John] Anderson and that he should wait 4–5 hours to see which way opinion went.' (See Harvey Diaries, 98). Twinning Eden with Anderson, a somewhat anonymous ex-civil servant, essentially a non-party figure, who served Churchill as Lord President and later as Chancellor of the Exchequer, could not have been very flattering to Eden.

54 Eden's complicated and often stormy relationship with Churchill may be followed in David Carlton, 1986; R. R. James, 1986; Elisabeth Barker; and *Harvey Diaries*, 87, 94, 98

55 See Addison, 1975, (1977 ed.), 106–07, 279–80 and Addison, 1992, 327–82; also Calder, 119–20

56 'Common Folk' quoted in Quentin Reynolds, 1941, 180; Attlee in Paul Addison in A. J. P. Taylor (ed.) 1976

57 Halle, 205

58 Churchill's comments in *Second World War*, IV, 861–62; Attlee's in Francis Williams, 1961, 57, quoted in Alan Bullock, 1967, ii, 228

59 See Addison in A. J. P. Taylor (ed.), 1976, 185

60 See *CSWC*, VII, 6755–65; also Addison, 1992, 369, 374

61 Quoted in Bullock, 1983, ii, 296

62 Quoted in P. Addison, 1975 (1977 ed.), 251

63 By-election results in P. Addison, *loc. cit.*, 230–31, 248–49

64 See *Channon Diaries*, 479, and *Amery Diaries*, ii, 998

65 Attlee on Churchill's Cabinets, *Observer*, 18; Martin on his work; Moran 240

66 Graffito incident, *Nicolson Diaries*, ii, 348

67 Greeting 1945, *Colville Diaries*, 550; and Conservative conference, *Channon Diaries*, 487

68 These quotations are from the four speeches and broadcasts that he delivered on 8 May 1945, Victory-in-Europe day. See *CSWC*, VII, 7153, 7154

69 Moran, 205

Chapter 21. The Great Commoner

1 *WSC*, VII, 649; Moran, 345

2 See *Cadogan Diaries*, 767, 769; and for 'bloody Poles', Moran, 308. For the Potsdam conference, see, *FRUS*, Berlin; *Second World War*, VI, 545–82; and *WSC*, VII, 60–104

3 Churchill's afterthought, *Second World War*, VI, 581–82; and under Stalin's 'spell', *Cadogan Diaries*, 764, and R. R. James, 1986, 307

4 Quotations in *WSC*, VIII, 78, *Cadogan Diaries*, 765, and R. R. James, 1986, 307

5 Churchill's achievements, *WSC*, VIII, 104; and *Cadogan Diaries*, 778

6 See W. K. Hancock and M. M. Gowing, 1949, 546–55; J. C. R. Dow, 1964, 14–15, and Hugh Dalton, 1962, 68–73

7 Churchill-Truman conversation in *Second World War*, VI, 546–47, and *WSC*, VIII, 67–68; Churchill on Truman, Moran, 296, 297

8 See CHUR. 2/3. Also Margaret Gowing in David Dilks (ed.), 1981, for an excellent summary of this topic; also her more detailed book, 1964. Churchill's initial reaction, *Alanbrooke Diaries*, ii, 374; other quotations in *Second World War*, VI, 551–52

9 'Lonely without a war' and 'no message', Moran, 277; hints of retiring, *Nicolson Diaries*, ii, 100, and *WSC*, VI, 1170, 1238; Clementine pressing him, Soames, 382

10 *Nicolson Diaries*, ii, 476, 480

11 'Booed' and 'a squib', Soames, 383; the Gestapo incident in Henry Pelling, 1980, and P. Addison, 1975 (1977 ed.), 265–66; and correspondence regarding the Laski controversy in CHAR. 2/552, and P. Addison, *op. cit.*, 266

12 'Crack-pot' opponent, Soames, 386; and declining the Order of the Garter, *WSC*, VIII, 109

13 Priorities wrong, P. Addison, 1975 (1977 ed.), 267; 'abuse', etc., Moran, 274,

275; Clementine's suspicions, Soames, 382–83; and expecting a majority, Wheeler-Bennett, 1958, 635

14 Warned off the turf, *Nicolson Diaries*, ii, 484

15 Sarah Churchill, 1968, 93

16 Soames, 389, 391, 397

17 See *WSC*, VIII, 179, 450–52

18 The holiday at Lake Como in Sarah Churchill, 94–104; and *WSC*, VIII, 143

19 Money melting, *WSC*, VIII, 308; and turning Chartwell over to National Trust, *WSC*, VIII, 255–57, 304, and Soames, 395

20 The details of the setting up of Chartwell Trust and his literary contracts for his war memoirs, in CHUR.4/41, 42; developing a property, Halle, 233; Luce, Korda, London Film Productions, and Columbia Studios in *WSC*, VIII, 255, 423–24, 1206–07. *My Early Life* was eventually screened as *Young Winston*. For an equivalent, at today's rates, multiply the numbers by 17.

21 His bank statements in CHUR.1/4, 109; also *WSC*, VIII, 255

22 Soames, 396

23 See *WSC*, VIII, 221, 344–45, 412–13

24 'My case', *WSC*, VIII, 315; using government records, *WSC*, VIII, 132, 234–35, 268–70; Kelly's notes, *WSC*, VIII, 344

25 Criticisms in *WSC*, VIII, 357, 392–94, 493–94, 626 and Graebner, 58–59, 68–69

26 *WSC*, VIII, 423; and information from Cassell and Houghton Mifflin.

27 For Macmillan's judgement, see Alistair Horne, 1988, 292

28 *Nicolson Diaries*, iii, 45

29 Moran, 339, and *WSC*, VII, 278

30 Churchill's speeches, *CSWC*, VII, 7365, 7437, 7739; 'magnificent animal', *Nicolson Diaries*, iii, 79; and *Channon Diaries*, 535, and devaluation speech, *CSWC*, VII, 7844–57

31 Cabinet decision of 25 Jan. 1944, CAB.65/45. The passage on Palestine, and quotations, is based on Rose, 'Churchill and Zionism' in Blake and Louis (eds.), 1993

32 Details of Indian Defence Council scheme in Nicholas Mansergh (ed.), 1970 vol. 1, docs. 77, 78, 79 (pp.124–27), 190(pp. 256–61), 196(pp.268–69); Draft Declaration to Indian Leaders, 30 March 1942, Mansergh, doc. 456(pp.565–66), published as Cmd.6350. Cadogan's and Amery's praise, *Cadogan Diaries*, 432, and *Amery Diaries*, ii, 768; and Churchill to King, John Wheeler-Benett, 1958, 703

33 Quotations in *Amery Diaries*, ii, 832, 842, 945

34 From his speeches to the Commons between 16 May 1946 and 6 March 1947, *CSWC*, VII, 7324–26, 7359–65, 7410–17, 7438–48

35 See *WSC*, VII, 332–33

36 *CSWC*, VII, 7500

37 Churchill to Nehru quoted in Sarvepalli Gopal

38 Text of speech in *CSWC*, VII, 7285–93

39 See Henry B. Ryan, 1979

40 For Eden's feelings, see Carlton, 1986, 265–66; and Macmillan's, Alistair Horne, 306; and for Churchill 'must go', *Nicolson Diaries*, iii, 79, 65

41 See Piers Dixon, 1968, 246

42 Quotations in *CSWC*, VII, 7286, 7379–82 (text of his Zurich speech), and 7537. For a general review of Churchill's European outlook, see Lord Beloff in Blake and Louis (eds.), 1993

43 *WSC*, VIII, 287–88, 424–25. From May 1946 until July 1951 Churchill delivered seventeen major speeches on European unity.

44 'Sludgy amalgam', *Colville Diaries*, 663; 'not be of it', quoted in Horne, i, 348

45 See CSWC, VII, 8681, 8696
46 See Harry S. Truman, 1955, 537–38, also 516–19, 522
47 WSC, VIII, 137
48 For teaching the Russians, WSC VII, 430–31, 432, 467–68
49 Election figures in Butler and Sloman, 1975, 184
50 His deafness, Moran, 362, 373–74; pneumonia, eye and skin complaints, ibid.,
     646; his 1949 stroke and 1950 spasm, ibid., 357–60
51 See Moran, 398, 401, 431, 434–45, 468, 483
52 Nicolson Diaries, iii, 242
53 Moran, 401, 407–08, and Colville Diaries, 642
54 'Profound changes', Moran, 407–08, and 'greatest asset', Colville Diaries,
     642
55 'Macaulay phrases', Channon Diaries, 564; at Margate, WSC, VIII, 897, and
     speech in CSWC, VIII, 8496–97; and to the House, Channon Diaries, 582,
     CSWC, VIII, 8499
56 See Moran, 562–66, and Shuckburgh, 158. For the speech, CSWC, VIII,
     8551–58
57 Observer, 57
58 Quotations in Moran, 552, and CSWC, VIII, 8219–20, 8315
59 For these issues, see Anthony Seldon; 1981, P. Addison, 1993, 412–13; and
     Roy Jenkins in Blake and Louis (eds.)
60 The most graphic description of Churchill's rearguard battle over Egypt in
     Charmley (ed.), 1986, for quotations see, pp.29, 75–78, 118, 127–28, 132, 148,
     165; also W. R. Louis, in Blake and Louis (eds.), and Eden, 1960, 243–47
61 Kermit Roosevelt, 1979, 206–07
62 Warmongering scare, Sheldon, 20–21; 'new prospects', from his speech to the
     Commons, 11 May 1953, CSWC, VIII, 8433
63 Churchill to Eisenhower, 11 March 1953, in Peter G. Boyle (ed.), 1990, 31
64 Colville Diaries, 676, 685–86, and 'world easement', Moran, 433; see also
     WSC, viii, 928–30, 959–60
65 Guildhall speech in CSWC, VIII, 8508; WSC, VIII, 759, 1015; and Truman
     unresponsive, D. C. Watt, 1984, 127
66 Quotations in Robert H. Ferrell (ed.), 1981, 222–24, 230
67 See Moran, 433, and WSC, VIII, 794
68 Boyle, 152–54
69 Cabinet minutes for 8, 9, 13, 23, and 24 July 1954, CAB.128/27. Also
     Colville Diaries, 701–02; Shuckburgh, 224–24, 227; WSC, VIII, 1030–36;
     and Sheldon, 47, 51
70 Boyle, 180–82
71 For Macmillan's role, Horne, 353–54, Colville Diaries, 701, and Soames, 449;
     'petrol running out', Butler, 175
72 Eden's health, R. R. James, 1986, 362–63; and Churchill's remark, Halle,
     245
73 Colville Diaries, 707–09; also Horne, 353
74 Cabinet minutes, CAB.128/28; on 'General X', quoted in Horne, 355; see also
     Colville Diaries, 705, and Moran, 676, 679, 681
75 CSWC, VIII, 6238
76 Moran, 692–93, and Soames, 454
77 Quoted in Halle, 241; also Soames, 428
78 For relations with Onassis, see CHUR.1/151, 152, 153, 154, and Moran, 806
79 Remaining Mr and Mrs Churchill, WSC, VIII, 822–23; receiving Nobel prize,
     Halle, 252, and WSC, VIII, 901; refusing a dukedom, WSC, VIII, 1123–24,
     and Colville Diaries, 709; and Churchill College, WSC, VIII, 1352
80 For Churchill's eightieth birthday and Sutherland incident, see Soames, 445–46,
     Moran, 647–48, 652, and WSC, viii, 1076, 1253

81 See his will of April 1944, CHUR.1/40
82 Hint dropped, Moran, 472; final decision, Churchill to Randolph, 3 Nov. 1960, CHUR.2/619; and Randolph's response, *WSC*, VIII, 1312–13
83 Advanced by the *Daily Telegraph* (serial rights), Heinemann (London), and Houghton and Mifflin (Boston). Randolph was put on a ten-year contract at £9,000 per annum; Churchill received £50,000 on signature of the agreement; and the Chartwell Trustees £15,000 as a down payment, acquiring the balance, some £266,000, when the work was completed. Details of contract, and note by Montague Browne, 5 June 1962, of his conversation with Randolph, in CHUR.2/619
84 See *Noel Coward Diaries*, 322–23; *Nicolson Diaries*, iii, 395; Montgomery's record, Soames, 479; Sarah Churchill 16–17
85 Moran, 741; preparations for state funeral, CHUR.1/137, 138; and not in Westminster Abbey, Halle, 285
86 For his ninetieth birthday, Howells, 164–76, and Soames, 488
87 Colin Coote, 38, 110
88 For his last days, Moran, 829–30, and Soames, 489–93
89 Rosebery, 1906, 72
90 *WSC*, VIII, 1363; and *Times* 1 Feb. 1965

Epilogue

1 *Colville Diaries*, 563
2 *Observer*, 61
3 Quotations in A. J. P. Taylor, *Bismarck* and CSWC, VIII, 8608
4 Quoted in Sarah Churchill, 15, and Boothby, 1978, 183–84
5 Quoted in F. W. Deakin, 1969. The story appears in *English Speaking-Peoples* (2nd ed., 1956), i, 90

Bibliography

Churchill's life has remained of perennial interest to scholars and to the general public for almost a hundred years. Works about him already fill volumes – see Frederick Woods, (1969 ed.) *A Bibliography of the Works of Sir Winston Churchill* – and every author who ventures into the field of Churchill studies must acknowledge his debt to those who have preceded him. This is particularly true of the Official Biography and its Companion Volumes (for details, see under Randolph S. Churchill and Martin Gilbert). Although the narrative biography has been completed, this mammoth project is still in progress with further Companion Volumes being prepared to cover the period after 1939. These volumes represent a published archival treasure-house, not only regarding the minutiae of Churchill's life but also for British and international politics in general. Like all students of Churchill, I have plundered it mercilessly, for profit and pleasure. Towards the end of my research I was granted permission to examine the Churchill Archive, located at Churchill College, Cambridge. Consisting of some 5,000 files, it contains approximately half-a-million pages of documentation. All CHUR, WCHL, CHAR citations refer to this collection. From even a cursory inspection of the archive, it became clear that much of the important material it held was included in the Companion Volumes, particularly those that deal with the inter-war period. I have, therefore, preferred to cite the Companion Volumes as references as these are more easily accessible to the reader at libraries.

References to other collections of private papers are listed in the Notes.

The Cabinet (CAB), Foreign Office (FO), Colonial Office (CO), and Premier (PREM) series of files are to be found at the Public Record Office, Kew; and newspaper references are located at the British Museum Newspaper Collection at Colindale.

I note in the bibliography only those works used directly in the writing of this book, or those that I found particularly useful in providing background material. The place of publication, unless stated otherwise, is London. Where an edition other than the first is cited, the date is included.

C. Abramsky and B. Williams (eds.), *Essays in Honour of E. H. Carr* (1976)

Christopher Addison, *Politics from Within* (1924)

—— *Four and a Half Years* (1934), 2 vols

Paul Addison, *The Road to 1945. British Politics and the Second World War* (1975; pb 1977)

—— *Churchill on the Home Front, 1900–1955* (1992)

—— 'Lloyd George and Compromise Peace', in A. J. P. Taylor (ed.), *Lloyd George: Twelve Essays* (1971, New York)

—— 'Journey to the Centre: Churchill and Labour in Coalition, 1940–5', in Alan Sked and Chris Cook (eds.), *Crisis and Controversy. Essays in Honour of A. J. P. Taylor* (1976)

—— 'The Political Beliefs of Winston Churchill', *Transactions of the Royal Historical Society*, 5th series, 30 (1980a)

—— 'Churchill', *History Today*, 30 (1980b)

—— 'Winston Churchill and the Working Class', in J. M. Winter (ed.), *The Working Class in Modern Britain* (Cambridge 1983)

—— 'Churchill and Social Reform', in Blake and Louis (eds.), (1993)

Countess of Airlie, *Thatched with Gold* (1962)

Stephen Ambrose, *Eisenhower* (New York, 1985), 2 vols

—— 'Churchill and Eisenhower in the Second World War', in Blake and Louis (eds.) (1993)

L. S. Amery, *My Political Life* (1953–55), 3 vols

Mark Amory (ed.), *The Letters of Evelyn Waugh* (1980; pb 1982)

T. H. Anderson, *The United States, Great Britain and the Cold War, 1944–47* (New York, 1981)

Christopher Andrew, *Secret Service. The Making of the British Intelligence Community* (1985)

—— 'Churchill and Intelligence', *Intelligence and National Security* (1988)

Timothy Garton Ash, 'In the Churchill Museum', *The New York Review of Books*, 7 May 1987

—— 'From World War to Cold War', *New York Review of Books*, 11 June 1987

Maurice Ashley, *Churchill as Historian* (1968)

Margot Asquith, *Autobiography* (1920–2)

J. B. Atkins, *Incidents and Reflections* (1947)

Earl of Avon, *The Eden Memoirs*. Vol. 1: *Facing the Dictators* (1962); Vol. 2: *The Reckoning* (1965)

David Ayerst, *Guardian. Biography of a Newspaper* (1971)

Robert Baden-Powell, *Indian Memories* (1915)

Victor Bailey, 'Churchill as Home Secretary: Prison Reform', *History Today* (March 1985)

Consuelo (Vanderbilt) Balsan, *The Glitter and the Gold* (1953)

Maurice Baring, *Puppet Show of Memory* (1922)

Elisabeth Barker, *Churchill and Eden at War* (1978)

John Barnes and Keith Middlemas, *Baldwin* (1969)

John Barnes and David Nicholson, (eds.), *The Leo Amery Diaries* (1980–88), 2 vols

Correlli Barnett, *The Collapse of British Power* (1972)

—— *Britain and Her Army* 1970

—— *The Audit of War* 1986

—— *Engage the Enemy More Closely* (1991)

Ethel Barrymore, *Memoirs* (New York, 1955)

Norman H. Baynes (ed.), *The Speeches of Adolph Hitler, 1922–39* (1942)

Lord Beaverbrook, *Politicians and the War, 1914–16* (1928)

——*The Decline and Fall of Lloyd George* (1966)

Anthony Beevor, *Crete. The Battle and the Resistance* (1991)

Hesketh Bell, *Glimpses of a Governor's Life* (1946)

Lord Beloff, 'Churchill and Europe', in Blake and Louis (eds.) (1993)

Tuvia Ben Moshe, *Churchill as Historian and Strategist* (1992)

—— 'Churchill's Strategic Conception During the First World War', *The Journal of Strategic Studies* (March 1989)

—— 'Winston Churchill and the "Second Front" – A Reappraisal', *Journal of Modern History* (December 1990)

Isaiah Berlin, *Mr Churchill in 1940* (1949)

Lord Beveridge, *Power and Influence* (1953)

Uri Bialer, *The Shadow of the Bomber* (1980)

Lord Birkenhead, *Contemporary Personalities* (1924)

Lord Birkenhead, *F. E. The Life of F. E. Smith* (1965 ed.)

—— *the Prof in Two Worlds* (1961)

—— *Halifax* (1965)

Robert Blake, *The Unknown Prime Minister. The Life and Times of Andrew Bonar Law* (1955)

—— *The Conservative Party from Peel to Churchill* (1970)

—— 'How Churchill Became Prime Minister', in Blake and Louis (eds.) (1993)

—— 'Winston Churchill as Historian', *British Studies* (Austin, 1990)

Robert Blake and W. Roger Louis (eds), *Churchill* (Oxford 1993)

John M. Blum, *Roosevelt and Morganthau* (Boston, 1970)

Wilfred Scawen Blunt, *My Diaries, 1888–1914* (1932)

Donald Graeme Boadle, *Winston Churchill and the German Question in British Foreign Policy, 1918–22* (The Hague, 1973)

Brian Bond, *British Military Policy Between Two World Wars* (1980)
—— (ed.), *Chief of Staff. The Diaries of Lieutenant-General Sir Henry Pownall* (1972–74), 2 vols
Brian Bond and I. Ray (eds.), *War and Society* (1977)
Violet Bonham-Carter, *Winston Churchill As I Knew Him* (1965; 1967 ed.)
Robert Boothby, *I Fight to Live* (1947)
—— *My Yesterday, Your Tomorrow* (1962)
—— *Recollections of a Rebel* (1978)
Andrew Boyle, *'Poor Dear Brendan'. The Quest for Brendan Bracken* (1974)
Peter G. Boyle (ed.), *The Churchill-Eisenhower Correspondence, 1953–55* (North Carolina 1990)
Timothy Boyle, 'New Light on Lloyd George's Mansion House Speech', *The Historical Journal*, 23, 2 (1980)
Piers Brenden, *Winston Churchill* (1984)
Maurice V. Brett (ed.), *Journals and Letters of Reginald Viscount Esher (1934–38), vols. II and III*
Carl Bridge, 'Conservatism and Indian Reform, 1929–39', *Journal of Imperial and Commonwealth History* (1974–75)
—— 'Churchill, Hoare, Derby and the Committee of Privileges, April to June 1934', *The Historical Journal*, 22, 1 (1979)
British Parliamentary Papers, Command Papers, Cd, and Cmd series
Michael and Eleonor Brock (eds.), *H. H. Asquith, Letters to Venetia Stanley* Oxford (1985)
Douglas Brownrigg, *Indiscretions of a Naval Censor* (1919)
Arthur Bryant, *The Alanbrooke War Diaries* (1958–9, 1965 ed.), 2 vols
Alan Bullock, *Hitler. A Study in Tyranny* (1952; 1969 ed.)
—— *The Life and Times of Ernest Bevin*: Vol. 2(1967); Vol. 3 (1983)
—— *Hitler and Stalin. Parallel Lives* (1991)
David Butler and Anne Sloman (eds.), *British Political Facts, 1900–1975* (1975)
J. R. M. Butler, *Grand Strategy* (1957)
—— *Grand Strategy* (1964), vol. III, part 2
Lord Butler, *The Art of the Possible* (1971; pb, 1973)
Angus Calder, *The People's War* (1969; 1971 ed.)
R. Calahn, *Churchill: Retreat from Empire* (Delaware, 1984)
C. E. Callwell, *Field Marshal Sir Henry Wilson. His Diary and Letters* (1927), 2 vols.
Peter Calvocoressi, Guy Wint and John Pritchard, *Total War. The Causes and Courses of the Second World War* (rev. ed. 1989)
John Campbell, *Lloyd George: The Goat in the Wilderness* (1977)
David Cannadine, *The Decline and Fall of the British Aristocracy* (1990)

—— 'Winston Agonistes', *New York Review of Books*, 15 June 1989

—— 'Churchill and the Pitfalls of Family Piety', in Blake and Louis (eds.) (1993)

David Carlton, *Anthony Eden* (1986)

—— 'Eden, Blum and the Origins of Non-Intervention', *Journal of Contemporary History*, vol. 6, no.3 (1971)

Michael Carver, 'Churchill and the Defence Chiefs', in Blake and Louis (eds.) (1993)

Richard Casey, *Personal Experience, 1939–46* (1962)

Anthony Cave Brown, *The Secret Servant. The Life of Sir Stewart Menzies, Churchill's Spymaster* (1988; 1989 ed.)

Dudley de Chair, *The Sea is Strong* (1961)

William Scott Chalmers, *The Life and Letters of David Beatty, Admiral of the Fleet* (1951)

Austen Chamberlain, *Politics from the Inside* (1937)

E. D. W. Chaplin (ed.), *Winston Churchill and Harrow* (1941)

John Charmley, *Duff Cooper* (1986)

—— *Churchill. The End of Glory. A Political Biography* (1993)

—— (ed.), *Descent to Suez. The Diaries of Sir Evelyn Shuckburgh, 1951–56* (1986)

Ron Chernow, *House of Morgan* (1990)

John Spencer Churchill, *Crowded Canvass* (1961)

Peregrine Churchill and Julian Mitchell, *Jennie, Lady Randolph. A Portrait with Letters* (1974)

Randolph S. Churchill, *Winston S. Churchill*. Vol. I: *Youth, 1874–1900* (1966) (Official biography)

—— *Winston S. Churchill*. Vol. II: *Young Statesman, 1901–14* (1967)

—— (continued under Martin Gilbert)

Companion Volumes:

—— (ed.) Vol. I, parts 1 and 2 (1967),

—— (ed.) Vol. II, parts 1, 2, and 3 (1969)

—— (continued under Martin Gilbert)

—— *Twenty One Years* (1965)

Randolph S. Churchill and Helmut Gersheim (eds.), *Churchill. His Life in Photographs* (1955)

Sarah Churchill, *Threads in the Tapestry* (1967; pb 1968)

Winston S. Churchill *The Story of the Malakand Field Force* (1898)

—— *The River War* (1899 pb 1964)

—— *Savrola. A Tale of the Revolution in Laurania* (1900; New York, 1956 ed.)

—— *Ian Hamilton's March* (1900)

—— *London to Ladysmith* (1900)

—— *Lord Randolph Churchill* (1906), 2 vols

—— *My African Journey* (1908)

—— *Budget* Issues (1909; 1970)a
—— *The People's Rights* (1910; 1970)b
—— *The World Crisis, 1911–1918* (1923; 1938 ed.), 2 vols
—— *The Aftermath* (1924; 1929 ed.)
—— *My Early Life* (1930; 1985 ed.)
—— *India* (1931)
—— *Thoughts and Adventures* (1932)
—— *Marlborough, His Life and Times* (1934–38), 4 volumes
—— *Great Contemporaries* (1937; 1949 ed.)
—— *Arms and the Covenant* (1938)
—— *Step by Step* (1939)
—— *The Second World War* (1948–1954), 6 volumes
   The Gathering Storm (1948)
   Their Finest Hour (1949)
   The Grand Alliance (1950)
   The Hinge of Fate (1951)
   Closing the Ring (1952)
   Triumph and Tragedy (1954)
—— 'Morning Thoughts. A Note on Post-War Security', 1 February 1943 in Michael Howard, *Grand Strategy* (1972), Vol. IV
—— *Secret Session Speeches* (1946)
—— *A History of the English-Speaking Peoples* (1954), 4 volumes
—— *The Collected Essays of Sir Winston Churchill*, see Woolf (ed.)
Anne de Courcey, *Circe. The Life of Edith, Marchioness of Londonderry* (1992)
Alan Clark (eds), *'A Good Innings'. The Private Papers of Viscount Lee of Fareham* (1974)
Ronald Clark, *Tizard* (1964)
I. F. Clarke, *Voices Prophesying War, 1763–1984* (1966)
Peter Clarke, 'Churchill's Economic Ideas, 1900–1930', in Blake and Louis (eds.), (1993)
Richard Cockett, *Twilight of Truth, Chamberlain, Appeasement and the Manipulation of the Press* (1989)
Michael J., Cohen, *Churchill and the Jews* (1985)
M. Cole (ed.), *Beatrice Webb Diaries* (1952–56), 2 vols
John Coleville, *The Churchillians* (1981)
—— *The Fringes of Power. Downing Street Diaries, 1939–55* (1985)
Alfred Duff Cooper, *Haigh* (1936), 2 vols
—— *Old Men Forget* (1957)
Colin Coote, *The Other Club* (1971)
George Cornwallis-West, *Edwardian Heydays* (1930)
Mrs George Cornwallis-West, *The Reminiscences of Lady Randolph Churchill* (1908)
Reginald Coupland, *India. A Re-Statement* (1954)

Maurice Cowling, *The Impact of Labour, 1920–24* (Cambridge 1971)
—— *The Impact of Hitler: British Politics and British Policy, 1933–40* (Cambridge 1975)
Gordon A. Craig, 'Churchill and Germany', in Blake and Louis (eds.), 1993
Martin van Crevald, *Hitler's Strategy, 1940–41: The Balkan Clue* (Cambridge 1973)
—— 'Prelude to Disaster: the British Decision to Aid Greece, 1940–41', *Journal of Contemporary History* (June 1974)
J. A. Cross, *Sir Samuel Hoare. A Political Biography* (1977)
Robert Dallek, *Franklin D. Roosevelt and American Foreign Policy, 1932–1945* (New York, 1979; 1981 ed.)
Hugh Dalton, *Memoirs* (1957–62), 2 vols
Edward David, *Inside Asquith's Cabinet. From the Diaries of Charles Hobhouse* (1977)
Bernard Darwin, *James Braid* (1952)
John Darwin, *Britain, Egypt and the Middle East Imperial Policy in the Aftermath of the War, 1918–22* (1981)
Michael Davie (ed.), *The Diaries of Evelyn Waugh* (1976)
David Day, *Churchill and Menzies at War* (1987)
—— *Britain, Australia and the Onset of the Pacific War, 1939–42* (1988)
F. W. Deakin, 'Churchill the Historian' (Foundation Suisse Winston Churchill, April 1970)
F. A. Dickenson, *Lake Victoria to Khartoum* (1910)
Dictionary of National Biography, 1961–1970
David Dilks, *Neville Chamberlain*. Vol. 1, *1869–1929* (1985)
—— (ed.), *The Diaries of Sir Alexander Cadogan, 1938–45* (1971)
—— (ed.), *Studies in Britain's Foreign Policy in the Twentieth Century* (1981), 2 vols
—— '"We Must Hope For The Best And Prepare For The Worst": The Prime Minister, The Cabinet and Hitler's Germnay, 1937–1939' *Proceedings of the British Academy*, LXXIII (1987)
—— 'The Twilight War and the Fall of France: Chamberlain and Churchill in 1940', *Transactions of the Royal Historical Society*, 5th series, 28 (1978)
Piers Dixon, *Double Diploma* (1968)
Documents of British Foreign Policy, 3rd Series (1949–55)
Documents on German Foreign Policy, Series D (1949–64)
Bernard Donoughue and G. W. Jones, *Herbert Morrison: Portrait of a Politician* (1973)
Lord Alfred Douglas, *Autobiography* (1929)
Reginald Doram-Smith, 'Recollections', *The Sunday Times*, 6 September 1964

J. C. R. Dow, *The Management of the British Economy*, (Cambridge 1964)

Blanche E. C. Dugdale, *Arthur James Balfour* (1939), 2 vols

Walter Scott Dunn, Jr., *Second Front Now – 1943* Alabama 1980

David Dutton, *Austen Chamberlain. Gentleman in Politics* (1985)

Charles Eade (ed.), *Churchill By His Contemporaries* (1953)

Robin Edmonds, *The Big Three. Churchill, Roosevelt and Stalin in Peace and War* (New York, 1991)

—— 'Churchill and Stalin', in Blake and Louis (eds.) (1993)

George T. Eggleston, *Roosevelt, Churchill, and the World War II Opposition* (Old Greenwich, Conn. 1978)

John Ehrman, *Grand Strategy* (1956)

—— 'Lloyd George and Churchill as War Ministers', *Transactions of the Royal Historical Society*, 5th series (1960)

Master of Elibank, *A Man's Life* (1934)

Richard Ellman, *Oscar Wilde* (1988)

J. T. Emmerson, *The Rhineland Crisis* (1977)

R. C. K. Ensor, *England, 1870–1914* (1930, 1960 ed.)

Carlo D'Este, *Fatal Decision* (1991)

Robin Fedden, *Churchill and Chartwell* (1968)

Keith Feiling, *The Life of Neville Chamberlain* (1947)

James Fergusson, *The Curragh Incident* (n.d.)

Robert Ferrell (ed.), *The Eisenhower Diaries* (New York, 1981)

Edith Finch, *Wilfred Scawen Blunt* (1938)

Sir Almeric Fitzroy, *Memoirs* (1925), 2 vols

—— *Foreign Relations of the United States (Paris Peace Conference, 1919)* (Washington)

—— *Foreign Relations of the United States* (Conferences at Washington, 1941–42, and *Casablanca, 1943*) (Washington)

—— *Foreign Relations of the United States (Conferences at Cairo and Teheran, 1943)* (Washington)

—— *Foreign Relations of the United States (Conferences at Malta and Yalta, 1945)* (Washington)

—— *Foreign Relations of the United States (Conference at Berlin, 1945)* (Washington)

Margery Forester, *Michael Collins, The Lost Leader* (1971; 1972 ed.)

R. F. Foster, *Lord Randolph Churchill. A Political Life* (Oxford 1981)

Peter Fraser, *Lord Esher. A Political Biography* (1973)

Gerald French, *The Life of Field Marshal Sir John French* (1931)

Michael G. Fry, *Lloyd George and Foreign Policy* (McGill-Queen's University Press, 1977)

Paul Fussell, *Wartime* (1989)

F. R. Gannon, *The British Press and Germany, 1936–39* (1971)

A. J. Gardiner, *Prophets, Priests and Kings* (1914)

—— *Certain People of Importance* (1926)

A. B. Gaunson, 'Churchill, De Gaulle, Spears and the Levant Affair, 1941, *The Historical Journal*, 27, 3 (1984)

Andrew Dewar Gibb (Captain 'X'), *With Winston Churchill at the Front* (1924)

Bentley B. Gilbert, *David Lloyd George. A Political Life* (1987)

—— *Evolution of National Insurance in Great Britain* (1966)

—— *British Social Policy, 1914–39* (1970)

—— 'Winston Churchill verses the Webbs; The Origins of British Unemployment Insurance', *The American Historical Review* (April 1966)

—— 'Pacifist to Interventionist: David Lloyd George in 1911 and 1914' Was Belgium an Issue?', *The Historical Journal*, 28, 4 (1985)

Martin Gilbert, *Winston S. Churchill*. Vol. III: *1914–16* (1971) (Official biography)

—— *Winston S. Churchill*. Vol. IV: *1916–22* (1975)

—— *Winston S. Churchill*. Vol. V: *1922–39* (1976)

—— *Winston S. Churchill*. Vol. VI: *Finest Hour, 1939–41* (1983)

—— *Winston S. Churchill*. Vol. VII: *Road to Victory, 1941–45* (1986)

—— *Winston S. Churchill*. Vol. VIII: *Never Despair, 1945–65* (1988)

—— Companion volumes (See also under Randolph S. Churchill)

—— (ed.) Vol. III, parts 1 and 2 (1972)

—— (ed.) Vol. IV, parts 1, 2, and 3 (1977)

—— (ed.) Vol. V, parts 1, 2, and 3 (1979) (See also under Randolph S. Churchill)

—— *Churchill. A Photographic Portrait* (1974)

—— *The Roots of Appeasement* (1966)

—— *Churchill's Political Philosophy* (1981)

—— 'Churchill and Roosevelt: The Background of the Relationship and its Testing Time', (Anglo-American Conference on the Second World War, Imperial War Museum, London, 29 July 1980)

—— 'The Origins of the "Iron Curtain" Speech', (First Crosby Kemper Lecture, April 1981)

—— 'Churchill and Intelligence', (The Hebrew University, 1990)

A. M. Gollin, *Proconsul in Politics. A Study of Lord Milner* (1964)

—— *Balfour's Burden. Arthur James Balfour and Imperial Preference* (1965)

Sarvepalli Gopal, 'Churchill and India', in Blake and Louis (eds.) (1993)

Gabriel Gorodetsky, *Stafford Cripps's Mission to Moscow, 1940–42* (Cambridge 1984)

—— 'Churchill's Warning to Stalin: A Reappraisal', *The Historical Journal*, 24, 4 (1986)

—— 'The Hess Affair and Anglo-Soviet Relations on the Eve of "Barbarossa"', *English Historical Review* (April 1986)

Margret Gowing, *Britain and Atomic Energy. 1939–45* (1964)
—— 'Britain, America and the Bomb', in David Dilks (ed.), *Studies in Britain's Foreign Policy in the Twentieth Century* (1981)
William Graebner, *My Dear Mr Churchill* (1965)
Ross Graham, 'Allied Diplomacy in the Second World War', *British Journal of International Studies* (October 1975)
David Green, *Blenheim Palace* (1951)
—— *The Churchills of Blenheim* (1984)
Viscount Grey, *Twenty Five Years* (1925), 2 vols
John Grigg, *1943: The Victory That Never Was* (1980)
—— *Lloyd George: The People's Champion* (1978)
—— *Lloyd George: From Peace to War, 1912–16* (1985)
—— 'Churchill and Lloyd George', in Blake and Louis (eds.) (1993)
P. Grigg, *Prejudice and Judgement* (1948)
Philip Guedalla, *Mr Churchill: A Portrait* (1941)
J. M. A. Gwyer, *Grand Strategy* (1964), vol. III, part 1
Aylmer Haldane, *A Soldier's Saga* (1948)
Richard Burton Haldane, *Autobiography* (1924)
Elie Halevy, *A History of the English Speaking People in the Nineteenth Century. Vol. VI: The Rule of Democracy, 1905–14* (Rev ed. 1954, 1961 ed.)
Kay Halle, *The Irrepressible Churchill* (1987)
William B. Hamilton, 'Churchill: Actor as Historian', *The South Atlantic Quarterly* (July 1951)
W. K. Hancock and M. M. Gowing, *British War Economy* (1949)
Maurice Hankey, *The Supreme Command* (1961), 2 vols
—— *The Supreme Control at the Paris Peace Conference*, 1919 (1963)
Hansard, Parliamentary Debates, 5th Series, Commons and Lords
Fraser J. Harbutt, *The Iron Curtain: Churchill, America and the Origins of the Cold War* (New York, 1986)
W. Averell Harriman and E. Abel, *Special Envoy to Churchill and Stalin, 1941–46* (New York, 1975)
José Harris, *William Beveridge: A Biography* (Oxford 1977)
Frank Harris, *My Life and Loves* (1964)
Wilson Harris, *J. A. Spender* (1946)
Roy Harrod, *The Prof. A Personal Memoir of Lord Cherwell* (1959)
Harrow School Songs (1987)
John Harvey (ed.), *The Diaries of Olivier Harvey* (1970–78), 2 vols
Christopher Hassall, *Edward Marsh. A Biography* (1959)
G. A. Hatham, *Guide to Harrow* (1929)
Robert Hathaway, *Ambiguous Partnership, Britain and America, 1944–47* (New York, 1989)
Cameron Hazlehurst, *Politicians at War* (New York, 1971)

Cameron Hazlehurst, 'Churchill as Social Reformer: The Liberal Phase', *Australian Historical Studies* (April 1976)

Nevile Henderson, *Failure of a Mission* (1940)

A. P. Herbert, *Independent Member* (1950)

C. Hill, *Cabinet Decisions on Foreign Policy, October 1938 – June 1941* (Cambridge 1991)

F. H. Hinsley, *British Intelligence in the Second World War* (1979–90), 4 vols

—— 'Churchill and the Use of Special Intelligence,' in Blake and Louis (eds.) (1993)

J. D. Hoffman, *The Conservative Party in Opposition* (1964)

Alistair Horne, *Macmillan* (1988–89), 2 vols

Richard Hough, *Former Naval Person. Churchill and the Wars at Sea* (1985)

Richard Hough, *Winston & Clementine* (1990)

Michael Howard, *The Mediterranean Strategy in the Second World War* (1966)

—— *The Continental Commitment* (1972)

—— *Grand Strategy* (1972)

—— 'Churchill and the First World War', in Blake and Louis (eds.) (1993)

Roy Howells, *Simply Churchill* (1965)

Emyrs Hughes, *Keir Hardie* (1956)

Ronald Hyam, *Elgin and Churchill at the Colonial Office, 1905–08* (1968)

—— 'Winston Churchill Before 1914', *The Historical Journal*, 12 (1969)

—— 'Churchill and the British Empire', in Blake and Louis (eds.) (1993)

H. Montgomery Hyde, *British Air Policy Between the Wars, 1918–39* (1976)

David Irving, *Churchill's War. The Struggle for Power* (Western Australia, 1987)

Lord Ismay, *Memoirs* (1960)

D. Jablonsky, *Churchill, The Great Game and Total War* (1991)

Marian Jack, 'The Purchase of the British Government's Shares in the British Petroleum Company, 1912–1914', *Past and Present* (April 1968)

Robert Rhodes James, *Gallipoli* (New York, 1965)

—— *Lord Randolph Churchill* (1959; 1969 ed.)

—— *Memoirs of a Conservative. J. C. C. Davidson's Memoirs and Papers, 1910–37* (1969)

—— *Churchill. A Study in Failure* (1970)

—— *Victor Cazalet. A Portrait* (1976)

—— *The British Revolution* (1978)

—— *Anthony Eden* (1986)

—— *Bob Boothby. A Portrait* (1991)

—— (ed.), *'Chips'. The Diaries of Sir Henry Channon* (1970 ed.)

—— (ed.), *Winston S. Churchill. His Complete Speeches, 1897–1963* (New York, 1974), 8 vols

—— 'Churchill as Parliamentarian', *Parliamentary Affairs*, (1964–65)

—— 'The Epic Concluded', *Encounter* (1988)

—— 'Churchill the Parliamentarian, Orator, and Statesman', in Blake and Louis (eds.)

William James, *A Great Seaman. The Life of Admiral of the Fleet, Sir Henry F. Oliver* (1965)

Kevin Jefferys, *The Churchill Coalition and Wartime Politics* (1991)

Roy Jenkins, *Asquith* (1964; 1967 ed.)

—— 'Churchill: The Government of 1951–1955', in Blake and Louis (eds.) (1993)

Douglas Johnson, 'Churchill and France', in Blake and Louis (eds.) (1993)

R. V. Jones, 'Churchill and Science', in Blake and Louis (eds.) (1993)

Thomas Jones, *A Diary with Letters, 1931–50* (Oxford, 1969)

Denis Judd, *Balfour and the British Empire* (1968)

Dennis Kavanagh, *Crisis, Charisma and British Political Leadership, Winston Churchill as the Outsider* (1974)

Eli Kedourie, *The Chatham House Version and other Middle Eastern Studies,* (1970)

John Keegan, *The Second World War* (1989, 1990 ed.)

—— 'Churchill's Strategy', in Blake and Louis (eds.) (1993)

John Kennedy, *The Business of War* (1957)

Paul Kennedy, *The Realities behind Diplomacy* (1981)

—— *The Rise of Anglo-German Antagonism, 1860–1914* (1980; 1982 ed.)

François Kersuady, *Churchill and De Gualle* (1981; 1990 ed.)

Warren F. Kimball, *The Juggler. Franklin Roosevelt as Wartime Statesman* (Princeton 1991)

Warren F. Kimball (ed.) *Churchill and Roosevelt. The Complete Correspondence* (Princeton 1984), 3 vols

—— 'Wheel Within a Wheel: Churchill, Roosevelt, and the Special Relationship', in Blake and Louis (eds.) (1993)

Martin Kitchen, *British Policy Towards the Soviet Union During the Second World War* (New York, 1986)

—— 'Churchill and the Soviet Union during the Second World War', *The Historical Journal*, 30, 2 (1987)

Jonathan Knight, 'Churchill and the Approach to Mussolini and Hitler in May 1940: a Note', *British Journal of International Studies*, II (1977)

G. Kolko, *The Politics of War* (1969)

Stephen Koss, *Lord Haldane. A Scapegoat for Liberalism* (New York, 1969)

—— *Asquith* (1985)

—— *The Rise and Fall of the Political Press in Britain* (1984) vol.II

—— 'The Destruction of Britain's Last Liberal Government', *Journal of Modern History*, 40, 2 (1968)

Walter La Feber, 'Roosevelt, Churchill, and Indochina: 1942–45', *American Historical Review*, 80 (1975)

François Lafitte, *The Internment of Aliens* (1940 rev. ed. 1990)

Richard Lamb, *Churchill as War Leader – Right or Wrong?* (1991)

Richard Langhorne (ed.), *Diplomacy and Intelligence During the Second World War. Essays in Honour of F. H. Hinsley* (Cambridge, 1985)

John Lavery, *The Life of a Painter* (1940)

J. M. Lee, *The Churchill Coalition, 1940–45* (1980)

James Lees-Milne, *The Enigmatic Edwardian. The Life of Reginald, 2nd Viscount Esher* (1986; 1988 ed.)

Lady Algernon Gordon Lennox (ed.), *The Diary of Lord Bertie of Thame, 1914–18* (1924)

Anita Leslie, *The Fabulous Leonard Jerome* (New York, 1954)

—— *Jennie. The Life of Lady Randolph Churchill* (1969)

—— *Cousin Randolph* (1985)

Shane Leslie, *The End of a Chapter* (1929)

—— *The Passing Chapter* (1934)

—— *Men Were Different* (1937)

—— *Long Shadows* (1966)

Hugh L'Etang, *Fit to Lead?* (1980)

Ronald Lewin, *Churchill as Warlord* (1973)

Basil Liddell Hart, 'Churchill in War', *Encounter* (April, 1966)

David Lloyd George, *War Memoirs* (1934–36; 1938 ed.), 2 vols

—— *The Truth About the Peace Treaties* (1938), 2 vols

Countess Lloyd George (Frances Stevenson), *The Years That Are Past* (1967)

Elizabeth Longford, *Pilgrimage of Passion* (New York, 1967)

W. Roger Louis, *Imperialism at Bay. The United States and the Decolonization of the British Empire, 1941–1945* (New York, 1978)

—— *The British Empire in the Middle East, 1945–51. Arab Nationalism, the United States, and Postwar Imperialism* (Oxford 1985)

—— 'Churchill and Egypt', in Blake and Louis (eds.) (1993)

W. Roger Louis and Hedley Bull (eds.), *The Special Relationship, Anglo-American Relations since 1945* (Oxford 1986)

Evan Luard (ed.). *The Cold War. A Reappraisal* (1964)

John Lukacs, *The Duel. Hitler vs. Churchill* (Oxford 1992)

Oliver Lyttelton, *Memoirs of Lord Chandos* (1962)

C. A. MacDonald, *The United States, Britain and Appeasement, 1936–39* (1980)

Norman McGowan, *My Years with Churchill* (1958)

John McGuire, 'Churchill made John a Cup of Coffee', *Sunday Post*, 25 February 1990

Ruddock F. Mackay, *Fisher of Kilverstone* (Oxford 1973)

Piers Mackesy, 'Churchill on Narvik', *Journal of Royal United Services Institute* (December 1970)

—— 'Churchill as Chronicler. The Narvik Episode', *History Today* (March 1985)

Roderick MacLeod and Denis Kelly (eds.), *The Ironside Diaries, 1937–40* (1962)

Harold Macmillan, *Memoirs* (1966–73), 6 vols

—— *War Diaries. The Mediterranean, 1943–45* (1984; 1985 ed.)

Nevil Macready, *Annals of an Active Life* (1924)

Philip Magnus, *King Edward the Seventh* (1964; 1967 ed.)

—— *Kitchener. Portrait of an Imperialist* (1968)

Ivan Maisky, *Who Helped Hitler* (1965)

—— *Memoirs of a Soviet Ambassador, 1939–43* (1967)

William Manchester, *The Last Lion, 1874–1932* (1983)

—— *The Caged Lion, 1932–40* (1988)

Robert Manne, 'The British Decision for an Alliance with Russia, May 1939', *Journal of Contemporary History* (July, 1974)

Nicholas Mansergh (ed.), *The Transfer of Power, 1942–47*. Volume 1, *The Cripps Mission* (1970)

James Marchant (ed.), *Winston Spencer Churchill: Servant of Crown and Commonwealth* (1954)

Arthur Marder, *From the Dreadnought to Scapa Flow* (Oxford University Press, 1961–70), 5 vols

—— 'Winston is Back', *English Historical Review*, Supplement 5 (1969)

David Marquand, *Ramsey MacDonald* (1977)

Edward Marsh, *A Number of People* (1939)

John Martin, *Downing Street. The War Years* (1991)

Ralph Martin, *Jennie. The Life of Lady Randolph Churchill* (1969), 2 vols

Lucy Masterman, *C. F. G. Masterman. A Biography* (1939)

—— 'Churchill: the Liberal Phrase. Part One', *History Today*, (November 1964); 'Part Two' (December 1964)

Vojtech Mastny, *Russia's Road to the Cold War* (New York, 1979)

W. N. Medlicott, *Britain and Germany: The Search for an Agreement, 1930–37* (1969)

R. Meinertzhagen *Middle East Diary, 1917–56* (1956)

—— *Diary of a Black Sheep* (1964)

Peter de Mendelssohn, *The Age of Churchill* (1961)

Keith Middlemas, *Diplomacy of Illusion. The British Government and Germany, 1937–39* (1972)

—— (ed.), *Thomas Jones. Whitehall Diary* (Oxford 1969), 2 vols

Stanlislaw Mikolajczyk, *The Rape of Poland* (New York, 1948)

Walter Millis (ed.), *The Forrestal Diaries* (New York, 1966)

Alan Milward, *The German Economy at War* (1965)

R. J. Minney, *The Private Papers of Hore-Belisha* (1960)

Phyllis Moir, *I Was Winston Churchill's Private Secretary* (New York, 1941)

Howard Moon, 'The Invasion of the United Kingdom. Public Controversy and Official Policy' (unpublished London Ph.D thesis, 1968)

R. J. Moore, *Churchill, Cripps and India, 1939–45* (Oxford 1979)

Alan Moorhead, *Gallipoli* (1956; 1965 ed.)

Lord Moran, *Winston Churchill. The Struggle for Survival, 1940–55* 1966; 1968 ed.)

David Morgan, *Suffragists and Liberals. The Politics of Women Suffrage* (1975)

Kenneth O. Morgan, *Keir Hardie. Radical and Socialist* (1975)

—— *Labour in Power, 1945–51* (Oxford 1985)

—— *Consensus and Disunity* (Oxford 1986)

Ted Morgan, *Churchill, 1874–1915* (1983)

—— *FDR A Biography* (New York, 1985)

John Morley, *Memorandum on Resignation* (1928)

Charles Mowat, *Britain between the Wars, 1918–40* (1955; 1968 ed.)

Arthur Murray, *Master and Brother* (1945)

Williamson Murrey, 'German Air Power and the Munich Crisis', in B. Bond and I. Ray (eds.), *War and Society* (1977)

Elizabeth Nel, *Mr Churchill's Secretary* (1958)

Harold I. Nelson, *Land and Power. British and Allied Policy on Germany's Frontiers, 1916–19* (1963)

Henry W. Nevison, *Fire of Life* (1935)

S. Newman, *March 1939: The British Guarantee to Poland* (Oxford, 1976)

Harold Nicolson, *Public Faces* (1932)

—— *Curzon. The Last Phase, 1919–25* (1934)

Nigel Nicolson (ed.), *Harold Nicolson: Diaries and Letters, 1930–39* [1966–68.] (1969 ed.)

—— (ed.), *Harold Nicolson: Diaries and Letters, 1939–45* (1970 ed.)

—— (ed.), *Harold Nicolson: Diaries and Letters, 1945–62* (New York, 1968)

Observer, Churchill By His Contemporaries. An Appreciation (1965)

Richard Ollard, 'Churchill and the Navy', in Blake and Louis (eds.) (1993)

Nicholas J. D'Ombrain, 'Churchill at the Admiralty and Committee of Imperial Defence, 1911–1914', *Journal of Royal United Services Institute* (March 1970)

Robert O'Neil, 'Churchill, Japan, and British Security in the Pacific: 1904–1942', in Blake and Louis (eds.) (1993)

Richard J. Overy, *The Air War, 1939–45* (1987)

—— 'The German Pre-War Production Plans: November 1936 - April 1939', *The English Historical Review* (October 1975)

—— 'German Air Strength 1933 to 1939', *The Historical Journal*, 27, 2 (1984)

—— 'Hitler's War and the German Economy' A Reinterpretation, *Economic History Review*, xxxv (1982)

—— 'Hitler and Air Strategy', *Journal of Contemporary History*, (July, 1980)

Frank Owen, *Tempestuous Journey* (1954)

Earl of Oxford and Asquith, *Memoirs and Reflections* (1928), 2 vols

Thomas Pakenham, *The Boer War* (1979)

R. A. C. Parker, 'Britain, France and Scandanavia in the "Phony War"', *Scandanavian Journal of History*, 2:29–51 (1977)

—— 'British rearmament, 1936–39. Treasury, trade unions and skilled labour', *English Historical Review*, 96 (1981)

Cecil Parrott, *The Tightrope* (1975)

Gerald Pawle, *The War and Colonel Warden* (1963)

—— 'Christmas with Churchill', *Blackwood's Magazine*, (December 1973)

Graham Payn and Sheridan Morley (eds.), *The Noel Coward Diaries* (1983)

G. C. Peden, *British Rearmament and the Treasury, 1932–39* (1979)

—— 'A Matter of Timing: The Economic Background to British Foreign Policy, 1937–39', *History* (1984)

Gillian Peele, 'Revolt Over India', in Gillian Peele and Chris Cook (eds.), *The Politics of Reappraisal, 1918–1939* (1975)

Henry Pelling, *The Origins of the Labour Party* (London 1960)

—— *Churchill* (1974; 1977 ed.)

—— 'The 1945 General Election Reconsidered', *The Historical Journal*, 23, 2 (1980)

—— 'Churchill and Labour', in Blake and Louis (eds.) 1993

A. R. Peters, *Anthony Eden at the Foreign Office* (Aldershot, 1986)

Charles Petrie, *The Life and Letters of Sir Austen Chamberlain* (1939)

Ben Pimlott, *Hugh Dalton* (1986 ed.)

—— (ed.), *Diaries of Hugh Dalton, 1918–45* (1986), 2 vols

Douglas Plummer, *Queer People* (1963)

Antony Polonsky (ed.), (1976) *The Great Powers and the Polish Question, 1941–45*

Antony Polonsky and Boleslaw Drukier (eds), *The Beginnings of Communist Rule in Poland* (1980)

Clive Ponting, *1940: Myth and Reality* (1990)

Richard Howard Power, 'Winston Churchill's Parliamentary Commentary on British Foreign Policy', *Journal of Modern History*, 26, 2 (1954)

Lawrence R. Pratt, *East of Malta, West of Suez. Britain's Western Mediterranean Crisis, 1936–39* (Cambridge 1975)

Robin Prior, *Churchill's World Crisis as History* (1983)

Martin Pugh, 'Asquith, Bonar Law, and the First Coalition', *The Historical Journal*, 17, 4 (1974)

John Ramsden (ed.), *Real Old Tory Politics, The Political Diaries of Sir Robert Sanders, Lord Bayford, 1910–35* (1984)

Herbert Read, *English Prose Style* (1952)

J. Redmond, 'Was Sterling Overvalued in 1925?', *Economic History Review*, XLII, 1 (1989)

P. G. Reid, *Townsman of Westerham* (1969)

David Reynolds, *The Creation of the Anglo-American Alliance, 1937–41* (1981)

—— 'Churchill and the British "Decision" to fight on in 1940: Right Policy Wrong Reasons', in Richard Langhorne (ed.), *Diplomacy and Intelligence during the Second World War*

—— 'Churchill in 1940: The Worst and Finest Hour', in Blake and Louis (eds.) (1993)

Quentin Reynolds, *The Wounded Don't Cry* (1941)

Lord Riddell, *Intimate Diary of the Peace Conference and After* (1933)

—— *War Diaries* (1933)

—— *More Pages From My Diary, 1908–1914* (1934)

Marvin Rintala, 'The Love of Power and the Power of Love: Churchill's Childhood', *Political Psychology*, v. 5, no.3 (1984)

—— 'Renamed Roses: Lloyd George, Churchill, and the House of Lords', *Biography*, v. 8, no. 3 (1985)

Keith Robbins, 'Konrad Henlein and the Sudeten Question and British Foreign Policy', *The Historical Journal*, 12, 4 (1969)

Andrew Roberts, '*The Holy Fox*'. *A Biography of Lord Halifax* (1991)

Esmonde M. Robertson (ed.), *The Origins of the Second World War* (1971)

Earl of Ronaldshay, *The Life of Lord Curzon* (1928), 11

Kermit Roosevelt, *Countercoup* (New York, 1979)

Norman Rose, *Vansittart. Study of a Diplomat* (1978)

—— (ed.), '*Baffy*'. *The Diaries of Blanche Dugdale, 1936–47* (1973)

—— 'The Resignation of Anthony Eden', *The Historical Journal*, 25 4 (1982)

—— 'Churchill and Zionism', in Blake and Louis (eds.) (1993)

Lord Rosebery, *Lord Randolph Churchill* (1906)

Andrew Rosen, *Rise up Women! The Militant Campaign of the Women's Social and Political Union, 1903–14* (1974)

Stephen Roskill, *Hankey. Man of Secrets* (1970–74), 3 vols

—— *Churchill and the Admirals* (1977)

—— *The War at Sea, 1939–45* (1954–61), 3 vols

—— *Naval Policy Between the Wars, 1919–39* (1968–81), 2 vols

—— 'The Ten Year Rule – The Historical Facts', *Journal of United Services Institute* (March 1972)

—— 'Marder, Churchill and the Admiralty, 1939–42', *Journal of United Services Institute* (December, 1972)

G. Ross (ed.), *The Foreign Office and the Kremlin: Documents on Anglo-Soviet Relations, 1941–45* (Cambridge, 1984)

A. L. Rowse, *The Churchills. The Story of a Family* (1966)

A. P. Ryan, *Mutiny at Curragh* (1956)

Henry B. Ryan, 'A New Look at Churchill's "Iron Curtain" Speech', *The Historical Journal*, 22 4 (1979)

Keith Sainsbury, '"Second Front in 1942" – a Strategic Controversy Revisited', *British Journal of International Studies* (April 1978)

Anthony Seldon, *Churchill's Indian Summer. The Conservative Government, 1951–55* (1981)

Felix Semon, *Autobiography* (1926)

Tony Sharp, *The Wartime Alliance and the Zonal Division of Germany* (Oxford 1975)

R. Shay, *British Rearmament in the Thirties* (Princeton 1977)

Robert E. Sherwood, *The White House Papers of Harry L. Hopkins (1948–49)*, 2 vols

Avi Shlaim, 'Prelude to Downfall: the British Offer of Union to France, June 1940', *Journal of Contemporary History* (July 1974)

Robert Skidelsky, *Politicians and the Slump* (1967)

—— *Oswald Mosley* (1975)

A. L. Smith, *Churchill's German Army: Wartime Strategy and Cold War Politics, 1943–47* (1977)

Denis Mack Smith, *Mussolini* (1983)

Malcolm Smith, *British Air Strategy between the Wars* (Oxford 1984)

—— '"A Matter of Faith": British Strategic Air Doctrine before 1939', *Journal of Contemporary History* (July 1980)

Mary Soames, *Clementine Churchill* (1979)

Edward Louis Spears, *Assignment to Catastrophe* (1954)

Eugen Spier, *Focus. A Footnote to the History of the Thirties* (1963)

Joseph Stalin: Correspondence with Roosevelt and Churchill (New York, 1965)

Zara Steiner, *The Foreign Office and Foreign Policy, 1898–1914* (1969)

—— *Britain and the Origins of the First World War* (1977)

Mark Stoler, *The Politics of the Second Front* (New York, 1977)

Anthony Storr, 'The Man', in A. J. P. Taylor (ed.) (1993)

Joseph F. Strange, 'The British Rejection of "Sledgehammer", An Alternative Motive', *Military Affairs* (February 1982)

James Stuart, *Within the Fringe. An Autobiography* (1967)

Lord Swinton, *I Remember* (1948)

—— (with J. Margach), *Sixty Years of Power* (1966)

A. J. P. Taylor, *The Origins of the Second World War* (1961)

—— *Bismarck* (1955)

—— *English History, 1914–45* (1965)

—— *Beaverbrook* (1972)

—— (ed.) *Churchill. Four Faces and the Man* (1969)

—— (ed.) *Lloyd George: Twelve Essays* (New York, 1971)

—— (ed.) *Lloyd George. A Diary by Frances Stevenson* (1971)

—— (ed.) *Off the Record: W. P. Crozier. Political Interviews, 1933–1943* (1973)

Viscount Templewood, *Nine Troubled Years* (1954)

The Times, The History of The Times, vol. IV, part II (1952)

Hugh Thomas, *The Spanish Civil War* (1961; 1965 ed.)

——*Armed Truce. The Beginnings of the Cold War, 1945–46* (1986)

Kenneth W. Thompson, *Winston Churchill's World View. Statesmanship and Power* (Louisiana, 1983)

Neville Thompson, *The Anti-Appeasers. Conservative Opposition to Appeasement in the 1930s* (Oxford, 1971)

Walter H. Thompson, *Assignment: Churchill* (New York, 1955)

Christopher Thorne, *Allies of a Kind. The United States, Britain and the War against Japan, 1941–45* (Oxford, 1979)

Philip Towle, 'Winston Churchill and British Disarmament Policy', *Journal of Strategic Studies* (December, 1979)

Harvey B. Tress, 'Churchill, the First Berlin Raids, and the Blitz: A New Interpretation', *Militargeschichtliche Mitteilungen*, 2 (1982)

G. M. Trevelyan, *Grey of Fallodon* (1937)

Harry Truman, *Memoirs* (New York, 1955–56), 2 vols

Richard Ullman, *Intervention and War* (Princeton, 1961)

—— *Britain and the Russian Civil War* (Princeton 1968)

Viscount Ullswater, *A Speaker's Commentaries* (1925)

Fred Urquart, *W. S. C. A Cartoon Biography* (1955)

Lord Vansittart, *The Mist Procession* (1958)

Brian Loring Villa, *Unauthorized Action. Mountbatten and the Dieppe Raid* (1990)

Neville Waites (ed.), *Troubled Neighbours: Franco-British Relations in the Twentieth Century* (1971)

Daniel Waley, *British Public Opinion and the Abyssinian War, 1935–6* (1975)

Wesley K. Wark, 'British Intelligence on the German Air Force and Aircraft Industry, 1933–1939', *The Historical Journal*, 25, 3 (1982)

Bernard Wasserstein, *Britain and the Jews of Europe* (1988)

D. C. Watt, *Personalities and Policies* (New Haven, 1975)

—— *Too Serious A Business. European Armed Forces and the Approaches to the Second World War* (1975)

—— *Succeeding John Bull, 1900–75* (1984)

—— *How War Came: The Immediate Origins of the Second World War* (1989)

—— 'Could the War in the Far East have been Prevented in November 1941?', (unpublished)

—— 'The Initiation of the Negotiations Leading to the Nazi-Soviet Pact: A Historical Problem', in C. Abramsky and B. Williams (eds.), *Essays in Honour of E. H. Carr*

—— 'Churchill and Appeasement', in Blake and Louis (eds.) (1993)

Evelyn Waugh, *The Sword of Honour Trilogy* (1978)

Charles Webster and Noble Frankland, *The Strategic Air Offensive against Germany* (1961), 4 vols

Beatrice Webb, *Our Partnership* (1948)

H. G. Wells, *Men Like Gods* (1923)

D. J. Wenden, 'Churchill, Radio, and Cinema', in Blake and Louis (eds.) (1993)

John Wheeler-Bennett, *King George VI. His Life and Reign* (1958)

—— (ed.), *Action This Day. Working with Churchill* (1969)

Francis Williams, *A Prime Minister Remembers* (1961)

Philip Williamson (ed.), *The Modernization of Conservative Politics. The Diaries and Letters of William Bridgeman, 1904–35* (1988)

S. R. Williamson, *The Politics of Grand Strategy* (Harvard 1968)

Ann Ruth Willner, *The Spellbinders: Charismatic Political Leadership* (New Haven, 1984)

John Wilson, *A Life of Sir Henry Campbell-Bannerman* (1973)

K. M. Wilson, 'The British Cabinet's Decision for War, 2 August 1914', *British Journal of International Studies* (July, 1975)

—— 'The War Office, Churchill and the Belgium Option: August to December 1911', *Bulletin of the Institute of Historical Research*, 50 (1977)

Trevor Wilson, *The Downfall of the Liberal Party* (1968 ed.)

—— (ed.), *The Political Diaries of C. P. Scott, 1911–22* (Ithaca, 1970)

—— 'Britain's Moral Commitment to France in August 1914', *History*, CVXI (1979)

J. M. Winter (ed.), *The Working Class in Modern Britain* (Cambridge, 1983)

P. G. Wodehouse, *The Swoop, or How Clarence Saved England: A Tale of the Great Invasion* (1909)

Frederick Woods (ed.), *Young Winston's War* (1972)

Llewelyn Woodward, *British Foreign Policy in the Second World War* (1970–76), 4 vols

Michael Wolff (ed.) *The Collected Essays of Sir Winston Churchill* (n.d.) 3 vols

Virginia Woolf, *Roger Fry* (1940)

Woodrow Wyatt, 'Churchill as Parliamentarian', *Encounter* (1954)

Daniel Yergin, *Shattered Peace* (1980)

John W. Young (ed.), *The Foreign Policy of the Churchill Administration 1951–55* (Leicester, 1988)

—— 'Churchill's "No" to Europe: The "Rejection" of European Union by Churchill's Post-War Government, 1951–52', *The Historical Journal*, 28, 4 (1985)

Kenneth Young, *Balfour* (1963)

—— *Churchill and Beaverbrook* (1966)

—— (ed.), *The Diaries of Sir Robert Bruce Lockhart* (1973–80), 2 vols

Robert J. Young, *In Command of France. French Foreign Policy and Military Planning, 1933–40* (Harvard 1978)

Philip Ziegler, *Mountbatten* (1985; 1986 ed.)

—— 'Churchill and the Monarchy', in Blake and Louis (eds.) (1993)

Index

Abdication Crisis, 226, 230–32
Abdullah, Emir of Transjordan, 156
Abyssinia (see also Ethiopia), 236
Admiralty, 83, 88–89, 98–99;
  lukewarm towards Dardanelles,
  117; criticized, 109–11
Agadir, crisis at, 86–89, 102
Air Defence Research Committee,
  and Churchill, 226–27
Aitken, Max (see Beaverbrook, Lord)
Alamein, El, battle of, 295
Albania, 247
Alexander, Albert Victor (Earl of
  Hillsborough), 271
Alexander, Field Marshal Harold
  (Earl of Tunis), 300, 326
Alfred, King, 346
Amery, Leopold ('Leo') Stennett,
  22, 171, 172, 174, 179, 188, 232,
  245, 251, 261, 266, 267, 319,
  320, 329, 351
Anderson, Sir John (Viscount
  Waverley), 318, 393
Anglo-Persian Oil Company,
  Churchill purchases shares of, 101
Anglo-Soviet treaty, 307–08
Antwerp, 111–12, 113
Anzio, landings at, 298
Arandora Star, 266
Ark Royal, 253
Ashley, Maurice, 45, 211, 213
Asquith, Henry Herbert (Earl of

Oxford and Asquith): Prime
  Minister, 63, 65; anti-suffragist,
  65; Churchill's patron, 103; too
  lethargic, 124; forms coalition,
  127–28; abandons Churchill, 128,
  132, 133; 'odious', 128, 133; 29,
  54, 56, 67, 70, 71, 72, 74, 77,
  81, 83, 84, 86, 88, 90, 93, 95, 98,
  105, 106, 107, 111, 112, 115,
  117, 118, 122, 125–26, 374, 413,
  354, 358, 360, 363, 366
Asquith, Margot, 56, 98, 108, 113,
  122, 128, 355
Asquith, Violet (see Bonham-Carter)
Astor, Nancy (Lady), 203, 254
Ataturk, (see Mustapha Kemal)
Atkins, John Black, 42
Atlantic, Battle of, 277, 296
Atlantic Charter, 288, 307
Atomic bomb, 323
Attlee, Clement (Earl), 1, 152, 194,
  266, 268, 284, 285, 288, 318,
  319, 324, 330, 331, 332, 335
Australia, 131, 290
Austria, and 1934 putsch, 235; and
  Anschluss, 240, 241, 242

Baldwin, Stanley (Earl of Bewdley):
  becomes Prime Minister, 168;
  Churchill influences, 184; 163,
  169, 170, 171, 172, 175, 176,
  177, 179, 180, 181, 185, 188,

189, 190, 224, 225, 226, 227, 228, 229, 230, 231, 269, 366

Balfour, Arthur James: charms Churchill, 90, 124; out-argues Churchill, 134; 17, 29, 38, 50, 52, 53, 54, 55, 74–75; 76, 77; 125, 133, 146, 169, 366, 370

Balfour Declaration, 156, 157, 370

Balkans Agreement (1944), 311–12

Balsan, Consuelo Vanderbilt (see Marlborough, 9th Duchess)

Banstead Manor, 14–15; 30

Baring, Maurice, 11

Barnes, General Reginald, 35, 36

Barrymore, Ethel, 60, 209

Baruch, Bernard, 187, 196

Battenberg, Prince Louis of, 99, 104, 116, 364

Beatty, Admiral Sir David (Earl), 100

Beauchamp, Earl of, 106

Beaverbrook, Lord (Aitken, Max): and relationship with Churchill, 195–96; 144, 129, 133, 136, 157, 158, 159, 163, 174, 184, 185, 189, 198, 231, 266, 307, 325, 333, 339

Belfast, 223

Bell, Sir Hesketh, 57

Berlin, and 1948 crisis, 333

Berlin, Sir Isaiah, 210, 214

Bermuda, and 1953 conference, 336

Bertie, Lady Gwendeline ('Goonie') (see also under Churchill), 59

Bevan, Aneurin, 317, 335, 343

Beveridge, William (Lord): Report of, 316, 319–20; 73

Bevin, Ernest, 318, 322

Birkenhead, Earl of (see Smith, Frederick Edwin)

Birla, Ghanshysm Das, 217

Bismarck, Prince Otto von, 54, 343, 345

'Black and Tans' (see Ireland)

Blackwood's Magazine, 43

Blandford, Marquess of (see Marlborough, George Charles, 8th Duke of)

Blenheim Palace, Churchill's affection for, 14, 204; 2, 3, 13, 61

Blood, Sir Bindon, 83

Blunt, Wilfred Scawen, 18, 50, 61, 355

Boer War (see also South Africa), Churchill's views on, 42, 43, 51

Bonham-Carter, Lady Violet, 67, 84, 98, 99, 131, 309

Bonnet, Georges, 250–51

Boothby, Robert (Lord), 178, 198, 231, 232, 267, 274, 345

Botha, Helen, 59

Brabazon, Colonel John, 27, 33, 34

Brain, Sir Russell, 334

Bracken, Brendan (Viscount): and relationship with Churchill, 196–97; 205, 232, 262, 266, 325, 328

Bridgeman, Admiral Sir Francis, 99

British Empire: forces menacing, 152–53; lost, 290

British Gazette, Churchill editor of, 177–78

Brockie, A., 92

Brooke, General Sir Alan (Viscount Alanbrooke): ascendancy over Churchill, 295; 272, 293, 296, 297, 298, 313, 323

Bruce, 2nd Lieut. Alan, 33, 34, 71

Budget, The 'People's', 180

Budget League, Churchill chairman of, 182

Bulganin, Marshal Nikolai, 338

Buller, General Sir Redvers Henry, 42, 43

Bullock, Alan (Lord), 213

Burns, John, 73, 105, 106, 173

Butler, Richard Austen ('Rab') (Lord), 261, 328, 332, 335, 337

Cadogan, Sir Alexander, 284, 298, 307, 313

Cairo, and 1921 conference, 416, 421

Callwell, General Charles Edward, 364

Cambon, Paul, 106

Campbell-Bannerman, Sir Henry, 63, 146

Canada, 412

Carden, Admiral Sir Sackville Hamilton, 115, 118–19, 120

Carson, Sir Edward (Lord), 91, 94, 96, 97, 107

Casablanca, and 1943 conference, 295, 296; and unconditional surrender, 310

Cassel, Sir Ernest, 97, 185

Cecil, Lord Hugh ('Linky'), and 'Hughligans', 52, 53, 54, 56, 62, 63, 262

Ceylon, 131

Chamberlain, Sir Austen, 93, 151, 159, 161, 163, 165, 169, 170, 171, 189, 226

Chamberlain, Joseph, 29, 38, 50, 52, 53, 54, 126, 354

Chamberlain, Neville: appraises Churchill, 170, 179; and Poor Law reform, 180–81, 372; fails to harmonize with Churchill, 181; Churchill warms to, 254; 46, 171, 172, 468; 185, 188, 221, 226, 227, 228, 229, 235, 241, 242, 243, 244, 245, 247–48, 249, 250, 251, 254, 259, 260, 261, 262, 264, 266, 267, 316

Chanak, confrontation at, 162–63

Channon, Sir Henry ('Chips'), 232, 334

Chant, Mrs Laura Ormiston, 28

Chaplin, Charles, 187, 193

Chartwell Manor: Churchill buys, Clementine disapproves, 167–68, 192–93; Churchill entertains at, 193; and Churchill's daily routine, 198–99; and Clementine runs, 204–05; during wartime, 281–82; turned over to National Trust, 326; expands, 327; 144

Chatfield, Admiral Sir Ernle, 374

Chequers, 282

Cherwell, Lord (see Lindemann, Frederick Alexander)

Chiang-Kai-Shek, 298

China, 298, 303

Churchill College, founded, 339

Churchill, John George, 187

Churchill, John Strange Spencer ('Jack'): pliant temperament of, 30; becomes a stockbroker, 98; and rumours that illegitimate, 351; 2, 12, 36, 44, 60, 128, 129, 343, 352, 187, 340, 365

Churchill, Lady Gwendeline ('Goonie'), 138, 146, 130

Churchill, Lady Randolph: gives birth to Winston, 3, 348; 'whirlwind romance' and marriage of, 3–4, 348; character of, 5–6; extravagant life-style of, 7, 353; remote to Winston, 7, 12–13; in Ireland, 8–9, loathes Blenheim, 13; marriage breaks down, 19–20; considers Winston frivolous, 22–23; changed relationship with Winston, 30; deft petitioning of, 30, 35, 39, 44; second and third marriages, 44, 166; dies, 166; 11, 27, 34, 61, 65, 98

Churchill, Lord Randolph Spencer: and birth of Winston, 3; 'whirlwind romance' and marriage of, 3–4, 348; education of, 6, 349; extravagant life-style of, 7; remote to Winston, 7, 29; banished to Ireland, 8–9; discovers Irish question, 9; rejects Winston, 12; Winston idolizes, 12, 20; storms English politics, 17–19; and 'Tory Democracy', 18, 68; resigns, 19, 351; dies from syphilis, 19, 29, 350; marriage breaks down, 19–20; berates Winston, 23–24; calmer relations with Winston, 29; Churchill to vindicate memory of, 29, 31; death of profoundly affects Winston, 29–30; 68, 161, 226, 168, 341, 378

Churchill, Winston Leonard Spencer (*see also separate Index references for specific topics*):
  Childhood: born, 7; and parental neglect, 7; in Ireland, 8–9
  Education:
    St George's preparatory school: 10–11; beaten, 10, 25; satisfactory grades, but bored, 10; reads for pleasure, 11
    Brighton: stabbed in chest, 12
    Harrow: enters, 15–16, 20; academic record at, 21, 23; as eccentric figure, 21–22, 24–25; lacks parental support, 24; departs from in haste, 26
    Sandhurst: enters, 26; suits his style, 27–28; craves university education, 32; involved in great scandals, 33–34
  Early Career (1896–1906): covers Cuban insurrection, 34–35; visits United States, 73–75; in India, 36–40; and self-education, 37–38; early political ideas, 38; adopts Tory Democracy, 38; criticizes Malakand and Sudanese campaigns, 39–40; discovers the Raj, 40; first political speeches, and fails to win Oldham, 41; views on Boer War, 42, 43, 51; becomes an authentic war hero, 42–43; but charged with dishonourable conduct, 43; elected M.P., 44; enters Parliament, 49–50; relives father's career, 50; antagonizes own front bench, 50, 51–52; and 'Hughligans', 50, 52; and maiden speech, 50–51; breaks with Tories, 52–54; elected as Liberal for North-West Manchester, 55; chasing Tory Democracy, 55
  Under-Secretary at Colonial Office (1906–08): 56–59; and South African settlement, 56–57; and imperial concept, 57–58; tours East Africa, 57–58; condemns Milner, 58; relationship with officials, 58–59
  President of Board of Trade (1908–10): elected for Dundee, 65; as a 'tepid' suffragist, 65–67; adopts social reform, 67–74, 358; collaborates with Lloyd George, 70–71; 'most extraordinary' period of career, 80–81; 63, 167, 171
  Home Secretary (1910–11): and reform of Lords, 75–76; Sidney Street siege, 77, 358; lacks party base, 77; and labour unrest (1910–12), 78–80; troubled relationship with Labour, 80, 81–82; 90, 95
  First Lord of Admiralty (1911–15): crossroads in career, 88–89; and naval estimates, 84–85, 92, 93, 102–103; enjoys post, 98; and naval reforms, 88, 99, 100–01, 103–04; reacts to Agadir crisis, 86–89; cooperates with Fisher, 100–01; offers Germany concessions, 101; and naval arrangement with France, 102; deficiences of Navy, 103, 363; 'bellicose' during July 1914 crisis, 104–107, 362; forecasts short and cheap war, 108; and Baltic strategy, 109, 115, 117; actions criticized, 109–11; and 'Dunkirk Circus', 111, 139; and tank, 139; and Antwerp, 111–12
  Dardanelles Operation: and Savrola, 113; as 'full of risk', 114; doubts about, 117, 119, 323; faith in, 118, 120–21, 122, 129, 365, 366; as 'legitimate war gamble', 121; affects political future, 121–22; calculates wrongly, 122; and

family pressures, 122–23; forced to leave office, 124; and damaged reputation, 129; 'intrigues' against government, 125–26, 366; fights to retain position, 127–28; as Chancellor of Duchy of Lancaster, 128; resigns from government, 131

In France (1916): with Royal Scots Fusiliers, 132–33; pines for politics, 133–34; astonishes House, 134; returns to government, 136–37

Minister of Munitions (1917–19): seeks grander entitlement, 139; fascinated with means of war, 139–40; and industrial relations, 140

War Office and Air Ministry (1919–21): resolves demobilization crisis, 141; implements cuts, 141–42; and 'Ten Year Rule', 141; and German settlement (1919), 142–43; runs anti-Bolshevik campaign (1919–20), 144–51; and fierce rhetoric, 146, 368–69; as Cold War warrior, 149; and future career, 149–51, 169

Colonial Office (1921–22): embarks on 'empire building', 153; proposes reconstruction of Ottoman Empire, 153–54; and Iraq settlement, 155; and Palestine settlement, 155–57; and Irish settlement, 158–61, 371; and Greek–Turkish imbroglio (1920–22), 161–63; and 'warlike policy', 163; moves towards right, 158

Out of Office (1922–24): 163; as Lloyd George's 'lieutenant', 164; and uncertain political future, 164–65; seeks political respectability, 165; rejoins Conservatives, 168, 170; rediscovers Tory Democracy, 169

Chancellor of the Exchequer (1924–39): appointed, 170–71; economic orthodoxy of, 171; and protectionism, 171–72; and social reform, 172–73; restores Gold Standard, 173–75, 373; attacks Labour, 169–70; and 1926 General Strike, 176–78; and de-rating scheme, 179–81, 373; prunes naval estimates, 182, 374; leaves office, 185

In Opposition (1929–39): tours North America (1929), 186–87; repudiates universal suffrage, 186, 188, 190; delivers Romanes lecture, 188, 374–75; opposes protection, 188; attacks Labour's Indian policy, 189–90, 191; breaks with Tory leadership, 190; supports 1931 National Government, 190; abandons Free Trade, 190; fights government's Indian proposals, 216–19; escapes assassination, 216; Indian 'chapter' closed, 218; warns against German menace, 219–20, 234–35; first impressions of Hitler, 220; advocates increased air rearmament, 221, 224–28; yearns for office, 226, 228–29, 230, 381; and Abdication crisis, 230–32; praises Mussolini, 236; and Ethiopian war, 236–37; and Rhineland crisis, 238; and Spanish Civil War, 239–40; and Anschluss, 241; and Czech crisis, 242–46; agrees with government, 225, 246, 247, 383; advocates Soviet alliance, 241, 248; joins War Cabinet, 250

First Lord of Admiralty (1939–40): appointed, 252;

repairing navy's shortcomings, 253–56; and Baltic, 257–58; and Soviet Union, 255, 258–59; and Norwegian campaign, 259–61

Prime Minister (1940–45): appointed, 262–63, 386; and compromise peace, 263–65; and Battle of Britain, 265, 386; consolidates political base, 266–67, 316; becomes a Superstar, 267–70, 387; as Minister of Defence, 271; and Greek campaign, 278–80; and Ultra, 280–81; supports Russia, 287–88; negotiates with Japan, 288–90; and wartime diversions, 282–83; securing 'proper respect' for Britain, 301; at Teheran, 297–98, 308–09; quarrels with Roosevelt, 301–03; plans for post-war world, 303–04, 305; recreates France, 304–05, 315; relations with Stalin, 306–08, 309, 312–13; persuades Poles, 309; and 1944 Balkans agreement, 310–11; at Yalta, 313–14; trusts Stalin, 314; appeals to Stalin, 315; saves half of Europe, 316; criticized, 316–18; prefers to delay domestic legislation, 319; and Beveridge Report, 319–20; expounds Four-Year Plan, 320; as electoral liability, 319–20; has 'no message', 320; at Potsdam, 322–23; and atomic weapons, 323, 333; and 1945 election, 324–25

Leader of the Opposition (1945–51): 'miscast' as, 328; 329–33; and Palestine question, 329; and Indian settlement, 329–31; and 'Iron Curtain' speech, 331–32; and European unity, 332

Prime Minister (1951–55); and

thermonuclear devices, 334–35, 336, 338; encouraged to retire, 335, 337; continues Labour policies, 335–36, 338; pursues summit conference, 336–37; doubts Eden's succession, 337–38

Retirement: receives honours, 339, 342, 344; official biography of, 339–40, 396; final years, 340–41; dies, 342; and state funeral, 1–2, 340, 341–42; as 'the greatest Englishman', 345; as symbol, 342, 345–46

Family: limited experience of women, 59, 377; conducts low-key flirtations, 59–60; 'no experience of Love', 60; and attitude towards women, 67; marries, 61–62, 356

Churchill (Hozier), Clementine: rumour that illegitimate, 60, 355; marries Churchill, 61–62, 356; tensions in marriage, 62, and why it survived, 63; character of, 62, 63, 206; ardent suffragist, 66; offers wise advice, 122–23, 134, 206, 231; overcome by grief, 129; mistrusts Lloyd George, 133; advises moderation over Ireland, 158; campaigns for Churchill, 164; and nervous exhaustion, 166–67, 205, 326; distrusts Tories, 168, 170, 267; dislikes Churchill's friends, 198; runs Chartwell, 204–05; relations with Churchill, 205–07, 325; presses Churchill to retire, 324; 35, 60, 68, 91, 98, 112, 122, 124, 128, 134, 140, 155, 169, 170, 189, 194, 195, 199, 203, 208, 209, 229, 266, 272, 281, 284, 285, 322, 328, 337, 339, 341, 344, 365

Churchill, Diana, 62, 123, 167, 207, 345

Churchill, Marigold, 62; dies, 166, 167

Churchill, Mary, 62, 164, 167, 207, 208, 324, 326, 344

Churchill, Randolph Frederick Edward: and relations with Churchill, 208–09, 325; as Churchill's biographer, 209, 339–40; fights and loses by-elections, 219, 229; 62, 123, 129, 167, 187, 189, 207, 227, 231, 233

Churchill, Sarah, 62, 112, 167, 207–208, 284, 324, 325, 326, 340, 345

Finances: shaky, 10; 'bankrupt', 36, 187–88, 202; spendthrift ways, 26–27, 30; amasses £10,000, 44; inherits windfall, 167; earns princely sums, 186, 202; becomes rich, 326–27; and investments, 327; 353

Foreign Policy Ideas: belief in balance of power, 148, 234, 304; attitude towards League of Nations, 148, 237; favours isolationism, 184; and collective security, 235; and Grand Alliance, 238, 241–42

Habits: work schedule, 63, 116, 272, 356; eating, drinking and smoking, 194, 283, 341; daily routine at Chartwell, 198–99; and archaic image of, 199

Health: a delicate child, 15–16; almost dies, 15, 25; and speech impediment, 23; 'cursed with feeble body', 25, 27; delicate skin, 49; physical energy, 128; and 'Black Dog', 124, 129–30; effects of appendicitis, 164; survives traffic accident, 191; weight problem, 192; during second world war, 283–85; suffers strokes, 333–34, 338,

341; and resilience of, 334; physical and mental decline, 334–35

Literature: first journalism, 22; influenced by Gibbon and Macaulay, 45; improves style, 99; and 1930s projects, 186; writes film scripts, 202; early writings, 209; brings 'true happiness', 210; as an historian, 211–12, 355, 378; and historical myths, 211, 345–46; methods of work, 212–14, 366; and style of, 214–15; possesses 'valuable properties', 326–27

Political Philosophy:
and National Coalition, 38, 52, 76–77, 105–06, 128, 150, 158, 163–64, 190–91, 335, 338, 344

and Anglo-American relationship (Unity of English-Speaking Peoples), 74–75, 148, 305; 256, 304, 336, 343–44; and wishful thinking, 275–76; myth of, 291, 303

and British Empire: his imperial outlook, 152, 210–11, 217, 268, 352; as obsolete, 343; loses imperial mission, 189, 190

and Whig beliefs, 37, 210, 211

Recreations: rifle shooting and fencing, 21; riding and polo, 27–28, 37, 199; collects butterflies, 37, 133, 187, 199; grows roses, 37, 199; hunting, 133, 203; gambling, 144, 199; painting, 130–31, 326, 328, 366; sing-songs, 132, 200; 'hates' games, 199; reading, 11, 200; Gilbert and Sullivan, 200; theatre and films, 200–01; and pets, 203; horseracing, 338

Religion: 37–38, 199–200

Rhetoric: first public speech, 28; influenced by Cockran,

35; technique improves, 41;
as rhetorician, 45–46; as
parliamentarian, 134–35,
165, 179, 184–85; and
inflammatory anti-Bolshevik
campaign, 146; as most effective
weapon, 165; as 'spiritualized
action', 199; and characteristic
mannerisms, 244

Personal Traits: favourite hymns,
2; phenomenal memory, 10,
24; precocious, 10; unpunctual,
11, 56, 203; 'greedy', 11;
self-glorification, 11, 26, 40,
49, 111; defiant, 11; unruly,
11; warlike, 21, 84–85,
87, 108, 112–13, 163, 177,
302; ambitious, 29, 42, 100,
124, 157, 164, 334, 344;
premonition of early death,
32, 36; dictatorial, 34, 198,
272; courageous, 25, 56, 124,
165, 351; as 'an egotist', 49,
59, 134, 194–95, 272; and
'noisy mind', 56; hedonist,
62, 202; optimist, 62, 257;
self-confidence, 58, 100; lacks
sensitivity, 58, 134; as 'pasha-
like', 63, 201; irresponsible,
134, 344; compassionate,
142, 344; interfering ways of,
99, 110, 138; inflexible, 165;
believes in own destiny, 36, 54,
57, 137, 165, 229, 262–63;
mischievous, 178; as bully,
178; as a survivor, 165; has few
friends, 195; possesses 'darting'
mind, 199; likes 'only the
best', 201–02; as idiosyncratic,
202–03; and sense of humour,
203; and style of dress, 62,
203–04; as English aristocrat,
204; and attitude to sex, 206;
rudeness, 272, 345; and 'Karsh'
look, 201, 376

Strategic Issues: cavalier approach
to, 28; early ideas on, 38, 51;

as 'little Englander', 84–85;
86–89; and Baltic strategy,
109, 115, 257–58; and 'eastern'
strategy, 115; and United
States as key to victory in war,
136, 290–91, 302; views on
attrition, 136; and ability of
German generals, 136; and Far
East, 182–83, 222, 240, 255,
316; faith in navy, 222–23;
miscalculates 'revolution' in
mechanized warfare, 223;
basic precepts of, 253–54; and
Balkans, 257, 295, 297, 298–99,
312; formula for victory, 273;
strategic bombing, 273–75;
fixation with Middle East and
Mediterranean, 277–78, 291,
301, 312; obsession with Italy,
277, 295–96, 297, 301–02; and
debate over second front, 287,
291–300

Works By:
Savrola, 8, 25, 113; as
autobiography, 46–47; 126,
212, 327
My Early Life, 16, 34, 44, 46,
186, 212
'The Scaffolding of Rhetoric',
45–46
From London to Ladysmith, 46
Ian Hamilton's March, 46
The Malakand Field Force, 46
The River War, 13, 46, 327
Lord Randolph Churchill,
begins writing, 50; publishes,
55, 355, 378
The World Crisis, 121; as
autobiography, 129, 254;
186, 211
*Marlborough, His Life and
Times*, 186, 212
Thoughts and Adventures,
186, 212
India, 186
Arms and the Covenant, 186
Step by Step, 186

Great Contemporaries, 186, 212
*A History of the English-
Speaking Peoples*, 186, 211,
282, 326, 345, 378
The Second World War, 211,
212; begins writing, 327;
making 'a case', 327–28;
published, 328; shortcomings
of, 328
Triumph and Tragedy, 303
Secret Session Speeches, 326
Citrine, Sir Walter, 230
Clemenceau, Georges, 387
Cockran, Bourke, 35–36
Collier's, 186
Collins, Michael, 159, 433
Colville, Sir John ('Jock'), 261, 278,
284, 310, 314, 334, 336, 339
Committee of Imperial Defence,
212, 354
Conservative Party: and Tory
Democracy, 18, 169; Churchill
breaks with, 53–54; Churchill
'hates', 55, 317; and debacle
of 1906, 177; Churchill moves
towards, 149–50, 158; as potential
leader of, 161; Churchill rejoins,
168, 170; loses 1923 election,
169; 'hates' Churchill, 170, 317;
loses 1929 election, 185; Churchill
castigates 'Tory hacks', 228;
Churchill as leader of, 267; loses
popularity, 319–20; loses 1945
election, 324
Cooper, Alfred Duff, 245, 266
Cornwallis-West, George, 44
Coward, Sir Noel, Churchill adores,
200, 340
Cox, Sir Percy, 155
Craigie, Sir Robert, 289–90
Crewe, Marquess of, 88
Cripps, Sir Stafford, 286–87, 307;
challenges Churchill, 316–17,
318, 330
Crowe, Sir Eyre, 105
Cuba, Churchill visits (1896), 35
Curragh: 'mutiny' at, 231–34

Curzon, George Nathaniel
(Kedleston, Marquess of), 38, 86,
133, 153, 154, 163, 166
Curzon line, 307, 308, 309, 311, 392
Czechoslovakia: and 1938 crisis,
240, 242–44

Daily Express, 149, 186, 378
Daily Herald, 186, 288
Daily Mail, 126, 163, 176, 186, 378
Daily Mirror, 317
Daily News, 360
Daily Telegraph, 39, 40, 149,
186, 326
Daily Worker, 198
Dakar, 277, 316, 386
Dali, Salvador, 339
Dalton, Hugh (Lord), 318, 393
Dardanelles: campaign at, 113–23;
and Savrola, 113; as 'full of
risk', 114; naval attack fails, 120;
no one exonerated, 121; under
investigation, 135; syndrome of,
162; 165, 168, 260, 272
Darlan, Admiral Jean François, 304
Davidson, Emily, 153
Davies, David (Lord), 229
Deakin, Sir William, 211, 213, 214
De Gaulle, General Charles: and
relations with Anglo-Saxons,
304–305, 312; 1, 277, 317
De Robeck, Admiral Sir John
Michael (Lord), 120, 365
De Valera, Eamon, 159
Defence Requirements Committee,
221
Denekin, General A. I., 145, 146
Deutschland, 253
Derby, Earl of, 218
Dieppe, raid at, 293
Dilke, Sir Charles, 168
Dill, General Sir John, 279, 293
Disraeli, Benjamin (Earl of
Beaconsfield), 9, 103, 169, 213,
216, 343
Ditchley Park, 282
Dixon, Sir Pierson, 332

Dodecanese Islands: and Churchill's humiliation, 297
Dollfuss, Englebert, 235
Dönitz, Admiral Karl, 296
Dreadnought, 84, 359
Dresden: destroyed, 274–75, 388
Dugdale, Blanche, 214, 232
Dulles, John Foster, 336
Dundee: Churchill represents, 150, 224
Dunkirk, 263, 265, 297, 338

East Africa: Churchill tours, 132–33; 131
Eden, Anthony (Earl of Avon): as a 'lightweight', 195, 234–35, 246; clashes with Churchill, 317–18; 322, 329, 332; as Churchill's successor, 337–38, 393; 1, 227, 239, 244, 261, 266, 269, 271, 275, 279, 284, 305, 307, 310, 311
Edward VII, King, 58
Edward VIII, King: abdicates, 230–32
Egypt, 76, 152, 153, 189, 335–36
Eisenhower, General Dwight D., 1, 284, 303, 336, 337, 338, 343
Elibank (Alexander Murray), Master of, 77
Elizabeth II, Queen, 1
Elgin, 9th Earl of, Colonial Secretary, 56, 58, 71, 355
Elliot, Walter, 245, 332
Esher, Viscount (Reginald Baliol Brett), 72, 84, 102, 137
Ethiopia, 237, 238
Evening Standard, 186
Everest, Elizabeth Ann: as surrogate parent, 7–8; 11; as Winston's confidante, 13; dies, 31–32; 15, 25
Ewart, General Sir John Spencer, 95

Far East: war in, 255, 276, 287, 288–90, 291, 298, 303, 314, 316, 323, 324, 374
Faure, Edgar, 338
Feiling, Sir Keith, 213

Feisal, King, 155
Finland, and Soviet war, 258–59
Fisher, Admiral Sir John (Lord): cooperates with Churchill, 100–01, 258–59; and Baltic strategy, 109; and Dardanelles campaign, 114, 115, 116–17; threatens resignation, 120; resigns, 126–27; 85, 110, 113, 121, 122–23, 128, 134, 252
Fisher, Sir Warren, 173, 180, 181, 221
Focus, and Churchill, 229–30
France: and 1904 *entente*, 85, 86, 104, 354; Churchill proposes alliance, 87, 89, 102, 143; and agreements with Italy, 235; and Union with Britain, 266; to be re-created, 304–05, 315
Franco, General Francisco, 234, 239, 240
Franz Ferdinand, Archduke, assassinated, 104
Free Trade: Churchill's ardour for, 37, 38, 52–54, 69, 75, 93, 169; Churchill abandons, 171–72, 190; 186, 188
French, Field Marshal Sir John (Earl of Ypres), 94, 95, 122, 125, 330
Fry, Roger, 10

Gallipoli (*see also* Dardanelles): landings at, 120; evacuated, 129; fabricating a 'new', 440; 116, 320, 489
Gandhi, Mahatma, 189, 190, 216
Gardiner, Alfred, 64, 79
Garibaldi, Giuseppe, 387
Garnett, Theresa: assaults Churchill, 151
Garvin, James Louis, 112, 125, 134
General Strike (1926), 174, 175–78
Geneva, and 1927 naval conference, 183
Genoa, and 1922 conference, 150
George V, King, 86, 104, 177
George VI, King, 291

Germany: and social reform, 70, 72; no threat to Britain, 85–86; and Agadir crisis, 86; ability of generals, 136; menaces Britain, 191, 220–28; breaks Versailles treaty, 236; attacks Soviet Union, 287; and partition, 304, 307; zoned, 310; and post-war settlement, 313, 317, 322

Ghana, 336

Gibb, Andrew, 133

Gibbon, Edward, 37, 45

Gifford, Walter, 337

Gilbert, Martin, 340

Giraud, General Henri, 304

Gladstone, William Ewart, 17

Gorst, Sir John, 17

Gort, General Lord, 351

Gough, General Sir Hubert, 94

Graf Spee, 253

Greece: war (1920–22) with Turkey, 161–63; 247, 295; and Balkan (1944) agreement, 312, 313; 316, 317

Greenwood, Arthur, 251, 266

Grey, Sir Edward, 63, 72, 87, 93, 105, 107, 111, 112, 118, 125, 328, 329–30

Grigg, Sir Percy James, 173, 174

Guest, Frederick Edward, 125

Guinness, Walter (Lord Moyne), 150, 206, 329

Gwynne, Howell Arthur, 126

Hackett, Mary, 59

Haldane, General Aylmer, 92, 353

Haldane, Richard Burdon (Viscount): and naval holiday, 101; 84, 85, 105, 112, 127, 366

Halifax, Viscount, 189, 190, 241, 244, 245, 256, 261, 262, 264, 266, 269, 316

Hamilton, General Sir Ian, 44, 113, 119, 120, 365

Hankey, Sir Maurice Pascal Alers (Lord), 100, 115, 117, 119, 133, 145, 163, 221, 225, 226

Harington, General Sir Charles, 163

Harris, Air Marshal Sir Arthur, 274, 275

Hearst, William Randolph, 186, 187

Henlein, Konrad: impresses Churchill, 243

Hess, Rudolf, 280

Hitler, Adolf, 220, 224, 227, 235, 240, 241, 242, 243, 244, 245, 246, 250, 259, 264, 270, 276, 277, 280, 287, 368–69, 393

Hoare, Sir Samuel (Viscount Templewood), 150, 169, 217, 218, 234, 236, 260, 316

Hobhouse, Charles, 54, 126

Hollis, General Sir Leslie, 291, 292

Hong Kong, 183, 412

Hopkins, Harry, 276, 288, 313

Hopwood, Sir Francis, 57, 58

Horne, Sir Robert (Viscount), 169

Hozier, Bill, 61, 62, 167

Hozier, Lady Blanche, 60, 61

Hozier, Clementine (*see under* Churchill)

Hozier, Colonel Sir Henry, 60

Hozier, Kitty, 140

India: Churchill's first experiences, 76–87; 152, 412; and proposed Dominion status for, 189–90, 191, 216–19, 290, 317; and post-war settlement, 329–31

Inskip, Sir Thomas, 228

Iran, 287, 323, 336

Iraq (Mesopotamia), 155

Ireland: and 1911–14 Home Rule crisis, 49, 89–90, 91, 92; Churchill at Belfast, 91; Churchill contemplates resignation over, 92–93, 228; Churchill adopts tough policy, 94–96; and Curragh 'mutiny', 94–96; Churchill calls for compromise, 96–97; Churchill infuriates all parties, 96–97; Churchill's role in 1921 settlement, 158–61; Irish Free State proclaimed, 160; 517

'Iron Curtain', 315, 316, 393
Ironside, Field Marshal William
  Edmund (Lord), 144, 182
Irwin, Lord (*see* Viscount Halifax)
Isaacs, Rufus (Marquess of Reading),
  361
Ismay, General Sir Hastings (Lord),
  260, 264, 271, 294
Israel, 329
Italy: and anti-German bloc, 235–36;
  and second world war, 287, 294,
  295, 296, 301–02

Jackson, Sir Francis, 171
Jackson, Admiral Sir Henry, 115,
  116, 117, 119, 364
James, Captain Walter Henry, 26
Japan: alliance with, 85, 354; as no
  threat, 182–83; and attempted
  rapprochement with, 221; and
  Anglo-American negotiations,
  288–90; 255, 314, 374
Jellicoe, Admiral Sir John (Earl), 99,
  100, 104, 110, 117, 313
Jerome, Jennie (*see* Churchill, Lady
  Randolph Spencer)
Jerome, Leonard, 4, 5
Jews (*see also* Palestine *and*
  Zionism): Churchill opposes
  anti-semitism, 44; and Bolshevism,
  147; National Home for, 157
Jones, Thomas, 177, 373
Jowitt, William (Lord), 318
July, crisis of 1914, 260–82

Karsh (Yousuf) of Ottawa, 376
Kell, Sir Vernon, 281
Kennedy, General Sir John, 299
Kennedy, Joseph, 248
Kenya, 154, 336
Keyes, Admiral Sir Roger John
  Brownlow (Lord), 99, 260, 261
Keynes, John Maynard (Lord),
  174, 373
King, Admiral Ernest, 292
King, William Lyon Mackenzie, 187
Kinsky, Count Charles Rudolph, 20

Kitchener, Field Marshal Herbert
  (Earl of Khartoum): Churchill
  criticizes, 39–40, 44; reputation
  fades, 124–25; drowned, 135;
  111, 112, 115, 117, 118, 119,
  121, 122, 126, 128
Kolchak, Admiral A. V., 145
Koniev, Marshal Ivan, 1
Korda, Sir Alexander, 202, 326
Korea, 333, 336
Krassin, Leonid, 405
Kristallnacht, 246
Kruger, Paul, 96

Labouchere, Henry du Pré, 34, 69
Labour Party: demonology of, 459;
  Churchill's stormy relationship
  with, 78, 81–82, 175, 178; and
  1945 government, 81; becomes
  main opposition, 141; Churchill
  attacks, 150, 189–90, 169–70;
  forms (1924) government,
  169–70; wins 1929 election,
  185; dominates Home Front in
  war, 318, 319–20; wins 1945
  election, 324
Labour Representation Committee
  (*see also* Labour Party), 70
Land and Water, 363
Laski, Harold, 324
Lavery, Sir John and Hazel, 130, 131
Law, Andrew Bonar: hostile to
  Churchill, 90, 168; extreme
  Unionist, 90–91, 94; forms
  government, 163; dies, 168; 93,
  95, 97, 99, 106, 126, 127, 128,
  133, 137, 195, 366
Lawrence, Thomas Edward,
  154, 193
League of Nations: Churchill lacks
  faith in, 148; applies sanctions,
  237; 156, 236, 240, 241
Lee, Arthur (Lord Fareham), 163
Leigh, Vivien, 193
Lend-lease: and being 'flayed alive',
  276, 303; cut off, 323
Leopold, King of the Belgians, 351

Liberal Party: Churchill joins, 54; forms 1906 government, 56; and social reform, 72; loses majority position in British politics, 74; Churchill not one of, 94; irrevocably split, 140–41, 170

Life magazine, 326

Lindemann, Frederick Alexander (Lord Cherwell): and relationship with Churchill, 196–98; 226–27, 233, 254, 266, 271, 274

Linlithgow, Marquess of, 217

Lloyd George, David (Earl of Dwyfor): first meets Churchill, 51; collaborates with Churchill, 70–71; 72, 73; and insurance schemes, 74, 357, 358; and reform of Lords, 75, 76; and national coalition, 76–77; and Mansion House speech, 86; and naval estimates, 92, 102–03; and Marconi scandal, 102, 361; and July 1914 crisis, 106–107; and Balkan strategy, 115; holds key to Churchill's future, 128, 134, 367; not to be trusted, 133; includes Churchill in government, 136–37; wins 'coupon' election, 140; checks Churchill's anti-Bolshevism, 148–49, 150–51; breach widens with Churchill, 157–58, 161; and Irish settlement, 158–61; and Turco–Greek war, 162; ousted from office, 163; 54, 62, 66, 67, 70, 77, 79, 81, 85, 88, 92, 93, 101, 108, 112, 122, 125, 126, 127, 135, 138, 139, 145, 153, 154, 156, 164, 169, 170, 171, 172, 174, 191, 195, 196, 203, 261, 267, 316, 320, 358, 360, 364, 371

Locarno, treaties, 238

Lords, House of: reform of, 178

Loreburn, Earl of, 79

Love, Mabel, 59

Luce, Henry, 326

Lytton, Countess of (Pamela Plowden), 58, 60

Macaulay, Thomas Babington, 21, 37, 45, 100, 211

McGuire, John, 132

McKenna, Reginald, 85, 126, 174, 473

Malaya, 412

MacDonald, Malcolm, 229

MacDonald, Ramsey, 195, 229

Macmillan, Harold Maurice (Earl of Stockton), 1, 179, 261, 319, 328, 332, 335, 337

McNeil, Ronald, 225

Macready, Sir Nevil, 159

Majoribanks, Dudley (Lord Tweedmouth), 22, 23

Malakand, 39

Malenkov, Georgy, 337

Manchester Guardian, 91

Marconi scandal, 102, 361

Marder, Arthur, 104

Margesson, David (Viscount), 261

Marlborough, Alberta, 8th Duchess, 14, 349

Marlborough, Charles ('Sunny'), 9th Duke, 44, 59, 210

Marlborough, Consuelo, 9th Duchess (*see also* Balsan, Consuelo Vanderbilt), 32, 349

Marlborough, Frances ('Fanny'), 7th Duchess: opposes Winston inheriting Blenheim, 14; 5

Marlborough, George Charles, 8th Duke, 14, 349

Marlborough, John Churchill, 1st Duke: builds Blenheim, 4; 79, 81, 89, 346, 396

Marlborough, John Winston Spencer-Churchill, 7th Duke: disapproves of Randolph's marriage, 3, 4; as 'Victorian prig', 5; 9

Marlborough, Sarah, 1st Duchess: builds Blenheim, 4

Marsh, Sir Edward Howard,

58–59, 61, 68, 122, 137, 213, 355
Marshall, General George, 291, 292, 294, 296
Marshall Plan, 333
Masterman, Charles and Lucy, 46, 54, 66, 68, 69, 73, 76, 77, 78, 188, 189, 191–92, 193
Maxse, Leo James, 63
Mayer, Louis B., 187
Meinertzhagen, Colonel Richard, 21, 154, 156
Menzies, Sir Robert, 1, 2, 316
Mers-el-Kebir, 266, 386
Middleton, Captain George ('Bay'), 60
Midway Island, battle of, 292
Mikolajczyk, Stanislaw, 311
Milbanke, John (Lord), 22, 25
Mills, Freddie, 193
Milner, Alfred (Viscount), 58, 151, 152
Molotov, Vyacheslav, 294, 309
Monckton, Sir Walter (Viscount), 335
Montagu, Edwin, 153
Montague Brown, Anthony, 340
Montgomery, Field Marshal Bernard Law (Viscount), 295, 300, 340
Moran, Lord (Charles Wilson), 68, 130, 212, 283–85, 320, 333, 334, 340
Morgenthau, Henry, Jr., 310
Morley, John (Viscount), 52, 63, 85, 93, 95, 105, 106, 212
Morning Post, 39, 41, 43, 51, 294, 364
Morocco, 208
Morrison, Herbert (Viscount of Lambeth), 172, 318, 319
Morton, Sir Desmond, 224, 225, 226
Mosley, Sir Oswald, 188, 191, 265, 351
Mossadeq, Dr Mohammed, 336
Mountbatten, Admiral Lord Louis (Earl of Burma), 1, 293
Mudania, convention at, 440

'Mulberry', floating harbour, 293
Munich: and 1938 settlement, 227, 240, 241, 244, 245, 246; 248, 249, 251
Murray, Alexander (see Elibank)
Murrow, Edward, 268
Mussolini, Benito: as anti-German, 235; regime falls, 296; 178, 236, 237, 244, 246, 247, 257
Mustapha Kemal, 161, 162

Napoleon: Churchill admires, 63, 72, 79; and Dardanelles, 113; and film script about, 187; 213, 357
National Review, 63
Nazi–Soviet Pact (1939), 248, 249–50, 253, 306
Nehru, Jawaharlal, 330–31
Nel, Elizabeth, 167, 272
Nelson, Admiral Horatio, 100, 114, 213, 252
New York Times, 326
News of the World, 186, 212, 378
Nicholson, Field Marshal William (Lord), 87
Nicolson, Sir Harold, 126, 245, 269, 277, 300, 320, 334, 340
Niemeyer, Sir Otto, 174
Nigeria, 336
Norman, Sir Montagu, 173–74, 175
North Africa: and second world war, 287, 292, 294; landings at, 295
North Atlantic Treaty Organisation, 333
North-West Manchester, 122, 127, 149–50
Northcliffe, Lord (Harmsworth, Alfred Charles William), 162
Northcote, Sir Stafford, 18, 109
Norway, 258, 278, 294, 385–86

Observer, 334, 378
Oldham: rejects Churchill, 41; elects Churchill M.P., 44; votes no-confidence in Churchill, 53
Oliver, Admiral Sir Henry Francis, 109, 363, 364

Oliver, Victor, 207, 272
Olivier, Sir Laurence, 193
Omdurman, 39, 211, 338
Onassis, Aristotle ('Ari'), 339
Orpen, Sir William, 326
Other Club, 196, 341
'Overlord': success of, 299; 292, 296, 297, 298, 301

Pact of Steel (1939), 247
Paget, General Sir Arthur, 94–95, 96
Pakistan, 330, 336
Palestine (*see also* Jews *and* Zionism): and Churchill, 155–57, 329; and 1922 White Paper, 156–57
Pankhurst, Emmeline, Christabel, and Sylvia, 66
Parnell, Charles Stewart, 134
Patton, General George, 302
Pearl Harbour, 276
Pearman, Violet, 201
Pétain, Marshal Philippe, 316
Philip, Terence, 206
Pim, Captain Sir Richard, 254
Ploegsteert, 132–33
Poland: and territorial changes, 307–08, 309, 314; 143, 247, 249, 250
Potsdam, conference at, 322–23, 324
Pound, Admiral Sir Dudley, 252, 259
Primrose League, 18, 65

Quebec, conference at, 297

Ramsey, Captain Archibald Henry Maule, 351
Rapallo, and 1922 treaty, 143
Read, Herbert, 214
Reade, Winwood, his *The Martyrdom of Man* influences Churchill, 37
Red Sea, 132
Redmond, John, 90
Repington, Charles à Court, 330
Reves, Emery and Wendy, 339, 340
Reynaud, Paul, 263

Richmond, Captain Herbert, 89, 117, 364
Riddell, George (Lord), 68, 88, 91, 93, 103, 122, 124, 125
Roberts, Field Marshal Frederick Sleigh (Earl), 43
Romanes Lecture, Churchill delivers, 188
Rommel, Field Marshal Erwin, 286
'Room 40', 363
Roose, Dr Robson, 11
Roosevelt, Franklin Delano: relations with Churchill, 275–76; quarrels with Churchill, 301–03; dies, 314; 244, 256, 271, 288, 291, 292, 295, 297, 298, 304, 307, 308, 309, 310, 311, 313, 314, 343
Rosebery, Archibald Primrose, 5th Earl of, 19, 29, 38, 52, 212, 341
Rothermere, Lord (Harmsworth, Harold Sidney), 194, 225, 339
Rothschild, Lord (Lionel Walter), 370
Rothschild, Lord (Nathaniel – 'Natty' – Mayer), 59
Roumania, 247, 249
Rowntree, Seebohm, and *Poverty*, 68, 69, 80
Royal Oak, 252
Runciman, Walter (Viscount), 44, 73
Russia (*see also* Soviet Union): and *entente*, 85; Churchill proposes alliance with, 87, 89; appeals for aid, 115
Rutherford, Ernest (Lord), 197

St Helier, Lady, 61
Sackville-West, Victoria, 269
Salisbury, 3rd Marquess of, 18, 19, 50, 111
Salisbury, 5th Marquess of, 334
Samuel, Sir Herbert (Viscount), 157, 176, 361, 370
San Remo, 1920 conference at, 157
Sandys, Duncan (Lord Duncan-Sandys), 198, 229, 233
Sarajevo, 260

Sargent, Sir Orme, 235
Savinkov, Boris, 145
Schuschnigg, Kurt von, 241
Schwab, Charles, 187
Scott, Charles Prestwich, 134, 135
Scrymgeour, Edwin, 371
Second Front, 287
Seely, John (Mottistone, Lord), 94, 95, 96
Semon, Sir Felix, 23
Sèvres, 1920 treaty of, 161, 162, 371
Shanghai, 131
Shaw, George Bernard, 356, 369
Shuckburgh, Sir John, 154
Sicily, 294, 295, 296
Sidney Street, siege at, 188, 202
Simon, Sir John (Viscount), 92, 106, 234, 316
Simpson, Mrs Wallis, 230–32
Sinclair, Sir Archibald Henry (Thurso, Viscount of), 133, 166, 231, 271
Singapore: Churchill and base at, 182; falls, 286, 290; 307, 329
Sinn Fein (see Ireland), 367
Smith, Adam, 37
Smith, Frederick Edwin (Earl of Birkenhead): 'drunk', 164; favours National Coalition, 76; and relationship with Churchill, 196; 76, 93, 105, 110, 133, 135, 157, 159, 160, 161, 163, 176, 177, 189, 194, 198, 212, 354
Smith, Sir Herbert Llewllyn, 73
Smuts, Field Marshal Jan Christian, 196, 332
Snowden, Philip (Viscount), 171, 175
Soames, Sir Christopher, 208, 326, 341
Socialism (see also Labour Party): Churchill attacks, 70, 147, 169–70, 190
South Africa, and 1906 settlement, 56–57; 152, 154
Soviet Union: recognition of, 150–51; invades Finland, 258–59; invaded by Germany, 287; decisive

victories of, 297; territorial demands of, 307, 309; 241, 288, 291, 303, 304, 305, 306; 317, 331, 332
Spears, General Sir Edward Louis, 164
Spender, John Alfred, 50, 110
Spier, Eugen, 229
Stalin, Josef Vissarionovich: Churchill's talks with, 294; relations with Churchill, 306–08; redraws map of Europe, 315, 392; 249, 286, 287, 288, 292, 296, 298, 305, 308, 309, 311, 313, 314, 322, 323, 336, 369, 393
Stanley, Beatrice Venetia, 127, 363
Stanley, Oliver, 260
Stevenson, Frances Louise (Countess Lloyd-George), 128, 151
Strakosch, Sir Henry, 193, 224
Strand Magazine, 57
Stresa, and 1935 conference, 235–36
Sudan, 72, 84–85
Suffragettes: oppose Churchill, 151, 157; escalate campaign, 153; 223, 224
Sutherland, Graham, and Churchill's portrait, 339
Sweden, 258
Swinton, Viscount, 227

Taranto, 278
Teheran: conference at, 297–98, 308–09, 311
Thomas, Hugh, 239
Thomson, Charlotte and Kate, 11
Thorneycroft, Peter (Lord), 332
Times, The, 66, 84, 125, 126, 211, 247
Tito, Josip Broz, 252, 312, 317
Tizard, Sir Henry, 226–27
Tobruk, falls, 286, 292
Tonypandy, Churchill and myth of, 78, 80, 175
Tory Democracy, 18, 38, 49–50, 55, 79, 198, 457
Trade Unions (see also Labour

Party): Churchill's soft spot for, 150; 164, 483

Transvaal, self-government for, 120

Tree, Ronald, 282

Trenchard, Air-Marshal Sir Hugh (Viscount), 142˙

Tribune, 317

Truman, Harry S., 315, 331, 333, 336, 343

Truman Doctrine, 333

Turkey: and 1920–22 war with Greece, 161–62; 278, 323, 336, 364

Ultra, and Churchill, 280–81; 296

United Nations, 314, 329

United States: secures Cuba, 35; Churchill visits (1896), and ambivalent attitude towards, 35–36, 275–76; as key to victory in war, 136, 290–91; as potential enemy, 183; refuses to cooperate, 221; and Churchill's war strategy, 278; and Soviet Union, 288; and Japan, 288–89; and second front controversy, 291–300; retreats from Europe, 314; and Cold War, 333; 303, 329, 331, 332

Vansittart, Sir Robert (Lord), 221, 224, 243

Versailles, treaty of, 143, 234, 238

Victoria, Queen, 19

Vienna, 299, 323

Wales, Albert Edward, Prince of (*see also* Edward VII, King): warns Churchill, 40; 8, 33, 97

Warsaw, uprising, 309–10

Washington: conferences at, 182, 291, 292, 296

Waugh, Evelyn, 209, 214, 269, 297

Wavell, Field Marshal Sir Archibald (Earl), 278, 279

Webb, Beatrice and Sidney (Lord Passfield), 71, 73, 77, 84, 178, 189

Wedgwood, Josiah, 261, 365

Weizmann, Chaim, 156

Welldon, Rev. James Edward Cowell, 16, 21, 22

Wellington, Duke of, 341

West Africa, 131

Wheeler, Sir Mortimer, 213

Wigram, Ralph Follett, 224, 225, 226, 235, 382

Wilson, Admiral Sir Arthur, 88, 89

Wilson, Harold, 343

Wilson, Field Marshal Sir Henry Hughes, 87, 88, 95, 145, 158

Wilson, Muriel, 59, 60

Wilson, Woodrow: blocks Churchill, 145

Wilton, Laura, Countess of: as Winston's deputy-mother, 27

Wimborne, Lady Cornelia, 137

Wolff, Sir Henry Drummond, 17

Wolff, Leonard, 356

Women's Social and Political Union (*see also* Suffragettes), 65

Wood, Sir Evelyn, 83

Wood, Sir Kingsley, 262

Woolton, Lord, 328

Wrangel, General Peter, 145

Yalta: conference at, 301, 313–14, 315

Yudenevitch, General N. N., 145

Zionism: Churchill's sympathy for, 155–56

Zurich, 332, 333